A New History of Documentary Film

A New History of Documentary Film

Second Edition

by

Betsy A. McLane

continuum

Continuum International Publishing Group
80 Maiden Lane, New York, NY 10038
The Tower Building, 11 York Road, London SE1 7NX

www.continuumbooks.com

Library of Congress Cataloging-in-Publication Data
A catalog record for this book is available from the Library of Congress.

ISBN: PB: 978-1-4411-2457-9

Typeset by Fakenham Prepress Solutions, Fakenham, Norfolk NR21 8NN
Printed and bound in the United States of America

For Jack C. Ellis
Friend and Mentor

Table of Contents

Preface

Like any account of history, this one is necessarily limited in scope. In this case, in addition to covering only nonfiction films there are two major delimiting factors:

1. This book is concerned with documentary films made in a particular part of the world: the UK, Western Europe and North America. These are the places where documentary film began.

2. After the silent era, the films considered are English language; even with that caveat, works from Australia, New Zealand, Ireland or other English language-speaking countries are not explored.

In recent decades documentary-making has become widespread, and with the use of mobile telephone cameras and the internet, documentaries are now made and seen regularly throughout the world. It is a marvel that documentaries seem to be everywhere. Even within the above limitations, there are far too many documentary films and filmmakers to include in this volume. Like Pare Lorentz's River, one drop became a trickle, a brook, a stream, a torrent, and now a flood that cannot be contained in two covers.

It remains important to understand that without the beginnings and the development described in this book there would not be a documentary tradition in the sense that we know it. The prevailing social hierarchies, the technologies, the finances, the conflicts and the distribution of personal and political power created the milieu in which the documentary developed. Sometimes it has been the films themselves that changed this order; documentaries are nothing if not a product of the shifting conditions of their own time. We today can learn much from these documentaries, not only about how reality was once recorded, but also about how to create change.

As do all writers, I write from the perspective of my own times and my own experiences. Although I believe that, like the best chroniclers of any history, I bring a conscientious factuality to my task, I am bound by my own understanding of the world. In terms of documentary film, my experience has been more munificent than anyone could hope. I am privileged to have seen, and to continuing seeing, tens of thousands of documentary films, and to know many people who dedicate their lives to creating, distributing, exhibiting and writing about them. I am especially fortunate to have known individuals who were important links in the chain of documentary history.

The first edition of this book was written with Jack C. Ellis, a scholar and teacher of great distinction. Jack and I agreed on many of the concepts expressed in that book, and disagreed on others. It was collaboration. With this second edition the concepts are mine alone, and although perhaps the poorer for lack of debate with Jack, I trust that they are as truthfully and thoughtfully presented as he would require.

A chronological organization remains in place in this book, although that structure is less rigidly imposed than in the first edition. Among the things that are different are: an expanded explanation of the intertwining of documentary and avant-garde that continues to the present; a look at the faux documentary as a subset of the form; a fine but consistent through-line that ties together the ways in which money, technology and artistry constantly interact with each other to determine what films get made and seen; and, of course, the book is up to date, with expanded information on documentary developments of the last decade. A change that is important to me is the addition and expansion of information on women in the documentary world, especially before 1970. There is little information available about the many documentary jobs taken on by women, and there is a great deal of research to be done. This book provides just a taste of what is yet to be discovered.

Jack Ellis' magnum opus is a magnificently detailed study of John Grierson and the Griersonian films and traditions. Jack spent time with John Grierson and many of the other men that worked with him. There is no one left alive now who has that first-hand knowledge. Grierson of course was great friends with Robert Flaherty and knew Frances Flaherty. The last living link to Flaherty was Ricky Leacock, who died in 2011, and although I met neither

Grierson nor Flaherty, I knew Ricky. So through Jack and through Ricky and through the gracious friendship of other documentarians, I feel deeply a part of this history. As a young film student I was welcomed into the documentary world by makers from older generations: Joris Ivens, Fred Wiseman, D. A. Pennebaker, Al Maysles, Robert Drew, Mel Stuart and George Stoney and others. The first documentary history class I took was taught by a man who had once worked with Leni Riefenstahl. There is a chain of human connection in documentary history, as well as a film record that ties it together.

There is nothing like hearing the first (or second)-hand colourful tales of documentary exploits and adversities from those who lived them. Of course, all the tales are not true, and it is the historian's job to try to uncover which bits are fact and which are fancy. This is this same challenge that makes creating and watching documentary films so valuable and so much fun. In the search for 'truth' in life and in documentary there are always unexpected developments and new discoveries. I hope that this Second Edition of *A New History of Documentary Film* will bring to its readers new information, and some small share of the enormous fun that I have had in writing it.

1

Some Ways to Think About Documentary

Documentary is one of three basic creative modes in film, the other two being narrative fiction and experimental avant-garde. Narrative fiction is well known as the feature-length and short story movies in theatres, on TV or computers, and now mobile phones and tablets. They grow out of literary, story-telling, and artistic and stage traditions. Experimental or avant-garde films are generally shown in nontheatrical film societies, in museums and art galleries, or are available in a few video anthologies; usually they are the work of individual filmmakers and the traditions of the visual arts and later aural experimentations mix with those of film.

Description

Traditionally, the characteristics most documentaries have in common, but that are distinct from other film types (especially from the fiction film), can be thought of in terms of: (1) subjects and ideologies; (2) purposes, viewpoints or approaches; (3) forms; (4) production methods and techniques; and (5) the sort of experiences they offer audiences, including actions that result from the films.

As for **subjects** – what they're about – documentaries for many decades focused on something other than the general human condition involving individual human feelings, relationships and actions; these were the province of narrative fiction and drama. For example, a British documentary made by Paul Rotha entitled *The Fourth Estate* (1940) is about a newspaper, *The* [London] *Times*, whereas Orson Welles' *Citizen Kane* (1941) is more concerned with a fictional character who is modelled on William Randolph Hearst, the powerful American press lord, than with the publishing of newspapers. The National Film Board of Canada's *City of Gold* (1957) made by Wolf Koenig and Colin Low from still photographs taken in Dawson City, in the Yukon Territory, in 1898 was set within a brief frame of live action in then present-day Dawson. In terms of library catalogue headings, *City of Gold* would be listed under 'Canada. History. Nineteenth century', 'Gold mines and mining. Yukon', 'Klondike gold fields', and the like. On the other hand, if Charlie Chaplin's *The Gold Rush* (1925) were to be similarly catalogued, it would be in the Cs (alphabetically by author) under the general heading Fiction, Comedy, Chaplin. Though its unforgettable recreation of the file of prospectors climbing over Chilkoot Pass is remarkably painstaking, *The Gold Rush* is not really about the Klondike Gold Rush as much as it is about loneliness and longing, pluck and luck, failure and success, friendship and love personified in an actor, in this case a world-renowned movie star. Generally documentaries are about something specific and factual; traditionally they concerned public matters rather than private ones. People, places, processes, politics, problems and events in documentary are actual, and, except for strictly historical work, are contemporary. Much of this categorical approach has been challenged in recent years, but to understand those changes it is necessary to understand the roots of documentary philosophy.

The second aspect – **purpose/viewpoint/approach** – is what the filmmakers are trying to say with their films. Today they record social, cultural and personal, as well as natural, institutional and political phenomena in order to inform us about these people, events, places, institutions and problems. In so doing, documentary filmmakers intend to increase our understanding of, our interest in, our sympathy for their subjects, and perhaps our future actions. They may hope that through this means they will enable lives to be lived more fully and intelligently. At any rate, the purpose or approach of the makers of most documentaries is to record and interpret the actuality in front of the camera and microphone in order to inform and/or persuade us to hold some attitude or take some action in relation to their subjects.

Third, **form** evolves from the formative process, including the filmmakers' original conception, the sights and sounds selected for inclusion, the artistic vision and the structures into which they are fitted. Documentaries, whether scripted in advance or confined to recorded spontaneous action, are derived from and limited to actuality. Hybrids continue to multiply, but documentary is based in reality. Documentary filmmakers limit themselves to extracting and arranging from what already exists rather than making up content. They may recreate what they have observed, but they do not create totally out of imagination as creators of stories can do. Though documentarians may follow a chronological line and include people in their films, they do not employ plot or character development as standard means of organization as do fiction filmmakers. The form of documentary is mainly determined by subject, purpose and approach. Usually there is no conventional three-act dramaturgical progression from exposition and complication to discovery to climax to denouement. Documentary forms tend to be functional, varied, and looser than those of short stories, novels, or plays. Sometimes they are more like non-narrative written forms such as essays, advertisements, editorials, or poems. More and more documentaries in the last decade blur the boundaries between the forms.

Fourth, **production method and technique** refer to the ways images are shot, sounds recorded, and the two edited together. Arguments can be made for exceptions, but a basic requirement of documentary is the use of nonactors ('real people' who 'play themselves') rather than actors (who are cast, costumed and made up to play 'roles'). Another basic requirement is shooting on location (rather than on sound stages or studio back lots). In documentaries sets are very seldom constructed. Other than lighting for interviews, lighting is usually what exists at the location, supplemented only when necessary to achieve adequate exposure. Exceptions to these generalizations occur, of course; but, in general, any manipulation of images or sounds is largely confined to what is required to make the recording of them possible, or to make the result seem closer to the actual than inadequate technique might. Special effects might be used to make clear a point, as in a science film for example, but technological effects are not a primary element of documentaries. Experimental documentaries are quite different, but their categorization is always difficult.

Finally, the **audience response** documentary filmmakers seek to achieve is generally twofold: an aesthetic experience of some sort, and an effect on attitudes, possibly leading to action. Though much beauty can exist in documentary films, it tends to be more functional, sparse and austere than the constructed beauties offered by fictional films. Also, much documentary filmmaking offers more that would be described as professional *skill* rather than as personal *style*; communication rather than expression is what the documentary filmmaker is usually after. Consequently, the audience is responding not so much to the artist (who traditionally keeps under cover) as to the subject matter of the film (and the artist's more or less covert statements about it). Generally the best way to understand and appreciate the intentions of documentarians is to accept the precept of the Roman poet Horace that art should both please and instruct. Another key factor is to understand for whom the film was made; in other words, follow the money.

Definition

Traditionally, the English-language documentary is said to start with American Robert Flaherty's *Nanook of the North*, shot in Canada and released in the United States in 1922. Flaherty wanted to show his version of the Eskimos – the people whom he had gotten to know in his travels – to audiences who had little or no knowledge of them. In the early twentieth century, few had seen a photograph or moving image of Eskimo life. To accomplish this goal he fashioned a new form of filmmaking. The worldwide success of *Nanook*, along with the influence of his wife Frances, drew Flaherty further away from exploring (which had been his profession) and still photography, and into filmmaking. His second film, *Moana* (1926), prompted John Grierson – then a young Scot on an extended visit to the United States – to devise a new use for the word *documentary*. Grierson introduced the word, as an adjective, in the first sentence of the second paragraph of his review in *The New York Sun* (February 8, 1926): 'Of course, *Moana* being a visual account of events in the daily life of a Polynesian youth and his family, has documentary value.' 'Documentary' film slowly developed as a stand-alone noun, due in no small part to Grierson's own efforts.

Fig 1 Nanook of the North *(US, 1922, Robert Flaherty). Museum of Modern Art Film Stills Library*

Documentary has as its root word *document*, which comes from the Latin *docere*, to teach. As late as 1800, according to the *Oxford English Dictionary*, *documentary* meant 'a lesson; an admonition, a warning'. When Grierson wrote that *Moana* had 'documentary value', he would have been thinking of the modern meaning of document – that is, a record which is factual and authentic. For scholars, documents are 'primary sources' of information; for lawyers 'documentary evidence' is opposed to hearsay or opinion. Perhaps Grierson was also thinking of the French use of *documentaire to* distinguish serious travelogues/ethnography from other sorts of early films that featured mere scenic views. In any case, he would move the term from his initial use of it partially back to the earlier one of teaching and propagating, using the 'documents' of modern life as materials to spread the faith of social democracy. Flaherty, for his part, continued to document the subjects of his films as he saw them and, to some extent, as they wanted to present themselves to the world and to posterity.

After meeting Flaherty, Grierson carried the word and his developing aesthetic theory and sense of social purpose back to Great Britain. His personal definition of documentary became 'the creative treatment of actuality'. Beginning with his own first film (the only one he personally directed), *Drifters*, in 1929, British documentary advanced to become an established movement. Most of the characteristics we associate with the term *documentary* and see evident in the films to which it is applied were present in the Griersonian films by the mid-thirties.

Documentary, then, as an artistic form, is a technique and style that originated in motion pictures. There are still photographic precursors and analogues, to be sure: the Civil War photographs of Mathew Brady, the remarkable photographic documentation of turn-of-the-century New York City by Jacob Riis, and the photographs made during the Depression years for the United States Farm Security Administration by Walker Evans, Dorothea Lange, Ben Shahn, and others. Documentary radio began in the early thirties in pioneering broadcasts of the British Broadcasting Corporation and in 'The March of Time' weekly series on the Columbia Broadcasting System; documentary television (which usually means documentary film or video made for television) became standardized, and later bastardized. In literature the concept of documentary established itself as the nonfiction novel (Truman Capote's *In Cold Blood* and Norman Mailer's *The Prisoner's Song*), and in newspaper reporting in the late 1960s and early 1970s as the 'new journalism' (Tom Wolfe's *The Electric Kool-Aid Acid Test*, Hunter Thompson's *Fear and Loathing in Las Vegas*, or Norman Mailer's *The Armies of the Night*). More recently, television courtroom and survival programmes and other 'reality' entertainments have become popular. In fact, the word *documentary* is by now pervasive, and much abused. But Webster's *New Collegiate Dictionary* offers as the primary meaning of documentary: '*n*. A documentary film.' Even the highly questionable validity of Wikipedia defines the term in its traditional sense.

Intellectual Contexts

Though various forms of nonfiction film preceded and existed alongside the story film, the latter early on became the main line of both film art and film industry. In aesthetic terms, the fictional feature film is an extension of nineteenth-century artistic forms: theatre, the novel, drama, and Pre-Raphaelite still photography. The documentary mode appeared, was invented in a sense, to meet new artistic and communication needs arising in the twentieth century. Documentary is purposive; it is intended to achieve something in addition to entertaining audiences and making money. This purposiveness is reflected in the four traditions identified by Paul Rotha in his seminal book of theory and history, *Documentary Film* (1935), as feeding into documentary: 1. naturalist (romantic), 2. newsreel, 3. propagandist, and 4. realist. These categories were adopted by many writers, and remain a valid starting point today.

According to Rotha, the beginning of the **naturalist (romantic)** tradition, exemplified by the films of Robert Flaherty (1884–1951), roughly paralleled the development of anthropology as a social science. Sir James Frazer, a Scot who lived from 1854 to 1941, was an anthropological literary pioneer. His monumental survey of the evolution of cultures, *The Golden Bough*, was published in 1890 in two volumes; the twelve-volume edition appeared between 1911 and 1915. Flaherty began to film the Eskimos in 1913.

Almost exactly contemporary with Frazer was Franz Boas (1858–1942), a German-born American anthropologist and ethnologist. Boas maintained that the immediate task of anthropology should be to record endangered cultures that might vanish. He stressed the specifics of each culture and taught that only after extensive data had been collected through fieldwork could any conclusions be put forward. Fieldwork has been the foundation of anthropology ever since. Though Flaherty had no training as an anthropologist, he approximated fieldwork more closely than any filmmaker preceding him, living with and observing the Inuit of the Hudson Bay region many years before filming them.

Boas' work was followed by that of Polish-born Bronislaw Malinowski (1884–1942). Malinowski's *Argonauts of the Western Pacific* was published in 1922 (the year *Nanook of the North* was released). It is about the people of the Trobriand Islands, located off the coast of New Guinea. Margaret Mead (1901–1978) published her *Coming of Age in Samoa* in 1928. Flaherty's *Moana*, dealing with Samoans, was released in 1926. What are accepted as the earliest academic attempts at film anthropology were undertaken by an 1898 expedition to the Torres Straits (a small group of islands near Northern Australia). The expedition was sponsored by Cambridge University and the four minutes of footage shot by the expedition's leader, Alfred Haddan, appear to be the first time that images purposefully intended for anthropological use were recorded in the field.

The **newsreel** tradition came out of the phenomenal expansion of journalism in the early twentieth century. The beginning of mass-circulation newspapers (and later of radio transmission) arrived at about the same time as the movies – 1896. The popular press, with its dramatization of the news, functioned not only as dispenser of information but also as informal educator for millions of avid readers. Newsreels appeared in movie theatres in regular weekly form from 1910 on. They were in some ways an extension into the motion pictures as the rotogravure (photographic) sections of the tabloids were to newspapers. Radio grew from its early pre-WW I military applications to an individual passion, to a mass medium. This trajectory from military technology developed for war then moving to industrial and wide consumer use is one that repeats itself throughout media history. It was present from the development of sound tape recording to the use of virtual reality.

The concept and term **propaganda**, Rotha's third tradition, goes back at least to the *Congregatio de propaganda fide* (Congregation for propagating the faith), a committee of Cardinals established by Pope Gregory XV in 1622. Interestingly, the purpose of this part of the Catholic Church remains responsible for establishing the Church in non-Christian countries and administering missions where there is no Catholic hierarchy. A subsequent use of propaganda grew out of the revolutionary theory set forth by German political philosopher and socialist Karl Marx (1818–1883). Film propaganda became a key concern of governments, especially Russian Communist leader Vladimir Ilyich Lenin (1870–1924). Following the Russian October Revolution of 1917, the new government – Union of Soviet Socialist Republics

– was the first to make sustained, extensive and coordinated use of film propaganda. Modern interest in propaganda is related to the intellectual disciplines of sociology, social psychology and political science, as well as proselytizing. The word has acquired a negative connotation over the years, but it is not necessarily derogatory.

Rotha's final tradition, **realist (continental)**, emerged as part of the European avant-garde of the 1920s, headquartered in Paris. One of its preoccupations was finding artistic means for dealing with the interrelatedness of time and space, thus the 'real'. Although 'real' is a slightly confusing and misused adjective here; Rotha's realist tradition became what today is called avant-garde or experimental. This modern understanding, originating in the physical sciences, was enunciated by Max Planck in his quantum mechanics, by Albert Einstein in his theory of relativity, and by others beginning about the turn of the twentieth century. Another preoccupation of the avant-garde was expressing the understanding of the unconscious human mind offered by Sigmund Freud, Carl Jung and others in the then new psychological science at about the same time. Thus Rotha's use of the word 'realist' referred to the emerging sciences.

Pre-Documentary Origins

Depending on how one defines documentary, it can be said to have begun with the birth of film itself. The filmed recordings of actuality in the experiments of technicians at the Edison laboratory in West Orange, NJ, might qualify. For example, the sneeze of an employee named Fred Ott was filmed in 1893, and two of the Edison workers dancing to phonograph music can be viewed during an attempt to synchronize sight with sound in 1896. Both of these are documents meant to be entertaining experiments. Closer in content and approach to subsequent documentaries are the first films produced by August and Louis Lumière and first projected for paying customers in a Paris café on 28 December 1895. Edison's use of a studio and very large camera is contrasted with Lumière's development of a relatively lightweight camera and outdoor shooting. The Lumière brothers' first films included *The Arrival of a*

Train at the Station, Feeding the Baby, and – most famously – *Workers Leaving the Factory*. A member of the audience at this showing is supposed to have exclaimed of the film being projected: 'It's life itself!'

In the very early following years of the motion picture, films were similarly brief recordings showing everyday life, circus and vaudeville acts, and skits. Only Georges Méliès used specially conceived narrative and fantasy to any extent before 1900, and even he began by recording snippets of life on the streets of Paris (*Place de L'Opéra, Boulevard des Italiens*, both 1896). Gradually, as the novelty of the moving photographic image began to fade, the subjects of actualities recorded by filmmakers were selected for extra-cinematic interest.

Foreign and exotic subjects had a strong appeal. Travelling projectionists and cameramen of the Lumière organization and other companies from England, Russia and the USA roamed widely, showing 'scenic views' of the Eiffel Tower and the Champs Elysées to audiences everywhere. In Russia they photographed troika rides and Cossacks, and in Spain Flamenco dancing and bull fights, to be shown to audiences in France and elsewhere. In addition

Fig 2 Workers Leaving the Factory *(France, 1895, Louis Lumière). National Archive Stills Library*

to such early travelogue forms – *Moscow Clad in Snow* (1909) is a French example (produced by Pathé Frères); *The Durbar at Delhi* (1911) a British one; *With Scott in the Antarctic* (1913) made by Herbert Ponting; *In the Land of the Head-Hunters* (1914) is a larger, more complex American film, produced by Edward S. Curtis. About the Kwakiutl Indians of the Pacific Northwest, it was the most ambitious experiment of its sort up to that time. Curtis was not only a professional photographer but also a trained and experienced ethnologist. Although working quite separately from Flaherty, he was headed in a somewhat similar direction. The Flahertys and Curtis met once in 1915 in New York City where they viewed each other's films.

The newsreel tradition may be said to have begun in France with Lumière's *Excursion of the French Photographic Society to Neuville*, 1895. Called 'interest films', the subjects quickly became events of greater newsworthiness. Many of them featured heads of state and ceremonial occasions. Examples include the crowning of a czar (*Coronation of Nicholas II*, 1896), the campaign of a presidential candidate (*William McKinley at Home*, 1896), and the final rites for a queen (*The Funeral of Queen Victoria*, 1901). Warfare was another frequent subject. The Spanish–American War (*Dewey Aboard the 'Olympia' at Manilla, Tenth US Infantry Disembarking*, both 1898), the Boxer Rebellion (*The Assassination of a British Sentry, Attack on a China Mission*, both 1900), and the Russo–Japanese War (*The Battle of the Yalu, Attack on a Japanese Convoy*, both 1904) had films made about them – though these were often re-enactments rather than actualities. In 1899 the great cameraman W. K. L. Dickson filmed the Boer War on location in South Africa. Among other examples that have lasted down to the present are *Launching of 'H.M.S. Dreadnought' by King Edward VII* (UK, 1906) and *Suffragette Riots in Trafalgar Square* (UK, 1909). Demand for war films was so keen that Harry Aitkin of Mutual Film paid Pancho Villa the enormous sum of $25,000 and a promise of net profit 50% for the exclusive right to film Villa in 1914 during the Mexican Revolution (1910–1920). The original contract still exists in a Mexico City museum. *The Life of Pancho Villa* also included many staged scenes with professional actors. The newsreel in weekly form was begun by Charles Pathé of France in 1910 with what became known as Pathé-Journal; newsreels made by Russians began in 1911.

Isolated examples of what might be called government propaganda films, in Rotha's sense of the term, appeared before the outbreak of World War I (1914). In the United States, the Department of the Interior produced and distributed motion pictures as early as 1911 to entice Eastern farmers to move to the newly opened land in the West. The US Civil Service Commission used a film, *Won Through Merit*, in a recruiting campaign in 1912. In the same year the city of Cleveland had a movie made as part of a programme to alleviate slum conditions.

WWI made film critical to victory. Training films were produced to instruct troops in warfare. Propaganda films were intended to instil in military personnel and civilians alike a hatred of the enemy and desire for victory. The multi-reel *Pershing's Crusaders* (USA, 1918), notable among these propaganda films, was meant to boost morale and the sale of war bonds, and such WWI documentaries were wildly popular in the US. Newsreels took on propaganda dimensions and the filmic documentation of warfare became much more comprehensive, skilful and actual than in preceding wars. *The Battle of the Somme* (1916), made by J. B. McDowell and Geoffrey Malins, and *The Western Front* (1919) are two British examples. Animated documentaries made their appearances during WWI. *Battle of the North Sea* (1918) is a completely animated diagrammatic account of the naval battle of Jutland. Silent, the film uses geometric outlines of cruisers, battleships, battle-cruisers, dreadnaughts, even radio waves and a zeppelin as they fight this inconclusive battle.

Perhaps the most important war documentary ever made is *The Battle of the Somme*. Long recognized as 'one of the jewels in the collection' of (England's) Imperial War Museum's Film and Video Archive, this opinion was formally endorsed in 2005 when the film became the first item of British documentary heritage to be accepted for inscription on UNESCO's 'Memory of the World' register. The reasons for this supreme honour are many. It is the first feature film to certifiably capture actual in-the-field combat and carnage during war, and is one of the most-seen documentaries of all time. This was, of course, at a time when commercial cinemas were the only place to see films. Shot by Geoffrey Malins and J. B. McDowell in June and July of 1916, *The Battle of the Somme* captures the grimness of filthy, pestilent, mud and poison

Fig 3 *Newsreel in wartime London (UK, 1917). From Strichting Nederlands Filmmuseum*

gas-filled trench warfare as the Allies and the Germans fought for five wretched months. The final result was a British advance of only about five miles. 420,000 casualties were suffered by the British (20,000 dead on the first day), 195,000 by the French and 650,000 by the Germans.

The film of this carnage was quickly edited and in August of 1916 released in thirty-four theatres across Britain. *The Battle of the Somme* shocked audiences who previously had seen only the 'Pack up Your Troubles in Your Old Kit Bag' glory of marching troops in newsreels. That the film was funded and endorsed by the British military was also significant. It laid bare the horrors and the human faces of war, a policy decision that governments from then until now have danced around. Scepticism about the authenticity of its battle scenes haunted the film for decades, but recent impeccable scholarship has proved that only about one minute and 12 seconds of a film running one hour and 14 minutes was faked.

Culturally and economically, filmmaking began as the exclusive province of white males from the upper and upper-middle classes, although the first audiences were mainly working-class. This was true in both fiction and documentary. It also began as a product of machine-age developments in Western Europe and North America, part of the breakneck rush to mechanical modernization that changed the world. Access to the new medium also required financial resources. Very few women and virtually no non-whites had access to the money or the technology needed for documentary-making. They existed merely as subjects in front of the camera. Although the same can be said to apply in other arts, the lack of non-white and female presence was more pronounced in film than in painting, literature, sculpture, or even still photography of the era, because films required large investments of money, and because filming required that its makers leave the confines of home.

During the silent era, a handful of women rose to prominence behind the camera in fiction filmmaking, and some blacks made movies, chiefly in the USA. The contributions of women to documentary filmmaking in its earliest years are themselves undocumented, and the exceptions have been glossed over by history. The best-known woman documentarian of the silent era, Frances Flaherty, would herself have never used the term filmmaker to describe her work, and she chose to spend her life building and promoting the

Fig 4 *'Mac' McDowell with a Moy and Bastie cine camera as he appeared during the Battle of the Somme. The 'head' mechanism which traversed and elevated the camera can be seen on the tripod. While he moved the camera on the tripod with his left hand, the right hand had to maintain a steady two revolutions per second. Information from Kevin Brownlow in the book* Ghosts of the Somme. *British Film Institute*

work and the myth of her husband Robert. The work of other notable women in silent documentary – Yelizaveta Svilova, Helen Van Dongen, Marguerite Harrison and Esther Shub – is described in this book to the extent that information is generally available. Van Dongen and a few others, among them John Grierson's sister Ruby, made films in the 1930s and 1940s, and a few women participated in experimental documentary-making in the 1950s and early 1960s. Hope Ryden was an important contributor to early cinema verité in America, as was Agnès Varda in France, but it was not until the late 1960s and 1970s that documentaries by women began to become more common. It was at this time, too, that people of colour began to have real access to documentary filmmaking, at least in the US.

In the four decades since then, much has thankfully changed. The triangular interaction of money/business, technology/equipment and artistry/aesthetics has shifted many times and continues to shift today. Thousands of people of every type raise money, make, and explore the world with documentaries. And whether one subscribes to, revolts against, partially accepts, or tries to escape from them, John Grierson's now 70-year-old 'first principles of documentary' remain part of the core of its history.

1) 'We believe that the cinema's capacity for getting around, for observing and selecting from life itself, can be exploited in a new and vital art form. The studio films largely ignore this possibility of opening up the screen on the real world. They photograph acted stories against artificial backgrounds. Documentary would photograph the living scene and the living story.'

2) 'We believe that the original (or native) actor, and the original (or native) scene, are better guides to a screen interpretation of the modern world. They give cinema a greater fund of material. They give it power over a million and one images. They give it power of interpretation over more complex and astonishing happenings in the real world than the studio mind can conjure up or the studio mechanician recreate.'

3) 'We believe that the materials and the stories thus taken from the raw can be finer (more real in the philosophic sense) than the acted article.

Fig 5 *John Grierson in the 1930s. Museum of Modern Art Film Stills Archive*

Spontaneous gesture has a special value on the screen. Cinema has a sensational capacity for enhancing the movement which tradition has formed or time worn smooth. Its arbitrary rectangle specially reveals movement; it gives it maximum pattern in space and time. Add to this that documentary can achieve an intimacy of knowledge and effect impossible to the shim-sham mechanics of the studio, and the lily-fingered interpretations of the metropolitan actor.'

(from Essays in the Winter 1932, Spring 1933 and Spring 1934 issues of 'Cinema Quarterly')

Books on Documentary Theory and General Histories of Documentary

Encyclopedia

Aitken, Ian, ed., *Encyclopedia of the Documentary Film*, Vol. 1–3. New York: Routledge, 2006.

Theory

Barsam, Richard Meran, ed., *Nonfiction Film Theory and Criticism*. New York: E. P. Dutton, 1976.

Coles, Robert, *Doing Documentary Work*. London: Oxford University Press, 1997.

Corner, John, *The Art of Record: A Critical Introduction to Documentary*. Manchester, UK: University of Manchester Press, 1996.

Grant, Barry Keith and Jeanette Sloniowski, (eds), *Documenting the Documentary: Close Readings of Documentary Film and Video*. Detroit: Wayne State University Press, 1998.

Grierson, John, *Grierson on Documentary*, ed. Forsyth Hardy. Berkeley: University of California Press, 1966.

Holmlund, Chris and Cynthia Fuchs, (eds), *Between the Sheets, In the Streets: Queer, Lesbian, Gay Documentary*. Minneapolis: University of Minnesota Press, 1997.

Hughes, Robert, ed., *Film: Book 1: The Audience and the Filmmaker*. New York: Grove Press, 1959.

Hughes, Robert, ed., *Film: Book 2: Films of Peace and War*. New York: Grove Press, 1959.

Levin, G. Roy, *Documentary Explorations: 15 Interviews with Film-Makers*. Garden City, NY: Doubleday, 1971.

Macdonald, Kevin and Mark Cousins, *Imagining Reality: The Faber Book of Documentary*. London: Faber and Faber, c. 1996.

MacDougall, David, edited and with an introduction by Lucien Taylor, *The Corporeal Image: Film, Ethnography and the Senses*. Princeton, NJ: Princeton University Press, 1999.

Nichols, Bill, *Introduction to Documentary, Second Edition*. Bloomington: Indiana University Press, 2001.

Nichols, Bill, *Representing Reality: Issues and Concepts in Documentary*. Bloomington: Indiana University Press, 2010.

Plantinga, Carl R. *Rhetoric and Representation in Nonfiction Film*. New York: Cambridge University Press, 1997.

Rabinowitz, Paula, *They Must Be Represented: The Politics of Documentary*. New York: Verso, 1994.

Renov, Michael, ed., *Theorizing Documentary*. New York: Routledge, 1993.

Renov, Michael and Jane Gaines, (eds), *Collecting Visible Evidence*. Minneapolis: University of Minnesota Press, 1999.

Rosenthal, Alan, *The Documentary Conscience: A Casebook in Film Making*. Berkeley: University of California Press, 1980.

Rosenthal, Alan, *New Challenges to Documentary*. Berkeley: University of California Press, 1987.

Rosenthal, Alan, *The New Documentary in Action: A Casebook in Film Making*. Berkeley: University of California Press, 1972.

Rothman, William, *Documentary Film Classics*. New York: Cambridge University Press, 1997.

Warren, Charles, ed., *Beyond Document: Essays on Nonfiction Film*. Hanover, NH: University Press of New England, 1996.

Winston, Brian, *Claiming the Real: The Griersonian Documentary and Its Legitimations*. London: British Film Institute, 1995.

Winston, Brian, *Lies, Damn Lies and Documentaries*. London: British Film Institute, 2008.

Wright, Basil, *The Use of Film*. London: John Lane, 1948.

History

Aufderheide, Patricia, *Documentary Film: A Very Short Introduction*. New York: Oxford University Press, 2007.

Baechlin, Peter and Maurice Muller Strauss, *Newsreels Across the World*. Paris: United Nations Educational, Scientific and Cultural Organization, 1952.

Barnouw, Erik, *Documentary: A History of the Non-fiction Film*. New York: Oxford University Press, 1993.

Barsam, Richard Meran, *Nonfiction Film: A Critical History*. Bloomington: Indiana University Press, 1992.

Barsam, Richard, guest ed., *Quarterly Review of Film Studies*, 7 (Winter 1982). Special issue on documentary.

Fielding, Raymond, *The American Newsreel, 1911–1967*. Oklahoma: University of Oklahoma Press, 1972.

Jacobs, Lewis, ed., *The Documentary Tradition*. New York: W. W. Norton, 1979.

Hertogs, Daan and Nico De Klerk, *Nonfiction from the Teens*. Amsterdam: Stichting Nederlands Filmmuseum, 1991.

Leyda, Jay, *Films Beget Films*. New York: Hill and Wang, 1964.

Manvell, Roger, ed., *Experiment in the Film*. London: The Grey Walls Press, 1949.

Orellana, Margarita *Filming Pancho Villa: How Hollywood Shaped the Mexican Revolution*. London: Verso, 2004.

Rotha, Paul in collaboration with Sinclair Road and Richard Griffith, *Documentary Film*. New York: Hastings House, 1952.

Waugh, Thomas, ed., *'Show Us Life': Toward a History and Aesthetic of the Committed Documentary*. Metuchen, NJ: Scarecrow Press, 1984.

2

The Work of Robert and Frances Flaherty

Between 1910 and 1915, at the time Edward R. Curtis was making *In the Land of the Head-Hunters* in western Canada, another American, Robert J. Flaherty, was exploring and mapping the Hudson Bay region of Canada. He was employed to search for iron ore by Sir William Mackenzie, Canada's railroad entrepreneur. Though Flaherty found some ore, the deposits were not rich enough to tempt anyone to try to mine and transport it. In the course of his travels Flaherty (re)discovered the main island of the Belcher group in Hudson Bay in 1914, and it was subsequently named for him. Flaherty often defined himself an explorer, and was very proud of his induction into the Royal Geographic Society of England for this discovery. But the most important discovery of his expeditions was how to make a new kind of motion picture. With this discovery he brought the life of the far North Country and its inhabitants, the Eskimos, to the attention of the world. And through this revelation, Flaherty forever put his personal stamp on documentary.

Robert Flaherty was born in Iron Mountain, Michigan in 1884, first son of an iron ore explorer whose family emigrated from Ireland. An early ability with the violin was taken as a sign of genius, if only the boy would discover 'discipline'. Despite such criticism, Flaherty continued 'playing' throughout his life; he applied real enthusiasm to his diverse interests, and photography especially grew to be a passion. He was determined to make 'beautiful pictures' even if it did mean lugging a bulky camera and tripod into turn-of-the-century homes, soda parlours and classrooms. Brilliant, but not cut out for long-term schooling, Robert went with his father on expeditions from an early age. He followed in his father's footsteps, in love with the wilderness, and developed a fascination for the people who lived there, beginning with the Ojibwa Indians.

Flaherty was already an acclaimed still photographer with gallery shows in Toronto, where he and his wife Frances lived at the time of making *Nanook*. He had photographed life and work in the North America wilderness since he was a teenager and was acclaimed for the portraits of American Indians and Eskimos on his expeditions. It was on his third expedition – 15 August 1913 to 3 October 1914 – that Flaherty, encouraged by then-affianced Frances and again funded by Mackenzie, supplemented his still photo kit with motion picture equipment to record what he saw. Supplies included 'a comprehensive motion picture and camera outfit including 1,000 pounds of chemicals, 25,000 feet of film and 2,000 dry plates' (a letter from Flaherty to Mackenzie). To prepare, he took a short course in camera operation offered by Eastman Kodak in Rochester, New York. During the expedition he shot hours of the Eskimos, their activities and their surroundings.

While editing this mass of material in Toronto, he dropped a cigarette onto a pile of film on the floor. Since it was the highly flammable cellulose nitrate stock of the time, it went up in a great flash of flame, nearly taking Flaherty with it. Though the original negative footage was almost totally destroyed, an edited positive work print survived and Flaherty, as usual prodded by Frances, screened it repeatedly throughout the US and Canada in attempts to secure funding for another filming expedition. At one point in 1915, the Flahertys met with Edward Curtis in New York. He showed *In the Land of the Head-Hunters*. They screened their work print of *Nanook*. Apparently this confirmed the Flahertys' sense that more human-interest storyline was needed in a new film.

Another novice might have given up filmmaking altogether following such an entry into the field; Robert and Frances not only persisted, they learned from the experience. In fact, some now speculate that the fire might not have been as much an 'accident' as a 'happy coincidence' that enabled a deeply flawed work to disappear. In this now-lost version, though, it seems Flaherty, ably assisted by the Eskimo crew, had faithfully recorded aspects of Eskimo

Fig 6 *Frances and Robert Flaherty as they appeared in Vancouver in 1908. The Robert and Frances Flaherty Study Center, Claremont School of Theology, Claremont CA 91711*

existence. Still, Flaherty's feelings for the people and their way of life was not expressed in a form that would permit audiences to share them. The film lacked emotion. When Mackenzie refused to finance any more expeditions

Fig 7 *Production still taken during shooting of* In the Land of the Head-Hunters, *aka* In the Land of the War Canoes, *Curtis is operating the camera (US, 1914, Edward S. Curtis). Thomas Burke Memorial Washington State Museum*

(after attending a screening of the first work print), Robert and Frances spent several years fundraising and, after many setbacks, obtained backing from the French fur company Révillon Frères for a return to the North to make another film. As such *Nanook of The North* is sponsored film. The name Révillon Furs was painted on a sledge, an early example of corporate promotion in a documentary, although audiences could not read it in the final film. (Morgan Spurlock was only fulfilling a documentary practice that was in place eighty-five years before he made *POM Wonderful: The Greatest Movie Ever Sold* [2011].) What resulted from Flaherty's shooting between 1920 and 1922 was the *Nanook of The North* we know.

In this unprecedented feature-length film ordinary people carried out and sometimes re-enacted things they did in everyday life – working, eating, sleeping, travelling, playing with their children – doing for the camera what they seemingly would have done if the camera hadn't been there. There are many scenes of the Eskimo working to survive, with a walrus hunt providing the most dramatic challenge. The shooting for *Nanook* was accomplished with a hand-cranked Akeley camera, weighing about sixty pounds, and by lugging a bulky fifteen-pound wooden tripod and quantities of 35mm film (which shattered in the sub-zero cold) across ice floes and frozen banks. Flaherty and Nanook almost starved during a trip to film bears. Very important to the film is the deep friendship that existed between Flaherty and some of the Inuit, and this quality is evidenced on the screen.

When the Flahertys took the completed *Nanook* around to distributors, one by one they turned it down. 'Who would want to see a movie about Eskimos,

Fig 8A & 8B *The Akeley camera revolutionized documentary filmmaking. Nicknamed 'Pancake' for its odd rounded shape, the camera featured a gyroscopic pan/tilt head so it could tilt straight up while the viewfinder remained in a fixed position. It had two lenses on the front: one a viewfinder, the other the film lens, which allowed for simultaneous focusing and filming. The Akeley also allowed the operator to change film magazines in less than 15 seconds. It was invented by explorer and big game hunter Carl Ethan Akeley 'The Father of Modern Taxidermy,' for use during his expeditions. Although not a manufacturer, he built this camera to suit his own needs, and it remained in production from 1917 until 1940. The shutter mechanism was another innovation. The pancake design allowed room for the shutter to travel all the way around its circumference; as a result, the shutter angle was 230 degrees. On right: Robert Flaherty continued technological innovations throughout his career. In his last major film,* Louisiana Story, *he worked with Ricky Leacock to create striking images of oil drilling in the bayou. Leacock is seen shooting high on the drilling rig. Robert and Frances Flaherty Study Center, Claremont School of Theology; Claremont, CA, 91711.*

a movie without story, without stars?', they seemed to be asking. It was Pathé Exchange, another firm with French origins, which eventually undertook worldwide distribution. No doubt much to the surprise of Pathé and perhaps to the Flahertys, this new kind of movie received an enthusiastic reception by critics and audiences. It became a substantial box office hit. Pathé's distribution deal, as often proved to be the case for documentaries, returned little to the Flahertys. Nanook himself, who received no compensation, became a recognizable face worldwide; he died of starvation less than two years after the film was released.

Following the success of *Nanook of The North*, Flaherty was approached by Jesse L. Lasky, head of Famous Players-Lasky (which later became Paramount Pictures), the first firm to have turned down distribution of *Nanook*. Lasky, not wanting to repeat a mistake, offered Flaherty what amounted to a blank cheque to make his next film. He was to go anywhere in the world and bring back 'another *Nanook*'. Flaherty had become interested in the peoples of the Southwest Pacific through the eloquent descriptions of Frederick O'Brien, who had written a popular book about the area, *White Shadows in the South Seas*. O'Brien urged Flaherty to go to Samoa to record the lovely culture of its gentle people before it was further eroded by the incursions of foreigners. With his wife Frances, three small daughters, their nursemaid, and his brother David, along with many filmmaking and family accoutrements including a piano, he set sail for the South Seas.

Flaherty was aware of what Hollywood expected from him – another box office success – and wondered what he would find in Samoa that could provide the drama of human survival contained in *Nanook*. Throughout his career he maintained a prickly relationship with the mainstream film industry. He sought money and on some levels craved its approbation; on the other hand, he refused to play by its commercial rules. Samoan existence seemed to provide no drama at all. Nature was munificent beyond belief; if one weren't hit on the head by a falling coconut one might spend life easily fishing and eating. For weeks, a dejected Flaherty sat on the veranda drinking apple beer, gloomily contemplating what form he might give to a film about Samoans. During this time, Frances, who learned photographic technique from Robert, took many beautiful still photographs, in a way creating a storyboard for a film. The role of stills artist was reprised by Frances on every subsequent Flaherty feature.

Through his informal investigations into the culture Flaherty learned of a ritual that interested him but was no longer practised. Formerly, young Samoan men had been initiated into manhood by undergoing elaborate and intricate tattooing over much of their bodies. Flaherty convinced himself that because there were few physical threats to their existence, the Samoans had invented a test of endurance involving considerable pain. He revived this custom for the purposes of his film and organized the narrative around the initiation of one Samoan youth named Moana. Preceding and paralleling the scenes of tattooing are scenes of the gathering of food – in the jungle, from the sea, and along the shore – the making of clothing and ornaments, the preparing and cooking of a feast, and the dancing of the Siva by Moana and his intended bride. When the tattooing was completed there was a ceremonial drinking of kava (a fermented beverage made from the crushed root of a shrubby pepper) by the chiefs, and a celebratory dance by the men of the village in honour of Moana's courage. In this resurrection of an old cultural practice, Flaherty was (most likely unknowingly) following in the footsteps of the first serious ethnographic film.

In his first two films – *Nanook of The North* and *Moana* – Flaherty's subjects and purposes led him into innovations in film form. In essence he was creating what would become documentary film. He found a means other than the plotted story, or simple topical organization of newsreels and travelogues, or even Curtis' work, to present real people and their everyday lives on the screen. Flaherty was intuitive and pragmatic, building his films out of long immersion in the culture of its subjects, and it is obvious from the films that he deeply respected them. He also was a true film artist and he made profound contributions to film aesthetic technique and to the uses to which films could be put. He experimented with film stocks and various lenses, spending days seeking the image he wanted. And Flaherty's body of work is the basis from which conversation about 'truth' 'reality' and 'illusion' in documentaries began.

The organizing structures of Flaherty's films involve loose narratives set within natural chronology. *Nanook of The North* extends through almost a year, during which time Flaherty never left the Eskimos. Beginning in late spring and ending in deep winter, *Moana* covers the period of its hero's initiation rites, from preparations to festive conclusion – somewhere between a month and six weeks. The separate sequences within the overall time spans describe the various kinds of work of each of these people: ceremony, children's play and other activities most characteristic and distinctive of their lives and culture. We see Nanook spearing fish, catching and rendering walrus, hunting seals, and building an igloo. Moana and his family are seen snaring a wild boar, collecting giant clams, gathering coconuts, capturing a huge tortoise, making custard, scraping breadfruit, and baking little fish. What Flaherty chose to show are traditional skills and customs that, while different from the 'civilized', modern ways of his era, are rooted in common sense all can appreciate. *Nanook's* kayak appears an extremely serviceable craft for navigating the ice-clogged waters of the far North. Flaherty asked the Eskimo to build what seems to be an efficient and comfortable igloo, even though it was constructed with a cutaway side to create enough light for the camera. In Samoa, clothing made from the bark of the mulberry tree and outriggers of carved wood and spars bound together with vines seem good use of what is readily available and well suited to tropical climate and rolling surf.

What Flaherty offers is beautiful visual description of then-unfamiliar human activities and artefacts, of exotic flora and fauna, and an emotional connection to nature – a perfect purpose for a maker of silent films. His films are all virtually silent. When sound became available, he used it essentially as secondary accompaniment to the images, filling in another sensory dimension of reality with natural sounds, adding emotional colour with music. Dialogue is used sparingly in Flaherty's two major sound films – *Man of Aran* (1934) and *Louisiana Story* (1948). Mainly it serves to characterize the timbre and style of his subjects' speech and to suggest their attitudes, more than to convey information or reveal psychological motivation.

Those who spent long evenings in Flaherty's company, whether in his youth or at the end of his life, remembered him as a teller of tales, a consummate raconteur with a sure sense of drama. In all his films, the dramatic conflict is achieved with man against – or at least in relation to – nature. In *Nanook of the North* it is family against the arctic cold and desolation. In *Moana*, amidst the warm soft abundance of a tropical paradise, it is man against invented, or at least man-made, pain. In Flaherty's later *Man of Aran* it is man and woman against the infertile rock of a barren island off the west coast of Ireland and the towering waves of the North Atlantic. And in *Louisiana Story*, with the most complex conflict of the four major films, it is still man in ecological relationship with nature – a boy and his raccoon moving amidst the secrets and dangers of a primordial swamp, and an oil drilling crew wresting commercial treasure from deep beneath its surface.

If Flaherty was a story-teller, he was also a teacher. His pedagogy employed mystery and suspense to arouse audiences' curiosity, to make them want to learn about the subjects that fascinated him. One of many instances of this method occurs early in *Moana* when Moana's younger brother, Pe'a climbs a palm tree. First we see him mid-frame, on a section of the trunk. He is allowed to climb up out of frame; then the camera tilts up to re-centre him. Pe'a again climbs out of frame and is again pursued by the camera. On the third climb-tilt the uppermost part of this majestic tree is revealed. By that time we are not only craving to see the top, we are prepared to accept this as the tallest palm in the world. Flaherty's visual exposition is splendid in its simplicity and clarity. Nanook's construction of an igloo is presented so clearly and simply we feel we could go out and build one. Much the same can be said for the making of soil in *Man of Aran*.

The dramatis personae of the Flaherty films are the nuclear family structured along conventional Western cultural lines. He did not acknowledge the polygamy practised in traditional Eskimo culture, nor the looseness of the Samoan family arrangement described by Margaret Mead in her seminal book *Coming of Age in Samoa* (1928). A Flaherty film family usually has a strong, mature father; gentle but heroic mother devoted to him, to their children, and to the concerns of the family; and a son who is learning his way into his cultural and natural surroundings. The women in Flaherty's films are supportive of the men in the struggle for existence, assisting them in domestic and ceremonial activities. Maggie, in *Man of Aran*, is the most forceful in her strength of character, independence, resourcefulness and bravery. The young boys of his films perhaps are surrogates for the young Flaherty himself. Water, boats and fishing are important in his films, as they were for the life of young Robert Flaherty, who grew up in isolated mining camps in the North Minnesota and Canadian wilderness.

The film families were artificially created for the films with considerable care given to the casting. Those selected to become father, mother, son, sister, and the rest are physically representative of the culture and also attractive – not necessarily handsome or beautiful, but 'best of type'. Nanook (which means 'The Bear') was played by Allarkariallak. Nyla's real name was Alice Nevalilnga. Community life is scarcely acknowledged; the family and the individuals are most important. The sudden appearance of numerous Eskimos, Samoans, or Aran Islanders for the trek to the fur trader's, the performance of a tribal dance, or the hunt for basking sharks is surprisingly within the prevailing intimacy and isolation of the central family. Ages and stages of life are present, but there are no human deaths or births in Flaherty films.

Fig 9 *Maggie in* Man of Aran *(UK, Robert Flaherty). International Film Seminars*

What he seeks out among his peoples are their consistent patterns of physical behaviour – activities related to obtaining food, clothing and shelter – rather than the aberrations of human psyches and antisocial actions which are the basis for Western fiction dating back to the Greeks. Flaherty may ultimately have been most concerned with the human spirit, but what he chose to show are its basic physical manifestations. He pays no attention to how his societies govern themselves, nor is there anything in his films about the spiritual life of the people. Religious beliefs and practices are absent – remarkable considering the importance of religion in the cultures he chose. We see neither anger nor grief. While affection is quite evident – of his subjects for each other and (implicitly) of the filmmaker for his subjects – there is no sex. (It has been verified that Flaherty did have an Eskimo female companion and fathered a son whom he neither saw nor acknowledged to the public on his sub-arctic expeditions.) Personal feelings – the emotions of individuals – are not central to Flaherty's concerns. Rather, more generalized notions of what a man, a woman and a child do are operative. What it means to survive, to exist in the culture and in the environment one is born into, are the archetypes of which his films are made.

Shooting in remote places in the way Flaherty did was fairly unique – at least in feature filmmaking up to that time – although at the same time in Scandinavia and Russia other explorers were using film to document their travels. Shackleton's 'Endurance' expedition (1914–1916) had been filmed. This venture – to be the first men to cross the Antarctic on foot – was extensively documented; even after their ship was crushed in an ice pack some eighty-five miles away from the continent, photography continued, and when, miraculously, all twenty-eight men survived, the cameraman, Frank Hurley, had the makings of a film. This became *South – Ernest Shackleton and the Endurance Expedition* (1919). But no one was developing and printing film on location, nor were they interested in and interpreting people's lives. Flaherty's methods of conception and production were especially original and unusual in two respects. One was what was characterized by Frances, constructor of what became the 'Flaherty Myth', as 'non-preconception'. Rather than approaching a society with an idea of the film they wanted to make, the Flahertys chose to live with and observe the people, to discover their essential story, like the Eskimo sculptor who cuts into the ivory tusk until he finds the seal figure it contains. The other, corollary characteristic was Flaherty's practice of shooting tremendous amounts of footage on the aspects of the people and their environment that struck him as significant, or beautiful, or interesting. That initial lack of fixed intention and seemingly random shooting were accompanied by long evenings of screening, looking for the essences of the culture in the images, seeking the particular rhythms and graces of the life being shown. As part of the editing process, Flaherty's subjects and members of his family and crew screened the uncut footage with him and discussed it for weeks.

As innovative as his production methods were, his initial use of film language followed accepted practice. Flaherty's camera was always mounted on a tripod. His nonactors were directed to re-enact things he had observed them do and to repeat their actions in multiple takes. The conventional continuity editing evidently rested on some sort of post-production script that formed in Flaherty's head during the repeated screenings. He seems never to have used pre-written scripts, only scribbled notes and Frances' magnificent photographic 'storyboards'. Though occasional differences are evident, the sequences are constructed with long shot-medium shot-closeup, matching action and sightlines, and consistent screen direction.

Shooting in out-of-the-way locations required considerable technological improvisation and ingenuity. Many technological advances in film technique have come about first from documentarians working outside the studio trying to get close to unaltered real life. Though he tended to profess ignorance of technological matters and worked with cameramen and editors, Flaherty seems to have been a natural and perhaps superb technician. He also surrounded himself with masters in the technical. From assistant cameraman Sam Sainbury on his northern expedition through editor Helen von Dongan and cameraman Ricky Leacock on *Louisiana Story,* skilled craftspeople always contributed to the film. And Frances' imprint is always there behind the scenes guiding and protecting his methods.

For his first filming in the North in 1913 Flaherty used a 1912 Bell and Howell studio camera, adapting it to his needs. Later he would use the Akeley, a sophisticated gyroscopic camera employed by newsreel cameramen, and then the Newman Sinclair, which became a standard camera for documentarians. On *Nanook of The North* he began his practice of developing and printing film in the field, necessary if he was to see what he was shooting while still on location. For this arduous task the Eskimo cut holes in the ice to obtain water for processing, carried it in barrels to the hut, and strained out deer hair and debris that fell into it from their clothing. The 'printer' was a rectangle of clear glass left on a window painted black. It corresponded to the 35mm film frame in size and dimension. Through it the low Arctic sun shone. That such a system of developing worked at all is amazing; that the quality of images in *Nanook* show little sign of the crudity of the 'laboratory' involved is even more astounding. The camera froze, the film cracked, the locations truly were dangerous, and Flaherty had no communication with the outside world during the long winters he spent with the Eskimo. Although *Nanook* is fully Flaherty's film, it is little noted that he had an Anglo assistant, Sam Sainsbury, who worked with him on the film, sometimes functioning as cinematographer, and helping with development as well as working to keep the equipment running in the freezing weather.

Flaherty was among the first to use Eastman Kodak's new panchromatic film on *Moana.* Though black and white (before practicable colour was available), panchromatic film is sensitive to all colours of the spectrum, unlike the orthochromatic film then in standard use. Orthochromatic film did not respond to red and was prone to harsh contrasts; *Moana,* shot with panchromatic stock, offers a Samoa of deeply rich and varied shades of gray. It was also on *Moana* that Flaherty first began to make extensive use of long (telephoto) lenses. Almost all of *Moana* was shot with lenses of six inches focal length and upward (two inches then being standard for most films). The use of such lenses had the obvious advantage of permitting the filming of distant and inaccessible subjects – the outrigger on the surf, for example. Also, Flaherty found that his subjects were less self-conscious and therefore behaved more naturally if the camera was some distance away from them. He also thought certain special photographic qualities resulted from the use of long lenses: 'The figures had a roundness, a stereoscopic quality that gave to the picture a startling reality and beauty,' he wrote, 'alive and real, the shadows softer and the breadfruit trees seemed like living things rather than a flat background.'

Man of Aran was Flaherty's first use of recorded sound. On the Irish island of Inishmore this would have been impossible with the cumbersome optical sound equipment then in use for fiction films (magnetic recording was not yet available). To solve this problem, Flaherty post-recorded in a London studio a soundtrack made up of music and noises and fragments of speech, laying it over the images in a complex and poetic blend. *Louisiana Story* was the first feature partly shot with the 35mm Arriflex camera, which had through-the-lens viewing capability (SLR) developed from the 16mm combat model used by the Germans in World War II. The Arri became one of the documentarians' favourite cameras. Some sound was also recorded on location, using a direct-to-disc method, with rather poor results.

The Flaherty Way

One aspect of Flaherty's overall significance is his special use of the film medium, which grew out of his creative impulse and began one main line of documentary. Stated simply, Flaherty used film to show people he loved and admired to the rest of the world. He was not an anthropologist; he idealized and interpreted as an artist does – a visual poet, in his case. The view he offers is his view, admittedly coloured by his own early life and the mores of the early twentieth century, but Flaherty's vision transcended the era in which he lived. At the 1904 Saint Louis World's Fair pygmies were exhibited in made-up 'villages' as curiosities, not considered fully human. Flaherty never condescended to or marginalized his subjects. In some respects his films are as much about him – his pleasures, his prejudices, his convictions – as about the people he was filming. Often he set them back in time to recapture and preserve cultures that were disappearing; and he always presented people at their finest, simplest and noblest, gaining their cooperation to achieve this presentation. *Man of Aran* especially – in which the hunting of basking sharks was recreated from past practices and the urgent contemporary economic problems of Aran were ignored – has been criticized for its 'distortions', but Flaherty did not invent or glamourize. His films were not created from make-believe or fakery; all that he shows did happen or had happened in the lives of the people and/or their fathers. (*Louisiana Story* is the exception; though based on actuality, it is a story, as its title announces.)

True, Flaherty usually stuck to peoples in far corners of the earth and dealt with the essentials of their traditional existence. But this is not exoticism à la 'Hollywood' (as in *Tabu*, 1931, on which Flaherty worked with F. W. Murnau in Tahiti but which became Murnau's sexualized film fantasy). In Flaherty's films there are neither 'colourful natives' nor 'native colour'. Instead, he was attempting to show how other cultures are like our own; how understandable, rather than how different and strange. This he shares with the developing field of visual anthropology, but unlike the distancing that characterized anthropology, *Nanook* ends with a closeup of Nanook's grinning face, and audiences may think: 'There's a man I've enjoyed getting to know. If I were in his situation, I hope I would be able to do things as well as he does.'

Simply to categorize Flaherty as a 'romantic', as Paul Rotha and others have done, misses the point. One can see what Rotha is thinking, in that the people and settings Flaherty selected and the way he chose to present them are linked with the noble savage of Jean-Jacques Rousseau and the idealized landscapes of early nineteenth-century painters. But Flaherty's films have little to do with

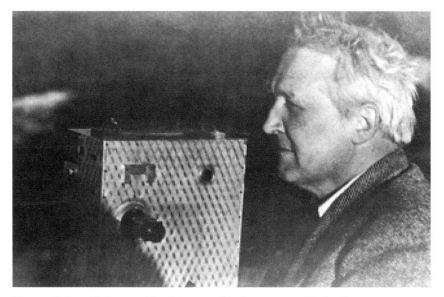

Fig 10 *Robert Flaherty with a Newman Sinclair camera, England, 1930s. Museum of Modern Art Film Stills Archive*

the romanticism of the 'romantic movement', resting as this does on individual imagination and heightened emotions. On the contrary, his work might be said to be 'classical', as the term is generally used in the romantic/classical dichotomy; it is spare and uninvolved with individuals' psychologies. Flaherty worked with what he understood and said what he had to say. Like many artists of substance this was essentially one thing reiterated throughout a career. The great French director Jean Renoir once remarked that a filmmaker spends his whole life making one film over and over again. What Flaherty said throughout his work was that humankind has an innate dignity, and that the world's meaning and beauty dwell in its patterns of existence.

The Flaherty Legacy

Though no school or movement ever formed around him, others who worked along similar lines have continuously followed Flaherty's example. *Nanook of the North* is a recognizable name even in the twenty-first century, and the idea of observing and recording people in their own milieu with a sympathetic eye continues to be a vital strand in documentary-making. Many also cite *Nanook of the North* as being among the first ethnographic films, and as anthropologists continue debate about the role of filmmaking (and ethnography) in their discipline, no one doubts that Flaherty holds a seminal place in it. The main strength of Flaherty's vision for ethnographic filmmaking lies in his refusal to pass judgment on his subjects. If his perspective sometimes sees quaint, it reflects more about the artistic milieu of the turn of the nineteenth century and perhaps the Pre-Raphaelites. Although this movement pre-dated Flaherty's work, it was the atmosphere in which his parents and Frances' parents lived. Since almost all of Flaherty's youth was spent in the wilderness, he was isolated from artistic trends in the early twentieth century and developed an aesthetic that reflected an earlier time. The films are about Flaherty's own unique poetic way of looking at life. For this his work is cherished, not only by visual anthropologists; but also by other kinds of filmmakers working today. For some detractors, Flaherty's lack of social comment was considered his downfall, perhaps even the antithesis of what they called documentary, but the films speak for themselves; the major work continues to resonate with audiences today.

During the same period as Flaherty's early work, one film by Merian C. Cooper and Ernest B. Schoedsack and their female partner, Marguerite Harrison (she secured the funding) deserves similar high praise. This film, the sweeping epic *Grass: A Nation's Battle for Life* (1925), records the migration of 50,000 Bakhtiari tribesmen in central Persia (today Iran) who cross a wide flooding river and climb a 12,000-foot mountain to reach pasture for their herds. Unlike Flaherty's work, the film does not focus on specific individuals, but rather captures the beauty and the dangers of a tribal culture from an almost objective point of view. The trio were the first white people to go with the Bakhtiari as they moved, carrying many pounds of gear on horseback. *Grass* is visually spectacular work that belongs in the pantheon of great documentaries. *Chang: A Drama of the Wilderness* (1927), which followed *Grass*, is Cooper's and Schoedsack's (without Harrison) concocted account of a family in the jungles of Siam (Thailand) struggling for survival against hostile animals – tigers, leopards, elephants. *Grass*, like Flaherty's films, remains compelling; *Chang* is a sentimentalized melodrama that exploits rather than respects native culture and environment. The two men subsequently had great success in Hollywood with *King Kong* (1933) and other fiction films. Harrison made no further films.

In the same ethical and artistic vein as *Chang*, in the 1930s the husband-and-wife team of Martin and Osa Johnson made several popular travel/expedition pictures with meretricious 'educational' trappings and condescending asides about the natives: *Wonders of the Congo* (1931), *Baboona* (1935), and *Borneo* (1937) are among them. Frank Buck, in much the same vein, filmed his expeditions to capture wild animals in Africa: *Bring 'em Back Alive* (1932), *Wild Cargo* (1934), *Fang and Claw* (1935). Set in the wild and using superfluous plots, these films are a stereotype of fiction film potboilers, and the antithesis of the Flaherty's work. The French also made films in the explorer mode, the most notable being *La Croisière Noire (Black Journey)*, a seventy-minute movie made in 1926 by Léon Poirier, which documents the Citroën Kégresse (a car race sponsored by Citroën) expedition in Africa.

Another offshoot from Flaherty's nonfiction form was the application of some elements by John Grierson and the British documentarians to purposes

Fig 11 *Marguerite Harrison in* Grass: A Nation's Battle for Life *(1925) She, with co-filmmakers Merian C. Cooper and Ernest Schoedsack, became the first Westerners to make the migration with the Bakhtiari tribe. The film follows Haidar Khan as he led 50,000 people across the Karun River and through a pass in the highest part of the Zagros Mountains in what is now Iran*

and subjects quite different from those of Flaherty. The British were concerned with people in an industrialized, interdependent and predominantly urban society. Their interests were social and economic, and political by implication. Grierson often publicly attacked Flaherty viciously. But, in a moving 'Appreciation' published in *The New York Times* at the time of Flaherty's death in 1951, Grierson said of his old friend and ideological adversary that perhaps Flaherty had been right after all in pursuing the timeless rather than the timely. In eulogy, Grierson wrote of Flaherty's seminal importance in the history of film, concluding with a quote from e. e. cummings in loving tribute to Flaherty:

> Buffalo Bill's
> defunct
>   who used to
>   ride a watersmooth-silver
>   stallion
> and break onetwothreefourfive pigeonsjustlikethat
>   Jesus

he was a handsome man

and what I want to know is

how do you like your blueeyed boy

Mister Death

Chapter Related Films

1919
South – Ernest Shackleton and the Endurance Expedition (UK, Frank Hurley)
1922
Nanook of the North (US, Robert Flaherty)
1925
Grass (US, Merian C. Cooper and Ernest B. Schoedsack)
1926
La Croisière Noire (The Black Cruise; France, Léon Poirier)
Moana (US, Flaherty)
1927
Chang (US, Cooper and Schoedsack)
Voyage au Congo (Voyage to the Congo; France, Marc Allegret and André Gide)

Chapter Related Books

Barsam, Richard, *The Vision of Robert Flaherty: The Artist as Myth and Filmmaker.* Bloomington: Indiana University Press, 1988.

Brownlow, Kevin, *The War, The West, and The Wilderness.* New York: Knopf, 1979.

Calder-Marshall, Arthur, *The Innocent Eye: The Life of Robert J. Flaherty.* London: W. H. Allen, 1963.

Carpenter, Edmund, ed., *Comock: The True Story of Eskimo Hunter as told to and by Robert Flaherty.* Boston: David R. Godine, 2003

Christopher, Robert J., *Robert and Frances Flaherty: A Documentary Life 1883–1922.* Montreal: McGill-Queen's University Press, 2005.

Flaherty, Frances Hubbard, *The Odyssey of a Film-Maker: Robert Flaherty's Story.* Urbana, IL: Beta Phi Mu, 1960.

Griffith, Richard, *The World of Robert Flaherty.* New York: Duell, Sloan and Pearce, 1953.

Holm, Bill and George Irving Quimby, *Edward S. Curtis in the Land of the War Canoes: A Pioneer Photographer in the Pacific Northwest.* Seattle: University of Washington Press, 1980.

Imperato, Pascal James and Eleanor M., *They Married Adventure: The Wandering Lives of Martin and Osa Johnson.* New Brunswick, NJ: Rutgers University Press, 1992.

McGrath, Melanie, *The Long Exile: A Tale of Inuit Betrayal and Survival in the High Arctic*. London: Fourth Estate, 2006.

Murphy, William T., *Robert Flaherty: A Guide to References and Resources*. Boston: G. K. Hall, 1978.

Rotha, Paul, *Robert J. Flaherty: A Biography*, ed. Jay Ruby. Philadelphia: University of Pennsylvania Press, 1983.

3

The Soviets and Political Indoctrination, 1922–1929

Paralleling the nonfiction films of Flaherty and others in the West in the 1920s were those of Russian Soviet filmmakers. After the Revolution in 1917 one of the first acts of the new Communist government was to set up a film subsection within the new Department of Education. An indication of the department's importance was the fact that it was headed by Nadezhda Krupskaya, wife of Vladimir Ilyich Lenin, principal architect of the Revolution. In 1919 the existing film industry was nationalized and the State Institute of Cinematography (VGIK) established in Moscow to train filmmakers. VGIK remains an important film school in the twenty-first century.

In Russian the word *propaganda* lacked the pejorative connotations it acquired in English. Soviets working in the arts and media understood that ideological bias operated in the selection and presentation of content in all information and entertainment, and that it was naive or hypocritical to pretend otherwise. In fact the filmmakers' goal was to create good Soviet propaganda, a goal they – at least at first – supported.

Lenin said – with remarkable foresight, given the uses of film up to that time and the negligible czarist film production: 'Of all the arts, the cinema is the most important for us.' He instructed Soviet filmmakers to revamp newsreels and other nonfiction short films. Western filmmaking companies were soon evicted. Key to Lenin's edict was the urgent need to communicate the experience and spirit of the Revolution to the still largely uninformed, often illiterate, poor and apathetic public. The country was exhausted and its human resources depleted by the harsh years of WWI and Revolutionary war. Three types of Soviet nonfiction films were prominent in the 1920s: newsreel-indoctrinational series, compilations of archival footage tracing recent history, and epic-scale celebrations of contemporary Soviet achievement.

Reportage/Newsreel

Among the most active and influential of the pioneer Soviet filmmakers was a young man who called himself Dziga Vertov. Dziga Vertov translates as 'spinning top', which characterized well his unstoppable energy; actually his name was Denis Arkadievitch Kaufman. He had two brothers who became filmmakers as well: Boris, a famous cameraman who later worked in the West with such directors as Jean Vigo, Elia Kazan and Sidney Lumet; and Mikhail, a cinematographer with Vertov and a documentary-maker in his own right. While Vertov's talent and originality are unquestionable, he seemed a whirling dervish to some, an eccentric fanatic to others. Before becoming a filmmaker Vertov had been an experimental poet and writer of fantasy and satire. In 1918 he joined the staff of *Kino Nedalia* (Film Weekly), which produced the first newsreel in Soviet Russia.

What attracted Vertov to cinema was what he saw as a close relationship between the filming process and human thought. Sergei Eisenstein would also develop much the same idea in his theories of montage. Also, Vertov saw human perception as having limitations compared with the more perfectible 'machine eye' of the motion picture camera. Flaherty, too, thought of the motion picture camera as a seeing machine, like the telescope or microscope, offering 'a sort of extra sight', albeit with a very different purpose from Vertov's. For both, the combination of technological developments and artistic desires played off each other to advance cinema in very different directions.

In his delight in the scientific and mechanical bases of cinema, Vertov was consistent with the great emphasis being placed on the machine in Soviet life and art. The government knew the urgent need to bring the Soviet Union up to a level of industrial production comparable with that of the Western

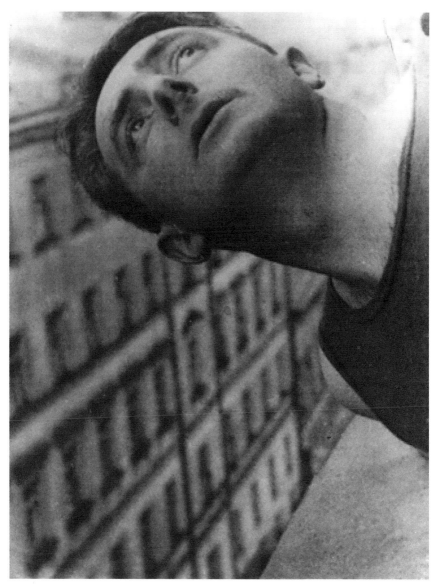

Fig 12 *Dziga Vertov in the 1920s. The Vertov Collection at the Austrian Film Museum*

nations, and to use modern technology to harness its vast natural resources since much of the country lived in the same ways that they had for generations. The constructivist artistic movement that become prominent in Europe in the early 1920s was also marked by an effort to give formal expression to the dynamic energy and quickly evolving movement of mechanical processes. This resonated with the artists in the new Soviet Union. It was adopted by some filmmakers, and thought to have a special relationship with the mechanics of film.

In 1920 the Russian Revolution was still being fought. The continuing conflict between the counter-revolutionaries (the Whites), who had supported the Czar or the Socialist Duma, and the Communists (the Reds) threatened the existence of the nation. Vertov at that time worked on 'agit trains' and made *agitka*. Agit is short for agitation; sometimes the term 'agit-prop' was used, for agitation and propaganda. *Agitka* were little political propaganda pieces that were 'agitated' in form as well as in their goal of agitating the population. agit trains were developed variously equipped with small printing presses, actors who gave live performances, filmmaking and processing equipment, and other means of entertainment and communication. These traveled to the far-flung battlefronts, mostly along the Trans-Siberian Railway, trying to instill the troops and peasants along the way with revolutionary zeal. There is no real way to measure the effectiveness of the agit trains.

In 1922 (the year *Nanook of the North* was released) Vertov began to produce the 'Kino Pravda' series of short films. *Kino Pravda* means, literally, 'film truth'; *Pravda* was also the name of the Soviet daily newspaper, central organ of the Communist Party. The series was released irregularly for twenty-three issues until 1925. It was, in that respect, a precursor to the 'The March of Time' series in the United States (1935–1951). In 'Kino Pravda' the newsreel and propaganda traditions merged with avant-garde art design and theatre techniques. Each issue, running about twenty minutes and frequently comprising three or more reports on separate subjects, was intended to inform and indoctrinate Soviet audiences about the necessity for and the values and progress of the Revolution.

The best-known example of 'Kino Pravda' contains six separate reports. The first is on the renovation and operation of the Moscow trolley system, with rails being laid, electric lines installed, meters measuring power, and trolley cars running. Second is the building of Khodinka Airport, with army tanks pulling graders to level the landing field. The third deals at some length with the trial of the Social Revolutionaries (i.e. the Whites who had been defeated by the Reds). Fourth is the organizing of peasants to form communes. Fifth is a sanitarium for crippled children at the town of Gelenzhik. Last is a report on starving children at the Melekes rail junction. The subject matter of all six reports is of a practical, immediate and concrete nature: social, economic and political problems being solved and outlines of things remaining to be done. 'Save the starving children!', a title in the last report exhorts.

Initially Vertov's production method did not involve recreation. Vertov confined himself, for the most part, to capturing what he could of undirected action as it was occurring: 'Life as it is' and 'Life caught unawares' were his slogans. 'All people must continue to act and function in front of the camera just as they do in everyday life,' he wrote. This strategy of shooting became a principle that has remained at the core of some subsequent modes of documentary filmmaking. Vertov insisted that the camera 'strive to shoot events "unnoticed" and approach people in such a way that the cameraman's work does not impede the work of others'. Conversely, the cameraman was not

Fig 13 *'Kino Pravda' newsreel series (USSR, 1922–25, Dziga Vertov). Museum of Modern Art Film Stills Archive*

to hide when people reacted to the camera even if they expressed displeasure at being photographed. Vertov did, however, plan the films beforehand. His equipment did not easily permit candid photography. He wrote complicated and detailed notes about where the camera should be placed, and about the artistic effects he sought to achieve. It is not an accident that the camera would be placed atop a building or in front of a train; a definite artist's view was expressed. Visual effects were also sometimes added in post-production, and the appearance of the camera and cameraman in his work marks a certain self-reflexivity.

In later editions of 'Kino Pravda' there are more exceptions to the unstaged ethos. In a sequence about the trial of the Whites, for example, the selling of newspapers on the streets and the reading of newspapers in a moving trolley obviously have been enacted for the camera. But even if Vertov generally confined himself to recording what was happening in front of the camera without intervention, he felt free to manipulate this filmed actuality in post-production. He edited extensively in order to make clear and emphatic the meanings he wished to communicate to his audience, often with rapid cuts. The brevity of the shots in 'Kino Pravda' may have been made more acute by the shortage of available film in the Soviet Union, which would have required the use of odds and ends of raw stock. On the other hand, the rapid cutting is consistent with the new editing theory and technique Vertov and Eisenstein were developing, and with the experimentation of constructivism.

Vertov's film practice was accompanied by his steadily developing written film theory. In a 1925 article, 'The Basis of "Film Eye" [*Kino Glaz*]', he explained his concept. Deciphering 'life as it is' begins with the direct recording of facts found in real life. 'Film Eye' had to act not through the medium of theatre or literature, since they were 'surrogates of life', but on its own terms. This bias stimulated Vertov's followers, called *kinoks*, to become antagonistic to drama and fiction, as well as – at least nominally – to 'pay little attention to so-called Art'. This authentic film material ('life facts') was then reorganized into cinematic structures ('film things') to give a new unity with a particular ideological meaning. According to the Marxist view, the world could not be known through naive observation because its operation is hidden. The empirical world is the starting place (the source of raw material) for the 'scientific' (that is, Marxist dialectical) analysis of the world. Vertov repeatedly pointed out that the 'deciphering' of life through cinema 'must be done according to the Communist view of the world'. Consequently, the 'Film Eye' method combined an aesthetic concept of unstaged, although manipulated, film with an ideological attitude towards art in general. The true Communist artist, Vertov claimed, must face reality 'as it exists', neither hiding from facts nor masking problems. Despite declarations of anti-aestheticism, the films remain compelling partly because they are highly contrived art.

The wife of Dziga Vertov, and a key member of the 'Cinema Eye' group, was Yelizaveta Svilova, who began work at age 14 as an assistant editor for Pathé in Moscow and in 1918 became an editor of features at Goskino. When they met in 1919, Vertov's early work inspired Yelizaveta; she alone of the editors he approached seemed able to understand his artistic vision. She joined the Cinema Eye studio and became the chief editor of all Vertov's subsequent films, including the *Kino Pravda* series, *Kino Eye* (1924), *Man With a Movie Camera* (1929), and *Three Songs of Lenin* (1934), later directing her own documentaries. Vertov and Svilova married in 1924. Her skill as an editor shielded her from Stalin's attacks, and she kept working throughout the 1930s, when Vertov was not permitted to make films. During World War II she was able to get him work on documentaries, and made notable films herself, including *Berlin* (1945), a compilation celebrating the Allied victory and one on the liberation of the Nazi concentration camps. Much like Frances Flaherty, Svilova devoted the later years of her life to protecting and enhancing her husband's reputation. She managed to smuggle a large part of his personal archive out of Moscow to Vienna, where they are now accessible.

Vertov's artistic impulse eventually proved stronger than his social one. He would probably have denied that the two impulses could be separated, and argued that his formal innovations were superior means of persuasion in support of the Revolution. Though maintaining their basis in recorded actuality, his films moved ever more toward aesthetic, psychological, even philosophical preoccupations. In his feature-length *Kino-Eye* (1924), opening titles announce it as 'The First Exploration of "Life Caught Unawares"' and 'The First Non-Artificial Cinema Object, Made Without a Scenario, Actors or a Studio'. What he created, though, is a succession of vignettes and anecdotes suggesting investigative journalism cut together to achieve a structural symmetry.

The following is one of Vertov's poetic manifestos about film:

Start 1917
Not like Pathé.
Not like Gaumont
Not how they see,
Not as they want.
Be Newton
To see
An apple.
Give people eyes
To see a dog
With
Pavlov's
eye.
Is cinema CINEMA?
We blow up cinema,
For
CINEMA
to be seen.

Dziga Vertov: *The Laboratory of Hearing*, 1917
(translation by Julian Graffy in *DZIGA VERTOV: The Vertov Collection at the Austrian Film Museum*, ed. Thomas Tode and Barbara Wurm)

Compilation

A major new type of documentary was introduced in Soviet Russia by Esfir (Esther) Shub. A consummate editor, she influenced Vertov and Eisenstein; she also learned from their work, insisting that she was 'in the final instance, Vertov's pupil'. Beginning in film in 1922, Shub was soon inspired by Eisenstein's full-blown use of montage in *Battleship Potemkin* (1925) to begin making compilation films. In her first three features she reconstructed recent Russian history by editing together shots taken from earlier newsreels, home movies, and other sorts of visual material. *The Fall of the Romanov Dynasty* (1927), the best known, covered the period 1912 to 1917; *The Great Road* (1927), 1917 to 1927; and *The Russia of Nicholas II and Leo Tolstoy* (1928), 1896 to 1912.

The Fall of the Romanov Dynasty is presented in four parts: pre-World War I; preparations for war; the war; and the Communist Revolution. Throughout, narrative intertitles in the past tense are used to identify images and give them emotional colouring, frequently ironic. It begins with 'Czarist Russia in the years of the black reaction'. There are short sequences on 'The Kremlin of the Czars', 'Moscow of the Priests', 'Police', and the legislative body: 'In St Petersburg the State Duma, obedient to the Czar, was in session.' We then see the prosperous-looking Russia of the clergy and landed aristocracy. There is one shot of village huts, with peasant women at a well, and a scene of 'Yoked peasant labour on the lands of the gentry'; but there is more footage of court nobility, senators and officials, and of army units and the fleet. In a sequence of pointed contrast between beautifully dressed aristocrats 'on an outing at sea'

Fig 14 The Fall of the Romanov Dynasty, *a compilation film (USSR, 1927, Esfir Shub). Museum of Modern Art Film Stills Archive*

dancing the mazurka aboard a ship, with images of labourers doing various sorts of manual work, a title makes a small joke about the sweating involved in each activity. *The Fall of the Romanov Dynasty* creates amazement and pleasure in its vivid sense of time and place, even of the personalities, caught by the camera. It is a visceral document, full of life and Shub's lively response to that life.

Even though she is clearly justifying the Revolution through showing the background out of which it came, the humanity of the people photographed comes through, regardless of which side they were on politically. A scene of an aristocratic celebration in Moscow of the 300th anniversary of the Romanov reign is fascinating for its interplay of relationships among family members and friends caught and preserved for decades, in some instances without any apparent awareness on their part that they were being recorded. Nothing like Shub's films had existed before them, and her work remains among the finest examples of the compilation technique.

Shub's contributions were influential in the United States. In the early 1930s leftist filmmakers made what they called 'synthetic documentaries' out of newsreels edited for propaganda purposes. Additionally, her techniques had a major influence on later experimental documentaries. Rapid montage filmmaking was also picked up and used later in 'The March of Time' (1935 to 1951) series, in the 'Why We Fight' (1942 to 1945) indoctrination series made during World War II, and in countless compilation documentaries made over the past hundred years. A seminal book by Jay Leyda devoted to this kind of filmmaking has the apt and engaging title *Films Beget Films* (1964). This work is discussed in Chapter 13.

Montages of very rapidly cut images and sounds later became a common technique in fiction films to represent, among other things, the passage of time. Serbian Slavko Vorkapich, a 'montagist', created both experimental films and documentaries. The most famous of the former is *The Life and Death of 9413: a Hollywood Extra* (1928), made with Robert Florey. Vorkapich was hired to use his montage technique in many Hollywood fiction features: *David Copperfield* (1935, George Cukor) and *The Broadway Melody of 1938* (1937, Roy DeRuth) are only two examples. 'Vorky', as he was nicknamed, became Dean of the film school at USC (1949–1951) and taught extensively in the US and Europe spreading the art of montage.

Epic

The final Soviet documentary pioneer to be considered here is Victor Turin. One film of his demands special attention: *Turksib* (1929), a large-scale feature about the building of the Turkestan-Siberian Railway. Prior to making it Turin had been sent by his well-to-do family to America, where he moved from the Massachusetts Institute of Technology to the Vitagraph Company in New York City, before returning to the Soviet Union. After the great success of *Turksib*, he was rewarded by being given a studio production post, organizing other people's films.

The introductory titles of *Turksib* set forth an economic-geographical problem. Cotton can be raised in Turkestan and 'cotton for all Russia' could be grown there if the wheat needed for the Turkestanis' subsistence could be shipped from Siberia (where cotton could not grow), thus permitting Turkestan land to shift from wheat to cotton production. However, Turkestan does not have enough water to grow cotton, so water must be brought in.

Shots of parched land are followed by a famous irrigation sequence as the snow melts in the mountains and water flows down into the valley. Trickles become streams, which become torrents. This sequence was echoed in King Vidor's fictional *Our Daily Bread* (1934), and in Pare Lorentz's documentary *The River* (1937). *Turksib* combines documentary ingredients already in use by others. It includes the distant and exotic, the Flaherty heroic struggle of man against nature. But whereas Flaherty recorded and celebrated indigenous cultural practices, Turin urged 'WAR ON THE PRIMITIVE!', as the large intertitle shouts. For Flaherty, technology represented a threat to what is most human; for Turin and the Soviets it was an extension of human power – 'forward the machines'.

Fiction and Documentary

It is sometimes impossible to separate documentary from fiction; hybrids have existed since the inception of cinema and continue to fascinate documentarians in the twenty-first century. Individual films, as well as certain national styles and movements, fall into an area containing both documentary and fiction.

The first recognized group of such films that fused fiction-documentary work are the Soviet silent features.

The basic factor setting all Soviet cinema apart from that of the rest of the world was its total support from the State. From idea, script, shooting, editing, distribution, exhibition, all financing and control was centralized. Filmmakers had to answer not to bankers, critics and the profit motive as they did in the West, but to government administrators and their presumed needs of the populace. This difference, if theoretically basic, may not have been as great in practice as it appears. Capitalist as well as Communist films all embodied ideologies. Both attempted to attract large audiences. The control of content and form in both instances was exerted by a 'front office', whether those behind the desks were called bosses or commissars. The success of Soviet films, however, was measured in terms of how well they conveyed the message – the extent to which they succeeded in affecting audience attitudes and behaviour in conformance with the Communist Party. In this respect they were profoundly different from films of the West, where market forces allowed for greater freedom.

The Fiction Films

The three greatest Soviet silent fiction film masters were Sergei Eisenstein, V. I. Pudovkin, and Alexander Dovzhenko. Eisenstein's work is the most influential of the three. It is also closest to documentary, and is therefore an invaluable example.

Eisenstein started his artistic career in the theatre, coming under the influence of renowned experimental director Vsevolod Meyerhold. He bounced out of theatre into film after he produced a play in 1924 entitled *Gas Masks*, performed by workers and staged in a real Moscow gas factory. Instead of replacing 'art' with 'life', as he had intended, Eisenstein found that the industrial setting and the performances of nonactors showed up the artificiality of conventions that would have seemed perfectly at home in the theatre. He thus turned to film as the medium in which art could be made out of materials much closer to life.

Fig 15 Battleship Potemkin, *a fiction film based on historical fact of the 1905 abortive Russian revolution (USSR, 1925, Sergei Eisenstein). Museum of Modern Art Film Stills Archive*

The documentary-like characteristics of Eisenstein's film are, first, that their subjects are all related to actual life lived or presently being lived. They are about people in relation to social institutions, a theme echoed many decades later in works by Frederick Wiseman and Roger Graef. Their concerns are large, economic and political. *Strike* (1925) deals with a labour protest and its smashing in Czarist Russia. *Battleship Potemkin* (1925) is based on the mutiny of the crew of an armoured cruiser in the abortive 1905 revolution. This was a mass uprising that sprang up in many parts of Russia, protesting against overwork, poverty, abuse and other government ills. It led to the founding of the Duma and a constitutional rather than absolute monarchy. *October/ Ten Days That Shook the World* (1928) is a recreation of the Bolshevik seizure of power in St Petersburg, the storming of the Czar's Winter Palace, and the takeover from the government. *The General Line/Old and New* (1929) is about an idealized agricultural collective in the new state; it is like an expansion of a 'Kino Pravda' report with the same emphasis on machines, in this case a tractor and a cream separator.

The purpose of these Eisenstein films, like Vertov's, is to inform and emotionally involve the Soviet public regarding: (1) the conditions and events leading to and justifying the Revolution; (2) the heroic struggle of the revolutionary forces during it; and (3) the positive and constructive efforts of the new state following it. Their aim is to persuade the people to support the efforts of their government, to make them think as Communists – for brotherhood, collective effort, and material progress, and against everything that stands in the way of those goals. Getting people to support the Bolsheviks was critical; real life in Russia was very grim and poor, often to the point of starvation, and the early USSR was not a stable nation.

Eisenstein shot on location and used nonactors. Though he started with actuality, he submitted it to extreme formalistic control and shaping. His work seems to represent a fusion of the contributions of two American pioneers: David Wark Griffith and Robert Flaherty. He acknowledged his indebtedness to Griffith; it is not known whether he saw Flaherty's films. But Eisenstein began with something close to natural material and morphed it with highly developed Griffith directing and editing technique.

According to his theory of *typage*, Eisenstein would select a person to play a priest, or a ship captain, or a foundry worker, whose appearance suggested most strongly that he might perform such a function. Eisenstein's definition of 'typage' is not the same as 'typecasting'. His purpose of typage was meant to present one aspect of a character, not a full psychological representation of that character. What Eisenstein needed was different from Flaherty's getting Nanook to play himself driving a dog sled. Performances in Eisenstein's films had to be created according to script requirements. Flaherty could capture his sort of action in sustained wide-angle takes. Eisenstein cut his nonactors' performances into bits and pieces, often using closeups. Montage, as Eisenstein conceived it, matches the Marxist dialectical process – shots cut together equalling thesis, antithesis, synthesis – rendering it ideal for polemical purposes. The aesthetic experience and social effects offered by Eisenstein's films finally move them outside the realm of documentary.

All of the Soviet silent films embrace the documentary impulse. If the art of Vertov, Shub, and Turin, of Eisenstein, Pudovkin, and Dovzhenko might include entertainment, it was intended ultimately to make a better-functioning country. The artists at that time were committed to building a perfect classless and centralized Communist Russia. Such loyalties shifted for some filmmakers as time passed. Eisenstein especially ran foul of Joseph Stalin's dictatorship. Sometimes his films were popular and in favour with the regime; at other times, after 1930, he was accused of being too formalistic, independent and elitist. Vertov, too, was later indicted as being too 'cosmo-politan' – a code-word for being too interested in art for art's sake and for being a Jew.

The relationship between government and documentary established in the USSR would be picked up later by Fascist Italy and Nazi Germany, and in the English-speaking democracies of Great Britain, the United States and Canada, as will be seen.

Chapter Related Films

1922–1925
'Kino Pravda' series (Dziga Vertov)
1924
Kino-Eye (Vertov)
1925
The Battleship Potemkin (Sergei Eisenstein)
1926
A Sixth of the World (Vertov)
Strike, Soviet (Vertov)
1927
The Fall of the Romanov Empire (Esfir Shub)
The Great Road (Shub)
1928
The Life and Death of 9413: a Hollywood Extra (Robert Florey, Slavko Vorkapich)
October/Ten Days That Shook the World (Eisenstein)
The Russia of Nicholas II and Leo Tolstoy (Shub)
1929
The General Line/Old and New (Eisenstein)
The Man with a Movie Camera (Vertov)
Turksib (Victor Turin)

Chapter Related Books

Feldman, Seth R., *Dziga Vertov: A Guide to References and Resources*. Boston: G. K. Hall, 1979.

Feldman, Seth R., *Evolution of Style in the Early Work of Dziga Vertov*. New York: Arno Press, 1977.

Hicks, Jeremy, *Dziga Vertov: Defining Documentary Film*. London: I. B. Taurus, 2007.

Kenez, Peter, *Cinema and Soviet Society*, 1917–1953. New York: Cambridge University Press, 1992.

Lawton, Anna, ed., *The Red Screen: Politics, Society, Art in Soviet Cinema*. New York: Routledge, 1992.

Leyda, Jay, *Kino: A History of the Russian and Soviet Film*. New York: Macmillan, 1983.

Leyda, Jay, *Films Beget Films*, 1976.

Roberts, Graeme, *Forward Soviet!: History and Non-fiction Film in the USSR*. London: I. B. Tauris, 1999.

Shlapentokh, Dmitri, and Vladimir Shlapentokh, *Soviet Cinematography, 1918–1991: Ideological Conflict and Social Reality*. New York: Aldine de Gruyter, 1993.

Taylor, Richard and Ian Christie, (eds), *The Film Factory: Russian and Soviet Cinema in Documents, 1896–1939*. Cambridge, MA: Harvard University Press, 1988.

Taylor, Richard and Ian Christie, (eds), *Inside the Film Factory: New Approaches to Russian and Soviet Cinema*. New York: Routledge, 1991.

Vertov Collection at the Austrian Film Museum. Wien, Austria: FilmmuseumSynema Publication, 2007.

Youngblood, Denise J., *Soviet Cinema in the Silent Era, 1918–1935*. Austin: University of Texas Press, 1991.

Zorkaya, Neya, *The Illustrated History of Soviet Cinema*. New York: Hippocrene Books, 1991.

4

The European Avant-Garde Experimentation, 1922–1929

It is a curious historical coincidence that at almost exactly the time Flaherty in America (*Nanook of the North*) and Vertov in Russia ('Kino-Pravda') began laying the groundwork for documentary, the avant-garde film was starting in Western Europe and to a lesser degree in the US. Thus, by the early 1920s documentary and experimental emerged alongside fiction to establish the three main aesthetic impulses of film art, its principal modes documentary, fiction and avant-garde. These Soviet and Western European films, along with Flaherty's, also became sources for the experimental documentary film as it would develop. And the avant-garde as well as documentary started as rebellion against the fiction film, which had quickly become the predominant artistic and commercial form.

Aesthetic Predispositions

What caused this rebellion was the feeling on the part of devotees of both new artistic tendencies that the conventions of the fiction film were limited and limiting. (This idea has surfaced many times in documentary, for example, with proponents of Free Cinema, cv/direct, and on-line filmmaking.)

Someone once remarked that the artistic experience offered by the Hollywood movie was equivalent to a performance by someone playing a grand piano with one finger, and throughout the course of film history new generations have continued to 'discover' this. The documentarians and avant-gardists of the 1920s shared a desire to explore more fully the capacities of film as a medium – to do what only film could do, or what only film could do best. They wanted to create films different from literary stories told through the theatrical means of actors and sets. They also agreed that the fiction film was telling lies about life. They did not agree on much else, however. For the documentarians, conventional fiction films were not realistic enough; for the avant-gardists, they were too realistic. For the most part the former wanted external (objective) facts, presented fully and accurately; the latter wanted formal (aesthetic) patterns and inner (subjective) truths, presented poetically.

The creative predilection of the documentarians extended out of the detailed verisimilitude the photographic image offered; the illusion of motion in the cinematographic image permitted the recording of yet more visible reality – more than was attainable through any other means of communication or form or art. With the motion picture, material and physical life could be captured as it was being lived, even more fully than still photography.

The avant-gardists, on the other hand, extended more out of emerging trends in design, architecture, poetry and painting. They valued the movement of the moving picture for allowing their visual imagery to become more complex and consistent with twentieth-century artistic and scientific conceptions of time as a fourth dimension. In addition, movement in time enabled the avant-gardists to follow the workings of the mind into dreams, hallucinations, fantasies, which jumble an incongruous succession of images in a stream of consciousness. Through film they could both present abstract patterns in motion and represent dream-like perceptions.

In the traditional arts the interrelationship of space and time was already being explored. In painting, Marcel Duchamp's 'Nude Descending a Staircase' (1912) offered an abstracted, stroboscopic view of a person and her activity. The practice of cubism, Pablo Picasso's 'The Violin' (1913), for instance, rests on the notion of an observer moving about to view a subject from various distances and angles; the separate views are then overlaid to try to suggest looking at the subject from different positions all at once. In literature, Marcel Proust, in his multi-volume *Remembrance of Things Past* (1919–1925), assumed that the past is always present, and that places experienced earlier join with places experienced later. James Joyce, in *Ulysses* (1922), intermingled what is happening to his characters in various parts of Dublin on 16 June 1904, cutting back and forth among them as a filmmaker would, trying to convey a sense of simultaneity and interaction of events and persons. The work of Vertov in 'Kino-Pravda' was rich in experimental design and the notion of placing self within film. The Dada and Surrealist movements with their emphasis on found objects, automatic writing, the importance of dreams, also found film to be a special medium. These last two movements in particular found their way into mainstream cinema.

Avant-Garde and Documentary

The first of the avant-garde films were along lines of abstraction and nonobjectivity. In 1921 two painter friends living in Berlin each began work on short films that might, aside from Vertov, be thought of as the beginning of avant-garde cinema. Influenced by such artistic movements as futurism and cubism, Viking Eggeling, a Swede, and Hans Richter, a German, had been attempting to bring a sense of motion approximating animation into their paintings. Their preoccupations led them from picture scrolls to the moving picture, and Richter's *Rhythmus 21* (1921) and Eggeling's *Diagonal Symphony* (1925) were the first results. 'Rhythm in painting' now painting on film is what they said they were after. Richter's film comprises an interacting set of square and rectangular shapes in white, gray and black; as they change sizes, they seem to be moving towards or away from the viewer. Eggeling's film consists of white abstractions shaped like lyres in shifting relationships with each other against a black screen. These two films might make one think of Piet Mondrian paintings in motion.

Some of Mondrian's nonrepresentational, geometric canvases resemble aerial photographs of a city taken from extremely high altitudes so that all we see is the grid of streets, a block of colour that may be a park, and so on. In 1921 two Americans, Charles Sheeler and Paul Strand – the first a painter, the second a photographer – made a film that offered a somewhat similar view of New York City: *Manhatta* (based on the Walt Whitman poem '*Mannahatta*'; the film version altered the spelling). In their *Manhatta*, shot mostly looking down from skyscrapers, the city becomes abstract. The streets and buildings appear as patterns of light and shadow. The people, flattened and seen at great distance, exist only as part of the design. Though shown little in the United States, *Manhatta* appeared in Paris in a Dadaist programme that included music by Erik Satie and poems by Guillaume Apollinaire. It was said to have received a shocked but enthusiastic ovation on that occasion. These films were an embryonic beginning of the 'city symphony', films that strongly link avant-garde with documentary, some experimental in intent. Very short actualities had been a staple of the earliest films, two notable examples being experimental or 'trick' films *Star Theater New York* (1901) and *Market Street San Francisco* (1906).

Another seminal film that could be added to the works of Richter, Eggeling, and Sheeler and Strand is one by the French painter Fernand Léger. With technical assistance from an American named Dudley Murphy, Léger made *Ballet Mécanique* (1924), exploring the rhythmic relationships of images in motion. In it, the capacity of film for mechanical repetition and its power to animate the inanimate (kitchen utensils, mannequin legs, Christmas ornaments, bottles, printed words, and geometric shapes) are strikingly exploited. Marcel Duchamp's *Anemic Cinema* (1926) is somewhat similar in its intentions. It was this type of filmmaking that led later into Len Lye's work in the UK and for the National Film Board of Canada, and to many experiments in graphics in motion.

The second line of avant-garde creation was inspired by psychoanalysis and Surrealism, with its preoccupations rooted in dream and the unconscious. In painting, Salvador Dalí, who subsequently worked occasionally and briefly in film, painted in the surrealist manner. This generally involved more or less realistic representations of objects and persons placed in strange juxtapositions with each other. In literature, Proust, though no surrealist, also relates to this psychoanalytic tendency, with the past affecting the present; as does Joyce, in *Ulysses*, especially in the use of stream of consciousness. In film, Luis Buñuel's and Salvador Dalí's *Un Chien Andalou* (1929), Buñuel's *L'Age d'or* (1930), and Jean Cocteau's *The Blood of a Poet* (1930) are celebrated examples of these dreamscapes. Freud's ideas about the unconscious were gaining public acceptance around this time, and the founders of the Surrealist movement were also deeply influenced by their traumatic experiences in WWI. This 'war to end all wars' was the first large-scale example of the horrors of highly mechanized warfare. It left these artists profoundly disturbed by its slaughter and violence.

Even in Rotha's realist (continental) precursors of documentary there is evidence of these two avant-garde styles. Abstraction appears in Joris Ivens' first significant film, *The Bridge* (1928). It is related to modernist movements such as cubism, futurism and constructivism. Like much of the later Vertov, whose work influenced Ivens, *The Bridge* converts machinery into art. Camera composition and movement, and edited relationships of shots are designed to bring out the functional and also aesthetic essence of an enormous railway bridge in Rotterdam. Few people appear in the film – a workman climbing a ladder and a bridge tender answering a phone and starting machinery that raises and lowers the bridge – and it ends with animated squares à la Richter's *Rhythmus 21*.

Surrealism is evident in Jean Vigo's *Jean Taris, champion de natation* (1931). This study of the aquatic style of a celebrated French swimmer is notable for its beautiful underwater cinematography in slow motion and a dive back out of the pool onto the diving board at the end. Jean Lods' *Le Mile* (1934), about a runner, employs 'ether music', slow motion, and superimpositions. Buñuel's *Land Without Bread* (1932) forces us to look at the devastating actuality, the poverty of the Las Hurdes region of Spain, in a way that might be described as having the intense irrational reality of a dream – that is, of being *sur*real. The mixture of 'real' and 'surreal' images makes this one of the more complex and fascinating avant-garde documentaries. It is also sometimes considered a beginning in 'reflexive' documentary – that is, narrative documentary in which the audience is made aware of the presence of the camera.

But it was a third line of avant-garde filmmaking, developing near the end of the twenties, that fed most directly into documentary. Its aesthetic *ism* was impressionism, and its origins went back to the French impressionists at the turn of the century. The style of impressionism also placed emphasis on the space/time relationship; impressionist painting was like looking at life from a

Fig 16 *A collage of images from* Berlin: Symphony of a Great City *(Germany, 1927, Walther Ruttmann). Museum of Modern Art Film Stills Archive*

fast-moving railway carriage, it had been said. (Of course, film provided this actual opportunity; see, for example, Jean Mitry's *Pacific 231* [1949], about a powerful locomotive rushing through the French countryside.)

The impressionist films resemble the paintings in their quick views and concentration on surfaces and light. What they offer mainly are collected glimpses of city life during a passage of time. Joyce's *Ulysses* might again be thought of as a literary precedent. Eisenstein wrote of that novel: 'What Joyce does with literature is quite close to what we're doing with the new cinematography, and even closer to what we're going to do.' He further said that if *Ulysses* were ever made into a film, the only men capable of directing it would be Walther Ruttmann or Sergei Eisenstein.

Ruttmann directed one of the early city symphonies, *Berlin: Symphony of a Great City* (1927). It was preceded slightly by *Rien que les heures/Only the Hours* (1926), about Paris, directed by Brazilian Alberto Cavalcanti. *Rain* (1929), Joris Ivens' film about Amsterdam, followed. What follows is an examination of these three seminal works: *Rien que les heures, Berlin, and Rain*. It must be acknowledged, however, that the line they started includes, among others, Jean Vigo's *À propos de Nice* (1930), a scathingly satirical study of the famous resort in the manner of Honoré Daumier paintings, Ralph Steiner's and Willard Van Dyke's *Manhatta*, Jay Leyda's *A Bronx Morning* (1931), Robert Flaherty's *The Twenty-four-Dollar Island* (1927), *The City* (US, 1939, to be dealt with in Chapter 6), Arne Sucksdorff's *Symphony of a City* (1947), about Stockholm, and John Eldridge's *Waverley Steps* (1948), about Edinburgh. Much later iterations of this mode came in Hilary Harris' *Organism* (1975) and Pat O'Neill's *Water and Power* (1989).

Three City Symphonies

Alberto Cavalcanti was a Brazilian emigré who became part of the Parisian avant-garde in the early 1920s. He began his film career as an innovative set designer for Marcel L'Herbier on such features as *L'Inhumaine* (1923), in collaboration with Fernand Léger, and *The Late Matthew Pascal* (1925), in collaboration with Lazare Meerson.

Rien que les heures is a curious and fascinating mixture of the aesthetic and the social. It deals with Paris from predawn to well into the following night – roughly twenty-four hours. Opening titles promise that we will not be looking at the elegant life but rather at that of the lower classes. Thus the social viewpoint is established. But a philosophical thesis concerning time and space is also introduced and reprised. At the conclusion of the film we are asked, after we have seen what the filmmaker has shown us of Paris, to consider simultaneously Paris in relation to Peking (Beijing). The titles assert that, though we can fix a point in space, arrest a moment in time, both space and time escape our possession – that life is ongoing and interrelated, and that, without their monuments, cities cannot be told apart.

The film is mainly devoted to contrasting scenes and changing activities of Paris during the passing hours. In early morning we see all-night revellers still out on deserted streets as well as the first workers on their way to work; later, workers are shown at labour; then lunchtime. In the afternoon some people are swimming; work ceases, rest and recreation occupy the evening. Among the views of unstaged actuality are brief, staged fragments. Three slight narratives are developed. The protagonists of all three are female – an old derelict (drunken or ill), a prostitute, a newspaper vendor – all of them pathetic figures. The overall mood of the film is a bit downbeat; there is a sweet sadness, a sentimental roughness about it.

Still, Cavalcanti's attitude may be one of detachment, perhaps cynicism: '*c'est la vie*', he seems to be saying. Though some attention to class distinctions and social matters is evident, the considerable number and variety of highly stylized special effects – wipes, rapid match dissolves, multiple exposures, fast motion, revolving images, split screens, freeze frames – seem to confirm that Cavalcanti's greatest interest was in artistic experimentation.

Like Cavalcanti, Walther Ruttmann came out of architecture and painting into avant-garde filmmaking in the early 1920s – specifically, in his case, to abstract, geometric forms in motion like those of his mentor, Viking Eggeling. A fascination with design is even more evident in *Berlin: Symphony of a Great City* than in *Rien que les heures*; and, incidentally, the former was released so soon after the latter that there can be little question of one influencing the other. Unlike *Rien*, *Berlin* emerged from mainstream commercial cinema. Produced for Fox-Europa Film, its scenario was written by Ruttmann and Karl Freund, based on an idea by Carl Mayer. (Mayer had written scripts for *The Cabinet of Dr Caligari* [1919], *The Last Laugh* [1924], *Tartuffe* [1925], and other notable German silent features.) The cinematography was supervised by Freund (who was director of photography on some of the great fiction films of the period including *The Golem* [1920], *The Last Laugh* [1924], *Variety* [1925], and *Metropolis* [1927]). Original music was composed by Edmund Meisel (who had created a famous score for the German exhibition of *Potemkin*). The editing was done by Ruttmann. Though the camerawork of *Berlin* is dazzling, it is above all an editor's film, and Ruttmann is credited as its director. We see Berlin, true enough, but it is Ruttmann's Berlin that we see.

The overall organizational basis is temporal; occasionally clocks show the time: 5:00, 8:00, 12:00. The major sequences comprise very early morning (the city coming to life), morning (work and general activity), lunchtime (eating and repose), afternoon (work ceases, recreation takes place), and evening (entertainment and various sorts of diversions). Intertitles indicate 'acts' up through four (though a fifth would seem to be intended), but they are much less clearly structured than the five acts of *Potemkin* or *Turksib*.

The criteria for selection and arrangement of material within these acts rest heavily on visual similarities and contrasts. Ruttmann is fascinated with the way things are shaped, the way they move. At any given time the organizing principle may be kinetic (things going up, things coming down; things opening, things closing) or shapes that look alike (people in a crowd walking, a herd of cattle moving, a troop of soldiers marching).

There are also topical groupings: workers going to work; children going to school; women cleaning and scrubbing; the various means of transportation; people eating lunch; animals feeding at the zoo. The pattern for each scene or subsection within the major sequences/acts is frequently that of an activity starting, increasing in tempo, then coming to a halt. The people are treated much as the objects; both are subjects for visual examination.

Some of the action is staged: a group of merrymakers in the early morning returning from a party; an argument between two men which attracts a group of watchers; a woman jumping from a bridge to drown, apparently. But mostly life is caught unawares. Much influenced by Vertov, Ruttmann did not follow Vertov's dictum about advancing a social point of view, though at the time he was identified with the political left.

In *Berlin* the rich and powerful are seen in contrast to members of the working classes, although no social comment is inferred. Much less attention is paid to individual persons in *Berlin* than in 'Kino-Pravda'. Machines are as important for Ruttmann as they are for the Soviets, but in *Berlin* they are not shown to have social utility as they are in *Turksib*. Instead, they exist as fascinating, intricate, moving objects. The film's opening proceeds from abstractions of water to what look like polarized images of fast-moving locomotive wheels and railroad tracks, beginning a protracted, elaborately cut evocation of a train's early morning approach to a Berlin terminus, which climaxes in a huge closeup of one of the engine's now stationary piston wheels after its arrival. Later, the image of a typewriter keyboard is set spinning and metamorphoses into a whirling animated design. *Berlin* strikes some viewers as brilliant and cold, an exercise in cinematic virtuosity.

The exclusively aesthetic concentration of Ruttmann represented a severe limitation, not only from the Soviet point of view but from that of subsequent British documentarians. Yet, *Berlin* may have more value as a *document* than do those *documentary* films made with more explicit social biases and programmes. Though composed according to artistic insights and intuitions and the requirements of form, what it offers essentially is a visual description. From this film we can learn a great deal about the appearance of life in Berlin in 1927.

Joris Ivens, like Louis Lumière, came out of the photographic business. His grandfather was a pioneer Dutch photographer; his father owned a chain of camera shops. After serving an apprenticeship at the Zeiss camera factories in Germany, Ivens returned to Holland in 1926 to become manager of his father's Amsterdam branch. His *Rain* (1929) and *The Bridge* (1928) are shorts (both run 10 to 15 minutes) and unlike *Rien* or *Berlin*, which are short features (45 and 70 minutes, respectively). Perhaps *Rain* is a city sonata. It presents Amsterdam just before, during, and immediately after a shower. Ivens' play with light and shadow and the compositional relationships of shots becomes much more important than in *The Bridge*. *Rain* is impressionist rather than cubist; lyrical rather than analytical. Its shapes and textures tend to be round and soft rather than straight and hard. It seems a very tactile film.

The film begins with shots of canals and harbour, roofs, sky, an airplane, streetcar and traffic, sheets hanging on clothes lines, and awnings. The first person we see extends his hand, palm up, to feel raindrops, then turns up his coat collar. An umbrella is opened; a window is closed. Throughout, Ivens seems to be asking us to examine images in everyday life – rain on

Fig 17 *A youthful Joris Ivens with editing equipment used at the time. Museum of Modern Art Film Stills Archive*

windshields, puddles in streets, umbrellas, reflections – to see the 'artistic' in the actual. Fernand Léger once observed that before the invention of the moving picture no one knew the possibilities latent in a foot, a hand, or a hat. Ivens makes something as commonplace as an umbrella or a bare window a thing of uncommon loveliness and significance.

The career of one of documentary's most brilliant early editors was launched in Ivens' shadow. Helen Van Dongen was also born in Holland. In her teens, she held a job with the firm owned by the father of Joris Ivens. She became deeply involved in Ivens' work, and with him. Her first screen credit came in 1931 with Ivens' *Phillips Radio*, although she worked uncredited on some of his earlier projects. She also studied in Russia with Eisenstein, Vertov and Pudvkin, and presumably with Esther Shub and Svilova, as did Ivens.

After moving to the US with Ivens, who soon abandoned her for another woman, she directed a Technicolor experimental film with stop-motion puppets for the 1939 New York World's Fair. Later during World War II she worked on films for both the Army Signal Corps and the Office of War Information. Other notable contributions were the editing of Ivens' *The 400*

Fig 18 Rain *(Holland, 1929, Joris Ivens). Museum of Modern Art Film Stills Archive*

Million (1938), about the Japanese invasion of China, and their last project together, *Power And The Land* (1941). Two remarkable collaborations editing with Robert Flaherty resulted in *The Land* and *Louisiana Story*. When the latter moved to the scoring stage Van Dongen supervised the music with its composer Virgil Thompson and Flaherty. *Louisiana Story* won the only Pulitzer Prize ever given for music. These films are discussed in later chapters.

Changes in the Avant-Garde

The energy of the first wave of film avant-garde diminished soon, in part because of the expense, complexity and cumbersomeness that sound added to the motion picture in the late 1920s. It was no longer easy for individuals or intimate groups of friends to shoot on weekends, registering images as they found or created them, cutting them together in the evenings using only a pair of rewinds and a splicer, and screening the completed film at a local ciné-club. Now the big studios, with sound stages and synchronous sound recording apparatus, exercised complete domination, and not only over production, but over distribution and exhibition as well.

Perhaps at least as contributive to this decline of the avant-garde were changing intellectual and artistic interests and attitudes. If the twenties were 'roaring' and frivolous, they also nurtured aesthetic innovation. The notion of art for the sake of art, with emphasis on formal experimentation, prevailed in influential circles. The intellectual preoccupations during the worldwide depression of the thirties, in contrast, were markedly social and political. This decade included not only depression, but also the rise of fascism, and other misfortunes that culminated in a second world war. In the thirties, art for the sake of society became a rallying cry, and the documentary film replaced the avant-garde film at the centre of intellectual and artistic life in a number of countries.

Before making *Rain*, Joris Ivens had been involved in the politics of the international student movement and had participated in workers' demonstrations, which strengthened his leftward leanings. In his subsequent films Ivens moved away from formal experimentation towards social problems posed in a realistic style. In 1929 and 1932 he visited the Soviet Union. From that point on his films would be made in support of projects on the political left. His work will be encountered again in subsequent chapters.

Ruttmann, too, moved from the avant-garde to the political, but in a different direction. In the late 1930s he lent his talents to the Nazi propaganda ministry. He served as adviser to Leni Riefenstahl on the editing of her massive *Olympia* (1938), which celebrated the Olympic games held in Berlin in 1936, the subtext of which supported certain aspects of Nazi mythology. In 1940 Ruttmann made *Deutsche Panzer* (German Tanks) and recorded on film the German occupation of France. The following year he was killed while covering the Russian front for a newsreel. Both brought to this later work the same artistic sensibilities as they did to their private projects.

Of the three city-symphonists, Alberto Cavalcanti is the most neatly symbolic figure of transition. He moved from the French avant-garde of the 1920s to the British documentary of the 1930s. Cavalcanti's documentary work is dealt with in the next chapter.

In its time, the emerging British documentary was considered avant-garde too, and included experimentation with new forms and techniques as well as with new subjects and purposes. If it is thought of as an artistic movement (as it can be), British documentary is remarkable within the history of twentieth-century art movements for lasting some twenty years, its influence spreading internationally and extending down to this day. The formal experimentation was encouraged partly to attract artistically talented young persons to documentary filmmaking, and partly to find ways in which social arguments could be made most appealing and persuasive. British documentary continued the avant-garde experimentation with shapes in movement, and the emphasis of the Soviets and their fascination with machines continued in Britain. Such experimentation was most evident in the works of Humphrey Jennings (the surrealist influence) and Len Lye (the abstract). The documentary avant-garde also grew in the United States during the 1920s and 30s but eventually the two forms took largely separate paths there.

Chapter Related Films

1921
Manhatta (US, Charles Sheeler and Paul Strand)
1926
Melody of the World (Germany, Walther Ruttmann)
Rien que les heures (France, Alberto Cavalcanti)
1927
Berlin: Symphony of a Great City (Germany, Ruttmann)
The Bridge (Netherlands, Joris Ivens)
1928
La Tour (The Eiffel Tower, France, René Clair)
1929
The Man with a Movie Camera (USSR, Dziga Vertov)
Rain (Netherlands, Ivens)
1931
A Bronx Morning (US, Jay Leyda)

Chapter Related Books

Aitkin, Ian, *Alberto Cavalcanti: Realism, Surrealism and National Cinemas*. Trowbridge, Wilts: Flicks Books, 2000.

Bakker, Kees, ed., *Joris Ivens and the Documentary Context*. Ann Arbor: University of Michigan Press, 2000.

Böker, Carlos, *Joris Ivens, Film-Maker: Facing Reality*. Ann Arbor, MI: UMI Research Press, 1981.

Delmar, Rosalind, *Joris Ivens: 50 years of filmmaking*. London: British Film Institute, 1970.

Ivens, Joris, *Joris Ivens: The Camera and I*. New York: International Publishers, 1969.

Manvell, Roger, ed., *Experiment in the Film*. London: Grey Walls Press, 1949.

Rees, A. L., *A History of Experimental Film and Video*. London: British Film Institute, 1999.

5

Institutionalization: Great Britain, 1929–1939

While documentary filmmaking was beginning in the 1920s – in America with films about tribal societies (*Nanook of the North* and *Grass*); in the Soviet Union with indoctrinational newsreels ('Kino-Pravda') and compilation films and epics (*The Fall of the Romanov Dynasty* and *Turksib*); and in Western Europe with the city symphonies (*Rien que les heures* and *Berlin: Symphony of a Great City*) – the conceptual origins of British documentary were also being formulated, but not exactly in Britain, and not in film. John Grierson later remarked that 'The idea of documentary in its present form came originally not from the film people at all, but from the Political Science school in Chicago University round about the early twenties.'

Background and Underpinnings

Grierson, founder and leader of the British documentary movement, was a Scot. Born in 1898 and raised near Stirling, he was strongly influenced from an early age by the Scottish labour movement emanating from the working-class district along the Clyde river in Glasgow. Most of World War I he spent in the Navy. When he was mustered out in 1919 he entered Glasgow University with other returning veterans.

Upon graduation in 1923 Grierson taught briefly in Newcastle-on-Tyne. While there he obtained a Rockefeller fellowship to pursue graduate research into public opinion and the mass media in the United States. He set sail for America in 1924. He had chosen the University of Chicago as his base because of its distinguished social science faculty. He also knew and admired the work of Chicago writers such as Sherwood Anderson, Ben Hecht and Carl Sandburg. He was fascinated by the newness and originality of American culture, and by the ways in which Europeans were being changed into Americans.

This assimilation of the foreign-born into American culture, and the role the popular press played in their education, occupied much of Grierson's attention. He spent more time on Halsted Street, with its polyglot population of Germans, Italians, Greeks, Russians and Poles, than on the Midway campus of the university, he liked to say. As Grierson came to understand the matter, the tabloid newspapers – the Hearst press, and its imitators – provided more of these immigrants' education into citizenship than did the schools, churches, or government.

A book that strongly influenced his thinking at the time was Walter Lippmann's *Public Opinion*, published in 1922. In it Lippmann described how the earlier ideals of Jeffersonian democracy had been rendered inoperative. Originally the Virginia gentleman sitting on his veranda reading the two-week-old newspaper brought by packet from Philadelphia could make up his mind about the issues facing the nation and vote for a candidate running for public office who would represent his views. Since that time, government had become big, distant and complex. The citizen, feeling he could not keep abreast of the information necessary to participate in the decision-making process, had dissociated himself from government. Lippmann thought education was the only solution to the problem, but that it was too late for it to take effect in time to keep the democratic system viable. Grierson postulated that what was needed was to involve citizens in their government with the kind of engaging excitement generated by the popular press, which simplified and dramatized public affairs. As he travelled around the country, Grierson eventually met Lippmann. It was Lippmann, Grierson frequently acknowledged, who suggested to him that, rather than the press, he look into the movies. Perhaps they were the form best suited to turn citizens' attention to the decisions that needed to be made in common, and to provide them with a basic education in the factors to be considered.

Clearly the entertainment film was not readily available for these purposes; two filmmakers and films not part of the Hollywood industry suggested to Grierson a way to harness the motion picture to the job of educating citizens. One filmmaker was Sergei Eisenstein. Though Grierson would not meet Eisenstein until a few years later, he did gain intimate knowledge of and respect for *Battleship Potemkin* (1925) by helping prepare it for American release. The other filmmaker, Robert Flaherty, Grierson met sometime in 1925. It was to Flaherty's second film, *Moana* (1926), that he first applied the term *documentary*.

When Grierson returned to England in 1927 he approached another man who would become enormously important in the development of the documentary film: Stephen Tallents, Secretary of the Empire Marketing Board (EMB). The EMB had been established in 1926 to promote the marketing of products of the British Empire and to encourage research and development among the member states. The broader purpose implicit from the outset was to substitute for the decaying military and political ties of empire the economic ones of a commonwealth of nations. Tallents saw quickly that the motion picture might be a valuable tool in this unique new governmental public relations endeavour, and that Grierson was exceptionally well qualified to initiate its use.

The System

Empire Marketing Board

Following Grierson's research into film activities of other governments and screening films for EMB, he and Tallents succeeded in talking the Department of Treasury into funding production of a film by the Empire Marketing Board. *Drifters* (1929) was the result, written, produced, directed and edited by Grierson. A short feature in length, it dealt with herring fishing in the North Sea. Rather than follow its substantial success with another and then another film of his own, Grierson chose to establish a collective filmmaking enterprise, a sort of workshop and schoolhouse, out of which the British documentary movement would emerge.

Fig 19 Drifters, *Grierson's first film (UK, 1929, John Grierson). Museum of Modern Art Film Stills Archive*

In 1930 the Empire Marketing Board Film Unit was established, with Grierson as its head. During the four years of its existence it made over one hundred films. Grierson's catchphrase for what the EMB films were designed to do was 'To bring the Empire alive'. He pursued this purpose by showing one and then another part of the Empire (one region of Britain, one of its colonies, one of its industries) to the rest. He hoped that films of this sort would help citizens of the Empire to more fully understand and appreciate each other, to perceive their interdependencies and value them, and to create a more coherent civic whole.

In the production of the EMB films Grierson involved dozens of young people, mostly upper middle-class and well-educated (many at Cambridge University), who were used to being listened to, as Grierson once put it. They learned not only filmmaking but also the sort of social commitment that motivated Grierson. What he wanted films to do was to make the state and the society function better. He thought that collective effort, cooperation and understanding could lead to a better world – not only better food and better housing, better teeth and better schools, but a better spirit – a sense of being part of a valuable society with space still left for individual satisfactions and eccentricities.

Those who came through this informal but rigorous schooling at the Empire Marketing Board included, roughly in the order of their hiring, Basil Wright, Paul Rotha, Arthur Elton, Edgar Anstey and Stuart Legg. Harry Watt came later, as did Humphrey Jennings. Alberto Cavalcanti joined the group as a sort of co-producer and co-teacher with Grierson. They were paid so little it was laughable (or perhaps weepable) at the time, but they were all caught up in the excitement of art put to social use. Each had special talents and interests: Wright's were poetic, Elton's technological and scientific, Legg's political, and so on. After absorbing what Grierson had to offer and developing deep and lasting loyalties to his causes and to himself, they could – and did – move out into the world filming for other sponsors, forming other units, training other filmmakers, while still working in common cause.

As well as creating filmmakers, Grierson was also concerned with creating audiences for his kind of film. Though documentaries were sometimes shown in theatres, theatrical showings were limited. The film industry resisted government filmmaking; distributors and exhibitors said the public didn't want documentaries. In answer, Grierson developed a method of nontheatrical distribution and exhibition. In order to build audience support, film critics on the major papers were recruited in behalf of the movement and Grierson and his colleagues wrote and lectured tirelessly. They were instrumental in founding and guiding three successive journals – *Cinema Quarterly*, *World Film News*, and *Documentary News Letter* – which served as house organs for the documentary.

If Grierson did not do it all himself, it was mainly his leadership and his manifold activities that brought British documentary into being and caused it to grow in its influence. The movement developed a powerful, coherent energy, with Grierson able to direct, to a remarkable extent, the uses to which that energy was put.

General Post Office

In 1933, at the depth of the Depression, the Empire Marketing Board was terminated on grounds of necessary government economy. Tallents moved to the General Post Office as its first public relations officer, on condition that he could bring the EMB Film Unit and the Empire Film Library with him.

A vast enterprise, the GPO handled not only the mail but the telephone, wireless broadcasting, a savings bank, and a whole host of government services. Here the subjects of the films were reduced from the exoticism and drama inherent in the far-flung reaches of empire available at the Empire Marketing Board to such subjects as the picayune detail of mail delivery (*Six-Thirty Collection* [1934]; *Night Mail* [1936]). 'One remembers looking at a sorting office for the first time,' wrote Grierson, 'and thinking that when you had seen one letter you had seen the lot.'

Designed to increase respect for the work of the GPO, by the population at large and by the GPO workers themselves, one approach the GPO Film Unit took to fulfil its obligations to its new sponsor was to stress the fact that post office services provided the means of modern communication. And some drama was found, though occasionally by stretching beyond what might properly be seen as post office concerns (*The Song of Ceylon* [1934]; *Coal Face* [1935]). Out of the more than one hundred films made by the General Post Office Film Unit came some lovely and lasting ones. Major British documentaries of the thirties will be discussed shortly.

Private Sponsorship

Growing restive within the constraints of government budgets and departmental requirements, Grierson began to reach out to private industry as an additional source of funding. He must have been remarkably persuasive in talking industrial leaders into taking his own broad view. Not only did he find sponsors, he convinced them to eschew advertising in favour of backing films in the public interest – that is to say, films whose subjects Grierson thought needed attention. The oil industry was especially receptive. Out of a report he made for Shell International on the potential uses of film came the

Shell Film Unit, highly regarded for its films on scientific and technological subjects. Edgar Anstey was first head of the Shell Unit. He was succeeded by Arthur Elton, who maintained a career-long connection with films sponsored by the oil industry, and developed great skill as a maker of expository films on technical subjects. Grierson also succeeded in getting the gas industry to back an annual film programme. The resulting group of films were intended to increase general awareness of problems of pressing concern, to provoke discussion of them, and to suggest attitudes that might contribute to their solutions (*Housing Problems* [1935]; *Enough to Eat?* [1936]).

With documentary growing apace, private units were being formed by alumni of the EMB and GPO units to make films for the emerging non-government sponsors. In 1937 Grierson resigned from the GPO to set up a central coordinating and advisory agency to put sponsors in touch with producers (and the other way around), oversee production, plan promotion and distribution, and the like. Film Centre was the organization he, with Arthur Elton and Stuart Legg, established for that purpose in 1938.

The British system of documentary financing, production and distribution became a model for subsequent developments in other countries. Many foreign visitors came to London to look into this new use of film – especially from the commonwealth nations and the colonies – and in 1937 Paul Rotha went on a six-month missionary expedition to the United States to show British documentaries and spread the documentary gospel. At the New York World's Fair of 1939 British documentaries were shown to sizeable audiences with evident success. One consequence of this exposure was the beginning of an association of documentary-makers in the US.

The Films

Some sixty filmmakers working within what is here called the British documentary system made over three hundred films between 1929 and 1939. Three main lines of subject/purpose/style emerged roughly in the order in which they are dealt with below. First, following *Drifters* (1929), were the documentaries which undertook to interpret one part of the Empire – or one region of Britain, one of its industries, or one of the government services – to the population at large. Often poetic and experimental, this group included such films as *Industrial Britain* (1933), *Granton Trawler* (1934), *The Song of Ceylon* (1934), and *Coal Face* (1935).

Drifters, Grierson's first film, was the only one of the hundreds of films with which he was associated in one way or another that he completely controlled creatively. It has a simple narrative structure. The herring fishermen board their trawlers in the harbour, sail to the North Sea banks, lay the nets, haul in the fish in the midst of a storm, and race homeward to auction the catch at the quayside. Rather than evidence of creative genius, it more nearly represents the work of a brilliant synthesist who had absorbed what was at hand to make the kind of film he wanted to see made. In it are reflections of Flaherty's *Nanook of the North*, with brave men eking out their existence in the face of the elements. Eisenstein's *Battleship Potemkin* is even more heavily called upon. In *Drifters*, the loving long takes of a Flaherty are cut up and banged together in Eisensteinian montage to provide a modern dynamism, and the individual accomplishments of Nanook are replaced by the collective efforts of a crew, as in *Potemkin*. It is unlike both sources in certain respects, however. Instead of the exotics of Flaherty or the heroics of the Soviets, the drama of *Drifters* is in the everyday workaday. By ending the film with the fish being sold at market, Grierson sets the fishermen's work firmly within the context of economic actualities of contemporary Britain. It was an unusual, perhaps unique, instance in British cinema up to that point in which work had been given this sort of importance, and members of the working class presented with dignity rather than as comic relief.

Industrial Britain establishes its thesis at the outset: though traditional ways of work have changed over the centuries, the success of British industry rests on the skill of its craftsmen. 'The human fact remains, even in this machine age, the final fact,' the commentator intones. To produce it, at the urging of Frances, Robert Grierson invited Flaherty to England. Though given a lot of film, Flaherty shot it all on the lovely images of traditional craftsmen (glass blowers) and ancient crafts (pottery). The individual faces and gestures that appear ('Look at those hands', exclaims the commentator) are like *Moana* in fragments. Then an intertitle in large letters, STEEL, advances towards us, accompanied by portentous music. This unexpectedly announces what becomes in effect a separate film, making the point of bigness, collectivity, and internationalization – clearly Grierson's contribution. If *Industrial Britain* represents the contrast between these two filmmakers' approaches, the commentator's stilted delivery and the clichéd stock music (including bits of Beethoven) are at odds with both. It was made before the film unit had its own sound recording facilities. Nonetheless *Industrial Britain*, along with *Drifters,* was one of the most successful and generally liked film to come out of the Empire Marketing Board.

The Song of Ceylon, Basil Wright the principal creator, is one of the accepted masterpieces of documentary. Sponsored by the Ceylon Tea Propaganda Board (Ceylon today is Sri Lanka), it is first of all remarkable in being so fully and freely a work of art while doing so little to sell the sponsor's product, perhaps even subverting their main goals. It may be even more remarkable, within the body of early British documentary, as a highly personal work which, furthermore, emphasizes matters of the spirit. It is a moving hymn to a native people, their work, their ways, and their values in conflict with imposed requirements of modern commerce. Though it contains exquisite images of a golden time and place, not unlike those of Flaherty's Samoa in *Moana*, Wright's discovered Eden has a discordant note accompanying it. Song of Ceylon remains a major film, a complex and sophisticated artwork in both form and content.

The commentary is drawn from a 1680 book on Ceylon by the traveller Robert Knox. It provides an appreciative description of traditional life, which we see and also hear in reverberating gongs, native music and rhythmic chanting to the dancing. In the third sequence, entitled 'The Voices of Commerce', the discord erupts. Images of the indigenous and traditional are here accompanied by deep whistles of seagoing freighters, Morse code beeping on the wireless, English voices dictating business letters and listing stock market quotations. This medley of sound, plus a musical score suggesting an Eastern modality composed and conducted by Walter Leigh, was supervised by Cavalcanti. In addition to Wright's principal role, Leigh, Cavalcanti and Grierson, to one extent or another, were all involved in the creation of the whole, which can astonish and delight audiences as much today as it did when first shown.

Fig 20 The Song of Ceylon, *Wright's account of the culture in the country now called Sri Lanka, is a work of art that perhaps subverts the sponsor's intended purposes (U.K., 1934, Basil Wright). Museum of Modern Art Film Stills Archive*

Coal Face, mainly Cavalcanti's creation, continued the formal experimentation with sound in relation to sight, though this time as an exalted tribute to the lives of British miners. Added to Grierson and Cavalcanti on its crew were the poet W. H. Auden and the composer Benjamin Britten, who worked together and separately on subsequent documentaries. *Coal Face* is an evocative combination of factual information laid over haunting images drawn from the coal-mining regions, of harsh modern music with piano and percussion prominent, of choral speech which at one point ascends into a kind of keening, and of snatches of miners' talk and whistling. The drabness and hardship that mark the men's lives are evident, along with their resilience, courage, and dignity – all heightened by the poetry of Auden recited and sung by a women's chorus. Though the commentary ends with the statement 'Coal mining is the basic industry of Britain', the last images we see are of an individual miner walking against a background of mining village and pithead at evening.

Fig 21 Coal Face *(UK, 1935, Alberto Cavalcanti). At a time when coal mining was the basic industry of Britain, Brazilian-born Cavalcanti offers a sense of the lives dependent on the mines in an experimentation of sight and sound*

The second line of British documentary, which began in the mid-thirties, consisted of calling public attention to pressing problems faced by the nation; of insistence that these problems needed to be solved; and of suggestions about their causes and possible solutions. Such matters sometimes involved differing political positions and in any case did not relate directly to the concerns of the Post Office. These were the films for which Grierson stepped outside the GPO to enlist sponsorship from large private industries. The subjects included slums (*Housing Problems* [1935]), malnutrition among the poor (*Enough to Eat?* [1936]), air pollution (*The Smoke Menace* [1937]), and the shortcomings of public education (*Children at School* [1937]). They consisted of reportage and argument. Making much use of stock shots and newsreel footage, they were given coherence and rhetorical effectiveness through editing and voiceover commentary.

Unlike the earlier British documentaries, these films are journalistic rather than poetic – they seem quite inartistic, in fact – yet they incorporate formal and technical experiments. Most notable among these is the direct interview – with slum dwellers in *Housing Problems*, for example – presaging the much later cinéma vérité method. Sponsored by the British Commercial Gas Association, *Housing Problems* was made by Arthur Elton, Edgar Anstey, John Taylor and Ruby Grierson (John's youngest sister). It begins by presenting the problems and what they look like – 'a typical interior of a decayed house' – with a housing expert commenting (voiceover) on how badly the housing functions. Then the film commentator (also voiceover) says 'And now for the people who have to live in the slums'. The man we see observes that where he lives they 'haven't room to swing a cat around' and describes how uncomfortable and unhealthy his apartment is; two of his children have died. A Mrs. Hill tells us 'the vermin in the walls is wicked [shots of cockroaches crawling on walls are cut in] and I tell ye we're fed up!' The use of commentary by the subjects without a narrator or interviewer and looking directly was a new concept.

The commentator says: 'The more enlightened public authorities have been applying themselves to clearing away slums with energy.' We see models of new types of housing, one of them of a development at Leeds. 'And now let's have a word with Mrs Reddington' who is living in one of the new housing developments. She tells us how pleased her family is with their new quarters; they especially like the new bathroom. Set forth in this bald way *Housing Problems* may not seem the innovation it in fact was. Its combination of voiceover housing authority and film commentator with onscreen interviews, of stock footage with models and fresh-shot material, established the basic format and technique of much later television documentary. The spoken word is used to provide information and analysis and to allow people to reveal themselves more fully and colourfully than was altogether possible in silent film. The intentions of *Housing Problems,* and certainly its effect, are quite different from those of *Nanook*.

Released shortly after *Housing Problems,* it was *Night Mail* (1936) that started the third trend: the narrative. Cavalcanti and Harry Watt were the leaders in this new tendency. Watt would go on in a direct line of increasing narrative elements. In *The Saving of Bill Blewitt* (1937) he shaped documentary ingredients of location shooting, nonactors and sponsor's

Fig 22 Housing Problems *(UK, 1935, Arthur Elton and Edgar Anstey). Museum of Modern Art Film Stills Archive*

message into plot, character and theme. With *North Sea* (1938) he reached a peacetime height in realistic use of story. This line led directly to the wartime British semidocumentary feature, a fusion of fact and fiction. Essentially a contribution of the 1940s, it is dealt with in Chapter Seven. Judging from the evidence of Watt's subsequent films, it is his directorial style that is dominant in *Night Mail*, though he shares director's credit with Basil Wright.

Night Mail is the most celebrated of Watt's pre-war films and one of the most famous in all documentary. Following the passage of a postal train from London to Glasgow, it is a prime example of 'drama on the doorstep', to use the Grierson phrase – everyday and close to home, yet engaging and lasting. It may be the ultimate blend of Grierson's ethic (social purposes) and aesthetic (formal properties). In any case, it is a paradigm of propaganda so intertwined with art that the viewer experiences pleasure while absorbing the message (painlessly, effortlessly, and probably even unconsciously). What this film is

Fig 23 Night Mail *1936 by Basil Wright and Harry Watt. The film documents the run of the night postal train from London to Glasgow. It may be the finest example of Grierson's ethic (social purpose) and aesthetic (formal properties). British Film Institute*

saying is simply that: (1) mail delivery is a large and complicated undertaking requiring the attention of the national government on behalf of all of us; (2) this government service is a splendid thing involving speed, efficiency, and intricate processes faultlessly learned and carefully regulated; and (3) the government employees who perform these multifarious and interesting tasks for us are a pretty good bunch – patient and caring, but not without an occasional irritability or a little joke.

Within this slight odyssey of a working journey, expository and poetic sequences alternate. The poetic interpolations include the rhythmic montage of mailbags being discharged and picked up by the speeding train, and the climb up into Scotland, 'Past cotton grass and moorland boulder, shovelling white steam over her shoulder'. These latter words are from bits of verse written by Auden. (Grierson himself speaks two sections after the train enters

Scotland, including the final one; Stuart Legg speaks the rest.) As in *Coal Face*, the words are combined with music by Britten; sound supervision is again by Cavalcanti. Interlaced with the very young Auden's poetry is a factual, statistical commentary, as if from the General Post Office itself, and the dialogue of the postal workers' conversations with each other while doing their jobs. This melange of sound, almost as diverse in its components and complex in its assemblage as that of *The Song of Ceylon*, accompanies the visuals in a manner that makes *Night Mail* a lively and seemingly effortless description and explanation of the workings of the postal train on its nightly run.

Grierson and Flaherty

In eighteenth-century England the essayist Joseph Addison, in his *Lives of the Poets*, complimented Alexander Pope by observing of his poetry: 'New things are made familiar, and familiar things are made new.' In the films of Robert Flaherty it seems clear that he was attempting to make the unfamiliar familiar; to discover and reveal, as he put it, what was distant and past. In the films produced under John Grierson, on the other hand, the attempt was to find new meanings and excitements in the familiar through applying the creative treatment of actuality, as Grierson said, to the close-to-home workaday modern world. Flaherty and Grierson represent two poles in the documentary tradition between which any documentary filmmaker still has to find a place. Incidentally, both men – the Irish-American, whom Grierson once described as 'a sort of handsome blond gorilla', and the small wiry Scot – had considerable personal magnetism and charm. How extraordinary, yet somehow appropriate, that these two should have become friends and antagonists, loving each other while hating each other's ideas. Their archetypal arguments were carried on in long evenings of talk and drink on what Grierson once described as 'a dialectical pub crawl across half the world'.

Flaherty, the artist, was a practical man in many ways. Determined and persuasive, he could talk big business and big government into financing his artistic statements. His concern was with showing the world as he saw it, which is one way of understanding the artist's job; it is sometimes argued to be the only thing the artist should be expected to do. The artwork may lead to social change but it is not created to effect that end. So it was with Flaherty. Grierson, for his part, said: 'I look on cinema as a pulpit, and use it as a propagandist.' He was, however, an extremely discerning and sophisticated propagandist who realized the utility of beauty in selling ideas – and recognized it when he saw it, incidentally. He early wrote about painting and his reviews of fiction films are exceptionally perceptive, well-informed and articulate, including especially those of popular Hollywood features. His own filmmaking, however, was primarily concerned with social engineering – with making the institutions of society function better on behalf of all of us – and he used every means available, including art, to achieve that end. Artistic creativity in British documentary of the 1930s appeared mainly when it could contribute emotional depth to intellectual argument.

Grierson's goals were always social, economic and political. He saw British documentary from the beginning as an anti-aesthetic movement. Art for him was 'the by-product of a job of work done'; not beauty as good in itself, or aesthetic experience as enriching and broadening. Nor was he much interested in documentaries that offered information or insights along with beauties, which, while they may have contributed to sympathetic understanding, did not attempt to lead the viewers to action.

Perhaps an understanding of the fundamental aesthetical divergence between the Flaherty and Grierson positions can be amplified by a short quotation from Frances Flaherty, acting as her husband's medium, summing up the relationship between Flaherty and himself as he saw it. Here is Mrs Flaherty:

> A Flaherty film is not a documentary, because a documentary film is preconceived. The great documentary movement fathered by John Grierson is all preconceived for educational and social purposes. Hollywood preconceives for the box office. None of these is simply and purely, freely and spontaneously, the thing itself, for its own sake. In other words he had no axe to grind.

It is interesting, of course, that the films of the man frequently called the father of documentary are dissociated from that mode altogether by Mrs Flaherty.

Like Flaherty, who had been a geologist and explorer, Grierson came to film from another field: social science. Whereas Flaherty wanted to use film to discover and reveal little-known people and places, Grierson wanted to use it to enlighten and shape the modern, complex, industrialized society in which he lived. Flaherty was a highly personal filmmaker who worked alone initially and always attempted to control every phase of the production of his few films. Grierson, who directed only one film himself, established documentary units within which dozens of others were created. In *Industrial Britain* (1933), the credits for which read 'Production Grierson-Flaherty', Flaherty came into brief contact with the early stage of British documentary. Then he went his individual way to make *Man of Aran* (1934) – a project Grierson helped set up, incidentally – leaving Grierson to the production and supervision of a host of other documentaries.

Grierson's Contribution

It is for his multifaceted, innovative leadership that Grierson is to be most valued. As a theoretician he articulated a basis for the documentary film, its form and function, its aesthetic and its ethic. As an informal teacher he trained and, through his writing and speaking, influenced many documentary filmmakers, not just in Britain but throughout the world. As a producer he was eventually responsible to one extent or another for thousands of films, and played a decisive creative role in some of the most important of them. And for most of his professional life he was an adroit political figure and dedicated civil servant. Even when not on government payroll, his central concern was always with communicating to the people of a nation and of the world the information and attitudes he thought would help them lead more useful and productive, more satisfying and rewarding lives.

More than any other person, Grierson was responsible for the documentary film as it developed in the English-speaking countries. The use of institutional sponsorship, public and private, to pay for his kind of filmmaking, rather than dependence on returns from the box office, was one key innovation. A second, which complemented the first, was nontheatrical distribution and exhibition

– going outside the movie theatres to reach audiences in schools and factories, union halls and church basements, and eventually on television.

The three hundred or so British documentaries made during the ten years between *Drifters* and Grierson's departure for Canada in 1939 and the system that spawned them became models for other countries. If many of those films were dull and transient in their significance (only the exceptions have been dealt with here), such an opinion would not have disturbed Grierson. His strategy involved a steady output of short films presenting a consistent social view. Each film dealt with a small piece of the larger argument. It may seem ironic that conservative institutions were talked into paying for what was overall and essentially the presentation of a socialist point of view, but the desperateness of the economic situation during the Depression had to be acknowledged even by the Tories in power. Perhaps the subject matter of the films about work and workers that Grierson talked them into sponsoring was, or was made to seem, obligatory.

The attitudes of those films were always positive; problems could be solved by combined goodwill and social action. Though never acknowledged publicly, it seems to be true that the films were seen mostly by middle and upper classes rather than by the working classes whom they were mostly about. Opinion leaders were thus reached who may have been persuaded, or at least encouraged, by the films to take a Griersonian view of the world.

One of the requisites for the success of the Grierson enterprise was the notion of consensus. The documentary films did not advance partisan political positions; they stayed within what the two major political parties, Conservative and Labour, might agree upon. Nor did the documentary filmmakers attach themselves publicly to a political party. At the same time, the subjects and viewpoints evident in the steady flow may have contributed to some extent to the sweeping Labour victory in 1945, at the end of the war.

In any case, Grierson once hinted that he thought documentaries of the thirties had helped prepare the British people for the collective strength soon to be required of them in wartime. Perhaps without the documentary movement there might have been responses other than the heroic national effort that began once the bombs started to fall. Before dealing with World War II in Britain, however, let's have a look at the parallel, if ultimately contrasting, documentary development in the United States during the 1930s.

Chapter Related Films

1929
Drifters (John Grierson)
1933
Aero-Engine (Arthur Elton)
Contact (Paul Rotha)
Industrial Britain (Grierson and Robert Flaherty)
1934
Granton Trawler (Grierson and Edgar Anstey)
Shipyard (Rotha)
The Song of Ceylon (Basil Wright)
Weather Forecast (Evelyn Spice)
1935
BBC – The Voice of Britain (Stuart Legg)
Coal Face (Alberto Cavalcanti)
Housing Problems (Anstey and Elton)
Workers and Jobs (Elton)
1936
Enough to Eat? (Anstey)
Night Mail (Harry Watt and Wright)
1937
The Saving of Bill Blewitt (Watt)
We Live in Two Worlds (Cavalcanti)
1938
North Sea (Watt)
1939
Men in Danger (Pat Jackson)

Chapter Related Books

Aitkin, Ian, *Alberto Cavalcanti: Realism, Surrealism and National Cinemas*. Trowbridge, Wilts.: Flicks Books, 2000.
Aitken, Ian, ed. *The Documentary Film Movement: An Anthology*. Edinburgh: Edinburgh University Press, 1998.
Aitken, Ian, *Film and Reform: John Grierson and the Documentary Film Movement*. London: Routledge, 1990.

Anstey, Edgar, 'Development of Film Technique in Britain', *Experiment in the Film*, ed. Roger Manvell. London: Grey Walls Press, 1949, pp. 234–65.

Arts Enquiry, The, *The Factual Film*. London: Oxford University Press, 1947.

Beveridge, James, *John Grierson: Film Master*. New York: Macmillan, 1978.

Commission on Educational and Cultural Films, *The Film in National Life*. London: George Allen and Unwin, 1932.

Ellis, Jack C., *John Grierson: A Guide to References and Resources*. Boston: G. K. Hall, 1986.

Ellis, Jack C., *John Grierson: Life, Contributions, Influence*. Carbondale: Southern Illinois University Press, 2000.

Grierson, John, *Grierson on Documentary*, ed. Forsyth Hardy. Berkeley: University of California Press, 1966.

Hardy, Forsyth, 'The British Documentary Film', *Twenty Years of British Film 1925–1945*, eds Michael Balcon and others. London: Falcon Press, 1947.

Hardy, Forsyth, *John Grierson: A Documentary Biography*. London: Faber and Faber, 1979.

6

Institutionalization: USA 1930–1941

In 1930 the (US) Workers' Film and Photo League (WFPL) was established in New York City. Its goal was to train filmmakers and photographers to produce material that would present the 'true picture' of life in the United States; that is, from their Marxist point of view – a picture not revealed by the news services, the newsreels, or the capitalist press. Among its listed advisors or associates were notables such as Margaret Bourke-White and Ralph Steiner, photographers; Elia Kazan, Burgess Meredith and James Cagney, actors; Slavko Vorkapich, film theorist and montage expert. The Film and Photo League (it dropped Workers' from its title, as did the League in London) produced such topical films as *Winter* (1931), *Hunger* (1932), and *Bonus March* (1932).

An increasing schism in this leftist group developed between those who wanted to stick to straight agit-prop newsreels and polemical films and those who thought the cause of revolution (or of social progress – political aims varied from person to person) could best be served by films with greater aesthetic value and emotional appeal. This latter group became more aligned with an avant-garde approach.

In 1934 three key members – Leo Hurwitz, Ralph Steiner and Irving Lerner – left the Film and Photo League to form Nykino (evidently a Russianized abbreviation for New York cinema; a leftist film organization named Kino also existed in London). Its *Pie in the Sky* (1934), by Elia Kazan, Molly Day Thatcher, Ralph Steiner and Irving Lerner, became its first publicized release.

Fig 24 *From left to right, Jacques Lemare, Henri Cartier-Bresson and Herbert Kline during the Spanish Civil War. For the New York Film and Photo League they filmed* Return to Life, Spain Will Live *and* With the Abraham Lincoln Brigade in Spain *(1938). This once 'lost' film chronicles the activities of American volunteer troops before and after their deployment to the front*

It is a whimsical spoof of the promises of religion for life in the hereafter in place of food for present hunger on earth. Nykino would subsequently become Frontier Films, whose work will be dealt with later.

In some ways the work of 1930s leftist documentarians presaged later developments in the 1960s, especially in the Newsreel Collectives. In the 1930s The Workers' Film and Photo League, unlike most of the later New Left groups, had direct ties to the USSR through the Communist Party in America. (Following the collapse of the Soviet Union, previously secret files were opened offering tantalizing glimpses into the organization and work of the WFPL.) From the 1920s through the start of World War II, the Communist Party USA sent copies of important documents to be filed for safekeeping in the Comintern's archives. Several of these files contain primary source material on the WFPL, though not all of the materials are legible. 2209 contains a four-page, unsigned document attempting to convince the CPUSA to systematically support the work of the WFPL. Dated December 16 [1932?], it summarizes the programme of the WFPL in its own words:

> Concretely: The next six months must witness the development of the WORKERS FILM AND PHOTO LEAGUE OF AMERICA into an organization capable of producing at least a thousand feet of workers' News weekly. By spring we must be ready to project films at open-air meetings on a wide scale; the issuance of a monthly organ for struggle against the bourgeois film and for the popularization and development of the workers' film movement; the forming of classes to train workers in the shooting of films with hand cameras. This is our immediate program and we are pledged to carry it forward to the conquest of the film! (Delo 2209, p. 18)

It is important to remember that the Communist Party is and always was a legal political party in the US.

The Film and Photo League was also briefly active on the West Coast. Departing from New York, Lester Balog, an editor and Ed Royce, an organizer for Workers' International Relief (WIR), after a crowded evening screening at the New York League headquarters, loaded into a car a projector, a print of Vsevold Pudovkin's *Mother,* and some New York Film and Photo League newsreels. Inspired by the Soviet agit trains, the two set off north, hitting Rochester and Buffalo then driving onto Detroit, Chicago and westward. Driving from one town to the next, they had showings in fifty-one locales across the country at workers' halls, ethnic clubs, community theatres and private homes. Along the way, Balog shot footage of strikes, demonstrations, the World's Fair in Chicago, and a trial of labour organizers in Utah. The trip served as a benefit tour for the WIR, raising money to support striking workers, as well as to keep the tour moving. The second half of their film tour was in California, where they travelled down the coast and back up the valley during the fall of 1933 at the time of the largest agricultural strikes in California. They set up shop in San Francisco at the Workers' Cultural Centre at 121 Haight Street, which functioned much like Workers' Centres in New York, Los Angeles, Chicago and other towns. Usually housing the Communist Party Headquarters as well as Workers' Schools, John Reed Clubs, bookstores, libraries, soup kitchens, Labour Sports Unions, workers' theatre groups, and Film and Photo Leagues, Workers' Centres were prominent in left cultural life of the period.

During their travels, they and colleagues encountered violent opposition from law enforcement officials, were put in jail and ultimately were shut down. In a 1933 crackdown, newsboys were arrested for selling the 'Western Worker', bookstores selling radical publications were shut down and their owners thrown in jail, street theatre players were beaten up. In July 1934, while Balog languished in jail, San Diego police arrested Louis Siminow of the Los Angeles Film and Photo League for showing a film. With San Francisco in disarray, and the local Film and Photo League darkroom and meeting space destroyed, the people who created the short-lived Film and Photo League movement on the West Coast disbanded. (This information is excerpted from: Leshne, Carla, 'The Film & Photo League of San Francisco', *Film History: An International Journal*, Volume 18, Number 4, 2006, pp. 361–73).

The March of Time

Unlike the Film and Photo League, another development, on the political right (or centre at least), stood apart from the mainstream of American documentary, but would be highly influential throughout the world – and to British and Canadian documentary especially. Entitled 'The March of Time', this monthly film series offered a new and distinctive kind of screen journalism, a cross between the newsreel and the documentary. Sponsored by Time-Life-Fortune, Inc., headed by Henry Luce, it was preceded by a weekly radio series of the same title. Louis de Rochemont was the principal creator of the film series. Luce himself said about it: ' "The March of Time" is fakery in allegiance to the truth.'

'The March of Time' had the most sustained popular success of any documentary-like material prior to television. It was announced on movie marquees, sometimes appearing above the feature title. At its peak, in the late 1930s and the years of World War II, it was seen in the US by over twenty million people a month in 5,000 theatres. It was distributed internationally as well.

Though originating from a conservative organization, the MOT became identified for a somewhat more liberal stance than *Time* magazine. This was particularly true on foreign affairs; on domestic issues the films tended to be more conservative or erratic. Still, while fiction features in the thirties largely ignored or dealt only covertly with the Depression, MOT acknowledged the bread lines and unemployment, as well as the political demagoguery it gave rise to (for example, *Huey Long* [1935]; *Unemployment* [1937]). While the European newsreels tended to avoid controversial political and military

Fig 25 *One of 5,236 theaters that presented 'The March of Time' to 12 million people every month during its heyday. From Raymond Fielding's book* The March of Time

developments, MOT reported the machinations of Hitler, Stalin, Mussolini and Tojo (as in *Nazi Conquest – No. 1* [1938]; *The Mediterranean – Background for War* [1939]).

Along with its energy, the success of 'The March of Time' was fuelled by the controversy it aroused and by its press agency. One of the most politically controversial films in the history of American cinema was MOT's *Inside Nazi Germany* (1938). In its sixteen minutes it examined in some detail the regimentation of the German people, the control and consolidation of national allegiances, and the preparations being made for future military and economic expansion. This was at a time when the majority of the American public was still strongly isolationist and the government maintained a careful impartiality.

The makeup for each issue of 'The March of Time' was worked out in its early years and varied little, regardless of subject. The fixed format may have been necessitated by the pressures of monthly production with modest resources. One of the most important ingredients was the voice and delivery style of its commentator, Westbrook Van Voorhis. His 'Voice of Time' was deep and commanding, ominous and reassuring at the same time. Spoken words carried the weight of the communication; the footage (largely stock), music (obvious and clichéd), and sound effects (sparse and highly selective) were cut to them. Often the images were given their meaning by the words as part of 'the dramatization of the news' that MOT practised. An extreme closeup of part of a face and a mouth at a telephone becomes 'An angry refusal' in *War In China* (1937). Editing was the key. The pace is fast, with a hard rhythmic impact; a great deal of information is presented dramatically to capture the attention of the popcorn-munching audience.

Structurally, every issue has four parts, with titles announcing each part. The first establishes the magnitude and urgency of the problem at hand. The second offers a historical survey of its origins and causes. Part three presents the immediate complications, confirming its newsworthiness. The concluding part looks to the future, stressing that the problem is a matter for continuing and serious concern.

No doubt, its unchanging style and approach had something to do with its eventual demise in 1951 (along with the competition of television and the rising costs of production). 'The March of Time' remains, however, a noteworthy phenomenon in the history of popular American culture. Its influence has extended to the documentary and public affairs programmes on television today.

Government Documentaries

The Film and Photo League and 'The March of Time' were precedents of sorts, but documentary in the institutional or Griersonian sense – engaging and educating citizens in the affairs of the nation – began in June 1935, in Washington, DC. At that time Rexford Guy Tugwell, head of the newly established Resettlement Administration, made a decision to use motion pictures to interpret its programme and objectives. Tugwell was one of the 'brain trust' assembled by President Franklin Delano Roosevelt to implement his New Deal. Roosevelt gathered around him the best minds he could find to help solve the problems presented by the Depression. Some have compared this style of Executive Branch composition with the methods of President John Kennedy and that of President Barack Obama. The Resettlement Administration was intended to aid those farmers who were being forced off their land by low crop prices compounded by the 'Dust Bowl' drought in the West and Southwest.

Into Tugwell's office came a movie critic named Pare Lorentz, whose wife was vaguely related to the president. Lorentz was a combination of New York liberal (where he was established) and West Virginia populist (where he had been born and raised). He convinced Tugwell that what was needed was a new kind of dramatic/informational/persuasive movie. Lorentz disliked the term 'documentary' and felt that much of Grierson's work in England was too school-teacherish. 'Films of Merit' was Lorentz's label for what he would produce. Out of that conversation came *The Plow That Broke the Plains* (1936), an indictment of the lack of planning that had caused the Dust Bowl. *Plow* shows the historical origins of the problem and its then current magnitude and urgency.

Lorentz, who had no prior film production experience, wrote and directed *Plow*. As cinematographers he hired Paul Strand, Ralph Steiner and Leo

Fig 26 The Plow That Broke the Plains *(US, 1936, Pare Lorentz). Museum of Modern Art Film Stills Archive*

Hurwitz. Strand and Steiner had backgrounds in still photography; all three had been active in the Film and Photo League. When they began shooting out in the field, with Lorentz remaining in Washington, they were frustrated by the lack of clarity in their instructions. To compensate for this, and to give themselves guidelines for shooting, they drafted a script. The film as they conceived it was to be about the devastation of the land caused by exploitative capitalism. This was not an economic-political stance Lorentz was prepared to take (nor one the government would have welcomed) and dissension and cross-purposes resulted. Lorentz hired an editor, Leo Zochling, to assist him, and with his help Lorentz learned to edit. He assembled the footage according to his own rough outline and began writing the commentary. Well-known composer Virgil Thomson was hired to compose the score. Working together, in hours upon hours of shaping and reshaping, they combined images and music with spoken words and sound effects. It was Thomson's idea that his music should have an operatic balance with the rest of the filmic elements. In fact, his score exists even today virtually as he wrote it for the film as a suite in standard orchestral repertoire.

Fig 27 *Pare Lorentz in the 1930s*

Unlike Grierson, who always determined in advance how his films would reach their audience, Lorentz failed to set up distribution for the completed film. He might have been forewarned of the Hollywood film industry's resentment of government film production by the resistance he had encountered in trying to obtain footage from fiction features. (It was finally only with the covert help of veteran director King Vidor that he obtained what he needed.) Accordingly, *The Plow That Broke the Plains* was not shown as widely as it might have been. What distribution it received was because of glowing reviews. The Rialto Theatre in New York City publicized its showing by proclaiming it 'The picture they dared us to show!'

Lorentz was discouraged by the inadequate distribution, exhausted from the hard work and frustration of production, and in debt for money he (and his wife) had invested in the film. In that dismal mood, he went to Tugwell's office to say goodbye. As part of his farewell he suggested another film he thought should be made – one about flooding in the Mississippi valley. Lorentz's enthusiasm for this project convinced Tugwell to allow him to produce another government film, *The River* (1937), backed by the Farm Security Administration.

While the Resettlement Administration, which had sponsored *Plow*, had intended to relocate people forced off their land, the Farm Security Administration was attempting to keep them on their farms. *The River* became a compelling plea for national flood control and soil conservation. The film also counteracted the public relations campaign being conducted by private utilities to keep government out of providing electric power. While it became generally agreed that the Tennessee Valley Authority was a remarkable and salutary instance of a government undertaking, it remains an experiment that has never been repeated. Perhaps if it had, the US would not have faced the extreme flooding and destruction at the mouth of the Mississippi that resulted

Fig 28 *A devastation scene in* The River. *Museum of Modern Art Film Stills Archive*

from Hurricane Katrina. *The River* screened with Spike Lee's and Sam Pollard's 2006 documentary *When the Levees Broke* provides remarkable comparison.

Lorentz wrote and directed *The River*. The cinematographers were Stacy Woodard, Floyd Crosby and Willard Van Dyke. Woodard had been producing a series of nature films entitled 'The Struggle to Live'. Crosby had worked on the Murnau-Flaherty *Tabu* (1931), would have a long association with Lorentz, and went on to fiction features (including *High Noon* [1952]). Van Dyke, who had studied still photography with Edward Weston, would become a fine documentary-maker in his own right. Though there was no political contention this time, there seems to have been the same uncertainty as to exactly what kind of footage was wanted. The score was again by Thomson, based almost entirely on hymns ('Yes, Jesus Loves Me'), folk songs ('Go Tell Aunt Rhody') and popular tunes ('Hot Time in the Old Town Tonight').

As in *Night Mail*, Lorentz's lyric commentary for this film became classic. Its blank verse litany of names of rivers and towns has often been imitated and sometimes parodied, but it is beautiful in itself. For example:

We built a hundred cities and a thousand towns:
St Paul and Minneapolis,
Davenport and Keokuk,
Moline and Quincy, Cincinnati and St Louis, Omaha and Kansas City ...

Or, again:

Down the Judith, the Grand, the Osage and the Platte;
The Rock, the Salt, the Black and the Minnesota;
Down the Monongahela, the Allegheny, Kanawha and Muskingum;
The Miami, the Wabash, the Liking and the Green;
The White, the Wolf, the Cache, and the Black;
Down the Kaw and Kaskaskia, the Red and Yazoo.
Down the Cumberland, Kentucky and the Tennessee ...

Lorentz this time took pains to set up proper distribution and the film was shown in more than 5,000 theatres. It has remained in active nontheatrical distribution ever since – not just as a historical curiosity but as a significant statement about an ongoing ecological problem, and as an epic poem. The only negative criticism is that following its moving evocation of the history of this big country, its people, and its natural resources, it adds a commercial. The last six minutes on the TVA are much weaker; even the photographic quality drops, with some stock shots being used. Unlike the best of the British documentaries, in which the propaganda becomes an indissoluble part of the whole, here the sponsor's message seems tacked on. Lavishly praised at the time of its release, *The River* has come to be considered a masterpiece of the screen.

On the basis of its success Lorentz was able to persuade the Roosevelt administration (with the backing of the President himself, who is reported to have loved the film) to set up the United States Film Service in 1938. It was intended to make films propagandizing the policies and activities of all departments of government. The first of the US Film Service productions was *The Fight for Life* (1940), produced for the US Public Health Service. Written and directed by Lorentz, it is about the work of the Chicago Maternity Centre in providing prenatal care for mothers, and delivering babies in the homes of poor families. It was photographed by Floyd Crosby. The music, composed by Louis Gruenberg (who shortly before had written the score for John Ford's *Stagecoach*), was innovative, including the use of blues. Its cast mixed nonactors with actors.

Feature-length, half-dramatic and half-documentary, *The Fight for Life* is what would sometimes be called a semidocumentary. In attempting to heighten the drama and engage the emotions, Lorentz inadvertently made childbirth a frightening experience. When the film was completed and rushed to the White House for viewing on New Year's Eve 1939, Franklin Roosevelt showed little enthusiasm for it. Eleanor Roosevelt is said to have remarked in her gentle way: 'Surely there's something good to be said about having a baby.' It was not very widely shown. In Chicago it was banned by the police censorship board, though it had been made there.

On the other hand, *Power and the Land* (1940), the next production, was distributed by RKO to nearly 5,000 theatres. It was so well received that it continued to be reissued nontheatrically into the late 1940s, with its maps being updated to show the continuing increase in the number of farms receiving electric power. It was produced for the Rural Electrification

Administration and the Department of Agriculture. Joris Ivens, the famous Dutch documentarian living in the US, directed, and Helen Van Dongen, his then wife and editor, edited. Cinematography was again by Floyd Crosby and Arthur Ornitz; the commentary was written by renowned poet Stephen Vincent Benet; musical score was by Douglas Moore.

Power and the Land pursues its objective of persuading farmers to organize rural cooperatives to obtain government power by showing a typical family, the Parkinsons, on their farm in southwestern Ohio. We see them at work, before they have electricity and then afterwards. The contrast in the greater ease and comfort electric power provides these decent and hardworking people is a simple and effective argument. At the same time, Ivens offers an affectionate picture of this family and their farm. With deft and poetic strokes he and Van Dongen document for other cultures and future generations a kind of life and economy that was fading into history.

The next production, *The Land* (1941), was conceived and directed by an even more famous documentary pioneer, Robert Flaherty, returning to America after a decade in Britain. It too was edited by Helen Van Dongen. Cinematography was by Irving Lerner, Douglas Baker, Floyd Crosby and Charles Herbert; the music by English composer Richard Arnell; the commentary written and read by Flaherty. Produced for the Agricultural Adjustment Agency of the Department of Agriculture, this became what the French would call a *film maudit* – a cursed film. Its initial purpose was along the lines of *The Plow That Broke the Plains* and *The River* – to encourage the careful and controlled use of agricultural resources. During its production, United States foreign policy shifted from strict neutrality at the beginning of the Second World War to support of the British. A lend-lease programme had been initiated and the US's promise to become 'the breadbasket of democracy' required that agricultural production be increased by every means available. *The Land* works against itself, and its message is confused. The visuals may in fact represent Flaherty's true uneasiness concerning what he had discovered about the land and the people on his first film about his own country.

In any case, before *The Land* was completed, Congress, now alienated from the New Deal by Republican victories at the polls in 1940, decided that government film production was needless and, indeed, un-American. The

US Film Service was not exactly abolished, since it had never really been approved. Now, not only were no funds for the Film Service appropriated by Congress, legislation was passed that forbade tucking film production costs into other budgets. *The Land* was never shown in theatres.

In summarizing Lorentz's highly significant contributions, a number of things can be said. He established American precedent for the government use of documentaries, which would be continued during World War II and afterwards. From Lorentz's efforts five large and important films resulted, the first three of which he directed: *The Plow That Broke the Plains, The River,* and *The Fight for Life.* In *Plow* and *The River* Lorentz developed an original personal style of documentary that also became a national style. In his two mosaic patterns of sight (carefully composed images shot silently) and sound (symphonic music, spoken words, selected noises). No one element works alone, but together they offer a form and content resembling epic poems. They seem close to the attitudes of American populism and are rooted in frontier tradition. The sweeping views of a big country and the blank verse

Fig 29 Power and the Land *was distributed to nearly 5,000 theaters by Hollywood studio RKO (US, 1940, Joris Ivens). Museum of Modern Art Film Stills Archive*

commentaries with their chanted names and allusions to historic events make one think of Walt Whitman. The use of music is quite special, with composer Virgil Thomson participating more fully than usual in the filmmaking process.

The closing of the US Film Service proved a great waste and inefficiency. Shortly after its demise, the United States entered World War II and government filmmaking on a vast scale had to be restarted from scratch, but in contributing two lasting masterpieces to the history of documentary, Lorentz joins a very select company: the artists of documentary.

Non-Government Documentaries

Paralleling the work of Lorentz and the United States Film Service and the 'March of Time' were the documentaries of private and commercial sponsorship. When, in 1937, Nykino (discussed at the beginning of this chapter) metamorphosed into Frontier Films, it represented those committed to art on behalf of social action. Among the persons associated with Frontier Films, either actively or as advisors, were notables such as John Howard Lawson, Elia Kazan, Leo Hurwitz, Herbert Kline, Ralph Steiner, Joris Ivens, Malcolm Cowley, John Dos Pasos, Lillian Hellman, Archibald MacLeish, Lewis Milestone, Clifford Odets, Willard Van Dyke and Paul Strand. The mainstays were Strand, Hurwitz and Steiner. Frontier Films intended to be an alternative to 'The March of Time'.

The non-government documentaries of the 1930s offer a catalogue of the most significant problems and issues of the time – with a bias to the left in their selection and treatment. International threats were a main subject. A number of films were made about the Spanish Civil War (1936-8), in which General Francisco Franco's legions, backed by Nazi Germany and Fascist Italy, were pitted against the Republican Loyalists aided formally by Russia and informally by volunteers from many nations. All of the American films supported the Loyalist cause. From Frontier Films came *Heart of Spain* (1937, Herbert Kline and Geza Karpathi) and *Return to Life* (1938, still photographer Henri Cartier-Bresson and Herbert Kline). From Contemporary Film Historians, Inc., formed by a group of writers that included John Dos Pasos,

Ernest Hemingway, Archibald MacLeish and Lillian Hellman, came *The Spanish Earth* (1937). The most ambitious and widely seen of the Spanish Civil War films, *The Spanish Earth* was a short feature in length (54 minutes). Directed by Joris Ivens, cinematography was by John Ferno and editing by Helen Van Dongen; narration was written and read by Ernest Hemingway; music arranged by Marc Blitzstein and Virgil Thomson, from Spanish folk melodies. The 1984 film *The Good Fight; The Abraham Lincoln Brigade in the Spanish Civil War* by Noel Bruckner, Mary Dore and Sam Sills offers a more modern, if somewhat simplistic view of Americans who fought in that war.

As for films dealing with China's defence against Japanese aggression, which began with the invasion of Manchuria in 1931 and continued until 1945, Frontier Films made *China Strikes Back* (1937). Harry Dunham directed; Jay Leyda and Sidney Meyers were among others involved in its production. This film offered sustained coverage of the Chinese 8th Route Army, the Communist force, with Mao Tse-tung among its leaders, its guerilla tactics, educational programme, relations with the peasants, and efforts toward the unity of Free China against the invading Japanese.

Films were made about the Munich crisis of 1938, when Prime Minister Neville Chamberlain of Great Britain agreed with Adolph Hitler that Germany could annexe the Sudetanland section of Czechoslovakia, without interference from Britain. *Crisis* (1938), produced and directed by Herbert Kline, was co-directed by the Alexander Hammid. The same pair created *Lights Out in Europe* (1938).

As for non-government documentaries on domestic subjects, most of those had 'progressive tendencies' and dealt with issues of particular interest to the political left. The 1930s were years of considerable labour unrest and progress, of union building and busting, and a number of films were made in support of unionism. For example, three were produced by Frontier Films. *People of the Cumberland* (1938) is about an isolated community of English and Scottish ancestry working in the coal mines of Appalachia and their emergence from poverty and backwardness to social consciousness and action. The feature-length *Native Land* was Frontier Films' magnum opus (and swan song). Production of it began in 1939 but it was not released until 1942. Based almost entirely on the investigation and conclusions of the US Senate Robert

Lafollette Committee on Civil Rights and other labour documents, it dealt with workers' rights and unionism, and was part-actuality footage and part-dramatization. Direction and script were by Leo Hurwitz and Paul Strand; cinematography was by Strand; music by Marc Blitzstein. Paul Robeson narrated.

Municipal planning was another subject. *A Place to Live* (1941) is a cogent little film about slum clearance in Philadelphia. *The City* (1939) is a trenchant large one. A hit at the New York World's Fair of 1939, it was produced for the American Institute of Planners by American Documentary Films, set up by Ralph Steiner and Willard Van Dyke, who co-directed and co-photographed the film. (When Van Dyke and Steiner left Frontier Films on ideological grounds this sponsored project left with them. That incident caused a serious and lasting breach among various filmmakers who had been involved with Frontier Films.) The scenario was by Henwar Rodakiewicz from an original outline by Pare Lorentz; the commentary was written by cultural historian Lewis Mumford and spoken by actor Morris Carnovsky, with music by Aaron Copland.

The City promotes the concept of the planned greenbelt communities detached from urban centres. It has a five-part historical organization: (1) In the Beginning – New England (a rural community dating from the eighteenth century); (2) The Industrial City – City of Smoke (Pittsburgh); (3) The Metropolis – Men into Steel (Manhattan); (4) The Highway – The Endless City (Sunday traffic congestion in New Jersey and the environs of New York City); (5) The Green City (shot in Radburn, NJ, and Greenbelt, MD). John Grierson, who was himself working on a film about city planning at the time (*The Londoners*), much admired the keenness of observation, the rhythm and the energy of *The City*. It is also part of the 'City Symphony' tradition.

Aesthetically and technically, Willard Van Dyke's *Valley Town* (1941) is remarkable for several reasons: the extraordinary force and effectiveness of its images for one; and its daring use of soliloquy, even sung soliloquy, in an effort to heighten the feeling of its contents for another. It makes one think of the words and music of Bertolt Brecht and Kurt Weill in *The Threepenny Opera* and their other music dramas with social meanings. Another, somewhat related film, *One Tenth of a Nation* (1940), is about the need for better

Fig 30 The City *was a hit at the 1939 New York World's Fair (US, 1939, Ralph Steiner and Willard Van Dyke). Museum of Modern Art Film Stills Archive*

schooling for the Southern Negro. It was the most widely seen of several films dealing with the problems of black Americans. Henwar Rodakiewicz and Joseph Krumgold co-produced and co-directed.

Conclusions

In concluding this section, a number of generalizations can be made about the nongovernmental American documentaries of the 1930s. First, the filmmakers often took bold positions on social matters, but they had continuing difficulty finding backing for their statements. The pattern was one of a big, fine film for which funding was somehow obtained, followed by inadequate distribution and exhibition, leading to the sponsor's disenchantment and the filmmaker's having to scramble to try to find sponsorship for the next film.

Second, because of the uncertainty of sponsorship, there was no steady flow of smaller films reaching interested audiences and little reinforcement of the ideas presented. Too frequently as still happens today, only those persons who already agreed with the filmmakers' positions saw the films or even learned of their existence.

Third – and related to the second point – rarely is the propaganda mixed with the artistic form in a smooth blend. The sponsor's message may obtrude. On the other hand, sometimes the pleasures of form seem to be working against the content and evident intention of the film. The liveliness and humour of the New York City sequence in *The City* is much more engaging than the blandness of its greenbelt sequence.

Though he never contributed to organizing American documentary filmmakers, Robert Flaherty may have been their unacknowledged bellwether. Certainly, all the filmmakers had seen his work. Documentary other than Flaherty didn't really take hold in the United States until seven years after documentary in Great Britain. American documentary did not grow out of British documentary, though it may not have begun when and how it did if there had not been the British precedent. Personal connections between the two national groups of documentary-makers were not made until the late thirties.

The major differences between American and British documentaries of the thirties seem to have grown mostly out of contrasting political positions. The American films are rooted in populism, the British in socialism. The populists, begun in the People's Party around the turn of the nineteenth century, felt that government should control tendencies toward monopoly, but that its function should end there. Populism began among American farmers in the country; socialism among factory workers in European cities. Agrarian subject matter and influence are very strong in the American films (this despite the fact that by the mid-thirties the majority of Americans were living in cities); urban and industrial subjects predominate in British documentary. In the American films, the importance of the people and the sacredness of the individual receive considerable emphasis. In the British films, collective effort through government, with government leadership, is stressed.

These American romantic and emotional tendencies led to the poetic rather than the expository. In general, American documentaries of the thirties may have been more 'aestheticky', to use a Grierson dismissive term, than the

British. 'The March of Time' is, of course, an exception to this generalization. Grierson seemed to value it (he imitated it, in fact, in films he produced in Britain and later in Canada) more than he did *The River* and *The City*. Another difference is that American documentaries tended to gravitate towards the historical and to use before-and-after arguments. *The City* moves from eight-eenth-century rural New England to twentieth-century urban Pittsburgh and New York; *Power and the Land* from the farm before electricity to the farm after it. Frequent reference is made to folk history and customs. Also, the New Deal, accused in some quarters of being a kind of creeping socialism, tended to attach itself to established American values and virtues, suggesting that the cooperation with government it embodied was as American as apple pie.

Finally, there are the sorts of aesthetic experiences and effects on social attitudes being offered. On the aesthetic side, the United States films *The Plow That Broke the Plains*, *The River*, *Power and the Land*, *The City*, and *And So They Live* are lovely and lasting. On the side of social and educational effectiveness, however, what Grierson called *propaganda,* perhaps none of these matched *Night Mail* or *Housing Problems*. On the other hand, Jennings and Cavalcanti in Britain saw themselves as artists.

Dénouement

At the end of the 1930s, some efforts were made to organize American documentary along British lines. Mary Losey (sister of feature-film director Joseph Losey) was a key figure in these. She was a researcher for 'The March of Time', and on a trip to London in 1938 which she undertook to study documentary, she met Grierson and was stimulated by his achievements. On her return she 'set to work after the Grierson pattern to organize the jangling sects of American documentary into a purposeful group', as Richard Griffith put it. An Association of Documentary Film Producers was established in New York City in 1939. The ADFP membership included, 'with the conspicuous exception of Pare Lorentz,' Losey noted, 'all the producers of documentary today' – some sixty full members, roughly the same number of documentary-makers as in Britain. Even Flaherty became part of this group on his return from Britain in 1939. Alas, those efforts were too little and too late. Following the United States entry into World War II in late 1941, the organization disbanded in 1942.

With the war, the groups on the far left that had culminated in Frontier Films lost their principal reason and means for being. The political situation was now that of a common cause, with the United States fighting fascism alongside Communist Russia. During the war, there was a virtual cessation of private documentary production, and documentary filmmakers instead made government films of one sort or another. In 1943, Frontier Films ceased to exist.

An Aside to Conclude

Though this history is mostly of the English-language documentary, we would be remiss here if we did not recognize some non-Anglophone developments – in this case, in Germany. Early in 1933, with curious simultaneity, Franklin Delano Roosevelt became president of the United States while Adolf Hitler, leader of the National Socialist Party, came to power in Germany. In Britain the Labour Party had been succeeded in 1931 by the National Government (made up of a coalition of the Conservative, Labour and Liberal parties), with Neville Chamberlain becoming Prime Minister in 1937. Paralleling John Grierson in Britain and Pare Lorentz in the United States was the equally formidable former actress, Leni Riefenstahl in Germany. In 1936 Grierson (and Watt and Wright) made *Night Mail*, Lorentz *The Plow That Broke the Plains*, and Riefenstahl *Triumph of the Will*. All three films were sponsored by their governments to try to rally support for current activities, programmes and policies. Politically the films could be characterized, implicitly at least, as socialist, populist, and fascist.

Triumph of the Will was made to commemorate the sixth Nazi rally in Nuremberg in 1934. Produced by order of the Führer, it was intended to show the German people the power of a resurgent Germany united under a Nazi party. The event was staged partly to accommodate the needs of filmmaking as a ceremony – a religious ritual – elaborate, powerful and penetrating, with mass emotion overcoming individual reason. Its key image is the moulding of tens of thousands of human beings into artistic patterns – stationary and solid masses in the huge stadium, or moving with deliberation and vigour in endless parades. What *Triumph of the Will* offers is the losing of self in the mass: in total dedication to an ideal of a strong and united nation, to supermen and super-state – a transcendence. Even today it retains terrifying power. Riefenstahl's other masterpiece, *Olympia* (1938), similarly edited from an enormous amount of footage covering a huge public event, the Olympic Games of 1936 held in Berlin, also – though more subtly – articulates Nazi ideology in cinematic terms. Taken in this light they can be seen as contributing to the *Zeitgeist* which accompanied the Holocaust and World War II.

Chapter Related Films

1935
'The March of Time' series began (Louis de Rochemont)
The Wave (Paul Strand and Fred Zinnemann)
1936
The Plow That Broke the Plains (Pare Lorentz)
1937
China Strikes Back (Harry Dunham)
The River (Lorentz)
The Spanish Earth (Joris Ivens)
1938
Inside Nazi German (de Rochemont)
The Four Hundred Million (Ivens)
People of the Cumberland (Elia Kazan)
1939
The City (Ralph Steiner and Willard Van Dyke)
Lights Out in Europe (Kline)
1940
Power and the Land (Ivens)
The Ramparts We Watch (de Rochemont)
Valley Town (Van Dyke)
1941
The Fight for Life (Lorentz)
The Land (Robert Flaherty)
A Place to Live (Irving Lerner)
1942
Native Land (Leo Hurwitz and Paul Strand)

Chapter Related Books

Alexander, William, *Film on the Left: American Documentary Film from 1931 to 1942.* Princeton, NJ: Princeton University Press, 1981.

Böker, Carlos, *Joris Ivens, Film-Maker: Facing Reality.* Ann Arbor, MI: UMI Research Press, 1981.

Bakker, Kees, ed., *Joris Ivens and the Documentary Context.* Amsterdam, Amsterdam University Press, 1999

Campbell, Russell, *Cinema Strikes Back: Radical Filmmaking in the United States, 1930–1942.* Ann Arbor, MI: UMI Research Press, 1982.

Delmar, Rosalind, *Joris Ivens: 50 Years of Filmmaking.* London: British Film Institute, 1979.

Enyeart, James L., Willard Van Dyke: *Changing The World Through Photography and Film.* Albuquerque, New Mexico: University of New Mexico Press, 2008.

Fielding, Raymond, *The March of Time, 1935–1951.* New York: Oxford University Press, 1978.

Ivens, Joris, *The Camera and I.* New York: International Publishers, 1969.

Lorentz, Pare, *FDR's Moviemaker: Memories of Scripts.* Reno, Nevada: Nevada University Press, 1992

MacCann, Richard Dyer, *The People's Films: A Political History of US Government Motion Pictures.* New York: Hastings House, 1973.

Rother, Rainer, *Leni Riefenstahl.* London: Continuum, 2002.

Snyder, Robert L. *Pare Lorentz and the Documentary Film.* Norman: University of Oklahoma Press, 1968.

Stufkens, Andre, *Cinema Without Borders: The Films of Joris Ivens.* Amsterdam: European Foundation Joris Ivens, 2002.

Zuker, Joel Stewart, *Ralph Steiner, Filmmaker and Still Photographer.* New York: Arno Press, 1978.

7

WWII

Part A: Great Britain

On 1 September 1939, German Panzer divisions rolled across the Polish border and Stuka dive-bombers took to the skies. On 3 September, Prime Minister Neville Chamberlain announced over BBC radio that a state of war existed between Great Britain and Germany. (His announcement was followed by the accidental setting off of air-raid sirens.)

Documentary, though relatively small in terms of money and audience, had established film as a means of social and scientific communication, with hundreds of short films of fact and opinion. It had prestige among the educated classes and fit in with thirties' ideas about art in relation to society. A movement with trained and skilled workers, it offered a distinct style as well as purpose, and innovations in form and technique that are arguably Britain's most important contribution to the development of the motion picture. Further, with the outbreak of war, when the needs of the country were paramount, British documentary's identification with government from its beginnings became especially significant. The film unit at the Empire Marketing Board and then at the General Post Office had been training ground and trend-setter, and had offered means of national expression in an exact sense. With the war, the GPO Film Unit became the Crown Film Unit, serving all departments of government. Wartime documentaries would be made by veteran documentarians plus new recruits.

Following the declaration of war it was some time before Britain was engaged in actual combat. There was a period of 'phoney war', as it was called

– the 'sitting war' or 'Sitzkrieg', as someone dubbed it in reference to the Germans' *Blitzkrieg* (lightning war). Poland was defeated before either France or Britain, bound to it by mutual defence treaties, could come to its aid. Six months passed between the fall of Poland and the beginning, in Denmark and Norway, of the German drive in Western Europe.

Early Days

The first film job, immediately evident, was to record the events of war. For that purpose the five English newsreel companies pooled their resources for what would soon become a mammoth task. This provided for the free exchange of material to limit redundancy in the use of personnel and permit a maximum amount of war activity to be covered. Exceptional work was done by newsreel and armed forces combat cameramen throughout the war. The casualty rate among them was high. In battle situations where troops could dig foxholes, those who had to move about above ground – platoon leaders, medics, and still photographers as well as cinematographers – were most vulnerable.

In September of 1939 the Ministry of Information was established to take overall charge of the creation and dissemination of news and propaganda. The film advisers to the Chamberlain government were distrustful of the documentary people because of their leftward tendencies. Instead of the documentarians, filmmakers from the entertainment film industry were called upon. The documentary group vented their frustration by grousing to each other and writing letters to *The Times*. Without any real authorization, let alone relevance to Post Office activity, the GPO Film Unit, on its own, made *The First Days* (1939) shortly after war broke out. Harry Watt, Humphrey Jennings and Pat Jackson collaborated on it.

When Winston Churchill became Prime Minister he named Brendan Bracken Minister of Information. Bracken in turn appointed Jack Beddington head of the Films Division. Beddington, public relations officer for the Shell Oil group, had been instrumental in the establishment of the Shell Film Unit. He understood the aims of the documentary movement and had a feeling for the film medium. His first act at the Films Division was to request a paper

Fig 31 *Britain's Ministry of Information, established in 1939, was responsible for the production of the Grierson units' wartime films and for exhibiting them to audiences throughout the country using vans such as this one. British Film Institute*

from Film Centre explaining how to use films in time of war. Former Grierson associates Edgar Anstey, Arthur Elton and Basil Wright wrote it.

After the summer of 1940, when France had fallen, the greater part of Western Europe was overrun by Germany. Britain was now a besieged island constantly under the threat of air attack. The documentarians reacted to these changed circumstances and became the interpreters of the British mood at war. A series of short factual films followed – half newsreel, half pictorial comment, and highly charged with the spirit of the time. *The Front Line* (1940), directed by Harry Watt, recorded life in the Channel port of Dover under air and artillery bombardment by long-range German guns. *London Can Take It* (1940) pictured life in the capital during the great night raids of the Battle of Britain. Directed by Watt and Humphrey Jennings, its commentary was written and read by American correspondent Quentin Reynolds. Cool images of actuality combined with hot journalistic prose are the basis of its style. Reynolds could say things about the English under fire that they couldn't modestly say about themselves.

The documentary old guard now fully entered the wartime filmmaking effort. *Squadron 992* (1940), produced by Alberto Cavalcanti and directed by Harry Watt, was made by the GPO Film Unit for the Air Force. About the training of a balloon barrage unit which then moves up into Scotland, it ends with a simulated German air raid on the bridge over the Firth of Forth. There is less attention to how things are done than is usual in documentaries, and more to mood and imagery, with lovely shots of the bridge, countryside and sea. The humour is noteworthy as well – including mild kidding of the Scots. (Watt was Scottish.)

As the war got fully underway, hundreds of training and orientation, scientific and medical films were produced for military and civilian audiences. There were films which enabled aerial gunners to test the accuracy of their aim, or which taught pilots the use of their controls. Short films encouraged civilians to conserve fuel and water (*The Burning Question* [1945], on fuel economy), to collect salvage (*Salvage with a Smile* [1940], paper for cartridges, household waste for pig food), and the like. Each month the MOI presented a fifteen-minute film on the progress of the struggle: the conquest and rehabilitation of Naples (*Naples Is a Battlefield* [1944]) or the devastation created in Walcheren by Allied bombing of the dykes (*Broken Dykes* [1945]), for instance. The scientific and medical films included one dealing with the National Blood Transfusion Service (*Blood Transfusion* [1942]), a film for doctors on diagnosis and treatment of a skin disease caused by parasites (*Scabies* [1943]), and another on a new antibiotic drug (*Penicillin* [1944]).

In addition to these more directly utilitarian films, three major types of British wartime documentaries emerged between 1941 and 1945. They were: (1) the semidocumentary indoctrinational features; (2) a continuation of the peacetime social documentary with new subjects and forms; and (3) the records of battle.

Indoctrination

Evidently the Ministry of Information decided that the best sort of support and inspiration for the population at large could come from showing British

Fig 32 Squadron 992 *(UK, 1940, Harry Watt). Museum of Modern Art Film Stills Archive*

men and women going about their wartime tasks with resolution, efficiency and quiet courage. In taking this approach, a main line of British indoctrination films moved toward Flaherty, and also toward fiction features, in depicting the drama of survival inherent in war. It was Watt in *Target for*

Tonight (1941) who created the prototype for the feature-length semidocumentary indoctrination films.

Target for Tonight concerns a Royal Air Force bombing mission into
Germany to destroy an oil refinery and storage and distributing centre at
Freihausen. After covering the preparation for the raid, it follows a Wellington
bomber and its crew. The bomber is hit by flak over the target, one of its crew
is wounded, and it limps back to base on one engine. The action is a composite
representation of how such an engagement would actually be carried out.
It has the real setting of airfield and airplanes and is acted by real airmen.
Through our direct involvement with the crew members, it comes alive in a
way usually associated with story films. The deft characterizations, dialogue
that seems to fit the men and the situation, and bits of wry humour are all
engaging. Watt was the first to depict the human undercurrents of war at a
depth documentary had not previously attempted.

Fires Were Started (1943), directed by Humphrey Jennings, is about the
work of the Auxiliary Fire Service during the devastating German fire raids on
London. By using the narrative device of a new recruit, Jennings saw through
his eyes the functioning of this fire-fighting service and the diverse and likable
personalities brought together in it. When the raid begins in the evening we
are able to follow the tactics of the fire-fighters without aid of commentary
through their actions and conversations, the phone calls from headquarters,
the maps with pins stuck into them, the lists of equipment chalked on a
blackboard. Among other things, *Fires Were Started* is a model of exposition
without didacticism. But its true greatness lies in the way it informs, persuades
and moves us, all at the same time. In this film Jennings succeeds in differ-
entiating and developing characters of his real/nonactor firemen. *Fires Were
Started*, together with two of his shorts – *Listen to Britain* (1942), an impres-
sionistic audiovisual poem about the country in wartime, and *A Diary for
Timothy* (1945), a fusion of the impressionist/symphonic approach with (in
this case multiple) narrative – comprise Jennings' masterpieces.

Jennings co-directed and co-edited *Listen to Britain* with Stewart
Macallister – his usual collaborator and editor of *Fires Were Started*. The film
is a masterpiece of visuals and sound; it uses natural sounds and music to
create the sound of Britain. The introduction, voiced directly to camera by

Leonard Brockington, touched many of Jennings' key themes in a way that invites the viewer to share. Indeed the invitation comes from outside of any narrative, directed straight at the audience. It creates an audio landscape of Britain during the war, with images both accompanying and conflicting with the multitude of sounds. Jennings' work as a Surrealist painter is evident here as he paints with both light and sound. His qualities as a filmmaker involve especially his formal experimentation, the intricate patterns of inter-woven sights and sounds. The individual images Jennings selected are rich in symbolic expressiveness, evoking peace as well as war, past as well as present, in combination and contrast. English tradition and English spirit saturate his films. Jennings celebrates cultural heritage with a warmth that encourages us to share his feelings.

Western Approaches (1944, titled *The Raider* in the US) was directed by Pat Jackson, who had assisted Harry Watt earlier (as had Humphrey Jennings before him). It is an account of the convoys of merchant vessels that left Halifax, Nova Scotia to transport supplies to Britain, and of the submarine warfare in the North Atlantic that they faced. It narrows down to the story of twenty-four men, survivors of a torpedoed freighter, who spend fourteen days adrift. Their lifeboat is used as bait by a lurking U-boat to attract an Allied ship. This is the largest in scale, the most ambitious, and the most technically difficult of the British wartime semidocumentaries. Along with the documentary essentials of nonactors, location shooting and description of process (how convoys and submarine attack and defence function), there is a high degree of skillfully handled artifice. The use of tightly scripted dialogue, synch-sound recording on location, and shooting with the cumbersome Technicolor camera on the high seas are all impressive. With its carefully plotted suspense and familiar characterizations, documentary here moves very close to fiction.

Two indoctrinational intentions of the British wartime semidocumentaries are apt to strike a viewer. One is their emphasis on togetherness. Over and over again the people are shown – civilians as well as military – working together to get the job done. Though microcosms of English society are frequently offered – with various identifiable regional and class accents, and a Scot or perhaps Canadian thrown in – no tensions between regions or among classes are shown. In fact, such differences, very real in Britain, are minimized.

Everyone is doing his or her work; all are working equally hard to win the war. The other distinctive characteristic is the lack of violence shown and the lack of hatred expressed in either dialogue or narration. Rather than digging coal or working for an advertising agency or attending university, the job now is to destroy the (unseen) enemy to keep them from destroying us. If bombs fall from the night skies, it's as if they were an act of God, a natural disaster like an earthquake. The thing to do is to put out the fires, clear away the rubble, attend the wounded, and bury the dead. While one might think these two attitudes were part of general wartime propaganda strategies, they appear to be very British – maybe even more specifically English. Nothing quite like them is present in the wartime films of Canada or the United States.

Social Documentary

Notwithstanding the national peril, the social documentary survived. In fact, some interesting innovations of subject and form were added to it. In the wartime social documentary a common goal was put forward: not simply that the war should be won, but that it should be won to some purpose; that life should hold better opportunities for everyone after it. This attitude even appears in Jennings' *A Diary for Timothy*. When the Welsh miner is injured in an accident, the commentary, written by E. M. Forster and read by Michael Redgrave, states: 'It's pretty shocking that this sort of thing should happen every day though we've been cutting coal for five hundred years.' As he is recuperating, the miner reminds his wife of the gains in health services made by Labour since the end of the First World War. 'Surely, if we can do that during that period,' he says, 'nothing can stop us after this war.' If post-war opportunity was a frequent theme in British wartime documentaries, it was probably at least partly a response to working-class feelings that their great sacrifices and losses of World War I had not resulted in sufficient benefits for them.

World of Plenty (1943), Paul Rotha's compilation film, begins with the breakdown in international food distribution before the war – surpluses in some countries, starvation in others. The system of fair distribution by rationing enforced nationally in Britain during the war is then presented. It is suggested as a worldwide model for the future. Rotha, firmly schooled in Marxist ideals, always insisted (as did Grierson less stridently) that documentaries had to deal with the economic underpinnings of any subject tackled. At the same time, economic abstractions are much harder to present in the language of motion pictures than are specific actualities. In attempting to solve this problem Rotha introduced a number of experimental elements. Diagrams, interviews and trick optical effects were added to stock footage. The remarkable animated representations created by the Isotype Institute add clarity and drama to statistics of food production and distribution. Especially original is the argumentative dialogue between an offscreen voice speaking for the audience to onscreen actors, and among onscreen actors, in roles of persons in various parts of the world, speaking to each other.

As a final example of the wartime social documentary there is *When We Build Again* (1945), about housing and city planning. Sponsored by Cadbury Brothers, Ltd., makers of chocolates, it was produced by Donald Taylor and

Fig 33 World of Plenty *(UK, 1943, Paul Rotha). Museum of Modern Art Film Stills Archive*

directed by Ralph Bond. Dylan Thomas wrote and read the poetic portions of the commentary. The film begins with a slight narrative of three returning servicemen. The music sounds like and is used in the manner of dramatic films. Inner city slums, suburbs and new towns (like the greenbelt town of *The City*) are surveyed. Interviews, statistics, visual demonstrations of existing housing and models for the future are employed. 'No private interest to stand in our way,' intones the commentator, who calls people 'the greatest capital – the future belongs to them.' This film could be thought of as *Housing Problems* ten years later.

Records of Battle

Desert Victory (1943) – with production by the Army Film and Photographic Unit and the Royal Air Force Film Production Unit, direction by Roy Boulting, and music by William Alwyn – is about the British Eighth Army's campaign in North Africa against the German forces under the command of Field Marshall Erwin Rommel. In this kind of filmmaking, with filmmakers working with miles of footage shot by combat cameramen, two creative problems are uppermost. The first is to give clarity to the mass of confusing, technical detail. The second is to give it dramatic form. These problems are the same as those faced by Esther Shub in *The Fall of the Romanov Dynasty* (1927), discussed in Chapter 3, and by all compilation filmmakers. In *Desert Victory*, the first problem was solved by the use of animated maps to establish the overall patterns and movement of the campaign, and by a carefully planned narration. As for the second, all of the nonartistic material with the irregularity of history inherent in it was organized into a coherent story told chronologically with beginning, middle and end. In addition, the sponsor's requirements – to show each branch of the armed forces, the civilian workers, the presence of US aid, and the like – were fitted into the whole without warping it out of shape.

Desert Victory starts at the lowest point of the campaign. The British, who had retreated across the Sahara pursued by the seemingly invincible Afrika Korps, are halted just sixty miles from Alexandria, deep inside Egypt. Then there is the fierce battle of El Alamein, with the British emerging victorious. From there the film follows the triumphant 1300-mile pursuit of the German army to the final victory at Tripoli. To organize these events so they would appear both clear and dramatic, the filmmakers contrived an alternation of cause and effect. To personalize the mass action, and gain empathy, a number of closeups of individual soldiers (some of them obviously recreated, particularly in the night attack sequences) are inserted. Generals Alexander, Montgomery and Wavell, and Prime Minister Churchill are introduced as well. In comparison with the indoctrinational semidocumentaries, which tended to make the violence of war part of a job of work to be done, *Desert Victory* is singularly bloodthirsty. Perhaps these filmmakers were not inclined to conceal their elation over this first major British victory following the battering Britain had received in the desert fighting and from the air blitz. It was hugely successful at home and abroad, receiving an Oscar as the year's most distinctive achievement in documentary features.

Fig 34 Desert Victory *(UK, 1943, Roy Boulting). Museum of Modern Art Film Stills Archive*

The True Glory (1945) was produced jointly by the British Ministry of Information and the US Office of War Information. It was co-directed by Englishman Carol Reed and American Garson Kanin, both fiction-film directors of considerable distinction. William Alwyn composed the score. It covers the final phase of the war in Europe, from the preparations for the D-Day landings in Normandy through the fall of Berlin, to the establishing of contact between the Western Allies and Soviet troops at the Elbe River. Made from 5.5 million feet of combat footage shot by 500 American, British and other Allied cameramen, it is a vast panorama, yet intensely human, even intimate at moments.

Emotional involvement is gained largely through the experimental use of commentary. The words are complementary to the images, sometimes in humorous or ironic counterpoint to them. Alternating with blank verse choruses are multiple voices representing soldiers involved with the particular

Fig 35 The True Glory *was a triumphant record and hymn to Allied victory in Europe. (UK and US co-production, 1945, Carol Reed and Garson Kanin). Museum of Modern Art Film Stills Archive*

action being shown. The generals' version, spoken by Dwight D. Eisenhower, supreme commander of the Allied forces in Europe, is irreverently interrupted by simulated voices of enlisted men who were there: New York cab driver, cockney Londoner, member of the French Maquis, and others. One marvellous moment occurs when a black American MP directing military traffic at a crossroads explains that the situation is tough, that the invasion forces are bottled up in the Caen Peninsula. 'Then we heard that the Third Army was taking off,' he says. 'They'd pulled a rabbit out of a hat – and what a rabbit! A rabbit with pearl-handled revolvers.' As he utters these last words a tank bearing an erect General George S. Patton roars by.

The True Glory was the final triumphant record and hymn to Allied victory in Europe. The occasion permitted a kind of boasting and self-congratulation without it appearing to be so. Pride is expressed in the massiveness and efficiency of the military machine, and in its democratic character. The participation of many nations is indirectly reiterated without explicit statement being required. The Allied attitude toward war is presented as being purposeful and matter-of-fact, its violence accepted as part of the job, as in the British semidocumentaries. Unlike the semidocumentaries, however, dislike and distrust of the German enemy are strongly stated. The horrors of what the advancing forces discovered at the Belsen concentration camp are included. An American GI, talking about guarding German prisoners of war, says: 'I just keep 'em covered … It wasn't my job to figure 'em out … But, brother, I never gave 'em more than the Geneva convention, and that was all.' Finally, though, it is the positive corollary of the GI's attitude that receives the strongest emphasis. What *The True Glory* is saying mostly is that this was a just and necessary war and that on the Allied side we can all feel proud of winning it.

The joint production ventures near the end of the war of the 'victory series' discussed in Chapter 8, culminating with *The True Glory*, were the final and most complete examples of this collaboration. The centripetal force exerted by war not only brought together documentaries and documentarians of three countries, it also pulled together documentary and fiction filmmakers within each country. Filmmakers of all sorts were working in common cause and sometimes on the same projects. Documentarians gained an unprecedented amount of theatrical screen time. The degree and kind of wartime pulling together in each country were different, of course. Differences among the films of the three nations will be examined in the final section of this chapter. The sections up to that deal with the four major types of wartime films – training, indoctrination, records of battle, social documentary – made in the US.

Part B: Canada

At the outbreak of World War II, Canada was something of a sleeping giant. In certain ways it was also a geographical and cultural anomaly which no orderly minded nation planner would have perpetrated. Larger in area than the United States, with a sparse population stretched across a 200-mile wide strip along its southern border, physically it represented a virtual extension of the United States up into the uninhabitable Arctic. Its prodigious breadth of forest and prairie, blocked at the western end by a fierce mountain range, took considerable conquering before the Atlantic was finally linked to the Pacific.

Considering the open nature of this border, it is easy to understand how both Canada and the US have always laid claim to Flaherty, since he lived and worked in both. In addition to the formidable size of its wilderness, Canadians had always faced a struggle for national identity. At first it was the matter of establishing independence from Great Britain. More recently, the gravitational pull of its powerful neighbour to the south was smothering Canada's distinctiveness. Economically and culturally, as well as geographically, Canada has to fight against becoming something of an extension of the United States.

When war broke out in 1939 the film situation in Canada was considerably different from that in either Britain or the United States. In Canada there was no production of fiction feature films, and theatrical distribution and exhibition were even more dominated by the Americans than in Britain. In fact, there was a negligible amount of Canadian film production of any sort. Britain had a firmly established documentary movement. If the United States' documentary efforts lacked the coherence and overall effectiveness of the British, it had distinguished documentary filmmakers and films it could point to with pride. War and documentary arrived together in Canada at the end of the thirties. A pioneer Government Motion Picture Bureau in Ottawa extended back to 1914, but it provided largely 'scenic and travel pictures' lacking the social relevance of the documentary. By the 1930s it had fallen badly out of touch with current realities, and the filmmaking techniques and styles it employed were quite old-fashioned. No image of productive, modern Canada appeared on the screens anywhere; no adequate acknowledgment was made of its role as a rising world leader with vast natural resources, agricultural and industrial potential. No sure sense of national identity was being given to the Canadian people through film.

Founding of National Film Board

By the mid-thirties, representatives of the Canadian government in London had become interested in the success of British documentary – its dynamic presentation of government services, British people and British problems. At about the same time, John Grierson was asked by the Film Committee of the Imperial Relations Trust, set up by the British government in 1937, to survey government film developments in Canada and other dominions. In 1938 he was invited to Canada, where he investigated, reported on, and made recommendations to the Canadian government regarding its use of film.

In his report Grierson, of course, recommended the creation of a new federal agency. It would produce films that would contribute to a greater sense of relationship among the Canadian people and present an accurate picture of Canada to the rest of the world. The acceptance of his recommendations followed; legislation establishing a National Film Board was passed by the Canadian Parliament in May 1939 and the search for the new Canadian-born Film Commissioner began, but no Canadian with adequate qualifications could be found. Grierson was chosen and accepted the offer in October 1939.

It is important to note that the Film Board was conceived in Canada's peacetime and for peacetime purposes. The legislation creating it decreed its principal mandate to be that of helping 'Canadians in all parts of Canada to understand the ways of living and the problems of Canadians to other parts of the world's'. This was the same goal as that pursued at the Empire Marketing Board ten years earlier by Grierson and Stephen Tallents in showing one part of the Empire to the rest. The Film Board's position as an autonomous government agency with its own budget and representation in Parliament came out of Grierson's frustrations with the limitations of sponsorship. The Board was also to concern itself with 'distribution of Canadian films in other countries'. The first six years of the National Film Board would, however, be focused to considerable extent on Canada's war effort – especially those films made for theatrical release.

Grierson began immediately to build the large and effective organization the National Film Board would become. In this he had the full support of Prime Minister Mackenzie King. Veteran ex-colleagues from Britain were brought over to assist, including Stuart Legg, already in Ottawa making two films for the Canadian government. Available documentary talent from other countries was hired as well: Irving Jacoby (screenwriter and producer) and Roger Barlow (cinematographer) among those from the United States; Joris Ivens and John Ferno from Holland; Boris Kaufman and Alexander Alexeieff (animator of the pinboard technique) from France. And hiring the young Canadians began, not unlike the hiring of young Britons in the earlier EMB and GPO days, except now in much larger numbers.

The production of hundreds and hundreds of films commenced. The first year closed in October 1940 with some forty pictures either in distribution, in production, or in script preparation; by fiscal year 1943-4 the annual rate of release had increased to 200. Two monthly series modelled on 'The March of Time' were distributed in the theatres and subsequently released to nontheatrical audiences. It was a newsreel war not a documentary war, Grierson said, requiring the crude immediacy of reportage rather than the considered refinement of art.

Theatrical Series

The first series was 'Canada Carries On', intended primarily to depict Canada's part in the war to its own people and to others. The initial CCO release was

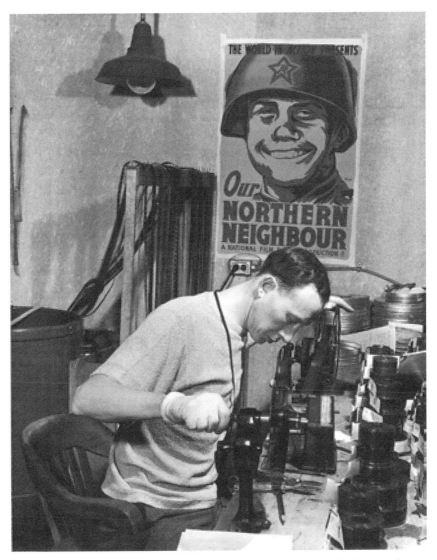

Fig 36 *Stuart Legg, the producer of 'The World in Action' monthly theatrical documentary series for the National Film Board of Canada, edits (1945, Canada, Stuart Legg). Canadian Government Photo Centre*

Atlantic Patrol (April 1940). It was about the work of the Canadian navy in protecting the huge convoys that sailed from Halifax to Britain from German submarine attack. *Churchill's Island* (June 1941), about Britain at war, won an Academy Award, one of the first given for best documentary.

The Canadian series demonstrated an uncanny knack for latching onto what was about to happen. *Warclouds in the Pacific* (November 1941), appearing ten days before the Japanese attack on Pearl Harbor, contained some borrowed 'March of Time' footage. de Rochemont tried to hold up its release to prevent it from scooping the MOT. *Zero Hour – The Story of the Invasion* (June 1944) was another scoop: the first account of the Allied invasion of Normandy to reach the screen. NFB personnel had assembled footage on D-Day preparations in Britain. Then they prepared more than a dozen different endings covering possible landing sites from Norway to the Mediterranean. When the invasion occurred, the appropriate ending was added and the film was released in the United States and Canada within three days.

If 'Canada Carries On' paid 'The March of Time' the compliment of imitation, the second, even more ambitious series began to compete with MOT in the world market, including the United States. Entitled 'The World in Action', it appeared two years after CCO had begun. With some exceptions, Stuart Legg wrote and directed every issue; United Artists distributed. Technically this Canadian series advanced in some respects from its American counterpart. Words and images were cut together in complex and artistic ways. The music, by Louis Applebaum, was subtler and more sophisticated. The commentator, Lorne Greene, had a deeper, richer voice than Westbrook Van Voorhis. (Greene would go on to play the father in the popular US television series *Bonanza*.)

Food – Weapon of Conquest (March 1942), the second release, is one example. *Time* magazine called it 'a blueprint of how to make an involved, dull, major aspect of World War II understandable and acceptable to moviegoers.' *Inside Fighting Russia* (April 1942) comprised mostly footage obtained from the USSR. Since the Soviets tended to be secretive, this represented quite a coup. *The War for Men's Minds* (June 1943) concerned psychological warfare. (Grierson took secret delight in being called 'the Goebbels of Canada', in reference to Nazi propaganda minister Josef Goebbels, though he thought Hitler the true genius of propaganda.) The most ambitious and intellectual of the WIA films, *The War for Men's Minds*, was also the first of the Canadian films to look ahead to peace.

The two series were distinctive in their departure from usual wartime propaganda emphases. There was very little hatred or violence in these films. 'World in Action' emphasis shifted from matters of immediate wartime preoccupations to those that would concern the post-war world. The international view and steady look ahead to peace were quite exceptional during wartime. Examples of internationalism would be *Labour Front* (October 1943) and, especially, *Global Air Routes* (April 1944). Grierson felt satisfaction in turning the globe upside down, as he put it, in the NFB films – putting Canada at the centre rather than the periphery of the world.

Nontheatrical Films

The great majority of those hundreds of films produced by the Film Board were for nontheatrical distribution rather than for the theatres, and were less likely to be war-related than the theatrical series. In fact, they dealt with a wide variety of subjects aimed at various audiences. These included intimate regional studies (for instance, on the life of a Quebec priest, or on Gran Manan Island), and the building of the Alaska Highway. There were also cultural shorts such as *Flight of the Dragon*, about the collection of Chinese art in the Royal Ontario Museum. Gudrun Bjerring, a woman, made a fifteen-minute film called *Before They Are Six*, intended particularly for mothers who ran a home and a factory workbench in a wartime plant.

Canada's comprehensive system of 16mm nontheatrical distribution and exhibition was unequalled and remained so for decades. It reported an annual audience larger than the national population. The films, in fact, grew out of the needs of the audiences to a remarkable degree; 'audience response' was the key term, uniquely important in the growth of the NFB. A network of nontheatrical showings was created by the Board (preceding television, of course), with rural circuits, national trade union circuits and industrial circuits being established. Showings were held by the women's club or library, for example, or by the YMCA or at a grange meeting. Sixteen-millimetre prints were borrowed from regional libraries. Volunteer projection services provided trained projectionists and taught others to operate projectors. Film councils formed, consisting of representatives from each of the local organizations using films. They would meet, once a month perhaps, to discuss and plan ways of improving the use of films'. So, a kind of decentralized leadership emerged and a feedback process started. It was not just the government telling the Film Board what it wanted films to be about. This strategy became the model for the development of the US system of nontheatrical, educational distribution.

Summary

The salient observation to be made about the National Film Board is that the kind of organization Grierson was able to construct in Canada was an unrivalled information system, the largest and best-coordinated government film operation in the world. By 1945, the end of the war, it was producing 300 films a year. Most of the Film Board releases reached an audience of roughly four million. It had a government paid staff of about 700 in production and distribution. All of this was achieved by a nation with a population of only twelve million.

The '5 1/2 films a week', as Grierson characterized the Film Board output when it had reached full speed, were often skilfully made, usually timely in subject matter (rather than timeless), quickly produced, and designed to reach as wide an audience as the subject and purpose permitted. In artistic terms, they had a roughness along with their urgency. Those films were valued by their audiences as well as by their producers for what they were – an almost television-like flow (before television) of information and coverage of important topics.

During the war a rift occurred between Grierson and his former British colleagues over the kind of documentaries that needed to be made. Grierson thought the British documentaries too soft and aestheticky. 'Sure London can take it,' he would say, in reference to the influential British documentary of that title, 'but can she dish it out?', paraphrasing dialogue from one of his favourite gangster movies, *Little Caesar*. Grierson saw early British wartime propaganda as reflecting a country preparing to go down with quiet heroism into defeat. There is an anecdote about Grierson preventing the young Canadians from screening a print of *Listen to Britain* so that they would not be distracted by its loveliness from the more vigorous style he wanted them to develop. Some of the British, for their part, found the Canadian films' illustrated lectures lacking in artistic sophistication, which infuriated Grierson.

Perhaps, finally, the sheer establishment of the National Film Board – which went on to other kinds of achievement, including aesthetic excellence, while the documentary movements in Britain and America faltered during the 1950s – is the great legacy of the wartime documentary efforts in Canada. It stands as the largest and most impressive monument to Grierson's concepts and activities relating to the use of film by governments in communication with their citizens. It became a model for national film boards established in New Zealand, Australia, South Africa, India and elsewhere. Grierson himself called the Film Board 'a tidy operation, the tidiest [he] was involved with'.

Part C: United States

In the US, the first two years of the 1940s were essentially an extension of the 1930s, but the extreme hardships of the Depression were gradually alleviated as the country backed into war. At President Roosevelt's request, Prime Minister Winston Churchill agreed not to send British wartime propaganda to the United States until the US officially entered the war. Roosevelt was concerned that such a clear indication of his administration's pro-British and pro-war stance would disturb the illusion of neutrality and provide American isolationists with evidence to use against him. Since no such agreement had been made with Canada, John Grierson, head of its National Film Board, saw to it that some British documentaries filtered into United States along with those of Canada. Britain's and Canada's early wartime documentaries may have contributed to moving America from sympathy to action on behalf of Britain. However, not until the Japanese attack on the US naval base at Pearl Harbor on 7 December 1941, followed by Germany's declaration of war, did the United States join the widening world conflict. Entry into the war had as profound an effect on documentary film in the US as it had had on America's allies, Britain and Canada.

The war brought English-language documentary together in ways and to a degree not true of any other period in its history. The people of Britain, Canada and the United States viewed each other's films about the war. Film materials were exchanged – stock-shot library footage, combat footage, captured enemy footage. Films about each other were produced to orient troops and civilians as to our differences as well as to our common ways and to the ways in which we each depended on the other for survival. The joint production ventures near the end of the war, culminating with the Oscar-winning co-production by Carol Reed and Garson Kanin, *The True Glory* (1945), were the final and most complete examples of this collaboration.

The centripetal force exerted by war not only brought together documentaries and documentarians of the three countries, it pulled together documentary and fiction filmmakers within each country. Filmmakers of all sorts were working in common cause and sometimes on the same projects, and documentaries gained an unprecedented amount of theatrical screen time. Newsreels played an even more important role than they had before. Only through newsreels was the public able to see live pictures of troops at rest and on the battlefront within weeks, sometimes days of the footage being shot.

Training

As with British wartime documentary, hundreds of 'nuts and bolts' films were made, on every conceivable subject. A random sample of those in the US might include the following: *Articles of War, Military Courtesy, Keep It Clean* (how and why to take care of a gun), *Resisting Enemy Interrogation,* and *Sex Hygiene*. In *Identification of the Japanese Zero* (1942) a young Ronald Reagan plays a flyer who mistakes a friend's P40 for a Japanese Zero and tries to shoot it down. In the end he gets a chance to down a real Zero. These training films were tested to be extremely effective pedagogically (see Hovland, Lumsdaine and Sheffield, *Experiments on Mass Communication*.)

Indoctrination – Why We Fight

Rather than using the 'un-American' terms *indoctrination* or *propaganda*, the US Armed Forces engaged in what it called *orientation*. Central to the massive effort directed toward converting more than nine million Americans from civilians into military personnel was the seven-part 'Why We Fight' series. The production of this series and of other important information and education films was entrusted to Lt. Col. Frank Capra. One of the most popular Hollywood directors of the 1930s (*It Happened One Night, Mr Smith Goes to Washington*), Capra had no prior documentary experience. (The same could be said of virtually all the Hollywood filmmakers involved with wartime documentaries.) He was assisted by Major Anatole Litvak and Captains Anthony Veiller and William Hornbeck – Hollywood veterans all; director, writer, and editor, respectively. Sgt. Richard Griffith (subsequently head of the film department of the Museum of Modern Art) did research. In addition to 'Why We Fight', the Capra group made other large-scale films designed to orient American troops to the foreigners – allies and enemies – with whom they were about to come into contact. Examples are *Know Your Ally – Britain* (1943), *Here Is Germany* (1945), and *Know Your Enemy – Japan* (1946).

'Why We Fight' was based on the assumption that servicemen would be more committed and able fighters if they knew about the events leading up to, and the reasons for, US participation in the war. The spirit of isolationism – still strong in America right up to the Japanese attack on Pearl Harbor – had to be counteracted. In this attempt, 'Why We Fight' presented a gigantic historical treatise from a particular point of view – that is to say, from the perspective of Roosevelt's New Deal Democratic administration, which became the predominant viewpoint during the war.

'Why We Fight' is most impressive in the scale of its conception and the virtuosity of its execution. Almost entirely compiled from existing footage, including newsreels, Allied and captured enemy records of battle, bits from fiction features, and Nazi propaganda films, through editing and commentary it presents a vast and coherent panorama.

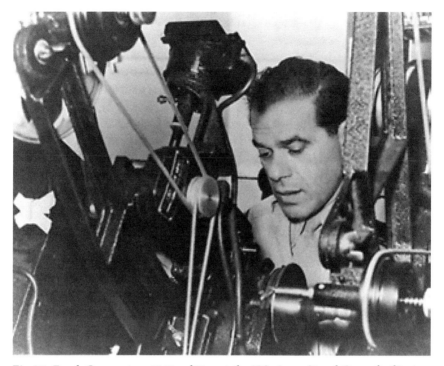

Fig 37 *Frank Capra, circa 1943, editing at the U.S. Army Signal Corps facility in Astoria, New York*

The first three films – *Prelude to War* (1942), *The Nazis Strike* (1943) and *Divide and Conquer* (1943) – cover the period 1918 to 1941. They document the increase in Japanese aggression in Asia, the growing menace of Hitler in Europe and, above all, the changing American foreign policy and public opinion between the end of World War I and US entry into World War II. *The Battle of Britain* (1943), *The Battle of Russia* (1943) and *The Battle of China* (1944) cover the efforts of the Allies who were in the war before the US and continued to fight alongside US troops. *War Comes to America* (1945) offered a recapitulation and even more detailed examination of changes in American attitudes over the preceding two decades, and of the conflicting impulses and ideologies that shaped them. Picking up and consolidating the themes of the first three films, it was made last but intended to be shown first.

The films, short features in length, were shown to servicemen; viewing of all seven was compulsory before embarkation for overseas duty. Though

Fig 38 *Theatrical poster for* The Battle of Russia *of the 'Why We Fight' series (US, 1943, Anatole Litvak). Academy of Motion Pictures Arts and Sciences*

designed solely for showing to military personnel. When their excellence and dramatic power were recognized by the War Department some of them were made available for civilian audiences through theatrical exhibition.

The chief artistic problem the makers of these films faced was one of giving structure to vast amounts of unstructured history. Dramatic form was given to each of the films, with exposition, mounting action, climax and denouement. They can be broken down into acts. *Divide and Conquer*, for example, has five acts, like classical tragedy. Act I contains exposition: Poland has been overrun by Germany; conquest of Britain is now its goal; German strategy is outlined; the theme of Hitler's lying treachery is sounded. The content of Act II is the successful German campaign against Denmark and Norway. Act III deals with the position of France, the Maginot Line, and French weakness. Act IV comprises the German conquest of Holland and Belgium. Act V is the fall of France. The various participant countries are given character; they become characters, like dramatis personae.

A considerable variety of visual and audio resources is used in these compiled documentaries – very nearly the full range conceivable. Visuals in *The Nazis Strike*, for instance, include, in addition to combat and newsreel footage, excerpts from the Nazi *Triumph of the Will*, bits of staged action (the victims of firing squads), still photos, drawings and maps, animated diagrams (the animation by Walt Disney Studio), newspaper headlines, and printed titles (Hitler's pronouncements). The soundtrack includes two narrators (Anthony Veiller for the factual, Walter Huston for the emotional), quoted dialogue (Churchill, and an impersonation of Hitler), music (by Dmitri Tiomkin), and sound effects. Dramatic conflict is obtained by painstaking manipulation of combat footage. Editing conventions of matched action and screen direction are maintained. German attackers always move from right to left. A synthetic assemblage of diverse shots is edited into a cause-effect order: German bombers in formation, bombs dropping from planes, explosions in villages, rubble. The result is almost as if all of this footage had been shot for these films under Capra's or Litvak's direction. Maps and animated diagrams give scope to the live-action sequences, clarify and relate random material to formalized patterns consistent with the actual movement. The animation takes on symbolic and rhetorical meaning; in *Divide and Conquer*, swastika termites infest the base of a castle, and python-like arrows lock around the British Isles.

Although 'Why We Fight' is greatly admired on technical and aesthetic grounds, there is some convincing evidence that it was not as effective indoctrination as hoped for and even thought to be (see Hovland, Lumsdaine and Sheffield, *Experiments on Mass Communication*). The problem, the social scientists inferred from their testing, was with the historical approach. It seemed to have the desired effects only on those with the equivalent of some college education; it appeared to be too intellectual and over the heads of a majority of soldiers tested. As film, though, 'Why We Fight' offers incontrovertible evidence of very great filmmaking skill and a remarkably full and varied use of film technique. It stands as a peak of achievement in the history of documentary, and influenced subsequent historical compilation films, especially the many which later appeared on television. Quite likely, it helped to win the war.

Records of Battle

As with the 'Why We Fight' series, others of the most prestigious wartime documentaries were made for the Armed Forces by Hollywood veterans. Among them were John Ford, John Huston and William Wyler.

John Ford's fiction features gave him a status at least as great as Capra's; his fictional films also emphasized American themes, though in his case usually historical (*Stagecoach, Young Mr Lincoln, Drums Along the Mohawk*). He enlisted in the Navy rather than the Army. Much of *The Battle of Midway* (1942) he filmed himself with a 16mm handheld camera, and he was seriously wounded during the filming. It won an Academy Award. It is early and unusual in using colour, which would come into documentary for the first time during the war. (Eastman Kodak had introduced the first practicable 16mm colour film for ordinary home movie use, Kodachrome, in 1935.) Ford's *December 7th* (1943) is a largely recreated account of the Japanese attack on Pearl Harbor using miniatures, rear screen projection, process photography, and actors. (It was shot by Gregg Toland, cinematographer of *The Grapes of*

Wrath and *Citizen Kane*.) Though the emotionalism of these two films may strike audiences today as excessive, they accurately reflect the feelings of many people at the time they were made.

John Huston (whose pre-war success included *The Maltese Falcon*) made some of the finest and most personal of the wartime documentaries. His subsequent filmmaking seems to have gained considerably from that experience. Many think *The Battle of San Pietro* (1945) is the finest American wartime documentary; it is among the most outstanding films made about men in battle. It is an engrossing account of a full week of savage fighting between American and German forces in Italy for the control of the Liri Valley. The taking of a small military objective becomes an indictment of modern warfare in general, with its incredible cost both in military and civilian casualties. This theme is underscored as we see bodies of soldiers being buried beneath dog tag markers. After the battle, the people of San Pietro return to their devastated village and must somehow find the strength to rebuild their shattered lives. The weary Americans will move on to 'more rivers, and more mountains, and more towns ... more "San Pietros", greater or lesser – a thousand more.' The commentary was written and read by Huston. *Let There Be Light* (1946), Huston's final wartime documentary, is discussed later.

William Wyler (director of *Wuthering Heights* and *The Little Foxes*) served in the Army Air Force. His *Memphis Belle* (1944) is, in a way, an answer to the British *Target for Tonight*. It is interesting that Hollywood director Wyler used candid colour footage of a real raid (one of his cameramen was killed while filming) with voiceover narration. The 'Memphis Belle' was a Boeing B17 'flying fortress' on its last bombing mission over Germany before its veteran crew was sent home. The world we see and hear is that of the airmen – refracted images of sky and enemy fighters seen through plexiglass, the drone of engines, and excited voices over the intercom. The film seems to come very close to the reality of their experience. The title of Wyler's *Thunderbolt* (1945, in colour) is what the P47 fighter-bomber was called. The film deals with the activities of the 57th Fighter Group in Italy destroying vital supply routes deep behind German lines.

In addition to combat documentaries identified with particular Hollywood directors were those made collaboratively by film crews of the various armed

Fig 39 *American troops on the attack in* The Battle of San Pietro. *Huston's original version, using the voices of dead men (recorded before battle) as narration over photographs of their bodies, was cut by the military authorities (US, 1944, John Huston). Museum of Modern Art Film Still Archive*

services. A notable group of these reported on warfare in the Pacific. *The Battle for the Marianas* (1944) concerns a joint Army, Navy, Marine and Coast Guard assault on Saipan, Tinian and Guam, the major islands of the Mariana group. In *Attack! The Battle for New Britain* (1944) explanations of the strategy are accompanied by comments about life in the jungle. *To the Shores of Iwo Jima* (1945) is one of the fullest and most skilfully made accounts of a combined operation. *Fury in the Pacific* (1945) is unusual in the number and intensity of the shots of Japanese and Americans being killed in battle, which is probably why it was not released until after the war. Nine cameramen fell while filming.

The Fighting Lady (1944) is about the final phase of the war in the Pacific (fought almost exclusively between American and Japanese forces). It is feature-length and in Technicolor. The title refers to an aircraft carrier, in this

Fig 40 The Fighting Lady, *made by de Rochemont after leaving 'The March of Time' (US, 1944, de Rochemont). Museum of Modern Art Film Stills Archive*

case the *Yorktown*. The action concerns defence against attacks of kamikaze pilots diving to their deaths, trying to take American warships with them. Directed by famed still photographer Edward Steichen, it was narrated by movie star Robert Taylor, both then in the Navy. It was produced by de Rochemont, who had left 'The March of Time' to become a producer at Twentieth Century-Fox, which distributed *The Fighting Lady* and was also then distributing 'The March of Time'.

Social Documentary

In 1940, before America's entry into the war, Roosevelt appointed Nelson Rockefeller as Coordinator of Inter-American Affairs (CIAA). This new agency was occasioned largely by US nervousness about the growing German presence in Latin America, through increased immigration and growth in trade. The conception of the CIAA was not unlike that of the earlier British Empire Marketing Board: government public relations working to increase economic and political interdependency and mutual support.

One film about Latin America made for the CIAA was *The Bridge* (1944), directed by Willard Van Dyke and Ben Maddow. It is about the economics of South America and the importance of air transport in connecting its countries with each other and with North America. A cluster of films for the CIAA were produced by the Walt Disney Studio. They are clever and imaginative, using animation for teaching and communication. *The Grain That Built a Hemisphere* (1943) is a historical survey of the importance of maize/corn in the nutrition and economies of the American continents. *Water – Friend or Enemy* (1944) offers basic education in the importance of uncontaminated water and methods for obtaining it. The Disney films were distributed widely in both Spanish- and English-language versions. The Disney Studio also made instructional films for the Armed Forces. *Cold Front* and *Fog*, both 1943, are two examples.

The most notorious of these films – although not a documentary – was Orson Welles' ill-fated *It's All True* (1941). Rockefeller, who was on the board of directors of RKO (the studio for which Welles was making *The Magnificent Ambersons*) requested that Welles make the film, but when Rockefeller left the board and the studio felt Welles was spending too much money, the project was cancelled. Welles had left *Ambersons* in the middle of editing and felt that it was butchered by the studio in his absence. *It's All True* was left unfinished.

In 1942, following United States entry into the war, the Office of War Information (OWI) was set up. This agency was equivalent to the British Ministry of Information and the Canadian Wartime Information Board. News commentator Elmer Davis was named head of the OWI. Its function was to coordinate all government information released to the media and to develop its own means of informing the public. The Motion Picture Bureau of the OWI was headed by Robert Riskin, scriptwriter for some of Frank Capra's most successful features. It established liaison with the Hollywood studios, primarily to ensure that entertainment films did not contain material harmful to morale or to US relationships with its allies. The Motion Picture Bureau also produced its own films.

The purpose of the Domestic Branch of the Motion Picture Bureau was to make films for American civilian viewing, somewhat along the lines of the British Crown Film Unit or the Canadian National Film Board. The Overseas Branch was to make films for showing to allies, neutral countries, and countries which had been under Axis occupation. It is characteristic of Americans' suspiciousness about government information directed at them that the Domestic Branch never succeeded in getting a production programme underway. The Overseas Branch, on the other hand, had a distinguished wartime record, its films made largely by documentary veterans. Though not as big, prestigious or expensive as the Armed Forces documentaries made by Hollywood directors, the OWI films, taken together, offer a broad and sensitive picture of diverse aspects of life in the United States. Among them were *Autobiography of a Jeep* (1943, Joseph Krumgold), a jaunty tribute to that product of American wartime technology. Following a showing in liberated France, the audience is said to have burst into shouts of 'Vive le jip! Vive le jip!'. *The Town* (1944, Josef von Sternberg) is about the contribution of many cultures to the United States as evidenced in the eclectic architecture, mixed population, and many religions of Madison, Indiana. *Pacific Northwest* (1944, Willard Van Dyke) describes and interprets the Northwestern states.

One quite singular film was *The Negro Soldier* (1944). The US Army used it as a means to convince African-Americans to enlist and to point out the contributions that blacks had made to the American military. It ultimately influenced army members and civilians of all races. The structure of the film is that of a black minister who preaches to his all-black congregation. He recounts the contributions of blacks in American military history, from Crispus Attucks and the Boston Massacre to the men who served in World War I, along the way touching on the War of 1812, the Civil War and the Spanish-American War. The film is a typical blend of archival footage and re-creations and even includes a re-creation of the destruction by the Nazis of a World War I monument in France to African-American soldiers. The second half is made up of graphic images of hangings, bombings and bodies; following the story of a young man through basic training; and wrapping up depicting African-Americans serving in all aspects of military life.

Let There Be Light (1946, John Huston), though produced by the Army Pictorial Service, was intended mainly for civilian audiences. It serves as a painful and moving reflection on the mental and emotional casualties of war. What had been called 'shell shock' in World War I became 'battle fatigue' in World War II; today it is known as 'post-traumatic stress syndrome'. Whatever called, the symptoms are equally debilitating. *Let There Be Light* examines the then current types of rehabilitation of the psychosomatically disabled at Mason General Hospital in Brentwood, Long Island. The psychotherapy is observed with close attention to particular cases. A GI who lost his memory during a shell burst at Okinawa is hypnotized and begins to recall his terror and fear of battle. Another soldier, who stutters, is given sodium amytol. He begins to speak and then to shout, half-sobbing: 'I can TALK! Oh God, listen! God, I can talk.'

It may seem overly dramatic and staged today, but at the time its impact seemed threatening. *Let There Be Light* was not released until almost forty years after it was completed. The Army said they were concerned about invasion of privacy of the men shown. Huston said they were concerned about showing the public the terrible and lasting psychological damage of war.

Comparisons: Great Britain, Canada, United States

A key aspect of wartime documentary in the three countries was that the films were all government sponsored, and related in one way or another to what was seen as needed in the national interest. Private sponsorship of nonfiction films virtually ceased during the war. Beyond that similarity, however, there were significant differences between the three countries, beginning with the context of documentary in each at the outbreak of war.

In Britain, before the war, documentary was a thoroughly established enterprise. It was not large in terms of amounts of money, numbers of filmmakers and films made, or total audience size, admittedly, but it had earned respect among opinion-leaders and gained a central relationship to matters of public concern. The British entertainment film industry, on the other hand, rested more firmly on the distribution and exhibition of American films than on the production of British ones. As a result, it was the documentarians who obtained the choice assignments and made the finest of the British wartime documentaries.

In Canada, little filmmaking of any sort had existed before the war. When the National Film Board was established, it became the main, almost the sole producer of Canadian wartime films. Its staff – consisting of a few documentary veterans from abroad and hundreds of Canadian tyros – made mainly documentary and related types of informational and instructional films.

In the United States, pre-war documentary had been individualistic and lacking power compared with monolithic Hollywood. It also tended toward left-wing politics. As a result, it was the Hollywood filmmakers who got the big Armed Forces projects and made some of the most valuable and lasting of the wartime documentaries. The American documentary veterans, for the most part, worked on smaller-scale projects for the Coordinator of Inter-American Affairs and the Office of War Information. These were closer to a continuation of the peacetime documentary, albeit with different themes, than were other American wartime documentaries.

The following is a comparison of wartime nonfiction films produced in the United States, Canada and Britain. Since the training films were generally alike, the comparison is confined to the indoctrination films, records of battle, and social documentary.

As one might expect, the greatest differences among documentaries of the three nations are evident in their **indoctrination films**. In Britain the most important of these took the form of poetic, sometimes experimental shorts and semidocumentary features. One noteworthy characteristic of all these British films is the lack of attention given to the violence and destructiveness of war, even less to vilification and hatred of the enemy. Instead, two themes are repeated, subtly and insistently. One is that Britain will survive – or, as put in the final words of 'The British Grenadier' (aka 'Rule Britannia'), which accompanies the conclusion of *Listen to Britain*, 'England never, never will be slave'. The other is that the British are all in this together; everyone is doing his or her job. The reason for the first of these two emphases is clear enough. Britain was facing German military might massed across a narrow Channel, and destruction rained down nightly from the skies. Survival was a matter of real and immediate general and personal concern. The second relates to class divisions persisting in England. Many of the working class had come to feel that their sacrifices in WWI had benefited the already privileged more than themselves. This time everyone is shown working with everyone else for everyone's post-war world.

Canadian indoctrination films took the form of the two 'March-of-Time'-like monthly theatrical shorts, 'Canada Carries On' and 'The World in Action'. These offer information about and interpretation of aspects of the world at war, showing their meaning for Canadians and Canada's relationship to them. There are two emphases here as well: one is that Canadians are doing their part; the other is that Canada is an important part of the world. The divisive issue of differences between French-speaking Canada (which did not fully support the war effort) and English-speaking Canada (which did) was avoided. Canadians are Canadians are Canadians in these films, whatever their ethnic backgrounds.

In the United States the main form of indoctrination films was the large historical compilation (short feature in length). The 'Why We Fight' series was the centrepiece. The emphases in them are, first, that our enemies (Germany, Japan, Italy) are unethical, sometimes even inhuman. Audiences today are shocked by the racism, chauvinism and incitement to hatred evident, but it was the accepted norm for that time. Second, that it is in America's interest to join the allies in helping destroy these enemies; if we don't, eventually they will invade and conquer us. This was a very real fear for many Americans.

British **records of battle** were mainly the large-scale feature-length 'victory series', which chronicled successfully completed campaigns. The series began with *Desert Victory* (North Africa) and concluded with *The True Glory* (Europe).

Canadians made few 'shot and shell' films, as Grierson called the accounts of combat. Strategy rather than tactics was the principal concern – the goals and progress of the war, the general problems which had to be resolved. Canadian films about warfare were mostly informational and analytical rather than descriptive and emotional; little battle was shown.

The Americans made a large number of battle films and became especially accomplished at this kind of documentary. They are, of course, full of violence and the attitudes expressed are jingoistic and frequently racist. The US was more distant from the war than were the British; more people were involved in it than were the Canadians (where a draft was never adopted). So there was felt to be a need for Americans to report back to Americans what war was really like.

Finally, there were continuations of the **social documentary**. British wartime documentaries frequently contain quite explicit references to what will be needed in the peace ahead, sometimes from what would seem a socialist point of view. The work of Paul Rotha in England is noteworthy here, especially *World of Plenty*, about international food distribution, and *Land of Promise*, about post-war housing.

The Canadian films are exceptional in their selection of subjects, having to do with peacetime needs and aspirations as well as with the wartime situation. Grierson said that everything that was built at the NFB in wartime was built for peacetime as well.

The American wartime documentaries continued peacetime subjects and themes only for special reasons. Those films produced for the Coordinator of Inter-American Affairs were directed at improving US relations with Latin American countries, and those for the Office of War Information were designed to present a favourable picture of American ways of life to neutral peoples and those who had been freed from occupation by the Axis powers. Admittedly what was shown was idealized, but the CIAA and OWI films reflect how a lot of Americans like to think about themselves. These films were made not only to counteract enemy propaganda, but also the overblown pictures of American life offered by Hollywood movies, with their gangsters and millionaires, materialism and glamour.

By the end of the war, documentary in Britain, Canada and the United States had reached a pinnacle. More money was being invested in documentary production, more personnel were making more documentary films than ever before. Vastly larger audiences were seeing documentaries and related types of realist and educational films in theatres and in greatly increased nontheatrical showings.

Chapter Related Films: Britain

1940
London Can Take It (Harry Watt and Humphrey Jennings)
They Also Serve (Ruby Grierson)
1941
Merchant Seamen (J. B. Holmes)
Target for Tonight (Watt)
1942
Coastal Command (Holmes)
The Harvest Shall Come (Max Anderson)
Listen to Britain (Jennings)
1943
Desert Victory (Roy Boulting)
Fires Were Started (Jennings)
The Silent Village (Jennings)
World of Plenty (Paul Rotha)
1944
Children of the City (Budge Cooper)
Tunisian Victory (Boulting and Frank Capra)
Western Approaches (Pat Jackson)
1945
Burma Victory (Boulting)
A Diary for Timothy (Jennings)
The True Glory (Carol Reed and Garson Kanin)

Chapter Related Books: Britain

Aldgate, Anthony and Jeffrey Richards, *Britain Can Take It: The British Cinema in the Second World War*. Oxford: Basil Blackwell, 1986.

Aitken, Ian, ed., *The Documentary Film Movement: An Anthology*. Edinburgh: Edinburgh University Press, 1998.

Arts Enquiry, The, *The Factual Film*. London: Oxford University Press, 1947.

Chapman, James, *The British at War: Cinema, State and Propaganda, 1939–1945*. London: I. B. Tauris, 1998.

Coultass, Clive, *Images of Battle: British Film and the Second World War*. London: Associated University Presses, 1988.

Hardy, Forsyth, 'The British Documentary Film', *Twenty Years of British Film 1925–1945*, eds Michael Balcon and others. London: Falcon, 1947, pp. 45–80.

Hodgkinson, Anthony W. and Rodney E. Sheratsky, *Humphrey Jennings: More than a Maker of Films*. Hanover, NH: University Press of New England, 1982.

Jennings, Mary-Lou, ed., *Humphrey Jennings: Film-Maker/Painter/Poet*. London: British Film Institute, 1982.

Lovell, Alan and Jim Hillier, *Studies in Documentary*. New York: Viking, 1972.

Manvell, Roger, *Films and the Second World War*. New York: Dell, 1974.

Powell, Dilys, *Films Since 1939*. London: Longmans, Green, 1947.

Rotha, Paul with Eric Knight, *World of Plenty: The Book of the Film*. London: Nicholson and Watson, 1945.

Sussex, Elizabeth, *The Rise and Fall of British Documentary: The Story of the Film Movement Founded by John Grierson*. Berkeley: University of California Press, 1975.

Swann, Paul, *The British Documentary Film Movement, 1926–1946*. Cambridge: Cambridge University Press, 1989.

Taylor, Philip M., ed., *Britain and the Cinema in the Second World War*. New York: St Martin's Press, 1988.

Thorpe, Frances and Nicholas Pronay, *British Official Films in the Second World War: A Descriptive Catalogue*. Oxford: Clio, 1980.

Vaughan, Dai, *Portrait of an Invisible Man: The Working Life of Stewart McAllister, Film Editor*. London: British Film Institute, 1983.

Watt, Harry, *Don't Look at the Camera*. London: Paul Elek, 1974.

Winston, Brian, *Fires Were Started*. London: British Film Institute, 2000.

Chapter Related Films: Canada

1939
The Case of Charlie Gordon (Stuart Legg)
1940
Atlantic Patrol ('Canada Carries On' series, Legg)
Hot Ice (Irving Jacoby)
Letter from Camp Bordon (CCO, Raymond Spottiswoode)
1941
Canadian Landscape (F. R. Crawley)
Churchill's Island (CCO, Legg)
Peoples of Canada (CCO, Gordon Sparling)
Strategy of Metals (CCO, Stanley Hawes)
Warclouds in the Pacific (CCO, Legg)
1942
Action Stations! (Joris Ivens)
Food – Weapon of Conquest ('The World in Action' series, Legg)
Geopolitik – Hitler's Plan for Empire (WIA, Legg)
13th Platoon (Julian Roffman)
West Wind (Crawley)
1943
High Over the Borders (Jacoby)
The War for Men's Minds (WIA, Legg)

1944
Look to the North (James Beveridge)
When Asia Speaks (WIA, Legg)
Zero Hour – The Story of the Invasion (CCO, Legg)
1945
Food – Secret of the Peace (WIA, Legg)
Listen to the Prairies (Gudrun Bjerring [Parker])
Maps in Action (Evelyn Lambart)
Music in the Wind (Jean Palardy)
Now – The Peace (WIA, Legg)

Chapter Related Books: Canada

Backhouse, Charles, *Canadian Government Motion Picture Bureau 1917–1941*. Ottawa: Canadian Film Institute, 1974.

Beattie, Eleanor, *A Handbook of Canadian Film*. Toronto: Peter Martin Associates, 1973.

Beveridge, James, *John Grierson: Film Master*. New York: Macmillan, 1978.

Ellis, Jack C., *John Grierson: A Guide to References and Resources*. Boston: G. K. Hall, 1986.

Ellis, Jack C., *John Grierson: Life, Contributions, Influence*. Carbondale: University of Southern Illinois Press, 2000.

Evans, Gary, *John Grierson and the National Film Board: The Politics of Wartime Propaganda*. Toronto: University of Toronto Press, 1984.

Feldman, Seth and Joyce Nelson, (eds), *Canadian Film Reader*. Toronto: Peter Martin Associates, 1977.

Grierson Project, McGill University, The John, *John Grierson and the NFB*. Toronto: ECW Press, 1984

Hardy, Forsyth, *John Grierson: A Documentary Biography*. London: Faber and Faber, 1979.

James, C. Rodney, *Film as a National Art: NFB of Canada and the Film Board Idea*. New York: Arno Press, 1977.

Jones, D. B., *Movies and Memoranda: An Interpretive History of the National Film Board of Canada*. Ottawa: Canadian Film Institute and Deneau Publishers, 1981.

Manvell, Roger, *Film and the Second World War*. New York: Dell, 1974.

McKay, Marjorie, *History of the National Film Board of Canada*. Montreal: National Film Board, 1964.

Nelson, Joyce, *The Colonized Eye: Rethinking the Grierson Legend*. Toronto: Between the Lines, 1988.

Chapter Related Films: United States

1943

The Autobiography of a Jeep (Irving Lerner)

The Battle of Britain ('Why We Fight' series, Anthony Veiller)

The Battle of Midway (John Ford)

Divide and Conquer ('Why We Fight' series, Frank Capra and Anatole Litvak)

High Plain (Jules Bucher)

The Nazis Strike ('Why We Fight' series, Capra and Litvak)

Prelude to War ('Why We Fight' series, Capra)

Report from the Aleutians (John Huston)

World at War (Samuel Spewack)

1944

Attack! The Battle for New Britain (War Department)

The Battle of China ('Why We Fight' series, Capra)

The Battle of Russia ('Why We Fight' series, Litvak)

The Bridge (Willard Van Dyke and Ben Maddow)

The Fighting Lady (Edward Steichen)

Hymn of the Nations (Alexander Hammid)

Memphis Belle (William Wyler)

The Negro Soldier (Capra and Stuart Heisler)

A Salute to France (Jean Renoir and Garson Kanin)

Steel Town (Van Dyke)

The Town (Josef von Sternberg)

Valley of the Tennessee (Hammid)

With the Marines at Tarawa (Marine Corps)

1945

El Agente Agronomo (The County Agent, Julien Bryan)

The Battle of San Pietro (Huston)

A Better Tomorrow (Hammid)

Capital Story (Henwar Rodakiewicz)

The Cummington Story (Helen Grayson and Larry Madison)

Fury in the Pacific (Army, Navy, and Marine Corps*)*

The Library of Congress (Hammid)

Thunderbolt (Wyler)

To the Shores of Iwo Jima (Navy, Marine Corps, and Coast Guard)

Tuesday in November (John Houseman)

War Comes to America ('Why We Fight' series, Litvak)

The Window Cleaner (Bucher)

1946

Let There Be Light (Huston)

Chapter Related Books: United States

Bohn, Thomas William, *An Historical and Descriptive Analysis of the 'Why We Fight'*
Series. New York: Arno, 1977.

Capra, Frank, 'Part III, The Great Struggle', *The Name Above the Title*. New York:
Macmillan, 1971, pp. 325–67.

Culbert, David, ed., *Film and Propaganda in America: A Documentary History*. Westport,
CT: Greenwood, 1990.

Hovland, Carl I., Arthur A. Lumsdaine and Fred D. Sheffield, *Experiments on Mass*
Communication. Princeton, NJ: Princeton University Press, 1949. Vol. 3 of *Studies in*
Social Psychology in World War II.

Look, ed., *Movie Lot to Beachhead*. Garden City, NY: Doubleday, Doran, 1945.

MacCann, Richard Dyer, *The People's Films: A Political History of US Government Motion*
Pictures. New York: Hastings House, 1973.

Manvell, Roger, *Films and the Second World War*. New York: Dell, 1976.

Shale, Richard, *Donald Duck Joins Up: The Disney Studio During World War II*. Ann
Arbor, MI: UMI Research Press, 1982.

Short, K. R. M., ed., *Film and Radio Propaganda in World War II*. Knoxville: University of
Tennessee Press, 1983.

8

Post-War Documentary, 1945–1961

The challenges of WWII brought documentary and fiction filmmakers closer together. Post-war, documentary in some ways drew closer to the fiction film than it had previously. One extreme example is *Benjy* (1951), a short produced for the Orthopaedic Foundation of Los Angeles, with the cooperation of Paramount Pictures, directed by Fred Zinnemann and narrated by Henry Fonda. Though it used acted performances, studio lighting and an opulent score to tell an authentic story of a crippled boy, it received the Academy Award for Best Documentary Short. A British 38-minute short, produced for the Central Office of Information (successor to the Ministry of Information, and still operating), *David* (1951) by Paul Dickson, used a full range of fictional techniques. The film lyrically describes the philosophy of the caretaker of a school in Wales, D. R. (David Rees) Griffiths, who is also a respected poet and brother of a powerful South Wales Miners Federation president. *David* brought Griffiths' importance as a poet and a role model to national attention. In the film he plays himself, thinly veiled, as 'Dafydd Rhys' and the film reflect much of his own story. Stylistically romanticized, the film defines the Welsh yin and yang of poetry and coal mining in a believable way.

In the United States, three of the biggest documentaries of the immediate post-war years were clearly nonfiction and narrative in structure. Using narrative obviously does not disqualify a film from being a documentary; it is one of many documentary tools. Robert Flaherty's *Louisiana Story* (1948) is about a Cajun family of father, mother, and a young son who paddles his pirogue through the bayous with his pet raccoon. An oil drilling rig enters this primeval wilderness to tap the riches beneath its surface. Shell Oil is the film's sponsor. The Flahertys had spent most of the previous two years touring oil rigs throughout the Southern US. In this search to find the perfect location, the Flaherty method continued, with Frances shooting hundreds of stills. Once again their enterprise was funded by a commercial company. In the film, two worlds come together, natural and technological, and a tentative affection develops between the boy and the drillers. As the title plainly says, this is a story. This disarms concerns about ethnographic accuracy, and reflects the then generally accepted assumption that drilling for oil was good for all. The cinematography, by the young Richard Leacock and Flaherty, is some of the most gorgeous ever created in documentary

The Quiet One (1949) was made initially as a nontheatrical promotional film for the Wiltwyck School in upper New York state. It was scripted and edited by Helen Levitt, Janice Loeb and Sidney Meyers. Levitt, a renowned still photographer, was one of the film's cinematographers. The narration was written by James Agee and is read by actor Gary Merrill. This school offered a home and rehabilitation to emotionally disturbed adolescent boys, most of them African-American, from the streets of Harlem. The film is about one such case, that of 'Donald', his painful past, the nature of his treatment, and the hopes for his recovery. *The Quiet One* was blown up from 16mm to 35mm and played with some success among art theatres in large cities. It was also widely shown nontheatrically. Oddly, as well as an 1948 Oscar nomination for Best Documentary, the film was nominated for Best Story and Screenplay in 1949, along with Federico Fellini for *Paisan*. These contradictory factoids are worth noting because they demonstrate not only the blurred line between documentary and fiction, but also the Academy's ongoing fluxuations in its documentary category.

All My Babies (1952) was an instructional film sponsored by the Georgia State Department of Health to demonstrate to midwives correct sanitary procedures to use in their deliveries. It was scripted and directed by George

Fig 41 *Images from* All My Babies, *George Stoney*

Stoney, himself a white southerner, who became sympathetically involved with the rural black people the film is about. Though it is a medical film and contains all the technical information required – some 118 points – it developed a length, a scope, and an emotional intensity that lift it out of the realm of the purely educational. Its protagonist, Miss Mary (Mary Francis Hill Coley), is not only a consummate midwife, she is a magnificent person commanding affection and respect. The 'Aunt Jemima' stereotype she might represent is exploded before our eyes. At first the official sponsors did not quite know what to make of the film; they were impressed (and surprised) when it was selected for showing at the Edinburgh International Film Festival. Because Miss Mary's skill in delivering babies was carefully recorded, the film was long afterwards shown in medical schools. The warm and wonderful feelings it contains – for birth, for people, for life – surely did the student doctors no harm. In 2007 Stoney returned to Georgia to record a 'reunion' in which over 150 people who had been delivered by Mrs Coley participated.

Efforts to hang onto the occasion provided by World War II to have documentary films playing in the theatres waned in the early fifties. The war years had marked a high point of documentary achievement. More filmmakers had made more nonfiction films for larger audiences than ever before. Given this vastly increased activity, with films being used in all sorts of new ways, it was assumed by some that the trend would continue in the post-war years. Instead, the documentary took different paths.

Personnel and Leadership

In the US during the war, not only had fiction film directors (among them John Huston, Anatole Litvak, William Wyler, Garson Kanin) been responsible for most of the major wartime documentaries, they had also been in positions of administrative leadership (Frank Capra and John Ford). When the war ended, these men returned to Hollywood. Some of them tended to make fiction features more closely related to social problems and/or more realistic in style, perhaps as a result of their wartime experience. Ford's *They Were Expendable* (1945), Wyler's *The Best Years of Our Lives* (1946), Huston's *The Treasure of Sierra Madre* (1948) and Litvak's *The Snakepit* (1949) could be cited. But neither they nor their films were any longer directly connected to documentary.

In Canada the situation was different. The NFB, which had almost a monopoly on Canadian production, was not making fiction features, but had other difficulties. Canadian documentary was profoundly affected by Grierson's resignation from the Board and departure from Canada at the end of the war. The number of NFB personnel was drastically reduced from the wartime high. As a result of this curtailment, some Canadian filmmakers went into other fields; others moved to other countries. Some observers charged that the Board was unjustifiably costly and extravagant, that it competed with private enterprise, that it harboured subversives, and that there was not need for it in peacetime.

One development in the immediate post-war years was that more people wanted to make documentaries. Most post-war documentary-makers were of a new generation. Many were young men who had received their training in filmmaking as a result of military service. The wartime recruits had been thoroughly trained technically, but ideologically emphasis was on a universal desire to defeat the enemy. Many lacked a common core of values and aspirations for peacetime filmmaking of the sort that had existed in Britain, Canada and the US in the 1930s and 1940s. Since the peacetime demand for films was much less great than it had been in wartime, competition for opportunities to make films led filmmakers to offer their services cheaply and with perhaps lowered professional standards.

Another, more complicated difficulty surfaced in the post-war years. Partly because of lessons learned during the war, a gap between the artist-filmmaker and the audio-visual educator widened. Elaborate and sophisticated social-scientific testing of the effects of films on learning had been done on an unprecedentedly large scale during the war. The results of this testing – for instance, that reported by Hovland, Lumsdaine and Sheffield in *Experiments on Mass Communication* – seemed to define and limit what films could be expected to do in relation to audiences. They seemed successful in teaching troops to assemble a pontoon bridge or clean and maintain the breech of a coastal gun – the so-called nuts and bolts films. Films used to teach desired attitudes, however – the so-called orientation films – seemed much less certain in their effect. For all its brilliance, *The Battle of Britain*, or the 'Why We Fight' series, did not appear to do much to move American servicemen towards a greater sympathy and appreciation for their British ally. In the post-war years, while the 16mm nontheatrical field expanded, with educational and industrial applications drawn from the inspiration and models provided by wartime use of documentary, such 'attitude-oriented' films languished. Some filmmakers moved further away from traditional documentary toward the experimental avant-garde.

The power of documentary and its unique ability to create social change is found in its fusion of social purpose with artistic form. It is worth remembering that the young tyros of British documentary had been well educated in the liberal arts before Grierson drilled them in his social philosophy. After the war in the United States and Britain, the social scientists and the technicians were predominant. Makers of classroom films usually worked from a formula:

tell the audience what you are going to tell them; tell them; tell them what you have just told them. It left little room for imagination, wit, or beauty. Makers of industrial films offered gorgeous compositions and perfect exposures, and left it to the sponsor to determine what would be said. Often neither the educational nor the industrial filmmaker was motivated to make emotionally or intellectually stimulating films. Documentary began to get a 'bad name' as something boring that had to be endured.

A successful theatrical documentary of this period was *The Sea Around Us* (1953). When Irwin Allen decided to make a film version of Rachel Carson's best-selling book of the same name, it must have seemed a natural money-maker, and a great way to jump-start the career of a Hollywood film producer. The book had, at that time, been on the best-seller list for more than seventy weeks, and Allen was building a filmmaking career in Hollywood, having only a couple of associate producer credits to his name. The film of *The Sea Around Us* went on to a healthy theatrical life as a second-billed title for its studio, RKO, and later became a staple of the 16mm educational market. According to studio press releases, Allen's original plan to shoot the film from scratch was untenable to RKO executives, who estimated the cost of such a production to be over $4 million. In response, he hit upon the seemingly simple idea to compile a film based on existing scientific research footage. By contacting over 2000 museums, scientific institutes, universities, individuals and the like, Allen was able to come up with over 300 hours of footage, which he and editors then cut to sixty-one minutes. He paid Carson $25,000 and paid no one for the filmed material, convincing the original makers that the prestige of being credited on the film version of *The Sea Around Us* was compensation enough.

Neither the book nor the film contains a storyline. Rather, episodes that describe the origin of the earth, the lives of various undersea creatures, the jobs done by fisherman and others who work with marine life, along with scientific explorations are presented in episodic style. The film links these episodes, which were originally shot mostly in 16mm and in a range of colour film processes, through special effects sequences designed by Linwood Dunn, then the resident wizard of optical effects at RKO. It features the booming voices of two 'Voice of God' (literally) narrators who explain what is going on onscreen.

The Sea Around Us was made some time before the films of Jacques Cousteau were seen widely, and its Technicolor wonders of the deep were revelatory to most of the public. It is also in many ways dated in its approach to the subject. The narration, written by Allen, continually refers to the 'limitless bounty' of the sea, as it celebrates the activities of salmon fishermen and the dragging nets of crab fisherman. In an astonishing sequence, the bloody harpooning of a whale from a small boat is captured closeup; a breathless drama unfolds as the whale is then attacked by other, killer whales, and the crew must respond so that 'all can share' in the catch. Much of this would be humorous, if we did not now understand the ecological peril that our whales and our oceans face today. Most egregiously, *The Sea Around* Us insists, like the later *March of the Penguins* (2005), on anthropomorphizing the marine life. By setting the sequences up in cute stories, the narration belittles the dignity carried in the images. All of this human-centric celebration of life is then creepily undone in an ending that brings back the Voice of God in a doomsday warning about the melting of the polar icecaps.

One long-lasting and important result of the influx of World War II veterans was the establishment and strengthening of college and university film programmes. Men who had been trained in filmmaking took advantage of the GI Bill and enrolled in schools across the US. It did not take long for their skills to be recognized by university administrations, and they were soon making educational films for science departments, etc. and shooting football games, thus creating classroom media and play-by-play study films. Soon they were training other interested students as assistants. Gradually formal film classes evolved. At places like USC where film schools previously existed, the new teachers modified curricula. At others, new departments were added. A new generation of young people began to be exposed to filmmaking and film-watching within university settings. Film societies began to become part of campus life, bringing the first taste of foreign and experimental films to these audiences. Some of these film students became the core of the generation who created important documentaries in the 1960s and 70s. As we shall see in chapters 13 and 14, it was they who carried on the social activist documentary tradition. Notable educators in the field who followed the path from armed service to college teacher included Bob Wagner at Ohio State, Jack C. Ellis at

Northwestern University and Herb Farmer and Dan Wigand at the University of Southern California.

The post-war period saw the end of British documentary as a Griersonian movement, although the type of structure he had developed continued. Crown Film Unit – successor to the Empire Marketing Board (1930–1933) and the General Post Office Film Unit (1933–1940) – was terminated in 1952. The grounds were that it cost too much, and that if films were needed by the government they could be made by private firms. No tradition of film training at university level developed in immediate post-war Britain as it did in the US.

However, in Britain another generation became active participants in documentary-making under the tutelage of Grierson veterans such as Arthur Elton and Edgar Anstey. Like their counterparts in the US, they made thousands of sponsored films, some good, some bad. For the most part, many of those filmmakers who worked in this field in both nations remain anonymous.

In Britain the Shell Film Unit was the most highly regarded documentary unit based within a private corporation. It was also especially long-lived, surviving many changes in distribution and technology – from 35mm film to 16mm to video. The combination of quality and subtlety evident in Shell's best films exemplifies a form of sponsored filmmaking, apparently more enlightened – or perhaps more insidious? – than direct advertising. From the start, it was designed to have a cumulative, but subtle, impact on the general public. Often released in theatres as well as screened nontheatrically, the films frequently avoided direct reference to the company or its products and services, focusing instead on processes and places. This methodology continues today; for example in 2011 General Electric, through its subsidiary CBS, announced the production of a series of short documentaries on the subject of 'innovation' to be made by such well-known filmmakers as Steve James, Barbara Kopple, Alex Gibney, Morgan Spurlock and Jessica Yu. Innovation is a buzz word for promoting GE.

In the US, what collective documentary leadership had existed on the political left or within the New Deal administration of Franklin Roosevelt ended as war broke out. After the war Pare Lorentz, head of the short-lived

US Film Service, lapsed into semi-retirement. Others were making indus-trially sponsored films. Willard Van Dyke, for example, in *American Frontier* (1953), produced for the American Petroleum Institute, retained some of the themes and style of his earlier work, but a prevailing blandness replaced the originality and conviction of *The City* and *Valley Town*.

Sponsorship

The established institutional sources that have always supported documentary are government, industry, foundations and associations. During WWII, governments were virtually the sole source of funding. The wartime Ministry of Information of the British government metamorphosed into the peacetime Central Office of Information, but the Labour government failed to back documentary-making. This profoundly dampened the spirits of the documentary people, most of whom were on the political left and Labour supporters. Second, the post-war years in Britain were ones of rigorous austerity; funds were lacking for many forms of government activity and film production could scarcely be regarded as essential.

In the US, the Office of War Information was eliminated altogether and sustained government support for filmmaking existed only in the Department of Agriculture (with a long and honourable record of using films to communicate with farmers through the county agents scattered around the country), the Armed Forces (which, of course, had available an enormous stockpile of films), and the International Motion Picture Division of the Department of State (IMPD).

USIA Films

In 1953 IMPS was absorbed into the new United States Information Agency (USIA), created to consolidate overseas information activities of the federal government into one programme. The first head of USIA was legendary broadcaster Edward R. Murrow, personally selected by President Dwight D. Eisenhower. IMPS operated in 135 offices in over fifty countries, through which 300 to 500 film titles eventually became available. It was said that these reached approximately 500 million people annually. The USIA was charged with disseminating ideas about American freedoms and the value of democracy to audiences abroad. In addition to its film service it operated 'The Voice of America' radio network. The USIA was officially disbanded in 1999, although Voice of America continues to operate. By law, USIA-produced films could not be screened publicly in the US. This restriction, intended to prevent the federal government from distributing propaganda to its own citizens, meant that Americans could not view the films at all. The law remained in effect until 1990, at which time the films became available twelve years after their production. This nondisclosure of the films led many to believe that they were strident propaganda about 'the American Way' and offered only the view of the federal government. This was true of many, but by no means all of the films, and they remain a little-studied, widely misunderstood sliver of documentary history.

Fig 42 *Walter de Hoog made the compilation film.* The Wall, *1962 about the human toll of the Berlin wall as part of the Marshall Plan*

Among the best USIA films is *The Wall* (1962) by Walter de Hoog. Clearly an anti-Communist propaganda film, *The Wall* is an emotional, factual account of the building of the Berlin wall and its effect on citizens on both sides. It is composed entirely of news footage, all shot from the Allied side, masterfully edited together by de Hoog. He was affiliated with Fox Movietone news and had easy access to the material. *The Wall* contains some of the most memorable images of Germany in this era: men, women, children, scrambling through barbed-wire fences that were the first stages of the wall; people jumping from second-storey windows in the East, caught by sympathizers on the West; families torn apart and waving to each other in code from one side to the other; and terrifying images of those shot and killed by German guards during escape attempts, are accompanied by a first-person narration spoken as if from the collective 'we' of West Berlin citizens. The overall effect of this short (ten-minute) compilation film is powerful. It crafted an inspirational message to West Berliners who were then living under the Communist blockade, demonstrated to the world the lengths people were willing to go to escape Communism, and remains one of the US government's most artful and informative documentaries. It was said to be such a favourite of Attorney General Robert Kennedy that he secretly showed it to visiting Soviet artists.

Launched by US Secretary of State George C. Marshall, the 'Marshall Plan' began in April 1948 when the US Congress created the Economic Cooperation Administration (ECA), which transferred over $13 billion of material and technical assistance to Europe – the equivalent today of around $90 billion US dollars. Europe desperately needed to be rebuilt after the disasters of WWII. In addition to supplies and technical assistance, the Marshall Plan housed an information programme whose mandate was to present a convincing picture of democratic values and vision of a future in which Europeans could aspire to prosperity, American-style. The plan included cooperative filmmaking between American makers and those living in war-ravaged Europe. The men who ran the Marshall Plan Motion Picture Section strongly believed in the potential of film to effect social change, and they also believed in representing stories from the points of view of the filmmakers living in Europe. German-born Lothar Wolff, who was picked to set up the film division, had been the long-time chief film editor at "The March of Time." Stuart Schulberg was recruited from American occupational government in Berlin, where, as head of the Documentary Film Unit of the Information Services Division, he had produced the feature-length official record of the Nuremberg Nazi war trials. He became the second person to head the Marshall Plan unit. During the course of its seven-year existence it produced at least twenty-five films in several counties that dealt with a range of social and personal issues affecting Europe's concerns. The best known of these films is *Nuremberg* (1948).

The famed Nuremberg war crimes trials accused a small group of Nazis of atrocities committed against humanity during WWII. In 1946 twelve were sentenced to death, three to life imprisonment and four to beween ten and twenty years in prison. Three defendants were acquitted, one committed suicide and one was too frail to stand trial. An official documentary about the trials was made by the US government. Pare Lorentz, who was then chief of Film/Theatre/Music for the US War Department's Civil Affairs Division, commissioned a treatment from Stuart Schulberg, who was awarded a contract by the US Department of War to write and produce *Nuremberg*. The result, completed in 1948, was a compilation documentary of trial footage and brutal images of Nazi horrors, including the first publicly shown scenes of people being gassed in the death camps. Some of this footage came from Yelizaveta Svilova's *Nazi Atrocities* (1945); Svilova also shot her own film about the Nuremberg trials, *Peoples' Trial* (1946). But while *Nuremberg* became mandatory viewing for the occupied German population, the film was not screened in theatres in the US. The public, outside of Germany, knew little or nothing of its existence.

The purpose *of Nuremberg* was to convince the German population that the blame for post-war decimation, poverty and national despair lay not with the Allies but with the deranged regime that had led their nation, and by extension themselves. The filmmakers also had larger goals. The Nuremberg trials presented a startling example of post-war global cooperation, with US Supreme Court Justice Robert H. Jackson serving as lead prosecutor alongside a team of British, French and Soviet colleagues. And as a giant media spectacle of judgment, the trials became the controversial model for the war crimes trials that continue today. The film was restored by Sandra Schulberg (Stuart's daughter) and Josh Waletzky and was released in a seventy-eight-minute version in 2010 as *Nuremberg: A Lesson for Today*.

Canada

Though the size of the National Film Board of Canada was cut, it survived and adjusted to the post-war needs of government and citizens. Government financial support for it would gradually increase. By the mid-fifties it had moved into new eminence with shorts that won awards for documentary, live action, and animation at major international festivals.

In Canada, production of sponsored films outside the Film Board increased, led by Crawley Films, which had begun with contracts from the Board during the war. Long-lived and often-ignored Canadian independent production company, Crawley Films deserves to be singled out. Frank Radford 'Budge' Crawley was thoroughly Canadian. He began making amateur films in the 1930s, and progressed into short nonfiction industrial work. For a time he worked at NFB. When WWII came, his filmmaking skills were urgently needed to make training films, so, turning a room in their home into a studio, he and his wife Judith built a business making sponsored films. By 1958, Crawley Films had built a studio and made a thirteen-part CBC documentary television series, 'The Saint Lawrence North'. Crawley later produced fiction features and the notable feature documentaries *Janis* (1974, about Janis Joplin) and *The Man Who Skied Down Everest* (1976), an adventure classic that won the Academy Award for Best Documentary Feature. This theatrically released film followed Japanese poet and world-champion skier, Yuichiro Miura as he and his team made the challenging climb up Mount Everest, carrying a 35mm Panavision camera. During the ascent an icefall claimed the lives of six members of the team. The remainder continued on to within 350 meters of the summit, where Miura tested his dream, with the camera recording the feat in Cinemascope. Using oxygen and a parachute to slow his speed, Miura skied 7,000 feet over sheer ice and rocks. Caught by gusting winds, he hit a boulder and fell 1,320 feet, smashing to his death, a finale that has been called by some the most exciting six minutes of film ever shot.

As noted, in the US and UK industry became a big sponsor of films. In all three countries, however, businesses and industries were now justifying every bit of money spent on films in terms of increased sales and obvious goodwill. There existed little industrial sponsorship of films in the general public interest in Canada, such as those sponsored by the oil and gas industries in Britain in the thirties. Flaherty's *Louisiana Story* is the most notable exception.

In Britain and in Canada, foundations and associations were less active sponsors of films than they were in the United States. And in the US the large foundations and national associations were soon limited in what they would spend their money on by growing pressure from the political right. This post-war right-wing reaction came to be known as 'McCarthyism'. Senator Joseph McCarthy (Republican, Wisconsin) headed congressional committees and used whatever other power he could muster to ferret out suspected Communists and Communist sympathizers wherever he saw them hiding. His work paralleled that of the House of Representatives Un-American Activities Committee, which was busy investigating Communist influence in the film and broadcasting industries. In its paranoia, McCarthy's investigations even attacked purported subversive influence in the Department of State and the Army. At the time of his death he was about to start on the large foundations, most notably the Ford Foundation, which were accused of sheltering 'reds' and radicals. As a result of this political climate, the foundations restricted their grants to existing and widely accepted institutions and activities. They did not sponsor films which might prove 'controversial' or might be made by filmmakers with a 'past' (involvement with organizations and causes on the left).

Subjects

It seems to be true that documentaries thrive on crisis and disaster, criticism and attack. Following the war the great documentary causes of the thirties (unemployment and rural poverty, conservation of land and water, housing and urban planning) and early forties (the fight against fascism) were no longer relevant.

Internationalism

The first years of peace saw a brief surge of international good intentions. The Axis powers (Germany, Italy, Japan) had been defeated by the Allies (British Empire, United States, Soviet Union, China). The United Nations was established to sustain and extend this victory, to try to make one world out of this war-torn globe. In this spirit, films were needed to interpret the meaning of the United Nations and its subsidiary organizations, and to show aspects of their services to the world at large. Also needed were films confronting particular post-war problems and the concerns of war-ravaged and underdeveloped nations.

The United Nations undertook some modest film production and distribution, making and circulating films for and about the UN and its related agencies. One of its films, *The Pale Horseman* (1946), written and produced by Irving Jacoby, was a grim and forceful survey of world devastation, famine, and the threat of pestilence. It took the stance that it was in US self-interest to combat this menace. In Britain there was a similar United Nations emphasis. As successor to his *World of Plenty* (1943), Paul Rotha made *The World Is Rich* (1947) for the Central Office of Information. Like the earlier film, it argues for more adequate international distribution of food by contrasting rich and poor nations.

Following the war, Britain used documentary to attempt to explain to its citizens (and the rest of the world) its changing conception of colonial stewardship. *Cyprus Is an Island* (1946, Ralph Keene) is a film with such a purpose. It is about deforestation and goatherds rather than the conflict between Greek and Turkish inhabitants that would erupt when Cyprus achieved independence in 1960. *Daybreak in Udi* (1949, Terry Bishop) concerns the progress of community education in Nigeria. It won an Academy Award for Best Documentary Feature.

In the world as a whole, the spirit of internationalism dwindled by 1948 with the outbreak of the cold war between the United States and the Soviet Union. The cold war subsequently changed political attitudes and military strategies throughout the world. Documentaries reflected this new paranoia.

Grierson's discovery that more seats existed outside the theatres than within them was a valuable one. Still, major documentary achievements had previously reached large audiences in theatres – *Nanook of the North, Night Mail, The River,* for example. Now the nontheatrical 16mm field was the main means for documentary distribution/exhibition. Nontheatrical films, the business begun in the 1920s by Kodak, were mainly used on behalf of industry or education. Subjects dealt with for the first time, or with a new frequency, were the arts, mental health, public health, and race relations. Films about the arts and those that used the arts to deal with other subjects became widely popular. Experimental documentary hybrids also relied on this arts audience. Sometimes experimental films were shown as shorts in the 'art theatres' specializing in European or otherwise non-mainstream feature films, and new film societies developed during these years, often being the only places to see foreign language movies.

Some documentarians had been trained in or were especially sympathetic to the arts. Willard Van Dyke, veteran American documentarian who had been a student of Edward Weston's, made a film about him entitled *The Photographer* (1948). Even Robert Flaherty shot material in 1947 for a study of *Guernica* and became involved in the promotion and distribution of *The Titan – Story of Michelangelo* (1950). The latter is a feature-length biography of Michelangelo using only contemporary architecture, interior settings and artworks as its visual material. Erica Anderson specialized in films about art. Her *Grandma Moses* (1950) received an Oscar nomination for Best Documentary Short, and she won an Academy Award for *Albert Schweitzer* (1957). Both films were made in collaboration with Jerome Hill. In Britain a similar interest in films about the arts was in evidence with documentaries such as Jack Howell's *Dylan Thomas* (1962) shot in Wales and London. With a first-person narration spoken by Richard Burton, this is a complex portrait in which Burton sometimes seems to become Thomas and vice versa. It won the Best Documentary Short Oscar in 1963.

More akin in subject and style to earlier documentary forms were documentaries about mental health. A profound difference between them and earlier documentaries on similar subjects was that the mental health documentaries now dealt with people in relation to themselves – their individual, interior lives – rather than with their relationships to society and to social problems. *The Quiet One* (US, 1948, Sidney Meyers), discussed at the outset of this chapter, is an example. If this film had been made in the 1930s, it might well have centred on the social, economic and political causes for the unhappy lives we see. Here, the Harlem ghetto and broken families serve as background for the disturbances in Donald's psyche.

Documentaries on matters of general public health became much more plentiful and effective than before. One film with which George Stoney was involved, *Feeling All Right* (1947), dealt with the detection and treatment of syphilis in a semidocumentary narrative form in Mississippi. Among the many noteworthy Stoney films about health problems is *Still Going Places* (1956, made for health professionals), about the care and treatment of the aged. The Museum of Modern Art recognized the importance of such films in a significant 1954 exhibition entitled 'The American Scene 1945-1953'. In addition to films by Stoney, it included sponsored works by Sidney Meyers, Irving Jacoby, Willard Van Dyke and others. In Great Britain, *The Undefeated* (1950, Paul Dickson) was about the therapy administered to permanently disabled World War II veterans.

Films about race relations were much in evidence in the US. This subject was dealt with using a number of styles and techniques in addition to documentary. In a rather bizarre theatrical short, *The House I Live In* (1945, produced by RKO Radio Pictures), Frank Sinatra sings the song of the title and speaks directly to the camera against anti-Semitism and racism. The song went on to become a classic Sinatra hit. A cluster of animated race-relations films began with the very popular *Brotherhood of Man* (1946), sponsored by the UAW-CIO. It was an early effort of United Productions of America (UPA), the talented group that broke away from the Disney Studio and went on to create Mr Magoo and Gerald McBoing Boing.

Norman McLaren, a filmmaker who worked with Grierson in England during the late 1930s, is best known as an animator extraordinaire. His work transcends boundaries and time, and some of his films are clearly animated political and experimental documents. McLaren's most famous film, *Neighbours* (1952) was made after McLaren joined NFBC in 1941, at the invitation of Grierson. *Neighbours* can be classified subject-wise with documentaries concerned with world harmony. A direct consequence of his experiences teaching in post-war China in 1949, it is a parable about two men who fight over a flower. The film uses pixillation of two live men to make a very strong anti-war, anti-racism statement that still resonates worldwide.

Approaches and Techniques

As for their formal aspects, the post-war films were freer and more varied in their techniques than were the earlier documentaries. More nonactuality was employed – fictional and dramatic elements – and structurally they tended to be organized as narrative or drama. There was an increased use of actors and performance and more location sound. Sound recording was made easier by the introduction of magnetic tape, developed in WWII by the Germans. It made recording outside the studio much more practicable than it had been with the optical system, but it still demanded large recording equipment and was not truly synched to the visuals. The narrative structures and use of dialogue coincided and complimented the tendency of these post-war documentaries to centre more on individuals than had the films of the thirties. In the post-war years even large-scale problems were dealt with in terms of how they affected individuals. The not-so-subtle influence of Sigmund Freud's increasingly adopted theories was also reflected in such films.

Observations

In the years between the end of World War II and the beginning of a world blanketed (or perhaps smothered) by television, mainstream documentaries were mostly industrially sponsored or classroom films. The oil, coal and steel industries provided funding for films using the arresting visuals of brilliantly burning furnaces and sparks flying in forges. This may have been because they had more money, or because of more need for improved public relations. In either case, they sponsored some noteworthy films during these years.

Among US-made classroom films, increased ambition and improving artistry were in evidence occasionally. Two examples, about city planning, were *The Baltimore Plan* (1953) and *The Living City* (1953). Both were sponsored by the Twentieth Century Fund, directed by John Barnes, and released by Encyclopedia Britannica Films. The latter was nominated for an Academy Award and was the first film shot by Haskell Wexler, who went on to become one of Hollywood's and documentary's renowned cinematographers. But such 'prestige pictures didn't pay the rent', as they said at Encyclopedia Britannica Films at the time, unlike those fitting more neatly into Kindergarten through Grade 12 curricula, so they remained exceptions.

National Film Board of Canada's Unit B, 1948–64

The National Film Board, too, was having to tailor its films to clearly identifiable informational and educational needs and nontheatrical distribution. But within that setting, in the late 1940s and early 1950s there developed an extraordinary array of creative talent identified as Unit B, which produced some brilliant and original work.

In 1948 the NFB was reorganized into four production units – A, B, C, D – reporting to an overall director of production. In 1951 Tom Daly, one of the earliest recruits to the Film Board, who had gained his experience working as Stuart Legg's assistant and researcher on 'The World in Action' series, was appointed executive producer of Unit B, charged with making sponsored, scientific, cultural and animated films. Eight Unit B films received Academy Award nominations, and some of its films remain documentary classics. Unit B ended in 1963 but its body of work remains as an extraordinary legacy and challenge for emulation.

Norman McLaren's *Neighbours* began Unit B's move into the spotlight, eventually reaching audiences worldwide, as did another animated film, *The Romance of Transportation in Canada* (1953). Curiously, this was a modest little (eleven-minute) documentary intended for classroom use. *The Romance of Transportation* broke out of the standard requirements of the educational film, however, sketching the history of Canadian transportation from snow shoes to jet planes with an appealing lightness and deftness, including spoofs of Hollywood cartoon clichés. Widely popular, it was nominated for an Oscar and won several international awards.

The Romance of Transportation in Canada brought together for the first time some of Unit B's key personnel – Colin Low (direction and animation),

Wolf Koenig and Robert Verrall (animation), Eldon Rathborn (music) and Tom Daly (production) – who would form the creative core of Unit B. In terms of live-action documentary, breakthrough films came the next year, including *Corral*, part of a 'Faces of Canada' series of short films. Directed by Colin Low, it was filmed on the Southwestern Alberta ranch where he had grown up. (Camera was by Koenig; music by Rathburn; editing and production by Daly.) The subject is a ranch hand working with a half-broken horse in a corral. There is a pairing of man and horse – a *pas de deux*, cutting back and forth between movements of man's feet and horse's front hoofs; hand-held moving camera in medium closeups predominates in the roping sequence. Finally the man mounts and rides off in long shot, horse and rider running out into the surrounding countryside with foothills in the background. Lyrical and wordless, the soundtrack consists solely of a guitar accompanying the images.

Among Unit B's most celebrated productions was *City of Gold* (1957). *City of Gold* concerns the Klondike Gold Rush of 1898, recorded in contemporary still photographs and brief live-action sequences that frame the main story of Dawson City in the mid-1950s. On the Yukon River, not far from the Arctic Circle, this was the jumping-off point for the journey north and the climb over Chilikoot Pass to the gold fields so gloriously staged in Charlie Chaplin's *The Gold Rush*. It was also the hometown of Pierre Berton, a well-known journalist, who wrote and read the narration, which is drawn from his remembered childhood in the 1920s.

The music used throughout is of an earlier time and place; it becomes part of the document. The intimate perspective of the narrator warms and gives life to the images. The immobile subjects seem so completely 'real' that we forget we are watching photos – we expect the people to move at any moment. To achieve this sense of liveness, a rostrum camera on an animation stand travels steadily and carefully over the photos as if it were actually at the scene. Direction is by Wolf Koenig and Colin Low. Transitions from the present-day live-action into the aged photos and out again are quite remarkable, especially in that they are almost imperceptible. For example, in the conclusion of the film viewers are brought back to present-day Dawson City by gradual degrees. First we are on photographs; then we are on a still-life scene in which we detect a tiny particle of matter dangling in a cobweb; then we have a still landscape with off-camera voices of children at play; and finally we are in the midst of a baseball diamond with all the usual shouting accompanying the game. This is the first time in the film that location sound is introduced. It appropriately breaks the spell of reminiscence, and returns us to the mid-twentieth century. In the 1980s this style of filmmaking came to be exemplified in the films of Ken Burns (discussed in Chapter 14), who was admittedly influenced by *City of Gold*. The 'Ken Burns Effect' of i-movie fame owes as much to *City of Gold* as it does to Burns' work.

The directorial pair Roman Kroiter and Colin Low did the strikingly different and equally original and inventive *Universe* (1960), again framed by live-action sequences. The film moves along an extraordinary probe

Fig 43 *A rare example of mythmaking in Canadian documentary,* City of Gold *created a paradox of living people and dead objects in a way that inspired the future work of Ken Burns (Canada, 1957, Colin Low and Wolf Koenig). National Film Board of Canada*

into the solar system, in which the filmic material consists largely of three-dimensional models of the moon and most of the planets. A second probe takes us beyond the solar system into our galaxy. A third and final probe asks the audience to imagine being able to 'move with the freedom of a god … so that a million years pass in a second'. We would come to 'an endless sea of night' dotted with islands of stars – galaxies – so immense 'that they have been observed slipping through one another like phantoms'. The animation consists of astonishing 3D constructions that create incredible and scary movements. (During the production of *2001: A Space Odyssey*, Stanley Kubrick bought several copies for his technicians to study.) The music is very dramatic and 'atmospheric', recalling Gustav Holst's *The Planets*. This film was one of the seeds which eventually germinated into large-format IMAX documentaries.

Paralleling these high-profile separate works was the 'Candid Eye' series of thirteen films of between twenty-four and twenty-eight minutes made for Canadian Broadcasting Corporation television, an early exploration of the possibilities of the cinéma vérité technique. The series began with *The Days Before Christmas* (1958), co-directed by Terence Macartney-Filgate, the first of many films in his distinguished career. *The Days Before Christmas* is both a city symphony of Montreal and a celebration of the holiday. Disparate images are cut together in a style not unlike Humphrey Jennings' in *Listen to Britain* or the experimental styles of city symphonies of the 1920s. Some of the sound is synchronous with the images, some not, but it is recorded on location and cleverly overlaid over non-synch footage. Montreal is presented as big, cosmopolitan, wintry: a melting pot, with cold, dirty winters; but also a sweet place where people live.

Another film of exceptional quality out of Unit B is markedly cynical. *Very Nice, Very Nice* (1961) is a seven-minute idiosynchratic work of one filmmaker, Arthur Lipsett, a member of the characteristically avant-garde Animation Unit. He made it solely from snippets of film and audio tape, out-takes culled from racks and bins in cutting rooms around the NFB. This cacophany of sights and sounds is perhaps intended to mimic and satirize the informational overload of modern (1960s) media life. Lipsett, who ultimately committed suicide, presents a bleak view of rampant commercialism and also seems preoccupied with bits of evidence suggesting that we may be mindlessly moving toward

Fig 44 Very Nice, Very Nice *was a film montage, without commentary – a first film by its maker that was nominated for an Oscar (Canada, 1961, Arthur Lipsett). National Film Board of Canada*

nuclear annihilation. *Very Nice, Very Nice* is also a key link for other avant-garde documentary filmmakers working in similar ways with 'found' material.

Chapter Related Films

1946
Cyprus Is an Island (UK, Ralph Keene)
The Pale Horseman (US, Irving Jacoby)
1947
First Steps (US, Leo Seltzer)
Journey into Medicine (US, Willard Van Dyke and Jacoby)
The World Is Rich (UK, Paul Rotha)
1948
Louisiana Story (US, Robert Flaherty)
Nuremberg (US German release only, Stuart Schulberg, Pare Lorentz)
The Photographer (US, Van Dyke)

1949
The Quiet One (US, Sidney Meyers)
Waverley Steps (UK, John Eldridge)
1950
The Titan – Story of Michelangelo (Switzerland, Curt Oertel)
1951
Benjy (US, Fred Zinnemann)
David (UK, Paul Dickson)
1952
All My Babies (US, George Stoney)
Neighbours (Canada, Norman McLaren)
1953
American Frontier (US, Van Dyke)
The Baltimore Plan (US, John Barnes)
The Living City (US, Barnes)
The Sea Around Us (US, Irwin Allen)
1954
Corral (Canada, Colin Low)
1957
City of Gold (Canada, Wolf Koenig and Low)
1958
The Days Before Christmas (Canada, Macartney-Filgate, Stanley Jackson, Koenig)
1960
Universe (Canada, Kroitor and Low)
1961
Very Nice, Very Nice (Canada, Arthur Lipsett)
1962
The Wall (US, Walter de Hoag)

Chapter Related Books

Beattie, Eleanor, *A Handbook of Canadian Film*. Toronto: Peter Martin Associates, 1973.
Bischof, Gunter, ed., Images of *The Marshall Plan in Europe*: Films, Photographs, Exhibits, Posters. Wiesbaden, Germany: Verlag, 2009.
Evans, Gary, *In the National Interest: A Chronicle of the National Film Board of Canada from 1949 to 1989*. Toronto: University of Toronto Press, 1991.
Feldman, Seth and Joyce Nelson, (eds), *Canadian Film Reader*. Toronto: Peter Martin Associates, 1977.
Film Council of America, *Sixty Years of 16mm Film, 1923–1983*. Evanston, IL: Film Council of America, 1954.
Jones, D. B., *Movies and Memoranda: An Interpretive History of the National Film Board of Canada*. Ottawa: Canadian Film Institute and Deneau Publishers, 1981.

Russell, Patrick and James Piers Taylor: *Shadows of Progress: Documentary Film in Post-War Britain*. London: Palgrave MacMillan, 2010.

Starr, Cecile, ed., *Ideas on Film: A Handbook for the 16mm. User*. New York: Funk & Wagnalls, 1951.

Waldron, Gloria, *The Information Film*: *A Report of the Public Library Inquiry*. New York: Columbia University Press, 1949.

9

Documentary for Television, the 'Golden Years', 1951–71

A Technical Note

English-language documentary films began and have remained a regular part of theatrical exhibition. The earliest actualities, as well as films such as *The Battle of the Somme and Nanook of the North*, were all made with the big screen in mind. At the time of *Nanook* and before, almost the only way to see a documentary, or any film, was in a theatre. Since film stock for these theatrical showings had a base of cellulose nitrate, which was highly flammable, it had to be projected from booths specially constructed in theatres in conformance with fire ordinances. Exceptions, like the projection vans used by the Soviets, were few. Audiences associated film with theatres; there was no other option.

In 1923, partly at the urging of educators, Eastman Kodak Company made available a 16mm film stock with a cellulose acetate base. Because it was nonflammable (it was called 'safety stock'), and had a narrower width, the use of lighter projection equipment was possible. Portable 16mm projectors could be set up in schoolrooms, church basements, union halls – almost anywhere. This also opened up another market for sales of Kodak film and its projectors. Still, theatrical exhibition of documentaries remained dominant.

With 16mm films available for rental and purchase, the nontheatrical field encouraged by the Griersonian approach became a force in the late 1930s. World War II caused an explosion in the use of films as means of informing and educating. Following the war the nontheatrical field, with industrially sponsored and classroom films predominating, expanded enormously. But the expansion of the nontheatrical field did not at first work to the advantage of documentary. The earlier classic documentaries did not fit comfortably into the rather narrow requirements of industrial sales or formal education. Nor did documentaries have the access to theatres they had had before and during wartime.

As theatrical documentary was slipping into the background, losing financial support and audiences, as well as its earlier subject matters and purposes, a new channel for distribution and exhibition was opening up. Thanks to television, more documentaries and related types of public information programmes were shown to larger audiences than at any previous time in history. The technical quality of early television did not require the visual clarity of 35mm, and 16mm production became the norm for television documentaries.

Historical Background

Telecasting began on an experimental and very limited basis in Germany, Great Britain and the United States before World War II, but military requirements of wartime stopped further development. After the war, regularly scheduled consumer television broadcasting began in Great Britain, the United States and Canada. By 1946 the British Broadcasting Corporation (BBC) had a schedule in place. A Documentary Department was established in 1953, with veteran Paul Rotha heading it until 1955. The BBC's first major documentary series was *Special Inquiry*, which ran from 1952 to 1957. Norman Swallow was its producer. But as a quasi-governmental organization supported by a tax on television sets, the BBC did not attract anything like the audience that would develop when commercial broadcasting was permitted to operate in the UK in late 1955. The Independent Television Authority

(ITA, initially; later called Independent Television, ITV) had a regular lineup of documentary programmes produced by a number of outside commercial companies. For example, from Granada Television, one of the original of four ITV franchises, came the long-running (1963–1998) *World in Action*, a public affairs and documentary series, the title for which was borrowed from the wartime National Film Board of Canada. Thames Television was another ITV franchise that existed from 1968–1992. Thames produced the outstanding twenty-six-part documentary series about World War II, entitled *The World at War* (1969). Scottish Television produced John Grierson's weekly television programme devoted to documentary and experimental shorts, *This Wonderful World*, later changing its title to *John Grierson Presents* (1957–1968).

The situation in Canada was anomalous. Though the Canadian Broadcasting Corporation (CBC), also a government-sponsored system, did not begin telecasting until 1952, most of Canada's population lived close enough to its southern border to receive US television earlier. Canada's bilingual culture was acknowledged by the CBC, with a French-language as well as an English-language network. The NFB continued to work more or less separately from CBC-TV, with little exchange between the two organizations.

Because American programming came to be the model for much of the world, most of this chapter focuses on the United States. 1946 was the year television was removed from the wartime freeze. In 1948 big-time TV was born. A network out of New York linked the major cities; the most popular shows were Milton Berle's *Texaco Star Theatre* and Ed Sullivan's *Toast of the Town*. By 1950, one hundred stations telecast to four million sets. In 1951 coaxial cable and microwave relay connected the country coast to coast. (Not altogether coincidentally, that was also the year 'The March of Time' ended.)

In the 1951–1952 season Edward R. Murrow's and Fred W. Friendly's *See It Now* (developed from their radio series *Hear It Now*) appeared on CBS. The 1952–1953 season also featured *I Love Lucy* and *Victory at Sea* (supervised by historian Henry Salomon, Jr, and edited by Isaac Kleinerman). *I Love Lucy*, a situation comedy about a married couple (starring a married couple) and the twenty-six half-hour films about US naval warfare in World War II (compiled from over six million feet of combat footage) are among the most successful and seminal television programmes ever shown. They are still televised today.

While dramatic and other entertainment programmes came from outside companies, production of documentaries and news was carried on primarily in-house by the networks and local stations themselves. Both the National Broadcasting Company (NBC) and the Columbia Broadcasting System (CBS) established units for that purpose, with personnel initially drawn from the ranks of radio and nontheatrical documentarians. American Broadcasting Company (ABC) documentary production was later and weaker, with a news emphasis. The main function of these units was the creation of special programmes, frequently non-sponsored, presented as prestige or public service features. At this time, commercial broadcasting took seriously its mandate to devote time to public service as mandated by Federal law.

In 1953 what is now the Public Broadcasting Service (PBS) began as National Educational Television (NET). This noncommercial network, supported by funds from the federal government, initiated and distributed substantial quantities of documentaries and public affairs materials. Its budgets were smaller than those of the commercial networks, but it made up for this by purchasing independently produced documentaries and importing many significant programmes and series from abroad, principally from Britain. The number of documentaries shown on commercial and public television networks from the fifties into the early seventies was very large and the shows were considered highly prestigious. ABC, NBC and CBS produced 447 individual investigative reports (not necessarily full documentaries) in 1962 alone.

Documentary Series

See It Now was the first regularly scheduled US documentary series. This is not surprising, since Murrow was the most-trusted, strongest voice of truth in radio reports during WWII. The fact that millions had listened as he broadcast live from a rooftop during the London Blitz created an aura of security for audiences that translated from radio to television. A sort of news magazine of feature stories in *The March of Time* tradition, *See It Now* had a much quieter and more intimate tone than newsreels, suitable for the living room, with Murrow as the on-screen host and commentator. At first *See It Now*, like 'The March of Time' and the present-day *60 Minutes*, presented several different stories in each half-hour programme. In 1953 that format changed to include only one story a week. Among the *See It Now* programmes best remembered are 'Christmas In Korea' (1953), made during the Korean War, the several programmes dealing with McCarthyism, including one in 1954 in which Senator McCarthy was given a follow-up programme for reply (consistent with an American broadcasting dictum called 'the fairness doctrine'), and a visit with nuclear physicist J. Robert Oppenheimer (1955). Like 'The March of Time', *See It Now* maintained consistent structural and stylistic characteristics in its format.

One programme, 'Argument in Indianapolis' (1953) presents opposing factions in that city when the American Civil Liberties Union, attempting to form a local chapter, is opposed by the American Legion post. One of the extraordinary things about this programme is its balance in handling a then controversial subject, no doubt necessary for it to be telecast. Depending on your sympathies, the Legion members become fascist monsters or upholders of true Americanism; the ACLU group, pleasant, sensitive intellectuals or dangerous radicals and subversives. The faces, speech and manner of the protagonists are caught more or less candidly, and this remarkable study offered diverse ideologies and personalities existing in uneasy relationship to each other.

In 1955 Alcoa (Aluminum Company of America) withdrew its sponsorship of *See It Now*. The show then changed from regularly scheduled weekly half-hours to hour-long programmes that appeared at intervals – 'specials' in effect. Media critic Gilbert Seldes quipped that it had become *See It Now and Then*. In 1958 *See It Now* was terminated, to be followed by *CBS Reports*.

CBS Reports developed its own excellence. Murrow's last programme for the series, 'Harvest of Shame' (1960) became one of the most celebrated. Examining the exploitation and hardships suffered by migrant agricultural workers, it was aired on Thanksgiving Day, shocking viewers with its examination of the poor. Subsequent notable *CBS Reports* made after Murrow left included 'Hunger in America' (1968, Martin Carr and Peter Davis), which is credited with facilitating the introduction of the federal food stamps programme. It was also criticized for containing a sequence of a baby, possibly incorrectly described as dying of malnutrition. 'The Selling of the Pentagon' (1971, Peter Davis) is a critical and controversial examination of the military's extensive public relations activities.

NBC responded to *See It Now* with the quite different *Project XX* series, begun in 1954. It grew out of the success of *Victory at Sea,* and its production unit included many of the same personnel. From the start, *Project XX* (pronounced Project Twenty) offered occasional hour-long specials. Like *Victory at Sea,* its programmes were compilation films devoted to recreating aspects of the history of the twentieth century using existing footage – newsreel, documentary and feature – and occasional re-enactments. Among those that attracted most attention were 'Nightmare in Red' (1955), which chronicled the rise of Soviet Communism, 'The Twisted Cross' (1956), which did the same for German Nazism, and 'The Real West' (1961). The latter, produced and directed by Donald Hyatt, used paintings and photographs,

Fig 45 *'Harvest of Shame' showed to critical outcry on Thanksgiving Day as part of the CBS Reports series (US, 1960, David Lowe). J. Fred MacDonald*

music and words of the era to capture the spirit of a particular time and place. It was one of the forerunners of the subsequent Ken Burns-type historical series. The commentary, spoken by Gary Cooper, took on a colloquial period flavour as well.

The NBC series comparable to *CBS Reports* was *White Paper*, begun in 1960, with Irving Gitlin as executive producer. For the most part it stuck even closer to current or recent headlines. 'The U-2 Affair' (1960) dealt with the Gary Powers incident that exposed US aerial spying on the Soviet Union. Other programmes also announced the currency of their topics in their titles: 'Angola: Journey to a War' (1961), 'The Death of Stalin' (1963), 'Cuba: Bay of Pigs' (1964).

The Twentieth Century, another weekly series, which began on CBS in 1957, was sponsored by the Prudential Insurance Company and produced by Burton Benjamin and Isaac Kleinerman. Its programmes were mostly half-hour. Many of these were historical compilations, such as 'Trial at Nuremberg' (1958) and 'Paris in the Twenties' (1960). The format of 'From Kaiser to Fuehrer' (1959) is typical. Host Walter Cronkite introduces the programme then retreats off-screen to voiceover commentary, the 'Voice of God' narration. Clips from German films of the thirties and forties are its main visual content; extensive use is made of Ruttman's *Berlin: Symphony of a great city* and *Variety* (1923) directed by Ewald Dupont, a fictional feature. The cutting pace is rapid and the editing skilful; a full orchestral score contributes to continuity and dramatic effect.

Other *Twentieth Century* programmes were on contemporary subjects and used freshly shot material and interviews: 'The Burma Surgeon Today' (1961), 'So That Men Are Free' (1962). Former Film and Photo League member Willard Van Dyke directed a number of *Twentieth Century* episodes. In 1966 *The Twentieth Century* became *The Twenty-First Century*. The new title was intended to suggest a shift in emphasis to scientific development and the future. Its final season was 1970–1971.

ABC distinguished itself with *Closeup!*, the first series using true cinéma vérité – more precisely, the American version of it called direct cinema. (This book uses the term cv/direct.) This radical technique made possible by new technology is the subject of Chapter Eleven. The idea for the series came from Robert Drew, who produced *Primary* and *On the Pole* (both 1960) for Time-Life Broadcast. These first synch-sound portable camera films were of the Wisconsin presidential Democratic primary contest between Hubert Humphrey and John F. Kennedy, and of the Indianapolis automobile race, following driver Eddie Sachs. They were initially shown on only four local stations owned by Time, Inc. ABC was sufficiently impressed to hire Drew to make four more one-hour documentaries for the *Closeup!* series: *Yanki No!* (1960), *X-Pilot* (1960), *The Children Were Watching* (1960) and *Adventures on the New Frontier* (1961). The first had to do with anti-Americanism in Latin America and was shot on location, including in Cuba. The subject of the second is the final test flight of a new airplane and the personality of the test pilot. The third was shot in New Orleans during one week of a school integration crisis, presenting the attitudes of white segregationists and their effects on a black family whose daughter is to be one of the first to attend a previously all-white school. *Adventures on the New Frontier* offers 'a day in the life' of John F. Kennedy in the White House.

Drew did not continue on *Closeup!* but the executive producer of that series, John Secondari did, and he made valuable programmes using direct cinema technique with his own personnel. Nicholas Webster was one of these. He made 'Walk in My Shoes' (1961). It presents the anger, resentment, and feelings of frustration of black Americans largely from their point of view. Webster's 'Meet Comrade Student' (1962) examines Soviet education after the launching of Sputnik, which had caused Americans to feel left behind in scientific knowledge and training.

Also ground-breaking was William Greaves, an African-American documentarian. After beginning as a stage actor, he spent a short time at the NFB in the early 1960s, working with the innovators of cv/direct there. He returned to the US and became the executive producer (after a controversy in which the white executive producer was removed) and co-host of the pioneering National Educational Television series *Black Journal* (1968–1976), with a mandate to produce 'by, for, and about Black people'. Greaves' best-known documentary television work is *Ralph Bunche: An American Odyssey* (2001), *From These Roots* (1974), an in-depth study of the Harlem Renaissance, and *Ida B. Wells: A Passion for Justice* (1989).

Fig 46 *William Greaves, co-host of the National Educational Television groundbreaking series Black Journal (1968–1976). International Film Seminars*

During this same period but following a far different track, producer David L. Wolper was pioneering a different type of television documentary. Like Drew, but unlike most of the others then producing television documentaries, Wolper did not work for any of the three networks, yet he wanted to sell his shows to them. In 1957, when a representative from Artkino, the official US

Fig 47 *Producer David Wolper and director Mel Stuart on the set of* Wattstax
(US, 1973). Mel Stuart

film distributor for the USSR, told him that he had actual footage of the Soviet
space missions to sell, Wolper conceived the idea of creating a documentary
on the rockets and the then-hot space race, and selling it to the networks as
a completed project. Financing it himself, he enlisted the help of friends Jack
Haley, Jr, and Mel Stuart to locate footage, shoot interviews, and create *The
Race for Space* (1958).

Wolper was not a documentarian but a man who had decided to be in the
entertainment business. His experience in film had mainly been selling old
Hollywood movies to individual television stations. This background paid off
handily with *The Race for Space*, since in these years the networks generally
refused to broadcast any documentary that was not made by their own
in-house production teams. Worries about the Fairness Doctrine and sponsor
accountability made network executives loath to buy from outsiders. Wolper
was able to convince individual stations, both independents and network
affiliates, to buy and air *The Race for Space*. It ran on various stations for one

week in April 1960, and proved to be a huge critical and financial success. It was even nominated for an Academy Award, the first made-for-television documentary to be so recognized. The Wolper empire and, more influentially, the huge American television syndication business was born.

Over the next forty years Wolper and his teams were responsible for fifty-eight television documentary specials and twenty documentary series consisting of 347 episodes – a prodigious output. With *Hollywood and the Stars* he was the first to create television celebrity biographies. (He is perhaps best known, though, for his fictional mini-series – fourteen of them at 108 hours, including *Roots* and *The Thorn Birds*.) He also produced twenty theatrical motion pictures, including successful documentaries. The Wolper company provided hands-on training for at least two generations of documentarians, and he won Oscars, Peabodys, and Lifetime Achievement Awards galore.

Documentary history has tended to pass over the importance of David Wolper's work for a number of reasons. He always asserted that he was in the business to make money, and at this he was more successful than any other documentary producer in history. He did not claim that his films could change the world, yet many of them deal compassionately with serious social and political issues. For example, it was Wolper who brought Jacques Cousteau to television. Wolper was located in Hollywood, rather than in New York City, the traditional centre of documentary production. He said that he didn't know his films were not supposed to be entertaining in addition to being informative. He was being a passionate and very adept salesman – a trait he shares with some of the most effective documentarians from Robert Flaherty and John Grierson to Ken Burns and Michael Moore. All of these men could sell their ideas to funders, their films to distributors, and themselves to the public. Wolper did, however, sometimes play fast and loose with history; it was rumoured that at a stack of Nazi uniforms was kept on hand, ready to be used when actuality film was lacking.

By contrast, Frederick Wiseman, one of the most skilled and talented makers of direct cinema, produced and continues to produce for public television. *High School* (1968), *Law and Order* (1969), *Hospital* (1970) and *Basic Training* (1971) were supported in varying proportions by the Public Broadcasting Service, WNET Channel 13 in New York City. After *Basic*

Training Wiseman contracted with WNET to do one documentary each year to play on the PBS network. His subjects have been various American institutions, the titles generally making clear which one. Wiseman's films are discussed in Chapter 11.

Among the television documentary news magazines the biggest success was CBS's *60 Minutes* (produced by Don Hewitt) which began in 1968. It brought documentary-like content and production methods into commercial television just as 'The March of Time' earlier had introduced its own kind of nonfiction forms and subjects into movie theatres. Like 'The March of Time,' *60 Minutes* developed a format that fit the medium within which it was received. Its origins are directly traceable to *See It Now* and *CBS Reports*. In *60 Minutes* the American journalistic term 'news story' is taken quite literally. The several stories of each programme – some light, some serious – use a combination of aggressive investigative reporting, personable on-the-air reporters (early-on Mike Wallace, Morley Safer, Harry Reasoner, Diane Sawyer) and tight narrative structures. It was successful not only in comparison with other television news, public affairs and documentary series, but reached the Top Ten among all television shows in ratings. Its success was also awarded the compliment of imitation, and the magazine format made up of short segments gradually began to multiply. *60 Minutes* still is produced and shown today.

Special Characteristics of Television Documentary

Many elements common to documentaries made for television can be traced to the new technological characteristics of this electronic means of distribution/exhibition, and to the new relationship with the audience sitting – as individuals or members of small groups – at home. Just as cumbersome equipment and theatrical exhibition dictated the form of documentaries from 1895 to 1945, the technology and financial base of television determined what subjects were covered and what form the documentaries took.

In regard to the content of documentaries made for television, three major types predominated throughout the 1950s and 1960s, and they correspond to emphases of the documentary series and specials discussed above. First is the documentary based on a current newsworthy subject, something that is of immediate, widespread interest. This is a mode in which TV is very effective. From its beginnings it could examine topics quickly, if not with today's immediacy. Second are the historical and often nostalgic subjects of the compilation series and programmes – *Project XX* and much of *The Twentieth Century*. Lastly there is what could be called 'human interest' – the curiosity people have about others, their personalities and their problems. This sort of content became most manifest in the use of cv/d, but later morphed frighteningly into the ubiquitous reality series.

The range of subjects of television documentaries was wider as well as different from that of earlier documentaries. A kind of 'entertainment documentary' emerged – the nostalgia and human interest categories – in which the issues no longer were of national concern or social significance. Lyman Bryson observed, in his essay 'Popular Art' (in *The Communication of Ideas*, 1948), that the function of the mass media, the experience they offer, is more like that of gossip than that of traditional art forms. Certainly television offers materials as diverse as those of a neighbour talking to us over the back fence – in our electronic global village, a concept another media scholar, Marshall McLuhan, suggested (in *Understanding Media*, 1964). Scandalous secrets are revealed, amusing anecdotes told, conundrums posed, local events recounted, and the like. This gossipy quality also reached its apex – or nadir – in the reality programming of the twenty-first century.

Television documentary tended to maintain a small-scale intimacy. In *The Twentieth Century*, for example, a programme on 'Gandhi' (1959) is as much about the man as about the magnitude of his accomplishments; it seems quite unlike *The River* or films of the 'Why We Fight' series. Television documentaries often centred not only on individuals but on values (ethical, spiritual, psychological) rather than on material concerns (work, housing, poverty), as did earlier documentaries. Perhaps this difference was due as much to changed post-war preoccupations as to the influence of television; but whatever the cause, the difference is evident.

Frequently in television documentary, the commentator was the star and appeared on camera. Except for pioneer Nancy Dickerson, all were male. In earlier documentaries, the narrator was usually anonymous and unobtrusive;

his voice was heard over the images, and he never appeared on screen. The few exceptions that occurred seemed awkward. With TV the commentator often appeared on screen. The images and sounds of television documentary were constantly there in the TV set, just as electricity was in the wires and water in the pipes, ready to be turned on at any time. The celebrity commentators of that era – Ed Murrow, Walter Cronkite, Charles Kuralt, Chet Huntley, Dan Rather, et al. – fed into and emphasized the quality of liveness. The audience tuned in to see what Ed Murrow was offering on a Friday night. He talked directly to us from the control room, his reporters were available to come in over the 'monitors' as he called on them. Actually, given the technology available at the time, they were filmed beforehand, the film was flown to New York City, processed in the lab, and edited before being aired. Still, *See It Now* was shot more as if events were live and undirected than they were in earlier documentaries. Today's celebrity reports and commentators continue this tradition. *360 with Anderson Cooper* is certainly nothing new. He tries to make everything look live, even when segments have been filmed beforehand.

From the 1950s until the mid-1980s the rule was that the commentator's own point of view was generally withheld, or balanced – or maybe just ambivalent, and therefore ambiguous. Exceptions to this rule sometimes created a furore. *Harvest of Shame* drew outraged protests from the agriculture industry. *The Selling of the Pentagon* provoked a congressional committee to investigate the fairness of the film and threatened to subpoena the president of CBS, Frank Stanton, to force him to turn over out-takes, sound recordings and production notes from the programme. This same issue surfaced again in 2010 with out-takes from Joe Berlinger's *Crude* subpoenaed by the oil company criticized in the film. *Sixteen in Webster Groves* (CBS Special, 1966, Arthur Barron) is an exceptional case. The citizens of Webster Groves strongly objected to its portrayal of their town. In a sequel, *Webster Groves Revisited*, parents and other residents of this posh suburb of St Louis were permitted to offer a counter-view to the one presented by the teenagers in the first programme.

In documentaries made for television there was an increased use of synch sound, especially talk, and interviews were used much more extensively. The spoken word carried at least as much content as the visual track, and the visuals, to say nothing of the music, were much less rich and interesting than in non-television documentaries. At its worst this became radio with pictures. As a result of this different balance between words and images, the *auteurs* of television were usually the producers, writers and commentators rather than the directors, editors and camerapersons, as was more often the case in films made for theatrical exhibition. A redundancy developed in the documentary made for television that permitted the viewer-listener to go to the refrigerator and still follow what was going on, or vacuum the living room carpet while keeping an eye on 'the tube' without missing much. And of course the commercial break dictated form. This was the financial underpinning of television. Making money by selling ads was, and largely remains, the force that determines what documentaries appear on television.

As already noted, television documentaries tended to appear in the context of a series. Before television this was true only in exceptional instances such as 'The March of Time' or 'Why We Fight.' Television documentaries also had and continue to fit into quite precise air times, down to the second, allowing pauses for and building structures to accommodate the commercial breaks. The running times of earlier documentaries varied and were determined, to considerable extent, by the form and content of each film: *The Spanish Earth* runs 55 minutes; *And So They Live*, 24; *London Can Take It*, 9; *Fires Were Started*, 72; and *Nanook* has been recut so many times by distributors and exhibitors that it is hard to name its exact length. The fixed times of television resulted in strains – insufficient time available to deal adequately with a subject, or padding to fill out the timeslot even though less time would have produced a better film. Unfortunately this latter factor has also affected the quality of many twenty-first century documentaries whose makers must meet restrictive time and commercial breaks or who feel that they need to exceed eighty minutes in length to be theatrically viable.

In the series context and in the daily flow of television programming, it may be difficult for documentaries to offer the best aesthetic experience, though they do reach many people more quickly. Television became virtually *the* mass medium, certainly as far as documentary was concerned. It was the best qualified of any form of art and communication then devised to quickly call large numbers of people's attention to various subjects. It established its ability to do that – and sometimes did it superbly.

Chapter Related Films

1952–53

Victory at Sea series (Henry Salomon and Isaac Kleinerman)

1953

Argument in Indianapolis (*See It Now* series, Edward R. Murrow and Fred W. Friendly)

Christmas in Korea (same as above)

1954

Dresden Story (*On the Spot* series, Julian Biggs)

Edward R. Murrow Talks on Senator McCarthy (same as above)

Segregation in Schools (same as above)

1955

Nightmare in Red (*Project XX* series, Salomon and Kleinerman)

1956

The Twisted Cross (*Project XX,* Salomon and Kleinerman)

Skid Row (Allan King)

1958

From Kaiser to Fuehrer (*The Twentieth Century* series, Burton Benjamin and Kleinerman)

The Population Explosion (*CBS Reports* series, Av Westin)

1960

Primary (*Closeup!* series, Robert Drew, Richard Leacock, Al Maysles, Terence Macartney-Filgate)

Harvest of Shame (*CBS Reports*, Murrow, Friendly, and David Lowe)

Paris in the Twenties (*The Twentieth Century,* Benjamin and Kleinerman)

The U-2 Affair (*White Paper* series, Wasserman)

1961

Angola: Journey to a War (*White Paper*, Wasserman)

The Real West (*Project XX*, Donald B. Hyatt)

Walk in My Shoes (*Closeup!*, Nicholas Webster)

1962

The Battle of Newburgh (*White Paper*, Wasserman)

Meet Comrade Student (*Closeup!*, Webster)

So That Men Are Free (*The Twentieth Century*, Willard Van Dyke)

1963

Crisis Behind a Presidential Commitment (For ABC-TV, Robert Drew, Richard Leacock, Hope Ryden, Gregory Shuker)

The Death of Stalin (*White Paper*, Len Giovannitti)

The Plots Against Hitler (*The Twentieth Century*, Benjamin and Kleinerman)

That War in Korea (*Project XX*, Hyatt)

The Vatican (*Closeup!,* John Secondari)

1964

Cuba: Bay of Pigs (*White Paper*, Fred Freed)

Cuba: The Missile Crisis (same as above)

1966
Sixteen in Webster Groves (CBS-TV Special, Arthur Barron)
1968
Hunger in America (CBS Reports, Martin Carr)
1971
The Selling of the Pentagon (CBS-TV Special, Davis)

Chapter Related Books

Bluem, A. William, *Documentary in American Television*. New York: Hastings House, 1965.

Curtin, Michael, *Redeeming the Wasteland: Television Documentary and Cold War Politics*. New Brunswick, NJ: Rutgers University Press, 1995.

Friendly, Fred W., *Due to Circumstances Beyond Our Control . . . .* New York: Random House, 1967.

Hammond, Charles Montgomery, Jr, *The Image Decade: Television Documentary 1965–1975*. New York: Hastings House, 1981.

Kendrick, Alexander, *Prime Time: The Life of Edward R. Murrow*. Boston: Little Brown, 1969.

Madsen, Axel, *60 Minutes: The Power & the Politics of America's Most Popular TV News Show*. New York: Dodd, Mead, 1984.

Murrow, Edward R. and Fred W. Friendly, *See It Now*. New York: Simon and Schuster, 1955.

Raphael, C., *Investigative Reporting: Muck Rakers, Regulators, and the Struggle Over Television Documentary*. Illinois. University of Illinois Press, 2005.

Sperber, A. M., *Murrow: His Life and Times*. New York: Freundlich Books, 1986.

Swallow, Norman, *Factual Television*. New York: Hastings House, 1966.

Wolper, David L., *Producer*. New York: Scribner, 2003.

10

British Free Cinema and New American Cinema 1953–60

As noted in Chapter Eight, in the late forties and early fifties traditional documentary in Britain had run down somewhat, as it had in the US and, to a lesser extent, in Canada following the wartime boom. Grierson and his old boys were locked into former subjects and purposes which no longer seemed as relevant to the needs of the society as they once had – not as urgent anyway, and certainly not as exciting. In part they were suffering from their success. Many still consider the Grierson films to be the high point of British cinema and Humphey Jennings is lauded as its Poet Laureate. British documentary films of the thirties could be seen as having pointed to the need for a more collectivized, socialized state. Now that state had arrived.

But beginning in the mid-fifties a kind of cultural revolution commenced that affected art in Europe and the US generally. In Britain, this new school first became manifest in film. With the advent of commercial television and a vitality in the political left that extended into all the arts, new popular values ('vulgar' they were thought to be an elitist quarters) came to the fore. Almost all of the Grierson people came from privileged backgrounds, and after WWII class continued to play a significant role in British documentaries. Although new emerging artistic trends remained partly the creative province of the middle and upper classes, working class people's lives were now viewed differently.

Expressing these new values was a group of novelists, playwrights and political essayists who were dubbed 'The Angry Young Men'. Some of these individuals had working- and lower-middle-class backgrounds. Prominent among these were Kingsley Amis and John Osborne, whose play *Look Back in Anger* became emblematic for the group. What they were angry about was the conformity, the ugliness, the lack of individuality present in what was being called a welfare state – the very sort of state that the Labour government and the earlier documentary films seemed to be seeking. Further, the Angry Young Men protested that even within this semi-socialist state the class system persisted, with the upper classes controlling government, business, education and the media, and that these upper-class people through these institutions were responsible for the flattening of the working class, for keeping the common people not only helpless but listless. A very important part of this agitation among young intellectuals and artists occurred in the documentary film. It took the form of a small but highly influential group of films and filmmakers who called their work Free Cinema. This was the first substantial reaction against the Griersonian main line since its beginning back in 1929.

Critical Background

The roots of Free Cinema lay in a critical position espoused by a group of young people at Oxford University in the late forties. What they started as *Film Society Magazine* in 1947 quickly became *Sequence*. Persons associated with *Sequence* would become extremely important in the British film scene. Later, *Sequence* became *Sight and Sound,* a still-venerable critical voice of film. Penelope Huston was its first editor, and Gavin Lambert her assistant editor. He later became a successful author of short stories, novels, biographies and Hollywood screenplays. Tony Richardson, Karel Reisz (the only male member of the original group not from Oxford; he was at Cambridge, from which a high proportion of the Grierson alumni had come), and Lindsay Anderson were three other principals. All three would later become fiction filmmakers of considerable distinction.

The editorial emphases of *Sequence* were clear-cut and contentious; it was strongly against some things, strongly for others. The British entertainment film industry was denigrated for being dominated by Hollywood and failing to produce films having a national character. British documentary was scorned for its didacticism, dullness, and collective (as opposed to personal) creation. Certain new European films and filmmakers were lauded, such as the Italian Neorealists and the French New Wave. A poetic cinema in Britain was called for that would also provide a national expression – a poetry of reality, and of the common man – not to be confused with the poetry of ships, machinery and trains prevalent in the Grierson documentaries. Whereas Grierson was inspired by Eisenstein and Flaherty, Free Cinema was inspired by contemporary European fiction films.

Lindsay Anderson was the leader of this group. Like Grierson before him, he began as a writer about film, was the articulate spokesman and the first to begin making films. While pursuing such artistic goals, he held jobs making educational films such as *Foot and Mouth* (1955), a short film about the danger of hoof and mouth disease in cattle. Also like Grierson, Anderson searched for precedents for the sorts of films he wanted to be made. He wrote seminal re-evaluations of the work of Jean Vigo, John Ford and Humphrey Jennings, finding in their films evidence of the poetic and of the expression of their respective cultures. The Free Cinema group were vigorous polemicists, as the Griersonians had been.

Free Cinema Films

Anderson, in addition to his work on *Sequence*, had been making sponsored films since 1948. It was this work that funded his first Free Cinema films. These first significant Free Cinema documentaries were originally seen by very few. *Thursday's Children* (1955), co-directed with Guy Brenton, celebrated the pupils and the loving, skilful teaching being done at the Royal School for Deaf and Dumb Children. It won an Oscar for best documentary short. *O Dreamland* (1953) castigated the dull and synthetic pleasures being offered to the bemused working class at a seaside amusement park; Anderson himself once described it as 'a horrid little film'. The cameramen on these two films would become principal technicians of the Free Cinema films: Walter

Lassally (who subsequently became one of the world's great cinematographers) and John Fletcher (who would concentrate on sound and editing). It was their invaluable technical and artistic work that was a key part of the films' aesthetics.

Karel Reisz and Tony Richardson made *Momma Don't Allow* (1956), about a lively London jazz club patronized by working-class teenagers. Lorenza Mazetti, the only woman in the Free Cinema group, made *Together* (1958), a semidocumentary, which deals with the emotionally impoverished lives led by two deaf-mute dock workers in London's East End. This dark and ultimately tragic portrait remains wrenching today. *Together* along with *Momma Don't Allow* and *O Dreamland* were the first films screened under the Free Cinema banner. The programme for this opening night at the British Film Institute (BFI) theatre included the following programme note:

> These films were not made together; nor with the
> idea of showing them together. But when they came
> together, we felt they had an attitude in common.
> Implicit in this attitude is a belief in freedom,
> in the importance of people and in the significance
> of the everyday.
> *As film-makers we believe that*
> *No film can be too personal.*
> *The image speaks. Sound amplified and comments.*
> *Size is irrelevant. Perfection is not an aim.*
> *An attitude means a style. A style means an attitude.*
> Lorenza Mazetti
> Lindsay Anderson
> Karel Reisz
> Tony Richardson

Of the subsequent Free Cinema films – there were only a dozen or so altogether – *Nice Time* (1957) was made by Swiss filmmakers Alain Tanner and Claude Goretta, who would return home to become well-known fiction filmmakers. *Nice Time* is about the people in Piccadilly Circus in London's West End on a Saturday night. Lonely and disconsolate by and large, they

Fig 48 Momma Don't Allow *(UK, 1955, Karel Reisz and Tony Richardson).*
Museum of Modern Art Film Stills Archive

are shown seeking pleasure and diversion among the movie theatres, the refreshment stands, the prostitutes, and the milling crowds of others like themselves.

Every Day Except Christmas (1957), by Lindsay Anderson, is about the Covent Garden produce market (which no longer exists). It is an elegiac observation of the workers and their culture – the look, the feel, the activities of the place – from early evening, as the trucks come in from the country with vegetables, fruits and flowers, until closing the following morning. *We Are the Lambeth Boys* (1959) is about 'teddy boys' – kids from a poor and tough part of London. At its social centre is an outing to a cricket match at a posh suburban school. It is a sympathetic and respectful view of these young people who the popular press were presenting as gangs of dangerous delinquents.

What did these filmmakers mean by Free Cinema? Essentially, independent: free from serving the sponsor's purposes, as in traditional British documentary; free from pandering to the demands of the box office, as in entertainment features. Gavin Lambert, in an article in *Sight and Sound* (Spring 1956), wrote about the three films shown at the first Free Cinema programme. Likening their spirit to that of D. H. Lawrence's writings, he noted that they 'sprang from non-conformism, from impatience with convention, sadness about urban life'. Like Lawrence's work, too, they represented 'a desire to regain contact with a more vital, individual force'. Lambert continued:

> In the broadest sense, they are films of protest; they are not conceived in sweeping terms … but the camera-eye they turn on society … is disenchanted, and occasionally ferocious and bitter … If compassion is explicit in Lorenza Mazetti's film [*Together*], implicit in Lindsay Anderson's [*O Dreamland*], it is the most rigorous, difficult and austere kind of compassion: not for the moment or the particular situation, but a kind of permanent temperamental heartache for the world and the people apparently lost in it.

A collusion apparent here between critic and creator is reminiscent of the Grierson documentary people who wrote about their own films in *Documentary News Letter*, which they had themselves established. Anderson, in his seminal essay 'Stand Up! Stand Up!', also published in *Sight and Sound* (Autumn 1956), demanded that film criticism also be socially committed. Commitment, individuality and poetry were key terms in the rhetoric of Free Cinema. The Free Cinema films observed workers and the working class, as

Fig 49 We Are the Lambeth Boys *(UK, 1959, Karel Reisz). Museum of Modern Art Film Stills Archive*

had the documentaries of the thirties, but rather than their work, Free Cinema was concerned with their personal lives. The films addressed the values of the people, their modest lives, their limited aspirations. They brought to light matters of social psychology and of the spirit.

The Free Cinema films are non-didactic, aesthetic rather than informative; they appeal to emotion more than to reason. The sluggish, unimaginative and flaccid are censured (*O Dreamland, Nice Time*); the lively, vigorous and idiosyncratic are extolled (*Momma Don't Allow, Every Day Except Christmas, We Are the Lambeth Boys*). They have in common a vaguely anarchic, nihilistic, iconoclastic air, yet were affectionate in tone. What they seem to be calling for is a reordering of society, one that respected the working class. They are implicitly revolutionary rather than actively evolutionary, as Grierson's work was.

The formal aspects of the Free Cinema films, especially their structural organizations, are reminiscent of Humphrey Jennings, who was much admired by Anderson. The Free Cinema films are distinctly not Griersonian. Though they employ a loose chronology, they follow feeling more than logic. Commentary is eschewed for the most part. (There is some in *Every Day* and *Lambeth,* but none in the other four examples cited.) Instead, the filmmakers' points are made through their choice and arrangement of sights and sounds. Juxtaposition of symbolic contrasts and counterpoint of the visible and audible abound. Considerable irony and wry humour result.

The production techniques and technology used grow out of the subjects and purposes of Free Cinema and vice versa. The filmmakers confined themselves to what could be seen and heard on location. Portable synchronous sound did not yet exist, so dialogue is sparse. The sights and sounds used are those that could be captured without studio equipment. Though bits of invented performance are inserted into *Momma Don't Allow*, as in some earlier as well as later documentaries, quite a lot of Free Cinema is candid – the subjects are unaware they are being filmed – hence the preponderance of places where people gather publicly: amusement park, dance hall, Piccadilly Circus, social centre. Early on the camera was hand-held, the black-and-white images grainy and underexposed. Ambient location sound, often of inferior quality, constituted the soundtrack. In essence, most of the people, excepting Anderson, were teaching themselves filmmaking. Between 1954 and 1959 there were increasing technological refinements, from non-synch sound to simulated synch, a so-called wild track that was recorded on location and later edited to match the available footage. The camerawork goes from candid to increasing awareness on the part of the subjects that a camera is present, to steadier and more carefully composed images. Editing is critical for both sound and image, and it is important to remember that most of the films were shot with a spring-wound Bolex 16mm camera with slow black-and-white film. Although portable and lightweight, the film reels limited the length of shots and needed strong lighting to capture images.

O Dreamland cost a few hundred pounds and was paid for by Anderson himself. The other three of the first four films received grants from the British Film Institute Experimental Film Production Fund. The last two listed were sponsored under an agreement with the Ford Motor Company.

As for the arguments between the Free Cinema newcomers and the old-line documentarians, the former were just as much propagandists as the latter, despite their attacks on earlier documentaries for attempting to manipulate viewer opinion. The ends were different – New Left vs. Old Left – as well as the techniques and styles used to advance those ends. Grierson predicted that Free Cinema would metamorphose into something else, and it very soon and very importantly filtered into the fiction feature film.

The documentary influence has also consistently contributed to some of the most interesting and distinctive cycles of British fiction production: wartime semidocumentaries, post-war Ealing comedies, social-realist features. It might be argued that the quiet genius of British cinema has always pointed most surely in the direction of realism and what John Grierson called the 'documentary idea'. For a while in the late 1950s and 60s the young people of Free Cinema came together with the young men and women of theatre and literature who had been tackling similar themes. The veracity of documentary detail was warmed and strengthened by the addition of story and character.

Free Cinema's end and metamorphosis into the social-realist fiction features, or what was sometimes called the British New Wave, was paralleled by similar, lesser-known developments in the US. These documentaries and experimental films eventually moved documentary closer to the dividing line between art and life. Called cinéma vérité in France and Canada and direct cinema in America, this development is the subject of Chapter Eleven.

The United States

Among the precursors in the US in the late 1940s was the renowned still photographer Helen Levitt, whose forte was documenting life on the New York City streets. She made two important documentary films with Janice Loeb and James Agee: *In the Street* (1948) and the previously described *The Quiet One* (1948). Levitt was active in filmmaking for nearly twenty-five years; her final film credit is as an editor for John Cohen's documentary *The End of an Old Song* (1972). Levitt's other film credits include the cinematography on *The Savage Eye* (1960), which was produced by Ben Maddow, Meyers, and Joseph Strick.

While in England it was Free Cinema that led the way to the literary and theatrical changes of the late fifties and early sixties, in the US film did not precede changes in other arts. The group of people making new kinds of film were influenced by their contemporaries, poets and painters living in New York City, a movement now known famously as the 'New York School', which included poets John Ashbery, Kenneth Koch, Barbara Guest, Frank O'Hara and James Schuyler. Abstract Expressionist painters Willem de Kooning, Jackson Pollock, Mark Rothko and Robert Motherwell were emerging at the same time. Not part of the 'New York School' rubric, but writing at the same time were others born in the 1920s, a generation various enough to include voices as dissimilar as Allen Ginsberg and James Merrill, Adrienne Rich and Robert Creeley. This was also the era that Dizzy Gillespie and be-bop shook the jazz world. Simultaneously what became known as 'The New American Cinema' was emerging. A number of noteworthy documentaries emerged during this period.

Among the most important of the independent documentaries from the post-war American independent scene was Lionel Rogosin's 1957 film *On the Bowery*. Rogosin's style and aims were similar to that of the Free Cinema makers. Shot on the street, the film is compassionate to its subjects, the denizens of New York City's skid row, and it sought to make a conscious break from previous documentary tradition. He called his work made 'from the inside' of ordinary people in their everyday surroundings, carrying out their lives as they would without the presence of a camera. Nominated for an Oscar for Best Documentary Feature, the film chronicles three days in the life of a drifter new to the dismal skid-row scene, Ray Salyer. Although he is still good-looking and well-spoken, Ray's life is lost to alcohol. Urged on by Bowery old-timer Gorman Hendricks, Salyer goes on two benders, quits twice, hops on a truck for a day job, but finally states: 'Me, I only care for one thing.' That thing is liquor, and Rogosin makes no apologies, no efforts at rehabilitation, nor gestures of charity. *On The Bowery* has been acclaimed as both a filmmaking inspiration and a look at a now-lost part of New York City. After seeing the film, Lindsay Anderson programmed it as part of the BFI Free Cinema series, and Martin Scorsese has called it 'a milestone in American cinema'.

Rogosin translated the style in a second film, *Come Back Africa* (1960), which was shot, in the Flaherty tradition, after a year of living among

Fig 50 On the Bowery, *1957. Lionel Rogosin's account of life on the streets of lower Manhattan.*

the people in South Africa. This film, more scripted and acted, is less a documentary than *On the Bowery.* Next, after three years of scouring the world for archival war footage, Rogosin made *Good Times, Wonderful Times* (1966). Inspired by Joan Littlewood's stage production of *Oh! What a Lovely War,* the film is a compilation of twentieth-century war footage, including scenes of the nuclear devastation of Hiroshima and Nagasaki. These archival pieces are contrasted with material shot at a posh London cocktail party where people are shown as representative of society's apathy and hedonism. Made at the start of the American War in Vietnam, *Good Times, Wonderful Times* was a success on college campuses and was one of first to help inspire the anti-war protest movement. Rogosin was one of the twenty-five filmmakers who joined together in 1960 as a 'free and open organization' called the New American Cinema Group, which soon became the heart of and the label attached to independent American experimental film.

New American Cinema sprang from some of the same feelings about society and its relationship to art that young artists were sharing in England,

Fig 51 The New York Times *wrote in 1964 of Jonas Mekas' film, 'The Brig is a raw slice of new American cinema filmed in an off-Broadway stage with such brutish authenticity that it won a Venice festival grand prize as best documentary'*

France, Brazil, Italy and elsewhere. As one of its founders and the key voice of the movement over the decades, Jonas Mekas, states:

> The year was 1960. New York was buzzing with dreams of a new cinema – a cinema that would reflect the sensibilities of 1960. Inspired by the New York School of Cinema – a term used at the Venice Film Festival to introduce the works of Morris Engel, Sidney Meyers, and Lionel Rogosin – the French Nouvelle Vague burst upon the screens of the world. In the United States, the avant-garde cinema of Kenneth Anger, Gregory Markopoulos, Stan Brakhage, Maya Deren, and Ron Rice was making its own waves. So was John Casavettes' *Shadows* (1959); Robert Frank and Alfred Leslie's *Pull My Daisy* (1959); Shirley Clarke's *The Connection* (1961); *Guns of the Tree* (1961) the film I made with Adolfas Mekas; and Bert Stern's *Jazz on a Summer Day* (1959) and Ed Bland's *Cry of Jazz* (1959).

Mekas has continued through today as a leading spokesman through the distribution company Filmmakers Cooperative and the screening venue Anthology Film Archive. These films are experimental in many respects, but documentary tendencies also play a significant role in them. Although many New American Cinema makers are best known as fiction and experimental filmmakers, much of the impetus for their work sprang from new documentary impulses being explored at the time.

A former dancer, choreographer and head of the National Dance Association, Shirley Clarke made a series of short films about dance, including *In Paris Parks (1954)* and *Bullfight* (1955). Moving on to other subjects, *Brussels Loops* (1957), a short work made for the 1959 Brussels World Fair, was co-directed by Clarke, D. A. Pennebaker, Wheaton Galentine and Ricky Leacock. The piece is a long series of film loops edited together beautifully, but without any obvious explanation. *Skyscraper (1959)* traced the construction of a building, used colour and black-and-white shots, and was made in collaboration with documentary stalwarts Willard Van Dyke and Irving Jacoby. It earned an Oscar nomination for Best Live Action Short Subject. *The Connection* is a film with New Wave sensibilities and a strong connection with beat culture. The film was banned because of obscenity and its frank depiction of drug culture. Based on a play, it is a fiction work that tells the story of junkies waiting for their dealer in a documentary style that captures the dark side of the era's counterculture. Clarke also made many other films, experimental, fiction, documentary and every combination of these forms. Her Oscar-winning documentary short *Robert Frost: A Lover's Quarrel With the World* (1963) was commissioned by President John Kennedy.

Pull My Daisy (1959) is a peculiar, interesting and not entirely successful twenty-six-minute film experiment that is very loosely based on a poem jointly written by Allen Ginsberg, Jack Kerouac and Neal Cassady. Each wrote one line then passed it on to another, and the film feels much as the poem does. Directed by photographer Robert Frank with artist Alfred Leslie, it is populated by an odd assortment of people who were then associated with the beat movement. Ginsberg, Gregory Corso and Peter Orlovsky play themselves, while painter Larry Rivers plays Neal Cassady (Milo), Cassady (Milo)'s wife Carolyn is played by a woman credited as 'Beltiane', who in reality was actress Delphine Seyrig. Painter Alice Neel and dancer Sally Gross also appear. Jack Kerouac later provided a voiceover narration that is meant to replicate one of his spontaneous writings. *Pull My Daisy* makes no pretence of being a documentary, but its existence is a fascinating document in itself and the film marks a key moment when the various filmmakers of that era moved in three different directions: the fiction feature, the purely experimental work and the documentary.

Jazz Dance (1954) is a wonderfully vital twenty-minute documentary film by Roger Tilton (who subsequently became a successful maker of large-screen Omnimax films) and Ricky Leacock. It documents a night at a New York dance hall in 1954. To the music of musicians Jimmy McPartland, Willie 'The Lion' Smith, Jimmie Archey, George Watling and Pee Wee Russell, Leacock's whirl of camera work and the film's editing takes the audience over, under and into the joy that fills the crowd. Although several cameramen had previously turned down the shoot, claiming that large cameras and studio lighting would be needed, Leacock was, as always, confident that he could do the job. As he said,

> So I agreed to try making this film the way we had filmed combat ... Roger and his editor Richard Brummer laid these fragmentary shots in sync with the four pieces of music selected for the film; slow, medium, fast and faster! It worked! On a big screen in a theatre, WOW! You were there, right in the midst of it and it looked like it was in sync... it was in sync! We couldn't film dialogue or sustained musical passages this way. But it gave us a taste, a goal.

The similarity of it to Karel Reisz and Tony Richardson's *Momma Don't Allow* (1957), shot by Walter Lassally, is unmistakable, Some have claimed that *Momma Don't Allow* was instrumental in changing the course of British cinema, and *Jazz Dance* is a jewel that continues to excite today's audiences. It is one of the most critical links to what would become cv/direct.

Chapter Related Films

1953
O Dreamland (UK, Lindsay Anderson)
1954
Jazz Dance (US, Roger Tilton and Ricky Leacock)
1955
Momma Don't Allow (UK, Karel Reisz and Tony Richardson)
1956
Together (UK, Lorenza Mazetti)
1957
Every Day Except Christmas (UK, Anderson)
Nice Time (UK, Alain Tanner and Claude Goretta)
On The Bowery (US, Lionel Rogosin)
1959
Pull My Daisy (US, Robert Frank and Alfred Leslie)
Skyscraper (US, Shirley Clarke, Willard van Dyke, Irving Jacoby)
We Are the Lambeth Boys (UK, Reisz)

Chapter Related Books

Dupin, Christophe, *Free Cinema*. London: British Film Institute, 2006 (note accompanying Free Cinema DVD set).

Durgnat, Raymong, *A Mirror for England: British Movies from Austerity to Affluence*. Faber and Faber, 1970.

Engelbach, Barbara, *Jonas Mekas*. Berlin: Walter Konig, 2009.

Gaston, Georg, *Karel Reisz*. Boston: Twayne, 1981.

Graham, Allison, *Lindsay Anderson*. Boston: Twayne, 1981.

Hedling, Erik, *Lindsay Anderson: Maverick Filmmaker*. London: Cassell, 1998.

Lovell, Alan and Jim Hillier, *Studies in Documentary*. New York: Viking, 1972.

Orbanz, Eva, *Journey to a Legend and Back: The British Realistic Film*. Berlin: Verlag Volker Spiess, 1977.

Sargeant, Jack, *Naked Lens: Beat Cinema*. Berkeley, CA: Soft Skull Press, 2009.

Silet, Charles L. P., *Lindsay Anderson: A Guide to References and Resources*. Boston: G. K. Hall, 1978.

Sussex, Elizabeth, *Lindsay Anderson*. New York: Frederick A. Praeger, 1970.

Welsh, James M. and John C. Tibetts, (eds), *The Cinema of Tony Richardson: Essays and Interviews*. New York: State University of New York, 1999.

11

Cinéma vérité, direct cinema 1958–70

In the late 1950s several major technological breakthroughs dramatically changed documentary as well as fictional and experimental filmmaking. These changes occasioned what can be thought of either as something new or merely as new ways of doing old things; technological advancement is always a bit of both. What these innovations permitted was the portable mobile synchronous recording of both sight and sound outside the confines of sound stages and studio lots. Many people, places and activities that were previously not filmable could now be captured almost anywhere with synch sound and 16mm film. These new technical possibilities were also driven by the types of film people wanted to make. Building on the work of Free Cinema and the New American Cinema, the desire for a different kind of creative work pushed technical advancement while the new technologies themselves offered opportunities for changes in both content and form. And, as always, money played a role.

As with the beginning of film itself in the 1890s, a general movement to create different kinds of documentary occurred simultaneously in many places. One of these breakthroughs was what Americans called direct cinema. Another was that of Frenchman Jean Rouch and his colleagues, echoing 'Kino Pravda', who coined the term cinéma vérité (film truth) to apply to their work. The Free Cinema group in England and some independent filmmakers in the US were also were heading toward similar goals. Brazilians too were experimenting with this style, influenced by the Swede Arne Sucksdorf, who held an influential documentary seminar in Sao Paulo in 1962. That country's Cinema Novo movement became another strong variation on the theme. This book does not deal much with non-English cinemas; the point is that the interest in a new kind of documentary with different subjects and made with new equipment surfaced in several places at about the same time.

Historical Background

Documentarians always seek technological modifications that permit them to film more easily under difficult conditions, and to better convey actuality to their audiences. The initial division between the creative impulses that led to documentary and those that led to fiction was caused at least partly by equipment. The first films made by the Edison Company in the 1890s were shot with the Kinetograph. This electrically powered camera was so large and heavy it was confined to a studio built to house it. Edison technicians recorded vaudeville and circus acts and bits of stage plays, performed in the Black Maria, as that studio was called, thus inaugurating the American theatrical/fictional mode of filmmaking. In France, Louis and Auguste Lumière designed a relatively lightweight, hand-cranked camera, the Cinématographe, which permitted them to record life on the streets, thus establishing the documentary mode. Making this distinction even early in film history has its contradictions. Edison was recording actual live performances, not, at first, making up new stories; and the Lumières used multiple takes and direction to get the effect they wanted, even in their very first film *Workers Learning the Factory* (1895). Still, the link between type of equipment and the distinct development of the two tendencies is a valid way to distinguish them.

By the 1920s, when documentary proper began to evolve, the cameras used were more portable than previously, but still cumbersome, requiring tripods to capture steady images. The comparatively insensitive film stock then in use – all of it black-and-white – needed lots of light. No sound was available until after 1927, except that provided in the movie theatres by live pianos, organs, or orchestras that played as films were being exhibited. Sound for location documentaries remained impossible even as studio fiction films with sound became the norm in the 1930s. Flaherty's descriptive sort of documentary, which showed the surroundings, physical appearances and outdoor activities of unfamiliar peoples, used existing visual technology to perfection. His work did not really require sound. Others – Grierson, Lorentz, the Film and Photo League, the WWII propagandists – all needed post-production sound to make their points.

In the 1930s, optical sound production equipment was so bulky that synchronous recording on location remained difficult to impossible. It was like Edison's big camera all over again, and most fiction filmmakers retreated into the studio. The standard documentary sound-film method became that of shooting silent pictures, subsequently adding to the edited footage spoken words, plus music, plus sound effects. To have documentary 'talkies', a voiceover commentary was almost obligatory, though sometimes artificial elements, commentary and music tracks did permit the addition of information and interpretation to visuals, and also explained complex contemporary issues.

Black-and-white images accompanied by post-synch sound thus remained the most common format for documentary-makers throughout the thirties, forties and fifties. The classic documentaries of this period – *The Song of Ceylon, The Plow That Broke the Plains, Night Mail*, the 'Why We Fight' series, and even the most experimental works – were all made within those limitations, even as filmmakers kept trying to come closer to capturing natural sound with natural scenes. This goal and the development of equipment to reach it were not confined to those with documentary interests (though they would win the race). Notable efforts occurred in avant-garde and fiction filmmaking as well.

The Italian Neorealists, especially Roberto Rossellini, made remarkable strides in adding audible reality to their images. Their sound was still post-synchronized, however; the dialogue was dubbed. Jean Renoir (who was a good friend of Robert Flaherty's in their later years) was another fiction filmmaker who disliked the confinement of the studio and the rigidity of the large and heavy stationary cameras standard in American studio shooting. In an amusing interview, Renoir likened the 35mm studio camera to a great metal idol to which humans are offered up sacrificially. Everything was done for the convenience of the camera and sound recordist. Actors had to move to chalk marks on the floor to be in focus, to turn their faces a certain way to catch the light. Renoir (and Flaherty) wanted, instead, the machine to be subservient to people – to follow them around, to attend to them.

Obviously, the lighter equipment of 16mm offered documentarians advantages over 35mm. Eastman Kodak had manufactured silent 16mm film since the 1920s. If desired, films shot on 16mm could be 'blown up' to 35mm for theatrical exhibition. Lionel Rogosin made *On the Bowery* (1956) and *Come Back, Africa* (1958) in this way, with some remarkable synch-sound actuality set within semidocumentary narratives. In 1960 John Cassavetes, in the fictional *Shadows*, allowed actors to improvise while their actions and words were recorded on 16mm equipment. Manufacturers also had a vested financial interest in perfecting 16mm. It was introduced by Kodak in 1923 as a home movie format, intended for the amusement of the wealthy. Streamlining the equipment and lowering costs meant that Kodak could sell the small Cine-Kodak camera, and charge for processing more film to middle-class consumers. Sixteen-millimetre projectors were made and sold by Bell & Howell by (1923). In addition to amateur use, these technical achievements inaugurated the modern professional nontheatrical field. Eastman Teaching Films was incorporated in 1928. Soon teaching films were a regular part of school curricula in the US, with hundred of films being produced regularly. This began to formalize the nontheatrical market, which became so important to documentary after World War II.

New Technology and First CV/Direct

With impetus from engineers, technicians and filmmakers, the key equipment that made direct cinema/cinéma vérité (cv/direct, as this book refers to it) possible began to be made. By substituting plastic for some of the metal moving parts, 16mm shoulder-mounted cameras became more lightweight and less noisy, no longer requiring blimps (i.e. casing containing acoustic insulation). The French Éclair NPR camera (Noiseless Portable Reflex), developed by André Coutant in 1961, and the German Arriflex SR (Silent Reflex) became standards. Cameras with reflex viewing (actually looking through the lens while shooting), plus zoom lenses, permitted cinematographers to alter the field of view – from closeup to long shot, for example – without having to stop to change lenses or to rack focus. The French Angenieux 12 to 120/mm zoom lens was commonly used, forever blessing and cursing the field with intense zooming in and out. Increasingly 'fast' film stock (that is, with emulsion very sensitive to light, thus needing little light) permitted shooting without adding illumination to that naturally available. Later, in the 1970s, Eastman Kodak 16mm colour negative was in widespread use, replacing the reversal processes (Kodachrome and Ektachrome) because of its superior qualities in low light. Added to faster film stock was a laboratory 'intensification process' which could push the sensitivity of a film to over 1000 ASA (American Standards Association; the higher the number the faster the film; standard colour negative had an ASA of 100) after it was shot.

For sound, 1/4' magnetic tape recorders were developed that synchronized with cameras first with a cable and eventually through use of an inaudible sixty-cycle pulse. The Nazis in the 1930s were the first to invent magnetic

Fig 52 *The French Éclair camera was part of the technical revolution that brought about cinéma vérité/direct, and changed documentary forever*

sound tape recording. In the WWII 'spoils of war' treaty between the Allies and the Axis, this technology became – like all German intellectual property (excepting atomic and other military knowledge) – free to the world. The Nagra, developed by Swiss engineer Stefan Kudelski in 1958, became the most common type in use. Around 1960 vacuum tubes, which were large and consumed a lot of energy, were replaced by transistors, and the weight of sound recorders was reduced from about 200 pounds to 20 pounds. When crystal synchronization was added later (first used in Drew Associates' *Primary* [1960]), there was no longer the need for even a cable between camera and recorder. This new technology permitted action to take place in front of the camera and microphone without the presence of extremely intrusive and cumbersome equipment. The camera could now move, creating a fresh way to see the world. A new generation of filmmakers was about to make the documentary its own.

In 1958 at the National Film Board, two young French Canadians, Michel Brault and Giles Groulx, using film left over from another project, shot more or less secretly *Les Raquetteurs* (*The Snowshoers*). The event with which the film is concerned – snowshoe races in Sherbrooke, Quebec – seems mainly to be the occasion for a parade and a party for the townspeople. The film records these activities but concentrates on the people and their relations with each other. The filmmakers seem to have entered into the sociability and evidently were fully accepted by the townsfolk.

Les Raquetteurs raised some hackles in official Canada, and concern was expressed about the non-official way in which it was produced. More serious was the question about the motivation of the filmmakers. Though they appear to be in affectionate, if amused, sympathy with their subjects, some French Canadians were made uneasy by the unprettified view of robust conviviality presented. Such a portrayal, it was alleged, helped to perpetuate the false stereotype of the crude and dull-witted 'Canucks'. This sort of controversy about cultural representation by outsiders is an ethical issue that continues today.

In 1960, in the US, *Primary*, a breakthrough in film, was produced by Robert Drew. Most of the shooting was done by Albert Maysles, Terence Macartney-Filgate and Richard Leacock. Many of the crew also worked on

Fig 53 The Snowshoers (Les Raquetteurs) *by Michel Brault and Giles Groulx for The National Film Board of Canada. National Film Board of Canada* (1958)

the editing; 18,000 feet (seven and one-half hours) of film was cut down to 2,000 (fifty minutes). During filming, two-man crews – one person recording sound, the other using the camera – operated autonomously, following and capturing their subject as they went through the day. This approach meant that there was no single 'director' present throughout filming. It was up to the two-man team to decide when to turn the camera on and off. Of course, no one saw any of the footage until weeks later when it had been developed. Drew then divided the editors into groups, each of which worked on separate sections while he supervised the whole.

Primary deals with the 1960 Wisconsin Democratic primary election contest between Senators Hubert Humphrey and John F. Kennedy. Not only does it follow each candidate through his public appearances and activities, intercutting between the two men, it also enters into the more private times when they are in hotel rooms or an automobile. Of the many remarkable moments the film contains, perhaps the most often mentioned is a seemingly

Fig 54 *John F. Kennedy on the campaign trail caught in a famous shot by cameraman Al Maysles in* Primary *(US, 1960, Drew Associates). Drew Associates*

uninterrupted shot, with synchronous sound, which follows Kennedy from outside a building into it, down a long corridor, up some stairs, out onto a stage, ending with a view of the wildly applauding audience. Maysles shot it holding the camera high above his head, never looking through the lens. The novelty at the time was breathtaking and the shot remains among the most famous in documentary. Another startling difference from documentaries of the thirties, forties and fifties was the absence of interviews; no people talked directly to the camera – unprecedented for that sort of subject. There was, however, a voiceover narrator. As one would expect, the new equipment often malfunctioned, and the crew spent many of their nights fixing it so it could be used the following day.

One could say that French cinéma vérité began in 1959 at a Robert Flaherty Seminar – an annual event started by Frances Flaherty and Robert's brother, David, which has met every year since. On that occasion French ethnographer Jean Rouch saw *Les Raquetteurs* and met Michel Brault, who would become

principal cameraman for *Chronicle of a Summer* (1961), directed by Rouch
in collaboration with sociologist Edgar Morin. *Chronicle* was first shown in
the US at another Flaherty Seminar, in 1963, along with Drew Associates' *The
Chair* and Albert and David Maysles' *Showman* (both 1962).

Chronicle of a Summer broke from tradition in ways different from *Les
Raquetteurs* or *Primary*. Its subject matter consists of a choreographed
sampling of individual opinions, attitudes and values of Parisians in the
summer of 1960. What the film offers is a chance to understand something
of the interviewees and of their culture, their positions within it, and their
feelings about it. The filmmakers' purpose and approach seem to be that
of interior discovery and revelation. The Parisians are modern, urban and
articulate. Their concerns, as well as those of the filmmakers, are about their
feelings rather than about the work they do or how they do it.

The overall structure of *Chronicle* is a loose narrative, as the title implies,
resembling an anthology of essays and short stories. Through it we get to

Fig 55 *Jean Rouch (left) and Edgar Morin in the conclusion of* Chronicle of a
Summer *(France, 1961). Museum of Modern Art Film Stills Archive*

know the Parisians directly from interviews: Marceline, who survived a Nazi concentration camp; Angelo, a factory worker; Marilou, a troubled Italian working in Paris; or Landry, a black African student. This is in contrast to *Primary* in which Humphrey or Kennedy are not interviewed. We are told by Rouch and Morin that part one of the film is intended to deal with the 'interior' lives of the subjects; part two is about the 'exterior', the more general world around them as they see it. Links among the sequences are made through groupings of persons and topics of conversation and the approach is persistently self-reflexive: the people on camera and the audience are continually reminded that a film is being made. The penultimate scene is of the subjects discussing themselves as they have appeared in the film they, and the audience, have just seen. Here the new synch-sound technology is used primarily for discussion and interview. There is a soliloquy in a famous sequence by Marceline strolling in the Place de la Concorde and Les Halles market, as she recalls painful episodes from her past. Angelo, the worker, gives a kind of improvised performance for the camera, pointedly ignoring its presence.

Throughout the film the cinematography of Michel Brault, Raoul Coutard and A. Vignier, though different from Flaherty's, is akin to his in skill and certainty. Their adeptness in moving smoothly and seemingly effortlessly with their subjects is clear, as was the case with the Drew cinematographers. Radically different from Flaherty or the Drew films, however, the two directors of *Chronicle* are frequently on screen, engaged in conversation with their subjects. This is a film being made by Rouch and Morin, they seem to be saying, and here we are so you can see how we are going about it.

The American use of the new equipment was pioneered by technicians and filmmakers, many of whom were at some point in their careers employed at Drew Associates. Its tenets were articulated most forcefully by Robert Drew and Leacock. The Drew approach falls generally within the reportage tradition, stemming from Drew's 'picture story' background in photo-journalism at *Life* magazine. A different element was added by Leacock's engineering training and experience as a WWII combat cameraman. D. A. Pennebaker also brought an engineering background, Al Maysles training in sociology, and Macartney-Filgate the Canadian perspective.

Cv/direct technique seemed to offer the possibility of an objective observer. While acknowledging that subjectivity occurs in selecting persons and situations and aspects of these, once those choices are made the filmmakers, in theory, do not direct or participate in, or even influence (it was contended) the scene in any way. It was felt that the presence of the camera was soon taken for granted by the subjects – ignored mostly, sometimes forgotten altogether. In this approach, the relationship between filmmakers and subjects had to be relaxed and trusting in order for the filmmaking to fit into ongoing action without affecting it. Leacock was particularly adept in winning confidence from the people he was shooting; an engaging person, he could be casual and very charming with his camera and the people in front of it. Maysles, with the gently inquisitive sociological approach of his training, was also able to get close to people with his camera, albeit in a different, softer way.

By design and in the course of the work, Drew discovered that their method functioned best if something important was happening to their subjects – if they were involved in an activity demanding their full attention and evoking a certain behaviour. This was the case in *Primary*. Humphrey and Kennedy were much more concerned with winning an election than with how they would appear in a film. They were attempting to win over people in order to obtain their votes, and public appearance was a normal part of their lives that the presence of a camera and microphone would scarcely alter. One visual convention in this film has become a fall-back shot for hundreds of later documentarians, in no small part because it provides movement in what would otherwise be static scenes. This is the in-the-car-sequences with Humphrey. Filmed by Leacock, Humphrey is seen from behind, the camera being in the back seat. He falls asleep. He occasionally turns to face the camera, but mostly he stares out the car window. As rain spatters against the windshield and the car wipers gently thump, Humphrey muses on life, not the political, but the wide empty landscape. Only some filmmakers today know that when they choose to film this type of shot, they are using a classic technique. Leacock himself did not realize the impact this sequence would have. He once said:

> I got into the car with Senator Humphrey and filmed with the tiny camera and recorder that no professional would be seen dead with. He probably

thought I was someone's uncle making home movies and he ignored me, perfect. He fell asleep, even better, then woke up and talked nonsense about how the snow brings nitrogen to the soil. We even filmed him in the men's room with the Governor as they planned their TV show.

Mooney vs. Fowle (1961, aka *Football*) climaxes with a high school football game in Miami, Florida between two rival teams. It concentrates on the players, coaches, immediate families, all completely preoccupied with this contest. *The Chair* (1962) centres on the efforts of a Chicago attorney, Donald Page Moore, to obtain a stay of execution for his client, Paul Crump, five days before it is scheduled to take place. *Jane* (1962), largely made by Hope Ryden and D. A. Pennebaker, concerns nineteen-year-old Jane Fonda in the production of a play, from the rehearsal period through the negative reviews following its Broadway opening and the decision to close it.

Fig 56 *Paul Crump faces execution in a shot by Ricky Leacock in* The Chair *(US, 1962, Drew Associates). Drew Associates*

As these examples suggest, those at Drew Associates also discovered that their films were more interesting if the situation chosen had its own drama (with beginning, middle and end), which would come to a climax within a limited time. Stephen Mamber, analyzing the films of Drew Associates in his book *Cinéma Vérité in America*, identified this as the 'crisis structure', a term that has stuck. When such a situation did not exist the films sometimes lacked point and force, Mamber felt. He gives as examples the Maysles' film made outside Drew Associates, *Showman* (1962), about movie mogul Joseph Levine, and Drew's *Nehru* (1962), about the then Prime Minister of India. Though these are interesting and significant figures, the days shown are cluttered and formless – nothing very dramatic happens, there is little understanding of either man, or of why he behaves as he does.

In 1963, Pennebaker and Leacock left Drew to form their own production firm. The partnership did not last long. Al Maysles also soon left Drew and began a new company, Maysles Films, with his brother David. After seeing a short film Pennebaker had done on jazz vocalist Dave Lambert, Bob Dylan's manager, Albert Grossman approached Pennebaker about filming Dylan while he was touring in England. The resulting film, *Don't Look Back*, became a touchstone in both film and music history. The opening sequence alone (set to Dylan's 'Subterranean Homesick Blues' with Dylan standing in an alley, dropping cardboard flashcards) became a iconic precursor to music videos. Pennebaker went on to make many more cv/direct films, many of which dealt with music and performance. Leacock continued with his own idiosyncratic career. The Maysles brothers also continued to produce many documentaries, some of which, like the series they made with the artist Christo and his wife Jeanne-Claude, are classics.

Direct cinema vs. cinéma vérité

Nowadays the term cinéma vérité is frequently used generically for non-directed filmmaking, but originally it was applied exclusively to the Rouch/French approach, to distinguish it from the Drew, Leacock, Maysles, Pennebaker, Wiseman (and others) American direct cinema. The differences between the two approaches are clear and significant, and worth discussing, but over the decades these differences have become so muddled that they seem almost irrelevant. Some films do follow one style faithfully, but a mixture of the two, often with other approaches added, is common today. Still, whether the distinction remains, is collapsed, or simply goes by another name, understanding the differences in the two points of view is vital to understanding documentary history, practical ethics, theory, and production approaches.

Cinéma vérité as applied by Jean Rouch to *Chronicle of a Summer* refers back to the Russian language equivalent, 'Kino Pravda', used by Soviet filmmaker Dziga Vertov forty years earlier. Rouch subsequently said that what he was attempting was to combine Vertov's theory and Flaherty's method. It is important to remember that Rouch was first and foremost an ethnographer. Anthropology, before and after he started making films, was his first interest.

Rouch denied that a filmmaker can achieve objectivity or that the camera can be unobtrusive. Since it is finally the filmmaker rather than the subject who is making the film, Rouch felt that filmmakers must have a strong attitude toward the subjects, must plan what to draw from them. In Rouch's films, and those of others following this approach, the subjects are not necessarily occupied with something more important to them than the camera and microphone. Virtually everything we see and hear in *Chronicle* is occasioned by the making of the film. In many instances the filmmaker is also the film. Examples include Chris Marker's *Le Joli Mai* (*The Lovely May*, 1963), Michel Brault's and Pierre Perrault's *Pour la Suite du Monde* (*Moontrap*, 1963), or the Maysles' *Grey Gardens* (1975), and most of Nick Broomfield's work. In these the camera acts as a stimulus. This approach is the root of even the serio-comic presences of Michael Moore and Morgan Spurlock. It causes people in the film and in the audience to think about themselves as they may not be used to doing, and to express their feelings in ways they ordinarily would not.

In 1963 in Lyons, France, a memorable meeting devoted to cinéma vérité and direct cinema was sponsored by Radio Télévision Française (the French national broadcasting system). Many of those present had contributed to the technology that made cv/direct possible, including André Coutant (Éclair camera) and Stefan Kudelski (Nagra tape recorder). While Coutant was displaying his camera he withdrew a fountain pen from his pocket and said: 'The camera is still not as simple to use as this, but we're working on it', ergo 'Camera Style'. Other attendees included Jean Rouch, Mario Ruspoli and

Edgar Morin from France; Robert Drew, Richard Leacock, Albert and David Maysles from the United States; Michel Brault from Canada.

The greatest excitement was said to be generated by a lively on-going debate between Rouch and Leacock, men noted for enjoying a good argument. Both of them were hoping to find 'the reality of life', 'the truth in people' hidden under the superficial conventions of daily living. Rouch sought to pierce the observable surface to reach this underlying truth by means of discussion, interview, and a performance sort of improvisation verité. Drew, Leacock, Pennebaker and the Maysles brothers sought reality by photographing people without intruding. Their subjects would reveal what they really felt and were like when unselfconsciously relaxed or deeply involved in some activity. Direct cinema sought to expose reality through capturing unguarded moments of self-revelation in the normal flow of life. Cinéma vérité wanted to explain the *raison d'être* of life, whereas direct cinema wanted to let life reveal itself.

Effects on Documentary Subjects and Styles

It seems quite appropriate that Ricky Leacock would be one of the pioneers of cv/direct. Working on Flaherty's *Louisiana Story* (1948), on which he and Flaherty both were cinematographers, made a profound impression on him early in his career and served as a foreshadowing of what was to come. Some of the most visually stunning moments of that film are at the beginning when the camera moves through the swamp, introducing the audience to the moving water, sky, trees in a perfectly composed and poetic study in black and white. Viewed in a correctly balanced film print, on a big screen, it takes away one's breath.

Flaherty's efforts to capture synchronous dialogue occurs when the father tells a story about a man who had his jaw bitten off by an alligator. The machine used to record sound was large and clumsy. Its use on location is one of the first such experiments in documentary, another instance of Flaherty's pioneering technical quests. The result is far from perfect, but demonstrates again Flaherty's interest in new technologies. The main synch-sound scene required time and complete concentration. According to the recollections of some of those involved, this occurred as camera and recorder were turned on merely for testing, but Flaherty let them run to preserve the telling of the story. Flaherty was so taken with the results that he included it in the film, though its non-directed verisimilitude is quite different in style from the other sound material. This was lucky happenstance – truly the thing itself, for its own sake, which is what Frances Flaherty later said her husband was after. She called it 'non-preconception'. From working with Flaherty, Leacock became even more committed to trying to arrive at portable synchronous sound equipment that would permit the recording of actuality in this way – without script, without direction, with scarcely any editing.

Cv/direct permitted relatively long continuous takes. A camera loaded with four hundred feet of 16mm film can be kept running for ten minutes. This may seem a short time compared with today's endless electronic takes. Short, though, is more difficult, and often better, than long. The act of cutting the thousands of feet of film that initially pass through the cameras into the final versions means that a highly selective point of view is operating. Overload of hours of video meandering can make this process even more difficult. However, synch sound in film prevents the breaking up and manipulation of shots as freely as is possible with footage shot silently. It is difficult to cut into a continuous soundtrack without the cut being noticeable; sound locks images into place.

The value of the long-take can be seen in the NFB film about Paul Anka, *Lonely Boy*. There is a scene in which Anka is singing before a huge audience at Freedomland amusement park in New Jersey. The camera panning a crowd of teenage girls screaming in adulation catches one face that seems to be dissolving in emotion. Just after the camera passes her it stops, pans back, zooms in, and refocuses on a closeup. One can almost hear the cameraman saying to himself as this image registers on his consciousness, 'Wow, look at that!', all the while maintaining synch sound. The implications of this technique became ever more evident as technology pushed on through video and digital documentary-making. Within synch-sound scenes the filmmaker is bound closely to the real time and real space of the events.

An even greater innovation in cv/direct was the way in which action is determined and who determines it. In *Nanook of the North*, Flaherty observed

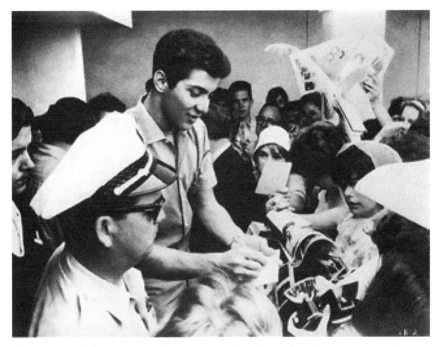

Fig 57 *Paul Anka, the teen idol in* Lonely Boy *(Canada, 1962, Roman Kroiter and Wolf Koenig). National Film Board of Canada*

what Nanook did. Subsequently – days, weeks, months later – he had him redo it for the camera. Flaherty might ask Nanook to do it a slightly different way, to do it again for another take, or for a shot from a different camera distance and angle. These shots would then be cut together to create an illusion of continuous action. In short, though Flaherty did not use written scripts, he 'scripted' in his mind and through still photographs and 'directed' Nanook according to that 'script'. Oppositely, in *The Chair*, the characters are essentially doing the 'directing', as their actions could not have been scripted or even anticipated. In the early direct cinema no one was asked to do something again or repeat an action.

Cv/direct has brought losses as well as gains to documentary. If it is not necessarily the cinema of truth, it originally did seem to keep filmmakers from lying too much – the 'Fly on the Wall' theory. But lying in this context may merely mean being as selective or as subjective as filmmakers may need to be. Cv/direct is less efficient or effective for some subjects and purposes than

Fig 58 *'Little Edie' in* Grey Gardens, *1975. Directed by Ellen Hovde, Albert Maysles, David Maysles and Muffie Meyer*

other techniques. It is not as good for history or poetry, which often require forms that are carefully controlled and fully shaped.

On the other hand, cv/direct pulls towards individuals, towards continuous recording of their words and actions, towards narrative – towards telling the sort of stories that are true, the kind of stories Flaherty told. Cv/direct is closer to narrative fiction films than to the descriptive, expository, argumentative, experimental, or poetic and experimental forms of documentary.

The technological bias of zoom lens and directional microphone that pulls cv/direct close to the individual also makes it an attractive technique for television and digital formats. It is no accident that cv/direct arrived after television and that its first substantial US successes, Robert Drew's in the *Closeup!* series, were designed for what was then called 'the tube'. This move toward apparent intimacy in documentary changed what audiences wanted to see. There has been a steady pressure to use the conventions of cv/direct to emotionally involve audiences, and what was once seen as a way to access unvarnished truth is now a style used to sell ideas and things, from ideology to soap. Techniques of cv/direct have been bastardized to the extent that they are accepted as a norm, even a faked convention in today's reality television and newscasts. It is interesting that at about the same time cv/direct was developing, in directly opposite techniques, and in response to the competition of television, wide screens and stereophonic sound offered Hollywood's equivalent of life more fully displayed, of less editing, more mise en scène and resultant spectacle and ambiguity.

Frederick Wiseman

Frederick Wiseman has made at least thirty-eight independent documentary features, most set in institutions within the United States. In the process he has become something of an institution himself. The new technologies that provided ways to enter situations without the distracting intrusion of lighting rigs, large sound recorders and bigger crews have served Wiseman's goals well. He often uses long telephoto lenses, creating a visual flattening of distance between the viewer and the subject. Long static takes are common, left uncut not only for their striking mise en scène, but to show people as part of groups. Both these visual choices occasionally place even the subjects in the position of watchers. The workings of the hospital, school or court being documented unfold without introduction or explanation, creating a feeling of slow discovery.

Wiseman's films are cited by some as the clearest examples of classic direct cinema, documentaries in which the filmmakers are never seen or heard, in which the camera is forgotten by subjects, which use no narration, musical score, or explanation outside the frame and ambient sound; films that thus offer the most 'truthful' of cinematic experiences. His films do give this impression despite the fact that he has worked almost exclusively with 16mm equipment, certainly a format no longer thought of as being invisible. He and his cameraman dedicatedly avoid interference with the action or its outcomes, choosing only to observe. He has said that his films' stories are never preconceived, presenting themselves only during editing, a process of viewing hours of footage, and emerging with a reputed shooting ratio of 30 to 1. The words, sounds and action onscreen do come across as real, totally unrehearsed, especially as a viewer spends the hours in front of the screen that is required by much of Wiseman's later work. *High School* (1968) is seventy-five minutes, *Near Death* (1989) is around six hours. Some critics maintain that Wiseman studies only the unfortunate, non-functional aspects of America and its social institutions. The infamous revelations of the treatment of the mentally ill in *Titicut Follies* (1967), the bleak struggle against life's end in *Near Death*, even the phoney glitz of *Model* (1981) or *The Store* (1967) may seem to undercut the values of fairness, caring, opportunity, equality and democracy that are meant to characterize the US. An audience – especially an international audience – may react to Wiseman's films as scathing critiques of American values. Different from other direct cinema films, Wiseman's institutional settings carry equal weight with 'closeup' of 'crisis structure' or the view of one or two people. His subjects are not so much revealed as individuals, as they are observed within an organization.

In each film, despite – or perhaps because of – the distance with which the subjects are observed, a respectful acknowledgement of the spirit of humanity emerges. Groups of people must work together within the institutions; individuals try very hard to help other individuals, and faith that circumstances can be made better prevails even when the systems and their arbitrary regulations make reaching such goals seem impossible. Wiseman's Americans carry on, believing that, faulty and heartless as they may be, institutions can be used to create caring and hope and to evince a democratic spirit. Perhaps even the institutions themselves, through a group of individuals, can be bettered, although Wiseman never offers such a 'feel-good' ending. It is up to the audience to take in the whole of a film's architecture, not to be caught up in the distractions of its parts. Enduring the dehumanization to which they are subjected, the occupants of the grim Bridgewater State Hospital for the criminally insane in *Titicut Follies* are not ashamed of their lives. Despite their bleak situation, they claim the variety show as their own, each participating within their own capability, despite what their warders or the viewer may think.

Another example of Wiseman's work, dissimilar in other ways from the bulk of his films, is *Model*, about the business of fashion modelling headquartered in New York City. Throughout, it alternates between fashion modelling (concentrating on a single agency) and life on the streets of Manhattan. The model business is based on glitz and illusion; real life is nitty-gritty and diverse. One intriguing sequence shows passers-by watching a commercial being shot on a residential street. Elderly women, construction workers, derelicts, young businessmen and dogs regard somewhat indifferently the sexy model, the high-tech equipment, and the Hollywood mannerisms of the crew. Another extended sequence concerns the production of a hosiery commercial which involves interminable takes (up to fifty-five on one shot). The sequence concludes with the thirty-second result of all this professional skill, perfectionism and gruelling work.

The myriad of detail offered by the film (it runs 125 minutes) can be read in at least two ways, probably many more. One is that *Model* is essentially a not-uncritical celebration of a bizarre, fascinating, glamorous and crazy institution in the Big Apple of American society. The other is as an exposé of exploitative, manipulative, frivolous and greedy people working at a profession that is the epitome of consumerism gone berserk. But the final sequence seems to confirm the first view. It is of the fashion-buyers' show, which is like, and is shot and edited like, a musical. Beautiful young women in high-style gowns pirouette down a runway to show tunes ('Strike Up the Band' among them). Unusual camera angles and dynamic cutting complete the choreographic effect. It ends with dancing and applause. The fact that the intent of the film can be argued – exposé or celebration – may suggest that the many snippets we are offered form a mosaic of, or a metaphor for, aspects of our culture, which, of course, is open to as many interpretations as there are cultural observers.

Conclusion

With the arrival of cv/direct the sharp distinctions between documentary and fiction became ever more blurred. Offering a close relationship to life as it is being lived, the classic cv/direct documentaries are preponderantly, almost automatically, narrative in form. They show something happening, followed by something else that happens, followed by yet another thing, and so on. *Eddie* (1961, Drew, Leacock, Albert Maysles, D. A. Pennebaker) is about a race car driver before, during and after a race (which he did not win). So is fiction feature *Red Line 7000* (1966, Howard Hawks), but they are very different kinds of film. *David* (1961, Drew, Gregory Shuker, D. A. Pennebaker, William Ray) is about a jazz musician who has sequestered himself in Synanon, a sanatorium on the beach in Venice, California, in an effort to rid himself of his addiction to drugs. *The Man With the Golden Arm* (1956, Otto Preminger) starring Frank Sinatra deals with the same subject of drug addiction.

Cv/direct did change documentary. Cv/direct did not revolutionize documentary. Even as its technology, ethical questions, subject matter and style were developing, audiences, critics and filmmakers alike were, quite rightfully, questioning the purposes and values of its approach. Such challenges to documentary are timeless. Robert Drew was criticized for showing candid footage of the Kennedys. They were not respectful enough. Robert Flaherty was, and seemingly always will be, criticized for exploitation of the Inuit. It is interesting to speculate what course the field of visual anthropology might have taken without him. John Huston was criticized for showing too much death in *Battle of San Pietro* and too much trauma in *Let There Be Light*. Arguments about filming even military coffins divide people. Michael Moore is criticized for harassment of his subjects in every film he directs, and Nick Broomfield for exploiting subjects for self-aggrandizement. Individuals today go to court to adjudicate violations of privacy carried out with mobile phone cameras. All of this is very important: documentary debate must remain alive. The development of its modes of financing and distribution, subject matter, form, artistic breadth and ability to move people to action are the very core of debates about what is a documentary, and more importantly, what does documentary do for individuals, for societies, for the world.

Chapter Related Films

1958
Les Raquetteurs (*The Snowshoers*, Canada, Michel Brault and Gilles Groulx)
1960
On the Pole (US, Robert Drew, Richard Leacock, D. A. Pennebaker, William Ray, Abbot
  Mills, Albert Maysles)

Plate 1 *An example of a poster from an early "travelogue."* Panama and the Canal from An Aeroplane ... in Six Parts. *"The Feature Film of the Century" Note the sales pitch and the size of the camera. The "daring flight," was made just before President Wilson's closing of the canal to such ventures, resulting in "a notable achievement in motion photography," Pilot, Bob Fowler and photographer, Ray Durem. Ray Durem, The Academy of Motion Picture Arts and Sciences. 1914.*

Plate 2 49 Up, *Michael Apted, The Academy of Motion Picture Arts and Sciences, 2005.*

Plate 3a *The Loud family in* An American Family *PBS, Graig Gilbert, Alan Raymond, Susan Raymond, 1971.*

Plate 3b *Morgan Spurlock in* Supersize Me, *Morgan Spurlock, 2004.*

Plate 4a *Gordon Quinn shooting with George Mitchell in the early 1960s. Kartemquin Films.*

Plate 4b No Crossover: the Trial of Allen Iverson *director Steve James and cinematographer Keith Walker shooting a basketball practice in Hampton, VA. Photo by Adam Singer, Kartemquin Films, 2009.*

Plate 5a *Kim Rivers Roberts and Scott Roberts outside their flood-damaged home in New Orleans in* Trouble the Water *by Tia Lessin and Carl Deal. Zeitgeist Films, 2008.*

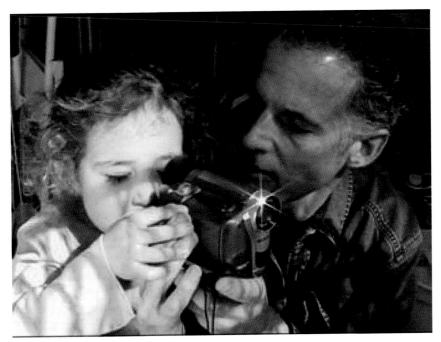

Plate 5b *Ella and Jay Rosenblatt experiment with hr camera in* Beginning Filmmaking, *Jay Rosenblatt, 2008.*

Plate 6a *Stuart Wilfe in* How to Fold a Flag, *Michael Tucker and Petra Epperlein, 2009.*

Plate 6b *Tim Hetherington and Sebastian Junger makers of* Restrepo, *a film account of the deployment of a platoon of United States soldiers in Afghanistan. Titled after Juan Sebastian Restrepo, a Colombian-born US medic killed in action. Hetherington (1970–2011) was subsequently killed while filming battle in Libya. National Geographic Films, 2010.*

Plate 7a If a Tree Falls, *an exploration of modern eco-terrorism in the United States¸ Marshall Tucker, Sam Cullman, 2011.*

Plate 7b *Posters on a Wall promoting* Exit Through the Gift Shop, *an artistically controversial film by Banksy. 2010.*

Plate 8 The White Diamond, *Werner Herzog, 2004.*

Primary (US, Drew, Leacock, Pennebaker, Terence Macartney-Filgate, Maysles)
1961
Football/Mooney vs. Fowle (US, James Lipscomb, Drew, Pennebaker, Bill Ray)
1962
The Chair (US, Drew, Greg Shuker, Leacock, Pennebaker)
Lonely Boy (Canada, Roman Kroitor and Wolf Koenig)
1963
Happy Mother's Day (US, Leacock and Joyce Chopra)
Pour la suite du monde/Moontrap (Canada, Brault and Pierre Perrault)
A Stravinsky Portrait (US, Leacock, Pennebaker)
1966
Don't Look Back (US, Pennebaker)
Meet Marlon Brando (US, Albert and David Maysles)
A Time for Burning (US, Barbara Connell, Bill Jersey)
1967
The Anderson Platoon (France, Pierre Schoendorffer)
Warrendale (Canada, Allan King)
1968
Birth and Death (US, Arthur Barron and Gene Marner)
The Endless Summer (US, Bruce Brown)
Monterey Pop (US, D. A. Pennebaker)
1969
Salesman (US, Albert and David Maysles, Charlotte Zwerin)
1970
A Married Couple (Canada, Allan King)

Chapter Related Books

Issari, M. Ali and Doris A. Paul, *What Is Cinéma Vérité?* Metuchen, NJ: Scarecrow, 1979.
Leacock, Richard with Valerie Lalonde, *Memoir: The Feeling of Being There.* Semeïon Editions, France 2011.
Levin, G. Roy, *Documentary Explorations.* Garden City, NY: Doubleday, 1971.
Mamber, Stephen, *Cinéma Vérité in America: Studies in Uncontrolled Documentary.* Cambridge, MA: The MIT Press, 1974.
Marcorelles, Louis, *Living Cinema.* London: George Allen and Unwin, 1973.
McElhaney, Joe *Albert Maysle.* Urban, IL: University of Illinois Press, 2009.
Seigel, Joshua and Marie-Christine de Navacelle, (eds), *Frederick Wiseman.* New York: The Museum of Modern Art, 2010.
O'Connell, P. J., *Robert Drew and the Development of Cinéma Vérité in America.* Carbondale: Southern Illinois University Press, 1992.
Rosenthal, Alan, *The New Documentary in Action: A Casebook in Film Making.* Berkeley: University of California Press, 1972.

12

The 1970s: Power to the People

The documentary impulse has always been inseparable from its social, political, artistic and intellectual environment. In the 1920s Flaherty's films reflected the beginnings of anthropology and popular interest in little-known cultures. Vertov and the Soviet filmmakers attempted to meet the needs of a new state, the first Communist society. The European avant-garde was experimenting with artistic means for expressing concepts coming to the fore in physical and psychological sciences, as well as reacting to the horrors of WWI. Documentaries in the 1930s were connected with economic and political upheavals, including the spread of socialism and unions. Totalitarian regimes employed them to gain the allegiance of their people. In Britain and the United States they were used to try to strengthen democratic societies in the face of worldwide economic depression and imperialist aggression. The 1940s were the years of World War II and its aftermath. During the first half of that decade documentaries were produced in unprecedented numbers by the Allied countries in their fight against the Axis powers. In the second half of the decade, the United States, and to some extent Britain and Canada, employed documentary in the Cold War against Communism. In the 1950s, in the US at least, many documentaries, but not all, were marked by conservatism and complacency; and, as it would subsequently appear, hidden uncertainties. New types of subjects and forms compatible with nontheatrical distribution and television were explored. The 1960s saw the beginnings of direct cinema and cinéma vérité, social and political unrest, and with them new debates about defining documentary.

For documentary, the transition from the 1960s into the 1970s was a vibrant era, a time of fruition and fullness. Independent 16mm funding, production, distribution and exhibition were on the upswing. The nontheatrical 16mm market place – schools, libraries, colleges and universities, film societies, even prisons, and later airlines – was substantial. In the US it provided a financial base that allowed considerable creative development for independent makers working outside traditional film and television establishments. In Canada most such production was controlled by the NFB. In the UK most documentary-making was meant for television, and was not as free-flowing.

The early 70s was also a time to pass the nonfiction baton. A new generation of documentary filmmakers, those who had not lived through the experiences of global depression and WWII, began to come into their own. The 16mm market base, the emergence of degreed film programmes, the artistic and social upheavals and protests of the 1960s, along with various personal explorations combined to make documentary filmmaking a leading means of creative expression for more people than ever before.

Some Established Filmmakers

Established and influential documentary-makers in North America remained active as the 1960s turned into the 1970s. Among these were Donald Brittain and Michael Rubbo working in Canada, Emile de Antonio and Frederick Wiseman in the US and Roger Graef in England. Drew Associates also remained formidable, as did other cv/direct pioneers, Maysles Films and D. A. Pennebaker.

Donald Brittain worked as a journalist until he joined the NFB in 1954 as a writer. He scripted most of his own films; frequently he collaborated on their direction. Brittain's 'writing' was really his matching of words and images; the creative process for him existed centrally in editing. In this respect he might make one think of Stuart Legg's work on 'The World in Action' series from the early days of the NFB. Brittain's approach was oblique and understated, yet involved his subjects in a way that makes them stick firmly in viewers' memories.

Ladies and Gentlemen, Mr Leonard Cohen (1966, with Don Owen) is an affectionate, non-adulatory portrait of the then-young Canadian poet/musician, who is allowed to participate fully in the presentation. Lest we take him or Brittain too seriously, Cohen himself offers an injunction for us at the end of the film, written on a steamy glass while he is bathing: 'caveat emptor: let the buyer beware.' Brittain died in 1989, a much-honoured figure who had made over a hundred films in his fifty-year career at the NFBC.

Emile de Antonio came to film after careers as a philosophy professor, longshoreman and art promoter. His documentaries, all feature-length, received some theatrical distribution. Consistently he advanced a sharply left-wing political view, using compilation – 'radical scavenging', he called it – in part to avoid copyright restrictions. 'De', as he was known, avoided cv/direct as well as standard voiceover narration. Like Esther Shub's, his documentary technique consisted in large part of obtaining footage from other sources, sometimes surreptitiously, and excerpting and editing it to make damning critiques of aspects of American politics and culture. He labelled his work 'the theatre of fact'.

De Antonio's first success was *Point of Order* (1963), which enjoyed an extensive theatrical run. It was made from 16mm kinescopes of the televised 1954 US Senate Army-McCarthy hearings. The title comes from an oft-repeated interruption of the proceedings by Senator Joseph McCarthy – 'Point of order, Mr Chairman' – and the film allows the Senator to damn himself and his methods without voiceover commentary. One hundred and eighty-eight hours of telefilm was recut and often chronologically reordered into a ninety-seven-minute film that was a scathing portrait of McCarthy.

In the Year of the Pig (1968) is a compilation about the history of the American War in Vietnam. It employs a mix of news footage, political propaganda, anti-war speeches, and other sorts of evidence and argument including the famous photograph of a young US soldier with 'Make War, Not Love' scrawled on his helmet. It is highly critical of United States involvement in the war.

De Antonio had important relationships with younger radical filmmakers. Perhaps the most potent example of this is *Underground* (1975, with Mary Lampson). In this remarkable document we see, from rear view or through gauze, most of the core group of the then-fugitive Weather Underground – Cathy Wilkerson, Kathy Boudin, Bernadine Dohrn, Jeff Jones and Billy Ayers. These young people had been responsible for five-and-a-half years of bombings at various locations: the Pentagon, the State Department, the US Capitol, and twenty-two other targets. Because of the need to keep their identities hidden, the majority of the film's visuals are shots of cinematographer Haskell Wexler reflected in a mirror. As they sit beneath a home-made quilt emblazoned with the motto 'The Future Will Be What We the People Struggle to Make It', they elucidate their philosophy for the camera, leaving us an indelible record from the most strident of the 'New Left' of the 1960s and 1970s. This film should not be confused with the 2002 film *Weather Underground*, an exploration of the same subject from a different, less personal point of view.

De Antonio died at the end of 1989. His final project was a self-reflexive biographical eulogy, *Mr. Hoover and I,* about the extensive FBI surveillance of De Antonio and his colleagues. Released after his death, it is fraught with the formalism of jump cuts and John Cage music. Like all of his work, it retains the mark of a dedicated 'Old Leftist' radical combined with the artistry of modernist sensibilities.

Michael Rubbo, an Australian painter and photographer with an education in anthropology, joined the NFB in 1965 after studying film at Stanford University. His best-known work is *Sad Song of Yellow Skin* (1970). *Sad Song* was shot in Vietnam in 1969. Rather than military action, then at its peak, Rubbo catches life on the streets of Saigon: the shoeshine kids; three idealistic young American journalists trying to help them; the opium lady, who died in the tomb she lived in while the film was being shot; and a little monk in saffron-coloured robes who takes a symbolic walk each day from 'Saigon' to 'Hanoi' and back. In talking about his work on this and other films, Rubbo said: 'These days I even make a virtue of being unprepared.' He then advanced a position that sounds rather like Frances Flaherty talking about her husband's 'nonpreconception', finding his story by living with his subjects. Rubbo explained:

Fig 59 *Emile de Antonio. Museum of Modern Art Film Stills Archive*

You go out with vague ideas about what you want and then just let things happen, trusting in your good instincts. I know it sounds dangerous, but life will inevitably serve up much better stories than you could ever think up beforehand. The trick is to get involved, to get in.

Frederick Wiseman, a leader of cv/direct who was formerly a lawyer, began filmmaking as producer of *The Cool World* (1964), a fictional feature directed by Shirley Clarke. Shot in Harlem and using many nonprofessional actors, it has semidocumentary characteristics. His first documentary was *Titicut Follies* (1967), co-directed with John Marshall (subsequently an important figure in visual anthropology, whose credit was later removed from the film after editing disputes). It is an examination of the Bridgewater State Hospital for the criminally insane in Massachusetts. The title refers to an annual variety show performed by inmates and employees. The film offers an unflinching look at the dreary day-to-day situation within the institution. Without doing more than showing the treatment the inmates receive and the attitudes and behaviour of all involved, the hopelessness of the sometimes-cruel care meted out becomes evident. The film became the subject of litigation, and the Supreme Court of Massachusetts banned its showing within the state; subsequently the film became a cause célèbre in the documentary world. In artistic approach and filmmaking philosophy it is very much like Allan King's *Warrendale* (1967).

Warrendale, like *Titicut Follies*, was never shown by its funder, CBC. The filmmaker spent twelve weeks in a Toronto treatment facility for disturbed children as they undergo a controversial treatment in which the children are encouraged to release their anger through near-hysteria as they are tightly held by staff members. The wrenching footage and the children's foul language, which King refused to edit out, caused CBC to cancel the broadcast. It went on to win a major prize at Cannes. Jean Renoir, a member of the jury, found *Warrendale* one of the most remarkable documentaries he had ever seen.

After *Titicut Follies* (and the justifiably famous *High School,* 1968) Wiseman continued to build an unbroken career making films that examine institutions. In *Law and Order* (1968), he did not present a picture of police brutality or corruption. Some violence, insensitivity, and perhaps racial prejudice are evident in the film, but only as part of a whole that is equivocal. In fact, the evidence offered in *Law and Order* could have served to counter the prejudices against the police that many held at the time. Wiseman is extraordinary in many ways, not the least being that all of his films are funded by and broadcast on public television, yet he retains full control and holds sole copyright. He continues to work today much as he always has, making one film per year and self-distributing through his own company Zipporah Films.

In England, American-born television documentarian Roger Graef, after beginning directing live theatre, has been producing and directing programmes for various British channels since the 1960s. Like Wiseman he is a proponent of filming without interference, has received most of his funding from broadcast television, and is interested in the everyday workings of institutions. The name of Graef's production company, Films of Record, sums up his own goals for documentary as unadulterated looks at reality. His earliest major series was *The Space Between Words* (1972) for BBC, which explores the processes of communication within various organizations. Graef's films in

Fig 60 Law and Order *(US, 1969, Frederick Wiseman). Photo by Oliver Kool, 1969. Zipporah Films*

the 1970s, mostly for Granada Television, are in the Wiseman vein, examinations of powerful institutions such as British Steel, Occidental Petroleum, the British Communist Party, and the European Commission.

One of his acclaimed series is *Police* (1981), about the Thames Valley Police force, shown on BBC between January and March of 1982. It foreshadowed Graef's continuing interest in the workings of law enforcement and the institutions of criminality. One episode, 'An Allegation of Rape', contains interrogation of a rape victim – shot over her shoulder, never revealing her identity – by three male police officers. Their apparently insensitive treatment of the victim led to public outcry, and ultimately to a change in the laws regarding police procedure in rape cases. In England, *Police* was second only to the American night-time soap opera *Dallas* in audience ratings during the three months it aired. Graef's brand of cv/direct involved an agreement with the subjects to film only what had been previously agreed upon, as well as no use of lights, staging, or interviews, along with straightforward camera angles. He subsequently made over thirty films involving criminal justice. His later work includes *Requiem For Detroit* (2010), for which he was executive producer. Julien Temple directed and narrated.

New Directions in CV/Direct

Criminal justice documentaries are a cv/direct staple. One landmark on that path is *Police Tapes* (1976), made by Alan and Susan Raymond. Like *Law and Order* and *Police*, it focuses on one police station, this time in the South Bronx. Perhaps best known for their intimate involvement (camera, sound, directing) in the groundbreaking US PBS series *An American Family* (1973), the Raymonds have made numerous significant films in the last forty years including the Oscar-winning *I Am a Promise, The Children of Stanton Elementary School* (1993). For *Police Tapes* they rode in patrol cars, Alan shooting video and Susan taking sound. Recording what they saw and heard, they also talked with the police about their work. What resulted is a matter-of-fact view of criminal activity in the city, and of public servants trying to do an impossible job. *Police Tapes* was also the direct inspiration for of the hit ABC television series *Hill Street Blues* (1981–1987). The first episode of *Hill Street Blues* is an almost scene-for-scene reproduction of the Raymonds' film, particularly in its use of naturally overlapping dialogue. *Blues* producer Steven Bochco was quoted as saying: 'We really stole the style of *Hill Street Blues* from something called *The Police Tapes* … It was one of the most arresting things I'd ever seen in my life. We said, "this is the feeling we want. We want to create something that gives the illusion of random event".'

Cv/direct methods continued to evolve in ever more complicated inter-twinings of reality and fiction. The generation of filmmakers who matured in the 1970s became interested in blurring the conventional distinctions between documentary, experimental and fictional films. In some cases this took the form of the 'staged vérité documentary'. Controversy about directing documentary participants to engage in activities outside their normal routines has raged from the work of Robert Flaherty onward. There is also the ongoing ethical question of how far a filmmaker should go in exposing the personal lives of her/his subjects. What was different from these straightforward documentary questions for a certain segment of 1970s filmmakers was their deliberate intention to confuse the audience about the veracity of the work.

An early and influential example is *David Holzman's Diary* (1968). It concerns a young man who begins filming his apartment, his girlfriend, the people in his neighbourhood, and every aspect of his life with his portable synch-sound camera rig. Initially the film appears to be a vérité documentary about himself. David Holzman is inspired by his conviction that the motion picture camera is capable of recording and representing 'truth'. But his obsession with trying to capture everything as it really exists, rather than leading him closer to reality, removes him from it. As the film progresses, the Éclair camera and Nagra tape recorder replace Holzman as protagonist. Further, when the credits appear at the end we discover that we have been subjected to a hoax. L. M. 'Kit' Carson plays Holzman (and also wrote much of the dialogue); James McBride directed; cinematography is by Michael Wadleigh. In short, this is a fictional film about documentary filmmaking – about reality and illusion.

...No Lies (1973, Mitchell Block), shot in vérité style, is a staged film about rape directly inspired by *David Holzman*. Appearing to be a documentary in the Rouch tradition, it plays upon many different audience assumptions until we discover at the end that what we wish had not happened in fact has not happened. Another filmmaker who worked in a similar vein is Michelle Citron. Her best-known film, *Daughter Rite* (1978), experiments with traditional modes in the process of exploring issues of central concern to women. It concentrates on the relationship between two daughters and their mother, and between each other. Citron's films are acted, but the roles and the dialogue are drawn from extensive research and interviews, as is the case with *...No Lies. Daughter Rite* and *...No Lies* look like cv/direct, complete with rack focus, rapid panning back and forth between people in conversation, not having the camera where the action is, natural light, and so forth. While the films are visually and aurally coded to be seen as documentaries, all are done with actors. *...No Lies* has created controversy throughout its long career. Used as a training film to sensitize law enforcement personnel to the issues around rape, audiences do not care if it is staged or 'real'. Feminist audiences have sometimes been outraged at what they see as duplicitous and manipulative.

Fig 61 David Holzman's Diary, *a classic of staged cinéma vérité (US, 1968, Jim McBride). Museum of Modern Art Film Stills Archive*

Fig 62 . . . No Lies, *with Shelby Leverington, plays upon documentary expectations (US, 1973, Mitchell W. Block). Direct Cinema Ltd.*

A documentarian who began in the 1970s and has successfully mined self-reflexive cinema since then is Nick Broomfield, though his route to self-interjection on camera is not accomplished through actors. A London-born graduate of Britain's National Film School, Broomfield started making films in England in 1971. It was when he teamed up with co-director Joan Churchill on a succession of documentaries that his work solidified. Their best- known early work together, *Soldier Girls* (1980), is a feature-length documentary in the cv/direct style that follows three female US Army recruits through the rigours of basic training. It focuses intimately on the women soldiers, a subject never tackled before. Like Wiseman's films it employs no narration, no subtitles, and no interviews. Unlike his *Basic Training* (1971), however, Churchill's and Broomfield's film centres on the personal more than on the institution of the army. It is a fully realized work following an emotional storyline from an observational point of view. Towards the end of the film the subjects acknowledge the presence of the filmmakers in an onscreen hug, a unique gesture in what is otherwise a classic direct cinema approach. This scene of filmmaker/subject interaction created a bit of stir in some circles.

Broomfield continued to create controversy with what some critics characterize as intrusive and unethical approaches to documentary. For example, he has been known to arrive to do an interview and begin shooting as an unprepared subject opens the door, creating a situation of adversity rather than trust between subject and filmmaker. His work, however, is consistently challenging and richly layered, always underpinned by a commitment to story.

Churchill, who is one of documentary's best cinematographers, has had a lifelong passion for observational filmmaking, which she described as 'a subjective camera style that throws the viewer into an intimate, first-hand experience with participants doing what they would have been doing if the camera wasn't there'. Part of a documentary-making family, Churchill is steeped in cv/direct camera tradition. She worked with the Maysles on *Gimme Shelter*, with Pennebaker and Leacock on *Monterey Pop*, and was a co-cinematographer on *An American Family*. She and Broomfield hooked up, both professionally and personally, while she was teaching at the National Film School. Her collaborations as a groundbreaking cameraperson and director have continued with many and various filmmakers for over thirty years.

Fig 63 *Privates Joanna Johnson, Jackie Hall, and Carla Tuten in* Soldier Girls *(US, 1980, Joan Churchill and Nick Broomfield)*

Broomfield's later films began to include more and more interaction between subject and filmmaker, challenging the objectivity of the filmmaker. Critical controversy raised by his insertion of self into the films reached boiling point when he is seen onscreen handing money for an interview to his leading subject in *Heidi Fleiss: Hollywood Madame* (1995). In part his work seeks to confront on deeper and deeper levels the dilemma of how the presence of a film crew can alter subjects' behaviour in cv/direct films. On the other hand, Broomfield became the 'star' of his own later documentaries, with his presence as agent provocateur creating serious tensions with the films' ostensible subjects.

A key shift in documentary-making in the 1970s was the increasing number of women filmmakers. Documentaries made primarily by women – notwithstanding the work of Frances Flaherty, Esther Shub and Yelizaveta Svilova in the 1920s, Leni Riefenstahl in the 1930s, Helen Van Dongen, Ruby Grierson in the 1940s – were few until the 1970s. In that decade women found an unprecedented and distinct voice in North American documentary on personal, political and professional levels. The documentary world changed, and women in the twenty-first century are equal players in the that world, a situation that is deplorably still not the case in fiction filmmaking.

Early films that came to be known as part of feminist documentary include *Nana, Mom, and Me,* made by Amalie Rothschild in 1974. It confronts some of the same issues of relationships between mothers and daughters as Citron's *Daughter Rite.* Rothschild's work is not acted by performers, however, but rather captures unscripted interaction among three real generations of women – Rothschild, her mother, and her mother's mother. Canadians Claudia Weill's and Joyce Chopra's *Joyce at 34* (1972) explores the conflicts Chopra faces as she juggles career, husband, and the prospect of a new baby. Both women later pursued careers in which they directed successful mainstream Hollywood fiction feature films. *Antonia: A Portrait of the Woman* (1974), by filmmaker Jill Godmilow and singer/songwriter Judy Collins, profiles the fascinating career of symphony conductor Antonia Brico, and her fight to be able to use her great talent in what remains today an almost entirely male profession. The film, in which we hear the voice of Godmilow and see Collins interviewing Brico, explores the career and artistic ambitions not only of the subject, but also of the filmmakers.

Political Emphases and Vietnam

Vietnam

The monumental event affecting the United States' society from the mid-sixties to mid-seventies, and the rallying point for much of the social unrest, was the American War in Vietnam. Documentary filmmakers were very much a part of articulating opinion about the war, particularly for those who opposed it. The repercussions of the war, both direct and indirect, became central topics for some of the best nonfiction work of the 1970s, but the subject was explored even earlier.

Letters from Vietnam (1965) is not an anti-war film by intent, but it becomes a questioning of US involvement, even at that early date. Made by

Fig 64 Nana, Mom, and Me *(US, 1974, Amalie R. Rothschild). Amalie R. Rothschild*

Drew Associates, with Gregory Shuker as correspondent and Abbot Mills as cameraman, it was shown on ABC television. The film follows a young helicopter pilot as he flies sixty missions over enemy territory; this was the first instance of synchronous sound film being shot in a helicopter. We learn his story through the device of the audiotape letters he sends to his girl back home, and come to feel his discomfort as he visits a Vietnamese orphanage and meets some of the child victims of the war.

Interviews With My Lai Veterans (1970) won an Academy Award for Best Documentary Short for filmmaker Joseph Strick. It is a deep indictment of a highly publicized and controversial US decimation of a whole Vietnamese village, the 'My Lai Massacre'. With interviews of five veterans of this encounter, shot by Haskell Wexler, the chaos of warfare is revealed not by showing what happened, but by letting the men involved relate emotions they felt during and after this tragedy of war. Peter Davis' *Hearts and Minds* (1974), released the year that the war ended, presents a detailed, compiled history of Vietnam going back to the French conflict following WWII using archival material of various types in the same contrapuntal way that Shub used, ending with a critical appraisal of the grievous hurt done to all sides by these wars.

Fig 65 *A famous shot of napalm victims in* Hearts and Minds, *released theatrically by Warner Brothers (US, 1974, Peter Davis). Museum of Modern Art Film Stills Archive*

The War at Home (1979, Glenn Silber and Barry Brown) is also largely a compilation work about the increasingly violent student protests against the war as manifested in bombings at the University of Wisconsin, Madison.

Newsreel Collectives

Like the Film and Photo League, which began in 1930, Newsreel Collective was started in New York in 1967 with similar aims of tackling social problems. It then spread to other cities: Boston, Chicago, San Francisco and Los Angeles. The groups quickly made many films, mostly short agit-prop pieces running from six to twenty-six minutes. To sympathetic audiences, often on college campuses, these seemed to be telling it like it was; to others they seemed merely crude and strident. For example: *Columbia Revolt* (1968) documented an occupation by students of the administration building at Columbia University with great support for the

Fig 66 *A young man burns his draft card in* The War at Home *(US, 1979, Glenn Silber and Barry Alexander Brown). Academy of Motion Picture Arts and Sciences*

student radicals. Filming from inside the buildings with the protesting students, the filmmakers were part of the takeover. As Roz Payne, now the keeper of the Newsreel archive, said: 'Our cameras were used as weapons as well as recording events ... [we] had a WWII cast iron Bell and Howell camera that could take the shock of breaking plate glass window.' The original goal of this small New York group was to make two films per month and get twelve prints of each film out to sympathetic groups around the US. There was never agreement on what constituted a 'correct' political line and the group splintered into many factions. In 1971 in the founding New York chapter, after a series of Marxist 'self-criticism sessions', Newsreel was renamed Third World Newsreel. It decided to focus its efforts on empowering people of colour, and added media training and audience development to its agenda. Produced during this transition by San Francisco Newsreel was Judy Smith's *The Woman's Film* (1971). Providing a sign of this new direction, it was one of the early feminist documentaries to deal with working-class women and their problems. Third World Newsreel continues to function in New York carrying on the progressive vision of the founders. California Newsreel, founded in 1968, is the other remaining pillar. It continues to make and distribute works on

'African-American life and history, race relations and diversity training, African cinema, media and society, labour studies, campus life, and much more'.

Feminist Resurgence

In the 1970s marginalized groups began to claim a rightful place in documentary. One institutional example of rising feminist power was the establishment in 1974 of Studio D at the NFB as a separate woman-oriented production entity. Under the leadership of Kathleen Shannon, Studio D proclaimed a strong mandate of serving women, the aged, youth, and non-whites, with a clearly articulated agenda of 'integrated feminism'. A link between Challenge for Change and Studio D is evident in the decision of both to put filmmaking into the hands of the previously disenfranchised. Shannon insisted that Studio D resources promote only women's perspectives, since she believed that other filmmaking entities already met the interests of white men. One of the studio's earliest successes was Beverly Schaffer's Academy Award-winning short *I'll Find a Way* (1977). This moving story of a young girl's struggle with the neurological disorder spina bifida was one of a ten-part series, 'The Children of Canada', all directed by Shaffer.

Not a Love Story: A Film About Pornography (1981) by Bonnie Sherr Klein both instigates and documents professional stripper Linda Lee Tracey's conversion to an anti-porn stance. Early in the film, Tracey performs her 'Red Riding Hood' act, which she claims is not to be taken seriously. Accompanied by conversations between Tracey and Klein, the film travels through the world of pornography in all its forms: porn shops, sex booths, live sex shows, hard-core magazines, photographs of women in bondage, etc. Sex industry workers speak about their jobs, social scientists discuss the connection between violent pornography and violence against women. The owner of a chain of pornographic magazines attributes the proliferation of hardcore pornography to the rise of the women's movement, and US and Canadian feminists analyze the phenomenon of pornography. As the camera travels through the red light district that then dominated New York's Times Square, Klein relates voiceover statistics on pornography:

- Pornography is an eight-billion-dollar business, now larger than the music and film industries combined.

- There are four times more pornography outlets than McDonald's restaurants in the US.

Throughout the film Tracey carefully considers the arguments against pornography, measures them against her own experience, and finally emerges as a convert to the anti-pornography crusade. *Not a Love Story* was extremely controversial among many different groups, those who attacked it for its raw content and compassionate depiction of life in the porn business, and also by feminists of the era, some of whom who felt, as B. Ruby Rich wrote, 'Not a *Love Story* is very much a National Film Board of Canada product: concerned, engaged, up to the minute on social questions, but slick, manipulative, avoiding all the hard questions to capture the ready success of answering the easy ones.' It is quite probably the most important film produced by Studio D and it remains a compelling document.

With films such as Lynne Fernie's and Aerlyn Weissman's *Forbidden Love: the Unashamed Stories of Lesbian Love* (1975) and Bonnie Sherr Klein's *Not a Love Story*, Studio D proved that documentaries by and about women could be funny, dramatic, emotionally wrenching as well as educational. Studio D went on to create important work in the 1980s and 1990s until being disbanded in 1996.

Perry Miller Adato is a documentary filmmaker whose work explores art and the creative process. Her biographies provide insight into a particular artist's life and work in a linear, lyrical way. Adato's first film was *Dylan Thomas: the World I Breathe* (1968), which creatively uses still photos in much the same manner as *City of Gold* and the later work of Ken Burns. She is known for applying this technique to works of art and for interviews with those who knew her film subjects that get to the heart of what made a particular person tick. Her films are jammed with visual information and use quick cuts. Each film 'has to arise from the style and the personality of the artist,' said Adato, 'I'm not interested in education, per se, but there needn't be a conflict between something that is entertaining and educational. You can take any subject in the world and make it fascinating, if it's done poetically, artistically and with relevance to people's lives today.'

As a young woman in 1950s New York City, Adato became passionate about documentary film, reportedly inspired by seeing 'Why We Fight' on TV. As she told *Ms. Magazine* in 1976: 'When the United Nations was looking for someone to compile an international catalog of social welfare films, I got the job easily. There wasn't much competition.' She subsequently became a top footage researcher at CBS and travelled through Europe, discovering documentaries at festivals, art houses and archives. Excited by the quantity and quality of what she saw, she determined to set up a centre for European documentaries and films on art in New York. Perhaps encouraged by Robert Flaherty in 1951, she founded the Film Advisory Centre in Manhattan. The centre introduced the films of Jacques Cousteau as well as many distinguished European documentaries on art to America. Adato is perhaps best known for *Gertrude Stein: When This You See, Remember Me* (1970), an evocation of not only the writer and her art collection, but also of the artistic and cultural milieu of Paris between the two World Wars.

Adato's biography of American Impressionist painter Mary Cassatt led to Adato becoming the executive producer of a groundbreaking seven-part PBS television series, 'The Originals – Women in Art', that included her film *Frankenthaler: To a New Climate* (1977). She was the first woman to be honoured with a Directors Guild of America Award for documentary directing for *Georgia O'Keeffe: A Life in Art* (2003), and she went on to win this award a total of four times. For *Georgia O'Keeffe* Adato interviewed the reclusive ninety-year-old O'Keeffe at her home in Santa Fe about her life, her art, her marriage and artistic collaboration with photographer Alfred Stieglitz. Stieglitz, in 2001, was himself the subject of *Alfred Stieglitz: The Eloquent Eye*.

Not a social issue filmmaker in the sense of many women documentarians in the 1970s and 80s, Perry Miller Adato is remarkable for establishing a career filled with artistic merit and wide distribution of her work, almost miraculously achieved by making films in her own style on subjects she loved. She was also responsible for reclaiming important parts of women's history with multifaceted portraits of women artists who, until her films, had been culturally marginalized.

Another influential institution reflecting the growing force of women documentarians was the start of the New York-based feminist film distribution company Women Make Movies in 1972, formed 'to address the under-representation and misrepresentation of women in the media industry'. While in Canada government subsidy enabled the NFB to allocate resources to female and other underserved documentary producers, in the US it was chiefly the marketplace of 16mm nontheatrical film that fuelled a burgeoning women's documentary movement. Both the Canadian and American entities embodied 'liberation' values of the 1960s and 1970s; and Women Make Movies continues to be important in the field, led for over twenty years by Debra Zimmerman.

New Day Films, another institution that continues to operate, is a distribution cooperative which grew from meetings at the Flaherty Film Seminars in the early 1970s. Co-founders included filmmakers Amalie Rothschild, Lianne Brandon, Julia Reichert and Jim Klein. Feminist in origin, later a more general haven for social activism, New Day is a distribution company collectively run entirely by and for filmmakers. In this it was a unique outgrowth of the empowerment movements of the era. Over fifty independents continue to use New Day to market their work.

Challenge for Change

In 1967 the National Film Board of Canada began a project called 'Challenge for Change' using documentary in a quite new way. In 1968 George Stoney, was hired as its head. The concept behind 'Challenge for Change' was the then-radical idea to provide citizens with access to the media to express their concerns and needs, and to create a dialogue with agencies of government involved in social programmes. This, of course, was close to the Griersonian idea of using documentary for social improvement. Grierson, after all, had been the first Film Commissioner of Canada. But, unlike Grierson, and any other prior programme, 'Challenge for Change' proposed that rather than communicating *to* the people, or even *for* the people, it would attempt to make films *with* the people. Eventually this led to enabling the *people* to make their own films. Grierson characterized this programme as 'decentralizing the power of propaganda'.

Out of the second 'Challenge for Change' project came a film entitled *You Are on Indian Land* (1969), an experiment putting equipment into the hands of the Indian non-filmmakers. The subject was the closing of a bridge across the St Lawrence River at Cornwall Island, Ontario. A treaty in 1794 had given the Mohawk Indians the right to duty-free passage across the river for any goods purchased, and they regularly used the bridge until the government decided to close it. The Indian filmmakers of 'Challenge for Change' took part in a protest demonstration against the closing. Screenings were held for the Mohawks, the Royal Canadian Mounted Police, the Cornwall police, the city administration, and representatives from Indian Affairs. This was the first time these groups had sat down together. Eventually the decision to close the bridge was rescinded. In subsequent 'Challenge for Change' work, following the introduction of portable 1/2' videotape recorders around 1970, documentary subjects were taught to use the equipment and made their own tapes.

Public Access Television

In 1970 George Stoney returned to the US to head the undergraduate film programme at New York University. One of his first actions there, with colleague Red Burns, was to set up an Alternative Media Centre to promote and support the use of public access cable television. New York City public access channels began operation in 1971. In 1972 federal legislation reserved public access television channels in all new cable installations in the hundred top markets in the country. It seemed to Stoney and other advocates that public access channels fit within the US tradition of freedom of speech for all the people and nicely accommodated portable video technology. He became the inspirational voice for community access in the US.

If Stoney can be called the 'grandfather' of community access, its 'godmother' is Dee Dee Halleck, long-time advocate of the populist voice in public media. Filmmaker and media activist, she was founder of Paper Tiger Television in 1981 and co-founder of Deep Dish Satellite Network. Among Paper Tiger's best-known programmes was *Herbert Schiller Reads the New York Times*, in which the UC San Diego professor delivers a funny and sometimes frightening interpretation of 'all the news that's fit to print'. Echoes of this approach ring through today's *Daily Show* with Jon Stewart. Halleck was involved in alternative media since her work in the 1960s with children making their own films, to a 1990s analysis of the media activist phenomenon exploding across the internet. Deep Dish continues today providing access to under-reported news and information and maintaining an active presence on Facebook.

Independent documentary video production specifically for community access, often directly inspired by Stoney's teaching, blossomed in the late 1960s and early 1970s. Frequently the work was conceived as an alternative to television shows of the time which, it was felt, had failed to illuminate critical social issues. Many of the alternative media operations were cooperatives bearing colourful names such as Videofreex, Video Free America, Raindance and Videopolis. Nearly all of these groups saw their mission as one of revolutionary scope – to inform and educate the public towards action and social change. In this sense they were the video successors to anti-Vietnam war 16mm filmmaking collectives like Newsreel and California Newsreel, described above, and the heir of the documentary legacies of Frontier Films of the 1930s.

Another activist documentarian, Jon Alpert and his wife, Keiko Tsuno started one of the country's first community media centres – Downtown Community Television Centre in New York City in 1971. Alpert bought a used mail truck for five dollars, installed TV sets and began showing his videotapes on street corners in Chinatown. At first nobody watched, but soon their tapes about local issues began to attract small crowds. From the beginning they had a commitment to sharing knowledge that had a direct relationship to the lives of people in underserved communities.

DCTV was the only place in New York City that offered production training and comparable services free. When funding from the New York Department of Cultural Affairs stopped for two years, the workshops went on. Even with the change in arts funding under the Reagan government in the 1980s, DCTV continued to offer free basic video training. Its goal to empower the community through media use has remained one of DCTV's top priorities. Alpert continues to be one of the most active documentarians working in the twenty-first century, both on grass-roots projects and larger, more commercial films for HBO. DCTV also continues, having been in operation for forty years, and having taught over 50,000 people the ins and outs of video production.

Other Emerging Organizations

One of the corollaries of 16mm and later video independent documentary-making was the emergence of regional media organizations across the US, which often made films on local, as well as national or international issues. In the early 1970s a climate of government support in the US, fostered to a certain extent by the remains of Lyndon Johnson's 'Great Society' programmes, was one of the conditions that made such efforts possible. These were never a formal arrangement like Canada's NFB regional units but rather very American social entrepreneurial efforts. Two examples, in different settings, point to the vitality of this grassroots media movement.

Appalshop, a media centre with strong local roots, was established in 1969 in Whitesburg, Kentucky, with support from the National Endowment for the Arts. An example of its early documentaries is the fourteen-minute black-and-white film by Ben Zickafoose and Dan Moan, *UMWA 1970: A House Divided*. It documents the time when W. A. (Tony) Boyle, president of the United Mine Workers of America, was under indictment for misuse of union funds, and suspected of the murder of Jock Yablonski (outspoken advocate for reform of the union) and his family. By intercutting a speech given by Boyle at a miners' rally in Virginia with scenes at a mine and interviews with miners, the film contrasts Boyle's statements with those of the reform movement then growing among the union rank and file. The film's point of view is clearly with the workers, and ties into another 1970s' populist documentary trend, elaborating on labour issues in America, past and present.

Two Appalshop films that were particularly successful are *Coal Mining Women* (1982) and *Strangers and Kin* (1984), the latter by Herb E. Smith. *Strangers and Kin* examines the stereotyping of 'hillbillies' through films, television shows, literature, and interviews with contemporary Appalachians. Elizabeth Barrett's *Coal Mining Women* is in the tradition of reclaiming women's history, with interviews revealing personal stories of the women who worked in this generally male world. Appalshop remains a viable production entity for regional media makers, with ongoing funding from the NEA. It continues to produce films and has trained hundreds of people from Appalachia to use many types of art and mass media to express and share their own life experiences.

In a second example, in Chicago in 1970 and 1971, Gordon Quinn and Jerry Blumenthal (as Blumenthal put it) 'began to gather into their hyperactive, flood-prone basement studio a small band of like-minded progressive-thinking sorts: filmmakers, organizers, teachers and students'. This became the Kartemquin Collective. Kartemquin's reputation and numerous international awards stem from works such as *Home for Life* (1967), its first film. It is a moving feature-length cv/direct record of two elderly persons entering the Drexel Home for the Aged and adjusting to the changes in their lives. Other noteworthy early productions include *The Chicago Maternity Centre Story* (1976), about the closing of this midwife service. Ironically, Pare Lorentz's *The Fight for Life* shows why midwives need to be created. *Chicago Maternity Centre* points out the mistake that local government is making by closing down midwife services. *The Last Pullman Car* (1983) is the story of the closing of Pullman Standard's South Chicago plant, the last factory in America to manufacture subway and railroad passenger cars. Working from an agenda of social justice and personal empowerment, Kartemquin has continued to successfully make documentaries, up to and beyond their most noted 1994 phenomenon *Hoop Dreams*, produced by Steve James, Frederick Marx and Gordon Quinn.

In 2004 Kartemquin made the ambitious series *The New Americans*, executive-produced by Steve James and Gordon Quinn. This truly cooperative series for PBS's Independent Lens used multiple filmmakers to document twenty-first century immigrants in the US. The stories and especially the music of people from Nigeria, Palestine, Dominican Republic, Mexico and India reveal the ways in which the cultural makeup of the US is rapidly changing through immigration. Kartemquin brought forty-plus years of experience in social issue filmmaking to bear with the same thoughtfulness and thoroughness that characterizes all of their work. The driving force of Kartemquin, Gordon Quinn, continued his documentary mission through 2009, when he stepped aside from his administrative leadership role. Kartemquin remains a force in regional filmmaking, continuing to function today.

By end of the 1970s, a fairly broad base of local grassroots film- and video-making groups existed across the US, such as Film Arts Foundation (FAF) in San Francisco, Pittsburgh Filmmakers, IMAGE in Atlanta, and the Association of Independent Video and Filmmakers (AIVF) in New York. The National Alliance of Media Arts Centres (NAMAC) was founded in 1980 by these and other activists who felt that by joining together they could create a national media organization that could support its institutional members and advocate for the field as a whole. This was a peak in government support for regional filmmaking in the US, but it was short-lived. By the late 1980s, national political support for independent regional media all but disappeared. NAMAC renamed itself The National Alliance of Media Art and Culture, partly in response to funding shifts, and continues to operate with a fluid agenda. AIVF disbanded in 2006, FAF was absorbed by the San Francisco Film Society in 2009. There remains a dedicated if under-funded history of populist activism through regionally based media-making but much has changed with defunding and the dramatic rise of internet filmmaking.

It almost seems that for the documentary world, the 1970s slipped into the 1980s unnoticed. Many interesting and important documentaries were being made as the decades changed, many still shot and shown on 16mm film. The aesthetic and ethical considerations of social issue documentary-making had been well-honed by filmmakers who came of age with cv/direct. This was the first generation to have grown up in a television-saturated world. The social issues that forged identities for these largely college-educated filmmakers from the mid-sixties onward – gay rights, black power, feminism, the American Vietnam War, spiritual enlightenment, rock'n'roll, environmentalism, drug use, and youth culture – were still the backdrop for many lives in North America and the UK. Documentary-makers learned ways to treat these and other themes in sophisticated films that demanded technical expertise. It required funding, cooperative work, planning, audience development, and a mastery of many crafts and skills to produce good documentaries. In North America especially, documentary-makers had achieved this goal, opening the way for previously unheard voices.

The 16mm documentary community, and its public, had established demanding aesthetic standards for image and sound quality, various editing techniques, music, usefulness of films for education and for entertainment value, originality and daring. Working with a medium that required intensive technical knowledge of cameras, lighting, sound recording, linear flatbed editing, optical effects, mixing and laboratory work, meant that documentary filmmaking was by no means a solo or a casual undertaking. Although video pioneers, like cable television community access users, Jon Alpert's DCTV, and Alan and Susan Raymond, were pushing accepted aesthetics with video, documentary was still basically the machine-based medium that Flaherty had used.

All of this changed dramatically in the 1980s. Video and then digital technologies seemed to sneak up on the documentary, hailed by its prophets and decried by classicists. Not as technically precise or aesthetically impressive, it began to open up documentary-making to different groups and individuals. Many things were gained in the shift away from the film medium, but other things that in many ways had become the true art of documentary were lost.

Chapter Related Films

1967
Warrendale (Canada, Allan King)
1968
Colombia Revolt (US, Newsreel Collective)
David Holzman's Diary (US, Jim McBride and L. M. Kit Carson)
1969
High School (US, Frederick Wiseman)
In the Year of the Pig (US, Emile de Antonio)
Law and Order (US, Wiseman)
1970
Gertrude Stein: When This You See, Remember Me (US, Perry Miller Adato)
Sad Song of Yellow Skin (Canada, Michael Rubbo)
1971
Angela: Portrait of a Revolutionary (US, Yolanda du Luart)
Interviews with My Lai Veterans (US, Joseph Strick)
The Murder of Fred Hampton (US, Michael Gray and Howard Alk)

1973
Attica (US, Cinda Firestone)
I. F. Stone's Weekly (US, Jerry Bruck, Jr)
...No Lies (US, Mitchell Block)
1974
Antonia: A Portrait of the Woman (US, Judy Collins and Jill Godmilow)
Hearts and Minds (US, Peter Davis)
Waiting for Fidel (Canada, Rubbo)
1976
The Chicago Maternity Centre Story (US, Kartemquin Films)
Harlan County, USA. (US, Barbara Kopple)
Police Tapes (US, Alan and Susan Raymond)
Underground (Emile de Antonio, Mary Lampson, Haskell Wexler)
Union Maids (US, James Klein, Miles Mogulescu, Julia Reichert)
1977
Men of Bronze (US, Bill Miles)
With Babies and Banners (US, Lorraine Gray, Lyn Goldfarb, Anne Bohlen)
Word Is Out (US, Mariposa Film Group)
1978
Daughter Rite (US, Michelle Citron)
1979
The Wobblies (US, Stewart Bird and Deborah Shaffer)
1981
Police (UK, Roger Greaf)
1982
Not a Love Story (Canada, Bonnie Sherr Klein)
The Life and Times of Rosie the Riveter (US, Connie Field)
Soldier Girls (US, Nick Broomfield and Joan Churchill)

Chapter Related Books

Anderson, Carolyn and Thomas W. Benson, *Documentary Dilemmas: Frederick Wiseman's Titicut Follies.* Carbondale: University of Southern Illinois Press, 1992.

Atkins, Thomas R., ed., *Frederick Wiseman.* New York: Monarch Press, 1976.

Beattie, Eleanor, *A Handbook of Canadian Film.* Toronto: Peter Martin Associates, 1973.

Benson, Thomas W. and Carolyn Anderson, *Reality Fictions: The Films of Frederick Wiseman.* Carbondale: Southern Illinois University Press, 1989.

Boyle, Deidre, *Subject to Change: Guerilla Television Revisited.* New York: Oxford University Press, 1996.

Ellsworth, Liz, *Frederick Wiseman: A Guide to References and Resources.* Boston: G. K. Hall, 1979.

Evans, Gary, *In the National Interest: A Chronicle of the National Film Board of Canada from 1949 to 1989.* Toronto: University of Toronto Press, 1991.

Feldman, Seth and Joyce Nelson, (eds), *Canadian Film Reader*. Toronto: Peter Morris Associates, 1977.

Fuller, Linda K. *The Power of Global Community Media*. London, Palgrave Macmillan, 2011.

Grant, Barry Keith, *Voyages of Discovery: The Cinema of Frederick Wiseman*. Champaign: University of Illinois Press, 1992.

Halleck, Dee Dee, *Hand-Held Visions: The Impossible Possibilities of Community Media*. New York: Fordham University Press, 2002.

Jones, D. B., *Movies and Memoranda: An Interpretive History of the National Film Board of Canada*. Ottawa: Canadian Film Institute, 1981.

Keller, Douglas and Dan Streible, (eds), *Emile de Antonio*, 'Visible Evidence' series, vol. 8. Minneapolis: University of Minnesota Press, 2000.

Kolomeychuk, Terry, ed., *Donald Brittain: Never the Ordinary Way*. Winnepeg, Manitoba: The National Film Board of Canada, 1991.

Nichols, Bill, *'Newsreel': Documentary Filmmaking on the American Left*. New York: Arno Press, 1980.

Rosenthal, Alan, *The Documentary Conscience: A Casebook in Film Making*. Berkeley: University of California Press, 1980.

Rosenthal, Alan, *New Challenges to Documentary*. Berkeley: University of California Press, 1987.

Siegal, Joshua and Marie-Christine de Navacell, eds, *Frederick Wiseman*. New York: The Museum of Modern Art, 2010.

Steven, Peter, *Brink of Reality: New Canadian Documentary Film and Video*. Toronto: Between the Lines, 1993.

Venstone, Gail, *D is for Darling: The Women Behind the Films of Studio D*. Toronto: Sumach Press, 2007.

Wood, Jason, *Nick Broomfield: Documenting Icons*. London: Faber & Faber, 2005.

13

Video Arrives

As the 1970s progressed into the 1980s, a major transition – sometimes threatening to mutate into a battle – took place as technology moved from film to video. Lighter, and easier to learn than 16mm, video did not have to be processed, generally required less light, handled more easily in difficult locations, was felt to be less intrusive in cv/direct situations, and could capture an image in a continuous shot for much longer than a load of film. Perhaps most important for the ever money-strapped documentarian was the fact that tape was much, much cheaper than film stock and laboratory processing. The US military, which, along with the National Football League, had for years been by far the largest consumer of 16mm stock, converted to video. The very serious drawbacks of video – lesser image quality and lack of long-term archival stability – did not seem to outweigh its cost-saving benefits, speed and ease of use.

Even though the first videotape recorder was demonstrated as early as 1956, it was not until the 1968 US presidential campaign that a portable video minicam was used in broadcast television. The 1/2' open reel portapak became available to consumers around the same time, but not until 1973 did a time-base corrector make 1/2' tape pictures acceptable for commercial broadcast. Video technology refinements continued throughout the 1970s and 1980s. In 1986 Sony introduced digital video recorders, dramatically improving ease of use and image quality. By the end of the twentieth century video had almost completely replaced film for most types of documentary-making.

Fig 67 *Sony introduced the world's first The Portable Battery Operated Video Rover in 1967, the first video portapack. It was black and white, reel to reel, record only. Recording time was 20 minutes on a 4-1/2 inch reel of 1/2 inch videotape. A small hand crank was stored in the unit's lid for rewinding the tape. Playback of tapes (after they were hand rewound) was on separate decks*

Development of digital editing systems, chiefly the Avid Media Composer, further revolutionized the field by replacing videotapes, which, like film, had to be moved back and forth, with randomly accessible images on digital hard disks. Fast, relatively simple, and cost-effective, Avid became the standard for digital nonlinear editing. At the end of the twentieth century over eighty per cent of US television commercials and prime-time programmes were edited on this system. These technological advances had numerous effects on documentary production practices as well as aesthetics. Shooting ratios expanded exponentially, since the cost of videotape was a fraction of the cost of film. Editors often faced hundreds of hours of videotape material, rather than the dozens of 16mm hours. This was particularly noticeable in cv/direct-style documentaries. Since it cost virtually nothing to let the camera run, why turn it off? In some cases this led to the capture of wonderful, previously unavailable moments; in others it led to overlong navel-gazing of the most boring sort.

The changes in distribution and exhibition brought by video were also dramatic, as technology, economics and artistry once again converged to rearrange documentary form and content. The nontheatrical educational field, which was built on a 16mm film marketplace, lost its economic under-pinnings to the low-cost availability of videotape. The sale and rental of 16mm films had created an economic base that from the 1950s until early 1980s generated enough money to support a group of distribution companies, which in turn returned royalties to filmmakers that helped them to continue producing documentaries. The profitability of this business was shattered when a film-user (teacher, librarian, film society programmer), who in 1976 had to pay $100 to rent or $800 to buy a 16mm print, could by 1986 purchase a similar videotape for $29.00. Pre-recorded home video was also a blow to art house and cinematheque exhibition, traditional venues for documentaries. So, although the means of production was more affordable and accessible, the economic returns generated by the distribution of video made profits, or even recouping costs, much more difficult.

A major factor in the transition from film to video was a significant change downward in quality of image and sound recording. Especially in early video work, the poor quality of these, compared with film, caused many serious debates about aesthetic values. From the vantage of the twenty-first century, when crystal-clear digital imagery is available virtually everywhere, it is difficult to understand the heated passion that surrounded the film vs. video debates. Advocates of film capture of images and sound were ardent in their beliefs that video degraded the form to an unacceptably low level. Video proponents were just as adamant about the ease of use, cost savings and portability of video formats. One of the big problems with video was its multiplicity of formats. New video, and later digital, technologies came (and continue to arrive) on the market in such rapid succession that makers, distributors and audiences all were often spinning in confusion.

The aesthetic effects of video, television and projected film images are all different, in terms of lighting, depth of field, aspect ratio, and even emotional tone, and discussion of these is important. What is just as important, especially for the documentarian, is a consideration of the archival stability of the medium. Earliest videos have in far too many cases simply disappeared, taped over for other purposes, or just disintegrated. Even when a video exists, the format with which it was recorded and/or shown may no longer exist. Salvaging original 2' television videotapes is a rarefied art form, and VHS is being phased out, heading the way of beta, 1' 1/2' and all the other previous formats. DVDs are being pushed out by downloads but neither is archivally stable. In fact, the only medium that has proven to last over a hundred years is film negative, stored in good conditions. For documentary, this is critical. Compilation films are made only when there is historical material to access, and any filmmaker who is producing a document which they hope will last beyond their lifetime needs to be constantly aware of preservation issues. Without conscious preservation efforts, no documentarian can claim that they are making a contribution to social history. Further discussion of this issue is in Chapter 16.

Cable and Satellite Technology

Another of the big changes to affect documentary-making in this period was the growth of multiple cable, later satellite, television channels that began in the 1970s and exploded in the 1980s. Cable, which originally was intended only to bring a television signal to areas that could not be reached by over-the-air broadcasts, soon presented the possibility of a hugely expanded number of special interest channels. Despite the growth of public-service cable access (described in Chapter 15), the profit-driven nature of US broadcasting assured that most channels, with the exception of public television, were devoted first and foremost to making money. By the end of the eighties there were speciality cable channels for children, every type of sport imaginable, animals, science, home care, history, movies and more. Documentaries and other varieties of nonfiction programming became more widely seen on television than ever before. Ultimately, the economics of this mode of distribution had an enormous impact on production. Like the advent of broadcast television (described in Chapter 12), cable television was both a boon and a bane for documentary. There were countless numbers of hours to fill on these new channels, but very little money to pay for product to fill them.

One of the more hospitable cable outlets for documentaries was, and remains, HBO. In 1972 HBO went on the air, originally transmitted via terrestrial microwave towers. In 1976 it became the first TV network to broadcast signals via satellite when it showed the 'Thrilla from Manila' boxing match between Muhammad Ali and Joe Frazier. Shortly after that, other networks also began satellite transmission. HBO, with its subsidiary Cinemax, has both produced and acquired a wide range of documentaries, including an extensive number of works from both emerging and established independents. Under the long-time leadership of executive Sheila Nevins, HBO has supported work by Al Maysles, Alan and Susan Raymond (*Children of War*), Rob Epstein and Jeffrey Friedman (*Paragraph 17*), and Jon Alpert, as well as Jessica Yu (*The Living Museum*), Rory Kennedy (*American Hollow*), Joe Berlinger and Bruce Sinofsky (*Brother's Keeper, Paradise Lost: The Child Murders at Robin Hood Hills*), Mitchell Block and Sarah Nesson (*Poster Girl*). Due in part to relatively lush production and marketing budgets, HBO helped to create a high television profile for serious documentaries in the 1980s and 1990s. At the same time, it became a cable home for some of the most innovative filmmakers in the US. HBO creates its share of cable 'potboiler' documentaries such as *Real Sex* but, unlike most other cable entities, it offsets these with pieces in which filmmakers retain a great deal of artistic control over their work.

In another vein, Ted Turner launched CNN in 1980, calling it 'America's News Channel'. At that time it reached only about 1.7 million households. By 1985 CNN reached more than 33 million households, nearly forty per cent of all US television homes. In that year Turner combined the US domestic signals of CNN and Headline News to put them on a global satellite system, creating CNN International. In doing so he created a commercial web, outside of old major network control, feeding news images to and from all parts of the world. CNN and TBS (Turner Broadcasting System) have been responsible for numerous documentaries, among the most notable being the continuation of the Cousteau legacy of undersea exploration begun by David Wolper.

The birth and growth of The Discovery Channel provides an interesting example of the shifting relationship between documentaries and television in the 1980s. It is representative of the mass of nonfiction programming that in the twenty-first century occupies most of the time on such networks as A&E, The History Channel, The Learning Channel, The Military Channel, House and Garden, American Movie Classics, and dozens of others. John S. Hendricks, founder, chairman and CEO of Discovery Communications, created the US Discovery Channel in 1982 as a cable network designed to provide documentary programming with a goal of 'enabling people to explore their world and satisfy their natural curiosity'. By definition, Discovery was all documentary all the time. In 2003 Discovery Channel reached over 86 million subscribers in the United States and was the most widely distributed television brand in the world, reaching over 425 million homes in over 155 countries. At least nineteen offices outside the US are part of its extensive infrastructure, enabling Discovery Networks International to create inroads in fast-growing markets from China to India to Mexico.

Although Discovery began as most cable channels did, by acquiring low-cost programming produced by others, it soon turned to in-house production to fill its ever-expanding schedule. One very early Discovery acquisition, for example, was *Justiceville* (1987), a half-hour video by Gary Glaser about homeless activists in Los Angeles. After Discovery's first months of operation, nothing remotely like this subject matter or its rough-hewn treatment (the soundtrack was by rapper Ice T) would make it into the channel's formula. Instead, Discovery's most successful audience-pleaser by far has been the relentless *Shark Week*. It is now a mega-business, having gone through many corporate restructurings, buying and selling of businesses, and the channel is one of many that are part of Discovery Communications Holding Corp.

The methods of production adopted by Discovery became the antithesis of the vision of an independent filmmaker with control over the form and content of his/her work. Rather than presenting a fully formed documentary piece in its entirety, Discovery became most interested in 'branding' itself as a cable 'destination', and 'repurposing' material contributed by filmmakers to create specifically targeted programmes for each of its international markets. In other words, a show about elephants might have one point of view and artistic perspective for audiences in North America, and the same material could be re-edited with a different soundtrack, aesthetic values and point of view for an audience in the Middle East. The documentary culture created by these practices is discussed further in Chapter 17.

Personal Essay Film

Some of the same technological factors that led to the production models at Discovery also contributed to the growth of very individualized films created for opposite reasons. Inexpensive video and the ease of use of digital media led many individuals who would otherwise never pick up a camera to create their own documentaries, as Pat Aufderheide, Director of the Centre of Social Media at American University, so clearly points out:

> First-person films – diaries, memoirs, home movies, therapeutic records, travelogues – have been part of the audio-visual landscape for decades. But it was not until the mid-1980s that the personal essay film became accessible beyond the reaches of film schools and art houses, and began to take a place in the programming diet of television. It was a period of rapid expansion of accessible video technology, and just-as-rapid cutting-back of public resources for

independent and experimental use of the medium. Personal essay documentaries were part of a trend in documentary work overall towards a more intimate approach, even in explicitly public affairs subject matter, with the goal of intervening in a shared understanding of meaning. In this documentary genre, the narrator takes clear ownership of the narration, at the same time that the narrator is a character. They are frankly, inevitably personal.

Ross McElwee is the filmmaker perhaps most acclaimed for (or accused of) initiating a flood of self-reflexivity that became known in the 1980s as personal diary or essay documentary. Like Michelle Citron, Mitchell Block, Jim McBride and Nick Broomfield, McElwee is another of the first film school-educated generation of documentarians. He began in 1975 as a graduate student at the Massachusetts Institute of Technology, when Ricky Leacock was leading the documentary film programme there. Ten years later McElwee made *Sherman's March: A Meditation on the Possibility of Romantic Love in the South During an Era of Nuclear Weapons Proliferation* (1986). In it McElwee retraces Union General William Tecumseh Sherman's destructive Civil War path, interweaving his journey with vignettes of seven Southern women. The film is not at all about General Sherman. Highly influential among other emerging documentarians of the time, and critically applauded, *Sherman's March* was followed by McElwee's continued self-reflection in *Something To Do With the Wall* (1991) and *Six O' Clock News* (1998). His films tend to be like *Bright Leaves* (2003), subtly comic, certainly self-deprecating, and appreciative of life around him. The vagueness and intensely personal subject matter in McElwee's films make them difficult to categorize. They are documentaries and yet they are profoundly subjective. McElwee completely exposes his family and friends to the audience in genuinely closed-lipped society of the South. McElwee the filmmaker/storyteller creates works which are both uniquely his and completely accessible.

Alan Berliner, another 1970s film school graduate, merged experimental art with documentary fact in a very personal manner. *Intimate Stranger* (1991) explores the extraordinary life of Berliner's maternal grandfather, a Palestinian Jew raised in Egypt, whose obsession with all things Japanese created confusion and conflict in his post-World War II Brooklyn home. Berliner has said:

Fig 68 *Ross McElwee in a North Carolina tobacco field with Aaton camera shooting* Bright Leaves *(US, 2004, Ross McElwee). Photo by Adrian McElwee*

The truth is I never actually 'decided' to become a filmmaker; somehow via a more arduous and circuitous route derived of inner necessity, I grew into one. Much of my adult life has been spent grappling with the conflicts and contradictions of family. With both the presences and absences of memory. When I came upon my family home movies … the images I had forgotten about suddenly became triggers for a flood of memories. Using them in my films became a kind of photo-therapy, perhaps, even a way towards healing some of the wounds of my childhood.

Compilation

For a time in the 1970s and 1980s, before many of the rights-holders realized the economic value of their footage, putting together 'clip shows' was relatively inexpensive. Part of the David Wolper empire, discussed in Chapter 12, was built upon popular themes such as *Hollywood and the Stars*, the 1963 clip-filled documentary 31 part mini series on NBC. Other filmmakers used the technique to explore more serious subjects.

America Lost and Found (1980) is a compilation by Tom Johnson and Lance Bird which conveys the impact of the economic and social collapse of the Great Depression in the United States. The filmmakers spent three-and-a-half years on research and production, assembling period film, photographs and sounds. Evocative commentary, written by John Crowley, reinforces the images of how the US reacted to the loss of its dreams of prosperity, and how those dreams were slowly rebuilt. This is a deeply psychological presentation of the effects of the Depression, offering persuasive yet emotional contrasts among the images, the hype, and the realities of the era. *The World of Tomorrow* (1985), also by Johnson and Bird and narrated by Jason Robards, is perhaps the most poignant historical film of the 1980s. Its use of home movies, many in colour, as well as promotional films from the 1939 New York World's Fair, captures a precious and precarious moment when the world stood poised between optimism about the fading of the Depression and foreboding occasioned by a looming World War.

Atomic Café (1982), by Jane Loader, Kevin Rafferty and Pierce Rafferty, is a serio-comic compilation elaborating on the ways that Americans' awestruck celebration of atomic weapons changed to pervasive fear of Soviet nuclear attack. When Rafferty found a catalogue of US government films in a San Francisco bookstore in 1976, he envisioned a film that would utilize such titles to create a satirical documentary on the subject of American propaganda. After six years of work, *Atomic Café* emerged as a successful theatrical feature, partly because the filmmakers abandoned narration and relied on the power of the footage and its often-ludicrous original soundtrack. The film's footage, much of it produced by the government, follows the development of the bomb through the atomic attacks on Japan to its central role in the cold war. Shown along with the infamous 'duck and cover' Civil Defence films are lesser-known clips, many of which are unintentionally filled with twisted black humour.

Other documentaries responding to the threat of nuclear warfare during these years were: *The Day After Trinity* (1980, Jon Else); *Eight Minutes to Midnight* (1981, Mary Benjamin, Suzanne Simpson, Baird Bryant); *If You Love This Planet: Dr. Helen Caldicott on Nuclear War* (1982, NFBC Studio D);

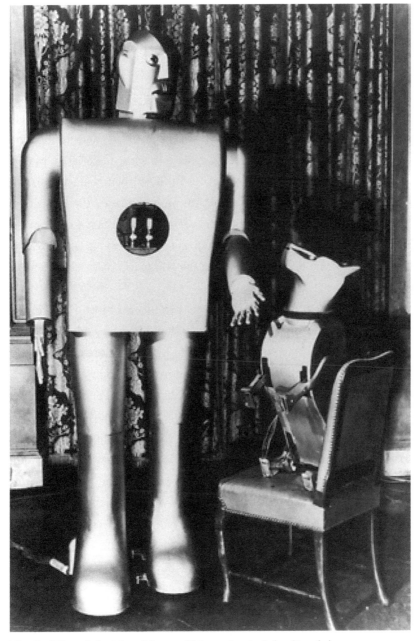

Fig 69 *'Electro' the Moto Man and his mechanical dog 'Sparko' were among the attractions at the 1939 New York World's Fair, documented in* The World of Tomorrow *(US, 1980, Lance Bird and Tom Johnson). Direct Cinema Ltd. 2005*

Half Life: A Parable for the Nuclear Age (1985, Dennis O'Rourke); *Radio Bikini* (1987, Robert Stone); and *Dark Circle* (1991, Judy Irving and Chris Beaver). Each of these films makes a strong anti-nuclear case, although in very different ways. Perhaps the most interesting in political terms is *If You Love This Planet*, produced by Women's Studio D at the National Film Board of Canada and directed by Terre Nash. In many ways it is simply a filmed speech by eloquent anti-nuclear activist Dr Helen Caldicott. But her message and the delivery of the film are very powerful, and United States nuclear policies are harshly criticized. Before winning an Academy Award as Best Documentary short, the twenty-minute film was labelled as 'political propaganda' by the Reagan-era US Department of Justice under the aegis of a 1930s-era law. Copies of the film print shown in the US were required to carry this warning label, creating a situation in which a documentary from the NFBC was discussed as enemy propaganda.

The career of one of the most successful producers of historical/compilation films, Charles Guggenheim, spanned half a century. He made over one hundred documentaries, was nominated for twelve Academy Awards, and won four of them. In 1954 he established his first production company in St Louis, where he produced a seminal film about the construction of the St Louis Arch, *Monument to the Dream* (1967). It won the Venice Film Festival's XI Gold Mercury Award, marking the first time in the festival's history that the award was given to an American. It was while in St Louis that Guggenheim won his first Academy Award, for the film *Nine from Little Rock* (1964), which tells the story of the Arkansas school integration crisis. Later he moved to Washington, DC, to work with George Stevens, Jr, who headed the film programme of the United States Information Agency (USIA) under Edward R. Murrow.

Guggenheim's second Academy Award came from *Robert Kennedy Remembered*, a film biography, which was made in a remarkable six weeks after the senator's assassination, in time for the 1968 Democratic Party Convention. The third Academy Award went to *The Johnstown Flood*, which included many re-enactment scenes of this 1889 disaster (commemorating its hundredth anniversary). His final Oscar was received in 1995 for *A Time for Justice*, a film about the Civil Rights Movement.

Despite acclaim, Guggenheim pursued his work with an almost private single-mindedness, developing an unadorned style that seemed to be a reflection of his own personality. In his later films, such as the Academy Award-nominated *D-Day Remembered* (1994), Guggenheim began to explore history from a singular point of view. The struggle and humanity of a few individuals thrown into harrowing circumstances beyond their control was the kind of story that interested him most. This was a theme that would lead him towards his most personal film of all – and his last.

Berga: Soldiers of Another War, made with his daughter Grace Guggenheim and his last film before his death in 2002, was the first film in fifty years of directing and producing in which Guggenheim included himself in the telling of the story. Many of the American soldiers caught in World War II's Battle of the Bulge were from his 106th Infantry Division. He could have shared their fate if he had not been injured in basic training. In his narration he remembers quietly: 'They went overseas, and I didn't. And some of them didn't come back. And I've been thinking about it for fifty years, wondering why it didn't happen to me. And that's why I had to tell this story.'

Strictly Political

The long tradition of using documentary to instigate political action continued in the 1980s and 1990s. Although his documentaries are not generally political, Charles Guggenheim was one of the first to create television promotion for American political campaigns, using documentary style in groundbreaking ways. Starting with the presidential campaigns of Adlai Stevenson, Robert Kennedy and George McGovern, he went on to shape the campaigns of many of the most prominent senatorial and gubernatorial Democratic candidates in the 1960s and 1970s. Unlike the 'slash and burn' techniques used in many of today's media campaigns, Guggenheim sought to reveal the character of his candidates in an affirmative way, and to let the issues speak for themselves. In a speech before Congress, he explained why, in the early 1980s, he had quit the business of political advertising: 'If you play the piano in a house of ill repute, it doesn't make a difference how well you play the piano.'

The new ease of use and low cost of video production of the 1980s made it easier for activists of many stripes to cover situations in remote places. The Central American insurgencies of that era, and US involvement in them, occasioned a number of impassioned exposés. As often happens in documentary, the desire to impress the audience with the importance and/ or urgency of the subject sometimes overrides the attention given to craft and artistry. Rarely does someone with the vision of Dziga Vertov use documentary to break aesthetic as well as political ground, but the following documentarians have at least well understood the use of film as political hammer.

Pamela Yates' work in war-torn Central America includes the Academy Award-winner *Witness to War: Dr Charlie Clements* (1985, made with David Goodman), as well as *When the Mountains Tremble* (1984) and *Nicaragua: Report From the Front* (1983). Her trilogy *Living Broke in Boom Times* (1990, 1997, 1999, made with Peter Kinoy) describes poverty in America in the 1990s. With Peter Kinoy, she completed *Presumed Guilty* in 2002, a study of the US criminal justice system seen through the eyes of Public Defenders. In 2011 *Granito* was released using the footage from *When the Mountains Tremble* to continue the story of genocide carried out against the Mayan people by the Guatemalan government.

Barbara Trent started the Empowerment Project, which uses agit-prop techniques to inform and motivate audiences to speak out. *The Panama Deception* (1992, with David Kasper) won the Academy Award with its blunt indictment of US policies in that country. Her other pieces include *Coverup: Behind the Iran Contra Affair* (1988) and *Destination Nicaragua* (1986). Trent's work continues into the twenty-first century with anti-globalism documentaries.

Long-time filmmaker and activist Robert Richter has worked in documentary since his days with the Edward R. Murrow team. His career has been dedicated to creating documentary exposés such as *Father Roy: Inside the School of Assassins* (1997), narrated by Susan Sarandon. This film exploring the inner working of the US Army's School of the Americas recounts the actions of Father Roy Bourgeois, a Vietnam War hero and leader in the campaign to close the school. Non-US operatives were trained at this school for work in

Latin America, and Richter documents human rights abuses committed by its graduates. Other productions include the short *School of Assassins* (1994), also narrated by Sarandon, which was nominated for an Academy Award, as was his *Gods of Metal* (1982), a short film about non-violent protests against nuclear proliferation.

Barbara Kopple is best known for her documentaries, two of which are Oscar-winners: *Harlan County, USA* (1976) remains the most famous, although she has made many more documentaries and also some narrative works. An early job was as part of the Winter Soldier Collective, a group of filmmakers who recorded the testimony of returning Vietnam War veterans in 1972. She then spent nearly four years with coal miners in Harlan County, Kentucky, recording the effects of a bitter thirteen-month strike and creating *Harlan County, USA*. This is a sympathetic record of coal miners and their families fighting big business. Also Oscar-winning is *American Dream* (1990), which again deals with a strike from the point of view of the workers, this time at a Hormel meat plant. Kopple's other documentaries include *Wild Man Blues* (1998–9), *Shut Up and Sing* (2006), *Woodstock: Now and Then* (2009).

Kopple's work clearly flows from a traditional political or sometimes simply humanistic perspective. She often uses editing selectivity to shape audience perspective, her positions becoming clear by allowing arguments to be stated by characters in the films and then be answered within the films. In some ways her work is as much about the process of creating public response as about investigating a situation. One of Kopple's latest films is *Gun Fight* (2011), narration-free film that combines interviews and visits to gun fairs and National Rifle Association conventions, along with news and archival footage. It takes no outright position but is clearly cautionary.

Racial and Ethnic Minorities

Exploring African-American history was Henry Hampton (1940-98), who established Blackside, Inc. in 1968, the largest African-American-owned film company of its time. As he chronicled political developments of the twentieth

Fig 70 *Barbara Kopple's* Harlan County, USA, *1976. Cabin Creek Films*

century, Hampton became one of the world's most respected documentarians. As executive producer, with Judith Vecchione as series senior producer, Hampton headed production of the massive PBS series *Eyes on the Prize*. The episodes, made over twelve years, followed the pattern of other historical compilations to make its points, using archival footage, interviews with participants, stills, and a strong period musical score. It remains a touchstone in television documentary history in its telling of the story of race relations in the United States.

Eyes on the Prize I: America's Civil Rights Years 1954–1965 (1987), narrated by Julian Bond, documents events that helped focus the nation's attention on the oppression of African-American citizens, such as the lynching of fourteen-year-old Emmett Till in 1955, and the Montgomery Bus Boycott. It also covers the key court case *Brown v. the Board of Education* and other milestones. *Eyes on the Prize II: America at the Racial Crossroads 1965–1985* uses the same formula of mixing present-day interviews and historical footage to examine those years of social unrest. Despite the critical and popular success of the first part, Hampton had difficulty raising the six million dollars needed to fund the sequel. The subjects of *Eyes II* – the rise of the Black Panther Party, the Nation of Islam, the Vietnam War, busing, and Affirmative Action – were considered too controversial by many potential funders. In a television interview, Hampton once said that he thought the civil rights movement was often overshadowed by the memory of Martin Luther King, Jr, and that *Eyes on the Prize* was an attempt to tell the stories of lesser-known civil rights activists. He wanted the series to be a testament to the power of ordinary people to effect great changes.

Blackside completed sixty major films and media projects, most exploring the worlds of the poor and disenfranchised. Among the dozens of filmmakers who worked with Hampton in making these films were Orlando Bagwell, Lillian Benson, Callie Crossley, Jim DeVinney, Jon Else, Louis Massiah, Sam Pollard, Judy Richardson, Terry Rockefeller, Paul Stekkler and Tracy Strain. Blackside titles include: *Malcolm X: Make It Plain* (1994), *America's War on Poverty* (1995), and *I'll Make Me a World* (1999).

Marlon Riggs' films explore various aspects of African-American life and culture, and earned him wide recognition before his early death in 1994. In addition to the intrinsic value of his work and his teaching, Riggs is remembered for the controversy surrounding the public television broadcasts of his highly charged *Tongues United*, which is discussed at the end of this chapter. *Ethnic Notions: Black People in White Minds* (1987) is a historical compilation examination of mass media stereotypes of African-Americans, much like Appalshop's review of hillbilly stereotypes in *Strangers and Kin*. Riggs' *Colour Adjustment* (1989) continued the themes of *Ethnic Notions* as it traces forty years of race relations through the lens of TV shows like *Amos and Andy*, *The Nat King Cole Show*, *I Spy*, *Julia*, *Good Times*, *Roots* and *The Cosby Show*. Riggs looks at these familiar favourites in a revealing examination of the interplay between America's racial consciousness and network primetime programming.

Other African-American documentarians of note include St Clair Bourne, who chronicled African life internationally by finding common links among people of African descent. Over twenty-five years he made more than forty films, including the feature-length *Half Past Autumn: The Life and Works of Gordon Parks* (2000) for HBO. With actor Wesley Snipes as executive producer, Bourne directed *John Henrik Clarke: A Great and Mighty Walk* (1996), a feature-length documentary about the respected historian and Pan-African activist. He also made *Paul Robeson: Here I Stand!* (1999). For at least forty years filmmaker Bill Miles has created documentaries such as *Men of Bronze* (1997), the story of the 369th Infantry regiment of African-American soldiers that fought under the French flag in World War I, *The Untold West: The Black West* (1994), and *Black Stars in Orbit* (1990), a film about the black astronauts.

In the UK, Black Audio Film Collective (1982-1998) was one of the film and video workshops set up in Britain in the aftermath of inner-city protests against institutionalized racism. Best-known and most controversial of the collective's work, *Handsworth Songs* (1986), directed by John Akomfrah, uses self-reflexivity and fragmentation to examine the history of contemporary black British experience. Shot in the aftermath of riots against discrimination and unemployment in Handsworth, Birmingham, the film uses images of the violence intercut with interviews with local residents. These are interwoven with archival footage of immigration into Britain, and mainstream media coverage of the riots, along with interior audio monologues. It is part of an emerging history of black people in England in its post-colonial eras. Other documentaries by Akomfrah include *Seven Songs for Malcolm X* (1993) and *Martin Luther King – Days of Hope* (1997). *Black and White in Colour* (1992), a two-part documentary produced by the British Film Institute and directed by Isaac Julien, details the role of black and Asian people in British television. It includes material on Akomfrah, who now also works with multi-media installations.

In documentary, one of the most successfully organized US racial minorities has been the various coalitions of Asian-Pacific filmmakers. The year 2010 marked the fortieth anniversary of Los Angeles-based Visual Communications, the thirty-fourth anniversary of Asian Cine Vision (both of these organizations sponsor large film festivals), and the thirtieth anniversary of the National Asian-American Telecommunications Association (NAATA). These organizations support Asian-American filmmakers and seek to address the need to raise social and cultural awareness of Asian-American experience and history. All three groups played a consistently important role in defining an Asian-Pacific documentary presence.

One of the well-known Asian-American documentarians is Arthur Dong, who is also claimed by the gay film community. His professional career began with *Sewing Woman* (1983), about the life of his grandmother, an immigrant seamstress. Dong's productions also include *Forbidden City USA.* (1989), a musical tribute to Asian-American nightclub performers in the 1940s, and *Licensed to Kill* (1997), a brutal look into the minds of murderers who killed gay men. *Coming Out Under Fire* (1994) chronicles the lives of nine gay and lesbian soldiers during World War II, when the US military established its first explicit anti-gay policies. *Hollywood Chinese* (2007) is an entertaining look at how Chinese are represented in American films. Dong is an interesting example of a filmmaker who has retained a great deal of independence by self-distributing all of his own work. This distribution income, coupled with grants funding, gives him an autonomy that is very different from that of producers for cable outlets.

Like many Asian-American documentarians, most of the work of Christine Choy deals with social issues directly pertaining to personal experience. Choy with Rene Tajima made a number of films, including their best-known, the Academy Award-nominated *Who Killed Vincent Chin?* (1988). This is about the murder of a twenty-seven-year-old Chinese-American, whose bachelor party turned into an ugly confrontation in a suburban Detroit bar, and later into Chin's fatal beating outside a fast-food restaurant. The incident, on 19 June 1982, was an almost perfect metaphor for the growing anti-Asian sentiment in America: it was ignorant (the attackers presumed Chin was Japanese); it was economically motivated (the two autoworkers blamed the Japanese – and, mistakenly, Chin – for the loss of US auto industry jobs); and the crime was horribly violent (a baseball bat was used as the murder weapon). The film presents this information in a dispassionate nightly-news manner which serves to make the facts even more shocking.

Other Asian-American documentarians who have left a mark include multi-Academy Award-nominated Freida Lee Mock, *Maya Lin: a Strong Clear Vision* (1995); Rea Tajiri, *History and Memory of Takiko and Takashige*

(1991); Jessica Yu, *Breathing Lessons: The Life and Work of Mark O'Brien* (1996); Dai Sil Kim-Gibson, *Silence Broken: Korean Comfort Women* (1999), about Korean victims of WWII Japanese aggression enslaved as prostitutes for Japanese soldiers; Loni Ding, *The Color of Honor* (1987), on the experiences of Japanese-American soldiers in WWII; and Stephen Okazaki, *Black Tar Heroin: The Dark End of the Street* (1999) and the Academy Award-winning *Days of Waiting* (1990). Spencer Nakasako has worked in the Southeast Asian community in the Tenderloin district of San Francisco for several years, training at-risk refugee teenagers in video production. He produced and co-directed *a.k.a. Don Bonus* (1994), a portrait of a Cambodian family devastated by the pressures of life in their adopted country.

Canadian Abenaki Indian Alanis Obomsawin has had a long career as singer, writer and storyteller, promoting the history and culture of her people. In 1967, after being seen in a television profile, *Alanis* (1965), she was invited by the National Film Board to act as a consultant, and has since divided her time between filmmaking and performing. In 1971 she directed her first film, *Christmas at Moose Factory*, a study of life in a small Northern settlement based on children's drawings. Between 1977 and 1994 she made ten films illustrating different aspects of Aboriginal life. Committed to the cause of justice for her people, she documented two major confrontations: *Incident at Restigouche* (1984) and *Kanehsatake 270 Years of Resistance*, her best-known work

In the United States – unlike Canada, where Indians use the term Aboriginal – the preferred term for American Indians is Native. The Native American Public Broadcasting Consortium was begun in 1974 by a group of six producers, with twenty-six public television stations. Its mission is to support and promote Native American culture through various media productions. Although it has been involved in numerous documentary works, its greatest successes have been with radio, and more recently internet development. In 1977 Frank Blythe opened a national office at the Nebraska Educational Television network headquarters in Lincoln, and was named Executive Director, a position he held for over twenty-five years.

In the Latino filmmaking community, noteworthy documentarians include Lourdes Portillo, whose *The Mothers of Plaza de Mayo* (1985) was the result

Fig 71 *Alanis Obomsawin. International Documentary Association*

of a three-year collaboration with writer/director Susana Muñoz and was nominated for an Academy Award. Her next film, *La Ofrenda: The Day of the Dead* (1989), is a charming look at cultural blending. *La Ofrenda* is set up to challenge the notion that, as Portillo puts it, 'documentary is always associated with injustice'. In it she celebrates the traditions of a colourful Mexican and Chicano holiday, the November 1st celebration of *el día de los muertos*. The film relies on a poetic structure that Portillo has used in other work. *Senorita Extraviada, Missing Young Woman* (2001) tells the haunting story of the more than two hundred kidnapped, raped and murdered young women near the maquilladores of Juárez, Mexico. Like others of the PBS Minority Consortium Groups, there is an organization of Latino Public Broadcasting, although much of its efforts have been focused on fiction works.

Repesenting Gay and Lesbian Culture

As an outgrowth of the social changes and the video technology of the 1970s, various previously disenfranchised groups began to make more documentaries speaking directly to their concerns. Homosexuals were one large group who found in documentary a powerful way to express a distinctive culture. Many of the advances in gay, later labelled queer, cinema were made in the documentary.

Word is Out: Some Stories of Our Lives (1977), an early landmark, was produced collectively by the San Francisco-based Mariposa Film Group: Peter Adair, Nancy Adair, Andrew Brown, Veronica Selver, Lucy Phenix and Rob Epstein. Following videotaped interviews with two hundred gay and lesbian people from across the United States, they focused on a selected group of these individuals. After more than a year of editing, they cut fifty hours of material to a final 135-minute version. *Word Is Out* is divided into three major sections: 'The Early Years', 'Growing Up', and 'From Now On' – although the interviews weave in and out among these with little formal structure. What emerges is a somewhat random, but often moving, collage portrait of the personal stories of gays and lesbians in mid-1970s America.

Fig 72 Las Madres: The Mothers of the Plaza de Mayo *(US, 1985, Lourdes Portillo and Susana Muñoz). Direct Cinema Ltd.*

Colleagues —
I hope this screening interests you. Would you pass it around + post it if you can?
Many thanks
Amanda Pope,
Peter Adair

ADAIR
F I L M S

Dear Friends,

WE WOULD LIKE TO INVITE YOU to attend an investors' screening of our documentary on gay women and men to be held on Saturday, June 4 at 10:30 A.M. at the Vanguard Theater, 9014 Melrose Avenue in Hollywood.

THE FILM is a series of portraits of twenty-two lesbians and gay men, edited from forty hours of color footage shot across the country during the past eighteen months. It is an exploration of the histories and variety of lifestyles of an emerging, but still mostly invisible, minority- ten to twenty million people in this country (according to Kinsey).

OUR PURPOSE is to begin to counter the pervasive negative images of "dykes" and "faggots" by presenting a series of intimate portraits of gay people as people- with all the joys and sorrows common to everyone. The film will help homosexuals, who themselves have accepted the negative mythology, begin to feel better about who they are and who they can be. It will also promote in the country as a whole a beginning air of acceptance of homosexuality as an alternative lifestyle.

OUR AUDIENCE will number in the millions. Following in the tracks of other recent theatrical documentaries (Harlan County, Pumping Iron, Antonia, The Sorrow and the Pity, People of the Wind, etc.), our movie will open first in theaters in large cities this Fall, then will be televised nationally this Winter (it has already been sold for four network broadcasts, which guarantees it a minimum exposure of four million), and then will be available for rental to colleges, graduate schools, feminist and gay groups, professional societies, etc.

FINISHING MONEY is needed in the form of investments. The film has been produced as a profit-making venture. There are no general films available about homosexuals, and there is now a tremendous and growing need for such material. Movies are very expensive to make. Our budget is $200,000- shoestring by industry standards for a film of this scope. We have already raised $92,000 from investors and $50,000 from the television sale. We need $50,000 more to finish. We're in the final stretch.

PLEASE COME to this hour-long screening of excerpts from our film, whether you can consider investing or not. If you are gay or not, judging from past audience reaction, you will be affected by the experience.

FEEL FREE TO BRING INTERESTED FRIENDS.

Yours,

2051 THIRD ST. • SAN FRANCISCO, CA 94107 • (415) 621-6500

Fig 73 *A fundraising letter for the film* Word Is Out. *(US, 1977, Mariposa Film Group). Academy of Motion Picture Arts and Sciences*

Before Stonewall (1984, Robert Rosenberg, John Scagliotti and Greta Schiller, narrated by Rita Mae Brown) chronicles the evolution of gay culture in the US from the early 1920s to the violence in 1969. In that year patrons of the Stonewall Inn in New York's Greenwich Village decided to fight back against ongoing harassment, transforming a police raid into three nights of

Fig 74 *The Mariposa Group of filmmakers who made* Word Is Out, *left to right: Lucy Phenix, Nancy Adair, Peter Adair, Rob Epstein, Andrew Brown, and Veronica Selver*

rioting that signalled the public nature of the new gay liberation movement. Using archival footage and photography from five decades, the film explores the gay underground of the twenties and thirties, the rise of gays in the military and workforce during WWII, and their persecution in the US State Department as 'subversives' and 'sexual perverts' by Senator McCarthy in the 1950s. *After Stonewall* (1999, directed by Scagliotti and narrated by Melissa Etheridge) explores gay and lesbian history from the 1970s through the 1990s. Like its predecessor, it covers a lot of ground in a short time, but since it deals with only three decades it is more concise.

Other important films of the era dealing in different ways with gay life include Academy Award-winning *The Times of Harvey Milk* (1984) by Rob Epstein and Richard Schmeiken. In 1978, Harvey Milk was elected to the San Francisco city council, becoming the first openly gay person elected to public office in California. One year later he and Mayor George Moscone were shot and killed by another council member, former police officer and fireman

Dan White. *The Times of Harvey Milk* recreates the story of Milk's grass-roots political organizing and election, through the murders and their repercussions. From the eloquent candlelight memorial joined by tens of thousands of San Franciscans on the evening of the assassinations, to the angry mobs who stormed City Hall, breaking windows and torching police cars in the aftermath of White's lenient sentencing, the film is a revealing analysis of democracy in America. As photographer Andrew Epstein said:

> Richard and Robert's vision was, of course, the bigger picture, the whole story in political terms. They reclaimed a queer political history that could have easily been forgotten. They recorded and bore witness. It was our assassination, our Kennedy, our King, our Malcolm X, our bullet.

Common Threads: Stories from the Quilt (1989) by Bill Couturié, Rob Epstein and Jeffrey Friedman, made for HBO, is one of the most hauntingly beautiful, and accessible to the public of many films concerning the AIDS crisis. Narrated by Dustin Hoffman, with a score sung by Bobby McFerrin, the film tells the story of the growth of the AIDS epidemic from its mysterious beginnings to the peak of the epidemic in the US.

Of the gay-identified filmmakers, experimental adventurer Barbara Hammer is probably the most prolific. Since the 1970s she has made over eighty films and videos, and is considered a pioneer of lesbian-feminist experimental cinema. Her work can be directly related to the experimental art documentaries of the 1920s. One early piece, *Dyketactics* (1974), was the first film about lesbian lovemaking to be made by a lesbian. Her trilogy of documentary essays on lesbian and gay history – *Nitrate Kisses* (1992), *Tender Fictions* (1995) and *History Lessons* (2000) – has been widely acclaimed. Hammer uses an evocative visual and aural style in which, although imagery may not always be instantly readable in a literal sense, its emotional and often sexual power is clearly recognizable. Her films are also laced with a sophisticated humour and sometimes-graphic eroticism.

Hammer's uncompromising work is far from mainstream, unlike that of African-American filmmaker Marlon Riggs, who pushed the boundaries of conventional network television. Before his death from AIDS in 1994, Riggs became one of the more controversial figures in recent documentary history.

Fig 75 The Times of Harvey Milk *(US, 1984, Rob Epstein and Richard Schmiechen)*

In his second film, *Tongues Untied* (1988), Riggs profiled urban African-American gay men with frank portraits of gay subcultures, complete with explicit language and sexual imagery. The film was partly financed by a $5,000 grant from the National Endowment for the Arts (NEA). When it was about to be broadcast nationally on PBS, descriptions of the film's subject matter touched off a heated debate about government funding of art that some labelled obscene. While artists argued for free speech, government policymakers, especially the politically conservative, engaged in a public discussion about the use of taxpayer money for the funding of such work. Adding to the controversy was the fact that the public television *POV* (Point of View) series which presented the film also receives general production funding from the Endowment. Leaders of conservative organizations, many of whom had not seen it, labelled *Tongues Untied* obscene. When a few public stations decided not to air the programme, this self-censorship added to the debate. Although most PBS stations did broadcast the film, controversy surrounding *Tongues Untied* played a key role in the future NEA decision to stop funding individual artists, including individual filmmakers.

Chapter Related Films

1980
The Day After Trinity (US, Jon Else)
From Mao to Mozart: Isaac Stern in China (US, Murray Lerner)
Garlic Is as Good as Ten Mothers (US, Les Blank)
1981
Not a Love Story (Canada, Bonnie Sherr Klein)
Eight Minutes to Midnight (US, Mary Benjamin, Suzanne Simpson, Baird Bryant)
1982
Atomic Café (US, Jane Loader, Kevin Rafferty, Pierce Rafferty)
The Brooklyn Bridge (US, Ken Burns)
Burden of Dreams (US, Les Blank)
If You Love This Planet (Canada, Terre Nash)
1983
The Profession of Arms (Canada, Gwynne Dyer, Michael Bryans, Tina Viljoen)
1984
The Times of Harvey Milk (US, Rob Epstein and Richard Schmiechen)

1985
Las Madres: The Mothers of the Plaza de Mayo (US, Susana Muñoz and Lourdes Portillo)
28 Up (UK, Michael Apted)
1986
Handsworth Songs (UK, John Akomfrah)
Sherman's March (US, Ross McElwee)
The World of Tomorrow (US, Lance Bird and Tom Johnson)
1987
Eyes on the Prize (US, Henry Hampton)
To a Safer Place (Canada, Beverly Shaffer)
1988
Lighting Over Braddock: A Rustbowl Fantasy (US, Tony Buba)
The Thin Blue Line (US, Errol Morris)
Tongues Untied (US, Marlon Riggs)
Who Killed Vincent Chin? (US, Rene Tajima and Christine Choy)
1989
Common Threads; Stories from the Quilt (US, Bill Couturié, Rob Epstein, Jeffrey Friedman)
Roger & Me (US, Michael Moore)
1992
Black and White in Colour (UK, Isaac Julien)
Brother's Keeper (UK, Joe Berlinger and Bruce Sinofsy)
Nitrate Kisses (US, Barbara Hammer)
1992
Berga: Soldiers of Another War (US, Charles Guggenheim)

Chapter Related Books

Boyle, Deirdre. *Video Classics: A Guide to Video Art and Documentary Tapes*. Oryx Press, 1986.

Crittendon, Roger with Cherry Potter, *Confronting Reality: Some Perspectives on Documentary*. Beaconsfield, Bucks: CILECT Review Clarendon Printers, 1985.

Goldsmith, David A., *The Documentary-makers: Interviews with 15 of the Best in the Business*. Switzerland: RotoVision, 2003.

Homlund, Chris and Cynthia Fuchs, (eds), *Between the Sheets, In the Streets: Queer, Lesbian, and Gay Documentary*. Minneapolis: University of Minnesota Press, 1997.

Rabiger, Michael, *Directing the Documentary*. Oxford: Focal Press, 1992.

Rosenthal, Alan, *The New Challenges for Documentary*. Berkeley: University of California Press, 1988.

Steven, Peter, *Brink of Reality: New Canadian Documentary Film and Video*. Toronto: Between the Lines Press, 1993.

Stubbs, Liz, *Documentary Filmmakers Speak*. New York: Allworth Press, 2000.

Waldman, Diane and Janet Walker, (eds), *Feminism and Documentary*. Minneapolis:
    University of Minnesota Press, 1999.
Zimmerman, Patricia R., *States of Emergency: Documentaries, Wars, Democracies*.
    Minneapolis: University of Minnesota Press, 2000.

14

Reality Bytes

The centennial of cinema, including the 100-year mark for the documentary, was 1995. The date of the first public projection of film, which took place on 28 December 1895 in Paris, is recognized by hundreds of film organizations around the world as the moment when cinema officially began. As described in Chapter 1, that now-famous Lumière Brothers exhibition at the Grand Café consisted of an approximately twenty-five-minute programme of very short – less than one minute each – films. In that first public screening, the dialectic between the 'real' and the 'staged', which is continuously included in discussion of documentary, was already in play. On that occasion, both 'actualities' and fiction-based vignettes were shown together without distinction. It is probably safe to say that no one from the Lumière organization stood up and announced: 'Here we have a selection of real, unscripted events, and other scenes which are acted for the camera.' In fact, those films in the programme long deemed 'actualities', such as *Workers Leaving the Factory*, on close examination appear to have been as rehearsed as the 'enactment' of the comic *The Hoser Hosed* (*L'Arroseur arrosé*). The Lumière workers were surely told to exit the factory gates as the camera was rolling, and not to look at the camera. Different 'takes' of this scene, possibly shot days apart, remain extant over a hundred years later. Still, the workers were nonactors, even if specially dressed for the occasion, and they engaged in an everyday activity as the Lumière camera recorded them. The people in *The Hoser Hosed* were play-acting a comedy.

Over the next hundred years, as suggested in this book, documentary and fiction filmmakers travelled mostly separate routes. However often the subjects and techniques of the two intersected, documentarians identified themselves as such, often by the social intent of their films. As with all rules, there were exceptions. Still, fiction filmmakers have generally created fictions, usually and primarily meant to entertain. The closing years of the twentieth century, the 'Century of Cinema', and the first years of the yet-to-be-named twenty-first century have brought cinema to a place where it is more and more difficult to separate documentary and fiction. Technology, economics and artistic experimentation continue to push and pull the documentary in new directions, and filmmakers themselves more openly challenge the label of 'documentarian'.

Business and Technology: The Bad and The Good

One of the major trends of the 1980s, the proliferation of cable and satellite channels, became even more pervasive in the 1990s. The consequences – ever more hours of television documentary programming, production cost per hour decreasing dramatically, decreased personal control by the individual filmmaker – all continued. What resulted was a marked decline in the overall quality of most televised documentary, even as the number of television hours devoted to nonfiction increased exponentially. This is not to say that there were not notable, even outstanding and groundbreaking works – there were – but the vast majority of television time devoted to nonfiction was taken up by product whose artistic quality was limited and whose veracity was sometimes questionable. This was increasingly true even before the millennial onslaught of reality TV. Hours were filled with recycled stock footage on every imaginable subject, accompanied by voiceover bland commentary, and the dullest kind of talking-head interviews. Point-of-view, investigative and artful filmmaking often went by the wayside as cable channels scurried to fill endless hours.

With advances in technology, anyone with a digital camera and a home computer could put together a documentary, and fortunately many more people did tell their own stories. At the same time, the professionalism of documentary craft and artistry, to say nothing of concern for ethical considerations, has suffered. The cost of professional small-format video is a fraction of that of older technologies. In the twenty-first century one or two people shoot major television documentary projects which once required substantial funding and numerous crew members. When shooting in 16mm, or even Betacam, it was common for makers to travel with several cases of equipment, film and supplies. The same technically sophisticated work can usually now be done in small-format, out of one small suitcase. This crush of quick, and above all cheap, work also considerably lowered the bar as to what television audiences accept as documentary. And this downward trend continues. The speed of this kind of filmmaking is low-cost and the fact that a person with almost no technical experience can perform it has opened the field of documentary-making to the entire world. Cell phone filmmaking, to be discussed in the next chapter, carries this approach further.

The need for low-cost programming affected not only documentaries shot mainly in the field. For some cable channels the exigencies of creating mass hours of programming about historical events led to disturbing developments. The slideshow approach, with narration and talking heads, was one consequence. Cost-conscious and inexperienced researchers sometimes substituted any available footage for actual shots of the events under discussion. For example, a stock image of a sinking ship has more than once been passed off as a specific sinking ship, whether or not the ship in the image had actually ever sailed in the same ocean that the documentary claimed. In all too many cases an astonishing disregard for factual rigour overcame historical compilation films. This problem became so widespread that the Association of Moving Image Archivists' newsletter published a column by archivist Jerome Keuhl listing misused footage. His watchful beast, known as the office cat, kept track of such misadventures and anachronisms, and reported to the community when an earnest film researcher asked for footage of Lincoln's 'Gettysburg Address' or the sinking of the *Titanic*, events never covered by a camera.

On the commercial front, when the merchandising of documentary tie-in 'branding' began in earnest, it became abundantly clear that some executives were far more interested in promoting the channels as profitable corporate commodities than in producing meaningful documentaries. A leader in the field was Discovery Communications, with its Discovery Stores. Using the

Discovery name and logos, along with those of its offshoot channels – Animal Planet, Discovery Health, Travel Channel, Discovery Kids, Wings, etc. – stores began to sell everything from plastic sharks to logo shirts to audio CDs, all loosely connected to documentary programming that played on the channels. Starting in 1997, Discovery.com's online store reached out to armchair adventurers with an e-commerce website to mirror the Discovery Stores found in retail malls. Eventually other channels joined in the trend at some level. *National Geographic* magazine redesigned its logo and opened www. shopnationalgeographic.com, and public television viewers were now invited continuously to shop the PBS Online Store. Ken Burns' *The Civil War* was one of the first PBS documentaries to deploy astute marketing tie-ins to books and recorded music. All of the bricks-and-mortar Discovery Channel Stores were closed in 2007, but the on-line site remains active.

There is nothing inherently evil in selling documentary-linked consumer products, nor in categorizing films by channel so that viewers can find the kinds of titles they like. And the cable and satellite channels were only adapting the long-time marketing techniques of Hollywood movie studios in selling theme-related goods. Practices that Hopalong Cassidy first began and Disney mouse ears continued were perfected by George Lucas and *Star Wars* in the 1970s. What is insidious for the documentary tradition is that the merchandise in these cases often became more important to the presenting channel than anything the documentarian might have to say on a subject. Yes, legend has it that chocolate-covered ice cream bars were first marketed as 'Eskimo Pies' or 'Nanooks' in the wake of the success of *Nanook of the North*. 'Eskimo Pie' was trademarked in 1922, the same year as *Nanook's* release; prior to that the frozen treat was called 'I-Scream-Bar'. However, it seems evident that selling ice cream had no bearing on future Flaherty productions, nor on the desire of audiences to watch his films.

Fiscal and artistic consequences have also resulted from the television industry's contractual practices with individual filmmakers. The majority of cable documentaries became works done for hire, in which the filmmakers retain little control and hold no rights to their films. This is not always the case for those producers who raise money independently and then license their work, but it is true for the majority of hours seen by cable viewers. Whereas independent producers in the 1950s to 1980s nontheatrical market could hope to recoup costs, make a small profit, possibly take some creative risks, and see their work shown in a form resembling the film they intended, these options, at least in the cable marketplace, are almost non-existent in the twenty-first century. Exceptions are HBO/Cinemax Documentaries, and more recently Sundance, IFC, HBO, the Documentary Channel and a few others. HBO is neither product nor advertising, but rather subscriber- and awards-driven. In a long-term economic sense, most independent producers are left with little clout. At one time a television mogul such as David Wolper chose the subjects and the forms, albeit highly commercial, in which he wanted to document them. He amassed capital by retaining the rights to rebroadcast, educational sales, and later home video. For example, to run the *Biography* series and create the Biography Channel, A&E turned to Wolper. The early cv/direct films were also more reflective of the filmmaker even when they went on television. Today's presenting channels demand control of these and any other ancillary rights, leaving most producers with no equity in their work.

On US television there are some alternatives, but not at the major networks. Fighting a defensive battle against the erosion of viewership by cable channels in the 1990s, the networks abandoned documentaries almost entirely. Except for the longstanding success of shows such as *60 Minutes* and its spin-offs, the end of the twentieth century brought the demise of what at mid-century had seemed the salvation of serious documentary-making. No one in network broadcast television was willing to take artistic or content risk, nor to uphold the investigative reporting traditions of Edward R. Murrow of CBS, or NBC's *Project XX* and *White Paper*. Even Jon Alpert and DCTV's twenty-year relationship with NBC ended with the First Gulf War in Iraq. 'We were the only independent documentary reporters in Baghdad during the war. But our footage documenting the death and destruction in civilian neighbour-hoods was a shocking message, so instead of broadcasting it, NBC killed the messenger,' he says. DCTV formed a new relationship with HBO, producing edgy one-hour investigative programmes such as *Lock-Up: The Prisoners of Riker's Island* (1994), *One Year in a Life of Crime* (1989), *Rape: Cries from the Heartland* (1992) and *High on Crack Street: Lost Lives in Lowell* (1995), the last two directed by Maryann De Leo. Community activist-based DCTV teamed up in 2003 with Discovery and its *New York Times*-linked DiscoveryTimes channel to produce programming such as *Off to War,* about the deployment of the Arkansas National Guard to the Second Iraq War. For the most part, socially critical documentaries were not the province of cable or network television.

Independent producers did create notable work. A five-part series, *Yugoslavia: Death of a Nation* (1996), made by the highly respected English documentarian Brian Lapping for the BBC and The Discovery Channel and narrated by CNN's Christiane Amanpour, untangled the political and military events which led to the dismemberment of the country that was Yugoslavia. It integrates video footage of council meetings and other events with interviews of the heads of all six states involved in the resulting war. The series explains how Serbian President Slobodan Milosevic systematically and brutally controlled an entire region. Amanpour continues to make documentary specials, which sometimes retain investigative power. Her presence as a respected journalist commenting on location and on-screen adds gravitas to a long-used format.

American Public Television

There remains public television BBC, CBC and PBS. Since its beginnings, US public television has struggled, usually desperately, for enough funds to stay in business. The original 1967 Corporation for Public Broadcasting (CPB) charter from Congress provided no guarantees of long-term financial support. This has left all three arms of public television – CPB, the PBS network, and the local stations – extremely vulnerable to the changing winds of politics in Washington, and to the vagaries of local tastes. (See the discussion of *Tongues Untied* in Chapter 13.) Pledge drives and corporate underwriting provide most of the money for station operation, while much of the production costs are also dependent on corporate or foundation funding.

In 1988, after years of lobbying by media activists (chief among them Larry Daressa and Larry Sapadin of California Newsreel, theoretical physicist/ media advocate Larry Hall, Dee Dee Halleck, and producer Mark Weiss),

Congress appropriated funds for an independent PBS production service. Part of that money went to create the Independent Television and Video Service (ITVS). Although it took several years to begin operating effectively, ITVS in the 1990s and into the 2000s has been responsible for some of the more daring programming available on American television. Officially, ITVS's mission is to create and present independently produced programmes that engage in creative risks, advance issues and represent points of view not usually seen on public or commercial television. ITVS is committed to programming that addresses the needs of underserved and under-represented audiences, and expands civic participation by bringing new voices into public discourse. It divides less than ten million dollars each year among a wide range of producers for all types of work, the majority of which are documentaries. As of 2004, ITVS had partially funded 325 documentaries; 304 documentaries with ITVS funding had aired on some part of the US public television system. Projects produced by minority and underserved makers have been emphasized. It has worked with the minority consortia of PBS (the Native American, Latino, African-American, Pacific Islander and Asian-American organizations described in Chapter 13) and has funded in whole or in part such noted gay-themed documentaries as Arthur Dong's *Coming Out Under Fire* (1995), Meema Spadola's *Our House: A Very Real Documentary About Kids of Gay and Lesbian Families* (1999), and Debra Chasnoff's *It's Elementary: Talking About Gay Issues in School* (1996).

ITVS-funded works that make it to national broadcast generally do so under the umbrella of one of two programming strands: *POV* (an acronym for point-of-view) or *Independent Lens*. These are limited showcases with twelve to fourteen premieres for *POV* and twenty-nine for *Independent Lens* each year. This means that on US national public television there are less than fifty one- to two-hour time slots open in any year to stand-alone documentaries made by independent filmmakers. All the other documentaries offered for national broadcast are commissioned to order by strands such as *Frontline*, *American Experience*, *American Masters* and *NOVA*, which is the longest-running documentary series on PBS. A big advantage of a PBS broadcast over commercial channels is that producers generally have much more creative control, and the rights to their films revert to them after a period of time. For documentarians seeking to effect social change, a national public television broadcast also delivers a much larger audience than any cable or satellite channel can. This remains true today.

Investigative reporting has remained alive on public television largely on another commissioned strand through the efforts of WGBH in Boston and producer David Fanning's *Frontline*. A native of South Africa, Fanning came to WGBH from the BBC to start the documentary series *World* in 1977. Fanning conceived, and has executive-produced, *Frontline* since it premiered in January 1983. For two decades it has remained America's only regularly scheduled public affairs documentary series on television, and has won every major US award for broadcast journalism. *Frontline* has tackled dozens of national and international issues.

Archival Documentary

Before many of the rights-holders realized the economic value of their footage, putting together 'clip shows' was relatively inexpensive, so the historical compilation film became a natural source of material for early television. Henry Salomon's twenty-seven-part series *Victory at Sea*, originally broadcast on NBC from 1952 to 1953, remains one of the most widely seen television shows ever. Its footage of the WWII naval war in the Pacific, combined with a recurring musical theme by Richard Rodgers, was made entirely of clips from US government combat photographers. CBS's *The Twentieth Century*, discussed in Chapter 9, was, in its first years, almost entirely a compilation series. Jay Leyda's important study of historical compilation film, *Films Beget Films: A Study of the Compilation Film*, was, interestingly, published in 1960, near the beginning of television's widespread use of the form. It was Leyda who first used the word 'compilation' in describing film. This kind of documentary is also sometimes called a Found Footage Film, especially when discussing experimental film. Of course, historical compilations go as far back as the Soviet work of Esther Shub in the 1920s, and have continued to the present. Part of the David Wolper empire was built upon popular themes such as *Hollywood and the Stars*, the

1963 clip-filled documentary miniseries on NBC. Other filmmakers used the technique to explore more serious subjects. This formula has remained a television staple for over forty years, perhaps reaching an inevitable overload with war on The History Channel and The Military Channel. Hitler and his friends never leave the screen, in large part because all Axis power films became the free property of the people of the world by law of the World War II Peace Treaty.

In Britain, in 1964, the BBC produced an archival footage-based mega-series. The twenty-six episodes of *The Great War*, narrated by Sir Michael Redgrave, marked the fiftieth anniversary of the outbreak of World War I, and helped launch a new channel in Britain: BBC2. Made at a time when many viewers could still recall this 'Great War', it evoked deep emotions about the First World War from Britons who were still recovering from the Second. It was the first well-researched mega-part war documentary, emerging from the combined resources of BBC, CBS, ABC (Australia) and the Imperial War Museum. *The Great War* remains a high point of historical documentary-making. It was updated, modified for a US audience (a process that meant cutting the forty-minute episodes to thirty minutes), and rerun on both BBC and PBS with great success.

There were other British archival film series; *The World at War* (1975), spearheaded by producer Sir Jeremy Isaacs and narrated by Sir Laurence Olivier, was another landmark in historical television. Using archival film, photographic and other still images, and interviews with eyewitnesses, it broke up historical events into smaller, accessible story lines. These are occasionally supplemented by the use of location shooting to establish atmosphere and to fill a gap where archive footage did not exist. *The World at War* won immense critical acclaim and was highly profitable for Thames Television, where Isaacs was the Director of Programming. It was purchased by broadcasters and shown throughout the world for over twenty years, demonstrating as did *The Great War* that a historical epic documentary series could be of high quality, attract a large popular audience, and make a great deal of money – very much like the 1950s' *Victory at Sea*. The popularity of both these British series continues in DVD sales and downloads.

Jeremy Isaacs has made mayor contributions to television documentary.

Born in Glasgow in 1932, Isaacs was educated at Oxford. He joined Granada Television as a producer in 1958, and worked for the BBC on the noted *Panorama* series. In addition to *The World at War* he produced some of the other most significant British television documentaries. For example, as the founding Chief Executive of Channel 4, Isaacs was also responsible for *Ireland: A Television History* (1981), and *The Cold War* (1998) made in conjunction with Turner Broadcasting. In 1993-4 he helped usher in the 'docu-soaps' phenomenon with a series of behind-the-scenes doings at the Royal Opera House, of which he was the Chief Executive, and thus a key subject of his film.

As an example of the importance of preserving film, in 1970 previously classified US government footage of devastation from the atomic bomb attack on Hiroshima and Nagasaki was revealed. This came to light due in large part to the work of noted media scholar Erik Barnouw and his colleagues at Columbia University. (The footage was originally shot by Japanese cameramen in 1945 for the Japanese government.) Suppressed for decades by the Pentagon, the document of destruction was almost unbelievable to audiences who had not seen this closeup horror. The film made from this declassified material, *Hiroshima-Nagasaki, August 1945* (1970), showed the intimate and shocking results of the atomic blast for the first time to the public. Images of charred human bodies and children with their skin peeling off have today become iconic, perhaps so familiar they cause no remark. In 1970 they made the world face the devastating results of the A-Bomb. This discovery was part of a long visual examination of nuclear war and nuclear power that has remained a continuing thread in documentary, albeit with some periods seeing more films than others. The young adults who began making documentaries in the 1970s were the first generation for whom nuclear annihilation was a serious possibility, if not an assumption, and nuclear holocaust – often incorporating archival film – became a strong theme in independent documentary in the 1980s.

Other filmmakers, also working independently of major television, turned to archival compilation to make social and political points. In the US, accounts of the labour movement and resurrecting women's history were a big part of this historical rediscovery, as newly politicized young filmmakers approached history with revisionist eyes. They looked back at the archival record of previous social change, and challenged how it had been traditionally presented. Some were inspired by the revisions of history Emile de Antonio popularized. The following are some examples.

From 1905 to World War I members of the Industrial Workers of the World (IWW), nicknamed the Wobblies, travelled across the US organizing workers into 'One Big Union'. The film *The Wobblies* (1978, Deborah Schaefer and Stuart Bird) integrates newsreel footage with music of the period and interviews with IWW members. Cultural, political and legal events of the time are carefully documented, creating an exceptional record of one of the most exciting periods in American labour history. Another union, the United Auto Workers, which was at one point one of the most powerful in the nation, rose from a series of auto plant strikes in Flint, Michigan in the 1930s. The women who participated in or supported participants in those strikes tell their story in Academy Award-nominated *With Babies and Banners* (1979, Lorraine Gray, Lyn Goldfarb, Anne Bohlen). Again, archival footage from the period of the strike serves to illustrate the women's stories. *Union Maids* (1977, Julia Reichert and Jim Klein), Academy Award-nominated, is about trade unionism, but it is even more about three extraordinary women. Their stories are intercut with each other and with period newsreel footage as they recall their lives as workers and union organizers in Chicago in the late twenties and thirties.

The Life and Times of Rosie the Riveter (1980, Connie Field) arguably became the most popular of these films of labour and women's history, perhaps because it dealt with a past that was then still alive in the memories of many in its audience. It re-examines the experiences of female war workers in America during the 1940s, especially their struggle for dignity and equality.

Historical documentaries tend to remain fresh. Their use of first-hand accounts from people who are no longer alive make them especially valuable as 'documents' and the facts they present can be 'rediscovered' by succeeding generations.

The Ken Burns Phenomenon

The biggest financial and audience success for PBS in the past thirty years has been the films made by Ken Burns and company under the Florentine Films umbrella. The multiple broadcasts of *The Civil War,* beginning in 1990, had deep and long-lasting effects on style, funding and audience development for PBS documentaries. The series changed the way the public thought about documentary, and it changed the way television executives thought about historical documentaries.

Burns had been making significant documentaries for over fifteen years before *The Civil War.* His first major film, *The Brooklyn Bridge* (1982), remains a graceful, reflective tribute to hard work by immigrants and engineering genius in America, and to many of the traditions of the historical documentary. Its evocative images of this iconic American symbol and meticulous detailing

Fig 76 The Life and Times of Rosie the Riveter *(US, 1980, Connie Field). OWI photo by Palmer, Direct Cinema Ltd.*

of the building of the bridge demonstrate the emotional power historical documentaries can have.

Burns' output follows in the footsteps of other notable historical documentary-makers discussed previously – Charles Guggenheim, Jeremy Isaacs, Lance Bird, Tom Johnson – particularly in their shared insistence on accuracy and respect for the integrity and beauty of the image. The film that most anticipates the Burns formula is the National Film Board of Canada's *City of Gold*, made by Colin Low and Wolf Koenig (see discussion in Chapter 9).

Like all of Burns' major work, *The Brooklyn Bridge* relies on stills brought to life with a swooping rostrum camera, stunning live-action 16mm cinematography, talking-head interviews with sympathetic experts, and a memorable soundtrack and score. Burns and a succession of very key co-producers and collaborators were to take this formula and refine it in films such as *The Statue of Liberty* (1985), *The Congress* (1989) and others – a total of seven titles, all shown on PBS before *The Civil War*.

Burns' combination of talent, sincerity and personality has put him among the small group of documentarians whose names are known to their contemporary publics. Like Robert Flaherty and John Grierson before him, Burns developed a bold public persona, which made him and his work fundable from different sources. Over the course of making his films he formed highly productive working relationships with his sponsoring PBS station, WETA, Washington, DC. He is one of the filmmakers most consistently funded by the US Federal National Endowment for the Humanities, which provides money for almost every Florentine Films production, and whose dictates about input from humanities scholars help shape the form of his work. Burns was also able to cultivate major corporate sponsorship. *The Statue of Liberty* (1984), for example, had funding from Liberty Mutual Insurance, and a later deal with General Motors guaranteed that it would put money into a series of productions following the success of *The Civil War*. Like Grierson or Flaherty, Burns has a strong mission, but his ultimate goal is not social change or even elegiac poetry. Rather, he considers himself a historian, documenting the social and cultural changes of American life through portrayal of its individuals and institutions.

Fig 77 *In* The Civil War *Ken Burns used photographs like this one attributed to Mathew Brady, and told an epic story by weaving into it many personal experiences (U.S., 1980, Ken Burns)*

The Civil War remains Burns' masterwork. His later, longer films – *Baseball* (1996), *Jazz* (2001), *The War* (2007), for instance – suffer somewhat from the lack of control that had been exerted by strong co-producers like his brother Ric Burns on *The Civil War*, his then wife Amy Steckler Burns on *Shakers: Hands to Work, Hearts to God* (1974), or Richard Kilberg on *Huey Long* (1985). Collaboration is an important part of Burns' filmmaking technique, and he uses a crack technical team, including editor Paul Barnes and sound mixer Lee Dichter. Lynne Novick has also become a notable contributor as producer. Part of the intrinsic beauty of Burns' work comes from an insistence on using film rather than digital capture, shot by Burns and highly gifted cinematographer Buddy Squires. Both were nominated as producers for an Oscar for *Statue of Liberty*. The visual and aural elegance of Burns' films set a high standard for the craft of historical documentary but, perhaps most importantly, they continuously succeed in engaging a mass audience in emotional nonfiction experiences. Upcoming films (at time of writing) include the five-and-a-half hour *Prohibition* (2011) and *The Dust Bowl* (2012). It is safe to say that Burns has enough projects in the works to carry him through the rest of his life.

Direct offshoots of Burns' approach from former collaborators include a number of important documentaries: Ric Burns' epic *New York* (1999) and *The Donner Party* (1992); Larry Hott's and Diane Gary's *Niagara Falls* (1985), *Sentimental Women Need Not Apply: A History of the American Nurse* (1988), *Tuberculosis in America: The People's Plague* (1995); Stephen Ives' *The West* (1996, executive-produced by Ken Burns). All of these films were made for PBS broadcast, and each bears the distinctive mark of its makers; still, they follow in the broad form of historical documentary made popular by Burns. Others have adopted the style with more or less success; the form becomes a documentary cliché.

Fig 78 *Theodore Roosevelt parades through Los Angeles in an example of the long tradition of historical compilation mixed with contemporary shooting in* The Indomitable Teddy Roosevelt, *made by Harrison Engle in 1986. Signal Hill Productions*

Canada Soldiers On

Throughout the 1980s and 1990s the National Film Board slowly shifted from a self-contained, government-sponsored production/distribution institution to a hybrid. In 1984 the Minister of Communications' National Film and Video Policy redefined the NFB's mandate. Substantial changes in production and distribution activities followed, with savings from distribution reinvested in production. The plan also suggested a reduction in permanent personnel and the increased use of freelance filmmakers. In 1982 the NFB, in collaboration with the Canadian Film Development Corporation, set up the Film Canada Programme to support private producers; by the end of the 1980s freelancers accounted for seventy per cent of production. This led in the early 1990s to works such as David Adkin's *Out: Stories of Lesbian and Gay Youth* (1994) and Aerlyn Weissman's and Lynne Fernie's *Forbidden Love: The Unashamed Stories of Lesbian Lives* (1992).

More restructurings – which reflected budget reductions, technological changes, and a 1996 Mandate Review Committee's report – again changed the form of the NFB. It slashed its infrastructure and, based on the report, a new long-range plan was put in place which re-emphasized co-productions with independent Canadian producers and international co-productions. It also reaffirmed the NFB's commitment to ethnic diversity, particularly to supporting work by Aboriginal peoples. Early in the twenty-first century, the Canadian Department of Communications dedicated $25 million for the NFB to undertake co-productions with independent producers. Additionally, it mandated that thirty-five per cent of funding go to new, emerging filmmakers.

Other opportunities for documentaries were principally on television. The History Channel in Canada is a completely separate entity from The History Channel in the US. The state-run Canadian Broadcasting Corporation (CBC) has long produced and shown documentaries. In 2000 the NFB joined with the CBC and several private partners to create The Documentary Channel, Canada, sold on the sly observation that 'Canadians have a special fondness for the documentary form'. TVOntario, a private television network, has aired many acclaimed social issue documentaries. It is difficult to categorize the shows on these channels since they are generally made by freelancers whose films use many different styles to cover many types of subject.

The documentary spirit of individual Canadian filmmakers has remained vital. Vancouver documentarian Nettie Wild has created a number of ardent political films. From armies in the Philippines and oppression in Mexico to confrontations over heroin use in Vancouver, Wild's films tend to focus on the flashpoints of social conflicts. Her work includes *A Rustling of Leaves* (1988), *Blockade* (1993), *A Place Called Chiapas* (1998) – perhaps the most telling document about the desperate situation of indigenous people in Chiapas, Mexico – and *FIX: The Story of an Addicted City* (2002). These are films in the investigative tradition that value social change over form.

In some ways Canadian documentary presents a middle ground between that of the US and the UK. Canada has a much stronger system of public funding support for its documentarians than does the US. The NFB, even with its many changes, along with the government-supported CBC, provides a base from which filmmakers can build a budget. In the US, public funding is almost non-existent. But like the US, Canadian documentary has embraced diversity in style, content, and in welcoming new kinds of filmmakers, particularly women. In the UK, where public funding is strongest, production has remained largely in the hands of the traditional white male media stake-holders. During the 1980s and 90s it is also fair to say that UK and Canadian filmmakers turned their attention to international topics far more than did their US counterparts. NFB in particular was noted for large budgets that encouraged overseas travel. Perhaps also, audiences in Canada and the UK were more open to international issues than the largely parochial, no-foreign-languages American audiences.

Developments in the UK

Unlike the often chaotic diversity of documentarians in the United States, many of the filmmakers working in the UK came from a common background, university education at the 'right' schools leading directly into apprenticeship programmes in television. This has been the case from Grierson through Free

Cinema and on, although somewhat less so today. This has led to a very high quality of craftsmanship and a rather consistent point of view.

The BBC government-supported broadcasting tradition in Britain does allow many socially critical documentaries to appear regularly on television. There are series such as producer Nick Fraser's BBC *Storyville*, which funds some works and acquires others, including some of the best North American independent documentaries. Fraser, a filmmaker in his own right, is one of the most astute and articulate of television's commissioning editors active in the twenty-first century. He works with a range of filmmakers, from venerable British documentarians to emerging talent.

Leslie Woodhead joined Granada Television as a graduate trainee in 1961, after Cambridge University, and in the mid-1960s worked on the series *World in Action.* During the early 1970s he pioneered the development of docudramas on British television, specializing in investigative reconstructions of major East European stories. His extensive filmography includes a documentary about the Iranian Hostage Crisis of 1979, the first on this subject shot inside Iran; a film about the Srebrenica Massacre, *A Cry from the Grave*; and the dramatized reconstruction *The Holocaust on Trial,* about the trial of Holocaust denier David Irving. Other recent films include a documentary about a Russian nuclear missile base, a film about Slobodan Milosevic, and the autobiographical *My Life as a Spy* for *Storyville*.

Clive Gordon is a prolific investigative television documentarian. His work ranges from the tragedy of *Children of Chernobyl* (1991) and the horrors of war in *The Unforgiving* (1993) or *The Betrayed* (1995), to the violence and misogyny of the Milwaukee, USA vice trade in *Pimp Snooky* (2000). In *The Mission* (2000), his third film about civil wars, Gordon focused on the conflict in Central Africa and exploitation of children.

John Pilger, Australian-born investigative journalist/documentarian who works in England, developed a reputation as a television polemicist. For example, his Carlton Television documentary *Palestine Is Still the Issue* (2003) analyzes the Israeli-Palestinian conflict, condemning Israel's injustices towards the Palestinians and arguing that Israelis were at the root of the Middle East conflict. The public outcry about this view was considerable. Pilger, a prolific writer and presenter, was previously in the spotlight for his anti-globalization work, *The New Ruler of the World* (2001), which links economic globalization with mass abuses of human rights. His style is direct confrontation of those with whom he does not agree. The works are didactic and uncompromising in their criticisms, even of his own role as journalist. Archival footage is used in counterpoint to head-on interviews in a style of investigative documentary that makes no attempt to be even-handed.

Among the few women who have penetrated the male domain of the British documentary is Molly Dineen. Born in Canada, she is a graduate of the UK's National Film and Television School and has made a series of documentaries that, in a self-reflexive mode, make evident the filmmaker in the making. The first of these, her student production, was *Home From the Hill* (1985), about retired soldier and safari operator Colonel Hook, returning from Kenya to England. She went on to make *My African Farm* (1988), a portrait of Sylvia Richardson and her servants on a farm in Kenya, and *The Ark* (1993), a series of four one-hour programmes about the London Zoo, filmed during a six-month period of internal crisis. More recent films include the sponsored promotional *Tony Blair*, a ten-minute portrait of Prime Minister Blair, screened across all four television channels just prior to the election campaign of 1997. (Dineen publicly disavowed support of Blair during the Second Iraq War.) *Geri* (1999) presents a portrait of the predicament of modern celebrity by following Geri Halliwell (Ginger Spice) in the three months after her departure from the popular singing group The Spice Girls.

Dineen is a recurring presence in her films, although not on camera. It is her voice, heard asking questions off-screen, which integrates the filmmaker in the works. In the earlier films, her questioning depicts the subject in ways that focus sympathetically on him/her, while later films contain more of the filmmaker. As some of the best cv/d makers do, Dineen sometimes spends months observing her subjects before filming, developing close relationships with them. This is perhaps most evident in *Heart of the Angel* (1989). It records forty-eight hours in the London Underground Angel station focusing on the female 'fluffers', women who clean dirt and detritus from the tracks. *The Lies of the Land* (2007) is her most overtly polemical film, attacking the UK ban on fox-hunting by examining how the law devastates the finances of small farmers. In 2003 the Grierson Memorial Trust presented its first

Fig 79 *The cleaning crew in* Heart of the Angel *by Molly Dineen, 1989. British Film Institute*

Trustees Award, which recognizes an outstanding contribution to the art of documentary, to Dineen, whose films also include *The Pick, The Shovel and the Open Road* (1991).

Nick Broomfield, one of documentary's most visible innovators, continued to press onward in the 1990s with the development of his own screen persona, to the extent of starring as himself in five Volkswagen television commercials. In this, and in other film projects, he and Joan Churchill occasionally collaborated professionally. Although his works sometimes veer over the top, a more insightful balance seemed to take hold with 2003's *Aileen: Life and Death of a Serial Killer*, made collaboratively with Churchill. This follow-up to *Aileen Wuoronos: The Selling of a Serial Killer* (1992) pulls back a bit from the filmmaker as subject to convey the banal horror of a woman facing execution. Broomfield is still there on-screen, but seems less sure of the moral righteousness of his presence than in his other films, especially in the face of a clearly unstable woman about to be executed. This film, in particular, offers new ways to think about the relationship between the maker and the subject. Still, at the close of the film, Broomfield holds a press conference in the parking lot of the state penitentiary as Wuoronos is executed.

From *Night Mail* onwards, the poetic documentary in Britain has had a long history. In the 1990s director Brian Hill collaborated with poet Simon Armitage in a number of unusual poetic works. *Drinking For England* (1998) is a documentary on alcoholism, and *Saturday Night* (1996) a commentary about nightlife in Leeds. These can be called 'film poems', which evolved from Armitage's writing. Some critics have called their later collaborations 'documentary musicals'. In *Feltham Sings* (2002), producer Roger Graef got Hill and Armitage access to Feltham Prison in the hope that their film might make the public look more closely at young criminals. Hill has said: 'Feltham is grim; youth crime is serious; some of these kids have very tragic lives. But I don't think doing it as a musical belittles the problem. And some of the lads at Feltham have more talent than a lot of people who've got recording contracts … I don't think any subjects are off limits.' The lyrics are by Armitage, who fashioned them from months of interviews with the inmates, although some prisoners insisted on writing their own songs. Most of the film was shot inside cells; all of it behind the prison's bars.

A steady champion of documentary, Michael Apted studied law at Cambridge before joining the BBC. He began his film career in 1963 with a Manchester-based training programme for Granada Television. He is a prime example of the English system for turning out filmmakers highly skilled in craft, who can move freely from one genre to another. (His fiction work ranges from *Nell* [1994] to the James Bond film *The World Is Not Enough* [1998] and *The Chronicles of Narnia* [2010].) One of his first assignments was to research a film entitled *Seven Up* for producer Tim Hewet, whose idea it was to take a survey of English society from the eyes of a group of seven-year-old children. Following the Jesuit saying, 'Give me the child until he is seven, and I will show you the man' as a theme, Apted spent three weeks selecting fourteen children from a range of class backgrounds. He has since returned every seven years to visit the same individuals, making his own films, and in the process has created one of the most remarkable documentary phenomena.

The films, known as the 'Up Series' – *Seven Up, Fourteen Up, Twenty-One Up, Twenty- Eight Up, Thirty-Five Up, Forty-Two Up* and *Forty-Nine Up* – have documented the personal and social changes in this small sample of English people for over forty years. The next instalment is expected in the spring of

2012. The only comparable documentary exercise is John Marshall's ethnography of the !Kung people, an African tribe whom he has revisited regularly for fifty years, recording the vast changes in their lifestyle. The characters of the 'Up Series' have not been subjected to the immense physical upheavals of the !Kung, but their stories weave both engrossing personal drama and a broad sociological tapestry. The 'Up Series' is one of recent documentary's most debated projects. Apted has also made other significant documentaries, among them *Incident at Ogallala* (1992), *Inspirations (Me and Isaac Newton)* (1999), *Married in America One* (2002) and *Two* (2007), and *Bring on The Night* (1985).

Apted is a special case among serious documentarians. In some significant ways the 'Up Series' changed the way that time is perceived in documentary. It is also one of the best examples of debate about filmmaker/subject relationship. In addition, its episodes provide one of the very few instances in which audiences eagerly anticipate new episodes. Faithful viewers identify with the lives of the characters, creating a unique bond. It would be foolish to understate the importance of 'Up' in the evolution of documentary, especially on television, since the series presents a sublime example of matching distribution with both form and content.

American Independents

Given the continuing lack of public and corporate funding for documentaries, American independents have resorted to a wide variety of means to make and exhibit their projects. The innovations that have emerged are as diverse as the many populations of the US. To write comprehensively about this explosion in documentary requires much more space than this book offers. The following represent major 1980s and 90s trends by focusing on selected bodies of work.

San Francisco Bay Area-based Les Blank is a man of few words and many films. It has been said by fans that in conversation with Les you get less. With over thirty largely self-made films to his credit, he has continuously explored American subcultures, finding revelation and celebration in life's ordinary details. Blank captures on film the sensual human spirit, often seen through the cultures of music and food. Born in 1935 in Florida, Blank attended film school at the University of Southern California. His first personal films were on Texas blues singer Lightnin' Hopkins (*The Blues Accordin' to Lightnin' Hopkins* [1970]) and the hippie subculture (*God Respects Us When We Work, But Loves Us When We Dance* [1968]). To finance these and other projects, he made industrial and promotional films, generally working as cameraman.

Blank's work continued with series of intimate glimpses into the lives of passionate people who are from often-overlooked segments of American society – an output that grew to include rural Louisiana French musicians and cooks in *Yum, Yum, Yum!* (1990), *J'ai Eté au Bal – I Went to the Dance* (1989), *Hot Pepper* (1973), and *Marc and Ann* (1991); Mexican-Americans in *Chulas Fronteras*, *Del Mero Corazon* (1979); New Orleans music and Mardi Gras in *Always For Pleasure* (1978); chef Alice Waters and other San Francisco Bay Area garlic fanatics in *Garlic Is As Good As Ten Mothers* (1980); filmmaker Werner Herzog in *Burden of Dreams* (1982) and *Werner Herzog Eats His Shoe* (1980); Appalachian fiddlers in *Sprout Wings and Fly* (1983); Polish-American polka dancers in *In Heaven There Is No Beer?* (1984); Serbian-American music and religion in *Ziveli!: Medicine for the Heart* (1987); Hawaiian music and family traditions in *Puamana* (1991); Afro-Cuban drumming and religious tradition in *Sworn to the Drum* (1995); East Texas bluesman Mance Lipscomb in *A Well Spent Life* (1972) and *Cigarette Blues* (1985) with Sonny Rhodes; and the charmingly personal *Gap Toothed Women* (1987).

Blank is perhaps the most independent American documentarian. His films have been financed by the sale of previous films through his distribution company, Flower Films; by lecture and screening fees; and by selling T-shirts and tapes from the trunk of his car. Every one of his works bears his own definitive stamp. The subjects are allowed to speak for themselves; the camera is respectful, not intrusive; the editing is not jarring or flamboyant; and the music flows naturally from the situation at hand. Blank is not an invisible filmmaker – the subjects often speak directly to the camera – but he is one who, like Apted, becomes a part of people's lives. His documents are important as ethnographic evidence, but they are just as important for the singular artistic worldview they create. If Ken Burns captures the realities of American history with the accuracy of detailed research and minute exactness, Les Blank captures it simply by witnessing.

Among the many independent American documentarians to begin creating work in the late 1990s and the earliest part of the twenty-first century, Judith Helfand is one who has combined the personal self-reflexive mode with a Griersonian dedication to education and social change. She co-produced and co-directed, with George Stoney, along with Susane Rostock, *The Uprising of '34* (1995), a documentary which draws on the hidden history of the General Textile Strike of 1934 to explore labour, power and economics in the South at the time. Her work is among the most clear in carrying on the tradition of America's 1930s' Film and Photo League tradition.

Helfand was working for other producers when, at twenty-five, she was diagnosed with DES-related cervical cancer. In 1963 Helfand's mother, pregnant with Judith, had been prescribed the ineffective, carcinogenic synthetic hormone diethylstilbestrol (DES), meant to prevent miscarriage and ensure a healthy baby. After a radical hysterectomy Helfand went to her family's home to heal, and picked up her camera. The resulting video-diary is an exploration of how science, marketing and corporate power can affect our deepest relationships. Shot over five years, *A Healthy Baby Girl* (1997) tells a story of survival, mother/daughter love, family renewal, and community activism. Continuing to combine the personal and the political, Helfand's *Blue Vinyl* (2002) addresses the complex issue of toxins in vinyl production by bringing viewers into her parents' home, recently re-sided with blue vinyl. Although her work employs a fierce investigative reporting style, it has been criticized for its lack of scientific accuracy. This problem becomes more and more acute as passionate filmmakers examine the increasingly complex scientific discoveries and revised hypotheses of our world. Helfand's latest film, *Everything's Cool* (2007), continues the homey, somewhat slapdash approach she brings to every topic, including a largely one-sided perspective.

Another example of the personal diary film that became a powerful public document is Deborah Hoffmann's *Complaints of a Dutiful Daughter* (1995). Nominated for an Academy Award, the film uses both humour and insight to explain how Hoffmann comes to terms with her mother's deterioration from Alzheimer's disease. A more traditional documentary made by Hoffmann, along with Frances Reid, *Long Night's Journey Into Day* (2000), follows the stories of four individuals whose cases come before South Africa's Truth and Reconciliation Commission following the abolition of Apartheid. This film, too, was nominated for an Academy Award.

Reid and Hoffmann are both documentary veterans from the Bay Area, as is Jon Else, another independent who believes firmly in using media for social change. Else, who was series producer and cinematographer for Henry Hampton's *Eyes on the Prize: America's Civil Rights Years*, teaches documentary filmmaking at the University of California at Berkeley's Graduate School of Journalism. He directed the first three parts of a visually stunning, meticulously crafted four-part PBS series *Cadillac Desert: Water and the Transformation of Nature* (1997), which examines the history and struggle for water in the American West. His Academy Award-nominated *The Day After Trinity* (1980) looks at the life of J. Robert Oppenheimer and the Manhattan Project at Los Alamos, while *Sing Faster: The Stagehands' Ring Cycle* (1998) views Wagner's operas from the point of view of stage hands. Else also has a career as an accomplished cinematographer, working on everything from commercials and music videos to feature-length documentaries such as John Korty's *Who Are the DeBolts? And Where Did They Get Those Nineteen Kids?* (1977) and Lauren Lazin's *Tupac Shakur: Resurrection* (2003). Frustrated with the amount of time and effort it requires an independent filmmaker to raise money through grant-writing (310 funding proposals for *Cadillac Desert*), Else launched a programme to make documentaries using very low-cost technology, providing access to a wide range of young would-be documentary-makers.

Formerly the co-curator of the Margaret Mead Film Festival, Jonathan Stack began his filmmaking career in 1991, forming Gabriel Films, 'an independent documentary film company that specializes in social issue story-telling'. His first production was *One Generation More* (1991) with the BBC, about the resurgence of Jewish culture in Estonia, and he has directed and produced more than two dozen films since then. He was nominated for an Academy Award for his documentary, produced with Liz Garbus, *The Farm: Angola USA* (1998), and was nominated a second time for *The Wildest Show in the South: The Angola Prison Rodeo* (1999), produced with Simon Soffer. Both of these films deal with Texas' Angola Prison, the largest maximum-security penitentiary in the US which houses around 5,000 men, three-quarters of whom are black and eighty-five per cent of whom die within its walls. Stack is a filmmaker who works very much in the Griersonian tradition of explaining social problems which general audiences might not fully understand, with an aim of bettering social conditions. He has revisited the workings of America's prisons in many works, taking audiences inside these complex, dangerous and controversial institutions.

It is also important to remember that many of the stalwarts of American independent documentary filmmaking remained vitally active in the 1990s and into the twenty-first century. Cv/direct pioneers such as Robert Drew, Albert Maysles (David Maysles died in 1987), D. A. Pennebaker and Frederick Wiseman all continued to make important contributions. For Pennebaker, the 1990s was a prolific time, greatly enhanced by his personal and professional partnership with filmmaker Chris Hegedus. Their film (with R. J. Cutler) *The War Room* (1993) was one of the most fascinating studies of a political campaign ever undertaken. It presents a classic vérité chronology of the 1992 presidential campaign waged by candidate Bill Clinton, and among other things made a media star of campaign manager James Carville. *Down From the Mountain* (2000), which Hegedus and Pennebaker made with Chris Doob, and photographed by Joan Churchill, is a concert documentary and historical document of American bluegrass music. In 2001, Hegedus, working without Pennebaker but with Jehane Noujaim, made *Startup.com,* which traces the rise and fall of a new media company during the 'dot.com' business craze of the 1990s. This film, sometimes amusing, sometimes bleak, is a revealing look at not only the vagaries of business, but also the emotions of driven young men. It is unique in the level of intimacy if offers, piercing the outer shells of its characters to reveal a roller-coaster of emotions. The male characters reveal themselves in ways they might not have done to a male film crew.

Al Maysles teamed with Susan Fromke and Bob Eisenhardt to make *Concert of Wills: Making the Getty Centre* (1997). Filmed over twelve years, it documents the conception, construction and completion of the Los Angeles 'Parthenon', the Getty Centre. Fromke and Maysles also made, with Deborah Dickson, the Academy Award-nominated *Lalee's Kin: The Legacy of Cotton*

Fig 80 *George Stephanopoulos and James Carville in* The War Room *(US, 1993, Chris Hegedus and D. A. Pennebaker). Pennebaker-Hegedus Films*

(2001). Robert Drew, often with his wife Anne, has never stopped making documentaries, with well over a hundred to his credit. Frederick Wiseman remained true to his format throughout a career that includes over thirty-five films. *High School II* (1994), *Ballet* (1995), *Public Housing* (1997), *Belfast, Maine* (1999) and *Domestic Violence* (2001) are only some of the more recent titles. Continuing to examine American institutions in his own distinctive style, and continuing to have his films broadcast on PBS, Wiseman has himself become something of an institution. And in 2011 Ricky Leacock died, still at work on an innovative multi-media autobiographical project.

Chapter Related Films

1989
The Heart of the Angel (UK, Molly Dineen)
1990
Berkeley in the Sixties (US, Mark Kitchell)
The Civil War (US, Ken Burns)

1991
American Dream (US, Barbara Kopple)
Brother's Keeper (US, Joe Berlinger and Bruce Sinofsky)
1992
Forbidden Love: The Unashamed Stories of Lesbian Love (Canada, Lynne Fernie and
    Aerlyn Weissman)
Nitrate Kisses (US, Barbara Hammer)
The Panama Deception (US, Barbara Trent)
1993
The War Room (US, D. A. Pennebaker, Chris Hegedus, R. J. Cutler)
1994
Hoop Dreams (US, Peter Gilbert, Steve James, Frederick Marx, Gordon Quinn)
Lock-Up: The Prisoners of Riker's Island (US, Jon Alpert)
1995
Complaints of a Dutiful Daughter (US, Deborah Hoffmann)
1996
When We Were Kings (US, Leon Gast)
Yugoslavia: Death of a Nation (UK, Brian Lapping)
1997
Cadillac Desert (US, Jon Else)
Concert of the Wills: Making the Getty Centre (US, Susan Fromke, Bob Eisenhardt, Albert
    Maysles)
Four Little Girls (US, Spike Lee and Sam Pollard)
A Healthy Baby Girl (US, Judith Helfand)
Licensed to Kill (US, Arthur Dong)
Waco: The Rules of Engagement (US, Dan Gifford and William Gazeccki)
1998
42 Up (UK, Michael Apted)
The Farm (US, Jonathan Stack and Liz Garbus)
Human Remains (US, Jay Rosenblatt)
A Place Called Chiapas (Canada, Nettie Wild)
1999
Belfast, Maine (US, Frederick Wiseman)
Geri (UK, Molly Dineen)
2001
Domestic Violence (US, Wiseman)
Startup.com (US, Hegedus and Jehane Noujaim)
2002
Dogtown and Z Boys (US, Stacy Peralta)
Feltham Sings (UK, Roger Graef, Brian Hill, Simon Armitage)
The Fog of War (US, Morris)
2003
Aileen: Life and Death of a Serial Killer (US, Nick Broomfield and Joan Churchill)

Chapter Related Books

Bullert, B. J., *Public Television: Politics and the Battle Over Documentary Film*. Rutgers, NJ: Rutgers University Press, 1997.

Bruzzi, Stella, *New Documentary: A Critical Introduction*. London: Routledge, 2000.

Corner, John, *The Art of Record: A Critical Introduction to Documentary*. Manchester, UK: Manchester University Press, 1996.

Edgerton, Garry R., *Ken Burns' America*. New York: St Martin's Press, 2001.

Goldsmith, David A., *The Documentary-makers: Interviews with 15 of the Best in the Business*. Switzerland: Rotovision, 2003.

Harris, Mark and Claudia Medina, *Wild at Heart: The Films of Nettie Wild*. Vancouver: Anvil Press, 2009.

Hogarth, David, *Documentary Television in Canada: From National Public Service to Global Marketplace*. Montreal: McGill-Queen's University Press, 2002.

Kilborn, Richard and John Izod, *An Introduction to Television Documentary: Confronting Reality*. Manchester, UK: Manchester University Press, 1997.

Singer, Bennett, ed., *42 Up: A Book Based on Michael Apted's Award-Winning Documentary Series*. New York: The Free Press, 1992.

15

Documentary Tradition in the Twenty-First Century

There are many fine examples of new films being made that fall sometimes more, sometimes less, into established documentary traditions. To follow are only a few examples, from the US mainly, but the quality and complexity of such work is evident in Canada and Britain, as well as in the rest of the world. It is interesting to note that at a time when the press continues to bemoan what it perceives as waning US world stature, the country's important social issue filmmakers are producing some of the most provocative, influential and well-made body of documentaries in the world. (A similar argument can be made for American's role as the foundation for music [hip-hop], art [graffiti and street art], internet innovation [social networking] and other cultural phenomena.)

In the politically motivated 1930s Film and Photo League vein is the 2011 documentary *No Contract, No Cookies: The Stella D'Oro Strike*. Made by longtime media and social justice advocate Jon Alpert with Matthew O'Neil. *No Contract, No Cookies* follows the struggle of 138 mostly immigrant women workers who go on strike to save their jobs at a famous bakery in the Bronx, New York after a private equity firm buys the company and demands wage and benefit cuts of up to thirty per cent. The film uses Alpert's interviews and cv/ direct technique to follow the eleven-month strike from its hopeful beginnings to its dismal epilogue. At the time, the *Wall Street Journal* reported on the case: ' "The accountability that frequently arises when a portfolio company acquired by PE firm, combined with the type of management attention that company receives, can create pressure that raises the bar for everybody", said the labour and employment law partner at Morgan Lewis & Bockius LLP. What does that language mean? More pointedly, *No Contract: No Cookies* begins eight months into a strike in which the workers, who originally came from twenty-two countries, tell their own stories of how their work lives of ten, twenty or thirty years in a family-run company are smashed by corporate greed. Says one worker, a Greek immigrant: 'When I see those cookies in the supermarket (now) I want to cry.' The struggles between labour and management never cease, and documentarians like Jon Alpert, and gatekeepers like Sheila Nevins at HBO, which backed the film, will hopefully never stop examining the problem.

Sheila Nevins and her team at HBO continue, through today, to provide a very important channel for independently made documentaries like *No Contract: No Cookies* to be made and seen. At any given time information about at least 225 major documentary films can be accessed on the HBO website: www.hbo.com/documentaries. Titles range from Nigel Noble and Daniel Jung's *The Killing of Sister Dorothy* (2008), about the 2005 murder of an American Catholic nun in the Amazon jungle and the subsequent trial of the suspects, to James Marsh's 2011 festival hit *Project Nim*, the story of a chimpanzee who in the 1970s became the focus of a series of unusual scientific experiments. Marsh also directed the Oscar-winning *Man on Wire* (2008).

HBO, never a network to shy away from the attraction of films affiliated with famous names, is responsible for getting the documentaries of Spike Lee, best known for his feature fiction work, on television. *When the Levees Broke: A Requiem in Four Acts* (2006) is partly a compilation film of news footage and interviews with which Lee, cameraman Cliff Charles and Lee's longtime editor (and filmmaker himself) Sam Pollard created a semi-poetic eulogy and testament to the struggle of New Orleans in the wake of Hurricane Katrina. Lee returned to the interviewees of *When the Levees Broke* in August 2010 when HBO aired his new documentary, *If God is Willing and Da Creek Don't Rise*, which chronicles how New Orleans and the Gulf Coast area have fared in the five years following Hurricane Katrina. *Trouble the Water* uses a different innovative technique to plumb the same subject matter in ways that speak

Fig 81 *HBO's Sheila Nevins left, with Susan Harris, a descendant of one of the 1911 fire's survivors at the premiere of* Triangle: Remembering the Fire, *2011 by Mark Levin and Daphne Pinkerson. Several other documentaries have been made about this tragedy, one of the earlier* The Triangle Factory Fire Scandal *was made by Mel Stuart in 1979. Michael Loccisano, Getty Images*

directly to audiences around the world. And watching these films side by side with Pare Lorentz's *The River* makes clear how little progress has been made in seventy years of US stewardship of its rivers.

Perhaps more meditative is Lee's *Four Little Girls* (1998), again made for HBO. His eleventh feature and first full-length documentary, it focuses on the 1963 bombing of the 16th Street Baptist Church in Birmingham, Alabama, an attack that left four young African-American girls dead. In the tradition of other historical documentaries, this film examines an event that proved to be a watershed in a time of radical change in American's racial landscape. The bombing unveiled a racist anti-black movement whose embrace of hate and violence was anathema to most Americans. Lee told CNN that one reason he made the film was that 'There's a legacy and I think it's a tragedy that we, as parents and as older generations, do not pass down to younger children.' As with many testament documentaries, Lee was motivated to make *Four Little Girls* in part because 'I think a dramatization would have cheapened it. Also, a lot of these people are very old, so when they go, their story goes.'

This same drive to tell the stories of passing generations has become a leitmotif in documentary filmmaking. As the people who lived through the World Depression of the 1930s, WWII, and especially the Nazi Holocaust die, the importance of a preserved documentary legacy heightens. The number of films recounting both individual and larger sociological accounts of the Holocaust has become uncountable and deserves a book-length study on its own. The depth of material on this and other historical events only heightens the need for awareness of the film preservation issues discussed more fully in Chapter 16.

In more recent war coverage, examples by Michael Tucker and Petra Epperlein are tandem films *Gunner Palace* (2004) and *How To Fold a Flag* (2010). These two films reflect documentary's continuous need to explore the reality, repercussions and meanings of war in their examination of the wartime and, in *How To Fold a Flag*, the post-war lives of a group of soldiers serving in the fierce battles of the second Iraq War. As a pair, these are remarkable in the long-term and personal revelations they provide, and are far different from the films from WWII, Korea and Vietnam that deal with veterans. A sobering perspective of a female US army vet is revealed in Sarah Nesson and Mitchell Block's 2010 Academy Award-nominated *Poster Girl*. This story of Robynn Murray's transformation from all-American high school cheerleader and ROTC advocate to scarred PTSD sufferer is an unflinching look at women and war today.

An important recent war film that justifiably received a great deal of attention is *Restrepo* (2010). Made by American journalist Sebastian Junger and British/American photojournalist Tim Hetherington, and produced for National Geographic Films, it chronicles a single US platoon on deployment in Afghanistan that arrives just as US Army General Stanley A. McChrystal is relieved of command following his comments critical of President Barack Obama's administration. It uses a non-narrative cv/direct approach to move from the frightening chaos of daily firefights to the backbreaking boredom of digging bunkers. It sits deep within the horror of war. Despite the high-tech equipment and the precision of high-flying bombers that define modern warfare, the film is a chilling reminder that much fighting is still done close enough to see the enemy's breath in the cold mountain air. The film shows that nothing about face-to-face war has changed much since WWI's *The Battle of the Somme*. The platoon depicted defending observation posts in *Restrepo* make this war personal. And the film's message of sacrifice was tragically realized when soon after it was released, Tim Hetherington was killed while covering combat in Libya.

Since documenting the up-close meaning of war has become so technologically accessible, expect more and more of these personal war and post-war stories to be turned into documentaries. This is especially true of studies of returning veterans' stories, and represents a change from earlier eras when such accounts were relatively rare. *Dear America: Letters Home From Vietnam* (1988) by Bill Couturié, *Winter Soldier* (1972) by the Winter Film Collective, *Letters from Vietnam* (1965) discussed in Chapter 12, WWII's *Let There Be Light* (see Chapter 7), and WWI medical study films reflect how attitudes about shell shock, battle fatigue and PTSD have shifted over decades.

Werner Herzog

Werner Herzog is a force, a genre, a mode, a style, a voice, a type all his own. An analysis of his film career would be psychoanalysis of the man himself, it is a career so long and unique. He has described his filmmaking as a quest for 'ecstatic truth'. The line between Herzog's stated contempt for cv/direct, 'the accountant's truth – the surface of facts that is not what cinema can really achieve' and his again self-stated desire 'to put the audience back into a position where they can trust their eyes and ears again' is self-servingly obscure. His films are more often opera-like than they are documentaries or fiction features; they are highly effective and can be, when they do not descend into 'soap', brilliant. Herzog generally narrates his documentaries, asks questions of himself and his participants, and sometimes appears on camera. Even though he appropriates self-reflexive styles, he always keeps a distance, and thus keeps the audience at a distance from his subjects and from himself. All are 'actors' playing on a stage that Herzog creates.

The recent fame and controversy of *Grizzly Man* (2005), which has far outstripped that of *Little Dieter Needs to Fly* (1997), is justified, but despite the outrage of bear eats man, it comes nowhere near the ethical unbalance of the latter. Dieter Dengler always wanted to pilot an airplane. From his WWII childhood in Germany, where he enviously watched the Allied bombers pummel his city, to becoming a US Air Force pilot fighting in Vietnam. His life is in itself fascinating. But for Herzog it gets better. Shot down, Dengler was taken prisoner by the Pathet Loa, then turned over to soldiers of the Army of North Vietnam. After a period of torture and starvation, chained to the bottom of a bamboo cage, Dengler escaped. Years later he allows Herzog to enter his life and probe the depths of his motivations. The bulk of the film consists of footage in which Herzog takes Dengler back to Laos and Thailand to recreate his wartime ordeal. Herzog hired locals to play the part of his captors and had Dengler retrace his steps while describing his experiences; Herzog films as Dengler crawls through the jungle again, reciting his own horrors. Dengler re-enacts his escape again rescued by air, and Herzog concludes the film with Dieter sitting happily home and safe, smiling at their mutual adventure. *Little Dieter Needs to Fly* goes further and deeper and creates visceral excitement more compelling than a traditional story might. Herzog even had the bravado (or the financial need) to remake *Little Dieter* into an unremarkable fiction feature film titled *Rescue Dawn* starring Christian Bale in 2007.

In the very different *The White Diamond* (2004) Herzog makes an almost typical science/nature documentary. Of course, it is still a Herzog film, and one of his most beautiful. He sets aside cruelty, although he still riffs on his recurring madman theme (there are no madwomen in Hertzog's universe). The main character, British aeronautical engineer Graham Dorrington, is still driven and over-reaching as he and his team struggle to build a teardrop-shaped balloon and send it gliding over the jungle canopies in Guyana. Dorrington remains haunted by memories of his friend who fell to death in a similar expedition 12 years earlier. But Dorrington's goals are benign; the film gives viewers a luscious dream that they might well share, and Herzog's cinematography is breathtaking. The balloon is a softly shining beacon, and one feels that the jungle canopy is touchable, just barely out of reach. Of course, being a Herzog film, there are indigenous tribespeople assisting. The main one of these, Marc Anthony Yap, when interviewed head-on says: ' It's beautiful up there flying around. I should've had my rooster here with me for the world to see. His name is Red. He has five wives, five hens. So, I get five eggs every morning. Yeah, my rooster's good.' It would be good if the rooster had glided in the balloon, and it would then be good to be that rooster.

That softer Herzog emerges in his most financially successful film to date. *Cave of Forgotten Dreams* (2011) was a runaway IMAX hit at the international box office, and at age seventy, Herzog well deserves that. The film offers a detailed look into the Chauvet-Pont-d'Arcave cave in southern France, which on its walls holds the earliest known artistic visions of humankind. In the film Herzog shows and tells the film audience how he fails to capture the full beauty of the cave because of severe (legitimate) restrictions on access. Included are 'mediated' interviews with the standard-type science experts and archaeologists before Herzog shows us the 'naked' cave, supposedly mediated only by him and his cameras. Herzog muses on the depth of time. At every turn he announces his cinematic failure, an aural device that becomes integral to the film. This use of monologue is another Herzogian convention, but one that works especially well here. *Cave of Forgotten Dreams* is beautiful; it takes audiences to a place they will never see, and with its mix of science and romance it gives the public, who might not otherwise watch a Herzog documentary, a wonderful – if not the best – example of his work. Whatever one thinks of his films, whatever forces drive him, Herzog continues to throw down welcome challenges for documentary.

Steve James, Alex Gibney, Davis Guggenheim

Years after *Hoop Dreams*, Steve James made *Stevie* (2003), a highly personal film about 'Little Stevie' whom James mentored in a Big Brother programme in rural Illinois. The documentary goes back to that eleven-year-old tie to find that Stevie is a troubled man, emotionally crippled and awaiting trial for molesting his eight-year-old cousin. *Stevie* becomes more about the Steve behind the camera than the Stevie before it in a fascinating self-reflexive manner. The film becomes a journey of self-discovery that manages to indict both America's healthcare system and the twenty-first century's 'me-first' society. *No Crossover: The Trial of Allen Iverson* (2010), which was part of ESPN's *30 for 30* television series, uses the same thematically and stylistically personal documentary, in which the director is much seen on camera. *No Crossover* re-examines the 1993 trial of Allen Iverson, then a teenage basketball star who was accused of harassing a white girl and starting a brawl. This case divided the Newport News and Hampton, Va. communities along racial lines. James, who is white and grew up there, returned to make the film, discovering that tensions, even within his own family, still run high when the black athlete's name is mentioned.

James was also executive producer, story director and co-editor of the PBS series *The New Americans* in 2005. *Reel Paradise* (2008) became his fourth film to premiere at the Sundance Film Festival. He co-produced and co-directed with *Hoop Dreams* collaborator Peter Gilbert *At the Death House Door* (2008), which traces the remarkable career journey of Protestant Minister Carroll Pickett, who served fifteen years as the death house chaplain in an infamous prison unit in Huntsville, Texas. During that time Pickett presided over ninety-five executions, including the very first lethal injection done anywhere in the world. In what became a ritual act of catharsis after each execution, Pickett recorded an audiotape account of the fateful day. These he stored and never again listened to them until the filmmakers prompt him to open the box. The scenes in which the camera observes Pickett hearing these tapes is a remarkable and painful moment of intimacy. The film also tells the story of Carlos De Luna, a convict whose execution affected Pickett more than any other. Pickett firmly believed the man was innocent, yet administered last rites and watched him die. *At the Death House Door* is a prime example of cases in which documentaries set out to tell one story (in this instance, that of one wrongfully executed man) and then discover and have the skill to follow a different storyline. The film's end reveals that Pickett, who had begun his job in the prison with approval of the death penalty, has become an anti-death penalty advocate. James' sixth feature documentary *The Interrupters*, made with writer Alex Kotlowitz, was released to wide acclaim in 2011. In it,

James returns to some of the same Chicago neighbourhoods featured in *Hoop Dreams* in an investigation of the unending violence that plagues American cities.

There are two remarkable things that stand out in James' career. The first is the way his work manages to combine deeply self-reflexive film essays with controversial social issues in a way in which neither takes precedence over the other. Even in those films in which he is not a direct participant, his presence can be felt behind the camera, yet it never overpowers the people and the arguments that the films explore. The second and almost more meaningful thing is James' longtime loyalty to the ideals of the Kartemquin 'collective' and to their model of distribution. Some filmmakers use documentary and its supporters as a platform for career advancement, and many have not stuck with the first funders, supporters and distributors that got them started. (Kartemquin's history and philosophy are discussed in detail in Chapter Twelve.) James is a filmmaker who has had offers to shift to bigger, more famous associates (he has also directed fiction features), but he continues to work with and support the grass-roots activism of Kartemquin. This loyalty is a testament to the people of that organization and to Steve James' strength of character.

Alex Gibney and Davis Guggenheim each seem to have established their own small production factories since 2000. In their cases this is a good thing. Each has produced a number of high-quality films, and more are arriving regularly. Both have achieved considerable success in the festival, review and theatrical areas, and they are part of the newer 'name-brand' documentarians.

After working for two decades in the documentary business as an editor and then a director, Gibney's personal break-out film was *Enron: The Smartest Guys in the Room* (2005). He followed this with *Taxi to the Dark Side* (2007), *Gonzo: The Life and Work of Dr Hunter S. Thompson* (2008), *Casino Jack and the United States of Money* (2010), *Client Nine: The Rise and Fall of Eliot Spitzer* (2010) and *Magic Trip* (2011), with more in production. He was also executive producer for *No End in Sight* (2007), an Oscar-winning film directed by Charles Ferguson. In addition to winning an Emmy, the Peabody, a duPont Columbia Award, and a Grammy, Gibney won an Oscar for *Taxi to the Dark Side*. Three things that all his features share is very careful attention to research and detail, a respect for the films' subjects, and impeccable craftsmanship. Whether he is working in a compilation style like *Magic Trip* or using interviews in balance with stock footage, the work is all compelling. Gibney is especially good at making very complex political and cultural issues understandable. In 2010, *Utne Reader* magazine listed Gibney as one of the '25 Visionaries Who Are Changing Your World'. If enough people watch his documentaries, that may become true.

Taxi to the Dark Side was part of a *Why Democracy?* series meant to present independent documentary filmmakers' personal perception of democracy. It was shown by forty-two different broadcasters worldwide in 2007, accompanied by a global interactive conversation that took place in real and interactive space. In this context, a personal side of Gibney's life is revealed at the close of the film. It is a historically investigative approach to

Fig 82 *Ken Kesey and driver Neal Cassady in Alex Gibney and Alison Ellwood's 2011* Magic Trip, *a freewheeling account of the Merry Prankster's fabled road trip across America in the 1960s in a bus named 'Further'. The Film Foundation helped fund the repair of damaged original footage at the University of California, Los Angeles film archive, a process which took over a over a year*

the decades-old battle about torture that led to the murder of an Afghan taxi driver, who was beaten to death by American soldiers while being held in extrajudicial detention at the Bagram Air Base. Unlike most of Gibney's work, it has many difficult-to-watch scenes of human degradation. *Taxi to the Dark Side* also presents a many-sided view of what was one of the US government and military's most appallingly controversial policies. Its sympathetic interviews with some of the ordinary soldiers who were incarcerated for this crime are especially surprising.

Davis Guggenheim is best known as the executive producer and director of *An Inconvenient Truth* (2006) and *Waiting for Superman* (2010). Although Guggenheim's credits include more television fiction work than documentaries, his documentary films merit attention, in part because two have generated loud public controversies. With *It Might Get Loud* (2009) Guggenheim is the only filmmaker to release three different films ranked within the top 100 highest-grossing documentaries of all time. All of these are entertaining and contemporary. Perhaps what they tell us about successful documentaries for large audiences in the twenty-first century is that these often feature famous people – Al Gore in *An Inconvenient Truth*, Jack White, Jimmy Page and The Edge in *It Might Get Loud,* and the entire U2 band in *From the Sky Down,* the 2011 opening night gala film of the Toronto Film Festival – or perhaps not. *Waiting for Superman,* about the sinking quality in US schools, is as far as one can get from celebrity.

The team of former Vice President Al Gore and director/producer Davis Guggenheim made waves in political and social arenas for *An Inconvenient Truth. Waiting for Superman,* an inquiry into the possibility of education reform through charter schools, also stirred debate. As Vice President Gore said about *An Inconvenient Truth,* 'Who would have ever thought that a slide-show about global warming would become a hit film?' While some quibble about the scientific and social evidence backing up the messages in *An Inconvenient Truth* and *Waiting for Superman,* there is no doubt that they present powerful examinations about urgent problems. And they demonstrate solutions to those problems, becoming truly social efforts in the Griersonian tradition.

Errol Morris, Sinofsky & Berlinger, Stanley Nelson

Errol Morris makes films that belong in theatres. He began filmmaking in the 1970s, and his total body of work becomes more important with each new documentary. The films have been distributed to wide critical acclaim, and he has a loyal following for his completely personal vision, one perhaps shaped by a distortion of sight in his one eye. This work includes *Gates of Heaven* (1978), *Vernon, Florida* (1981), *The Thin Blue Line* (1988), *A Brief History of Time* (1992), *Fast, Cheap and Out of Control* (1997), *Stairway to Heaven* (1998), *Dr Death: The Rise and all Fall of Fred E. Leuchter, Jr.* (1999), *The Fog of War: Eleven Lessons from the Life of Robert S. McNamara* (2002), and *Tabloid* (2011). Morris is drawn to often-eccentric people who talk candidly about their lives while doing what they normally do. In an interview he explained that he is asked endlessly whether his films are documentaries:

> The answer is 'yes' and 'no'. There are elements of fiction and nonfiction in all filmmaking. I use real people. They're not reading a prepared script. They're attempting to talk about themselves. That's real. But I do other things that are closer to fictional, like I storyboard for instance.

As a graduate philosophy student, Morris spent much of his time at San Francisco's Pacific Film Archives watching movies. After making *Gates of Heaven* and *Vernon, Florida*, he spent two years working as a private detective. This job may have given him a sharp forensic capacity to evaluate evidence and put fragments of a narrative together. Morris' talent for investigating the implied truth and for appreciating how people reveal themselves to the camera is at the heart of his art. His first two films became cult favourites. Critic Roger Ebert said about *Gates of Heaven*:

> I believe it is one of the greatest films ever made. Ostensibly a documentary about two pet cemeteries in Northern California and the people who owned them, it is in fact one of the most profound, and funniest, films ever made about such subjects as life and death, success and failure, dreams and disappointments, and the role that pets play in our loneliness.

It was the theatrical release of *The Thin Blue Line* that brought Morris wide popular recognition. The film follows the case of Randall Dale Adams, a man who, it seemed, was falsely accused of the highway murder of a Texas police officer. Morris uses repeated dramatizations of the murder, multiple points of view, visual effects, talking-head interviews, and telephone conversations, in concert with Philip Glass' almost eerie score, to create the overriding impression that justice was not served. The film makes a strong case that prejudice and possibly tainted testimony persuaded the jury to find Adams, a drifter from the Midwest, guilty. The 'thin blue line' of police officers separating the public from chaos – as the judge, quoting the DA in the case, describes them – is shown as ineffective. The police, courts and prisons are seen as putting people at the risk of injustice as often as they protect them. After serving time for a death sentence commuted to life imprisonment, Adams was freed, in no small part due to the film. He died in 2011.

Most recently Morris completed *Tabloid* (2011), the story of a woman whose high jinks became a tabloid newspaper sensation in the late 1970s. This film prompted Morris to rethink some documentary precepts. Where once a single documentary (or book, or piece of journalism) could provide focus and a filter for a story, there are now many thousands of public views about every incident. Speaking of how tabloid journalism dominates the news, Morris commented on society's over-saturation of information from television, the internet, print, and every other source:

> Now, there are so many sources of information that you lose track. You really do. I don't know how else to describe it. Maybe other people can deal with this glut of information differently, but I forget now where I heard things. There's a hall of mirrors where people are reporting on other people reporting on other people reporting. The connection of all this sea of information, this glut of reality, is sometimes lost. Where did all this stuff originate?

Morris acknowledges the importance of his films as documentary innovations. About the *Thin Blue Line* he says:

> I did use movies in a different way, I think, than they had been used before … I investigated a murder with a camera – an oddity in and of itself, it

was not telling a story about a murder investigation, it was the investigation – and evidence was accumulated with that camera … One of the lessons about the Adams case is that, if it had happened now instead of 1988, when the movie came out, Randall Adams would in all likelihood have been executed [because there would be too much information and dis-information circulating about the case].

Interesting documentaries have also been made by the team of Joe Berlinger and Bruce Sinofsky. Previously best known for the intriguingly odd portrait film *Brother's Keeper* (1992), they transformed a tragic and lurid story into the 1996 HBO documentary *Paradise Lost 2: The Child Murders at Robin Hood Hills*. It explores the deaths of three boys, all second-graders who were found mutilated and murdered in a West Memphis, Arkansas ravine. The killings were dubbed the 'Robin Hood Hills murders', after the neighbourhood where the killings took place. Three youths who wore black T-shirts and listened to heavy metal music were arrested, tried and convicted in what the prosecution called 'ritualistic, satanic cult' killings. That trial was filmed by Sinofsky and Berlinger (who began work in advertising and later worked with Maysles Films.) Not only did it expose why poor people without adequate legal representation often end up on death row, it seriously cast doubt on the trio's guilt. *Paradise Lost* 2: *Revelations* was made in 2000. In it the filmmakers revisit the legal case, then mired in appeals for the imprisoned youths. The two films created a wave of popular support for the accused, Damien Echols, Jason Baldwin and Jesse Misskelley. In 2011, while they were editing the final cut on *Paradise Lost 3: Purgatory*, news came that the accused, known as the 'West Memphis Three', would be freed. Berlinger and Sinofsky flew to Arkansas and shot a new ending for the third film they, as filmmakers, now firmly a part of the story. There are echoes of *The Thin Blue Line* and Nick Broomfield's Aileen Wuornos films in the *Paradise Lost* trilogy, all of which demonstrate that documentaries can play an important, potentially life-or-death part in contemporary social discourse.

Stanley Nelson is known for historical documentaries that illuminate critical but sometimes overlooked parts of history, often that of African-Americans and other minorities. Before becoming an independent filmmaker,

Fig 83 *Filmmakers Bruce Sinofsky and Joe Berlinger flank one of the accused 'West Memphis Three' in the HBO trilogy* Paradise Lost: The Child Murders at Robin Hood Hills *1996,* Paradise Lost 2: Revelations *2000,* Paradise Lost 3: Purgatory *2011. The films and the cause célèbre created by them had an impact on the ultimate release of Jason Baldwin, Jesse Misskelley and Damien Echols in 2011.*

he was a producer for Bill Moyers at PBS. Nelson's feature documentary work includes *Wounded Knee (2009), Jonestown: The Life and Death of Peoples Temple (2006), Marcus Garvey: Look For Me in the Whirlwind (2000)* and *The Murder of Emmett Till.* (2003). This last film had the remarkable impact of reopening the inquiry into the murder of fourteen-year-old Emmett Till. His brutal killing was the result of Till's 'crime' of whistling at a white girl in Mississippi while he was visiting from Chicago in 1955. The young Till did not understand that he had broken the unwritten laws of the segregated South. Although his killers were arrested and charged with murder, they were both acquitted by an all-white, all-male jury. Shortly after, the defendants sold their story to a journalist, including a detailed account of how they murdered Till. The murder and the trial, along with the killers' subsequent boasts about the murder, horrified the world.

Nelson's films are usually made for PBS's 'American Experience' series, and the productivity of his relationship with PBS is topped only by Ken Burns' long-term support from the network. His work includes *Black Press: Soldiers Without Swords* (1998) and *A Place of Our Own* (2004), a semi-autobiographical look at the African-American middle class. *Sweet Honey in the Rock: Raise Your Voice* (2005) documents the African-American female a cappella ensemble as it traces the group's deep musical roots to the sacred music of the black church – spirituals, hymns, gospel – as well as jazz and blues. Nelson produced and directed *Wounded Knee* (2010), one of the five films that formed part of the 'We Shall Remain' series for PBS's 'American Experience'. Nelson's efforts in community outreach are realized through Firelight Media, a non-profit company dedicated to telling the stories of people, places and issues that are under-represented in popular culture. Firelight Media also provides training and support for emerging filmmakers who might otherwise be unable to make films.

His *Freedom Riders* (2010) recounts the powerful and inspirational story of six months in 1961 that changed America forever. Over four hundred black and white Americans, many young college students, risked their lives and endured savage beatings and imprisonment for travelling together on buses and trains as they journeyed through the Deep South. Deliberately violating the American South's Jim Crow laws, the Freedom Riders met with bitter racism and mob violence along the way, testing their belief in non-violent activism. The film's impact was enhanced by a web series, and a re-enactment of the freedom rides for the historic event's fiftieth anniversary. Nelson's work sits firmly in the tradition of historical interview and compilation films. His choice of subject matter, skill and thoughtfulness make him one of the twenty-first century's most notable documentarians working in this form.

Women Documentarians

There are no women documentarians in the above section. There are about the same number of women as men making English language documentaries, at least in the US, in the twenty-first century, but only a few have sustained bodies of work with films appearing regularly over time. Fewer still have public profiles. As a cinematographer, Joan Churchill's career stands out for its longevity as well as for its artistic triumphs. She has been shooting acclaimed documentaries for over forty years and continues to grow creatively, yet only a few times has she been the producer or director of the films. Jessica Yu steadily makes very solid documentaries beginning with the Oscar-winning documentary short *Breathing Lessons: The Life and Work of Mark O'Brien* (1996). Her first hard-hitting social issue documentary is *Last Call at the Oasis* (2011), about the world's drinking water crisis, and she often directs television dramas. Her one-time employer Frieda Lee Mock also has an extensive filmography that includes five Oscar-nominated films. Women with high-profile names (as do men with high-profile names) have a bit more access to documentary-making and a shot at substantial careers. Alexandra Pelosi's (the daughter of US House Representative Nancy Pelosi) *Journeys with George* (2003) presented a homey and approachable portrait of George W. Bush on the campaign trail, and she has now made several films.

Chris Hegedus is a strong filmmaker in her own right, and in partnership with D. A. Pennebaker for thirty years, she commands great respect within the documentary community, but their films are less often referred to as Hegedus' than they are as Pennebaker's. Interestingly, she was drawn to documentary by seeing Drew Associates' *Jane*, described in Chapter 11. Hegedus' films with other filmmakers include *Startup.com* (2011) with Jehane Noujaim, a film about two young men who fail to get their internet start-up company off the ground. Possibly its candid intimacy of failure shared among young men is achieved only because it was made by two women. Reminiscent of Helen Van Dongen/Joris Ivens is Anne Drew, who has produced alongside Bob Drew for decades, and the work of Victoria Leacock or Valerie Lalonde, both of whom made films with Ricky Leacock in his later years. Lynne Novick has produced regularly with Ken Burns since 1989, but few know her name. Oppositely, Oscar-winners Susan Raymond and Alan Raymond are always referred to as just that: Alan and Susan Raymond, as is another husband-and-wife team Larry Hott and Diane Garey. Karen Goodman and Kirk Simon (also Oscar-winners) and Tia Lesson and Carl Deal are other successful male/female producing/directing teams.

348

A New History of Documentary Film

A woman filmmaker with a substantial number of credits as producer and director is Rory Kennedy who, often with producer/director Liz Garbus, has made over twenty-five documentaries since 1992. *A Boy's Life* (2004) is a portrait of the troubling forces that shaped the character of a seven-year-old boy from an impoverished region of Mississippi. The documentary follows two years in the life of Robert and his younger brother, Benji, as their grandmother, Anna, struggles to raise them. Their mother, who got pregnant as a teenager as the result of a rape, feels that she cannot care for her sons. The film recalls the feel of *Lalee's Kin: the Legacy of Cotton* and *Portrait of Jason* in its sympathetic approach to a child's ongoing problem. Kennedy also directed and produced *Pandemic: Facing AIDS* (2003), going to Uganda, Russia, Thailand, Brazil and India to show the wide differences between how these nations view the disease, the services they offer, the quality of life and chance for survival within each. Her other credits include *American Hollow* (1999), *The Changing Face of Beauty* (2000), *Thank You, Mr President: Helen Thomas at the Whitehouse* (2008) and *The Nazi Officer's Wife* (2003). *American Hollow*, made with Nick Doob, reveals a deep sympathy with the heart of Appalachian culture in the Eastern US. It tells the story of Tree Bowling, sixty-eight years old and mother of thirteen, who discusses life in the hollow through interviews and footage of her and her large family. Tree and her family are stuck in century-old traditions that have turned them into a family suffering from poverty and unemployment due to lack of opportunities and the crutch of government welfare. Many of her grandchildren dream of leaving once and for all, aware they are giving up a time-honoured heritage. *American Hollow* is another of Kennedy's many HBO productions.

Barbara Kopple has the most long-lived record of steady documentary-making success and public recognition, a feat in itself. Some of her company, Cabin Creek Films' credits include: a portrait of Woody Allen as a jazz musician, *Wild Man Blues* (1998); *Shut Up and Sing* (2006); *Bearing Witness* (2005), the story of combat photographer Molly Bingham, who was held prisoner at Abu Ghraib at the start of the Iraq War; *Woodstock Now and Then* (2009); a film for ESPN's prestigious sports documentary series 'Thirty for Thirty', *The House of Steinbrenner* (2010); and for HBO *Gunfight* (2011). None

Fig 84 Number Our Days *(1977) is an elegiac study of the aging members of the last remaining synagogue on the boardwalk in Venice, California by director Lynne Littman and producer Barbara Myerhoff. It won an Academy Award for Best Documentary Short*

of these has the raw power of her debut film *Harlan County, USA*, but her work is a testament to dedication, indomitable passion and persistence that Kopple brings to her films.

Shut Up and Sing is one of Kopple's best. In 2003, with anti-Iraq War feeling running high, the top-selling Texas-based band the Dixie Chicks (Natalie Maines, Emily Robison and Marcie Maguire) played a gig in London, during which Maines told the crowd that she was embarrassed that US President George W. Bush was from Texas. The comment was reported by a British paper and picked up by the US media, who lost no time in branding the Dixie Chicks as traitors, banning their songs from radio and turning them into figures reviled by right-wing political conservatives. Despite death threats and mounting pressure from their record company and corporate sponsors, the women refused to apologize. Instead they took a stand for free speech, eventually turning their experiences into a new, politically charged album. Directors Barbara Kopple and Cecilia Peck were granted classic cv/direct access to tell this story – the cameras are backstage with the women as the story breaks and there are many intimate moments. The film uses as a structural basis a cutting between the growing media furore in 2003 and the Dixie Chicks' older, wiser reunion in 2005.

Even as women and people of colour create more styles of documentary films on a wide array of subjects, most of their work generally gets less high-profile attention than that awarded to films made by men. This reflects the standard thinking of mainstream Hollywood media in which women directors and producers, along with people of colour, remain a minority. For most of the twenty-first century, of the roughly 13,400 members of Directors Guild of America, only about 1,000 (7%) are listed as female directors. Total female membership in the DGA, which includes people on the directing team such as assistant directors and unit production managers, is about 3,000 (22%). In 2003 Caucasian males directed more than 80% of US television episodes; of the 860 total episodes studied in 2002-3, Caucasian males directed 705 (82%); women directed 92 (11%); African-Americans 43 (5%); Latinos 14 (2%); and Asian-Americans directed 8 episodes (1%).

Admittedly, the documentary world is a far different place than episodic television. By nature, and continuing decades of tradition, many people who make documentaries embrace a social consciousness that welcomes minorities and women. In documentary pretty much anyone who can raise the money can get their film made, but completing any documentary accomplishes only two-thirds of the process – that is, funding and production. Distribution and exhibition are often daunting tasks, as Robert Flaherty learned but never took to heart, and which John Grierson mastered. In the international television market many documentary decision-makers are women. Not only at HBO/Cinemax, but in the US at POV and ITVS, PBS's long-running strands 'American Masters', 'American Experience' and The Discovery Channel, A&E, Bravo, Sundance, Lifetime and IFC, women often hold key decision-making positions. A big part of the reason for this is that after the 'golden years' of network television documentary in the 1950s and early 60s, nonfiction-making became a less visible, less profitable and less prestigious arena. Women were allowed into the 'ghetto' of documentary television since it was perceived as secondary to fiction and entertainment TV. When cable programming began, more women got jobs, accepting the low budgets and low salaries offered by the cable start-ups. Now some of them are in key executive positions and nurture younger women.

Experimental Documentary

A filmmaker whose work might be placed among documentary experiments is Chuck Workman, best known for the short *Precious Images* (1989). Commissioned to celebrate the fiftieth anniversary of Directors Guild of America, this glorious pastiche takes audiences on a whirlwind-of-editing trip through the history of American feature film. It is the soundtrack as much as the visuals, taken from movie soundtracks, that makes *Precious Images* stand apart. It won an Academy Award for Best Live Action Short Subject, but it is more rightly a documentary. This influential film played in thousands of theatres around the world, has been used as part of museum installations and continues to thrill audiences whenever it is seen. Workman has made dozens of these montage experiments, or 'clip shows' as the Hollywood industry calls them. His style, rooted in compilation film, is much imitated by others to create mass emotion-based entertainment. Other documentary work includes *Superstar: The Life and Times of Andy Warhol* (1990) and a summary of the early avant-garde in the US, *Jonas Mekas, and the (Mostly American) Avant Garde* (2009). He has a list of television credits for both documentaries and compilations; it is the latter at which he excels.

Jay Rosenblatt continues to break new ground not only with the compilation films previously mentioned, but also with a series of short live-action films that have documented his relationship with his young daughter and her filmmaking. These self-reflexive personal essay/experimental films originated when two-year-old Ella said she wanted to be a filmmaker. Turning four, her dad gave her a video camera for her birthday. *Beginning Filmmaking* (2008), another HBO film, takes the audience through one year of trying to teach a pre-schooler how to make a film. Ella rises to the challenge of filmmaking on her own terms. The joys and frustrations of being a parent and of being a child are chronicled, with one result being the message that everyone does have to be careful what they wish for. More experimental in nature are Rosenblatt's provocative compilation films *King of Jews* (2000), the most personal *Phantom Limb (2005),* and *Human Remains* (1998). The last addresses the horror of evil in a completely innovation way. Irony and occasional humour are threaded throughout a rapid montage compilation that brings to light the banality of evil by creating unusual portraits of five of the twentieth century's most reviled dictators. The film disturbingly unmasks the personal lives of Adolf Hitler, Benito Mussolini, Joseph Stalin, Francisco Franco and Mao Tse Tung. Historically accurate, but mundane, details of their everyday lives – their favourite foods, films, habits and sexual preferences – are the only subject of the documentary. There is no mention of their public personae or of their place in history, but Rosenblatt's intentional omission of the unspeakable acts for which these men were responsible becomes clear in a repeated closeup image of a shovel digging earth.

Su Friedrich has made more than a dozen films and is generally typed as an experimental filmmaker. She has been mixing forms for over thirty years with work such as *The Odds of Recovery* (2002), *The Head of a Pin* (2004), *Seeing Red* (2005) *and From The Ground Up* (2008). Her words about documentary vs. experimental films are worth noting:

> Of course, I run into problems naming what I do when I do something that relates to documentary, so I (sometimes) use the term begrudgingly. I don't know whether anyone could ever coin a term that would be large enough to embrace the huge range of work made under this current name, but I still have to say I dislike and disavow it.

Tarnation (2003), a first feature documentary by Jonathan Caouette, is very much an experiment. It is a critical darling and financial wonder created from Caouett's family home movies and found footage on Apple's i-movie system for a reported $187.00 or $218.32, depending on which publicity one reads. It exemplifies the mesh of self-reflexive documentary and experimental film in the early twenty-first century. Caouette was thirty-one when he morphed the surreal and shaky pieces of his regularly filmed life into a riveting self-reflexive documentary. Using self-filmed diary footage that stretches back to his 1970s childhood, along with re-enactments, collages of commercial films and other material, *Tarnation* presents the story of a schizophrenic mother, Renee, who was once a child-model and her son who is shuttled through abusive foster homes and who grows up gay in the middle of nowhere, USA. Through the intervention of established fiction filmmakers Gus Van Sant and John Cameron Mitchell, the film had its technical edges polished and became a sensation at Sundance, Toronto, the New York Film Festival and Cannes. *Tarnation* is perhaps the most narcissistic documentary ever made, at least in terms of the amount of screen time and reflection taken up by Caouette's image. *(David Holtzman's Diary* could top it, but see Chapter 12 for an explanation of that film's exempt status.) Roger Ebert, always the documentary champion, proclaimed it: 'A TRIUMPH! A film of remarkable power. One of the best documentaries of recent years.' The film is also charming in its matter-of-fact explanation of various family horrors through simple on-screen text. Spanning a twenty-year filmmaking period, *Tarnation* is an emotional, craftily edited pastiche that is made more powerful through its pop and rock score. (Did the $218.00 include the cost of music clearances?) A sequel to *Tarnation, Walk Away, Renee* is said to be forthcoming, but in 2011 Caouette claimed that he wanted to make no more documentaries.

Fig 85A

Fig 85A and B *In* Gimme Shelter *the 1970 film by Albert Maysles, David Maysles and Charlotte Zwerin, Keith Richards and Mick Jagger are being filmed. In the second picture a flatbed editing machine monitor reflects Jagger's face back at him as he watches. During the editing, Jagger is confronted with the image of the murder of a spectator by the Hell's Angels that took place while the Rolling Stones were onstage during a free concert at Altamont, California*

An aside about theatrical success and cv/direct ethics via rock documentaries

From 1961, when the National Film Board of Canada produced *Lonely Boy*, to Berlinger's and Sinofsky's 2004 psychological exposé of heavy metal stars Metallica in *Some Kind of Monster*, rock'n'roll and pop music have fascinated documentary-makers, and musicians have loved to be filmed. Notable music documentaries are not fiction films that use rock'n'roll, or straight-ahead filmed concerts, nor are they simply records of performances. These are fully realized creative efforts. Filmmakers such D. A. Pennebaker *(Don't Look Back,* Bob Dylan, 1967), Martin Scorsese *(The Last Waltz,* The Band, 1979), Taylor

Hackford *(Hail, Hail, Rock and Roll,* Chuck Berry, 1987), Penelope Spheeris *(The Decline of Western Civilization,* the punk movement, 1981), Jonathan Demme *(Stop Making Sense,* Talking Heads, 1985), Michael Apted *(Bring on the Night,* Sting, 1985), Wim Wenders *(Buena Vista Social Club,* 1999) and Jason Priestly *(Barenaked in America,* Barenaked Ladies, 2000) are only some of the well-known names who have made notable music films. There are dozens of such films, up to and including Davis Guggenheim's latest *From the Sky Down* (2011).

For many years the most financially successful theatrically released documentary – rock, music, or otherwise – was Warner Brothers' *Woodstock* (1970) by Michael Wadleigh. The film devotes almost as much screen time to the audience encamped on Yasgur's farmland in upstate New York as it does to its now-legendary musical performances. *Woodstock* thus is an informal sociological study of hippie culture. Its many split-screen images, its (for the time) thundering soundtrack, and the lure of its carefree approach to 'Peace, Love, and Music', as well as sex and drugs, made it a landmark and an inspiration for millions of young people. The iconography of *Woodstock* remains powerful. New versions of the concert have been staged and new documentaries made about those events, notably Barbara Kopple's *My Generation,* which began as a documentary of Woodstock '94. As she finished editing her Woodstock '94 footage, Woodstock '99 occurred: 'I took a deep breath and went and did '99 with a really small crew – one 16mm camera and two DV cameras', she has said. The result was a cross-generational look at all the factions that participated in the various Woodstocks. Wadleigh's original, which continues to generate income in revamped re-release and home video and DVD sales, remains as a seminal event in the history of American culture.

Wattstax (1973) is a bold documentary directed by Wolper alumnus Mel Stuart, produced by Wolper for Warner Brothers. This film of a concert staged in the summer of 1972 that drew over 100,000 people to the Los Angeles Coliseum featured performances by Stax Records soul stars such as Isaac Hayes, Albert King and the Staples Singers, as well as an appearance by Jesse Jackson. Intercut with the musical numbers are two contrapuntal threads: one of a group of black men discussing life questions in a local bar, another of raw standup comic newcomer Richard Pryor. *Wattstax* is an unusually frank and hip look at the mores and the problems of urban black Americans in the mid-1970s. Stuart achieved this insider's perspective by using a crew made up of as many black filmmakers as he could find (an almost unheard-of situation for a studio-backed film) and the result is a real-deal celebration of giant afros and swinging dashikis.

The flip side to *Woodstock*'s sunny view of the world (even during a downpour) is Albert and David Maysles', Charlotte Zwerin's and Muffie Meyers' *Gimme Shelter* (1970). Ostensibly the study of a free concert by the Rolling Stones at Altamont Speedway in Northern California, *Gimme Shelter* invokes the darkest moments of rock'n'roll as an enormous crowd surges out of control in response to Mick Jagger's 'Sympathy for the Devil' persona. At Altamont two people died in a hit-and-run auto accident, another drowned, and captured on film is the knife murder of an 18-year-old black spectator by the Hell's Angels, who were hired to provide concert security. Later in the film we see the filmmakers screening, rewinding and focusing in on this bit of footage as Jagger watches it on a flatbed editing machine. We, the film viewers, watch as the performer watches his performance and the filmmaker watches his own work, while an unknown someone is killed in front of us all. The murder becomes part not only of the filmed record, but also of a work of art. In this, it presages many controversies about capturing brutality and death on film and so-called reality television.

Michael Sragow, writing in 1990 for the magazine of the International Cinematographers Guild *ICG*, made the point that 'Pauline Kael and Vincent Canby led the [critical] charge against *Gimme Shelter* as an opportunistic snuff film, essentially saying that the filmmakers were complicit in the murder by having photographed it and subsequently profited from its theatrical release.' Their main criticism was that the concert was staged specifically to be filmed – and irresponsibly so. While conceding that the filmmakers had caught Jagger's 'feral intensity' with acute 'editing of the images to the music', Sragow quotes Kael writing that 'the filmed death at Altamont' was part of a 'cinéma vérité spectacular'. She condemned the movie with rhetorical questions: 'If events are created to be photographed, is the movie that records them a documentary, or does it function in a twilight zone? Is it the cinema of fact when the facts are manufactured for the cinema?'

Theatres and Festivals

There are many more documentaries seen in theatres in the twenty-first century than ever before. This book has noted that there are more of all types of moving image media available, but it is true that the percentage of documentary features playing in cinemas, measured against the number of fiction films in cinemas, has increased. Documentary shorts, however, remain in distribution/exhibition limbo. The following section details how a huge increase in film festivals, cultural institutions and theatrical documentaries are related.

The increased screening of documentaries in commercial theatres owes not a little to the rise in the number and quality of film festivals that showcase the form. There is a natural symbiosis between the popularity of documentaries and the popularity of documentary films in festivals. One feeds the other. From around 1995 with the success of *Hoop Dreams*, a pattern for launching 'big' documentaries became established, and a growing popular and critical interest in documentaries swept many titles from film festivals into multi-plexes. The late 1990s and early 2000s saw an exponential growth in the sheer number of festivals worldwide, and in the United States in particular. It is possible to be at a film festival in some part of the globe every day of the year. It is probably possible to be at a film festival in the United States every day of the year. These festivals in themselves create a niche market for documentaries, since every festival programmer is competing with others to have the premiere showing of any given film. And many festivals are now dedicated only to documentaries.

To use festivals and other public platforms to gain a theatrical release, the plan is this: (1) get the film accepted into a festival that provides high visibility for documentaries; (2) have a successful festival screening, audience 'buzz' and great reviews; (3) be acquired by a theatrical distributor, hopefully one that will pay an acquisition fee up-front, offer a reasonable percentage, and not require the filmmaker to put up money (for blowups, prints, promotion, etc.); (4) hope that the distributor prepares a good advertising and PR campaign; (5) personally become involved in the theatrical distribution strategy, i.e.

get the film opened in the right theatres in the right places, get more good reviews; and (6) receive royalty cheques from the distributor. Then move on to television sales, the educational market, and DVD/download sales. This all assumes that the filmmaker has a spectacularly good film that audiences want to see. The chance that events will play out as described above is almost nil. Most documentaries never make it past the first hurdle, and of the handful that do, most return very little money to the filmmaker.

There are variations on the theme: self-distribution, a gruelling business proposition that takes up to two years of grass-roots work (after the film is completed); or acquisition by a distributor who learns about the film prior to a festival screening, moving into theatres following success in the nontheatrical market.

Documentaries have been part of film festivals as long as there have been film festivals. There have also long been festivals devoted to documentary. Nyon, Switzerland was one of the first modern festivals to focus on the documentary. Originating in the trend for ciné-clubs, the Nyon Festival started in 1969, and by the end of the 1970s was well established. Other important festivals for documentary in the twentieth century were Rotterdam, Holland, and in the US the Margaret Mead Film Festival, held at New York's Metropolitan Museum. Although the focus of the last is the anthropological film, it was a serious showcase for many varieties of documentary long before other film festivals celebrated the form, and it remains an important venue.

In the past two decades in the United States, no festival has been more responsible for the explosion of interest and commercial exposure for documentaries than Sundance. Robert Redford, its founder, has always supported, talked about and embraced documentaries. Sundance eventually provided the same legitimization and commercialization to documentaries that it earlier bestowed on independent fiction films. In 2004, Stacy Peralta's *Riding Giants*, an exploration of surfing culture, was the first documentary ever to be the Sundance opening night film. Peralta had a previous hit at Sundance and in theatres with *Dogtown and Z Boys* (2002), his homage to the skateboarding culture of his youth in Santa Monica, California. The 2004 opening night event was another signal that the documentary had arrived in terms of Hollywood's independent film scene. And in 2011, the Toronto

Film Festival opening night was for the first time a documentary, Davis Guggenheim's U2 film *From the Sky Down*.

Sundance is only one of the proliferation of film festivals around the world that are known for their documentaries, or exclusively screen documentaries, but it provides an example of the type, form and content of the documentary in relation to film festivals today. Approximately 862 documentaries were submitted to Sundance in 2010, sixteen were selected for the main competition, and a handful more played out of competition. That means that each year hundreds of feature-length documentaries are floating around seeking a festival home. There are other important festivals for documentaries of course: Toronto, Cannes, SXSW, New York, Tribeca and Silver Docs, Berlin and Full Frame.

An example of a documentary greatly helped by Sundance was *Capturing the Friedmans* by Andrew Jarecki, which was awarded the grand jury prize for documentaries in 2004. Later it was shown on HBO and released in theatres with limited success. Because it deals with the sensitive issue of child molestation in an ambiguous, reflexive, non-traditional way, the film was not a likely candidate for theatrical release. Its somewhat controversial approach, in which the filmmaker does not take a clear stand on the guilt or innocence of the convicted child molesters, led to critical debate in the press. 'Winning the prize [Sundance] got the film invited to other festivals. And it hiked up the profile a notch, which is very important for difficult films with difficult subjects that are hard enough to sell,' said Jarecki. The list of significant North American documentaries that have premiered at Sundance is impressive. It includes, among others, Ross McElwee's *Sherman's March* (1987), Al Reinert's *For All Mankind* (1989), Mark Kitchell's *Berkeley in the Sixties* (1990), Barbara Kopple's *American Dream* (1991), Joe Berliner and Bruce Sinofsky's *Brother's Keeper* (1992), Terry Zwigoff's *Crumb* (1995), Leon Gast's *When We Were Kings* (1996), Kirby Dick's *Sick* (1997), Liz Garbus and Jonathan Stack's *The Farm* (1998), Morgan Spurlock's *Super Size Me* (2004), James Marsh's *Man on Wire* (2008), Davis Guggenheim's *Waiting for Superman* (2010), Jeffrey Friedman's and Rob Epstein's *Paragraph* 175 (2000), Chris Smith's *Home Movie* (2001), Doug Pray's *Scratch* (2002), Steve James' *Stevie* (2003) and others which, like many of the other documentaries that premiered there, have been little seen since their opening.

The most significant documentary festival in Europe in the twenty-first century is the International Documentary Film Festival Amsterdam, most ably run by Ally Derks. It is a huge, comprehensive world festival that attracts public and professionals alike to almost two weeks of screenings in several theatres. It also includes an important film market and the original 'Forum' pitching sessions. In Asia, Yamagata, held every other year in Japan, is perhaps the most prestigious. The leading documentary film festival in South America is called 'It's All True', headed by Amir Labaki. It is held in Brazil in Rio do Janeiro and Sao Paulo. Hot Docs is the leader in Canada and in England, it is Sheffied Doc Fest. There are literally hundreds of film festivals around the world that feature documentaries almost exclusively. The most charming name – and one that brings documentary history full circle – Flahertyiana in Perm, Russia.

Fig 86 *Robert Flaherty wearing his Borsalino hat, near the end of his life.*
International Film Seminars

Chapter Related Films

1978
Gates of Heaven (US, Errol Morris)
1988
The Thin Blue Line (US, Morris)
Precious Images (US, Chuck Workman)
1996
Paradise Lost: The Child Murders at Robin Hood Hills (US, Joe Berlinger and Bruce
    Sinofsky)
1997
Little Dieter Needs To Fly (US and Germany, Werner Herzog)
1998
Four Little Girls (US, Spike Lee)
Human Remains (US, Jay Rosenblatt)
1999
American Hollow (US, Rory Kennedy and Nick Doob)
2000
The Eyes of Tammy Faye (US, Fenton Bailey and Randy Barbato)
Paradise Lost 2: Revelations (US, Berlinger and Sinofsky)
2002
The Fog of War: Eleven Lessons from the Life of Robert S. McNamara (US, Morris)
2003
Capturing the Friedmans (US, Andrew Jarecki)
Journeys with George (US, Alexandra Pilosi)
Shut Up and Sing (US, Barbara Kopple)
2004
Gunner Palace (US, Michael Tucker and Petra Epperlein)
The White Diamond (US, UK, Herzog)
Tarnation (US, Jonathan Caouette)
Super Size Me (US, Morgan Spurlock)
2005
Murderball (US, Henry Alex Rubin and Dana Adam Shapiro)
Enron: The Smartest Guys in the Room (US, Alex Gibney)
The Power of Nightmares: The Politics of Fear (UK, Adam Curtis)
Grizzly Man (Herzog)
2006
An Inconvenient Truth (US, Davis Guggenheim)
When the Levees Broke (US, Lee)
Shut Up and Sing (US, Kopple)
2007
No End in Sight (US, Charles Ferguson)
Taxi to the Dark Side (US, Alex Gibney)
2008

Beginning Filmmaking (US, Rosenblatt)
Man on Wire (France, US, James Marsh)
2009
It Might Get Loud (US, Guggenheim)
2010
Waiting for Superman (US, Guggenheim)
How to Fold a Flag (US, Tucker and Epperlein)
Restrepo (UK, US, Sebastian Junger and Tim Hetherington)
Inside Job (US, Ferguson)
Crude (US, Berlinger)
If God is Willing and Da Creek Don't Rise (US, Lee)
Poster Girl (US, Sarah Nesson and Mitchell Block)
Freedom Riders (US, Stanley Nelson)
2011
Cave of Forgotten Dreams (Herzog)
No Contract, No Cookies: The Stella D'Oro Strike (US, Jon Alpert)
Sarah Palin: You Betcha (US, Nick Broomfield and Joan Churchill)

Chapter Related Books

Bloom, Livia, ed., *Errol Morris: Interviews*. Mississippi: University of Mississippi Press, 2010.

Cronin, Paul and Werner Herzog, *Herzog on Herzog*. New York: Faber and Faber, 2003.

Levy, Emmanuel, *Strange Than Fiction: Michael Moore, Barbara Kopple, Errol Morris and the New Documentary Filmmakers* (not yet released)

McCreadle, Marsha, *Documentary Superstars*. New York: Allworth Press, 2011.

Rothman, William, *Three Documentary Filmakers: Errol Morris, Ross McElwee, Jean Rouch*. Albany, NY: State University of New York Press, 2009.

16

Now and When

During its long journey from a single screening to a world now blanketed – perhaps smothered – by moving image information and opinion, documentary has given voice to both charlatans and truth-tellers; it has gathered acolytes and debunkers, shaken up populations, and kept them in line. It has changed the lives of individuals and the course of society. All the while, it has recorded the actual sounds and images of the world. The history of documentary is far from simple or straightforward, even though this book presents a historically organized chronicle of major works and trends that shaped the field. The complexity of that field has become ever more pronounced in the twenty-first century. There are so many types of work laying claim to the term 'documentary', so many practitioners of the form, and so many ancillary 'documentary' activities, that the more one examines it, the more confused the label might seem. In this, documentary is much like other aspects of our post-post-modern world: extremely rich in data and nuance that sometimes falls into the bathos of self-importance.

Documentary films are different from other media because the force driving the most dedicated documentarians has always been, and remains, a deep desire to shed light on the very issues, people, places and processes that make the world so complex. Grierson or Flaherty might not recognize the technology or the politics at work, but they would certainly identify with filmmakers' motivations in the twenty-first century. They knew that as individuals who belong to an increasingly global society, we can best affect what we best understand, and we bear an increasing responsibility for the ways our personal actions affect the entire world. In terms of promoting social change, documentary film remains one of the most effective ways to enhance understanding on a mass level. Nothing else can so fully reveal one part of the world to another. Documentary also provides its own singular aesthetic and emotional pleasures. For these reasons, and others, it is worth the effort to make sense of the documentary now, to linger on the history that shaped it, and to speculate on its possible future.

Even though this book deals mainly with Great Britain, the United States and Canada, documentary has long been a more global form than suggested by these geographical/political entities. Globalization has made what was always an international movement the province of every part of the earth. Worldwide access to documentary is due in no small part to advances in technology and economic changes – the same factors that drove every phase of cinema's growth.

Rapid changes have also affected funding, distribution and exhibition. High-definition cameras and screens, hundreds of cable and satellite channels, internet exhibition, and video-on-demand are all realities. At the same time that Hollywood spends more and more millions for special effects spectacle in simplistic fiction features, documentaries of all kinds are made at much lower cost. Some, on the level of 2004's theatrical success *Super Size Me*, are produced for $100,000 or less, and screen at festivals, in cinemas, and in homes. Many others, made with much smaller budgets, reach smaller audiences, but all are giving voice to makers who have never before been heard.

As access to equipment for production, distribution and exhibition becomes more universal, the documentary world expands and reconfigures in surprising ways. Just as many developing countries skipped the second stage of the telecommunications chain – jumping from no telephones at all to mobile phones, without ever stopping at landline phones – some filmmakers leapt from no access to media-making to complete access to a world stage. In 2004, Arab Muslim terrorists filmed the beheading of foreign hostages and put the images on the internet for all to see, creating a few moments of 'actualities' indeed. It is absurd to think of these terrorists having the access or ability to do the same with 35mm or 16mm cameras, or without the internet as a distribution mechanism. Because of the presence of mobile phone cameras, the 2009 death of Neda Agda-Soltan during the Iranian election process instantly became a worldwide story and human rights cause. It was called by *Time* magazine 'The most widely witnessed death in human history'. The downside of these reports is that they are in no way documentaries. They are not journalism. They are actuality documents much like early silent film actualities, some of which later become parts of fully realized documentaries.

Another interesting sidelight to the world's big technological leaps is the fact that in the USSR the domination of the top-down Soviet system of centralized filmmaking from the teens through the 1980s dictated that documentaries intended for theatrical release were made with 35mm equipment. Professional documentary, education, production, distribution and exhibition were supported by the Communist systems, and beautiful, meaningful, and occasionally subversive films were made and seen. After the dissolution of the USSR the technical leap was from 35mm to portable video with little stopover at 16mm. Television used some 16mm, but the vast output of Soviet regional documentaries in gorgeous 35mm will never be repeated.

It always takes some time, and much trial and error, to find the best uses for new equipment and new means of expression. Most internet documentaries have progressed little further than snippets – thankfully most are more productive than terrorist acts. And the internet is vital now to documentary. Working documentarians and many individual films have their own websites supporting, and in some cases surpassing, the usefulness of the primary film. A recent trend is online fund-raising through social media sites. Historically, no new technology immediately begets great artistry, but better online documentaries are coming, hopefully building on long-tested documentary practices, as new ideas are explored.

Aesthetics and Content

The aesthetic questions that always arise with the introduction of new technologies also continue to shift. It is often claimed that much is lost – visually, aurally and artistically – with the cheaper, easier-to-use equipment. This is true. *Super Size Me* feels more like a home movie than a finished work meant to be screened in theatres, although it was successful there, grossing over $7 million. Perhaps the cute and catchy home movie aesthetic was the intention of the filmmaker, Morgan Spurlock. Probably the story – of the consequences of its maker eating nothing but fast food from McDonald's for a month – would not have been made without the cheap technology. Would it have been better not to tackle this issue at all than to have it exist in a rough form? Is it better to drink wine from a poor vintage than to drink no wine at all? The answer perhaps is that every vintner must take care to do the best job possible with the grapes at hand, and every consumer must make their own valuation. In the case of *Super Size Me*, audiences embraced the film, both for its comedy and its social comment. McDonald's does now post its exorbitant calorie counts on its menus, but the number of its customers and its corporate profits continue to grow. The danger for the documentary lies not in using the newest, most accessible technologies, but in being careless with their use. Just because something seems simple does not mean that it does not deserve to be used with care and respect. It is possible, for example, to light beautifully for mini-DV, just as it is possible to shoot without any regard for the lighting. Unfortunately most people choose the latter, easier route.

Audiences have been conditioned for several generations to accept certain aesthetic qualities as part of documentary. They are unlikely to reject a nonfiction film combined with the techniques of fiction film simply because it has less than perfect image quality, sound or editing techniques, or because it promotes a first-person point of view. However, aesthetically ugly images increasingly dominate as audiences come to accept low quality. Documentaries have long been victim of being judged solely for their content rather than for their skilful use of film techniques. It is almost axiomatic that the perfectly produced documentary on a less-than-emotionally compelling subject will be bested in competition for prizes and audience acceptance by the less well-made film that moves an audience to tears. The best documentaries, just as the best fiction films, manage to combine high-level skill with story and emotion. Although Grierson sometimes decried the artifice of technique, documentarians such as Humphrey Jennings and Alberto Cavalcanti, even when they worked for him, tried very hard to combine the best available technique with a passion for their subject. Experimental film also continues to push boundaries within documentary. Jay Rosenblatt, especially with his remarkable compilation shorts *Darkness & Day* (2009) and *Human Remains* (1998), has moved the classic compilation technique past historical comparison, past pastiche, and into a realm of art that pulls at the darkest of human thought.

Content-wise there have been shifts towards worldwide democratization of documentary. In some cases this has meant a move to better understanding of the complexities of our linked globe. *FRONTLINE/World* (1998–2010), for example, was a US public TV series that profiled countries and cultures seldom seen on American television. Springing from the original WGBH *FRONTLINE*, each episode of *FRONTLINE/World* featured two or three short stories told by an ethnically diverse group of video-journalists. With portable digital cameras, these correspondents roamed the world, observing and filming, sometimes surreptitiously. This idea has been reiterated recently by the Current TV channel. ITVS International, with its mandate for diversity, launched the 'Global Perspectives' project in 2005. This is a two-way exchange that brings documentaries from other nations to US audiences and delivers independent US documentaries to audiences abroad through public and cable television, online and outreach partners. More than eighty fiction films and documentaries have been partially funded through this programme.

In other cases, globalization of documentary has meant little to increasing understanding among cultures. The subjects most easily transported to all parts of the world are often those which are least offensive to mass audiences. Nature documentaries, because they rely on no human language, have an international currency that transcends any border. This can translate into advantages for some 'message' films, as was the case with the anti-dolphin killing *The Cove* (2009), but can be rather meaningless in a case such as *March of the Penguins* (2005), in which animals become anthropomorphized Disney-like characters. Stories of adventure, ancient civilizations, natural wonders, unexplained phenomena are also easier to sell cross-culturally, and fascination with every detail of WWII seems to permeate society, sixty-five years after conflict ended. It is the politically and personally challenging analyses of recent historical and current events that are hard to explain across cultures. Documentaries on these subjects create the most controversy, if they get seen.

Finance

International co-production became a buzzword in the documentary field of the 1990s. In most cases the term meant international co-financing rather than actual production. In its simplest form, television entities from various countries invest money with a production company (usually based in one country) to buy the rights to telecast a film that has yet to be made or is in some stage of production – in effect, presales. The finished documentary takes shape depending upon the amounts of monies involved and the varying power of the investors and the production company. In Europe this system was a fairly natural outgrowth of the meshing of separate countries into the European Union. The NFB has, as it tends to do, institutionalized the globalization trend with a mandate decreeing that a specific percentage of all its productions be made with international co-financing monies. Canada is now well known for its co-production efforts.

For US producers, operating independently, the challenge is greater. While European co-productions are facilitated by European Union economic incentives, documentarians in the US are both aided and penalized by international co-production. Some enterprising producers are savvy enough to find financing from any place on earth, but the trade laws and cultural quotas of other nations do not facilitate the funding of US productions. Many nations mandate that the majority of their media funding go to 'native' producers. Conversely, US television entities, even public television, have no restrictions about paying for programming from foreign sources. These policies make sense in the Hollywood-dominated fiction world. The hegemony of such US media giants is obvious, and fought by those who wish to retain separate cultural identities. However, the same exclusionary formulas are also often applied to independent US documentarians who do not have the same clout nor the same objectives as major corporate producers.

The market for completed documentaries on television internationally is fairly large. Networks and stations around the world buy thousands of nonfiction shows. According to the trade publication *The Hollywood Reporter* in October 2003, prices to license documentaries (of all types) for broadcast ranged from $2,000 to $5,000 in the Middle East, $1,000 to $7,500 in Eastern Europe, $5,000 to $15,000 in Japan, and a high of $25,000 to $50,000 in the UK. The films are sold by a variety of individual producers, sales representatives, television networks and large production entities at markets like Docs For Sale at IDFA (International Documentary Film Festival Amsterdam) and Sunny Side of the Doc in Marseilles. The traditional international television market MIP, which takes place each year in Cannes, added a special separate two-day MIPDOC session in the mid-1990s specifically for the buying and selling of documentaries. Many of these are nature films and other types of nonfiction that might well not be categorized as documentary (cooking shows or travelogues, for example), but important social issue documentaries, too, ultimately make money when sold to international television. International television sales are often the largest source of revenue for any documentary from any English language-speaking country.

Today's international documentary scene also includes a large number of public pitching events and conferences designed to help filmmakers co-produce their work with partners from different countries. These emerged in the late 1980s from events such as the Amsterdam Forum, running within IDFA, and from the three International Documentary Congresses organized in the late 1990s by the Academy of Motion Picture Arts and Sciences and the International Documentary Association in Los Angeles. There are documentary training initiatives funded by the European Union's MEDIA (e.g. Eurodoc), Discovery Campus Master schools, the Banff Television Festival in Canada, etc. The original pitching forum was so popular in Amsterdam that it successfully expanded to a sister forum at the Hot Docs Festival in Toronto, Canada. There are also specialized for-profit multi-day conferences for history documentary producers, science documentary producers, wildlife documentary producers, and the like.

There is a flip side to the argument that an increasingly global culture and international funding results in a healthier production landscape for documentaries. Leslie Woodhead, in a critique for the website Docos.com in 2001, said:

> In his remarkable series of diaries recording the subtle corruptions of daily life in Nazi Germany, Victor Klemperer notes how curious it is that

at the moment when modern technology annuls frontiers and distances (flying, wireless, television, economic interdependence) the most extreme nationalism is raging. They (these words) were written more than 60 years ago, in 1938. At the beginning of the 21st century, it is hard to avoid the evidence that those same forces of new technology and international business, far from extending our understanding and our tolerances, are shutting down our horizons. More and more, it seems, the Global Village is patrolled and ring-fenced by the Global Market. The evidence for that mounting insularity is clear and disturbing in the tough new environment for television documentary. Commissioners and schedulers regret that international stories don't get the big audiences; ratings-hungry networks gorge on the overnight returns for material, which exploits the most intimate doings of the people closest to home. In a time when even the most public-spirited broadcasters seem frozen in the headlights of ratings and profits, the space for documentary to explore difficult issues in faraway places shrinks every year.

Documentary Un-reality

As has been pointed out, examples of faux documentary are found throughout its history. The purposes and techniques involved in making such films vary, but there have been many attempts to fool audiences, to comment on documentary technique and the authenticity of moving images, to surprise audiences and to let them in on a joke. And while they have generated serious debate and comic comment over the decades, these films are today a widely accepted cinema subset, regardless of whether they are called fake documentary, staged documentary, pseudo-documentary or faux documentary, or in the sometimes cruel spirit of the twenty-first century, mockumentary, even shockumentary.

One name that does not apply to this sort of film in this book and in our era is docudrama, particularly when discussing work in Canada and the US. Docudramas are fiction films that are based on events that occurred or were imagined to have occurred in the past; and they are fully scripted, cast, acted, and often do not use documentary styles. When they do employ documentary styles, the makers are not trying to create something that will be perceived as anything other than a partly or wholly fictionalized account of events that happened or to people who live/d. In other words, the makers do not intend the audience to believe that the dialogue or costuming, for example, are authentic. Docudramas often do contain factual information and references, and they sometimes include employing nonactors as participants or shooting at authentic locations. It is sometimes difficult to draw a line between docudrama and faux documentary, and debate over definitions continues, but in this context faux documentaries are categorized as belonging to the documentary tradition and docudramas are not. Docudramas have stronger links to fiction films and should be considered in a category of their own. In the UK, the documentary drama is a somewhat different animal, partly because of a history rooted in using television as a dramatically staged educational medium that contrasts with the often-melodramatic needs of North American commercial networks.

At the end of the nineteenth century, faking events for short actualities was common. In January 1898, the battleship *USS Maine* was near Cuba to 'safeguard American interests', even as Secretary of the Navy, John D. Long insisted that it was only making a friendly call. A mysterious explosion destroyed the *Maine* while it sat in Havana harbour, killing many aboard. Although the cause of the explosion was unknown, America became bitten by war fever, and blamed the Spanish in Cuba for the attack (this despite the fact that many Spanish ships sent out lifeboats to rescue survivors of the explosion). The young film industry immediately began to exploit the drama inherent in this event and thus furthered public outrage in order to sell more films to theatre owners. The Biograph Co. reacted to the sinking by taking their existing film *Battleships 'Iowa' and 'Massachusetts'* (December 1897) and simply retitling it *Battleships 'Maine' and 'Iowa'* (February 1898). This retitled version was described in the Biograph sales catalogue: 'This scene embodies probably the only moving picture extant of the ill-fated battleship *Maine* blown up in Havana harbour. It was taken, together with the *Iowa*, in the Brooklyn Navy Yard but a few days before the *Maine*'s departure for the South. Most of the men shown in the picture were killed by the explosion under the

Maine.' In other words, Biograph renamed the ship in their existing actuality footage to fit the immediate need for a 'documentary' about the sinking of the *Maine*. Biograph lied; audiences watched, but we do not know if they questioned.

War against Spain was declared by the US Congress in April 1898, and the Vitagraph Company, eager to be a part of growing war film frenzy, produced *Tearing Down the Spanish Flag*, clearly a staged event. The film was simply a closeup of the hand of Vitagraph executive J. Stuart Blackton pulling down a Spanish flag and hoisting the US flag in its place. 'It was taken in a 10 x 12 studio room, the background a building next door,' Blackton explained in a lecture at the University of Southern California in 1929. 'We had a flagpole and two 18-inch flags. [Albert E.] Smith, another Vitagraph executive operated the machine and I, with this very hand, grabbed the Spanish flag and tore it down from the pole and pulled the Stars and Stripes to the top of the flagpole. That was our very first dramatic picture and it is surprising how much dramatic effect it created … the people went wild.' *Battleships 'Maine' and 'Iowa'* was a faux documentary; *Tearing Down the Spanish Flag* was a drama.

Early in the conflict Biograph cameramen, including Billy Bitzer, were sent to Cuba to film the scenes of the war. Actual footage of marching troops, the *Maine* wreckage, and other non-combat scenes were shot. Bitzer, beginning what in the future became a modus operandi for some war zone cameramen, apparently spent much of his time on William Randolph Heart's press yacht being entertained by Hearst and his entourage of young ladies. Blackton and Smith also went to Cuba, where they followed Teddy Roosevelt and his Rough Riders on the 'charge' up San Juan Hill. At one point the filmmakers realized that the sound overhead was sniper bullets, not the buzzing of tropical bugs as they thought, and they soon returned to the US. According to the Library of Congress website, 'The risk was far too great for cameramen to film actual battles in the Spanish-American War but the studios capitalized on the public's interest by filming re-enactments of the conflicts.' National Guard troops recreated several scenes in New Jersey, including an attack on a Spanish scouting party in *Cuban Ambush* and Spanish soldiers executing Cuban rebels in *Shooting Captured Insurgents* (both1898).

The difficulties of capturing combat footage have made re-enactment of battle in documentaries a subject of debate in every ensuing decade, from

WWI (see the discussion of *Battle of the Somme* in Chapter 1) through WWII (*The Battle of San Pietro* in Chapter 7) to present-day questions about terrorist website posts. Most of what is presented as documentary combat footage is just that, brought to audiences in spite of the obstacles of unwieldy equipment and great personal danger, first by cameramen and, since the 1980s covert US wars in Central America, camerawomen, both those officially working for a government and those filming without authority.

Fake documentaries are not limited to the subject of war; they exist on a myriad of topics. According to Raymond Fielding, in his book *The March of Time, 1935–1951*:

> For every genuine news film photographed under difficult and sometimes dangerous conditions, an equal amount of energy was spent by the same producers to fake outstanding news events of the day … realistically staged re-creations of famous events, based upon reliable information and duplicating insofar as possible the location, participants, and circumstances of the original. These films were generally designed to deceive audiences.

In films other than combat, though, faux documentaries often are not meant to directly deceive, rather they contain a strong element of self-consciousness that seeks to subvert documentary conventions. While using the stylistic techniques of documentary, they often seek to question the 'truth' of all documentary films. Sometimes these films are parodies, 'a work that broadly mimics a characteristic style and holds it up to ridicule'. One of the best of these parodies is the famous 1957 April Fool's Day BBC *Panorama* television series segment by cameraman Charles De Jaeger and producer David Wheeler about the bumper Alpine spaghetti harvest. As the camera shows the harvesting by local girls, presenter Richard Dimbleby notes, in his sonorous BBC announcer's voice, that 'After picking, the spaghetti is laid out to dry in the warm, Alpine sun'. Recently treehugger.com, a website of the slow food movement, posted tongue-in cheek: 'One of the earliest and most important documentaries on local food and cultural practices was this classic, one of the first studies of the importance of climate (there was a really mild winter that year), culture and food, rolled into two minutes of cinematic history.' BBC has followed up on reactions to the spaghetti trees segment for decades and reports from viewers who thoroughly believed the film can be found on its website. Any artistic form can be parodied. Mel Brooks mastered the western in *Blazing Saddles* and the monster movie in *Young Frankenstein*. Similarly Woody Allen parodies science fiction in *Sleeper* and the documentary in *Zelig*. Parodies like these are meant to make audiences laugh, and on that level the finest documentary parody is *This Is Spinal Tap* (1984).

As its premise, young filmmaker and Spinal Tap fan Marty D. Berg sets out to capture, in his words, 'the sights, the sounds, and the smells' of a workhorse British rock band named Spinal Tap. With a small crew by his side, Marty films the group during their first US tour in six years. The result of Marty's vision is a documentary that is humorous, shocking, and completely made-up. *This Is Spinal Tap* is actually Rob Reiner's directorial debut. After having been granted unprecedented access to the band's tour, Marty captures the day-to-day grind of what it means to be fading rock stars on tour. In addition to concert and behind-the-scenes footage, Marty interviews the three principals of Spinal Tap: lead singer David St Hubbins (Michael McKean), guitarist Nigel Tufnel (Christopher Guest) and bassist Derek Smalls (Harry Shearer), all three of whom are the film's co-writers. *Spinal Tap* even includes 'archival images' of earlier incarnations of the band from better days in the 1960s and 70s. *This Is Spinal Tap* is constructed to resemble a genuine low-budget rock music documentary, except that the tone, instead of being earnest, is gently mocking. Spinal Tap became a cult band with a power to live on in the 'real' world, spawning a fan base, websites and merchandize. Christopher Guest went on to appropriate its mock-documentary form successfully in *Best in Show* (2000), *Waiting for Guffman* (1996) and *A Mighty Wind* (2003), documentary parodies of dog shows, community theatre and folk music, respectively.

Other fiction feature films and many television programmes that have appropriated documentary's aural and visual conventions for various enter-tainment objectives include: *The Rutles* (1978), which parodies the Beatles, *Hard Core Logo* (1996), *The Blair Witch Project* (1999), *Borat: Cultural Learnings of America for Make Benefit Glorious Nation of Kazakhstan* (2006), and *Incident at Loch Ness* (2004), in which Werner Herzog archly attempts to parody his own filmmaking style. These and many others are similar in their use of documentary form to create films that audiences are expected to understand are faked and are expected to enjoy with a grain of salt. Other faux documentaries operate on more serious levels and intend other results.

Peter Watkins

The films of Peter Watkins are among the most challenging ever made in documentary, or any other cinematic form. At least since *The Forgotten Faces*, his 1961 short, through today, his films challenge convention and they do it in a very deliberate reasoned way that represents his own highly structured and iterated media theories. All of his films have either been documentary or drama presented with documentary techniques, sometimes portraying historical occurrences and sometimes possible near-future events, as if contemporary reporters and filmmakers were there to interview the participants. Watkins pioneered this technique in his first full-length television film *Culloden* (1964), which portrayed the Jacobite uprising of 1745 (the attempt by Charles Edward Stuart to regain the British throne) in the then-contemporary style of a news broadcast about the Vietnam War. With the success of *Culloden*, the BBC commissioned him to make what became his best-known film, *The War Game*, which was released theatrically and won the 1966 Academy Award for Best Documentary Feature. In this film Watkins places the viewer in the subjective position of the confused soldiers, who have no real idea of how the battle is going. Using medium closeups of soldiers' faces and few establishing long shots, he refuses to provide a clear overview of the action. This form, which is also the basis of *The Forgotten Faces*, allowed Watkins to place the action in a context that could not be signposted by familiar landmarks of place or time. The incongruous presence of news cameras on an eighteenth-century battlefield became irrelevant as viewers were drawn into the conflict. Watkins continues to use this aesthetic throughout his work, filming events from the past, the present, and the possible future as if they were contemporary news events. *The War Game* (1965) is Watkins' most emotionally powerful use of these techniques. Viewers see vague, often hazy or grainy long shots that could be from any number of locations, medium closeups of individuals, little traditional cross-cutting and preference for random events over psychological character development.

The War Game was banned by the BBC, which refused to broadcast it until 1985. Due to this and other instances of what he characterizes as black-balling by the television and critical establishments, Watkins has lived and worked in self-imposed exile from England since the mid-1960s. Great public debate surrounded the cancellation of the film's broadcast. Although the BBC is, by charter, free from government influence, it receives this charter and its funding from central government. *The War Game* was screened for government representatives prior to the broadcast date, and pressures were brought to bear to prevent its being shown. Other private screenings were held from which came varied opinions, specifically that the film was too powerfully shocking for audiences to handle and that it played into the hands of England's anti-nuclear activists who were very prominently in the news at the time. Over the years, the BBC did make the film available to film societies, limited theatrical release, educational and festival screenings.

Official distress over *The War Game* came not only from the realistic treatment of horrific events. The British government maintained and maintains a pro-nuclear weapons defensive strategy. *The War Game* is adamantly anti-nuke. The film also portrays the response of the official agencies and individuals as laughably inadequate, and the information given to the public as lies. In this it is similar to the 2005 BBC fictional production *Dirty War* that dramatizes the inadequacies of response to the explosion of a terrorist bomb in London.

The charges of censorship and suppression may have moved members of the Academy to award an Oscar to *The War Game* as much as did its shocking content and challenging form. Obviously, the nominating committee knew that the events portrayed never actually occurred. In recognizing Watkins' work as a documentary, they took a chance at broadening the definition of the term. There was probably also a sentiment that this is one of those films that everyone should have the chance to see and that the award would facilitate that. Although it is not a Soviet Union vs. NATO war, the twenty-first century world faces a continued, possibly less manageable, threat from nuclear war. The lack of government preparedness for catastrophic events is more apparent than ever in the mid-1960s, when many people harboured complacency about the ability of our bureaucracies to handle any problem. The disaster of the official response to Hurricane Katrina has shown that this faith, like that of the survivability of nuclear war, is false. Amazon.com used the appalling term 'shockumentary' in its headline description of the *The War Game*. It is not that. Nor can it be classified with most of the other recent films in which documentary conventions are used to trick, ridicule or dramatize life. Almost none of these contain the sophisticated comment on media itself that characterize Watkins' work. His films comprise a body of original cinematic works that are hard to categorize.

Watkins has struggled to have his films seen, as well as to continue making films. He spent many years developing a critical manifesto against what he calls 'Monoform', the dominant media language of film, television and the web in which audiences are pummelled by endless sounds, images and rapid, seamless editing. He continues to evolve a stylistic critique that questions the 'reality' of media images; even to the point of having performers in his later films question the director about the purpose of the work.

The staged documentary, using conscious reflexivity and self-reflexivity, has been explored and reworked dozens of times since Watkins made *The War Game*, among them Watkins' own *Punishment Park* (1971) and his overly theoretical and rather tedious *La Commune* (2000). Other notable films that can be grouped with them include *Daughter Rite, ...No Lies* (discussed in Chapter 12), Orson Welles' *F for Fake* (1973), Peter Greenaway's *The Falls* (1987), William Greaves' *Symbiopsychotaxiplasm* (1968) and its sequel *Symbiopsychotaxiplasm: Take 2 1/2* (1998), Barry Spinello's *Rushes* (1979), Mitchell Block's *Speeding?: A Film About Driver Safety* (1978), and Eleanor Antin's *From the Archives of Modern Art: A Documentary Fiction* (2005).

Intimate Doings of Reality

It has been posited that part of the wide audience enthusiasm for documentaries in theatres beginning in the 1980s lies in the fact that commercial television so embraced 'reality' shows like MTV's *Real World, Survivor, Big Brother,* and on downward to *Extreme Makeover*, that a ready-made audience accepted the conventions of Michael Moore and other first-person documentarians as ordinary entertainment. There is a devolving and skewed road leading from the founders of cv/direct to the frenzy of TV reality shows, with many stops of self-reflexivity on the way. An example of such a trajectory begins with Frederick Wiseman's *Law and Order* (see Chapter 15), plus Jon Alpert's 1969-70 series of cv/d films on the Pittsburgh Police Department, and continues with Alan and Susan Raymond's *Police Tapes*, which foreshadows Malcolm Barbour's and John Langley's *Cops*. Wiseman looks at the institution of the police with his distanced vérité approach. *Police Tapes* is a serious, yet character-driven, personal and sobering vérité view of the very real threats to policemen. *Cops*, on the other hand, earned an online review in which it was observed that 'Cops is always more fun when you are a tad inebriated yourself; this collection (*Cops: Caught in the Act*, 1989) can be enjoyed simply for the fact that some people can be very, very stupid, and, as a bonus, these people are not you.' *Cops* has played successfully on the Fox network for over twenty-five years, and has generated numerous spin-offs and copycats around the world. *Cops* is often cited as the progenitor of reality shows, but it sprang from a documentary impulse. One of its creators and its long-time executive producer, John Langley, came to the documentary world with a master's degree in English. He always had an interest in crime documentary. Langley and partner Malcolm Barbour happened to pitch the *Cops* concept to Fox at a time when the network was new and very hungry for inexpensive programming. *Cops* continues.

It sometimes seems that every boundary of documentary ethics has been breached by reality TV. Following the success of its US broadcast of the BBC's *Victorian House* (a show in which middle-class people from the twenty-first century attempt to dress and live as Victorians), PBS got into the reality show business with a series that began with *Frontier House* in 2003. This eventually produced the spin-off *Colonial House* (2004), in which rich and famous television talk show host Oprah Winfrey arrived via rowboat at the colony, fully dressed in Colonial garb. Few would claim that this is documentary, and today we are regaled, or nauseated, by the antics of the Kardashians and the *Real Housewives* – an overblown version of the American dream. The 2011 suicide of a cast member of *Real Housewives of Beverly Hills* shows the heartless 'reality' to which so-called unscripted television has sunk.

Cheap and easy-to-produce reality shows have joined the globalization and spawned a particularly hollow and exploitative kind of 'celebrity'. The cross-cultural reality series *Worlds Apart* generated in 2004 for the US National Geographic is an example. Plopping urban American families into remote locales around the world for ten-day periods, it aired in the UK, Brazil, the Middle Eastern channel Al-Hurra, Goodlife Channel in Israel, Australia's ABC, and National Geographic Channel Canada. Promoting the show, Gary Lico, then President and CEO of CABLE ready, said: 'The drama caused by the intermingling of cultures in *Worlds Apart* has proven to have wide appeal around the globe. Viewers in North and South America, the UK, the Middle East and Australia will be able to see these entertaining examples of how people overcome their differences to eventually arrive at enlightenment.' This series combines reality television, globalization, new technology and perhaps, despite itself, a now-warped traditional documentary impulse to explore people. *Alien Wife Swap* anyone?

Academic Approaches

Intellectual debate and discussion of ethical and theoretical issues surrounding the documentary has continued since Grierson first used the 'D' word in 1926. Grierson and Flaherty, Drew and Leacock, George Stoney and all his students spent hours in debate and discussion over issues of documentary form and purpose. Michael Moore and Werner Herzog are self-contained documentary contradictions. As a rule, documentarians love to gather to discuss their work and the work of others. After all, these are people who have strong opinions about the subjects of their films and very strong opinions about the ways they should be made. As is evident in this text, the British documentary movement founded by Grierson compared with the observational approach of the Flahertys has received the most attention in critical and historical writings, followed later by debates about the nature of cv/direct, self-reflexivity, and onward. Discussion of practice, impact and ethics by serious documentarians continues today with vigour, forever moving into new realms, and occasionally marginalia.

For much of its early history, film was written about chiefly in the form of popular criticism in general interest publications. The notable exceptions, Vertov and Eisenstein, Grierson and Rotha, Jay Leyda and later Lindsay Anderson, set forth their opinions in writing as well as practice, and a body of literature began to slowly accumulate. While film theory in general grew slowly as a field of serious study in 1970s and throughout the 1980s, it was not until later that documentary studies emerged as a sub-category in the newly academicized field of film theory. Feminist and Marxist approaches were among the first to turn their attention to the subject, in part because documentary was a field in which many women and minorities gained access to filmmaking as early as the 1970s. Today there is lively scholarly debate about documentary theory in academic journals and specialized conferences.

Teachers and writers who helped to shape the emerging field include Jay Ruby, Cal Pryluck, Henry Breitrose, Ernie Rose, Raymond Fielding and, especially, Brian Winston in England, who succeeds both as a filmmaker and a scholar. Winston's keen, witty and adversarial writings are perhaps the most challenging and entertaining in the field. Much credit for the strength of documentary theoretical thought in the twenty-first century goes to Bill Nichols and Michael Renov, two scholars whose wide-ranging writings and work have influenced many others. Nichols has an 'organic' approach to the development of various kinds of documentaries that sees new works growing out of existing examples in the categories he calls Expository, Observational, Interactive, Reflexive, and Performative modes, suggesting a chronology of linear development. His work is continuously cited by others. Renov argues that documentary is the cinematic idiom most actively promoting the illusion of immediacy insofar as it forswears 'realism' in favour of a direct, ontological claim to the 'real'. This approach has also influenced the way that many recent film theorists attack the problems of documentary. Both also have substantial influence because of their respected academic positions and influence on students.

Women have added significantly to the development of documentary theory. Among them are Jane Gaines, Patricia Zimmerman (especially with her work at the Flaherty Seminar) and Pat Aufderheide, whose controversial positions on copyright and fair use seek to settle the irreconcilable debates about using work made by others. English scholar Stella Bruzzi has produced an argument in contemporary documentary theory that involves a polemic against some of the traditional ways of discussing the form. She advocates an analysis of newer films, which are 'familiar and relevant', rather than the canon of older classics.

However useful they may be for students seeking a deep understanding of the films, the academic writings of film theorists are not very much a part of the world of documentary-making and watching. It is without a doubt fascinating and instructive to think about, read about, and discuss film theory. Its impact on the vast majority of documentaries made and seen is relatively minor, because it is a specialized field with its own language, its own arguments, and its own self-limited audience. There are working documentary-makers, such as Jay Rosenblatt, Jill Godmilow, Barbara Hammer, Dennis O'Rourke in Australia, Chris Marker in France, Peter Watkins and Peter Forgács in Hungary, who employ preconceived formal theoretical constructs in their work. Most makers, however, are driven principally by issues that put documentary theory, when it is considered, in service to a larger idea.

Emergent Technologies

The media response to the 2001 terrorist attack on New York City's World Trade Center, because it was unexpected and took place in a world media hub, became the most-documented event in human history. Some of the twentieth-century trends of documentary development reached a natural apotheosis in coverage of the attack and aftermath. Not only was the technology portable, lightweight, intimate and immediate, the event was observed by hundreds of individually owned professional- and amateur-operated still and motion cameras. Access to many versions of the visual record of this attack could not be effectively limited by anyone; there were just too many people with too many cameras for authorities to control. Many recorded their own reactions to the events in an unselfconscious outpouring of self-reflexivity.

It was the financial and production resources of HBO that focused this mass of imagery to produce a new version of the compilation film with *In*

Memoriam: New York 9/11/01. When the World Trade Center was attacked within view of HBO's mid-town Manhattan headquarters, Sheila Nevins and her team created a response that aided the development of new ways to analyze documentary. This film is especially relevant because the 9/11 attack was recorded on film and video from hundreds of perspectives, all of which were made within the same timeframe of a few hours. Never before had any event been photographed from so many angles by so many different kinds of people with different kinds of camera. Still and moving images were edited together with a soundtrack by the HBO team, to create a record of the shattering events of that day. The 'Rashomon Effect' was realized in a way that fiction-makers could never equal.

Social Media

Anyone today can call themselves a filmmaker; smart phones with cameras and internet connections make that obvious. As noted, this material is mostly snippets of reportage, sometimes of questionable veracity, almost never analyzed journalistically, let alone for its documentary content. The power of social media is about access, the enabling of ordinary individuals to tell and disseminate their own stories. It is happening worldwide, and it is happening now. This change in the way factual information is shared will change the nature of documentary, just as surely as the coming of sound, the technical developments of cv/direct, the advent of television and the use of videotape changed the form. An excellent explanation of this process at work is the Academy Award-nominated documentary *Burma VJ: Reporting from a Closed Country* (2009), directed by Anders; Anders but sometimes credited as being made by 'The Cooperative', the anonymous activists who risked their lives to get the images.

Composed partly of mobile phone images taken during the 2007 uprisings against the government in Burma, it is framed with reconstructed footage that provides the film with a storyline centred on one individual whose ruminations weave together the disparate on-the-ground reports. This 'character' provides emotional connection and logic for the audience. To get the original anti-government videos out of Burma, they were uploaded to a Swedish server and sent out to the world. Despite the nitpicking of some few who continue to argue that staging is not documentary, this film explains the power of mobile phones and social media within the framework of traditional staged documentary form.

An example of emergent technology use from the UK is the *One Day on Earth* project, in which amateur and professional videographers shot footage during one twenty-four-hour period in October 2010. This idea is nothing new; 'one day in the life of...' projects have existed in multiple forms for decades. What is different in this experiment is that it evolved into an online community that plans to document social issues around the globe. One of its projects was called *Libya: True Story*, a multi-platform-based way to record activists' struggle to free the country from the Gaddafi regime. Brandon Littman, the executive producer of *One Day on Earth*, states that: 'Though what we are making is a traditional documentary in that it will follow a linear storyline, the project will also involve content that sits online within a social community so that the documentary can be organic and interactive, too.' On Facebook its page is called 'A Crowd-Sourced Documentary'. It is covered on other sites such as Babelmed, which defines itself as 'The leading independent website on Mediterranean issues'. It is free, totally independent and put together by a multicultural network of journalists from the whole Mediterranean; it exists in multiple languages, and the videos seem to be uncensored. This site, like *One Day on Earth*, promotes varied political propaganda. Through the immediacy of many internet links, people now see these kinds of diverse opinions and styles from thousand of places, created by thousands of people and groups, all with unique philosophies and agendas, when audiences have the time and energy to engage with it.

To date, the piecemeal style of such projects remains similar and largely informed; still, all it takes is one person to share with another. *18 Days in Egypt* aspires to do just that. Phase two of this project is about assembling the gathered content in a variety of ways across different platforms. Based on on-the-ground reports, a documentary will be compiled to mark the first anniversary of the Egyptian uprising. This is a reiteration, like HBO's *911*, of compilation film techniques whose finished product stems from Esther Shub's work. The form, the actual content and the meaning of the finished product always reflect the editors' choices and points of view.

A similar idea carried out on a large corporate scale is *Life in a Day* (2011), jointly distributed by National Geographic Entertainment, YouTube and Cine Digital Cinema Corp. Called the first 'user-generated feature-length documentary', it was edited together from footage shot by anyone who cared to participate during a twenty-four-hour period on 24 July 2010. Well-known directors/producers Kevin McDonald and Ridley Scott collaborated to edit over 4,500 hours from 81,000 YouTube submissions. The rules for submission were 'Tell us your story, tell us what you fear and show us what you have in your pocket'. The film premiered at the 2011 Sundance Film Festival, where it was well received.

Immediacy, worldwide reach, diverse opinions, on-the-ground reporting and extreme economy are the pluses of such evolutions of documentary form. It is part of the natural historical progression of the media interplay between money (not much capital necessary, small amounts of funds accessible to millions), technology (the digitization of the world) and content (the human desire to capture a timely situation). On these levels this is different from the traditional evolution of documentary.

Commitment to History

To these advantages of emergent technology, there are distinct minuses, some of them heartbreakingly detrimental. One major downfall is the loss of craft. Lighting, composition, sound quality and every other technical aspect of filmmaking are imperilled. Devaluation of the work becomes easier, and the artistry of documentarians is diminished. The ability to make a living making worthwhile films is jeopardized when television audiences accept the crudity of anyone's free 'street reportage' and when video piracy is rampant. Documentary ethics, including a commitment to veracity and obligation to one's subject, are often thrown away, especially by individuals who have little sense of documentary history. These problems have been debated for decades by serious documentarians. They must remain part of any discourse if the form is to retain respect. Today ethics and artistry seem to be very secondary to the pull of here-and-now.

One of the most critical of the minuses is that the digital information cannot be well preserved. This book is not meant to be an explanation of the state of digital storage, the existing means of film preservation and restoration, the morass of videotape loss, a recounting of the possibilities of future preservation techniques, the benefits of media migration, nor especially the cost of preservation. All of these discussions exist elsewhere. It is a fact that negative film stock is still the only medium known that can save our moving image media. We are able to look at the images from the very first moving picture. Without those experiments of the Lumière brothers and the other enduring millions upon millions of feet of documentary film so hard won, so painstakingly made since 1895, our world would be very different. Imagine a world without any moving images of Theodore Roosevelt or FDR, Winston Churchill, Joseph Stalin, the opening of the Nazi concentration camps, Marion Anderson at the Lincoln Memorial, John and Robert Kennedy, Martin Luther King, Leonard Bernstein conducting, or the Rolling Stones in concert. Our artistic and social heritage would be bereft. The lives and the souls of those to come would be much poorer.

Much of our early film history, especially nonfiction footage, even that shot on film, has vanished because people did not recognize or care enough to save it. And worse happened. From the invention of videotape through the digital age, until today, we have lost an incomprehensible amount – the majority, in fact – of our moving image history, especially our documentary, part of the 'orphaned' works. Work created and distributed digitally is most at risk. How many websites have come and gone? How are mobile phone images being preserved once they are shared? What will happen to the visual record of the Arab Spring, or to the stories created and stored in drives, discs or clouds, about our grandmothers and our children? Documentaries not preserved result in a world in which coming generations will not be able to see today through our eyes. That is happening hourly. Every person who makes, aspires to make, or who finds value in watching documentaries must personally engage with the enormity of this problem. To assume that someone else is taking care of it is a mistake. To leave the record of today at risk, despite any cost, is to commit a criminal act against the future. If you are not saving your film for others to see in five, fifty or a hundred years, why are you making it?

And what might be considered irrelevant and uninteresting now – people walking out of a factory, for example – may become vitally import in a hundred years. Who are we to make that judgement?

Even before pictures moved, the US Civil War photographs of Mathew Brady shook contemporary audiences with their vision of death, and they continue to haunt viewers today. A recent example of the importance of preservation is the 2009 documentary by James Chressanthis, *No Subtitles Necessary: László and Vilmos*. This follows the lives of renowned cinematographers László Kovacs and Vilmos Zsigmond, telling the story of their escape from the 1956 Soviet invasion of Hungary to the present day. As film students in Hungary, the two friends shot footage of the Russian invasion of Budapest – the tanks, the riots, the murders – and then smuggled it out of the country. Barely escaping with their lives, they fled, eventually arriving in Hollywood. Both rose to prominence in the late 60s as cinematographers on *Easy Rider, Five Easy Pieces, McCabe and Mrs Miller, Deliverance, Paper Moon, Close Encounters of the Third Kind* and many others. Their film of the Hungarian uprising exists. In 1956 there was no way for audiences to see it immediately, and their story did not affect the situation. Yet they filmed at great risk, and the footage changed the way history interprets the brutal power of 1950s USSR. We have the images today, still on film, for our documentary record.

Conclusion

Our history of documentary is a story of determined individuals who overcame every kind of obstacle to put their messages on the screen. That message may be one of artistic experimentation, the world's beauty, political consciousness, personal triumph over adversity, self-revelation or historical record. Documentarians can choose among dozens of available technologies and techniques to get their messages seen and heard. However, what was once a manageable number of documentary films to see and evaluate every year is now a cacophony of sounds and images, often relentless. There are animated documentaries, computer-generated documentaries, IMAX documentaries, internet documentaries, scripted documentaries, video diaries, cv/direct

Fig 87 *This 1956 image of freedom fighters celebrating during the Hungarian Revolt against Soviet rule is attributed to Vilmos Zsigmond, ASC. It is a frame from 35mm footage of the Russian invasion of Budapest in the 2009 documentary* No Subtitles Necessary: László and Vilmos *directed by James Chressanthis ASC. This film follows the lives of László Kovacs and Vilmos Zsigmond who barely escaped from Hungary with their lives and the footage. They fled to America, eventually becoming renowned cinematographers of films such as* Easy Rider, Five Easy Pieces, McCabe and Mrs. Miller, Deliverance, Paper Moon *and* Close Encounters of the Third Kind. *Their 'student-shoot' footage of the revolution has immeasurable value as an archival record in its own right. Because of the later artistic contributions of the men who shot it, it is doubly valuable.* No Subtitles Necessary *is a special example of the importance of saving documentaries and the reliability of film as the best preservation medium. Had the images of the revolt been shot on video, it is almost certain that they would no longer exist. BBC / CBS 'Revolt in Hungary', Walter Cronkite*

documentaries, fake documentaries, investigative news documentaries, and all of their hybrids. And these forms multiply exponentially around the world every day.

In the twenty-first century documentary is livelier and more complex than ever. This book devotes one full chapter to WWII, basically ten years in a 110-plus-year history. The number and types of films from the 1940s is small enough to be discussed in detail. And fortunately almost all of them remain to be screened and studied. Today, thousands of English-language documentaries premiere on television, in theatres, or at festivals every year, and thousands more are made in other languages and posted online. Analyzing this number is impossible in any one book. And not only do more people make documentaries, more people than ever before watch and talk about documentaries. Perhaps this is inevitable simply because there are many more people, but it is also due to worldwide access to production, distribution and exhibition mechanisms – and, more importantly, to the strength and flexibility of the 'documentary impulse'.

Fig 88 Streetfight *(2005) by Marshall Curry is emblematic of one way that 21st Century documentary filmmakers are adapting traditional forms and subjects. This film, which traces the mayoral campaign of Corey Booker in Newark, New Jersey shows black people judging other blacks for not being "black" enough. Curry was nominated for an Academy Award for* Streetfight *(2005), his first documentary, and was also nominated for his third,* If a Tree Falls: The Story of the Earth Liberation Front *(2011), (made with Sam Cullman and Matt Hamachek) Curry's ability to create narrative and reveal personality makes him the direct heir of the American cv/direct techniques.*

Although there is always discussion about and debunking of documentary, many, many people want to make documentaries. It has been suggested, more than once, that the term is obsolete and the form too defiled to have meaning. The ongoing and sometimes heated debates about documentary indicate that the term is too meaningful and too powerful to abandon. People are always interested in seeing their own, and other, realities reflected back to them. The proof is in the history of the form. From the astonishing importance of the Lumières' *The Arrival of a Train at the Station*, Flaherty's *Nanook of the North*, Capra's 'Why We Fight', Grierson's enormous influence, Murrow's *Harvest of Shame*, Drew's *Primary*, Pennebaker's *Don't Look Back*, IMAX's *To Fly*, Burns' *The Civil War*, Moore's *Fahrenheit 9/11*, Guggenheim's *An Inconvenient Truth* and Herzog's *Cave of Dreams*, among many others, we know that people love documentaries. Filmmakers will continue to produce, audiences will watch, the world will debate, and our culture will remain richer, not only for the magnificent legacy of this form that tries to explain some truths, but also for its present and its future. Our world today without the debate of documentary is hard to imagine, and a future without its questioning energy is a place where few of us would want to live.

Fig 89 *A secret service officer and Michael Moore confront one another in* Fahrenheit 9/11 *(US, 2004, Michael Moore). Dog Eat Dog Films*

Chapter Related Films

1898
Battleships Maine and Iowa (US, Biograph Company)
Tearing Down the Spanish Flag (US, Vitagraph Company)
1964
Culloden (UK, Peter Watkins)
1965
The War Game (UK, Peter Watkins)
1984
This Is Spinal Tap (US, Rob Reiner)
2009
Burma VJ: Reporting from a Closed Country (Andres; Andres)
No Subtitles Necessary: László and Vilmos (US, James Chressanthis)
2011
Life in a Day (Kevin McDonald and Ridley Scott)

Chapter Related Books

Bruzzi, Stella, *New Documentary: A Critical Introduction*. London: Routledge, 2000.

Hogarth, David, *Documentary Television in Canada: From National Public Service to Global Marketplace*. Montreal: McGill-Queen's University Press, 2002.

Juhasz, Alexandra and Jesse Lerner, *F is for Phony: Fake Documentary and Truth's Undoing*. University of Minnesota Press, 2006.

Kilborn, Richard and John Izod, *An Introduction to Television Documentary: Confronting Reality*. Manchester, UK: Manchester University Press, 1997.

McCreadle, Marsha, *Documentary Superstars: How Today's Filmmakers Are Reinventing the Form*. New York: Allworth Press, 2009.

Sights of the Turn of the Century: New Tendencies in Documentary Cinema, lectures CILECT, 1996.

Renov, Michael, *The Subject of Documentary*. Minneapolis: University of Minnesota Press, 2003.

Rhodes, Gary D., *Docufictions: essays on the intersection of documentary and fictional filmmaking*. Jefferson, NC: McFarland & Co., 2006.

Roscoe, Jane, *Faking it: Mock-documentary and Subversion of Factuality*. Manchester: Manchester University Press, 2001.

Waldman, Diane and Janet Walker, (eds), *Feminism and Documentary*. Minneapolis: University of Minnesota Press, 1999.

Zimmerman, Patricia R., *States of Emergency: Documentaries, Wars and Democracies*. Minneapolis: University of Minnesota Press, 2000.

Appendix One

Academy Awards for Best Documentary Feature

THE WINNER IN BOLD

1942
The Battle of Midway
Kokoda Front Line!
Moscow Strikes Back
Prelude to War
no winner

1943
Desert Victory
Baptism of Fire
The Battle of Russia
Report from the Aleutians
War Department Report

1944
The Fighting Lady
Resisting Enemy Interrogation

1945
The True Glory
The Last Bomb

1946 – none given

1947
Design for Death
Journey Into Medicine
The World Is Rich

1948
The Secret Land
The Quiet One

1949
Daybreak in Udi
Kenji Comes Home

1950
The Titan: Story of Michelangelo
With These Hands

1951
Kon-Tiki
IO Was a Communist for the FBI
The Sea Around for the FBI
Kokoda Front Line!
Moscow Strikes Back
Prelude to War

1952
The Sea Around Us
The Hoaxters
Navajo

1953
The Living Desert
The Conquest of Everest
A Queen is Crowned

1954
The Vanishing Prairie
The Stratford Adventure

1955
Helen Keller in Her Story (aka **The Unconquered**)
Crévecoeur

1956
The Silent World
Where Mountains Float
The Naked Eye

1957
Albert Schweitzer
On the Bowery
Torero

1958
White Wilderness
Antarctic Crossing
The Hidden World
Psychiatric Nursing

1959
Serengeti Shall Not Die
The Race for Space

1960
The Horse with the Flying Tail
Rebel in Paradise

1961
Sky Above and Mud Beneath
La grande olimpiade

1962
Black Fox: The Rise and Fall of Adolf Hitler
Alvorada

1963
Robert Frost: A Lover's Quarrel with the World
Le Maillon et la chaíne
The Yanks Are Coming

1964
World Without Sun
14–18
Alleman
The Finest Hours
Four Days in November

1965
The Eleanor Roosevelt Story
The Battle of the Bulge...The Brave Rifles
The Forth Road Bridge
Let My People Go: The Story of Israel
Mourir á Madrid

1966
The War Game
The Face of a Genius
Helicopter Canada
The Really Big Family
Le Volcan interdit

1967
The Anderson Platoon
Festival
Harvest
A King's Story
A Time for Burning

1968
Journey into Self

Note: At the 41st Awards ceremony on 14 April 1969, *Young Americans* was announced as the winner of the Documentary Feature Oscar. On 7 May 1969, it was revealed that the film had played in October 1967, which rendered it ineligible for a 1968 Award. The first runner-up, *Journey Into Self*, was awarded the statuette on 8 May 1969.

A Few Notes on Our Food Problem
Legendary Champions
Other Voices

1969
Arthur Rubinstein – The Love of Life
Before the Mountain Was Moved
In the Year of the Pig
Olimpiada en México
The Wolf Men

1970
Woodstock
Chariots of the Gods
Jack Johnson
King: A Filmed Record...Montgomery to Memphis
Say Goodbye

1971
The Hellstrom Chronicle
Alaska Wilderness Lake
Le chagrin et la pitié
On Any Sunday
Ra

1972
Marjoe
Bij de beesten af
Malcolm X
Manson
The Silent Revolution

1973
The Great American Cowboy
Always a New Beginning
Journey to the Outer Limits
Schlacht um Berlin
Walls of Fire

1974
Hearts and Minds
Antonia: A Portrait of the Woman
The Challenge...A Tribute to Modern Art
The 81st Blow
The Wild and the Brave

1975
The Man Who Skied Down Everest
The California Reich
Fighting for Our Lives
The Incredible Machine
The Other Half of the Sky: A China Memoir

1976
Harlan County, USA
Hollywood on Trial
Off the Edge
People of the Wind
Volcano: An Inquiry Into the Life and Death of Malcolm Lowry

1977
Who Are the DeBolts? And Where Did They Get Nineteen Kids?
The Children of Theatre Street
High Grass Circus
Homage to Changall: The Colours of Love
Union Maids

1978
Scared Straight!
Mysterious Castles of Clay
Raoni
Le vent des amoureux
With Babies and Banners: Story of the Women's Emergency Brigade

1979
Best Boy
Generation on the Wind
Going the Distance
The Killing Ground
The War at Home

1980
From Mao to Mozart: Isaac Stern in China
Agee
The Day After Trinity
Front Line
The Yellow Star – The Persecution of the Jews in Europe 1933-45

1981
Genoicde
Against Wind and Tide: A Cuban Odyssey
Brooklyn Bridge
Eight Minutes to Midnight: A Portrait of Dr. Helen Caldicott
El Salvador: Another Vietnam

1982
Just Another Missing Kid
A Portrait of Giselle
After the Axe
Ben's Mill
In Our Water

1983
He Makes Me Feel Like Dancin'
Children of Darkness
First Contact
The Professional of Arms
Seeing Red

1984
The Times of Harvey Milk
High Schools
In the Name of the People
Marlene
Streetwise

1985
Broken Rainbow
The Mothers of Plaza de Mayo
Soldiers in Hiding
The Statue of Liberty
Unfinished Business

1986(tie): **Artie Shaw: Time Is All You've Got** and **Down and Out in America**
Chile: Hasta Cuando?
Isaac in America: A Journey with Isaac Bashevis Singer
Witness to Apartheid

1987
The Ten-Year Lunch
Eyes on the Prize
Hellfire: A Journey from Hiroshima
Radio Bikini
A Stitch for Time

1988
Hôtel Terminus: The Life and Times of Klaus Barbie
The Cry of Reason: Byers Naude – An Afrikaner Speaks out
Let's Get Lost
Promises to Keep
Who Killed Vincent Chin?

1989
Common Threads: Stories from the Quilt
Adam Clayton Powell
Crack USA: County Under Siege
For All Mankind
Super Chief: The Life and Legacy of Earl Warren

1990
American Dream
Berkeley in the Sixties
Building Bombs
Forever Activists: Stories from the Veterans of the Abraham Lincoln Brigade
Waldo Salt: A Screenwriter's Journey

1991
In the Shadow of the Stars
Death on the Job
Doing Time: Life Inside the Big House
The Restless Conscience: Resistance to Hitler Within German 1933–1945
Wild by Law

1992
The Panama Deception
Changing Our Minds: The Story of Dr. Evelyn Hooker
Fires of Kuwait
Liberators: Fighting on Two Fronts in World War II
Music for the Movies: Bernard Herrmann

1993
I Am a Promise: The Children of Stanton Elementary School
The Broadcast Tapes of Dr. Peter
Children of Fate
For Better or For Worse
The War Room

1994
Maya Lin: A Strong Clear Vision
Complaints of a Dutiful Daughter
D-Day Remembered
Freedom on My Mind
A Great Day in Harlem

1995
Anne Frank Remembered
The Battle Over Citizen Kane
Hank Aaron: Chasing the Dream
Small Wonders
Troublesome Creek: A Midwestern

1996
When We Were Kings
The Line King: The Al Hirschfeld Story
Mandela
Suzanne Farrell: Elusive Muse
Tell the Truth and Run: George Seldes and the American Press

1997
The Long Way Home
Ayn Rand: A Sense of Life
Colours Straight Up
4 Little Girls
Waco: The Rules of Engagement

1998
The Last Days
The Dancemaker
The Farm: Angola, USA.
Lenny Bruce: Swear to Tell the Truth
Regret to Inform

1999
One Day in September
Buena Vista Social Club
Genghis Blues
On the Ropes
Speaking in Strings

2000
Into the Arms of Strangers: Stories of the Kindertransport
Legacy – Tod Lending
Long Night's Journey into Day
Scottsboro: An American Tragedy
Sound and Fury

2001
Murder on a Sunday Morning
Children Underground
LaLee's Kin: The Legacy of Cotton
Promises
War Photographer

2002
Bowling for Columbine
Daughter from Danang
Prisoner of Paradise
Spellbound
Winged Migration

2003
The Fog of War
Balseros
Capturing the Friedmans
My Architect
The Weather Underground

2004
Born into Brothels
The Story of the Weeping Camel
Super Size Me
Tupac: Resurrection
Twist of Faith

2005
March of the Penguins
Darwin's Nightmare
Enron: The Smartest Guys in the Room
Murderball
Street Fight

2006
An Inconvenient Truth
Deliver Us from Evil
Iraq in Fragments
Jesus Camp
My Country, My Country

2007
Taxi to the Dark Side
No End in Sight
Operation Homecoming: Writing the Wartime Experience
Sicko
War/Dance

2008
Man on Wire
The Betrayal
Encounters at the End of the World
The Garden
Trouble the Water

2009
The Cove
Burma VJ
Food, Inc.
The Most Dangerous Man in America: Daniel Ellsberg and the Pentagon Papers
Which Way Home

2010
Inside Job
Exit Through the Gift Shop
Gasland
Restrepro
Waste Land

Appendix Two
The National Film Registry

Under the terms of the United States National Film Preservation Act, each year the Librarian of Congress, Dr James Billington, names twenty-five 'culturally, historically or aesthetically significant motion pictures to the Registry. The list is designed to reflect the full breadth and diversity of America's film heritage, thus increasing public awareness of the richness of American cinema and the need for its preservation. The films are not selected as the 'best' American films of all time, but rather as works of enduring significance to American culture.

'Taken together, the 550 films in the National Film Registry represent a stunning range of American filmmaking – including Hollywood features, documentaries, avant-garde and amateur productions, films of regional interest, ethnic, animated, and short film subjects – all deserving recognition, preservation and access by future generations. Despite the heroic efforts of archives, the motion picture industry and others, America's film heritage, by any measure, is an endangered species … The Library of Congress – with the support of the US Congress – must ensure the preservation of America's film patrimony,' says Billington. 'The National Film Registry is a reminder …that the preservation of our cinematic creativity must be a priority because about half of the films produced before 1950 and as much as ninety per cent of those made before 1920 have been lost to future generations.'

It is safe to say that the figures for lost documentaries are higher. The following is a list of the documentaries included in the list in order of year of release.

Documentaries Selected for the National Film Registry:

1893
Thomas, Edison: *Blacksmithing Scene*

1901
President MacKinley Inauguration footage

1904
Bitzer, G. W.: *Westinghouse Works*

1906
A Trip Down Market Street
San Francisco Earthquake, April 18, 1906

1910
Jeffries-Johnson World's Championship Boxing Contest

1913
Preservation of the Sign Language

1914
Curtis, Edward S.: *In the Land of the Head-Hunters* /aka *In the Land of the War Canoes*

1920
American Red Cross: *Heros All*

1921
Scheeler, Charles; Strand, Paul: *Manhatta*

1922
Flaherty, Robert: *Nanook of the North*

1925
Schoedsack, Ernest B.; Cooper, Merian C.; Harrison, Marquerite: *Grass: A Nation's Battle for Life*

1928
Fox Movietone Newsreel: *Jenkins Orphanage Band*

1930
Ames, Alfred: *From Stump to Ship*

1931
Leyda, Jay: *A Bronx Morning*
Marvin Breckinridge Paterson, Mary: *The Forgotten Frontier*

1934
Lorentz, Pare: *The Plow That Broke The Plains*

1935
Republic Steel Strike Newsreel footage

1936
Chevrolet Motor Company: *Master Hands*

1936–1939
Mead, Margaret: *Trance and Dance in Bali*

1937
Lorentz, Pare: *The River*
Hindenberg Disaster Newsreel Footage

1938
de Rochemont, Louis: *March of Time: Inside Nazi Germany*

1939
Marian Anderson: The Lincoln Memorial Concert
Steiner, Ralph; Van Dyke, Willard: *The City*
Cologne: *From the Diary of Ray and Esther* (home movie)

1940
Bryan, Julien: *Siege*
Tacoma Narrows Bridge Collapse footage

1941
Water, Lee H.: *Kannapolis, N.C.*

1943
Wyler, William: *Memphis Belle*

1943–1945
Capra, Frank; Litvak, Anatole; Veiller, Anthony: *Why We Fight (series)*
Topaz (home move footage taken at Japanese American Internment Camp)

1943–1946
George Stevens' World War II

1944
Mili, Gjon: *Jammin' the Blues*
Heisler, Stewart: *The Negro Soldier*

1945
Huston, John: *Battle of San Pietro*

1946
Huston, John: *Let There Be Light*

1948
Levitt, Helen; Loeb, Janice; Agee, James: *In the Street*
Flahety, Robert: *Louisiana Story*

1951
Rizzo, Anthony: *Duck and Cover, US Federal Civil Defense Administration*

1953
Stoney, George: *All My Babies*
Federal Civil Defense Administration: *House in the Middle*

1956
Rogosin, Lionel, *On the Boweny*
Disneyland Dream

1957
Marshall, John: *The Hunters*
Algar, James: *The Living Desert, Walt Disney Studios*

1959
Avakian, Aram; Stern, Bert: *Jazz on a Summer's Day*

1960–1975
Core, Dwight Sr., Ingmire, George: *Think of Me First as a Person*

1960
Drew, Robert; Leacock, Richard; Maysles, Al; Macartney-Filgate, Terence: *Primary*

1963
Zapruder footage
Drew, Robert; Shuker, Greg; Leacock, Richard; Lipscomb, James; Ryden, Hope: *Crisis*

1964
Warhol, Andy: *Empire*
Blue, James: *The March*
Gardner, Robert: *Dead Birds*
de Antonio, Emile: *Point of Order*

1966
Jersey, Bill: *A Time for Burning*
Brown, Bruce: *The Endless Summer*
Anderson Mike; Benally, Susie; Clah Al: *Through Navajo Eyes (series)*

1967
Pennebaker D. A.: *Don't Look Back*

1968
Sanders, Dennis: *Czechoslovakia*
Bass, Saul and Elaine: *Why Man Creates*
Wiseman, Frederick: *High School*

1969
Wadleigh, Michael: *Woodstock*
Maysles, Albert and David: *Salesman*

1970
Wiseman, Frederick: *Hospital*
Lumet, Sidney: *King, A Filmed Record*

1971–1972

Klein, Jim; Reichert Julia: *Growing Up Female*

Mekas, Jonas: *Reminiscences of a Journey to Lithuania*

1974

Block, Mitchell: *...No Liesi*

Godmilow, Jill and Collins, Judy: *Antonia, Portrait of a Woman*

1975

Appalshop: *Buffalo Creek Flood*

1976

Hovde, Ellen; Maysles, Albert; Maysles, David; Meyer, Muffie: *Grey Gardens*

Blank, Les: *Chulas Fronteras*

Kopple, Barbara: *Harlan County, USA*

MacGillvray, Greg: *To Fly*

1980

Blank, Les: *Garlic is as Good as Ten Mothers*

Field, Connie: *Life and Times of Rose the Riveter*

1986

Workman, Chuck: *Precious Images*

McElwee, Ross: *Sherman's March*

Morris, Errol: *The Thin Blue Line*

Strand, Chick: *Fruitcake Factory*

1989

O'Neill, Pat: *Water and Power*

1994

James, Steve; Marx, Frederick; Gilbert, Peter: *Hoop Dreams*

Index

An 'f.' after a page number indicates a figure.

HEARTBREAKER

PART ONE

ITCHY FEET

1

Gemma Adderley had had enough.

She had taken everything she possibly could, endured everything that had been slung at her, and was scared, humiliated, broken, hurt. Hurt above all. In so many ways.

As the front door slammed, shutting out the outside world once again, Gemma looked round the house. At her possessions. At her life. What was it Robert De Niro had said in that film she had watched once when Roy was out? Never get attached to anything you wouldn't walk out on in thirty seconds if you had to. Something like that. She sat at the kitchen table and looked at the walls, the floor. The cooker he had wanted her chained to. The fridge he had told her to keep fully stocked, even if she didn't always have the money to do it. They weren't her possessions. He had bought them. Had tried to make them possess her. There was nothing in the room – the flat – she wouldn't be able to walk out on. That she didn't want to walk out on.

Except Carly. And that was why she was taking her daughter with her.

Heart thumping, Gemma stood up, went into the living room. Thought once more of Roy. What he would say to her if he knew she was planning this. Do to her. The sins she would be committing. The punishment he would inflict – no, not him, not his punishment, God's, for daring to go against His will. And knew she wouldn't face that again. Never again. She

3

opened the door, gripping the handle, trying not to notice how much her fingers were trembling.

Carly was lying on the floor watching TV. Some unreal reality show. The kind she could only watch when Roy was out. She turned as Gemma entered, her eyes as usual wide, head and body flinching. Expecting God's wrath. Expecting to go straight to hell. Gemma's heart broke every time she saw her daughter do that. She had wondered where she had seen eyes like her daughter's before and the answer had come to her one night when she was watching the news. They'd shown footage of some war zone in the Middle East, tortured refugees making their way slowly out of the city, trying to forget what they had seen, trying to carry on, and she'd seen the same things in the children's eyes that were in Carly's.

A war zone. Just about sums it up, thought Gemma. Straight to hell. How could you fear going there when you were already living in it?

'Hey,' she said, trying to keep her voice light, 'we're going out.'

Carly sat up, looked round nervously. She had heard the door slam shut as well. It was usually a sign for them both to relax. Get together, find a shared strength to keep them going. But this was new. This was unheard of for the little girl. What her mother was proposing was against the rules. And she knew there would be punishments.

'But . . . ' Carly's eyes darted to the door. 'We can't . . . '

'We can,' said Gemma, hoping she sounded calm and in control, fearing she didn't. 'And we are. Come on.'

Carly stood up, dumbly obeying, even if it was against the rules. 'Where . . . '

Gemma summoned up a smile for her daughter. Only for her daughter, she thought. It had been a long time since she had smiled for herself. 'Somewhere nice. Somewhere safe.'

4

Carly said nothing.

'Come on,' said Gemma, holding out her hand for the girl to take.

Carly, clearly not happy but not wanting to go against her mother's wishes, walked towards her. Then turned back to the TV. 'I'd better turn it off. If I don't turn it off . . . '

'Leave it on,' said Gemma.

Carly stared at her.

'Yeah, leave it on.' Gemma smiled. That little act of rebellion had emboldened her. With Carly she turned, left the room.

She had already packed their bags, hidden them under the bed. She pulled them out.

'Are we . . . are we going on holiday?' asked Carly.

'Yeah,' said Gemma, 'that's right. A holiday.'

'Where?' asked Carly, excitement building despite her fear. 'Somewhere hot and sunny? Like Benidorm?'

It was one of the seven-year-old's favourite programmes. Something Gemma let her stay up and watch if Roy was out. Which was most nights.

'Not Benidorm, petal, no. But somewhere nice. Somewhere we'll feel . . . ' What? What could she say to her daughter, tell her about where they were going? 'Safe. Happy. Somewhere happy. Come on, get your coat on.'

Carly turned to go to her own room, stopped, came back. 'Can I bring Crusty?'

Her toy bear. She took it everywhere.

'He's already packed. We won't forget him. Now come on, we've got to go.'

But Carly didn't move. A thought had occurred to her. Gemma stood, waited. She knew what the child was going to say. Had her answer prepared.

'Is . . . is Daddy coming with us?'

'Not, not just yet, petal. D'you want him to?'

'He's Daddy.' Her voice flat, monotonous. The words like something learned by rote at school. 'We're his family. He's the head. In charge. Just like God. He has to know what we're doing all the time.'

'That's right. He's Daddy.' Not dwelling on the rest of her daughter's words. Hoping she was young enough to forget all that stuff in time. 'Well, look. We'll get going and he can come and join us later if we want him to. How does that sound?'

Again those wide war-zone eyes. Carly nodded.

Gemma knew she didn't mean it, knew she had done it more out of fear of disagreeing than because she wanted him to join them. She knew also the conflict that would be raging inside her daughter, tearing her apart. But it had to be done. It had to be.

'Good,' she said. 'Right, just a couple of things to do before we go.'

She took out her phone, dialled a number she had memorised. Waited.

'Gemma Adderley,' she said when someone answered. 'Safe Haven, please.'

The voice on the other end of the line asked her where she was. She told them. She was given directions, told where to be.

'The car'll be with you in ten minutes. Is that okay?'

'Yeah,' said Gemma, hardly believing that she was actually doing this. After toying with it for years, wanting to but not having the strength, the courage to actually do so, she was leaving Roy. And with him would go all the pain, hurt and suffering that she and her daughter had endured for so long.

'Yeah,' she said again. 'That's fine.'

'The driver needs to give you a word so you know it's from us. The word is strawberry. If they don't give you that, don't get in, okay?'

6

'Okay.'

'See you soon.'

Gemma ended the call, looked down at Carly. Her daughter had her coat buttoned up and was staring up at her, trying to be excited but unable to hide the fear in her eyes. In that moment Gemma thought it wasn't possible for her to love another person more.

'Come on, petal,' she said. 'Let's go.'

They reached the front door.

'Oh,' said Gemma, 'one more thing.'

She went back into the living room, took the book – Roy's only book – from pride of place on the shelf. The Bible. The family Bible, a source of guidance and prayer. A template to live your life by. She felt the edges. Hard leather, scuffed and indented where it had struck her and her daughter. A weapon of anger, of fear.

She felt rage build inside. Wished she had a fire so she could throw the book on it, watch it burn away to nothing. Instead had to content herself with opening it up at random and ripping out pages, throwing them round the room in a frenzy.

Eventually she wore herself out, dropped the book on the floor, knowing it would serve as a goodbye letter, and went to join her daughter.

She looked at the front door once more. He never locked it when he went out but she knew she was expected to remain inside. Imprisoned not by lock and key but by fear. Of what would happen if she dared to be out when he returned. If she dared to even think about leaving. Well, now she was. Leaving for ever. And it had taken her longer than she could remember to build up the courage to do that. To walk out of her open prison, never to return.

Gemma and Carly held hands as well as they could with their bags; left the house together.

As Gemma closed the door behind her for what she hoped would be the last time, another Robert De Niro quote sprang to mind. Something about life being short and whatever time you got was luck. That was what she was having now. Luck.

She had been given this chance for a fresh start, and from now on, Gemma Adderley was going to create her own luck.

2

Nina felt the air on her face, cool and welcome. Closed her eyes and kept walking.

The club had been good, she had to admit. Itchy Feet night at Lab 11. Just one room with bare brick walls and a bar, kind of damp-smelling, but it played good music for a club night. Not the usual stuff all the other places played. Fifties music, swing. Retro. Just what she liked. And she'd enjoyed herself, mostly. It hadn't been her idea to go but she didn't want to seem like the odd girl out or the killjoy who held all the others back. Especially as they hadn't known each other long and were still bonding as a group. The first uni semester was like that. Just as she'd expected it to be. She wanted to make friends with the rest of the group she had been put in halls with, and this seemed to be the best way of doing it. Also, she suffered from serious FOMO. She hadn't heard the phrase before she had arrived at uni, but it had stuck in her mind ever since. FOMO: Fear of Missing Out. And now that naming it made it officially a thing, she was relieved to admit it was pretty strong inside her.

She opened her eyes, still walking, looked at the others she was with. Andrew was from Manchester, gay and mouthy. She'd had a friend like him in sixth form. She hoped he could be her surrogate. Every girl needed a gay best friend, she had decided. Laura was the other girl in the group. Nina could see herself gravitating towards her too. They seemed to have lots in common and they were on the same course. The other two boys were Mark and John. Lads. That was all she could think of to say about them. They were good fun; bright, funny, but not really on her wavelength. Good lads, though, happy to be seen out with girls and didn't stigmatise Andrew for being gay. A great bunch to be with and it seemed like they all got along together. Early days, but that was a good sign.

Mark and John were clowning as they went. Loud, laughing like everyone was watching.

'Oh,' said Andrew, 'you and your laddish fun . . .'

This seemed to be a pattern, fooling around as soon as they got a drink inside them. First time away from home, experiencing that nervous, giddy freedom. Nina wasn't like that. She was cautious, careful. Took everything as it came, in her stride. Tried not to have fixed expectations. That way she wouldn't be disappointed. That was what she'd always told herself. But she smiled at them. They were funny.

'Did you see that guy?' asked Andrew.

'Which guy?'

'Looking at you. That guy. Dark hair. Big eyes. Like Jared Leto.'

Nina knew exactly which guy he meant. She had fancied him but didn't want to admit it. Not in the game plan, she'd told herself. Do the degree, have fun, get out. Don't get lumbered.

'Nah,' she said. 'Must have missed him.'

Andrew's eyes rolled and widened in stage shock. 'Missed him? How could you? My God, if you didn't want him, I was going to have a go.'

Nina smiled.

Her ears were still ringing from the BPMs in the club, but she let Andrew go on, not really listening to him, pleased with the constant buzz. It was light now, early Saturday morning.

10

They had gone into town quite late and Nina had paced herself with her drinks. Always bottles, always in her hand, making sure she knew who had bought them, ensuring no one could have tampered with them. Always in control. The way she liked it.

'Where are we?' asked Laura.

'Digbeth,' said Nina. 'Birmingham.'

'Yeah, I know that. But where are we? How do we get back home?'

Nina looked round. All the streets looked the same in Digbeth. Run-down warehouses and factories supposedly having had the cultural magic wand waved at them. The new hip and edgy part of town. All cool bars and vintage clothes shops. She could see the silver-spotted undulating form of Selfridges in the city centre off in the distance. Like a massive science fiction slug had just died there.

'Head for that, I suppose,' she said. 'Get a cab.' If we've got any money left, she wanted to add. She had budgeted carefully for the night. She hoped the rest of them had. She didn't fancy walking all the way to Edgbaston.

'Nah,' said Andrew, 'let's—'

'Guys.'

They stopped talking. Up ahead, Mark and John had stopped walking, John turning to them, serious expression on his face.

'Guys,' he said again, gesturing towards a doorway, suddenly no longer drunk. 'Come here, guys, come here . . .'

Nina moved forward, caught up with them. The other two followed. She looked to where John was pointing. There, huddled in the doorway, was a little girl.

The child looked away from them, curled herself into a foetal ball, eyes screwed tight shut; if she couldn't see them, they wouldn't see her. Her clothes were dirty but not rags, her face

11

equally grimy; tears and snot had left tracks down it. She clutched hard at a teddy bear in her hands, pulled it towards her chest. She looked like she had been living rough on the street. She looked, thought Nina, like the kind of kid you saw on the TV news from a war zone.

Looking round to see what the others were doing – nothing – Nina knelt down in front of the girl.

'Careful,' said Andrew, 'she might have something—'

Nina turned, gave him a hard stare. He said nothing more.

'Hello,' she said quietly. 'What's your name?'

The little girl didn't reply, just screwed her eyes up tighter.

All sorts of thoughts tumbled through Nina's head. She'd been trafficked, she'd run away from somewhere, she'd been abandoned. She might not even speak or understand English.

'I'm Nina,' she said. 'What's your name?'

The little girl started to cry. 'Go away,' she said, clutching her toy like it was a life raft.

Nina edged forward. 'What's your name? Look, we can help you.'

Nothing.

Andrew knelt down next to Nina, wanting to help. The little girl flinched, seemed as if she was about to cry again. Wide-eyed, he moved back. Nina stayed where she was.

'Where's your ... your mum? Where do you live? Do you know?'

The girl shook her head.

'Look, we'll get help. We won't leave you, okay?'

The girl still said nothing. Held on harder to the bear.

'Can you tell us anything?' said Nina, sensing that words were now futile and they should phone the police. 'A name? Anything.'

The little girl looked up at them, her eyes wide with ghosts.

12

'Why are you here? What happened?'

The girl seemed about to answer but stopped herself. The enormity of what was behind the words too much for her. She looked away from them again, eyes down.

Whatever she had been about to say was now locked up firmly within her.

3

'Hello.'

Psychologist Marina Esposito smiled, sat down on a chair that was way too small for her. She looked at the little girl in front of her.

'I'm Marina. What's your name?'

The girl looked up briefly, eyes wide, then away again. Back to the bear in her hands. Clutching it tightly.

Marina kept her smile in place. 'You've had a horrible thing happen to you, haven't you? I'm here to help you get over it.'

The girl didn't look at her. Marina looked at the bear in her hands. It was filthy but she knew the girl wouldn't give it up. Hadn't given it up since she had been found.

'What's your bear called?' asked Marina.

'Crusty,' the girl replied.

'Crusty. Nice name. And has he been with you all the time?'

The girl nodded.

'And what's your name?' Marina knew – it was in the report – but she still had to ask.

The girl kept staring at the bear.

When she had received the call, Marina had told them this wasn't her area. She didn't usually deal with children, no matter how traumatised. 'I'm a criminal psychologist,' she had said on the phone. 'Unless she's committed a crime, I don't think I can be of much help.'

'She's been the victim of one,' said Detective Sergeant Hugh Ellison, 'or at least we think her mother has. She's disappeared. And the daughter's the only witness.' He paused, letting that sink in, went on. 'Normally we would go with a child psychologist, but your particular skill set makes you a better fit for this. And you come highly recommended.'

'Right.' Marina nodded even though he couldn't see it. She knew who had recommended her. Her husband, Phil Brennan, was a detective inspector with the West Midlands Major Incident Squad based in the centre of Birmingham. She had worked with him on cases before. Helped.

A shiver ran through her as she thought of him. He couldn't help her now. Not any more. And that was a wedge driven between them, because she doubted he ever could again.

And she couldn't give him the chance.

'Anyway,' DS Ellison had continued, 'she was found on the street in Digbeth. Said she'd been going on holiday with her mother but her mother had gone off without her. Thrown out of the car, left on the street. Found by some students.'

'What's happened to her mother?'

'That's what I'm hoping you can find out.'

And the call had ended.

Marina had agreed – with some reluctance – to try and help the girl. She had read every report presented to her. The girl had given her name – Carly – but little else. She wouldn't tell them where she lived and she looked terrified at the prospect of talking about her mother. Marina suspected that the two things weren't connected, but the responses suggested some kind of trauma related to each. There had been no missing persons report answering her description, so that was all she had to go on.

Now she found herself at the special reception centre where the girl was being treated and cared for. The walls were bright,

15

colourfully painted with murals of cartoon characters. But even that didn't disguise the institutional feel of the place.

'You're Carly, aren't you? I got your name from Lesley who's been looking after you.'

The little girl nodded.

'How old are you, Carly?'

'Seven.'

Marina nodded. 'Good age. I've got a little girl. She's a tiny bit younger than you. Her name's Josephina.' She looked at Crusty. 'She's got a favourite teddy she never lets go of.'

The girl just stared at her. Marina wasn't sure, but she saw the beginnings of interest, a tentative kind of trust building within, reaching out to her.

'So where's your daddy, Carly?'

Something dark seemed to flutter over the girl. She had almost made eye contact with Marina. Instead she looked away.

'At home,' she said.

'And where's home?'

'Home.' Her eyes guarded, downcast.

'Do you want to tell me how to get there, Carly?'

She kept staring at the bear. Shook her head.

'Why not?'

'Mummy said we were going away. On holiday. Not Benidorm, but somewhere nice, she said.'

'Benidorm? Why Benidorm? Did you want to go there?'

Carly nodded. 'Like on the telly.'

On the telly? Marina thought, puzzled. Then it came to her. A comedy. Of sorts. All bright sun and broad acting. She smiled, nodded. 'The programme. You like that, do you?'

Carly nodded. 'Mummy lets me stay up to watch it. When Daddy's not—'

She stopped herself, eyes scared, guilty, once more.

16

Marina studied her. 'When Daddy's not what? Home?'

The girl said nothing. Clutched the bear, knuckles white.

Marina leaned forward. Just enough to be seen, not enough to invade the girl's personal space. 'You want to know something, Carly? About your teddy? And about my daughter Josephina's teddy?'

The girl looked up once more, wary but interested.

'They protect you. You hold on to them and they protect you. When things get bad, they're always there for you. Sometimes you have to do things you don't want to do. And you have to be strong to do them. That's when teddies help.'

Carly kept staring at her. Marina, sensing she had the girl hooked, continued. 'My little girl, Josephina, when she was even smaller, she . . . she had to be brave. She had to be strong.'

'What happened?' asked Carly, interested despite herself.

'Well, she . . . ' *Was kidnapped. Held to ransom. And I had to go after her, hunt down the kidnappers and bring her home.* 'She . . . there were some bad people. And they wanted me to do something for them. So they took her away from me.'

Carly's eyes widened. 'Did . . . did she come back?'

Marina smiled. She hoped it was reassuring. 'Oh yes. I got her back. She came back home with me. But you know what? When things got bad for her, really bad, she had her teddy to cling on to. All the time, all the way. And he protected her. Made her feel strong. Just like Crusty is doing for you now.'

And it was me that got her. Brought her back. Not Phil, me.

Carly looked at the bear, back at Marina.

'So no matter what happens in here,' and to emphasise the point, Marina gestured round the room, 'you're safe. Whatever you say, whatever you do, you're safe. Because your teddy's with you. He won't let anything bad happen to you.'

Carly gazed at Marina, her eyes wide, desperate to believe, to trust. Not yet able to take that final step.

17

'Is . . . ' She glanced down at the teddy, looked once more at Marina. 'Is Josephina safe now?'

Marina smiled. Hoped it was convincing.

'Of course she is.'

Hoping the girl wouldn't notice the lie. Hoping she wouldn't be able to read her mind, know that nowhere was safe for Josephina – or Marina – now. Not any more. Not since . . .

She put those thoughts out of her head. She would deal with them later. She knew what she was going to do. But now she had to concentrate on Carly.

'So we're safe in here, Carly. You're safe. And we can talk. That's all. Just talk. Would you like to talk? To me?'

Carly took a long time to make up her mind. Then nodded.

'Yes,' she said.

Marina smiled. 'Good,' she said. 'That's good.' She arranged her posture into her least threatening, most open and responsive pose. 'So tell me what happened.'

Carly looked at the teddy, studied it for a long time, as if it was relaying information to her, giving her the will, the strength, to speak. Eventually she looked up. Said one word.

'Strawberry.'

PART TWO

SATURDAY BRIDGE

4

Rain lashed down, incessant and hard, washing away the life from the city, draining the colour from the afternoon, turning daylight to premature dusk. It was borne on a chill wind that when it swirled and strengthened made the cold wet drops into razor-ice projectiles, reminding everyone, if they needed it, that summer was only a distant memory and autumn was on its last legs.

Not the best kind of day to be out for any length of time.

Not the best kind of day to discover a dead body.

Detective Inspector Phil Brennan of the West Midlands Major Incident Squad stood on Saturday Bridge in Birmingham, looking down on the nearly drained locks of the Birmingham and Fazeley Canal from underneath an umbrella, waiting to be given the signal to approach. The two-tone crime-scene tape stretched across the footpath, demarcating where the normal world ended and the other world – the dangerous, murderous, tragic and brutal other world – started. Phil stood with his back to the tape. He had been here enough times. He knew which world was his.

The rain kept all but the most persistent rubberneckers away. The white plastic tent erected on the bank of the canal ensured that those who remained wouldn't be able to see anything anyway. Phil ignored the watchers, avoided eye contact and feigned deafness with the few reporters and TV crews who had braved the elements to chase a story. Shut out everything that was taking up valuable real estate inside his head, just concentrated on what was before him.

The hand holding the umbrella barely shook. That was something. His unshaven look could be explained away as fashionable stubble. His clothes, never very smart, might just look particularly shabby because of the rain. The sunken red eyes with the sleep-deprived black rings around them were harder to explain, though. He just hoped no one noticed. He sucked on an extra-strong mint, focused.

Even with the white tent erected, he knew that the chances of preserving the crime scene in the face of this whipping rain were, unless they were miraculously, religiously lucky, slim to none. But procedure had to be followed. He walked down the raised metal squares of the common approach path, stood at the entrance to the tent.

'You ready for me yet?' he called in to Jo Howe, a short, round, middle-aged woman and the leading crime-scene investigator.

Jo was kneeling on the ground, checking all around, careful not to touch the body in front of her. 'I'll call you when I'm ready. Get in the pub with the others,' she said without looking up.

He wanted to say, *I just want to be doing something. I need to be doing something.* But didn't. Instead he turned, walked away. Doing as she had suggested.

His wet jeans moulded themselves to his legs like a second skin, constricting his movement in the most unpleasant way possible as he walked back up to the bridge. His leather jacket kept out most of the water, but it still ran down his umbrella-holding hand and up his sleeve, down the back of his neck. He should change his clothes as soon as possible. Might get a cold or flu. Part of him didn't care.

He pushed through the small crowd, dodged the media, crossed the road and made for the pub. The Shakespeare had been on the same spot in Summer Row for years. Victorian and resolutely old-fashioned, it maintained a sense of tradition beside the more fashionable bars and kitchens that had sprung up next to it.

Phil went inside, flashed his warrant card at the barman, who beamed back. 'What can I get you?' he asked.

Phil knew the type. Eager to get bragging rights for assisting the police and hoping that some of the glamour of a major investigation would rub off on him. Glamour. *Tell that to the dead person on the canal towpath*, thought Phil.

'Coffee, please,' he said. 'I'll be in the back room.'

They had temporarily taken over the pub. Uniforms, plain clothes and SOCOs gathered around, sheltering from the rain until the temporary incident unit arrived. Phil saw two members of his team, Detective Sergeant Ian Sperring and Detective Constable Imani Oliver, sitting silently at a table underneath a bust of Shakespeare. He went over to join them.

'Heard somebody in here once asking if they were brothers,' said Sperring, pointing to the bust above his head, then to an identical one on the other corner. 'Shakespeare. Wondered if one did the writing and one did the, I dunno, acting or book-keeping or something.'

'And what did you tell them?' asked Imani, a glint of humour in her eye.

Sperring shrugged. 'Told them what they wanted to hear,' he said, expression liked a closed fist.

There was no love lost between the two officers, but Phil had insisted that since they were part of his team, they had to work together. Detective Constable Nadish Khan, the other imme-diate member of the team, was away on a training course. Sperring, ten years older than Phil and many pounds heavier, was ensconced in the corner, his bulk at rest, looking like he was going nowhere. Imani, keen and alert, was on the stool opposite.

Phil had been settled in Colchester, happy with his position with Essex Police. But when events had taken a near-terminal turn for the worse, the area hadn't seemed as welcoming, so he and Marina had decided on a change of scenery and picked Birmingham, the city of Marina's birth, as a destination. It had taken Phil some time to be accepted by his team. And for him to accept them. But out of that animosity had evolved a way of working they could all accept. The team had even begun to respect Phil's methods, even if they weren't in a hurry to adopt them.

He took off his leather jacket, slung it over the padded chair and sat down beside them. The pub was warm. He could almost feel the steam rising off his soaking legs. The front of his plaid shirt was wet through, the T-shirt underneath likewise.

Phil never wore a suit for work. He dressed as he pleased. A combo of Red Wing boots, heavy Japanese selvedge denim, a Western shirt and a leather jacket was the nearest thing he had to a uniform. This approach had brought him into conflict with other officers over the years, most recently his own team. He believed that creativity in dress led to creativity and intuition when it came to the job. His views weren't embraced, but he was tolerated. As long as he kept getting results.

'They ready for us yet?' asked Sperring, barely glancing up from the mug of industrial-strength tea he was stirring.

'They'll call us when they want us,' replied Phil.

'Why you been standing out in the rain?' asked Sperring, looking up.

Phil looked at his junior officer. Sperring had been stabbed on a case a few months previously and it seemed to have aged him. Not that he would admit it; he had wanted to come back to front-line duties the first opportunity. Phil admired his tenacity.

'Just . . . waiting,' he said.

Sperring studied him, eyes unusually compassionate. About to say something else. Thinking better of it.

Phil's coffee arrived. He thanked the barman, put his hand in his pocket.

'On the house,' the barman said.

'No,' said Phil, 'let me pay.'

'Won't hear of it. Anything I can do to help our boys in blue.'

The barman loitered in front of them, grinning, hoping to pick up some titbit of information, something he could tell his mates about. Or more likely a reporter.

'Well, thank you,' said Phil, dismissing the man. Once he was out of earshot, he turned to the other two. 'Hate it when they do that.'

'What?' said Sperring. 'Hang around trying to eavesdrop?'

'No, not let us pay. Like we're trying to get something for nothing.'

Sperring shrugged. 'Precious few perks in our line of work,' he said. 'A free cuppa now and again's neither here nor there.'

'That's how it starts,' said Phil. 'Anyway, who called it in?'

'Uniform,' said Imani. 'Got a call from a dog-walker this morning.'

'Not a dogger?' said Sperring. 'Get our fair share of those round here.'

'Must be committed to be out in this weather,' said Imani. 'Or need committing. No, this dog-walker saw the body in one of the locks. Supposed to be drained. No chance in this weather.'

'Did they give a statement?' asked Phil.

Sperring nodded, thought about having a sip of his tea. Thought better of it. 'Yeah. Don't think we've got much there.

25

Didn't see anyone else, anyone acting suspiciously, running away. Nothing. Spotted something in the lock. The dog almost went in looking at it. A woman. Mid to late twenties, as far as we can tell. That's all we know at the moment.'

Phil nodded. 'What else do we know about this dog walker?' he asked.

'Office worker in the city. Little dog, yappy kind, lives in those posh flats over there by the roundabout. Exercising it so it doesn't crap all over the carpet while she's out at work. Didn't seem the kind to be involved.'

'They never do,' said Phil.

At that moment his phone rang. Phil jumped, his heart skipping a beat. He took it from his jacket, almost dropping it in his haste to look at the display. He sighed. *No*, he thought. He put it to his ear, listened, nodded. Ended the call.

'That was Jo,' he said to the other two. 'She's ready when we are.' He stood up. 'Come on.'

The other two did likewise, Sperring not without difficulty.

Phil felt the wet denim tightening against his legs once more as he moved towards the door. Even worse than when he had entered. The wall of cold air hit him as he stepped outside, but he was chilled from more than the weather. He crossed the road, not looking forward to the sight that was waiting for him.

5

'So what have we got?' asked Phil.

Jo Howe straightened up, stared down at the body in front of her. The rain high-hatted on the plastic-sheeted roof, a never-ending irritating drum solo, especially inside Phil's head. 'Look for yourself,' she said. 'Ask Esme. Her department.' The way she phrased the words told Phil she was glad she didn't have to deal with that side of things.

Kneeling beside the body was the pathologist, Esme Russell, arrived while Phil had been over the road. Young, pretty, her hair scraped back into a ponytail, she looked and sounded to Phil more like a debutante at her coming-out party than a professional corpse-prodder at a crime scene.

'Hey, Esme,' he said. 'Good to see you.'

She glanced up at him, nodded, went back to examining the corpse. 'We'll have to stop meeting like this. Someone will talk.' She gestured to the body in front of her. 'Not this poor creature, though.'

Phil came over, his paper-wrapped boots already threatening to dissolve, clanking wetly on the raised metal CAP. He knelt down beside Esme, as near as he dared to go to the body. His first instinct, even after all his years as a front-line detective, was to look away. Not out of horror. Perhaps decency. But he knew that wasn't the correct approach, the professional one. Resurrecting this person as a living, breathing human being would come later. Right now, whoever this had been was, just for a few moments, not as important as who – or what – the body was now. A mass of clues. A way in. The climax to a story that he had to write the beginning to. A whodunnit for him to solve.

'Jesus,' he said. 'She didn't go easily . . . '

'No,' said Esme. 'Let's see what we've got. Female. Perhaps in her twenties, thirties, judging by what's left of her.'

Phil studied the body as dispassionately as he could. 'Yeah,' he said. 'What's left. Not to mention what the water's done to her.'

'And the things in the water,' said Esme. 'Where exactly was she found?'

'Just outside. In the lock, floating. Someone called us.'

'Good job she was lying face down,' said Esme, 'or whoever found her would have lost their breakfast.'

'Can you work out what's been done to her pre- and post-mortem?'

'Do my best,' she said. 'But it'll take time.'

Phil nodded in agreement, studied the body. It was difficult to differentiate between what her killer had done to her and what had happened in the water. Difficult but not impossible. He made some preliminary judgements.

The woman was white, or had been. Death had discoloured her, the water bloated her. Her face looked bruised and purple. Small chunks of flesh were missing, ragged holes all over.

He pointed to the marks. 'Rats?'

'And whatever else was in the water with her.'

Phil shuddered, tried to convince himself it was just the cold and the damp.

Her legs and arms were cut and scored. He peered closer. Small round patches on her skin.

'What are they?' he asked Esme.

28

'Look like burns to me,' she said examining them. 'See here, on her thighs and arms. Mostly her inner thighs.' She looked closely. 'I'll run some more tests later, but it looks like they've been allowed to scab over then been burned open again. Hard to tell, everything's so wet.'

Phil felt his stomach lurch. He swallowed it down, concentrated on the professional, analytical part of his brain.

'So this was done, what? Over time?'

Esme shrugged. 'Looks that way.'

'Can you—'

Esme smiled. 'I know what you're going to ask me. And no. I can't give you a time of death. Not yet. I couldn't even hazard a guess.'

'Worth a try,' said Phil.

Another smile, equally as grim as the first. 'You should know better than to ask by now.'

'I know.' He turned his attention back to the body. 'What d'you think caused those?'

The other wounds on her arms and legs were deep, straight slices.

'A knife, I would say. Straight blade, sharp. No serrated or jagged edges. Swift cuts. All done with force, and judging by the depth of the wounds – that one cuts right down to the bone –' she indicated the right arm, 'there was a degree of emotion behind the thrusts.'

'I can guess what kind of emotion,' said Phil. 'And what about that?'

Finally. He had kept the biggest till last.

There was something about the body that neither of them had yet mentioned, but it was the one feature they couldn't ignore. The defining one of the woman's fatal injuries. The gaping hole in the centre of her body.

'Well,' said Esme, 'I'd say her heart's been removed.'

'Yeah,' said Phil, distracted by the sight. 'I agree. And it certainly wasn't the rats.'

'No,' she said. 'Not unless they were strong enough to crack open her ribs, bend them back and cut the heart out.'

Esme sat back, exhaled. Phil kept staring at the body, hoping it would give up its secrets. He became aware that Esme was watching him. He turned to her. She smiled.

'Any news?'

Phil frowned, surprised. 'How did you . . . '

'Oh, come on. It's all over the station. Everyone knows, I'm afraid. Sorry.'

Phil said nothing.

'How are you?'

Phil felt another shudder inside him that was definitely nothing to do with the cold or the body. 'I've got my work,' he said. 'I'm fine.'

She straightened up, face just beside his. 'If you want to . . . ' She sighed, almost shook her head, but continued. 'If you'd like a drink one night, or . . . I don't know, dinner . . . just as, you know. Just as friends. Or . . . ' A shrug. 'Friends.'

Phil dredged up a smile. 'Thank you, Esme, but—'

'Can we come in yet?'

They both turned. Sperring and Imani were standing at the flap of the tent, getting drenched. The umbrellas they held seemed ineffectual.

'Sorry,' said Phil, standing up as if he had been caught doing something he shouldn't. He was aware of Esme moving swiftly away from him. 'Got caught up. Careful where you stand when you come in.'

They entered, saw the body.

'Jesus,' said Sperring, 'Deep breaths all round.'

'Oh my God . . . ' Imani screwed her eyes tightly closed.

'Look at it out of the corner of your eye,' said Sperring. 'Like

30

stargazing at night. That's the way you see constellations and that.'

They all stood in silence, taking in the sight before them.

'Suppose ID's a bit too straightforward to hope for,' said Sperring.

'There are a couple of tattoos on the body,' said Esme, 'One looks like a name. Perhaps her? Or a child?'

'We'll check with MisPers,' said Phil. 'See if they've got anything outstanding that might fit.'

'So,' said Imani, 'what kind of person we looking for? The man that did this?'

'You think it's a man?' asked Phil. 'Jumping to conclusions.'

Imani shrugged. 'Well ... if it is a man, it's a man who ...' She couldn't finish.

Phil kept staring at the body. Nodded. 'Yeah,' he said, eyes never moving from that gaping wound. 'Whoever they are, they certainly hate women.'

6

Janine Gillen took a seat slowly, lowered herself carefully. She failed to quell her shaking as she crossed her legs and placed her hands on the armrests. Then she quickly, jerkily smoothed down the front of her blouse. It was Primark but good. Clean, well looked after. She always liked to look her best coming here. Liked to have something to dress up for, to take pride in her appearance. Even this. She took a couple of deep breaths. Tried to relax, or at least look relaxed. Failed.

The man in front of her, Keith Bailey, smiled. Janine relaxed slightly, finding the smile comforting.

'Just you this time?' asked Keith.

Janine nodded. 'I ... I tried to ... ' She snuffled, drew in a ragged breath through her nose. 'Just me.'

'Okay then.' Keith nodded, smiled once more. Casually dressed, a soft plaid shirt and chinos, blonde hair nicely styled. Glasses. He had notes on his knee but he didn't consult them. He was familiar enough with Janine's story. She had been seeing him for a few weeks now. Mostly on her own, which wasn't ideal, but ... that was the way it went sometimes. Unfortunately.

'So ...' Keith paused, allowed Janine to gather herself before the talking began in earnest. 'How are things with Terry?'

Janine sighed. The shaking in her hands began again. 'The ... the same. He ...' She took her hands off the armrests, uncrossed her legs. She hugged her arms close to her body, aware of the increasingly violent trembling in her hands, especially the left one. Always the left one. 'He . . . ' She sighed. 'I . . . I thought things would get better. After, you know. After he came here.'

Keith nodded. He had heard these words – or similar ones – before. Too many times.

'But he . . . he . . . Well, things were okay for a few days. After, you know. The first time. He was . . . mindful of things. Of me and the twins. He . . . would think before he . . . he did things.'

Keith nodded, shifted slightly in his seat. 'And did he ever seek counselling on his own? Contact the therapist I gave him the number of?'

She shook her head. 'No. He, he said he would. And I think he meant to, I really do. But he . . . he didn't.'

'Right.' Keith nodded, made a couple of notes on the pad in his lap. 'Right. And how is he with the twins?'

The trembling in Janine's left hand increased. She pushed it tight against her body. 'He . . . he started to get angry with them again.'

Keith leaned forward, professional concern in his eyes. 'Has he hurt them? Attacked them in any way?'

She shook her head. 'No. Not . . . ' Another shake of the head, more emphatic this time. 'No.'

'You sure?'

She nodded, not making eye contact.

Keith sat back. He had been a marriage counsellor long enough to know when someone was lying to him. And not just lying, covering something up. Something unpleasant. 'Are you sure, Janine?'

Still she couldn't make eye contact.

'Janine?' Again Keith leaned forward. His voice dropped. 'Has he hurt the boys?'

33

She shook her head. 'No.'

Keith sat back, understanding. 'Has he started hitting you again, Janine?'

She nodded. And that was when the tears, long dammed, erupted.

Janine Darvill had thought she had found the perfect man when she met Terry Gillen. Tall, dark and handsome, with a glint of the roguish bastard twinkle in his eye. As she eventually found out, it wasn't just a twinkle. And she wasn't the only one to fall for it. Unfortunately, she was married and pregnant by then.

It had sounded quite romantic, or at least she had made herself believe it was. Meet a handsome man, have kids, be happy ever after. Her friends had stayed on at school, got A levels, gone to college or even, in a few cases, university. And Janine had intended to do that, or something like that. Go to college. Learn hairdressing or beauty, whatever. Get trained. Get a job. Meet a man, have kids ... She had done that all right. A mother at seventeen, married at eighteen.

Terry was the first real boyfriend she had ever had. He was a few years older than her and had been around a bit, but she knew that. Liked it even; it made her feel special that such a man of the world had chosen her.

Except he hadn't. Once the twins were born, he was back out at nights, drinking, disappearing for days on end sometimes. He was a roofer by trade, when he was working, and he sometimes 'forgot' to leave her housekeeping money.

Janine was spending more time on her own. Or rather on her own with two squealing babies that she didn't know how to look after, barely more than a kid herself. And no friends to turn to. They were all in work or at college.

Her mother would help when she could but she also had to look after her stepfather, who was on long-term sick. Janine

34

knew it was alcohol and obesity-related diabetes but her mother insisted he had been injured at work.

Janine couldn't cope. She had told Terry he had to stay in more, take more responsibility. And that was when he first hit her.

She didn't know what had happened. He had smacked her across the face, told her to shut her whingeing fucking mouth. She was so stunned that she burst into tears and just lay there. Terry had stormed out. Later, when he returned, he was drunk and tearful. Told her he didn't know what had happened, that he had never hit a woman before and that he never would again. That men who did that were the worst kind of scum. He begged and begged her to forgive him. So she did. And things got slightly better.

Until he did it again.

And again.

The same treatment, the same drunken remorse afterwards.

And as everything spiralled downwards, Janine tried to work out how her life had come to this. How her romantic ideal had come crashing down around her. She wondered what she had done wrong, how she had displeased him. Couldn't find anything but knew there must be something. Eventually she told her mother, who said she had to leave him.

She tried. Told him she was going, taking the kids with her. He hit her again, even harder. Told her that she was his, and not to forget it. And hit her again, harder than ever this time. That was the first time the police were called.

After that, things changed. For a while. Knowing that the police would be keeping an eye on him, Terry agreed to marriage counselling. He started to come with Janine to see Keith. And things seemed to be better. But deep down Janine knew it wasn't peace. It was just the pause before reloading.

And then he started getting angry again.

*

'So . . .' Keith was saying, 'he doesn't hurt the children.'

She shook her head.

'Is that because he's taking it out on you instead?'

She felt that she could tell Keith anything, that he would understand. He was a reasonable man, a *good* man. She wished all men were like him. Or at least the one she had married. She nodded.

'Right. And is there a pattern to this behaviour of his? Is he drunk when he does it?'

'Usually.'

Keith sighed.

They talked for nearly an hour, the whole of the session, Keith being as professionally concerned as he could, Janine sobbing over what had happened to her life. Eventually he opened the file on his lap, took out a card, handed it over.

'Here,' he said. 'Take this.'

Janine took it, looked at it. Safe Haven, it said. And a phone number.

'Legally I'm bound to tell the police. And social services. There's a crime being committed and your children are in danger.'

'No, please . . .' she said between sobs. 'Please don't. That'll just . . . just make things worse.'

'Perhaps in the short term, but in the long term it'll make things better. In the meantime, you need to get out of that house. It's a toxic environment for you and the kids.' He looked straight at her, steel in his eyes. 'You don't have to put up with this. You deserve better. You've got your whole life ahead of you.' He sat back. 'Think about it. Think about it hard.'

She nodded, clutching the card close to her.

It was time for her to go. They both stood up. Janine was reluctant to leave the room, to go back to her life.

'Call that number,' Keith said. 'They can help you.'

'Thank you.' Almost sobbing again.

'And do it straight away. Things aren't going to get better with Terry. He's not going to change. Get out of there as quick as you can.'

Janine nodded once more and the tears started again.

She waited until they had subsided, then, aided by copious amounts of tissues from the often-replenished box in Keith's room, made her way outside, the card clutched tightly in her hand.

Terrified, but ready to make a positive change to her life.

7

Seedy. It was a word that Phil had, of course, often heard and often used. He knew its original meaning – gone to seed, no use any more – and its more recent connotation – the above but with an added layer of sleaze – but he had never seen such a perfectly apt example of both definitions sitting in front of him.

Short and round almost in proportion, Detective Sergeant Hugh Ellison looked like he came from a planet with a denser gravity than Earth. Despite being younger than he looked, he appeared to Phil like the kind of detective who was waiting for the seventies to return, with all that decade's swagger, corruption and political incorrectness. A relic of a bygone age he was too young to remember. Amongst other things, the moustache – clearly not grown ironically for any charitable purpose – gave him away. He was thinning on top, his suit a remnant from when he was a couple of sizes smaller, his shirt collar unable to meet round his neck, his tie overdue for a clean. Eyes darting, shifting. Gambler's eyes, always calculating the odds, working an advantage.

Seedy.

It had been relatively easy to find out the dead woman's identity. That was one thing Phil felt he should be grateful for. He had phoned the Missing Persons Unit, asked if they could run a search on women, twenty to thirty, missing fairly recently, with tattoos, one saying 'Carly', one an inscription in a foreign language, possibly something Arabic. That in turn led him down to Digbeth nick on the High Street.

When he had first arrived in Birmingham, Phil had been sent to Steelhouse Lane, the main station. Backing on to both the magistrates' and crown courts, it looked like a faux-Gothic castle. He wasn't naive enough to think they would all look like that but had nevertheless been surprised at the differing stations in the city. He had been amazed to find that Digbeth was actually a functioning police station. It looked from the road like a closed and shuttered mansion or private school, litter and street detritus gathering in its main doorway, faded posters in the wall-mounted glass display. The blue lamp still hung outside, seemingly never lit since the fifties. But a quick walk round the side showed how deceptive first appearances could be. Patrol cars, vans, people carriers and unmarkeds were all parked up alongside. He had gone in asking for the name of the person he had spoken to on the phone.

Now, in an office that boasted the best of office-surplus chic, Phil was shaking hands with Detective Sergeant Hugh Ellison. The man sat at his desk surrounded by detritus, making Phil think of a spider at the centre of a dirty, cluttered web.

'Sit down,' said Ellison, pointing to a black object that had been an office chair in a previous life. He noted Phil's trepidation. Smiled. His teeth matched the rest of him. 'Budget cuts,' he said. 'Not that glamour boys like you would know anything about that.'

Phil was slightly taken aback. Was that meant to be an insult? Or maybe a test, to see how he would react. He kept a straight face, didn't rise to the bait. 'Nothing glamorous about finding dead bodies. Thought we were all on the same side.'

Ellison just shrugged, like he didn't care if Phil was offended or not.

39

'So you want to see me about Gemma Adderley,' said Ellison.

'That's the name I was given.'

Ellison nodded. 'Think it's fair to say we're thinking of the same person.' He reached forward, grabbed a folder from the desk. 'Could have just emailed you all the stuff, but here's a copy of the file. Nice to do it the old-fashioned way sometimes.' Another smile, another reminder for Phil to book a dentist's appointment.

Phil took the folder. 'Thank you. Sure it's her?'

Ellison nodded. 'Worked the case myself. Stuck in my mind. Course, the tattoo's the thing. Soon as you mentioned that, I knew.'

Phil skimmed the notes in the folder. 'What can you tell me about her?'

Ellison shrugged, looked at the Tesco Value sandwich on his desk. Phil presumed it was a signal for him to leave so the two of them could spend some time alone, but he hadn't finished so he stayed where he was.

'Went missing from her home in Hollywood,' said Ellison when he realised Phil wasn't going anywhere. 'About a month ago. Exact date'll be in there. Without her husband. Disappeared.'

'Right. Okay.' Phil was already formulating plans, means of approach.

'Don't you wanna know the rest?' A glint in Ellison's eye now.

'The rest? Yeah. Go on.'

'There was a daughter.'

'Carly?' asked Phil. 'The tattoo?'

'That's the one. Found wandering the streets in Digbeth by some students coming out of a club. Couldn't get much out of her, poor kid. In shock. Had to bring in a professional to help.'

40

'Right,' said Phil.

Ellison grinned. 'Your missus.'

Phil stared. Said nothing.

Ellison laughed. 'Yeah, I know who you are, mate.' He nodded. 'Your DCI, Cotter, recommended her. And she was good, too, Marina.' The look on his face and the relish in pronouncing her name indicated that he was making more than a professional appraisal of Phil's wife.

'Good?' Phil barely got the word out.

'With the kid. Carly. Got her talking. But then when you've got kids yourself, you know how to talk to them. I've got three.' He gave a guttural laugh. 'That I know of.'

Phil didn't join in.

'That's how we found out so much about Carly's mother. And the father.'

Phil swallowed back everything that the thought of Marina had put into his head, concentrated on Ellison's words. 'Tell me.'

'The kid said they were going on holiday. Just her and the mother.'

'And were they?'

'Dunno. Nothing was booked. At least not in her name. Her mobile never turned up either, so we don't know if she made any arrangements on that.'

'Just her and the mother?' asked Phil. 'What about the father? You questioned him, I take it?'

'Yeah, we liked him for it. But ...' Ellison shrugged once more. 'Couldn't get anything to stick. And we tried. By God we tried. The kid was thrown out of a car. Didn't get a good look at the driver, didn't hear his voice. She didn't think it was her father but we didn't rule it out. She was in shock. Memory plays tricks.'

'What about—'

'Him hiring someone, were you going to say?'

Phil nodded.

'Nothing in his bank account. But again, that doesn't rule it out.'

Phil looked at the file in his hands, suddenly anxious to leave. The cramped room was becoming oppressive. He felt like he couldn't breathe.

'Well, thanks. I'll be—'

'One more thing,' said Ellison. 'About the husband.'

'What?' Phil waited.

'Still reckon it was him, but . . . ' Ellison brought his hands together in prayer, looked heavenwards, mock piety in his eyes. Then he looked at Phil, laughed. 'God on his side. Good luck, mate.'

Phil took that as his cue to leave, and turned, walked down the corridor away from Ellison.

Feeling sure eyes were boring into his back all the way out.

8

Birmingham Airport sat outside the city centre on a flat sub-urban stretch of land, a collection of huge metal and glass huts with added overhead noise pollution.

Phil Brennan flashed his warrant card on the way in and parked his Audi in the staff car park. He and Sperring asked for directions, then made their way to the administration building.

'I'm looking for Roy Adderley,' he said to the woman on the desk. 'Is he about?'

The woman, small, round and Afro-Caribbean, with perfectly made-up hair, stared up at him, eyes wide in alarm. He knew what she was thinking. Police. Terrorist.

'Can I ask what this is concerning?'

Phil gave her what he hoped was a reassuring smile. Reassuring, yet hard enough to stop her asking any further questions. 'I'm afraid it's a personal matter.'

Head down, the woman began pressing keys, checking her screen. Eventually she looked up. 'He's working at the moment.' Like that was an end of it.

'Could we see him, please? This is important.'

Again she looked down, then back up. 'I'll need to get you an escort.'

'Thank you,' said Phil.

A security guard came to take them across to where Roy

Adderley was working. First he checked their warrant cards again and asked the nature of their business. Phil wasn't very forthcoming.

'Just take us to Mr Adderley.' He was losing patience.

The security guard stared at him, clearly not used to having his authority questioned. 'I don't have to, you know. If you want to be unpleasant, I can just refuse. We take security very seriously here. Can't let just anybody wander about.'

Phil turned to him, glared like he wanted to do him some damage. 'And I take having my time wasted even more seriously. We're on official police business. We're doing our job. You do yours.'

The guard reluctantly backed down, led them out of the admin block and across the tarmac, never speaking once, striding so quickly they had to almost run to keep up. Eventually he came to a stop, gestured towards another low-level building, this one with less glass and more metal, of the corrugated variety.

'He'll be in there.'

'Right,' said Phil. 'Thank you for your cooperation.'

'I'll tell him you're here.'

'We can mange,' said Sperring, wheezing from the brisk exercise.

Phil joined him as the security guard walked away, muttering audibly under his breath.

'You all right?'

'Fine,' said Sperring in between gasps for breath.

'Don't exert yourself. Remember what the doctor said. Give your body time to heal fully.'

'Nothing wrong with me,' said Sperring. 'Fuck's the matter with you?'

Phil bristled. He knew what was coming. 'What d'you mean?'

'You know what I mean. Talking to that security jobsworth the way you did. Thought you were going to leather him one.'

'Officious little twat,' said Phil. 'Deserved it.'

Sperring frowned at Phil. 'What happened to Mr Liberal? Sorry, Detective Inspector Liberal? Usually it's me doing the bad cop routine and you telling me not to be so hard on him because he's on minimum wage and his mum didn't buy him a pet dog when he was little, or some such bollocks.'

'Yeah, well,' said Phil, looking straight ahead and not wanting to be drawn into conversation. 'Just the way it is.'

They approached the hangar. It had huge double doors at the front, a glass-fronted entryway beside them. They went into the reception area. Beyond the window was a small room with uniformed people sitting round on worn-out easy chairs. A sink area in the corner. Through another door Phil could see that the main part of the building was full of buses. This was where the passenger transport was coordinated from.

'Roy Adderley,' he said to the woman behind the desk, showing his warrant card once more. 'Detective Inspector Brennan and Detective Sergeant Sperring.'

'Is this about his wife?' asked the woman. She was quite young, white, heavily made up, with a figure that had crossed the line between curvaceous and morbid obesity.

Here we go again, thought Phil. 'Just get him, please.' His tone perhaps more brusque and irritable than usual.

She turned to the room behind her, gestured. 'He's in there.' She looked between the pair of them, eyes wide, looking scared. She stood up. 'I'll go and get him.'

'No thanks, we can—'

But the woman was off her seat and straight through to the other room. Phil and Sperring followed. They arrived while she was still speaking.

'Roy,' she said, 'it's the police. They want to see you . . . '

A uniformed man on the other side of the room stood up. Medium height, medium build, sandy hair, he had once been good-looking, but various forms of self-abuse seemed to be taking care of that.

'The police, Roy,' the receptionist said again.

Roy Adderley looked between the three of them.

Then turned and ran.

9

Marina Esposito checked her watch. It was nearly time.
She looked out of the window, up and down the street, both sides, stayed there until she was sure no one was loitering, hiding. Scanned the windows opposite for signs of movement, sudden or otherwise, light glinting off anything behind them. Any unfamiliar cars that she hadn't seen before, number plates that didn't match those on the lists she had already made. She repeated this procedure once more before she was satisfied that there was no one in the street who shouldn't have been there. Then she picked up her keys, checked her pockets and made her way out, making sure she triple-locked the door behind her.

It was her routine, her system.

Still in her gym gear – she barely seemed to be out of it these days – she ran down the road, knowing that the blade was in her pocket, hoping she wouldn't have to use it but knowing that if she did, she would do so without a second thought. Scanning all the time, alert for any signs of danger.

She reached her destination, stopped running. She was barely out of breath. Her time at the gym and her regular self-defence classes had left her in good shape.

Her route was timed; she knew exactly how long it would take. She also knew how long she would have to spend there – at least roughly; there were always fluctuations that she couldn't control – and how long the walk back would be. She didn't speak to anyone else, had nothing to say to them. Sometimes she offered a smile so as not to draw attention to herself. To look as normal as possible. But mostly she just did what was expected of her. Her job, almost.

She stood by the gate until the noise level on the other side began to increase, then readied herself. Another glance round – behind her, to the side, nothing out of the ordinary – and then she turned her attention straight ahead. Locked on, focused, determined to let nothing and no one come between them.

The afternoon school run.

'There you are, precious.'

'Hello, Mummy!'

Josephina Esposito-Brennan ran towards Marina, smile on her face like she didn't have a care in the world. Marina knelt down and hugged her, as she always did. Then straightened up, holding her hand and glancing round, checking. Like she always did.

'You had a good day, sweetheart?'

Josephina began to tell her mother about her day while they walked. Marina listened, eyes alive for threat all the while.

'Can Krista come round to play?'

'Sorry, sweetheart. Not today.'

The little girl looked momentarily sad. She was used to being given that answer but it didn't stop her from asking. She glanced up at Marina, face expectant.

'Is Daddy home tonight?'

'No, sweetheart, I'm afraid he isn't.'

'Why not? Why do I never see Daddy any more?'

'Because . . .' Marina sighed. *Because he can't protect us, sweetheart. He can't keep us safe any more. Not like I can.* It wasn't the first time that question had arisen and it wouldn't be the last.

48

Marina tried to be honest with the little girl, but there were still some things she couldn't tell her.

And hoped she would never have to.

'He's . . . still busy. Sorry.'

'Is he still away?'

'He is, yes.' She hated lying but knew she had no choice. She changed the subject. 'Shall we bake some biscuits when we get home? You and me?'

The disappointment at not seeing her father slid off the little girl's face, to be replaced by a tentative excitement at what lay ahead when she got back to the flat. She nodded vigorously.

'That's my girl. Come on, I've got everything we need ready in the kitchen.'

They hurried back to the flat, Marina scanning the streets constantly.

They made it to the front door without mishap. *Dodged another bullet*, Marina thought, and went inside, checking the lock for signs of tampering. Everything looked fine. Thankfully.

She ushered Josephina into the kitchen, gave her some juice, got her set up for baking.

Always busy, she thought. That was the best thing. Always keep busy. Something to do, someone to protect. Work. Push herself. Don't stop to think. Because if she did that, she might just fall apart.

'Right,' she said, summoning up a smile, 'chocolate or peanut butter? Or both?'

Before Josephina could answer, Marina's phone rang.

She excused herself, went to answer it. Checked the display. Work.

'Marina Esposito.' Her voice strong, capable.

'Afternoon,' said a voice she had come to know quite well in the last month. Know, but not necessarily like.

'Hello, DS Ellison, what can I do for you?'

'Hugh, please, I've told you. No need for such formality when we're work colleagues.'

She could imagine the leering smile as he spoke those words and felt a nausea in her stomach.

The Carly Adderley case. Marina had talked to the girl, managed to coax facts out of her about her mother's disappearance. Comforted her when she had broken down repeatedly in tears. Then tried her best to put her back together again, even arranging treatment to hopefully minimise what she had gone through. If that was possible.

Ellison had been impressed with her work. And, Marina strongly suspected, impressed with her in a less than professional capacity. It happened from time to time. She just ignored it, carried on. Let Carly Adderley break her heart.

'So what can I do for you, DS Ellison?' Ignoring his exhortation.

A pause, then he continued. 'Just wanted to give you a heads-up, that's all. You might be back on the case.'

'Which case? Carly?'

'That's the one. Her mother's turned up. Well, her body, anyway. Or what's left of it.'

A shudder ran through Marina. 'Oh, God.'

'Yeah, I know.' Ellison's voice sounded anything but empathetic. 'Murder, they reckon. So I just wanted to let you know that you might be asked for your thoughts.'

'Right. Thanks. Well, I have—' She stopped short as another thought occurred to her. 'Who's . . . who's investigating?'

Ellison could barely keep the relish out of his voice. 'Your ex.'

'He's not my ex,' she said quickly, heatedly. 'We're . . . separated.'

'Right,' said Ellison, with some degree of disappointment. 'Well, like I said, I just wanted to let you know.'

'Thank you.'

50

'And if you ever want some . . . assistance or—'

'I'll let you know.'

She hung up as quickly as she could, threw the phone on to the sofa as if it were contaminated.

Shit, she thought. *Shit, shit, shit.*

'Are we going to make biscuits now?'

Marina turned. Josephina stood at the living room door, concern on her face.

'Yes,' she said absently. 'Yes, darling, we are.'

She ushered her daughter into the kitchen. Tried to find a smile for the child. One that told her everything was all right, that her mother was there for her and everything was going to be fine.

Hoped she succeeded.

10

Straight through the inner door, out into the main bus hangar, Adderley ran, Phil right after him.

Adderley knew his way round better, knew which corner to duck round, where to run ahead. He ran between parked buses, doubled back, down the other way. Phil, fast but often wrong-footed, kept chase.

Adderley broke into the open, made for the main doors. Phil could sense him flagging, saw him trip, stumble, but keep going. He reached the doors, went outside. Phil after him. Immediately all sound was taken away by the roar of a departing plane, right overhead. Adderley kept running, down the tarmac, towards the perimeter fence. Phil felt anger burning inside him. Who the hell was he to run? Who did he think he was?

Adderley was weakening. He stopped ahead of Phil, bent double, hands braced on his thighs, back heaving with heavy, deep breaths. As Phil approached him, he turned, looked up. Shaking his head slowly from side to side, he began to speak.

Phil was on him. Head-butting him right in the middle of his face, knocking him flat on the ground. He bent down, grabbed Adderley by the front of his uniform, pulled him up. The man had trouble breathing, the fall having knocked all the air from his lungs. That didn't stop Phil from his task. Neither did the blood that was now spurting from Adderley's nose.

He set him on his feet, ignoring his protestations, his waving arms, the wheezing, groaning sound he was making.

'Roy Adderley,' said Phil, 'I want a word with you.' He looked at the damage he'd caused. Smiled.

'Right, boss, I'll take it from here.'

Phil barely heard the words. It wasn't until he felt a forceful hand on his shoulder that he turned round. Sperring was behind him, the woman from reception next to him. Another plane boomed overhead. The rain poured down.

'Let's get back inside that hangar,' said Sperring, 'shall we?'

The room with the worn-out chairs had been cleared. Roy Adderley sat hunched over, the majority of a roll of toilet paper applied to his face. The paper was more red than white. The receptionist sat next to him, her hand on his arm, concern in his eyes. She kept firing darts of pure anger at Phil. Until she saw his expression. Then the looks became more fearful and her eyes would flutter and drop.

'Can I have a word?' asked Sperring at Phil's side.

Phil turned to him. 'Not now,' he said.

Sperring kept staring at him, clearly with plenty to say.

'Later,' said Phil. He turned his attention to Adderley. 'Mr Adderley. You ready to talk now?'

Adderley looked up, eyes as fearful as the receptionist's. 'What did you do that for?'

'Why did you run?' asked Sperring, lowering himself into an armchair opposite Adderley, then instantly regretting it as he wondered how he would get out of it again, 'We only wanted to talk.'

Adderley's eyes darted from side to side. Getting ready to lie, Phil thought.

'I didn't know who you were,' he said. 'I thought . . . thought you were . . . I don't know.'

'We identified ourselves as police officers, Mr Adderley. There was no doubt as to who we were.'

Adderley just shook his head. 'What did you want to talk about?'

Phil glanced at the receptionist. 'Might be better if you hear this on your own.'

Adderley shook his head. 'You can say what you want in front of Trudi,' he said. 'I don't mind.'

'And if I'm not here as a witness, you might hit him again,' said Trudi, feeling braver now.

'I didn't hit him,' said Phil. 'Force was used but it was used proportionately and appropriately.'

She didn't reply.

'Mr Adderley,' said Phil, sitting down. 'It's about your wife. About Gemma.'

Adderley took the red-crusted paper away from his face. The blood had dried on his skin, giving the appearance of an all-over birthmark. 'You found her?'

'We have, Mr Adderley.'

'Where is she then? Where's she been? She left me, you know. Ran off and left Carly too.'

'She didn't, Mr Adderley.'

Adderley leaned forward, feeling braver now. 'Oh yes, she did.'

'No, Mr Adderley, she didn't. She was murdered.'

Adderley looked from one to the other. 'Murdered?'

'I'm afraid so.'

Phil studied the two of them. Trudi seemed the more upset. Adderley blinked hard and fast, like his eyes were doing calculations behind his eyelids.

'We'll get a family liaison officer to contact you,' he said. 'In the meantime, we're going to need you to answer some questions.'

54

'What, here? Now?'

Phil raised his hands, looked around. 'Why not? If you don't mind doing it in front of Trudi, of course.'

A look of cunning entered Adderley's eyes. Cunning interlaced with fear. 'No,' he said. 'Not here.'

'Why not?' asked Sperring.

Adderley's eyes darted once more. 'Because ... I'm not going to say anything without a solicitor present. That's why. Not going to answer anything.' He sat back, looking quite relieved.

Phil scrutinised him. 'Why did you run?' he asked again.

Adderley said nothing.

'In my experience,' said Sperring, 'only guilty people run. Why did you run, Mr Adderley?'

'I'm ... I'm not saying another word until I speak to a solicitor. I know my rights.'

'I'm sure you do, Mr Adderley. And I'm sure you have a solicitor handy.'

Adderley narrowed his eyes. 'What's that supposed to mean?'

'We checked your file before coming here,' said Phil. 'Seems you have quite a history where your wife was concerned.'

'Nothing was ever proved,' Adderley said.

'No,' said Phil. 'Complaints were made against you by Gemma, but she always dropped the charges, didn't she?'

'What's this?' asked Trudi.

'Lies,' said Adderley. 'Said I was ... hitting her.'

'And were you?' asked Phil.

'We had arguments, yeah. Like all couples. But that was it, that was all. I'm not ... not like that. Not that kind of person. I'm born again.'

'Right,' said Phil. 'And does your God know you go about hitting women? Or was he the one who told you to do it?'

Adderley reddened, looked angry. Phil stared at him. He didn't reply. Silence fell.

'Don't you want to know any of the details?' asked Sperring. 'About your wife?'

Adderley glanced between the pair of them like it was a trick question and he didn't know what the right answer would be. 'When my solicitor's there,' he said.

'And that's that, is it?' said Phil.

'Yeah,' said Adderley. 'That's that.'

Phil and Sperring exchanged a look. 'Well,' said Phil, 'in that case, we'll be off.' Behind him, he heard Sperring noisily trying to extricate himself from the armchair.

They made their way to the door. 'We'll see ourselves out,' said Phil.

Sperring paused before leaving. 'I hope you'll be very happy together,' he said. 'And that God approves.' He followed Phil out.

The rain was easing, the clouds thinning. But no sign of the sun. Dark soon.

Sperring stopped walking, stared at Phil, mouth open. 'What the bloody hell was all that about?'

Phil tried not to make eye contact with him, keep walking. Sperring wouldn't let him. 'Nothing.'

'Nothing? Nothing? You nutted that bloke. He could sue you.'

'Let him try. He ran. Had to stop him somehow.'

'If it is him, and if this case somes to court, a good brief could have it thrown out. Jesus Christ, what's the matter with you?'

Phil looked at Sperring. Really looked at him. 'I'm fine,' he said.

Sperring studied his boss's features. He seemed about to say something but thought better of it. The anger was draining from him, to be replaced by something else. Compassion, Phil thought. The last thing he wanted.

'I said I'm fine.'

Sperring stepped back, still looking at him. 'You'd better be.'

They reached the car and drove away. Phil thought about the lies he was telling people. The lies he was telling himself.

11

Janine Gillen could barely breathe. She was on the verge of a panic attack, she knew it, recognised the signs from the previous ones. And it wasn't her fault. None of it. *None* of it. But she knew she would get the blame. She always did.

The Metro train was stuck on the track. Hadn't even reached The Hawthorns yet. No word from the driver other than an apology for the delay and a hope that they would be on the move shortly.

Janine glanced round the carriage, checking everyone else's expressions, trying to find answers. Clues as to how long they would be there, comfort that it wouldn't be long till they were moving again. All the while trying not to let her terror show, communicate to the others. She didn't want any of them asking if she was all right. She didn't want to answer that question.

Her twin boys were with her sister. They always went there when she was in town. Terry didn't know she was still going. No idea. He had told her what he thought of the counselling sessions, of Keith, in no uncertain terms, and that was that. End of story. He wasn't going again, therefore she wasn't going again. And she knew what she would get if she defied him.

Yet still she went. She didn't know how or where she had found the strength to defy him, but found it she had. And she kept going because she drew comfort from the sessions. Keith made her think of her life before she met Terry. The silly, romantic girl with her hopes and dreams. Thinking that she didn't need an education, not if she had a good man to love and take care of, and who would love and take care of her in return. Keith didn't make her feel stupid for thinking those things. Like he said, he gave her permission to feel like that, to think like that.

There was one other thing the sessions had taught her, and it was something she couldn't stop saying to herself: *It's not my fault.*

Because it had been. For years. Her fault. Always her fault. Whatever happened. If it was bad weather and Terry couldn't work, her fault. If one of the twins was ill and off school, making a noise coughing while Terry was sleeping off a hangover, her fault. If she herself was ill and couldn't make Terry his dinner exactly the way he wanted it, when he wanted it, her fault. Everything. Her fault.

She would hurry home – like she was trying to do now – and if she was late for some reason then it would be her fault. And Terry would punish her for it. Sometimes it would just be a slap to the face or a punch to the stomach. But the punishments crept up depending how late she was. Sometimes he had taken off his belt and lashed her across her back with it. Sometimes he had just contented himself with banging her head off the dining room wall.

And then he would sober up and the apologies would start. And she would look at him, cringing, weeping, begging, and something would be touched inside her. That spark of emotion – of love, even – that she used to feel for him would be slowly fanned back into life. And as the pain subsided and the bruises and welts healed, she began to feel hope for the future.

Until the next time.

After a while, Terry hadn't even bothered to beg for forgiveness. Hadn't even been drunk – or not too drunk – when he hit her. He had told her it was what she deserved, what she should expect. She was worthless. Ugly. Stupid. And after a while, she had started to believe it.

She shook her head, looked round the carriage once more. Still no sign of movement.

How had she got to this point? How had it happened? If it hadn't been for the counselling, she didn't know where she would have ended up. *It's not your fault.* Her personal mantra, said over and over in her head, every day, so she wouldn't forget it. Not her fault. It was Terry's. No matter what he said, how forceful he was, it wasn't her fault. Keith had told her about some cases, strong, independent women who'd ended up in her situation. And they couldn't believe what had happened. How the man they had loved – still loved, in most cases – had turned out to be the way he was. And turned them into the person they were. But it wasn't the end. It could be stopped.

She felt inside her pocket once more. Her fingers curled round the card that Keith had given her. The refuge. The phone number. All she had to do was call.

So why hadn't she? Why didn't she just do it?

Because . . . She didn't know. Not really. She found reasons, although she thought they were probably just excuses. The twins needed her. That was a lie. They loved their father. Probably more than her. She could see it in their eyes. The same look he had. Growing up, growing up into two copies of him.

Maybe that was it. Maybe she should stay, fight him. Make sure they turned out all right. No. She knew that was stupid. So why was she going back? When she knew what was waiting for her?

Because . . .

Because.

Because she didn't have anywhere else to go.

60

She kept hold of the card. Yes, she did. She did have some-where to go.

But it wasn't just that. It wasn't easy to walk out on a mar-riage even when it was going as horribly wrong as hers. It was admitting defeat. Telling the world – and yourself – that you were wrong all those years ago. That you'd made a huge mis-take with your life. It was inviting ridicule and laughter. Hatred, even. That was how she felt. Keith had insisted that it wasn't like that, that no one would be judging her. But still the feeling persisted.

And she was also inviting her children to hate her. If she took them with her, they would resent her for leaving their father; if she left them, they would grow up hating her in her absence. And that was a horrible burden for a mother – any mother, she thought – to bear.

But she had to do something. She had to take that leap of faith Keith was always talking about. She had asked him once about his own life. She knew she wasn't supposed to, but she couldn't help it.

'You're married,' she had said, looking at the gold band on his finger.

'I am, yes,' he said almost shyly.

'What's your wife like?'

He had hesitated before answering.

'Sorry. I know I shouldn't ask.'

'No, no,' he had reassured her, 'that's all right. My wife's . . . ' He had smiled to himself. 'Lovely. A strong woman. A great person. Great mother, great wife, the lot.'

Janine nodded. Jealous of their relationship. 'Not like me, then,' she'd said, trying to smile.

Keith had leaned forward then. 'She'd been in an abusive relationship before she met me. Very bad, had to escape. Like I said, it can happen to the strongest of women.'

'And you saved her.'

Keith had shaken his head. 'She saved herself. One of the things I love her for.'

With a jolt, the train started moving again.

Janine sighed. Looked out of the window. It was still raining. And she knew what that meant. No work. Terry would have spent the day in the pub with his mates. Roofers can't work in the pissing rain, he had told her on many occasions. Except he could, she had thought. If he wanted to badly enough. But she had never dared to say it.

So that meant he would be home already. Waiting. Angry. And she knew what would be in store for her.

Her stomach turned over in dread at the thought.

The train stopped. The Hawthorns. Two more stops and she would be home. Home. Or whatever she called it.

She looked at the open space beyond the door.

She felt the card once more.

So easy. She could just get off the train now, call that number. She could . . .

The doors closed.

One last chance, she thought. She owed it to that romantic girl who had believed in everlasting love. One last chance.

The train moved forward.

Janine tried to have hope, to be strong.

Tried to ignore the terror that gripped her.

12

'That was quick,' said Phil into his phone. 'Must be a new record.'

'Oh, you know how it is,' said Esme Russell in reply. 'Sometimes we have quiet days.'

There was a pause. The silence threatened to become deafening until Esme said, 'You coming over, then?'

Phil checked his watch. It was almost time to call it a day. Shift's end. He looked round the Major Incident Squad office. The team were working on the murder of Gemma Adderley: writing reports, checking and cross-referencing databases. They knew their jobs. There didn't seem to be anything more that he could do at present. If he went to see Esme he couldn't claim it as overtime. He checked his watch again. That was fine. It wasn't like he had anywhere to be.

Anyone waiting at home for him.

'Yeah, okay,' he said.

'I'll hang on for you.'

He hung up, leaving the day's earlier awkwardness between them hanging in the air. Ignored. Or perhaps just unacknowledged, even welcome.

Phil, getting up and heading for the door, wasn't sure which was better and which was worse. Which he wanted and which he didn't.

Just a post-mortem report, he told himself. That's all.

He left the office.

'It's only preliminary,' Esme Russell said once Phil had arrived at the mortuary, deep in the bowels of Birmingham's Selly Oak Hospital. 'But it seems quite comprehensive.'

The air in the mortuary was chill, but still carried on it the ghosts of spoiled meat with an underscore of preserving chemicals and a faint dirty copper tang of blood. The smell always reminded Phil of what a butcher's shop would be like if it set up in a hospital. Which, he thought wryly, was exactly what it was.

The body was no longer in sight. He knew its fate. It would have been rendered down to its base components, organs removed and weighed, measurements and samples taken. Gemma Adderley's death reduced to a series of chemical and biological puzzles to be answered.

Music was playing. Something Phil didn't know. Something classical. A bottle of chilled white wine was open on Esme's desk. Two glasses. One almost full, sipped from.

Esme saw him looking. 'I always do this at the end of the day. Little ritual. Care to join me?'

Phil looked at the bottle of wine, condensation running down the glass. He didn't want to think about what had been in the fridge with it.

'No thanks,' he said.

'Still on duty?'

'Not much of a white wine drinker, that's all.'

'Right.' Esme smiled, took a sip.

Phil looked at the report she handed him. 'Talk me through it,' he said. He had seen enough reports to know what they meant, but he always asked for a description too. His eyes weren't as well trained as those of a pathologist. He couldn't pick up what was important as well as she could.

64

'Well,' she said, putting her glass down, moving close to him and looking at the report he held in his hand, 'it's pretty much as we surmised. Tortured: burnt with cigarettes, as far as I can make out, cut. The knife was sharp. Kitchen knife, medical blade, perhaps, although the size of the cuts would suggest something large.'

'Any degree of medical accuracy?' asked Phil.

'Not really. Just random cuts, it seems. Deep, though. Lot of weight behind them.'

'Man or woman?'

'If it was a woman she would have to be huge. No, the angle and weight of the blade suggests a man. Left-handed, too, I think.'

Phil wrote that down. 'Pre or post?'

'Pre. She was very much alive when this was happening.'

'Jesus. Raped?'

'No evidence of semen or DNA but some degree of vaginal tearing. Either he was very careful or he used substitutes. Large ones.'

'Punishment? Humiliation?'

Esme smiled. 'Your department, I think. Ligature marks on the wrists and ankles. Had her tied up somewhere for quite some time.'

'Right. Did he know the woman?'

'Your department again.'

'No, I meant are there any signs of what you could infer to be intimacy? Would a stranger have done this, or would it be someone she knew? Like I said earlier, it's clearly someone who hates women. I'm just wondering if he hates all women, or just this one.'

'I don't know. Good question, but I really couldn't say.' She pointed at something in the report. Phil noticed that she was wearing perfume. And make-up. 'She wasn't killed at the scene. And she'd been in the water for some time.'

'Time of death?'

'Can't say. She'd been in there long enough to have attracted rats but not long enough to have any flora growing inside her. Lividity and decomposition suggest she was dead for a while before he put her in the water. Stomach contents back that up. I don't yet know what kind of place she was kept in.'

'She'd been missing a month, how does that sound?'

'About right.'

'The hole in her chest,' asked Phil. 'Pre or post?'

'Post.'

'And no sign of the heart?'

She shook her head. Phil was aware of her perfume once more. He was getting used to it now, even quite liked it. 'None. I checked the area. Jo and her team did likewise. But we didn't really expect to find it there.' She looked at the report once more. 'The injuries, the torture, although they're extreme, I can't find any evidence of one fatal blow. Maybe she just died of shock. Or of the cumulative effects, even.'

'He still killed her, though.'

'Undoubtedly. Any suspects?' she asked.

'At the moment, the husband. History of spousal abuse. Got a new girlfriend. Ran when I tried to question him. Won't talk to us without a lawyer.'

Esme took the report from his hands, put it down on her desk, turned to him. Faced him. 'Quite a day.'

'You're not wrong.'

Another silence fell between them. Of awkwardness or anticipation, Phil didn't know. He couldn't read his own emotions at the moment , never mind anyone else's.

'Look, erm . . .'

Phil waited.

'I'm sorry about what I said this morning. About . . . I didn't want you to get the wrong . . . Oh, you know what I mean.'

'I know,' said Phil, not altogether sure if he did.

'But ...' Esme shrugged. 'I know you've not had a good time of it lately. With everything that's happened. I just thought ... Are you free tonight? A drink? Dinner? Just a chat.'

He looked at her. Thought of all the times he'd done the right thing for the wrong reasons. And the wrong thing for the right reasons. And sometimes just the wrong thing for reasons he couldn't even explain to himself. Or didn't want to explain to himself.

'Okay,' he said. 'Where did you have in mind?'

13

He opened the box. Looked inside. Stepped back. Feeling pride, or something like pride. He wasn't sure what the exact word was, the exact emotion. But pride would do until he could think of a better one.

He kept staring. At it. Beyond it. Back. Doing what it was supposed to do. What he had collected it for. His ritual. His exorcism. Cleansing the past. Enabling the present to become the future. A clean future.

Back. He kept staring. It started to work. He started to see. To hear.

I don't know where you think this is going. There it was. Her voice, back again after all those years. Lorraine Russell. He'd never forgot her name. Never.

What d'you mean? But he knew what she meant. Had known she was going to say this all along. This or something like it. The end result would be the same.

You. Me. This. Looking around, gesturing, taking in the city. He had never understood that bit, when she did that. It hadn't been about the city. Never about that. Only the two of them. Only ever the two of them. Down by the canal. The lock. Saturday Bridge. Before the gentrification, years ago, when it was still run-down, dangerous. The only ones who ever went there. *I mean, it's not like this is it, is it? Forever.*

The words piercing like an arrow through his heart. It must

have shown on his face. She responded with an expression that looked compassionate yet contained hints of a mocking smile. Yes, both. He had thought about that for years, gone over it in his head. Over and over it. And yes. Compassion, yet a mocking smile. He was right. Remembering it like it was yesterday.

The autumn air. Cold. Brown leaves blowing. Summer dying. She was wearing his denim jacket, the collar turned up. The room was cold but it was the memory that made him shiver.

What? she said next. *You thought it was?*

Yes. The only world he could think of. His words had dried up. Before that, before they had stopped, he had said plenty. Told her his plans for the future. Their future. He had thought of nothing else. Worked the whole thing out. And now this. Compassion, yet mocking.

Sorry. No.

Why not?

This was . . . never meant to go anywhere. It just got out of hand, that's all. I know what you want. Marriage and kids and that. But I'm still at university. I've got my third year coming up. I can't do all that.

I'll . . . I'll wait.

That look again. Compassion, yet mockery. He tried once again to work out the percentages.

Look, I'll . . . I'll come with you. When you go back to Exeter. It's not far.

I'm a student. What will you do while I'm at uni?

I'll . . . I'll get a job. Work. Find . . . find our home. You need never have to . . . I'll take care of you. You . . . you won't need to work or anything. I'll do that. I'll look after you.

A sigh then. A shake of her head. And in that one movement his heart split open once more. The pain that was always with him, buried somewhere, came bubbling to the surface like dark, black, bad blood from a fatal injury.

I don't need looking after. I'm doing a law degree. It looks like I've got a job lined up at the end of it. A career. Why would I give that up? Especially for someone here, without a job. That's what I've worked towards all these years, that's what I want, more than anything.

Anything? Unable to keep the pain from his voice.

Anything.

He walked away then, three paces, three and a half, then turned back to face her.

And that's . . . that's it. We were just fun, were we? Something to fill the time before you went back to uni. Anger tingeing his voice now.

She shrugged. *It was fun, though, wasn't it? You have to admit that.*

He waited a while until his words, his breath, were under control. Then spoke. *So this is . . . it? The end?*

She laughed. *No need to be so melodramatic. God, it's not like we're the love of each other's lives or anything. I'll see you at Christmas. We can go for a drink, maybe.*

And that was when the split happened.

The reality, remembered. He looked at her. Really looked at her. Saw her for the first time, what she really was. And there was no compassion. Only mockery. That was all there had ever been. Mockery. And pity. That was all he had been to her. A pity fuck. A common kid to occupy her time with until she went back to uni and surrounded herself with her posh friends. Something to tell the others about over drinks in the union bar: *Well, I had a common kid this summer. That's one thing ticked off the bucket list . . .* Rage rose up inside him, threatened to spill out. He wanted to grab her, shake her, hurt her. He wanted her to love him. But he did nothing. Just accepted her words. He mumbled something and walked away. Left her there.

He never saw Lorraine Russell again. He spent years twisted

70

up by the pain of her rejection. He attempted suicide, needed therapy to sort him out, just get him functioning again.

The reality of what happened.

But now, standing in front of the box, came the exorcism. The chance to make things right after all those years, those long, painful years. A time of atonement.

He closed his eyes.

In this version, Lorraine Russell never sees the knife. Neither does anyone else. It's like they're apart from everyone else. Alone. What few passers-by there are are just ghosts. They don't stop to interfere.

Her eyes widen, her mouth falls into a rigid O. Like a long-haired Munch *Scream*. Then she goes to scream herself. No one hears her. Nothing comes out, like a dream scream. He grabs her. Pushes her against the heavy wooden lock gate, holding her by the throat, bending her over backwards. Smiling all the time. Knife glinting.

You know what you've done? he screams at her. *You know?*

She tries to shake her head. She's about to speak. He stops her.

Shut up. Listen. I'll tell you. You've taken my heart. That's what you've done. My heart. I gave it to you. You've got it. And you've fucking killed it . . .

She just stares at him. He's aware of her breathing becoming restricted. His hand on her throat, her body bent backwards.

So now . . . He shows her the knife. *Now I'm going to take yours . . .*

He gets to work. Rips open her jacket – his jacket – then her blouse. Then snaps her bra in two with a swish of the blade. Her breasts are exposed. Her beautiful milky-white breasts. How he loves those breasts . . .

The knife goes in. Blood bubbling up and over the blade, covering those magnificent breasts. He pushes it in further. More blood.

The look of terror on her face is exquisite.

He gets to work. Hacking, cutting, sawing. The blade is sharp, never lets him down. And it's easier than in real life. His hands, arms, body, are covered in her blood. He luxuriates in it. Imagines he is bathing in it. Eventually he throws the knife aside, plunges his hands in. Finds what he is looking for.

Her heart.

He pulls. It's reluctant to leave her. But he is stronger than she is. And soon he stands over her, her heart in his hands. He smiles. But she is already gone.

He was back. In front of the box. Looking into it. Seeing his latest trophy. The heart.

He breathed deeply. In, out again. Smiled. Tried to place himself back in his room. Tried to work out how the exorcism had made him feel. Good, he decided. Centred. Calm. At peace.

The exorcism had worked. Lorraine Russell was gone. Forever. All he had to do was close the lid and that part of his life was over. All that hurt and pain, all those wasted years gone. Banished.

He closed the lid.

And felt a warmth spread throughout his body.

He looked at the other boxes. All empty. All soon to be full.

He pulled off his gloves. Heard voices calling.

'Daddy ... Daddy ... dinner's ready ... '

'Coming.'

He took one last look at the box. Smiled. Left the room.

14

He couldn't protect us. He just couldn't protect us.

The words ran laps round the inside of her head, over and over, again and again, a mantra to keep the rhythm going.

Josephina was in bed. Asleep, hopefully, but Marina knew from experience that wasn't always the case. She was worried that taking Josephina away from her father might damage the child, but it was a risk she had had to take. She spent as much time as she could with her daughter, made her feel as loved and wanted as possible. Since Ellison's phone call, she had done that even more, keeping busy, trying not to think about what she had just heard. Or anything else. And she had just about succeeded. She had become so lost in the world of her daughter that – just for a short while – she forgot why she was in that house and what she was supposed to be doing and allowed her guard to drop. Just for a while. But, like a terminal diagnosis or incessant pain, she could never relax for long.

Nights were the worst. That was why Marina was working out. The house belonged to a work colleague from the university. He had taken a year-long sabbatical accompanying his much better renumerated wife on a business venture abroad, and let her stay for as long as she liked. The house was beautiful; detached, so anyone approaching it could be seen, with alarms and security systems, in a discreet part of Edgbaston. But the thing she liked best about it was the home gym. Small, but useful. Very useful. Physical activity that would tire her out, make her able to sleep. But not only that: exercise that would build her muscle, sharpen her reflexes. Keep her prepared. Ready.

No matter what she did, though, she knew that as soon as she closed her eyes, that face would be there again. Those eyes. The smile. Those taunting words:

Goodbye. Although it isn't really. I'll be seeing you again very soon.

And when Marina had countered that:

You're wrong, Marina. Very wrong.

And then the words that had chilled her then and still did so now:

Give Phil my love.

Fiona Welch. Or the woman who had called herself that. The woman who had split Marina and Phil up.

She had engineered the murders of several women in East Anglia and escaped from a high-security hospital for the criminally insane, killing one of Marina and Phil's closest friends in the process. She wasn't really Fiona Welch. The real Fiona Welch was a twisted, murderous, insane individual whom Phil had watched plummet to her death several years previously. They didn't know who this woman really was. But she had behaved just like the real Fiona.

Then there was that night. Never far from Marina's mind. The night she came home and found Phil unconscious on the floor, beaten. He had come round, in pain, and told her what had happened. The woman who called herself Fiona Welch had been there. Except she wasn't calling herself that any more. She wanted to go by another name.

Marina's.

She had been in their bedroom. That was bad enough. But she actually been in their bed, waiting for Phil to return home. And after the fight she had gone, taking some of Marina's clothes with her. Leaving Marina feeling violated in so many ways. And leaving that final message relayed to Phil:

I'll be seeing you again very soon.

A description of the woman had gone out to police forces all round the country. But any reported sightings of her had turned out to be false. They still didn't know who she was or what her motivations were. And they were no nearer to finding her. It was like she had just vanished into thin air. All they had was the threat that she would return. And that had been more than enough.

In the aftermath, Marina and Phil had talked. Marina was terrified that the woman would return. Phil had to be too, but Marina decided he was better at keeping the fact hidden.

'Look,' he had said, 'I'll call in some favours. Get the house watched. Bodyguards for Josephina. I'm police. There's things we can do.'

And she had to admit he had sounded convincing. But things still gnawed away at her. 'You can't keep that up. If she doesn't show up any time soon, the threat'll be downgraded. And Cotter has to balance the books. We won't be guarded for ever. And when all that's gone, when we're alone and vulnerable, that's when she'll come back.'

'And we'll be waiting for her.'

They had agreed to face whatever was coming together, and that worked for a while. But when the unmarked car was no longer watching the house and Josephina had no bodyguards to escort her to and from school, the unease that she had initially suppressed began to resurface.

She told Phil. 'It's fine,' he had said. 'We're aware. Both of us. Let's not show that she's got to us. Let's just live our lives. Get on with things. We can't live in fear of her all the time.'

But Marina wasn't convinced. She *was* living in fear. Over

the last few years their work had brought them – and their daughter – into danger. Real, life-threatening danger. And she had dealt with enough criminally unhinged people to know that this madwoman couldn't be easily dismissed.

Once again she confided her fears to Phil. Once again he tried to manage them. 'Don't give in to her,' he said. 'That's what she wants.'

'What she wants?' Marina could contain herself no longer. 'I know what she wants, Phil. She wants *you*. She wants *my life*. Phil, she was in our bed. When she left the house that night, she took some of my clothes with her. She's insane. No, beyond insane.'

'And that's your professional opinion?'

He had only been trying to make a joke, lighten the tension. She knew that. She had thought about it long enough after-wards. But the months of living looking over her shoulder, of dreading stepping outside the door, of fearing what she might find when she picked Josephina up from school, all of that had taken its toll on her.

'I can't do this any more,' she said, tears coming as they so often did.

He hugged her. 'It's okay. We'll get through it. We'll be fine. She might never—'

'She will, Phil. She will.' Pulling away from him as she spoke. 'And if she doesn't? I don't want to spend the rest of my life looking for her. Seeing her everywhere. Terrified to move in case she's there. I can't stand this any more. I . . . I'm heading for a breakdown.'

He tried to hug her again. She stopped him.

'No,' she said. 'No. We have to . . . have to do something. We can't keep on living like this.'

'What do you suggest? I'll try to take some time off, maybe we can go away somewhere.'

Marina shook her head. 'Run away? And what if she's there, waiting for us? No, Phil. That won't do.'

Phil stepped back, looked at her. Like he was seeing her for the first time. 'What, then?'

She regarded him the same way. As though a naked, truthful light was shining on him. 'You're . . . you can't protect me, Phil. You can't protect our daughter.'

'What d'you mean? Of course I can. Of course I will.'

The conversation she had had with Carly Adderley came back to her. The look on the child's face when she'd told Marina how her mother couldn't protect them. And what had happened as a result. Then the image of Phil lying there outside their bedroom, defeated, broken, almost paralysed. The sheer helplessness in the face of something greater, something darker.

'No, Phil,' she said, her voice small but firm, 'you can't.'

He tried to speak again. She didn't let him.

'I'm going away. I . . . It's better if I'm not here.'

Phil stood there, stunned. Waiting for her words to sink in. Eventually he tried to speak. She stopped him.

'No. Don't say anything. Don't try to talk me out of it. Phil, I love you. More than anyone else I've ever known. But I can't keep going like this. Every time I look at you, I see her. What she did. What she'll do again.'

Again he tried to talk. Again she stopped him.

'It's all arranged. I'm taking Josephina with me. She doesn't deserve to be put in danger. She's been through enough over the years. Don't ask me where I'm going. I'm not going to tell you. Don't try to contact me.'

She couldn't say any more. The tears had started again. She ran from the house.

Soon she had run from his life.

*

77

Marina counted reps in her head, reached the number she wanted, put the weights down. She slumped to the floor, exhausted, sweat covering her whole body. She stretched out a still-shaking arm, admired it. The sinew and muscle. The leanness of it. She made a fist, pulled it back, let it go. Hard. Imagined Fiona Welch's face on the end of it, connecting, breaking.

'I'm ready for you, bitch,' she said, her voice a hoarse whisper. 'I'm ready.'

15

'So is this your local?'

Phil took a sip from his pint of San Miguel, looked round. The Plough in Harborne was a neighbourhood boozer that had gone the upscale gastropub route. Not the kind of place he would usually come to, but he had to admit he liked it.

Esme Russell took a sip from her wine, sat back, looked round also, then back at Phil. 'I suppose so. If I have a local. I like it here. Good place to meet friends.'

'Harborne. Nice.' Phil was being polite, looking for things to say. And things to avoid saying. 'I wonder who decided that all pubs should now be full of mismatched rustic furniture and bits of industrial salvage? It's like the back room at an auctioneer's.'

Esme laughed. 'Don't you like it?'

'I do, actually. Bet they've got craft beer, as well. A hundred and forty different varieties that all taste the same.'

Esme laughed again and he enjoyed that feeling. Making someone laugh. Pleased to be with him. He had missed that.

'I like it here,' she said. 'Harborne. Like a village, almost. It's got that feel. You can forget you're so close to the city centre.'

'And so close to work, too.'

Esme smiled. 'With what we do? You know as well as I do that it can happen anywhere.'

'True.' Another mouthful of lager. Phil settled back in his

metal chair. It was surprisingly comfortable for something that looked like it had come out of the canteen of a fifties steel-works.

'So.' Esme replaced her drink on the table, leaned forward. Phil said nothing.

'How are you?'

The good feeling of a moment ago dissipated. 'Fine,' he said, almost cutting off her question in his haste to answer.

Esme looked down, toying with the stem of her wine glass. 'I mean . . . everything.'

'This a professional enquiry? Has Cotter put you up to this?'

Esme pulled back, removing her fingers from the stem of her glass. 'No. I . . . I'm just concerned about you. That's all.'

Phil looked at her. Esme couldn't meet his eyes. He studied her. She was a very attractive woman. Not really his type, if he was honest. Tall, slender; long, straight blonde hair. An accent so posh it could cut glass. But attractive. He had never really noticed it when they had met professionally. Or if he had, he had subjugated his feelings. For obvious reasons.

And maybe she was concerned about him. For professional reasons. But he didn't think so.

'I'm . . . coping,' he said. 'I'm sure I'm not the first man whose wife has left him.' But I might be for the reasons she gave me, he thought.

'I know. But you seemed so happy together. So . . .'

'Yeah, well,' said Phil, reaching for his pint to hide behind, 'it happens.'

Esme nodded. 'I'm just saying,' she said, reaching across the table, 'you've got friends.'

He nodded. Made no attempt to remove his hand.

They sat in silence, each waiting for the other to make the next move.

'Are you hungry?' asked Esme eventually.

'I'm okay,' said Phil.

'No, you're not,' she said. 'You've lost weight and you don't look healthy. If you don't mind me saying so.'

'Thank you.'

She smiled. 'I'm a professional. I'm good at spotting those kind of things.'

She took the opportunity to remove her hand and reach for the menu.

'Their pizzas are very good. And burgers.'

'I'll have a burger, then.'

'Sorted. My treat.'

Before he could say anything else, Esme had jumped up from the table and crossed to the bar to place their order. Phil watched her go, his mind performing emotional somersaults.

Why was he sitting here? What was he doing? Esme was attractive, yes. No denying that. And if he thought about it, if he allowed himself, he was attracted to her. And she laughed at his jokes, which counted for a lot. But he was still married. Even if Marina was gone and he didn't know where she was. And it wasn't just that. He still loved Marina. He didn't want anyone else.

So why was he here? Why was he with Esme? He knew the answer to that. Because he was lonely.

She returned to the table. Smiled at him.

'Thank you,' he said. 'You didn't need to do that.'

She shrugged his words off.

At that moment a waiter appeared with more drinks.

'I didn't . . . '

'I took the liberty.'

'I've got to drive.'

Esme didn't answer.

The food arrived. The burger looked bigger than Phil's head. He started on it, pecking at it, but felt full very quickly. Esme on the other hand devoured her pizza. He wondered where she put it all. Maybe she was the kind of woman that other women hated, who could eat anything they wanted and never put on weight. Or the kind Marina hated, anyway.

Marina. There she was in his head again.

'Not hungry?' Esme looked down at Phil's plate. He had pushed it away. 'You've barely touched it.'

'Sorry,' he said. 'Thought I was. Mustn't have been. I've wasted your money. Sorry.'

He noticed that his second pint of lager was almost gone.

'Thirsty, though,' said Esme. 'I'll get you another.'

'No, I'm fine,' he replied. 'I don't think . . . '

She gestured to the waiter. Another lager arrived. The plates were cleared away.

'You trying to get me drunk?'

Esme sighed. 'Life's too short, Phil. Too short to be unhappy, anyway. I've discovered that from experience. And it's been a hard lesson to learn.'

He said nothing.

'You're not the only one to have a relationship break up. A relationship that you thought was going to last for the rest of your life.'

He nodded. And realised in that moment that he didn't really know anything about Esme. Beyond work, anyway.

'I was married once. And I thought he was the love of my life. He didn't share my feelings, however. Result: one messy divorce. Years of heartbreak, thinking I was unattractive, wasn't good enough to have a man in my life. Years and years of that. And then one day I just woke up and thought, fuck it.'

Phil's eyes widened. It was the first time he had heard Esme swear.

'Yes,' she said, smiling grimly. 'Fuck it. Life's too short. I'm not unattractive and I deserve to be happy.' She shrugged. 'And that was that. It's been my philosophy ever since.' She sat back, wine glass in hand. Looked at him, waiting for a response.

Phil knew what kind she wanted.

He sighed. Couldn't give it to her.

'Thank you,' he said. 'For dinner. And the drinks. But I think I should be off.'

He stood up. She looked at him, sadness in her eyes. 'I'm sorry.'

'No,' he said, shaking his head. 'I am. I'm a . . . bit of a mess at the moment. I don't want to do something tonight that I'd regret. That we'd both regret. In the morning. Whenever.'

She was clear-eyed as she looked at him. 'I wouldn't regret it.'

He nodded. Made his way to the door, weaving as he went.

Not sure if he'd made the right decision or the wrong one.

16

Janine Gillen opened the door as slowly and carefully as she could. As though if she didn't disturb the atmosphere, her actions couldn't ripple out and cause any kind of disruption in the rest of the house.

'Where the fuck have you been?'

Too late.

He came towards her. Terry Gillen, her husband. Angry, as usual. Like it was his natural state of being, his default setting. She wondered whether it was more from habit than anything else, angry with her because that was what he did. What he had always done.

But it wasn't what he had always done. How he had always been. Not at first. Just the way he had become. Or maybe he had always been like that and their courtship was just some temporary blip. Being nice to lure her in. She had been thinking about that a lot lately. Keith had asked her questions and in turn made her question. But she hadn't found the answers.

Whatever, another part of her brain said. That was later. Now she had to think how to get past him, how to make it through another night. How to avoid a beating for something she had either done or not done, or any permutation of the two.

'Hello, Terry,' she said.

He loomed before her in the hallway. The house was small

and he seemed too big for it. Like it was keeping him constrained. A too-small cage for a large wild animal.

'I said, where the fuck have you been?'

'Out. In . . . ' She felt her heart palpitate once more. 'In the city.'

His eyes narrowed. Suspicion in them. 'Why? Where?'

'I . . . ' This was it. Should she lie or tell the truth? Which would be easiest? 'I . . . went to see Keith. We had an appointment. I thought you would be there. You said you would.'

'I said nothin' of the sort.'

'But you did, you said—'

He grabbed her then, his big meaty hand gripping her neck, pushing her up against the wall.

'I said nothin' of the sort. You deaf? I told you I don't want to see that interferin' fuckin' faggot ever again.' He tightened his grip. 'Ever. Again. And I don't want you seein' him either. Puttin' fuckin' ideas into your head. Fuckin' faggot.'

'But he's not a . . . not gay.'

Terry's eyes became glowing hot coals. His grip tightened further. 'Oh, he's not, is he? And how would you know, eh? You fuckin' him, that it? That where you've been? Fuckin' your gay-boy boyfriend?'

Janine tried to shake her head. Couldn't. 'Terry, I—'

'You want to argue with me, that right? You want to answer me back, do you, you useless fuckin' bitch? Yeah? Do you? You know what that'll get you, don't you?'

Janine felt her whole body start to shake. She knew it was better not to reply. She cast her eyes to the floor.

His grip loosened slightly. 'That's better.' Nodding. 'That's better. Now. Where's my fuckin' dinner?'

'I . . . I'm sorry, Terry. I . . . '

'You brought anythin' in with you?'

She shook her head.

His hand was back at her throat again, harder this time, tipping her head back, pulling it away from her body. She felt her throat being stretched, breathing becoming harder. He moved even closer to her. She could smell alcohol and sweat coming off him. Knew then that he hadn't been to work today.

'What kind of a mother are you, eh?' he said, sour beer breath right in her face. 'What kind of a fuckin' wife are you? You don't have to answer. I'll tell you. A shit one.'

She tried to speak. Could find no words. She felt she was about to piss herself.

'You know what day this is, don't you?'

Janine tried to think, tried to order her mind into something rational. Couldn't. Terry answered for her.

'Stupid cow. It's Monday. The Villa are at home and I'm takin' the boys. I picked them up from your sister's. You forgot that, didn't you? While you were in the city fuckin' that faggot.'

'I wasn't, Terry, I—'

'You'd better fuckin' not have been.' Face pushed right into hers. 'If I find out you have, well. Your life'll be fuckin' over.'

She moved her mouth but no words would emerge.

He relaxed his grip on her. 'Too late to have anythin' to eat now. We've got to go out. I'll have to get the kids somethin' at the ground. More fuckin' expense. And all your fault. That's less money you'll be gettin' off me next payday.'

He turned, walked away from her. Called for the boys to get their things, they were going.

Janine didn't move. Couldn't move. She stood trembling up against the wall, her mind reeling. She watched Terry's retreating back as he went towards the kitchen.. Allowed herself a sigh of relief. At least he hadn't hit her. At least she wasn't physically hurt.

He must have read her mind. In that moment he turned back into the hall, arm raised, so fast she didn't see him coming, didn't have time to think, to move out of the way. He slapped her right across the face, the force of the blow sending her sprawling on the floor, the noise reverberating all round the house. He stood over her, stared down at her prone body. Breathing like he was in the middle of a lengthy fight or a bout of strenuous lovemaking.

'Fuckin' useless bitch.'

The boys appeared on the stairs, stopped dead when they saw the scene before them.

'Come on,' Terry said to them. 'We're going.'

He went to the front door, the boys following mutely. Janine tried to look up at them, plead for ... What? Sympathy? Help? Support? She didn't know. She got nothing. They just stared at her, expressions blank of anything but contempt, fledgling versions of their father.

Terry turned to her. 'They'd better fuckin' win. Because there'll be hell to pay in here if they don't.'

He slammed the door behind them.

Janine tried to get up. Couldn't move. Just lay there, numb, staring at the ceiling. Trying to imagine that this wasn't her on the floor. That all this was happening to someone else. Someone who deserved it.

It was over a quarter of an hour before she could get up.

It wasn't until then that she noticed the puddle of urine she was lying in.

17

Phil hadn't gone home. Couldn't face going home. Not after what had just occurred. Not now. Not on his own.

But he had nowhere else to go. He had run through a few options in his head: cinema, walk, pub, back to work, even. But none of them worked, nothing grabbed him. He couldn't concentrate on a film, didn't want to be alone with his own thoughts on a walk, couldn't face sitting in a pub on his own and watching everyone else in couples or groups, and he didn't want to go back to the station and just sit there, unable to think clearly enough to do any work.

No. He knew where he wanted to be. And who he wanted to be with.

Marina.

Anywhere, as long as Marina was with him.

He put the bottle to his lips, took another swig. The beer had given him a taste for alcohol, and a mellow buzz that he didn't want to let go of. He had stopped at an off-licence on the Hagley Road, driving back into the city; bought a bottle of Maker's Mark. He wasn't much of a spirit drinker, but he was quite partial to a good whisky or bourbon. And Maker's Mark was his favourite. Expensive, and something he only bought himself as a treat, for special occasions. Well, he thought, this counts as a special occasion. Although there's not much in the way of a treat about it.

He had parked up a few streets behind the row of shops he had bought the bottle from. Next to a tall brick tower. The locals had told him that Tolkien had used it as inspiration for one of his books. Phil neither knew nor cared if that was true. It was just somewhere convenient to sit. And think.

Marina was the love of his life. He knew that. Had felt it almost from the first time he met her. Like there had been some kind of electrical spark between them. Like she knew him, could see him as no one else had ever seen him. And he felt the same with her. Phil had thought the concept of a soulmate was something for trashy supermarket magazines. But meeting Marina changed his mind. Both damaged, both missing something, they completed one another. He had thought he would never leave her. Never lose her. And certainly not like this.

He could understand why she had gone. That was the worst of it. He could understand. After what they had been through together over the years, the threat of this Fiona Welch woman was just too much for her. She had reached breaking point. Something had to give. He just hoped she felt safe now, wherever she was.

Now he was alone. And lonely.

He had been tempted by Esme. He could admit it to himself. Very tempted. Even if it had been for all the wrong reasons. If they were in fact the wrong reasons.

She was attractive. Undeniably. Vivacious, fun to be with. Entertaining. And he had been very close to taking up her offer. Going back to her place. Having sex. Part of him had wanted to. A big part. Just for the connection that being close, intimate, with someone else gave. For the opportunity to take himself out of himself, even for a short while, to let another part of his brain take over. Even just to hold another body next to his.

But he couldn't. Because he was still married to Marina.

I still love you, Phil. She had said that as she was walking out on him. *I still love you.* And he had held on to those words, believed in them, even while knowing that hope was the cruellest of all emotions. One day she would be back. One day they would be together again.

Hopefully.

And he had to keep believing that. *Had to.*

But now, tonight, sitting in his car, hope wasn't enough. He had to talk to her, listen to her. Connect with her. Even though it was against the rules, even though he knew what the response would be, he had to try.

He took one more swig, for courage, and took out his phone. Hit her number. Waited.

Nothing. The phone just rang and rang, eventually going to voicemail. His heart fluttered at the thought that he might hear her voice, even if it was just a recording. But that was denied him too. Her voice was no longer there. She had replaced it with a generic service-provider speech, reiterating the number and asking him to leave a message after the tone.

The tone sounded loud and harsh in his ear. His mouth moved but nothing emerged beyond a couple of strangled, mangled sounds, halfway between syllables and sobs.

He ended the call.

The phone fell from his suddenly useless fingers, slid to the floor. He brought his head down on the steering wheel, slumped and breathless, like he had just run a marathon. Tears racked his frame.

He rode the tide of tears out. Sat back, wiped his eyes. Reached for the bottle, ready to take another swig. Checked the level. Nearly half gone. No. Not the way.

He threw the bottle back on the passenger seat. Thought.

That anger was still inside him. Anger and self-pity. He had to do something, get rid of it somehow. He thought for a few moments.

Then he had it. Just the thing. Yeah. Just the thing. He knew he was breaking all his own rules, not to mention the rules he was supposed to uphold as a police officer, but he had to do something. *Something.*

'Right, you fucker,' he said, and started the car up. 'Coming to get you.'

He drove unsteadily away, Warren Zevon cranked as loud as he could stand it. So he didn't have to listen to his own thoughts.

18

He loves me. I know he does. He loves me. That's why he's doing this, that's . . .

Janine Gillen sighed, closed her eyes. Leaned her head back against the hard tiled wall, her legs straight out, her shoulders against the cold porcelain, even colder in contrast to the hot water she lay in. Tried to let the bubbles soothe and comfort her, her cares and worries rise and disappear like the steam all around her.

He loves me. I know he does. He . . .

Tried not to cry any more. Couldn't.

The tears came again, shaking and shuddering the water, making the bubbles vibrate and quiver. It would have been comical if it hadn't been so sad.

He loves me. I know . . .

She replayed the events of earlier over and over in her mind. The way Terry had touched her. Hurt her. The look on his face while he did so. The humiliating effect it had on her. And the way her boys had looked at her. God, the way the boys had looked at her . . . She shivered, despite the warmth of the water.

And then started crying again.

No, she thought; she might even have said it out loud, *this isn't love. Nothing remotely like love . . .*

Instead of stretching her body, she curled it up as tight as she could. Made herself as small and insignificant as possible.

Like a hedgehog fearing attack. She felt the muscles stretch and contract as she did so, thought of all the times he had hit her, taken out on her whatever had made him angry that day. She kept her eyes tightly closed, imagined all those beatings she had taken, the casual slaps and punches, the everyday abuse, like a map on her body. Leading from where she had started to where she had ended up. Her final destination. It had taken her a long time to realise that that was what it was, a long time to allow herself to actually use the word *abuse*, but she did so now. And she never wanted to stop doing it. Call it what it was, take the power of the word, of the abuser, away. But that didn't stop her crying. In fact, the realisation of who and where she was, of how she had ended up, just made her cry all the more.

Eventually the tears subsided and Janine began to uncurl herself. She stretched out once more, the water now carrying a chill when she moved about in it. She lay back, staring at the ceiling until she could no longer look at it. Then she put a flannel over her face, closed her eyes.

In that moment she could have been anywhere. Lying in a bath in a beach hut in Mauritius, tired from the exertions of a day spent swimming in the purest blue sea, relaxing on a white beach, drinking the finest cocktails and eating the best seafood of her life.

Or in a Russian ice hotel, having a quick soak before heading down to the bar, surrounded by the most exquisite ice sculptures, wearing a gorgeous evening dress, drinking vodka cocktails and making sparkling, charming conversation with the most beautiful and handsome people in the world, all thinking she was so funny and profound, all loving her for who she was.

She moved her legs. Noticed that the water had become even colder. It brought her back to where she was: in a characterless, charmless housing estate in West Bromwich. Each street like the wing of a prison. Each house like a spur on that wing. Each room in the house as small as a cell. And she was trapped in the middle.

Reluctantly she opened her eyes, took the cloth off her face. The bathroom light, cold and stinging, hit her like reality flooding back after a dream. Even more reluctantly she began to drag herself from the bath. She reached for a towel, wrapped it around herself, pulled out the plug. She stood and stared, watching the water flow away, until there was nothing left. Then she straightened up, walked into the bedroom.

It was gone. All of that was gone. Who she was, who she could have been. Who she had ended up as. Gone.

No more.

Her features impassive, eyes set hard, she took the suitcase from the top of the fitted wardrobe, threw it on the bed, opened it. Stared down at it. She turned back to the wardrobe, opened the doors, looked at her clothes hanging there. She suddenly hated all of them, didn't want them touching her skin any more. But she knew she didn't have the money to get new ones and she knew she had to wear something, so she pulled as much as she could from the hangers, crammed it into the case. As she did so, her face barely registered emotion. Like a blank mask in a Greek tragedy.

The suitcase as full as she could make it, clothes and shoes and coats and cosmetics crammed in, she pushed down the top, zipped it closed. It was heavy to pull from the bed and she was glad that it had wheels underneath.

Dressed, she wrestled it downstairs, checked her watch. She had about an hour or so until Terry and the boys came back from the football. A little pre-programmed shiver ran through her: I hope they win. She had always thought that, even praying to a God she had long since stopped believing in. That way,

94

Terry wouldn't take out the inadequacies of his team on her body like he usually did. She smiled. It didn't matter any more. Because by the time he returned, she would be gone.

She sat on the sofa, having one last look around the place she couldn't call home. Her arm accidentally rested on the remote, turning on the TV. She jumped at the sudden noise. The local news. A woman's body had been discovered. Missing over a month. Janine shuddered. They showed a photo of the woman and her husband. Smiling. They looked happy. Something sank within Janine. Happy and still murdered.

Then the face of a stout, slightly sleazy-looking man filled the screen. He was greasy and sweating, but something in his eyes said his sweat hadn't been honestly achieved. *Detective Sergeant Hugh Ellison*, a caption read underneath. He talked about the case before the screen gave way to a woman police officer, DCI Alison Cotter, who seemed altogether more capable and knew what she was talking about.

Janine turned it off. She didn't want to hear any more.

She stood up, made her way to the coat rack. Pulled on her coat, felt in the pocket. The card was still there. Thank God. She knew, rationally, that it would be, but that still didn't stop her worrying. While she was packing, she had even begun to imagine that she had made the whole thing up. That Keith hadn't given her the card, hadn't given her those all-important words of encouragement, of self-esteem. She had even begun to worry that Keith wasn't real. That she had imagined him as well. That happened a lot to her. Events that she could clearly remember would be contradicted by Terry, even ones that he hadn't been at. When she tried to point out that he was wrong in his recollection, she would receive a smack for her trouble. And if she persisted in pointing it out, she would receive another. And another. Until yes, Janine would agree with him. He was right. She must have been mistaken.

But not this time. She took the card out, took out her phone, too. Dialled the number.

Then stopped. Stared at the screen.

Just one little tap of the button, that was all it would take. One little tap. And she would never see Terry again. Never be hit, never be hurt, never be humiliated again. One little tap. That was all.

And never see her children again. A pang of loss passed through her at the thought. Her children. What kind of mother gave up her children? And then she thought about the boys. What they really were. Not hers. Never hers. They were Terry's. She had just borne them for him. Dispensed food to them, cleared up after them. There was no joy in the relationship, either way. She was nothing to them.

She looked round: the hallway, the kitchen beyond that. The staircase. The door to the living room. Her house. Her world.

And she hit the button as hard as she could.

A woman's voice answered. 'Safe Haven.'

'I . . . ' Janine sighed. The voice waited. 'I think I need . . . no, I need, yes, I need to come to you . . . '

And the tears started again.

19

The bottle was now two thirds empty and Phil had the acid burn from his throat to his gut to match.

He picked it up from the passenger seat of the Audi, put it to his lips. Felt the liquid there but didn't open his mouth. *No,* he thought. *No more.* He fixed the lid, tightening it hard, and threw the bottle on to the passenger seat once more, where it settled with a final, atonal slosh.

He looked instead at the house before him. Tried to convince himself he was doing something positive, something good. Something worth risking his licence for – his career, even. He had to squint to see it, covering one eye to throw the house into relief. He bit his lip at the same time, checking. If you can feel your teeth, someone had once told him, when it hurts if you bite, then you're not drunk. Phil bit down on the corner of his lip. Hard. Harder. Ground his teeth, jaw straining with the effort. He felt something in his mouth then. Old pennies. Dirty money. Blood. *Yeah,* he thought. *I'm sure I felt that. Yeah.*

'Fucking God-botherer . . . ' he mumbled, good eye on the lighted front room of the house. 'Wife-beating fucking God-botherer . . . '

After his aborted call to Marina, he had driven out to Druid's Heath, driven around until he had found Roy Adderley's house, parked up in front of it. Doing something good, he thought. Yeah. Thanking a God of his own that he hadn't had an accident or been picked up by the police.

Boxy and redbrick, on an estate of identical red boxes, it had probably looked modern sometime in the late sixties. There had been attempts at expansive individuality all down the street. Polite bay windows, Georgian front doors. The inhabitants trying to make the most of their homes, their lives. But the modest back and side conservatories didn't enlarge the houses, just made already tiny gardens look even smaller.

Adderley's house was unremarkable in every way. But Phil was experienced enough to know that a dull exterior was no disguise for what was going on inside.

He had checked Adderley's file; the case of his wife's disappearance, now murder. Adderley had claimed he was out at a church meeting the night she disappeared. However, cursory questioning revealed this to be a lie, prompting him to then become a person of interest. Eventually Adderley had admitted that he was at the flat of his girlfriend, Trudi. She had vouched for him, and with no body, there had been nothing to charge him with so they had reluctantly let him go. Now that Gemma's body had turned up, Adderley was again of interest. And he knew it, which was why Phil could only talk to him with a solicitor present.

But it didn't stop him doing this. Not harassment, though. Just parked up somewhere for the evening. Should anyone ask.

The alcohol had deadened any questions that Phil might have had about his actions. Both the cause of them and the effects they might have. And that was good. The less time he had to think, the more he just had to do, the better.

It was cold, both outside and inside the car. But Phil didn't feel it. Or told himself he didn't feel it. He wouldn't put the heater on in case it ran down the battery. The same for the CD player, although he was in the kind of mood that he could never find music to accurately reflect. Warren Zevon had been fine for driving, but there was nothing in the glove box for just sitting. So he sat in silence, with only an unacknowledged, crystalline anger and the emptying bottle for company. And that, he thought, with a bitterness in his mind to match that in his body, was fine by him.

The curtains of Adderley's living room had twitched a few times while he had been sitting there. Phil took a cruel solace from that. Someone was watching him. Or was at least aware that he – or someone – was there.

'Good,' he said as the curtains twitched again, reaching for the bottle.

The front door opened.

Phil sat immediately upright, attention as focused as it could be. Roy Adderley stepped outside. Scanned the empty street. Spotted the car.

A rush of adrenalin went through Phil. *Come on*, he thought, *come on. Over here, make something of it, come on . . .*

He smiled, gave a little wave.

Even in the darkness, even across the street, he could see how the gesture enraged Adderley. Enraged but, Phil reckoned, scared him as well. Adderley walked over to the car. Phil flung the door wide, tried to square up for confrontation. But the drink had affected his legs, and he found that he had to stagger to his feet.

Adderley stopped before him. 'You're that copper from the airport.'

'Yeah,' said Phil.

'You're pissed.'

Phil managed a smile. 'Yeah,' he said, his words tumbling and slurring, 'but in the morning I'll be sober. And you'll still be a wife-beating little shit.'

Adderley sprang back as if he had been struck. 'I don't have to take this from you. I could have your job for this.'

Phil attempted a shrug. 'Really?'

'This is harassment.'

Phil looked round with what he hoped was a nonchalant swing of the head but was actually a loping drunken swagger. 'Public property here. Can park where I want.' He took a step closer to Adderley, who flinched. 'Why, you got something to hide?'

Before Adderley could answer, Phil saw another figure appear in the doorway. He recognised her straight away. Trudi, from the airport. He turned his attention back to Adderley. 'You didn't waste any time.'

Adderley turned, saw what he was looking at, turned back to Phil. 'Carly needs a mother. A woman round the house.'

'Doesn't your good book say something about living in sin?'

'We've got . . . separate rooms. If it's any of your business.'

Phil gave a snort of laughter. 'Separate rooms? What, till your daughter goes to bed?' He shook his head. 'Fucking hypocrite.'

'You've got no right to—'

'Aw, shut up,' said Phil, waving his hand dismissively, staggering slightly from the effort. 'You're a fucking hypocrite. Admit it. Beating your wife, then going to church and asking for forgiveness. Then coming home and doing it all again. Hypocrite. Weak . . . spineless . . . little . . . hypocrite . . .'

Adderley looked like he didn't know whether to hit Phil or run from him. Instead, he spoke. 'I'll have your job for this. Just you wait.'

Phil pointed a finger, having to squint in order to do so. 'Yeah? Not if I have you first.' He leaned in to him, Adderley recoiling from his lethal breath. 'You're scum, you. You know that? Scum. The kind of man the police hate. The kind that's too fucking scared to attack other men so he takes it out on women and children. Scum. That's what you are.'

Adderley said nothing.

'And I'm going to have you. One way or the other. Fucking have you . . .'

'I'm going to call the police,' said Adderley, turning to go.

'Yeah, you do that, mate,' said Phil, attempting another laugh. 'Tell them what I said and why I'm here. Tell them how handy with your fists you are when it comes to your wife. Sure they'd love to know that.' He looked over to the house once more. 'She know what she's got coming, does she? The lovely Trudi? Is it going to be her we're looking for in a couple of months' time?'

Adderley walked away.

Phil watched him go. Then, convincing himself that his actions had been victorious, he made his way back to his car.

And passed out.

20

'Call the police, Roy, you've got to . . .'

Trudi stood in the hall beside Adderley, waiting for him to respond in some way. Instead she saw him do something she had never seen before. He twisted his face, contorting it into several shapes, all of them unpleasant. She watched, fascinated and a little scared, as his lips started moving. He was talking to someone, but not her. Someone who wasn't in the room with them.

He turned away, his conversation going on without her. Eventually he nodded. Mind made up.

Trudi watched him. 'Roy?'

He turned to her, eyes unfocused, mouth curled into a snarl. 'Shut up, just . . . shut up . . .' He turned away, paced up and down the hallway, a trapped animal in a too-small cage. 'I'm . . . thinking . . . Got to think . . .' He resumed his one-sided conversation.

Trudi stepped back, watched him. She had never seen Roy like this before. Happy, sweet and, she had to admit, sexy Roy. This was a different side to him. Scared. Angry. And slightly unhinged. Watching him, seeing that animalistic snarl, she could suddenly believe some of the things she had heard about him. She felt a frisson run through her. Not an altogether unpleasant feeling.

He stopped walking, went into the living room. She followed. He crossed to the window, looked out.

'He's still there. Just, just sitting there . . . '

He sighed, turned away, shaking his head.

'Got to get out . . . got to get out . . . '

'What, now?' asked Trudi. 'Where you going?'

He turned back to her. And there was that animalistic look in his eyes again. But this time there wasn't anything of the snarling, aggressive beast about it. Just something feral and trapped, ready to spring loose, take out anyone or anything who tried to stop it.

'You questioning me?'

'What?' Something in his voice, his eyes, made Trudi instinctively step back. This wasn't like the aggression of a few moments earlier. This was something else.

His eyes flicked to a Bible on a shelf. It was just about the only book in the house, apart from the Argos catalogue. Though given the scarring and tears on its heavy leather cover, the missing and torn pages sticking out, it looked like it had been used as more than just a book. A shiver went down Trudi's spine at the thought.

At that moment, for the first time, she felt scared to be alone with him.

Adderley reluctantly tore his eyes from the Bible, walked over to Trudi. Faced her, unblinking. 'I've made my judgement,' he said, voice small and hard, like a rock that could crack open to reveal white-hot lava. 'And when I've made my judgement, you don't question me.'

He walked into the hallway, grabbed his car keys from the table, opened the front door.

'But what am I—'

'You're staying here. You're doing what you're told. Know your place.'

'But I—'

'Don't question me, woman . . . '

Another step towards her, his hand raised this time. That was enough. Trudi cowered away from him, really scared now. He stood like that before her, arm raised, heavy but suspended. She closed her eyes, waiting for the blow, anticipating the pain, already flinching away from it.

But the blow never came. Roy let his arm drop, reluctantly, to his side. She studied his eyes. It was like there was something else living inside him, another identity fighting for dominance. He tore his gaze away from her. She wasn't sure, but she might have glimpsed a shudder of fear or revulsion in them as he did so.

'Roy . . .'

He didn't look at her, didn't reply, just strode out, slamming the door behind him.

Trudi stood there staring at the door. From upstairs came the sound of Carly crying; suddenly, like a wound-up air raid siren.

'Mummy . . . Mummy . . .'

Trudi, looking one way then the other and feeling unexpectedly tired, just stood there.

21

Janine stepped outside. The night was cold, dark, the threat of rain hanging heavy in the air. But she didn't feel any of that. All she could feel was the freedom.

She closed the door behind her. It hit the frame with a satisfying final thump. The sound of something ending. She grabbed hold of her suitcase, pulled it along behind her.

As she walked, she felt a pang of regret over the boys. What kind of mother was she to walk out like this? But when she remembered the look her sons had given her as they passed her on the way out with their father, the hatred and contempt, she didn't feel so bad. She would have to hang on to that image, that memory, every time she felt she had done the wrong thing. Put it in the forefront of her mind. Never forget.

Clive Street was deserted. Janine, walking quickly, idly wondered why. Was everyone behind their front doors? Locked away from the rest of the world? The pubs in the area were losing money, haemorrhaging customers, so they weren't there. But she'd read somewhere that TV viewing figures were down as well. So what else was there to do? They couldn't all be at the football like Terry. She felt a pang of envy. They would probably be having better times, better lives, than she had had with Terry. All of them.

Unless . . .

Unless they were putting up with the same thing.

She gripped the handle of the bag, walked faster. Sang a couple of bars of a song her dad used to sing when she was little. Some country song about not knowing what went on behind closed doors. It didn't matter now. Not to Janine. Because that was the old her, the old life. She was about to embark on a new one, a better one.

She walked the few streets to her allotted pick-up spot. The corner of Milton Street and Garrett Street, just by Oakwood Park. How anyone had the nerve to call it a park was beyond her. A tree-lined plateau rising from the road hid a wide, flat expanse of grass and a basketball court held within a chain-link fence. In the centre of the grass stood a small clump of trees. And that counted as a park.

Janine checked her watch. She was early. As she put her arm down, she looked along the street. A car was moving slowly towards her, headlights off, side lights only, hard to make out in the shadow of the trees. Like it had been parked there, waiting for her. She felt giddy, suddenly, stomach flipping, light-headed. This was it, she thought. No going back now. The car crawled closer. Janine readied herself.

It drew alongside her. The driver's window slid down. She waited, remembering what the voice on the phone had said. *Let the driver say the word. Don't prompt her.* She bent down.

'Strawberry,' said the driver, sitting back, features hidden in shadow.

Janine gave a tired, taut smile. 'Oh,' she said. 'Yes. Strawberry.'

'Get in.'

She opened the back door, put her bag on the seat, climbed in after it. The car began to pull away.

Janine looked in the mirror, saw the driver's eyes. Puzzlement crept over her face.

'Wait,' she said, 'you're not a woman. You're—'

'Just be quiet,' he said. 'Everything will be fine.'

Janine frowned. 'But—'

'I said be quiet.' The voice sharp, commanding.

This wasn't what she had been expecting. Not at all.

She looked round, suddenly worried. This wasn't how she had imagined it. She began to feel uneasy.

'I . . . I think I've made a mistake.'

The driver didn't reply.

'I think I want to get out now.'

Nothing.

'I want to get out now,' she said, her voice stronger, louder, tinged with panic.

'Just stay where you are.'

Janine looked round in a panic. The car hadn't got up much speed yet. The driver was still creeping along the side of the park, head going side to side, like he was trying to see if anyone had spotted him.

'I want to get out . . .'

They pulled to an abrupt stop. The driver turned to her. Anger flared in his eyes. He jabbed his finger at her. 'Just stay where you are. Do as you're told.'

Janine sat back, eyes wide. Stunned not only by the words and the tone, but by something else.

'I—'

She didn't finish her sentence. Just grabbed the handle and pushed the door. It opened. A hand appeared over the back of the front seat, trying to grab her. It missed. She managed to get out of the car. And ran.

She didn't know where she was going. Streets that she had lived on or around all her life suddenly seemed alien, unfamiliar. She just ran as hard and as fast as she could. Behind her she could hear the sound of the car turning round in the street, coming after her.

Oh God . . .

Not looking back, she ran even faster.

The car sped up. Not full speed – the driver still didn't want to be observed – but fast enough to catch up with her. Janine looked round. Houses on one side. Park on the other. Her mind whirled furiously. She could knock on a door, ask for help, get them to call 999. If they were in. If they answered the door at night. And what if they weren't, or they wouldn't? Would she be able to try another house? She doubted it. Park on the other side. Without stopping to think, she ran up the tree-lined slope on to the grass.

Once there, on the unlit stretch of dark green, she allowed herself time to get her breath back. But he could run up here, she thought. Run after me, catch me . . .

She looked round. No one. Deserted. Not even the few teenagers who occasionally congregated. For once she would have been glad to see them.

Then from behind she heard a familiar sound. The car. She turned. Headlights made their way upwards and through the trees as the driver managed to negotiate a route for himself. The engine revved, the car appeared over the brow, then on the flat of the green.

Oh shit . . .

Heart pounding so much she feared it would jump from her chest, legs aching and stomach ready to heave from the exertions, Janine ran once more.

The car didn't bother to keep its speed down or its lights low now. It was on a course for Janine. There was no way she could outrun it. She tried to put her hand in her pocket as she ran, bring out her mobile, call 999, but she didn't dare slow down enough to do so. So she ran. Blindly on.

The noise of the car increased and the grass ahead of her was suddenly starkly illuminated. He was on her.

Janine turned. The car hit her, almost breaking her in two, sending her spinning over the bonnet and windscreen.

She landed with a thud on the green.

She opened her eyes, looked down. Pain coursed all round her body like infected electricity. Her legs were the wrong way round.

She looked up once more. The car was bearing down on her.

She tried to crawl out of the way but her body wouldn't work.

The last thing she saw were the headlights hammering towards her.

Then pain.

Then nothing.

He reversed and went over her twice more.

But Janine was long gone by then.

22

Phil only woke up when the near-empty bourbon bottle rolled off his lap and on to the floor, spilling its remaining contents on him as it went.

He looked round, not knowing where he was, or, for a few seconds, who he was. He managed to refocus. He was still sitting in his car outside Roy Adderley's house. He checked the house: darkness. He checked himself: his jeans and shirt front were now soaking wet and stinking of booze. It just added to his disorientation. His mouth felt thick, sickly and sour, his head swirling and spinning like a waltzer, his stomach a combination of the two.

'Oh God . . .'

Groaned more than spoken. A plea more than a prayer.

He sighed. Checked his watch. Nearly three.

He sat back against the car seat. What was it that someone had said about three o'clock in the morning? In the dark night of the soul it's always three a.m. Something like that. And who had said it? Hemingway, Faulkner, Fitzgerald? One of them. Someone like that. Whoever it was, they were bang on.

That was just how Phil felt. The dark night of the soul. Body and mind addled and curdled from so much more than just the booze. And, like a hook in his flesh, drawing his mind away from his problems, drawing the attention of the pain he was feeling, the case he was working on. Gemma Adderley. And her husband Roy.

He checked the house once more. Still no movement. Decided it was time to do the thing he had been dreading most, putting off. Time to go home.

He turned the engine over. Band of Horses immediately began singing about a funeral. He switched it off, head pounding even more. Took a few seconds to steady himself, focus on the road ahead, to see only a single one, and begin to pull out.

As he did so, he became aware of headlights coming along the road behind him.

He checked his own car: he hadn't yet turned on the lights. He still looked stationary. He turned the engine off immediately, checked the rear-view mirror. Roy Adderley was driving back to his house.

Phil stayed where he was. Slumped down in his seat, pretended to be asleep. With one eye open. Watching.

Behind him, Adderley drove slowly to the front of his house. In his wing mirror Phil watched him turn the car's engine and lights off, get out, quietly close the car door and turn in his direction. This was it. He couldn't give himself away now.

Adderley watched Phil for what seemed like hours but was only really seconds, or at the most, minutes. Satisfied, he turned, went into his house. Closed the front door behind him.

Phil waited. When nothing more happened, no lights, no sound, no movement, he knew it was safe to drive away. He did so quietly, not putting on his lights until he was in the next street and on the way home.

He drove slowly, not wanting to attract attention to himself, not wanting to get pulled over. That would be highly embarrassing. He could probably get away with it, that wasn't a problem. Rank saw to that. But the whispers would start, word would spread. Phil's reputation would be compromised. And that was something he couldn't allow to happen.

So he drove as carefully as he could, thinking all the time, wondering just where Roy Adderley had been. Wondering what answers he would give when he was questioned properly.

Anything to avoid thinking about what was most on his mind.

PART THREE

THE SOFTEST BULLET EVER SHOT

23

The room was still spinning. Phil looked down at his feet, immediately wished he hadn't. It spun some more. He looked up. Slowly. Carefully. Tried to breathe, focus. The morning briefing was just about to get under way.

He hadn't slept, just endured a brief state of uncomfortable unconsciousness. He hadn't even made it to bed. Woken by his phone's alarm in the living room armchair, he had showered and changed clothes, but the previous night's beer and bourbon, combined with the stress he was already under, ensured he felt even more tired than previously. Not to mention hungover. Severely, nauseously hungover.

DCI Alison Cotter was standing before the room. Phil's boss and nominally the head of the inquiry, she delegated most of the work to the members of her team. Phil, as the chief investigating officer on the case, would normally be expected to address them. But Cotter had seen the state he was in and decided to take over. He knew she would be having words with him later.

'Okay,' she said to the assembled throng. 'Another day, another chance to get it right.'

Not Phil's words, hers. Her briefing, not his. He sat by her side, tried to fix an expression of intent listening to his features. Hoped he was successful.

'So I suppose I should start by asking, where are we?' She turned to him. 'Phil?'

He stood up, found his legs were made of water. Summoned imaginary ballast to them, strength to stand still and upright.

'Right,' he said, clearing his throat and closing his eyes as the room spun. He swallowed. His mouth was full of putrescent gravel. 'Gemma Adderley went missing over a month ago. We can be a hundred per cent sure that the body found is hers. Esme Russell' – he coloured slightly mentioning her name; stumbled on it – 'has done a preliminary PM. She gave me the results last night.' He paused, realised that what he had said could be misconstrued. He glanced furtively round the room. No one seemed to have picked up on it. Grateful for that, he continued. 'She says Gemma Adderley was kept alive after her abduction. She was tortured before she was killed.'

'Raped?' asked Cotter.

'Looks that way,' said Phil. 'Or at least it was attempted. Either by him being very careful or by using something else.'

'Maybe he couldn't get it up,' chimed in Sperring.

'It's a thought,' said Phil. 'Then he cut out her heart before dumping the body.'

'Was that the cause of death?' asked Cotter.

'Probably not,' said Phil. 'Her body just gave up under all the abuse, it looks like. The heart-cutting took place post-mortem.'

'Find the heart, find the killer,' said Cotter.

Phil nodded, even though he could have done without the interruption.

'So far,' he said, 'we've been looking at the husband, Roy Adderley. DS Sperring and I paid him a visit at his place of work, Birmingham International, yesterday. He ran when we tried to question him. Now he'll only talk with a solicitor present.'

'Feelings?' said Cotter.

'Seems like a good fit. He's got previous for assault and actual bodily harm. There's also been a history of disturbances at the Adderley household, and while there were no charges, he's been cautioned for spousal abuse and domestic violence. But he says that's all in the past and he's found God now.'

Sperring put his hand up. Phil nodded at him. It hurt to do so.

'Now he's just battering for Jesus,' said Sperring. 'I spoke to DS Ellison yesterday, who handled the initial MisPer inquiry, and he fancied him for it too. The daughter was a witness but she was inconclusive as to whether he was the one who drove her mother away. We can't rule out the idea that he could have paid someone to do it.'

'Has he an alibi for the night of Gemma Adderley's disappearance?' asked Cotter.

'Said he was at a Bible study group for his church,' said Sperring again. 'But that was a lie, may God forgive him. He was with his mistress. I'll talk to him today, see if he can elaborate on that.'

'He still looks the likeliest suspect at the moment, but we can't rule out someone else,' said Phil. 'The body must have been dropped in the canal sometime on Sunday night. We've set up a mobile incident room on site, but so far no one's come forward.' He turned to a young Asian woman sitting by a computer. 'How's the CCTV going, Elli?'

Elli looked slightly nervous to have all the attention of the room focused on her. She was even more relaxed in her dress than Phil, taking the laissez-faire he had introduced to an extreme. It was tolerated because she was the team's resident expert on all things computer-related. Today's T-shirt was advertising a 1950s Bela Lugosi movie, *Bride of the Monster*. The garishly rendered monster on the front was a visual representation of how Phil felt.

'Slowly,' she said. 'I've requisitioned all the footage from cameras in the area, but nothing so far. We're still looking for vans.'

'Or a boat,' said DC Imani Oliver.

Phil looked over to her. She was young, local, black and ambitious. But not ambitious in a political, careerist manner, just to be the best detective she could be. Working-class, university-educated. That dedication to the job had made her enemies in the department. But Phil liked her – and more importantly, trusted her – enormously.

'Good point,' he said.

'Thank you,' said Imani.

Phil nodded in acknowledgement, making the room spin once more.

'This sounds like the work of a full-on nutter,' said Imani. 'Ripping the heart out, taking a boat down the canal, or a van, all that. I mean, he must have somewhere he's taken the victim to . . . do what he gets up to. That takes planning, forethought. Would it help to have a psychologist on board to give us a profile, or at least some clues on how to proceed?'

Phil didn't answer. Couldn't answer. He shivered, his stomach tumbling from more than the hangover.

In the silence, Cotter answered. 'Good idea, Imani. Might be helpful, but for the moment we'll keep on with what we're doing.'

Imani nodded in response.

'Right,' said Cotter. 'There is one other thing that I was only made aware of just before this briefing.'

She looked round the room, ensuring she had everyone's full attention.

'There was a killing last night in West Bromwich.'

She paused. Sperring was about to go for a funny remark, so she cut him off.

'And there may be a connection with Gemma Adderley.'

'What d'you mean?' asked Phil.

Cotter drew herself up to her full height, looked at the team once more. 'A young mother. Janine Gillen. Killed in what seemed like a hit-and-run. But the car was used more as a murder weapon. She was chased off the road into Oakwood Park, where the driver seems to have deliberately targeted her. Mowed her down, and then, just to make sure she was dead, ran over the body several times.'

A ripple of disgust went round the room.

'So how does that link in with this case?' asked Imani.

'The on-duty pathologist noticed something odd about the body,' said Cotter. 'Despite the extreme damage, the driver seems to have gone back and removed something. Guess what?'

'The heart,' said Phil.

'Right,' said Cotter.

Phil felt that thrill run through him. He knew this was something, the strands of the inquiry knitting together. His pulse quickened; adrenalin kicked through the nausea. 'A car,' he said. 'Any idea what time?'

'Last night sometime,' said Cotter. 'No more details yet.'

Phil could almost feel his body vibrate with excitement. 'It's him,' he said, barely able to get his words out.

'Who?' asked Cotter.

'Adderley. Definitely. It's him.'

She turned to him, a genuinely quizzical expression on her face. 'Why d'you suppose that?'

'He went out in his car last night,' said Phil. 'Didn't come home until after three in the morning.'

'And how d'you know this?'

Phil looked round the room. The team were waiting for an answer. He paused, thought up a more convincing answer than the one he had been about to give.

119

'I . . . got someone to follow him. Find out where he went, what he did.'

Silence from Cotter. Phil felt himself reddening once more.

'After yesterday, I thought . . .' He shrugged, tried to make it natural. 'He was a person of interest. Maybe even the prime suspect. So I got someone to follow him. That's all.'

'Who?' asked Cotter.

'A . . .' Phil thought quickly once more. 'Confidential Informant. Owed me a favour. Got him to sit outside Adderley's house, see if anything happened. Good job too.'

'What state was the car in when it came back?' asked Imani.

'Don't know,' said Phil. 'We can send someone over to assess it after we bring him in.' He looked at Cotter hopefully.

She returned his look, but it held more questions than answers.

Phil swallowed hard. Like rocks in his throat. 'Shall we, then?' he said. 'Bring him in?'

'Do it,' said Cotter. 'But don't jump to conclusions. And remember, he'll have his solicitor with him. We don't want the interview stopped before it's started.'

'Thank you, ma'am,' said Phil. He turned to his team. 'Right. Here we go. Imani, you go to West Bromwich, see what you can find out about last night.'

Imani nodded.

'Ian, you're coming with me. We're going to pick up Mr Adderley for a little chat. Elli, keep on keeping on. See what you can turn up.' He looked at the rest of the team. 'Right. Let's get this guy.'

'Remember what I said,' said Cotter. 'Find the heart, find the killer. Bear that in mind. And quick. Once the press makes the connection – even if there isn't one – between these two murders they're going to be all over us. The last thing we need.'

Orders given, the team moved their chairs back, made ready to get on with the day. Cotter looked at Phil.

'A word, please,' she said. 'In my office.'

Feeling nauseous all over again, Phil followed her.

24

It was useless. No, worse than useless. There was no connection. It meant nothing to him at all. Nothing.

He held the heart in his latex-gloved hands, stared at it.
Crushed and broken, the blood congealed and hardened on its
surface. He felt nothing for it at all. Might as well be some
butcher's offal.

He scanned the room, searching for the right box, the correct final resting place for the heart. But nothing spoke to him.
The one he'd had planned, a dark wooden Indian box deco-
rated with carvings and inlaid ivory, wouldn't do now. He had
chosen that box specifically. The right box designed to invoke
the desired memories. He had then planned to work as he usually did. Acquire the body, spend the right amount of time
preparing it, remove the heart, leave the body in the correct
place and alignment, then, once alone, undertake the breaking
ritual. And afterwards experience what the ritual intended: the
healing.

But not this time.

He looked round his room. The boxes were all in their
places on the shelves. All hand-chosen, carefully considered.
Some were already filled. But many more were still awaiting
their contents. And that was understandable. Because this room
held his life, his inner life. His *real* life. All his fears and rejec-
tions, his darkest secrets and disappointments. And he hadn't

finished dealing with them yet. Hadn't finished working through them.

And now this. West Bromwich. West fucking Bromwich. What had that place to do with him? Ever? Nothing. No connection at all. Totally wrong.

He had panicked, that was what had happened, what he had to admit to himself. He had seen her body lying there and had thought quickly. His car had made plenty of noise, leaving the road and taking to the park, and her screams had been shrill and plentiful. Both those noises would have eventually brought people over, no matter how reluctant most of them were to step outside their doors at night. So he had knelt down and got to work.

A few cuts, some deeper incisions. Wasn't hard this time. Wasn't much of her left. His car had done the job for him. She looked more like a carrier bag of badly wrapped butcher's meat, crushed, dripping and splitting all over the place, than a human being. Her ribs smashed where the wheels had gone over her torso. He had snapped on the latex gloves, pushed inside her body. Her heart, or what was left of it, came out easily.

Then in his car and quickly away before anyone came. He had scanned the windows as he drove out of the park once more. Nothing out of the ordinary, no one watching. Or no one that he could see. He had kept his lights off and driven slowly. Coming quietly down the grassy ridge, finding a space in a row of parked cars. Well away from the street lights, he had parked up, watched.

Nothing. No one. Either he hadn't been heard, or no one wanted to get involved. Knowing human nature, he knew which one he believed.

Once he was certain he wasn't going to be discovered, he simply put his lights on and drove carefully away. The car was a bit of a mess, though. The front bent and bashed where he had hit her, the wheel wells and sides blood-splattered. He would have to get it cleaned. Repaired, even. Or perhaps just dump it, torch it and report it stolen. For now it was garaged, but he'd have to take it out at some point. He needed time to think about that. For now, he had more pressing matters to attend to.

The police, for one thing. What had he left at the scene? No fingerprints, as he was wearing gloves. Fibres? DNA? Could he have done that? He was always so scrupulous, so controlled about every aspect of his work, hated to let anything get out of hand, hated any variables he couldn't account for. Everything was meticulously planned.

Usually.

But last night . . . Had he done the right thing in taking the heart? Maybe he should have just left it there. Let them put her death down to a hit-and-run. Okay, a chase, hit and run, but nevertheless. Had he left footprints in the blood? On the grass? Could they get prints from that? Catch him from it? What about his car tyres? He didn't know. Didn't know anything.

He felt himself becoming agitated. No, he told himself, keep calm, keep controlled. He closed his eyes. Think. No matter what they had, witness statements or DNA, they had to find him first. Make a match. And he wasn't on file. That was the thing to keep in mind all the time. Plus his face had been covered. And his number plate was obscured and unreadable. Precautions. Control. He was all about that. And he had to keep reminding himself of that when the other moods threatened to take over.

He looked at the heart in his hands once more. Then at the box he had prepared for it. He had to do something, had to try . . . He closed his eyes. Tried to summon up the memories, the images, get the ritual started.

Nothing.

He sighed, opened his eyes. Felt anger rising within him. This wasn't right. Wasn't right . . .

Closed his eyes, tried again.

Waited, waited . . .

Nothing.

Anger welled inside him once more. Typical. Bloody typical. Just like all women. Leading him on, getting him to make mistakes. Even when they were dead . . .

'You coming?'

The voice came from outside the room. It hit him as swift and hard as a wrecking ball swung into his chest.

'I . . . I'll be along in a minute.'

'Well, hurry up, then. You know what the traffic's like at this time in the morning. Shall we take my car?'

'Yes.' Too quickly. He took a breath, calmed himself. 'That's fine. We'll take yours.'

Reluctantly he placed the heart in the box allocated for it, then stripped off his gloves, dropping them in the bin.

'Mustn't keep her waiting,' he said, feeling that familiar nub of anger inside him once more. 'Mustn't keep that cunt bitch waiting . . .'

He turned off the lights, locked the door and, forcing himself to stay controlled, made his way back into the real world.

25

'Come in. Close the door behind you.'

Phil did so. He eyed the seat before Cotter's desk, but, tempting though it looked, didn't sit down on it.

Cotter seated herself behind the desk, looked up, noticed Phil was still standing. 'Sit down, then.'

He did so.

Cotter had the senior office, the corner office. The room was a reflection of her personality: sleek, uncluttered, efficient. The only traces of a life beyond work were an unostentatious framed photo of herself and her partner, Jane Munnery, a city lawyer, and a squash racquet and gym bag in the corner of the room.

She regarded Phil with the kind of scrutinising stare she usually reserved for the interview room. In his fragile state, he felt himself begin to wilt under it.

'I was going to ask how you were,' she said, 'but I can see that for myself.'

Phil didn't reply. Just looked at his feet. This room wasn't spinning quite so much as the previous one, but it was still enough to make him feel queasy. That and the expectation of what Cotter was going to say.

'You were a shambles out there,' she said, pointing to the main office. 'You stink of booze and you can barely stand upright. And you're white as a sheet.' She scrutinised him further. 'Are you white? Or are you green?'

'I'm sorry, ma'am,' said Phil, as steadily as he could. 'I've . . . had a few personal issues to take care of.'

'I'm well aware of that. And I'm not unsympathetic. You've got some leave coming up. I think you should take it.'

The words, while hardly unexpected, still hit Phil hard. 'But I'm in the middle of an inquiry. I'm CIO.'

'Look at you. Stumbling all over the place—'

'I had a bad night.'

'Don't interrupt me.' Cotter's eyes shone darkly. 'Look at the way you're dressed. I've always given you a certain leeway in regard to this department's dress code, but you've gone too far. A T-shirt and jeans? And when was the last time your face was acquainted with a razor?'

Phil sighed, found he couldn't answer back to anything she had said. 'Sorry.'

'I should imagine you are.'

He held up his hand. 'Could I just say something?'

Cotter sat back, waited. Clearly she had been expecting this. 'Go on.'

'In there.' He gestured to the main office. 'The briefing. Was I out of order? Did I handle it badly?'

'You looked terrible. You smelled drunk. That's unprofessional.'

'With respect, ma'am,' said Phil, choosing his words carefully, 'I'm not the first copper to turn up hungover and I definitely won't be the last.'

'True.'

'So did I handle it badly? The look and the smell aside, of course.'

Cotter thought. 'No. I suppose you didn't. Overall. Other than a little slurring of words.'

Phil said nothing.

Cotter leaned forward. 'Look, Phil. You're a bloody good detective. One of my best. You're unconventional at times and, Ian assures me, a pain in the arse. But I tolerate that because you get results. But not this time. Take time out, Phil. Get some help. We can provide you with someone through the department. Work things through. Then, when you're ready, come back to work.' Her words were straightforward; her voice, while professional, was not unkind.

'But like you said,' said Phil, 'I was all right in there. In the briefing.'

'Yes, all things considered, I suppose you were.'

'Last night was bad. I drank too much. But I'm still focused on this case. I'm still in charge. I can still do it.'

Cotter was about to reply, but Phil cut her off.

'Please. You know what's happened.'

'Yes, I know.'

'I'm pouring everything I've got into this job to try and stop myself thinking of anything else. To keep me going. The job is all I've got. Please.' Phil felt a pleading tone enter his voice. He tried to stop it, but it had crawled there of its own volition. 'Don't take it away from me.'

Cotter sat back, thoughtful. Phil said nothing. Eventually she leaned forward again.

'Who was your CI?'

'What?' It wasn't what he had expected her to say.

'Your CI. The one who followed Roy Adderley last night. Who was it?'

'Erm . . . it—'

'Because I received a complaint from Roy Adderley's *friend*' – she spoke the word in speech marks – 'saying that you were round there last night harassing him.'

Phil felt himself reddening. 'Ah. Well . . . '

128

'I'm waiting.'

Phil shook his head. No point in lying. 'Yeah, it was me. After the way he was when Ian and I went to see him yesterday, we thought there must be more to him. So I . . . parked outside his house. And he saw me. Came out. There was an argument.'

'And you drove away.'

'One of us did.'

Despite the nature of the conversation, Cotter's copper instincts were still working. 'Where did he go?'

'I don't know.'

'Why not?'

Phil shrugged, apologetic.

'You passed out.'

He looked uncomfortable.

'And presumably his return woke you up.'

'Yeah. Kind of a coincidence, really.'

Cotter sat back once more, shaking her head. A smile almost appeared at the corners of her lips. 'On the one hand, that's good police work. On the other, you were a drunken, angry slob out looking for a fight. And there's no place for people like that in my team. No matter what's happened to them.'

'Yes, ma'am.'

Cotter sighed. 'Not to mention how you got there. Were you driving drunk?'

Phil said nothing. Just looked ashamed.

Cotter shook her head, mouth curling in distaste. 'Jesus Christ . . . One last chance to pull it together, Phil. Otherwise you're out of here until you can convince me you're fit to return. Got that?'

Phil felt something positive stir within him. 'Thank you.'

'Don't make me regret this. The case has been upgraded to high priority. Go on, bring Adderley in for questioning. But Phil, I want you focused. Not fixated.'

'Right.'

'He's the prime suspect, but if it's not him, you keep an open mind.'

'Okay.'

'And if it does turn out to be something more, we may – and I stress may – get some psychological help in. And you would have to be all right with that.'

Phil didn't reply. Just nodded.

'Good.' Cotter sat back. 'On you go, then.'

Phil thanked her once more, got slowly to his feet and left the office. A reprieve. Nothing more than that.

He was standing on the edge of the abyss. He just hoped he had the strength not to be pulled in.

26

'Not much chance it was an accident, then.' Detective Constable Imani Oliver stared at the crime scene in Oakwood Park.

It looked like the garden party from hell. Most of the grassed area had been taped off, giving it an air of exclusivity, while the ubiquitous white plastic tent had been erected over Janine Gillen's final resting place. Instead of caterers, paper-suited crime-scene investigators moved about. Behind barriers at a distance, the usual collection of rubberneckers were watching, along with the media.

'Thought you'd have screens up,' said Imani. 'Stop that lot from getting too much footage.'

'Screens?' Detective Constable Avi Patel laughed. 'Wish we had the budget. Anything beyond the plastic tent has to be begged for.' He looked at Imani, smile still on his face. 'Must be different over in the big city.'

Not being unkind; just banter, thought Imani. That was how she would take it. He seemed naturally cheerful. She hoped she hadn't misread that. 'Big city? We're only down the road.'

Patel nodded. 'Yeah. And we might be handing this one over to you, from what I've heard. Could be a link with that body in the canal?'

'That's what I'm here to find out. You identified her?'

'Janine Gillen. Her wallet was still in her coat pocket. Wish they were all that easy.'

'Know anything about her?'

Patel took out his notepad, read from it. 'Quite a bit. Wife of Terry Gillen. He's been on and off our radar over the years. Bit handy with his fists, that sort of thing.'

A shudder of something like recognition ran through Imani. 'Against his wife?'

'And others.' Patel checked his notebook once more. 'Yep. Cautioned. That's all.' He looked up and the earlier cheerfulness was absent. 'Fucking scum, they are. Wife-beaters.' He realised he had been talking to a woman. 'Sorry. 'Scuse my language.'

Imani smiled. 'You'll hear no argument from me.'

Patel looked relieved, continued. 'I know we get sent for training, go on courses for how to deal with this, but ... ' He glanced round at his colleagues. 'Most of them? Not high on their list of priorities. Slap on the wrist, don't do it again, that sort of thing. Or even worse, when uniforms agree with the husband. Women need a smack now and again, keeps them in line. All that shit.' He shook his head, looked like he had something unpleasant in his mouth, wanted to spit.

Imani gave a short laugh. 'You sure you're actually a copper?'

He smiled, slightly shamefaced, reddened. 'Sorry. Bit of a pet hate. Just tell me to shut up.'

'No, I'm glad to hear it.' Imani found herself smiling once more. Maybe there was more to DC Patel than met the eye. 'So what's the husband got to say for himself?'

'He was out last night. First thing he said, wanted us to know it. And he's got a watertight alibi. With his kids. Watching the Villa.'

'Poor bastards,' said Imani, then looked up hurriedly. 'Sorry.'

'Don't worry,' said Patel. 'More of a cricket man myself.'

'That's okay,' said Imani. 'It's just I come from a family of Villa fans. I can remember what it was like at home when they lost. My dad wasn't worth being around.'

'Did you know that when a football team loses, the rate of domestic attacks in that area rises? What does that say about us?' said Patel. He looked at her sheepishly once again. 'Sorry. They told us that on one of our courses. Couldn't get it out of my head ever since.'

'I'll bear that in mind.' Imani looked back at the murder scene. The body was long gone, but the aftermath of the act still hung in the air. Phil Brennan always likened it to a stage set in a theatre after the actors and audience had gone home, and she could see what he meant, but for Imani it was something different. It was as though all the incidents in Janine Gillen's life, no matter how large or small or seemingly insignificant, had led her to this point. Everything. Imani didn't believe in predestination or anything religious, but there was something about moments like this, settings like this, where the forcible absence of life had occurred, that made her understand spirituality, the need for there to be something else, even the desire to take pilgrimages to certain sites in the hope that something mystical might occur. Some answers be found. Even here.

'So this husband,' she said as they walked towards the white tent. 'How did he take the news?'

Patel shrugged. 'Not that bothered really. Maybe he was in shock and it hadn't quite hit him yet. Just moaned that he couldn't take time off work to look after the kids.'

'Where does he work?'

'Roofer.' He smiled when he said it. 'Kind that doesn't bust a gut if the weather's bad.'

'What's your feeling about him? Think he did it?'

Patel stopped walking, gave the question some thought. 'Don't think so. I mean, I know he wasn't all that bothered, and of course he was a bastard to her at home, but I didn't get a murderer vibe from him. Not deliberately, anyway. Not like this. One thing he said, though. They'd started seeing a therapist, a counsellor together.'

'Really? Doesn't sound the type.'

'Don't think he was. Marriage was rocky, though. Apparently his brief told him to do it.'

'So next time he hit his wife he could say he was working on being a changed man.'

Patel gave a grim smile. 'Exactly. Anyway, he didn't last long at it. But I think Janine kept going. Became something of a bone of contention between them.'

Imani gestured towards the white tent. 'Enough to . . . ?'

Patel shrugged. 'And there's the question of the car as well. Terry Gillen was driving his last night. We looked it over. Not a mark on it. Well, no new ones, anyway. Nothing to match this.'

They stopped walking, in front of the tent now. Imani could see the ruts left by the tyre tracks, deep and muddy. The grass seemed to have almost been ploughed, the driver had gone backwards and forwards so much. She could also make out where the earth was much darker in colour than in other places. She knew what had been there. Or rather who.

'Body was in a right mess when we got here,' said Patel, no trace of a smile now. In fact his mood seemed to have changed the nearer he got to the murder scene, any earlier humour now completely gone. 'Some dog walker just about brought up their breakfast. Body was all over the place. Bottom half on back to front, ground into the . . . well, ground, I suppose. Horrible. Horrible way to go.'

Not that there's ever a good way, thought Imani. She liked this young DC. His attitude, his thought processes, his commitment. Or at least that was what she told herself.

134

'There was one other thing,' said Patel. 'She had a card in her purse. For a refuge.'

'A women's refuge?'

Patel nodded. 'It's been bagged and taken as evidence, but I wrote the details down.' He tore a page out of his notebook, handed it to her. 'Here.'

She read it, looked up. 'Safe Haven,' she said. 'D'you know them?'

'Not my area, really. I'd just started asking around about them. Hadn't got very far.'

Imani smiled. 'Considering what little time you've had, I think you've done a great job.'

Patel blushed, looked away. 'Thanks. You know ... So you think it's connected with your case, then?'

'Could be. Some strong links there. Need to do a bit more digging. But thank you.' She held out her hand. 'I really appreciate the help.'

'No problem,' he said, taking it and holding it for a moment too long after shaking it.

'Why don't you come with me? I want to check out this refuge and the counsellor. And there's someone I want to bring in who might be able to link the two cases together. I'll give her a call on the way. You up for it?'

Patel smiled. 'Off to the big city?'

'If you think you can handle it.'

'Why not? It'll look good. Bit of joint enterprise, if you like. Engendering relationships across the forces. Sharing good practice. All that bollocks.'

Imani smiled. 'Another training course?'

Patel laughed. 'Paperwork'll be a bastard, though,' he said.

'You can deal with that.'

She walked away towards her car, Patel following.

27

The interview room held stories. And the ghosts of stories. They hung in the air like stale coffee-coated breath, clung to the hidden dusty corners where no cleaner could reach. They lay amongst the dead fly carcasses in the strip-light casings. Clung to the walls, refusing to be washed away by paint or paper. And in more tangible form, the table held the marks of those who had sat there previously. The names of the players, guilty and innocent and everything in between, their illiterate litanies recorded forever, biro upon biro, carving upon carving. Threats to the guilty for stitching up, grassing, all violence and horror and bloody retribution. Prayers for the innocent and invocations of despair. Heartfelt and real and often the only honest sentiments ever expressed in that space.

From that side of the table at least.

Phil sat on the other side. The clean, unmarked side. Sperring alongside him. Their story in front of them, hidden in the binding of a manila folder. About to add it to the room's collection.

Opposite sat Roy Adderley and his solicitor, Lesley Bracken. She looked professionally stoic, bored even. Adderley had the look of a man who had gone to hospital to have his bunions looked at only to be told he had something inoperable and terminal. He looked like he was about to melt into a pool of sweat. The closeness of the room amplified it, gave the atmosphere a rank edge.

'Thank you for sparing the time to come and see us, Mr Adderley,' said Phil, unable to keep the smile from his face.

'My client wishes to state that, for the record, he came here voluntarily and of his own free will,' said Lesley Bracken, the words said so often she could probably have recited them in her sleep.

'And we're very grateful,' said Phil. 'Saves us the trouble of doing this under caution. And this way nothing gets put on tape.' He opened the folder in front of him, studied it. Or pretended to. He knew exactly what he was going to say, the approach to take. Before he could start, Bracken spoke again.

'My client would also like it known that as a gesture of good will, and to demonstrate his innocence, he will not, at present, be pressing charges arising from your behaviour towards him yesterday, Detective Inspector Brennan.'

'Kind of him,' said Sperring, finding something on the wall fascinating.

'Your client ran when we identified ourselves as police officers. That what innocent men do?' Before she could say anything further, Phil continued. 'But let's get down to business.'

He stared at the words and pictures before him, playing a waiting game, making Adderley's unease rise even higher.

Eventually he looked up, straight at the nondescript man before him. Didn't look like a wife beater or a murderer. But then they very rarely did. 'Not the first time you've been in here, is it, Roy?' he said, face blank.

Adderley didn't respond. Just gave his solicitor an imploring look.

Bracken jumped in. 'Is that relevant?'

'We'll see when he answers the question,' said Phil. He turned once again to Adderley. 'Do you want to answer the question? Or shall I just tell you?'

137

'That . . . that was different,' said Adderley, voice small.

'Not so different,' said Phil. 'Assault. Bodily harm.'

'I was never charged,' said Adderley. 'It's not relevant.'

Phil smiled. 'That phrase,' he said. 'Never charged. Never proved. Not "I never did it", not "I was innocent". No. Just never charged. The refuge of the unproved guilty, that phrase. Well, you *were* charged. You were cautioned and no further action was taken. Your victims all withdrew their complaints.'

'All women,' said Sperring, before Bracken could raise an objection. 'Your victims.'

Phil leaned forward. 'Like hitting women, do you? Gives you a thrill, makes you feel big? Like a real man?'

Adderley looked down at the table, shook his head. There were things being said that even his solicitor couldn't help him with.

'You've got previous for violent attack as well, haven't you?' said Sperring. 'Against men this time.'

'Years ago,' said Adderley. 'All in the past.'

'Yeah,' said Sperring, looking down at the report in front of him. 'Looks like you always came off second best, an' all.' He glanced up. 'They used to hit you back, the other blokes? Hurt you too much?'

'I . . . ' Adderley sighed. 'That was years ago,' he repeated. The words dried up and blew away as soon as they left his lips.

'Right,' said Phil. 'So now you only hit women.'

'That's not fair,' began Bracken.

'You're right,' said Phil. 'Not fair at all.'

'I . . . I'm a different man now,' said Adderley. 'I . . . don't do things like that any more. The Lord gives me strength now.'

'The Lord?' asked Phil.

'God. I worship God now. He gives me strength.'

Phil looked at him, a mocking expression on his face.

'Look,' said Adderley, 'I know I've had problems in the past.

138

Trouble with my temper an' that. But ever since I gave myself up to the Lord I've been a much better person. A much calmer one. At peace. Contented. I've put all that behind me.' He looked at Phil. 'You should try it.'

'I'm not quite that desperate,' said Phil. He opened the folder. 'May I?' Didn't wait for a response. 'Here's a transcript of an interview with Gemma Adderley, your wife. This is from . . . let's see. Two years ago. Nearly three. A complaint she made to the police about you. She gave her statement to a constable while she was in A and E. Remember? Or do they all blur into one after a while?'

Adderley dropped his gaze, bowed his head.

'Here we go. *He would hit me*, she says. *Like this time. He would get angry because I hadn't done something right, or he'd come in from work and the table wasn't set the way he wanted it or I'd made something for dinner he didn't want. Something like that. Or Carly was making too much noise playing with her dolls. Then he'd get angry with me, start to shout. Prayers and stuff. Then he'd get the Bible down. This big old book, massive and heavy, really thick, and hit me with it. All over, my arms and legs, my body. Shouting all the time, bits from the Bible, prayers. Then my head. Sometimes I'd pass out. But this time it's really bad. And he hit Carly this time. So I came down here.* There's a bit more, then she says: *It was always the same. If I go back now he'll be on his hands and knees praying for forgiveness, in tears. It always happens. Every time. And I go back to him because he promises to be better. But not this time.*' Phil looked up, put the paper down. 'But she did, didn't she? She did go back to you. Shame, really, because if she hadn't, she would probably be alive now.'

'So that's the kind of strength your God gives you, is it?' asked Sperring.

'That was a long time ago. I'm a changed man now. He saved me,' said Adderley.

'Didn't save your wife, though,' said Sperring.

Before Bracken could interject once more, Phil jumped in.

'Which brings us to last month. October the sixteenth, in particular. The night your wife went missing. The last time anyone saw her alive.' He checked the notes in front of him once more. 'The detective in charge of Gemma's case, DS Ellison, initially interviewed you. You said you had no idea where she might have gone. They tried to talk to her friends, but she didn't have any. You wouldn't let her have any. Apart from the other women at church, and Gemma hated going. Wouldn't go. I'm sure she paid for that. So no one knew if she was going anywhere. And then she was gone.'

It looked like Adderley was fighting back tears.

Phil ignored him. 'So. The night she disappeared. You initially said you were at Bible study. But you were actually with your new girlfriend. Why the lie?'

'I ... '

'Did you think it would make you look suspicious? Is that it?'

'Something ... something like that ... '

Bracken spoke. 'My client was visiting his girlfriend, who has subsequently moved into the family home and is helping him to bring up his daughter.'

Phil looked straight at Adderley. 'Couldn't wait to get rid of one before you moved the other one in, eh? What does the Bible say about that?'

'My client realises this isn't a flattering portrait of him,' Bracken continued, 'but in light of subsequent events he thought it best to tell the truth.'

'Better late than never,' said Phil. 'And where were you last night, Roy?'

Adderley looked up, his expression an angry, hurt sneer. 'You should know.'

Sperring looked at Phil. Phil knew he was frowning.

140

'Just answer the question, please.'

'You were sitting outside my house. Watching. You should know.'

'That could be construed as harassment, Inspector,' said Bracken.

'No, it couldn't,' said Phil. 'Your client is a suspect in his wife's murder. Having his house watched is proper procedure.'

'But my client says you were drunk.'

'His word against mine,' said Phil, feeling anger rise within him.

'Nevertheless—' began Bracken, but Phil kept going.

'So, Roy, you got in your car and drove away. Came back about three in the morning. Where'd you been till then?'

Adderley looked to his solicitor once more.

'This would be inadmissible in court, Detective,' said Bracken. 'Whatever you're trying to prove—'

'There was another murder last night,' said Phil. 'Another woman, about Gemma's age, build, type. She was killed about the same time as Roy here went out for a drive.' He leaned forward. 'So I'll ask again. Where were you last night?'

Adderley stared round the room, looking for ways of escape. His mouth worked but no sound emerged.

'Janine. That was her name. Janine Gillen. Know her?'

'Inspector, I don't think this is—'

'You know how she died, Roy? Hit by a car. Repeatedly. How's your car today?'

'Inspector—'

'We'll need to take a look at it, of course. See what kind of state it's in today.'

Adderley dropped his head to the table, began to cry.

Bracken stood up. 'That's quite enough, Detective Inspector Brennan. My client came here today of his own free will to assist the inquiry into his wife's death. Instead, you've accused him of murdering not only her but another woman as well. Where's your evidence?' She stared at him. Silence.

'Sorry,' said Phil. 'I thought it was a rhetorical question.'

'I don't appreciate your attempts at flippancy,' she said.

'I wasn't trying to be flippant,' said Phil. 'You want evidence? We'll get evidence.'

'Should you do that,' Bracken said, picking up her bag, 'then we'll be back. But please don't harass my client again, or attempt an illegal seizure of his car. Or we will take matters further.' She turned to the door. Adderley rose as if in a dream, not believing he could actually leave. He meekly followed her out.

Phil sat back, expelled a heavy whisky-soaked breath. Rubbed his eyes. 'How . . . fucking . . . dare she . . . '

'Thanks for coming,' said Imani. 'I appreciate that this is short notice, that you've got plenty of other things you should be doing. Your day job, for a start.'

Marina sat back, gym bag next to her work bag at her feet. Listening. 'No problem. Luckily I'm not teaching any classes today. Just admin that I'm glad to get away from. What can I do for you?'

The Six Eight Kafé on Temple Row in the heart of the city. An independent coffee shop, all chalkboards and stripped blonde wood. The antithesis of Starbucks. Marina was sitting opposite Imani and Avi Patel. The police officers sipped various milky coffees. Marina had ordered fruit juice and water. Two manila folders lay on the table in front of them. Unopened.

'Well,' said Imani, 'I'm sure you can guess.'

Phil was her first thought. Something had happened to him. Something bad in a next-of-kin-notified kind of way. The distress must have shown on her face.

'It's work,' said Imani. 'The job you did with the child last month? Carly Adderley? I don't know if you've seen the news, but her mother's body has been discovered.'

'Yes,' said Marina. 'I'd heard. That poor kid.' She remembered the little girl. Lost, abandoned. Literally.

'Right,' said Imani. 'There's more. DS Patel here is involved in the case of another dead young woman and there are similarities.'

'You think it's the same person?'

'That's what I'm hoping you'll be able to tell me.'

'No pressure then,' said Marina, a small smile in place.

Imani returned the smile, even smaller if anything.

'Does Cotter know about this? About you asking me?'

'Not yet. I put it to her and she thinks you should be brought in if you're needed. I'm just sounding you out, getting your opinion. I think the two deaths are related.'

'What makes you say that?'

'I'll give you the files to look at. In the meantime, what d'you think about the husband? Roy Adderley, was it?'

'You mean do I think he did it?'

Imani nodded.

'Gut feeling? I didn't like him. Felt there was something off about him. Carly was returned to him once he was located but I always felt it was too soon. That there was something more the girl could have told us. That she needed more help.'

'Couldn't you do anything?'

'I voiced my opinions,' said Marina, trying to put distance and professionalism into her words. 'I'm sure they were noted down somewhere.'

'What did the CIO on the case say?'

'Hugh Ellison?' Marina suppressed a shudder. 'Tried to push the husband but couldn't get anywhere. To be honest, I don't think he was the most incisive of interviewers. Eventually had to let it go.'

Imani nodded.

Marina leaned forward, her voice dropping involuntarily, face as blank as she could make it. 'I take it Phil's running this one?'

'He is,' said Imani.

144

'And was this meeting his idea?'

'Definitely not,' said Imani. 'He knows nothing about it. This is all coming from me.'

Marina smiled, relief apparent on her face. 'So you're running an investigation within an investigation?'

'I'm just using my initiative, that's all.' Her features inscrutable. 'Like any good copper would do. I don't think there's any money in the budget for this, not at this stage. But I'll see what I can do.'

'So this is just a favour?'

Imani looked apologetic. 'At the moment, yes. Sorry. I know it's unorthodox, but if I'm right and these two cases are connected, I think it's safe to say you'll be on the payroll. And I wouldn't want anyone else to do it. You're uniquely placed for this. You're already involved in the investigation.'

Marina said nothing. Was Imani abusing their friendship for the sake of her investigation? Trying to look good at Marina's expense? Did she think there was a genuine need for Marina's services? Was she telling the truth? Or the worst option: was this about getting her and Phil back in close proximity again in the hope of a reconciliation?

'What d'you say?'

Marina kept thinking. Weighing things up. Part of her felt disloyal to Phil to even be considering doing this. Especially when she thought of what had happened to him after their separation. How he had seemingly not heard her words, understood her concerns and fears; how badly he had taken it.

But there was another part of her mind whirring away inside her. The part that was thrilled to be engaged on a case, to be active in pursuing criminals, using her skills to stop them. She had always found it difficult to say no, whatever the circumstances.

She looked at the manila folders on the table in front of her.

And suddenly couldn't wait to open them, see what was inside. Phil or no Phil. Money or no money.

'Okay then,' she said, reaching for them.

'Thank you,' said Imani. 'Just look them over, let me know what you think. Similarities, differences. Your hypothesis. I'd be very grateful.'

'Fine.' Marina put the folders in her work bag. 'When d'you need this by?'

'Soon as.'

'Okay. Well, like I said, it's a light work day today. I'll get straight on to it.'

'Thanks.' Imani stood up. Taking his cue, Patel did likewise. 'I really do appreciate it. You know where to find me when you've finished.'

They said their goodbyes and left the café. Marina sat and watched them go, the files burning a metaphorical hole in her bag, her mind. She would get straight on to them.

After she'd had a session at the gym.

29

Sperring turned to face Phil. Both were still in their seats in the interview room. 'So all that about a CI was bollocks, was it?'

'Yeah.' Phil sat forward, controlling the temper inside him. Trying to shake away the near-constant rage he felt. 'After what he did yesterday, the way he ran, his lying, I knew there must be something iffy about him. So I sat outside his house to see if he moved.'

Sperring just looked at Phil, shook his head.

Phil stopped rubbing his eyes, turned to him. The anger was still there. 'What? Like you've never done that.'

Sperring started to answer, but Phil stood up, began walking round the room. His body containing too much energy to remain seated. 'How many times have we had words about you taking off on your own, mavericking about? Doing stuff that's borderline illegal to get information? And now you're taking the moral high ground for what? Because I sat outside his house last night?'

'The difference is, boss,' said Sperring, staying where he was, 'I do it with scumbags who know the score, play the game. I don't do it with suspects who go crying to their solicitors. You knew he was getting his brief in here; why d'you go antagonising him?'

Phil walked round to the other side of the table, placed his fists on it, stood where Adderley had sat, faced his junior officer. 'He was out last night at the same time Janine Gillen was being murdered. In his car. We have to get a warrant, see that car.'

'You heard what his brief said. You've made it impossible now. Might even give him enough time to get rid of it.'

'So there's our proof of guilt. We'll have him then.'

'Yeah,' said Sperring, 'because that's how it works. We always arrest someone with no evidence.'

Phil just stared at him.

Sperring shook his head. 'You think it's him then? Definitely?'

Phil turned away from the table, resumed pacing. 'Course it's him. Who else would it be?' He held up his fingers, counting off. 'Means, motive, opportunity. He's got the lot.'

'And how does he know this Janine Gillen?'

'For us to find out, isn't it?'

'So he was out last night,' said Sperring. 'Right. It's still a bloody big jump for him to be Janine Gillen's killer as well. You're usually spot on, boss, but I reckon you're off on this one.'

'But look at him,' said Phil. 'He gets down on his knees and prays after he beats up his wife. He's got previous. He's got a temper on him.' He shook his head, as if confirming the truth of his words to himself. Gesturing as he walked. 'The bloke's a nutter. A dangerous, violent nutter. We have to stop him from doing it again.'

Sperring didn't reply. Phil, feeling suddenly weary as the withdrawal of adrenalin hit, sat down in Adderley's seat, facing his colleague. Sighed.

'Listen, boss,' said Sperring, his voice not unkind.

Phil looked up. He wasn't used to hearing sympathy or concern from Sperring. Usually the opposite.

'I think . . .' Sperring stopped, unsure how to proceed. 'Why don't you take a bit of time off?'

'I don't need time off. I just need to get this bastard off the streets.'

'I don't mean a lot of time, just . . .' He sighed. 'Look, all I'll say is don't mix the personal and professional. Don't bring your home life to work.'

Phil stood up once more, anger rising with him. 'You're lecturing me? You're fucking lecturing me?'

'Somebody has to,' said Sperring, raising his own voice now. 'You're heading for a breakdown the way you're going. Not only that, but you're going to make a mistake on this job and then the shit's really going to be spread. We'll all be for it.' He stood as well. 'Get a grip. Get yourself sorted. Not later, now.'

Phil stared at him, about to argue. He saw that Sperring was ready to argue too.

'I don't want a fight,' said Sperring. 'Not with you. Not about this. But if that's what I have to do to make you see sense, then I will.'

'You're going to take me on, are you? Really?'

Sperring stood his ground. 'If I have to, yeah.'

Phil stared at him until he could hold his gaze no more. He wanted to charge at Sperring, pummel the anger out of his system. But he didn't. Instead he just sighed. His head dropped. The adrenalin withdrawal was flatlining in his system now, leaving him wearier than he had ever felt. He closed his eyes. As he did so, an image of Marina appeared before him. He smiled at her, his heart breaking all over again.

'Boss?'

Phil opened his eyes. 'Yeah.' He nodded. 'Yeah.'

'What?' Sperring, wondering which way Phil's mood was going, was still ready to fight.

'Maybe I . . . ' Another sigh. 'Could you hold the fort for a while?'

'Course.'

'Follow up whatever you can on—'

'I said of course. Do what you've got to do.'

Phil nodded, looking at Sperring once more. He opened his mouth to speak but the first-choice words couldn't make themselves heard. 'I'll be back later,' he said.

Sperring nodded, understood.

Phil left the room.

30

He sat in the toilet cubicle even though he didn't need the toilet. Head in hands, eyes closed tightly. Rocking slightly, backwards and forwards. Hands pressed into his face. Blocking out the world around him, refocusing, repositioning his mind. Thinking. *Thinking.* But it was no good. No matter what he did, what he said, what he thought, he could only think about the previous night.

He was trying to say the right thing, do the right thing. But he couldn't. And he could tell it was wrong from the way it was received. He found himself distracted. Making mistakes. And if he kept on like that, it would be noticed. Normally that wouldn't bother him. He'd just shrug it off. A bad day. Everybody had them. But not him. Not today. Too much suspicion.

He still couldn't stop his mind from drifting back to the night before. He relived it over and over again. The conversation in the car. Janine's unease. Unease that blossomed into panic.

Panic. That was the word. The one he kept coming back to. The whole night summed up in that one word. Panic.

The chase. Then the eventual capture. Over and over again in his mind. He hadn't stopped to think while he had been driving; just acted on impulse. She couldn't be allowed to get away. Not with what she'd seen. That had been his overriding impulse. And then when her body lay there, mangled under the wheels of his car, he had tried to salvage something.

151

He still didn't know whether he'd been right to do that. In a sense it didn't matter. Not any more. Because he done what he had done. And now he had to deal with the consequences of that.

He kept telling himself what he had thought earlier. No DNA. Nothing on file to make a match even if he had left any. He had got away with it.

And yet . . .

That niggling voice in the back of his mind. Trying to trip him up, pull him down. Put obstacles in the way of his more rational thoughts. Guilt? Was that it? No. He had no guilt about his actions. None whatsoever. It was therapy. And it had been *working*, before this. But it had to go on. Had to. Because it mattered. It was the only way he could be well again. In his mind. Free of everything – everyone – that had been holding him back. Stopping him becoming the person he should be. His therapist had given him the clue.

'You've got to find a way to put all this behind you,' he had said. Sitting in his armchair, dressed casually and relaxed, legs crossed as usual. Calm and knowledgeable. Sun streaming in through the windows behind him. Like a different, better world being glimpsed outside. 'Something that works for you. Take all the individual hurts and upsets, the scars and the tragedies, and box them away. They won't be gone for ever. You'll know they're there, but you won't be tempted to reopen them. Just acknowledge their existence and move on.'

And that was exactly what he had done.

He had thought long and hard about it at first. About who had hurt him, had made him the way he was. And he knew straight away. Women. Not men, never men. Just women. And not all women, either. Just the ones he had been in contact with.

His mother had been the first. But the box he had put her in

152

was so large and complex and so deeply buried that he could never think about her. If he was ever tempted to mentally exhume her, he knew the effort would be so much, the consequences so dire for himself, that it wasn't worth it. So that particular part of his past would have to stay buried. No matter what.

But the others. That was different . . .

All the girls who had broken his heart, had thought him weird, had called him names, shamed him, humiliated him, made him want to kill himself . . . they were fair game. More than that: they were necessary. But he couldn't do it with the actual women. No. For one thing he didn't know where they were, and for another, if he could find them, the police might link their deaths to him. And he couldn't have that. So after much thinking he had settled on his plan. Surrogates. That was what he needed. And he knew where to get them.

It was simple. So simple. Find the right girl. A damaged one, so she would empathise with what he had been through. Then take her. Keep her safe until she was in the correct state of mind and body. Then take her heart. Once he had that, it was a simple matter to evoke the particular memory. They were never far from his mind. Then perform the ritual. Box the heart up. Seal it. And that was that. Another part of his past put firmly away. One step closer to moving on completely. To becoming a full person. To letting his inner man become his outward one too.

His therapist would have been proud, he thought, that he was taking his advice so literally.

And it was working, he could feel it. As each heart was safely boxed away, he felt something inside him lift. A stone, a great weight. He felt he was inching his way to being like everyone else. If not happy, then at least normal.

He heard someone come into the lavatory, try the door to

the cubicle. Heard a mumbled *sorry*, then the retreat of feet. The action brought him out of his reverie. He took his hands away from his face, blinked as the light hit his eyes. Then rubbed his face, like he was trying to wake himself. He stood up. Pulled himself physically together.

Something would have to be done. He knew that. Because he'd panicked last night, because he'd spoiled the ritual and the memory was still stuck within him, he would have to rectify the situation. Sooner rather than later. And the thought of that – the promise of that – would have to be enough to keep him going. For now.

But first, he had the rest of the day to get through.

31

Marina entered her office, closed the heavy wooden door behind her, waited for the click of the lock. She put the overhead light on, then her desk lamp. Checked every corner and shadow in the room. Satisfied that she was alone, she crossed to her desk, sat down in her chair and closed her eyes. Exhaled.

She opened her eyes, sat forward. Her hands were shaking from her time in the gym. Thirty minutes with the bag in two-minute sessions, interspersed with one minute of aerobic jumps and jabs. Hard, pounding. Relentless. Just let anyone try something. She was ready for them.

She reached down into her bag, drew out the two folders Imani had given her. Ran her hands over them, feeling that familiar thrill once more. The sense of delving beyond the surface, turning the academic into the real, slipping out of one world into another. Marina knew that on one level it was probably wrong to feel this way. For the sake of decency to the dead. But she couldn't look at it like that. Despite everything that had happened in her own life, she still had to know, had to dig deeper. Find the skull beneath the skin. And the mind within it.

But she didn't even have time to open the folders before there was a knock on the door.

Marina froze. No one knew she was here today. She stood up, her gym-hardened body ready for whoever it could be.

Another knock.

She waited.

A voice. 'Hello?' Small, timorous. But male. Definitely male. Not female.

'Yes?'

'Could I . . . could I come in, please? I need to see you.'

Marina's body began to relax slightly. A student, that was all. Come to see her about work. Or just to moan about the course and use her as a surrogate mother. The usual.

'Just a minute,' she said.

Leaving the folders where they were, she walked to the door, turned the lock, opened it.

And there stood Phil.

Marina was too stunned even to slam the door.

'Hi,' he said, waiting for her familiar response. It didn't come.

She found her voice. 'How did . . . '

'How did I get in?' Phil edged himself just over the threshold. 'Police ID. Warrant card. Just asked. Can I come in?'

She was still staring as he moved forward. She made to close the door on him, but he was already too far in. It slammed harmlessly against his chest. She began to get angry.

'That your police tactics, is it? What you do with suspects when you call on them? Just barge your way in?'

'Look, Marina, I know you're angry, but please. Stop shouting. Or at least close the door.'

He stepped fully inside. The door closed behind him. She walked across the room to her desk. Once there, she turned to him, her anger becoming fury.

'You just walked in. Just showed your card and walked in. Just like that.'

156

'Just like that, I suppose, yeah. But Marina, I—'

'Don't you *but Marina* me.' Her voice hissing out like a sudden leak in a high-pressure hose. Before he could say anything more, she started on him. 'If you could do it, she could too, couldn't she? Just walk in here, get into my office when I'm alone. It wouldn't take much, would it? To find a warrant card, do that. She could . . . ' She ran out of breath, of words, of anger. Even as she spoke, she doubted it was true. If that woman had found her way in, Marina would have been ready for her. It was one of the places she expected to be attacked. But she wasn't ready for Phil. She was still too raw, too mixed up in her own head about what they had been through, what she was going through now, to have him near her again. Not yet.

'I just wanted to talk to you, that's all. Please.' Phil's voice was plaintive. 'I need to talk to you. To see you.'

He crossed the floor to her desk. She saw him coming, opened a drawer. Took out a letter-opener. The blade glinted under the overhead lights. She pointed it at him.

'Don't,' she said. 'Just stay where you are.'

He did so. 'Marina . . . '

'Don't.'

He looked at the letter-opener. 'I could have you for possession of a dangerous weapon.'

'Try it.' Again her voice hissed. 'I know the law. It's not counted as a dangerous weapon. It serves a purpose.'

'It looks sharp.'

'It is,' she said, 'it has to be. In case I need to use it.'

Phil sighed. 'Look,' he said, 'I'm tired of this. And from the look of you, you are too. Let's talk. Let's . . . find a way through this. Come on, we have to. We need to.'

Marina looked at him then, seeing him properly for the first time since he had entered her room. He was unshaven, his hair greasy and standing up even more than usual. His eyes looked like they had been hollowed out from his face and his clothes seemed to have been slept in. There was also the faint tang of something unpleasant around him. Stale sweat and alcohol.

In that second her heart broke. She missed him so much, wanted him, desired him.

Phil moved forward. 'Marina, you're just causing us more pain . . . '

'Shut up. Don't throw all this on me. And stay where you are. Don't . . . ' The letter-opener brandished once more.

Phil stopped moving. He stared at her. His eyes fell to her desk. He saw the folders.

'What are those? How did you get them?'

'Something I'm working on for Imani,' she said. 'Unpaid.'

He stared at her, unconvinced. 'That's . . . that's my case . . . '

'It's from Imani, not you. Nothing to do with you.'

He seemed to be about to answer back, argue further, but his face fell. Collapsed.

'I can't live without you,' he said. 'Or our daughter. It's not right to keep her from me. You can't . . . I can't . . . ' Tears formed in his eyes. 'I'm not right without you . . . '

'Stop it,' she said.

'No,' he said. 'You know what I mean. You complete me. I know that sounds like bullshit but you know it's true. You're my missing part. I'm yours. That's how it's always been. Two sides of the same coin, you said. Both damaged in different ways, healing each other. That was our life. But I can't . . . I can't function without you . . . '

She couldn't bear to see him cry in front of her. She didn't know whether she would resent him for it, think him weak, or whether it would make her want to join in. Either way she couldn't face it. 'Just . . . stop it.'

'Please . . . please, Marina. We can face this together. We can. We're stronger together than apart. Just . . . come home. Please, we can sort it . . . '

She sighed. It would be so easy. She knew that. Just to say yes and go. Do as he was asking. Take Josephina. Go forward together.

But she remembered what it had been like before she left. What she had been like before she left. Every day lived in fear, in desperation, just waiting for that woman to turn up, to destroy everything and everyone she loved, everything she held dear in the world. Every time she looked at Phil, she saw the same thing in him reflected back at her. That waiting. And she couldn't bear it any longer. But there was more than that: with it came the knowledge of his inability to protect her and their daughter. That was why she'd had no choice but to leave. To save herself and Josephina, and to perhaps save him as well.

'Please go,' she said, her voice almost breaking.

'Marina . . . '

'Please, just . . . go. Now.'

Phil stared at her, unable to comprehend what he was hearing. 'Couldn't we just—'

'Leave. Now.'

He didn't move. 'So is this it, then? Is this the end?'

Marina turned away from him. Couldn't answer. Knowing that if she did, she might well say yes to him. Return to him, take their chance. And she couldn't. *She couldn't.*

She heard movement behind her, and she knew that Phil was making his way to the door.

She heard the door open and softly close. Even then she hoped he would come back in, that he wouldn't take no for an answer, that he would make her come home. But she knew he wouldn't do that. And really she knew it wouldn't be right. If he did that, she would always feel as if she had been forced. And

159

every time she looked at him there would be the ghost of that decision always between them.

So she stood there. Alone. Her back to the door. Telling herself she had done the right thing, made the correct decision. Waiting until she was sure he had gone.

And then the tears came.

32

'Feeling better?'

Lesley Bracken sat behind her desk. Roy Adderley came back into the office and resumed his seat, hands still wet from where he had washed them in the lavatory.

'Thanks,' he said, absently.

Rage was simmering inside him now. He had run the gamut of emotions since leaving the police station, had tried to sort things out in his head and had thought he had succeeded. But he hadn't. Now he was just left with anger.

'You're breathing rather heavily,' said Bracken, concerned. 'Sit back, take some deep breaths.'

'I'm not going to have a heart attack, if that's what you're thinking,' he said. 'Wouldn't give Brennan the satisfaction.' *And wouldn't want you to not be paid*, of course, he thought sarcastically.

He knew he wasn't having a heart attack. It wasn't his time yet. God had other plans for him.

He stood up once more. 'He has no right, no right . . . '

'No,' said Bracken, 'he doesn't. That's why we . . . '

Adderley tuned out. There were two kinds of law. God's law and man's law. He had seen man's law in action, been at the wrong end of it. And it wasn't remotely concerned with justice. Just revenge. So he didn't answer her, just let her talk. And while she talked, he thought.

'I said,' said Bracken, realising he wasn't listening, 'he was out of order to bring up your past like that.'

Adderley nodded. A plan forming in his mind. God's law. Pure law.

While she spoke, he prayed for guidance.

And received it.

He stood up. 'I'm going now. I've got things to do.'

Bracken, mid-sentence, just stared at him. He ignored her, walked out of the building and drove away. Off to gather the materials he needed for the test that lay ahead.

He sat, arms against the steering wheel, steadying himself with a few words of prayer. He heard God's voice telling him that what would come next was the right thing to do. The *just* thing to do. And he replied saying he wouldn't let Him down. That he would shine like a light in the world.

He felt his breath catch when he thought those words.

He opened his eyes once more, took in his surroundings. The Pentecostal church he attended was right before him. An old converted hall in a poor area of Handsworth, it was where he had found God. Or rather, where God had been waiting for him to enter.

He could remember the day vividly. He still didn't know what had made him walk into the church. He had been out all afternoon with friends, drinking and watching the football in a pub. His wife was at home, Carly was only four. He had thought that married life would suit him, settle him. Hoped it would. But it hadn't. All his life he had felt like he didn't fit in. Not at school, not at home. His father constantly reminded him of that, telling him he wasn't the son he wanted, favouring his brother instead. His father had been the kind of post-war petty tyrant who ruled the home with an iron fist. His mother was almost a ghost, like subservience had worn her away. And Roy had always blamed her for being weak, never forgiven her for that.

He had been, even from an early age, a failure. Not sporty at school. Not intelligent enough to do well either. Not physically robust enough to follow his father's footsteps into factory work. Not like his brother. Never like his brother.

So Roy had played up to it. If he was the idiot son, he would act like it. He got drunk, took drugs. Went looking for trouble round the city centre bars and clubs. Frequently found it. Managed to get a job, several jobs, but never held them down for long. As for women, it was just frustration after angry frustration. And then he met Gemma.

They moved in together when she was pregnant. By the time Carly was born, Roy had a job at the airport and was trying to stay on the straight and narrow. But it was hard. He missed his friends. He missed the fights, if he was honest. The raw feel of fist upon flesh, of grappling muscle on muscle, the crack of bone as his opponent went down. Usually his opponent. Sometimes himself. But he missed it. It was the time he felt most alive.

He supposed that was what had brought him into the church that Sunday three years ago.

He had sat on a chair and listened. And watched. All the people around him had seemed so content. All sharing stories about how good Jesus was, how happy he had made them, the strength they had drawn from him. They made him sound like the best friend a person could ever have. And Roy wanted some of that. When he left to go home that night, there were tears streaming down his face.

He went back. Again. And again. Soon he was asking to be baptised. He had watched them do it to others, a full pool at the front of the church, the person totally immersed in the water. He wanted that more than anything. That cleansing of body and soul. And he got it. And that, he had thought, was that.

Except it wasn't.

Yes, he had accepted Jesus into his life. And he now had God to help him cope. But other things hadn't changed. Gemma, for one thing. She seemed to be living her life in a way that wasn't taught at his church. She wasn't showing subservience to her husband, like the Bible said she should. She was arguing with him, telling him when he was wrong, defying him. That wasn't the way she should be behaving. Not her. Not his *wife*.

She was dressing immodestly. When he complained, she looked at him uncomprehendingly. This was how he liked her to dress, she said. How she had dressed when they first met. He told her he had moved on since then. And she would have to as well. He didn't like the way she was bringing up Carly, letting her watch inappropriate things on the television. Ungodly things. Licentiousness and worldliness.

One day he had had enough. Enough of Gemma defying him, answering him back, telling him he was wrong. Just another woman disappointing him. Enough. So he took the Bible down from the shelf and, rage blinding him, let her have it across her head.

Afterwards he was in tears, sobbing and praying and begging for forgiveness. Not only from Gemma but from God himself. Gemma forgave him. God, he felt, did too.

But that was only the first time. There were others. More and more frequent. Gemma needed to be taught a lesson. She needed God beaten into her. And he, God had told him, was the one to do it. To bring her under the obedience of her husband in a Christian manner.

And all that had led him to this.

He got out of the car, went to the boot. Took out the things he had bought, put them on the pavement, closed the car, locked it. Then picked them up, went into the church.

Praying all the while.

33

'Thank you for seeing me at such short notice.' Imani Oliver sat down in the consulting room easy chair, Avi Patel in the one next to her.

'Not a problem. Anything I can do to help.' Keith Bailey sat opposite them, one leg thrown casually over the other.

The two of them had come straight to the Relate office in the centre of Birmingham. Hidden behind a seventies strip mall of cheap clothes and phone shops and fast food outlets just off Colmore Row, it had barely any markings and no advertisements as to what went on behind the shuttered store front. Imani wasn't surprised by that: no one wanted to broadcast their marriage troubles to the world.

She had phoned ahead, checked that Keith Bailey was in. He was. He sounded young on the phone, open and pleasant. Like she imagined a counsellor would be. In person he lived up to his voice. There was something engaging about him. She felt immediately he was the kind of person she could open up to, tell her problems to. The receptionist had said he was popular with the clients. She could see why.

And he looked like she imagined too. Sandy-blonde hair, perhaps less of it than he wanted, swept over his head, parted, falling boyishly to one side. A red plaid shirt and jeans. Some kind of jewellery, metal and leather, poking out from under his right sleeve. Trainers. A heavy silver ring on his wedding finger.

Metal-framed reading glasses. Like his whole wardrobe came from Fat Face or Mantaray at Debenhams. A bookish lumberjack who'd never cut down a tree.

The room was bare. Some pre-school toys in the corner; three chairs. A couple of boxes of supermarket paper tissues sat on a small table between the two police officers and Keith Bailey. Imani nodded to them.

'I imagine they get used a lot, Mr Bailey.'

He smiled. 'Constantly. Should have shares in Tesco.' The smile faded. 'Can I ask what this is about, Detective . . .'

'Oliver,' she said. 'And this is my colleague, Detective Constable Patel.'

Patel nodded, then settled back in his chair. Just like a married couple, she thought. Except we've jumped straight to the bad bits.

'I believe you have a client called Janine Gillen.'

Keith Bailey glanced between the two of them, a slightly worried look on his face. 'Should I be discussing my clients with the police?'

'I'm afraid she's dead, sir,' said Patel. 'And we're investigating her murder.'

Bailey's eyes widened. 'Dead?' He looked at them once more, mouth open in shock, eyes eventually settling on the tissues, as if the answer lay there. 'But . . . I just saw her yesterday . . .'

'It happened last night,' said Imani. 'Very suddenly. Very nastily too, I might add.'

Bailey shook his head. 'Dead . . . Oh my God . . .'

Imani shared a look with Patel. *Get him going*, her eyes said.

'We realise this must be upsetting for you,' said Patel, 'but if you could just give us a few details about Janine Gillen, we'd really appreciate it.'

'Of course, yes . . .' Bailey still looked like he wasn't listening properly. 'Anything I can . . .'

'What did you talk about at your session yesterday, Mr Bailey?' asked Imani. 'You did say you saw her yesterday?'

'I . . . I did, yes. She was . . . ' He looked up, quizzical. 'Should I be talking about this? Client confidentiality and all that?'

'I don't think that comes into it now, sir,' said Patel.

'Oh yes. Yes. You're right.' He rubbed his chin, eyes staring off into the distance once more.

'So what kind of things did you talk about?' Imani again.

'Well, she . . . ' Bailey shrugged. 'I don't know. I'd have to get her notes. She was . . . unhappy at home. I used to see both her and her husband. Thought they were making good progress together. So did she. But I think her husband had other ideas.'

Imani leaned forward. 'In what way?'

'Well, he . . . ' Bailey moved about, as if the seat had become suddenly uncomfortable. 'He wasn't supportive of Janine seeing me. Of the whole process, really.'

'And he let you know?'

'He did. Very vocally. One session he just walked out. Effing and blinding. Awful. Never came back again.' He shrugged. 'But you get that sometimes. You tend not to see people at their best in this job.'

'But she still came to visit you after that? Janine?'

Bailey nodded.

'Did her husband not mind?' asked Patel.

Bailey's voice dropped, became conspiratorial. 'I don't think he knew. Or if he did, she tried to sugarcoat it somehow. Told him it was good for her. I don't know.' He became silent then, pensive. Shook his head. 'So she never reached the refuge, then.'

'Refuge?'

'Yes, Safe Haven. I could tell she wasn't happy with her home life. An abusive husband, and it sounded like he was turning her children against her too. There wasn't a lot more I could do for her really. It was a toxic environment and things clearly weren't going to get any better. So I suggested a way out. But I was too late. He got her.'

Neither Imani nor Patel answered. Bailey looked between the two of them, his expression quizzical. 'He did . . . do it, didn't he?'

'We're keeping an open mind at the moment, Mr Bailey,' said Patel.

'This refuge,' said Imani, before Bailey could speak again. 'Have you any details?' She took out her notepad, noticing that Patel had done the same.

'Er . . . yes,' he said, and got up, crossed to a filing cabinet behind him. He took out a card, handed it over. 'This is it. A phone number and an address. Obviously they'd appreciate discretion when you go to call.'

'Of course,' she said.

'Is there anything else you can tell us, Mr Bailey?' asked Patel.

He frowned. 'I . . . don't think so. That's just about everything from yesterday.'

'Did she mention any other men?' asked Imani. 'Friends, boyfriends, even?'

'No,' he said. 'No one. She was very lonely, really. Quite isolated, I thought.' He sighed. 'I felt sorry for her. Sweet girl. Just married the wrong man.' He shook his head once more. 'Not alone there, sadly.'

Imani and Patel shared a glance. Imani stood.

'Well, we'll not take up any more of your time, Mr Bailey. If you do think of anything more, please don't hesitate to get in touch.' She handed him her card.

He took it. 'Thank you. I will.' He sighed. 'Poor girl. Times like this, makes you wonder why you bother.'

'I'm sure you did what you could to help her. We'll see ourselves out.'

Out on the street, Imani took a deep breath. She turned to Patel. 'What did you think?'

'What a depressing place. Suppose it would be, though.'

'Not much laughter in there.' She looked at the card in her hand. 'Fancy a trip to a refuge?'

He smiled. 'Who's doing the paperwork for all this?'

'Toss you for it,' she said.

His smile widened. 'Got a better idea. Tails, you do the paperwork. Heads, I do the paperwork. And I get to buy you dinner.'

'If it's tails, don't I have to buy you dinner?'

He shrugged. 'Only if you want to.'

She smiled. 'And I suppose now's the time you tell me you've got a two-headed coin.'

He returned her smile. 'You're too clever for me.'

34

By the time Phil drove up in his Audi, Wheeler Street in Handsworth, the home of the One True Church of God Pentecostal church, had been cordoned off.

Phil pulled up by the police tape, got out. Walked over to the nearest uniform, showed him his warrant card.

'DI Brennan,' he said. 'I'm expected.'

The call had come in just after he had left the university. He had sat in his car for what felt like years, trying to pull himself together after his abortive attempt to talk to Marina. His first thought was to take the rest of the day off. Find a pub somewhere and drink the daylight hours away. Then the night-time ones too. But he stopped himself from doing that. It wasn't easy, and it took a huge amount of willpower, but he managed it. He patched himself up, at least as far as facing other people went, talked himself into being as functional as possible, and drove towards the station.

He never got there. A call came in for him, reporting a disturbance at a church in Handsworth. Someone had barricaded themselves inside, taken hostages. And they would only speak to Phil.

'Who is it?' he had asked.

'Roy Adderley. Says you've been questioning him.'

Phil's heart sank. 'Yeah. On suspicion of murder.'

The sergeant on the other end of the phone laughed. 'I think this is what you might call an escalation of the situation.'

Phil drove straight to Handsworth. The afternoon was drawing to a close as he got there. The clouds threatening to let loose once more. The darkness of early dusk creeping over the city.

The uniform led him through the barrier towards the church. A mobile incident van had been set up in the middle of the street. He headed straight for it. Sperring was already inside.

'Here he is,' said the DS.

Another man was sitting with Sperring, a bank of CCTV and communication instruments before him. They all showed the outside of the church.

'You Phil Brennan?' said the man, rising.

Phil identified himself, shook his hand.

'Mike Battersby. Hostage Negotiation Unit. He's been asking to speak to you and you only.'

'Lucky me,' said Phil. 'What's happening in there?'

Battersby was tall, stocky and black. Dressed in a suit and shirt, no tie. 'Went in a couple of hours ago, from what we can gather. Closed the place up. Couple of cleaners in there, local community volunteers. Both women. Had a couple of jerry cans with him. Full of petrol.'

'Oh God,' said Phil. 'I can see where this is going.'

'You're not wrong. Poured petrol all over himself and got the two women as hostages. Won't let them go, won't leave, won't do anything until you talk to him.'

Phil sighed. This was all he needed, he thought, suddenly weary beyond belief. 'He given any reason for this?'

'Apart from the fact he's mental?' said Sperring.

Battersby gave him a sour look. 'Nothing. Wouldn't go into details until you got here.'

'How d'you contact him?'

171

'Mobile.'

Phil nodded. 'Okay then. Give him a call. Tell him I'm here.'

Battersby dialled. Waited. 'Mr Adderley?' he said eventually. 'I've got Detective Inspector Brennan for you.' He handed Phil the phone.

'DI Brennan here,' said Phil. 'What's going on, Roy?'

'Detective Brennan?' Adderley's voice was shrill, tinged with madness. 'I want to talk to you.'

'So talk.'

Battersby gave Phil a sharp look. That clearly wasn't the tone he was supposed to take.

'Not here.'

'Where, then? Shall we make a date? Cosy little bistro, bottle of wine?'

Silence on the line. Phil was aware that Battersby was gesturing at him. He ignored him.

'Just insults,' said Adderley eventually. It sounded like he had been crying. 'That's all I get. No respect. Just accusations. Insults.'

Phil sighed. 'Let the women go, Roy. Then we'll talk.'

'No. they stay here. If any of your armed police try to storm this church, I'll use my lighter. Then we'll all go up. Got that?'

'Got it. So what d'you want to do, Roy?'

'Come inside,' said Adderley.

'Into the church?'

'Yes.'

Beside him, Battersby was shaking his head vigorously, trying to attract his attention.

'Just a moment, please,' said Phil. 'I have to put you on hold.' He covered the mouthpiece with his hand, turned to Battersby. 'What?'

'No,' said Battersby. 'Under no circumstances are you going in there.'

172

'He wants to talk to me,' said Phil.

'Are you being deliberately stupid?' said Battersby. 'He's volatile, in an unpredictable state. He needs calm handling, not provoking. We don't know what he'll do next. He could kill himself and take the two women with him.'

'He could,' said Phil. 'But he might not. Could be bluffing.'

'You going to take that chance? I'm telling you. Under no circumstances are you to go inside.'

Phil listened, said nothing. Then put the phone back to his ear. 'You still there, Roy? Sorry about that. Should have had some music to play for you. Wind you up a bit more.'

Battersby shook his head again, turned away.

'You want me to come in?' asked Phil.

'Yes,' said Adderley. 'But just you. And unarmed.'

'I never carry a gun,' said Phil. 'Hate them. Not even firearm-trained. Okay. I'll be in. Put the kettle on.' He broke the connection.

Battersby turned to him, furious. 'What the fuck are you playing at? Didn't you listen to a single word I said to you?'

'Yeah,' said Phil, taking off his leather jacket. 'And don't worry. You'll get to try your way if my way doesn't work.' He walked towards the door.

Battersby looked about to explode. 'For the record,' he said, his gaze bouncing between Phil and Sperring, 'I want nothing to do with this. You're acting on your own. Against rules and regulations. Against my better advice. If anything happens to those hostages, it's entirely down to you. D'you understand?'

'Whatever,' said Phil.

'Boss?' said Sperring.

Phil pretended he hadn't heard him.

Just stepped out of the incident van, headed straight for the church.

Trying to wipe the image of Marina in her office from his mind.

35

Imani looked at the building again. A nondescript house in a nondescript street. Somewhere in Kings Heath. The houses were all big, Edwardian and Victorian, the majority of them turned into flats. The refuge seemed at first glance to be no exception.

She got out of the car, walked up to the front door. Patel stayed in the car. No men allowed. She rang the bell. A voice came through the intercom. Imani introduced herself.

'Right,' said the voice. 'There's a camera just above your head. Could you hold your identification up to it, please?'

She looked up, saw the camera, held up her warrant card.

'Thank you,' said the voice, and the door was buzzed open.

The hallway was bright and trying to be cheery. Homely. Pictures and posters. Some that looked like they'd been done by children. The woman who stood before Imani was medium height, blonde hair pulled into two long plaits. She was dressed casually in jeans and a peasant-type blouse. If Keith Bailey, the counsellor, was Fat Face man, this, Imani decided, was Fat Face woman.

'Could I see your identification again, please?' she said.

Imani had expected that, still held her warrant card in her hand. She passed it over. The woman examined it carefully, returned it.

'Thank you.' She gave a tight smile. 'Can't be too careful.'

'Quite agree,' said Imani.

'I mean, obviously we deal with the police on a day-to-day basis, but I've never seen you before, Detective Constable Oliver.'

'No, I'm with MIS. Major Incident Squad.'

The woman's eyes widened. 'Oh dear.' She braced herself for bad news.

'Is there anywhere we can go to sit?'

'Come into the office.' She walked along the hallway to the back of the house. There was a kitchen with a door off to the side. They went through it. Inside was a desk with a chair behind it, a couple of filing cabinets, shelves two old armchairs and not much else.

'Pull up a chair,' said the woman, sitting behind the desk.

Imani dragged one of the armchairs over, sat down. 'Sorry,' she said to the woman, 'I didn't get your name.'

'Haven't given it yet. Claire Lingard. I run this place.' She didn't smile as she spoke.

Imani wasn't getting much warmth from her. But that, she thought, was to be expected. This was a woman who would be naturally wary of everyone.

'Then it's probably you I need to talk to,' said Imani. 'Have you heard of a woman called Janine Gillen?'

Claire Lingard thought for a moment. Shook her head. 'No. Should I?'

'What about Gemma Adderley?'

'Rings a bell,' she said. She thought some more. 'Wasn't that the name of the woman who was found dead in the canal?'

'That's her.'

Understanding dawned on Claire Lingard's face. 'And that's what you're working on.'

'That's right. Janine Gillen was found dead this morning. We don't know yet whether there are links between the two, but it's a line of enquiry we're following.'

'So what has it got to do with us here?'

'Janine Gillen was found with your card in her purse. It was given to her by a counsellor at Relate.'

Claire Lingard smiled. 'Bet I know which one. Keith Bailey?'

'That's right. D'you know him?'

'Should do. I'm married to him.'

Imani's eyes widened in surprise. 'Oh.' Then she thought about it. Fat Face man and Fat Face woman. Yes, she could see that.

'Our work tends to overlap sometimes. When he gets someone he thinks can go no further with their domestic situation, or is in real danger, he gives them our number.'

'Is that how you get all your referrals?'

'No,' she said, sitting back, stretching. On her own territory now. 'There's lots of ways. They can look at one of the websites, Refuge, Women's Aid, the city council, even, and phone one of the numbers on there. Depending who they are, where they are and what their needs are, they'll get put through to whoever can help them best.'

'Their needs?'

'Birmingham has a very big Asian population. Muslim women who are forced into arranged marriages, or home slavery, or even FGM, may not feel comfortable going to a refuge with other cultures there. Especially because what they've experienced is so integral to their own culture. So we know who to put where.'

'Okay,' said Imani. 'So I'm presuming that the location of this place is secret?'

'The locations of all the refuges in the city are secret.'

'Right. So how would someone get here, then? Say they phone the helpline. What happens then?'

'Well, as I said,' a slight note of irritation crept into Claire Lingard's voice, 'they would be put through to the place or person that could serve them best.'

'Assuming it was this place.'

'Well, assuming it was this place, we would tell them to be at a prearranged spot and a car would come to pick them up. We'd give them a particular word that they would expect the driver to say so they would know to get into the car. Then they'd be brought here.'

'Right.' Imani looked round the room once more. It gave as much away about the refuge as its boss was giving away about herself. Virtually nothing. 'And then what?'

'The refuge is divided up into flats, so the women can lock their own door and feel safe. Once they're here, we sort out counselling, help with money, childcare, education, whatever's needed.'

Imani nodded, thinking. 'Could someone intercept the calls? Be there to pick the women up instead of your arranged driver?'

Claire Lingard's features hardened. 'Definitely not. Are you saying someone from here did it? Definitely not.'

'No, I'm not saying that. I'm just wondering if the system could be hacked in some way, that's all. Whether that was a way this person was meeting these vulnerable women.'

Claire Lingard relaxed slightly. Imani seemed to have said the right thing.

'I couldn't think of a way. But then I'm not computer-minded.'

Imani smiled. 'Me neither. Can barely work my iPad. Did you have any calls last night?'

'I wasn't on duty,' Claire Lingard said, features impassive. 'I don't know offhand.'

177

'Right. Do you keep a list of the names of the women who contact you?'

'If they give their names. Some give false ones. Some of them prefer not to give any name at all. We always ask for one, just so we know who we're talking to. It's up to them what they say. Remember, we provide a confidential service. But there's a transcript made of each call. Notes are taken. We can use those notes as a basis to assess their needs.'

'D'you keep recordings of the calls?'

'No, just the transcripts.'

'But you log the calls. Keep a list.'

'Yes, of course.'

'Could I have a copy of that list, please? And a copy of the transcripts?'

Claire Lingard sat back once more. 'I don't know. I'd have to talk to my superiors. I'm sure you understand.'

'Oh, I do,' said Imani. 'Definitely.' *She's a tough one*, she thought. *Harder to crack than a walnut at Christmas.*

'Thank you.' Claire Lingard spoke as if Imani was being dismissed.

Imani didn't move. 'Look, I understand about your client confidentiality. I really do. But I'm investigating two murders. And if there's a link between these two dead women and your refuge, it's best if we all know about it, don't you think? Then we can deal with it. All of us. Together.'

Claire Lingard realised what Imani was saying. She nodded, face held tight like a mask. 'I'll get a printout for you.'

She stood up and left the room.

On her own, Imani looked round once more. She saw something on the wall behind the desk that she had overlooked before. She stood up, crossed to it. A poem. She read the title: 'The Softest Bullet Ever Shot . . . '

Then the rest of the poem.

You hurt me and chained me
Humiliated and raped me
Spoke hate to me, taunted me
Tried to kill me inside
The bullet hit slowly
Fired year after year by you
Got right in the heart of me
Spread its fire all around
But I wouldn't let it
I found I was stronger
I ran and I healed and
I built myself up again
And now I grow stronger
And stronger and stronger
And the best thing of all
Is that you're out of my head
For ever.

'The title comes from a Flaming Lips song.'

Imani jumped, turned. Claire Lingard was standing in the doorway. Imani immediately felt shamefaced, like she was a schoolgirl who had been caught in the headmistress's office.

Claire Lingard smiled, entered the room, a bundle of paper in her hands.

'You wrote that?' asked Imani.

'I was a fan of the band. Had to get the title from somewhere.'

Imani looked again at the poem, then back to Claire. 'So you . . .'

She nodded. 'It was the album I kept playing. When I was in . . . somewhere like this. The poem was my therapy. Or part of it. Now I keep it there to remind myself of how far I've come. And why I do what I do. Every day.'

179

'It's beautiful.'

'And necessary. It'll stay there until I go. Or until it's not necessary. Whichever happens first. And I think I know. Unfortunately.'

Imani understood the woman now. And began to warm to her. 'But your story had a happy ending.'

'Keith? Yes, it did. I was lucky to meet him after what had happened. We understand each other. Know what we've both had to go through to be happy. But not everyone is so lucky. Here.' Claire handed over the papers. 'I didn't know how far back you wanted to go. Is six months okay for you?'

'That's fine, thank you.' Imani took them off her.

Claire Lingard stood there, seemingly thoughtful.

'Two women, you say?'

'We think so.' Imani gestured to the paper. 'Hopefully no more than that.'

'You looked at the husbands?'

'It's where we always look first. We're still looking. Nothing's off the table yet.'

Claire nodded.

They shook hands.

'Let me know what happens.'

'I will.'

Imani said her goodbyes and made her way back out to the car. Patel was asleep when she got there, the radio blaring. She rapped on the window with her keys. He jumped up, startled. She smiled, got in.

'What you got there?' he asked.

Still smiling, she turned to him. 'You know how you said you would do all the paperwork for this job?'

He looked at it.

'Aw, no . . . '

180

36

'St-stay where you are. I'm . . . I'm warning you . . .'

Phil had opened the doors of the church, walked straight inside. He took it in immediately, made judgements, decisions, just as he had been trained to do. The building was old, originally a community centre. A concrete and plasterboard exterior gave way to a bare and uninspiring interior. No adornments, a minimum of religious trappings, just rows of wooden chairs, a slightly raised stage at the front and space for an electric keyboard at the side. A simple wooden cross was on the wall, a doorway to the left.

There had been an attempt at cheering the place up, with vases of flowers dotted round the windowsills. Stalks and petals were strewn on the floor. Phil surmised that the two elderly black women cowering in the front row, clutching each other in terror, had been engaged in flower-arranging when Adderley arrived.

'I said, I'm warning you . . .'

Adderley stood on the raised stage, soaking wet, squinting. Two large jerry cans beside him, the floor wet also. A cheap lighter in his hand.

'Stay where you are . . .'

Phil kept walking, slowing his pace only slightly. 'What's this about, Roy?'

'I'm . . . I'm innocent . . .' Adderley's eyes were almost closed.

The air stank of petrol; Phil could feel the sting of it in his own eyes, light-headed from the fumes. He stopped walking, looked at Adderley.

'So simple,' he said. 'Just click and burn and it's all over . . .'

Adderley frowned: not the words he had been expecting, not sure if they were actually directed at him.

Phil continued. Tried to wipe that image of Marina away, the hopelessness that accompanied it. 'All that pain, gone. Forever . . .'

He started walking again.

'Stay back . . .'

Phil spoke louder this time. 'I said, why did you want to see me? Why me?'

'Because. Because you think I did it . . .'

'So? You think this is going to change my mind?'

'I'm innocent . . .' Screamed at him, a cry of pain torn from Adderley's body. Then softer, 'I . . . I didn't kill her . . .' He looked at Phil once more, focusing through the stinging fumes. Noticed how near Phil was to him. 'Stay there, stay back . . .' He moved his thumb over the lighter. 'I'll . . . I will . . .'

Phil stopped walking. 'So if you didn't kill her,' he said, 'why all this?'

'To make you . . . make you listen to me . . .'

Phil sat down on the nearest chair. 'You want to talk to me?' He folded his arms, crossed his legs. 'Talk.'

Adderley stared at him, suspecting some kind of trick.

'Come on, Roy,' said Phil with a sigh. 'Can't wait all day. I'm sure these ladies have somewhere they'd rather be.'

The two cowering women looked up at him then. Phil saw a flicker of hope in the eyes of one of them.

'I'm waiting, Roy. Convince me that you didn't kill your wife. The one you used to regularly beat up.'

'I . . . I . . .'

Adderley looked at the two women. It was clear that they knew him. Phil was sure that disapproval was now mixed in with their fear. Adderley dropped his head, shame on his features.

'She . . . she wouldn't do what she was told . . .' he said weakly.

'So you assaulted her. Repeatedly.'

'I . . . She had to learn that a . . . a wife's place is in the home. She . . . she had to—'

'Really? You mean when she wouldn't do what you told her, when she demonstrated independent thought, you hit her, is that it?'

'It says in the Bible, a woman must . . . must submit to her husband.'

Phil stood up. Adderley flinched, held the lighter aloft once more.

'You sick bastard,' said Phil. 'You weak, pathetic little man.' He began walking forward again.

'Stay back . . .'

Phil ignored him. 'What about your new girlfriend? Does she know her place?'

'Don't . . . don't bring her into it . . .'

'Oh, she's a good girl, is she? Does as she's told?'

'It's different, different . . .'

'Right,' said Phil, still walking. 'Of course. It's different. It would be, because you're making this shit up as you go along, aren't you? Whatever it takes to justify what you do. Blame it on the Bible. Women are either saints or whores, is that it? Nothing in between? That what your book tells you?'

'I . . . I . . .'

'And when women, when human beings, don't fit into those roles, you get angry, is that it?'

'I . . . I didn't kill her . . .'

183

Phil had reached the two women. He looked down at them. 'You can go now,' he said. He looked at Adderley. 'Can't they?'

Adderley said nothing.

The women hadn't moved. 'He's not going to do anything,' Phil said. 'He's not going to hurt you. He never was. Just go. Now.'

The two women, dazed and confused, as if they were being told to leave a car crash that they thought had been fatal for them, got to their feet and moved hurriedly down the aisle and out the door.

Phil turned to Adderley. Smiled. 'Alone at last.'

Adderley kept brandishing the lighter. 'Stay . . . stay back . . .'

'Why? You scared of me? Because I'm bigger than you? Because if you hit me, I'll fight back?'

'I . . . didn't kill her . . .'

Phil reached the small stage. He looked at the jerry cans once more. One of them seemed to be quite full. He stepped up on to the stage. 'You know what? I don't fucking care.'

'Don't . . . don't swear in the house of the Lord . . .'

'Fuck you,' said Phil, still walking. He suddenly felt tired. Beyond tired. 'I don't care. I don't care about you, or your God, or your dead wife, or whether you think you're innocent or guilty or whether you were fucked by your uncle when you were a kid. I don't care about any of it.' He stood right beside Adderley. The man seemed to visibly shrink before him.

Phil reached down, picked up one of the jerry cans.

'I don't care whether my wife hates me because I can't make her feel safe, or that I'll never see my daughter again . . . I just want some peace, that's all . . .'

He held the can over his head, upended it until it was empty, soaking himself completely. His eyes were stinging.

He threw the can to one side, looked at Adderley. The man

184

was cowering away from him now, trying to reach the back of the stage, look for the door behind them. Phil grabbed him.

'Where you going?'

He grabbed the lighter. Adderley screamed.

'Thought this was what you wanted,' said Phil.

'Don't,' sobbed Adderley. 'Please don't . . . '

'Come on, Roy, don't be like that.' Phil pulled Adderley close to him. Above the smell of petrol, he realised that the man had pissed himself. 'This is what you wanted . . . '

He held the lighter high, moved his thumb back . . .

The armed response unit burst in.

Phil heard noise, confusion, shouting. He was grabbed, pushed to the floor, the lighter taken forcibly from his hand.

He didn't resist, didn't complain. Said nothing.

Just lay there smiling.

37

Imani had taken Patel back to the incident room and, introductions made, the two of them and Elli settled down to work.

'This is the list Claire Lingard gave me,' said Imani, hand on the pile of paper. 'From Safe Haven. They log all the calls, take a few details, that sort of thing. They're rough transcripts of the conversations. It's a long shot, but let's see if we can match some of the names with missing persons. Start with last night, go a couple of months back.'

It was hard going, as Claire Lingard had predicted. Sometimes all that had been given was a first name, and they had no way of knowing if it was false or not. But they started with Janine – not a false name; at least they knew that – and worked back from that.

'Let's look at the ones that say they want to come to the refuge,' said Patel. 'That should narrow it down a bit.'

They read. Cross-referenced.

It made for depressing reading. Imani knew that the other two were thinking the same thing. So many sad, blighted lives. So many men who hated women.

Patel shook his head, leaned back, rubbing his face and sighing. 'My God . . . Never stops, does it?'

'Tip of the iceberg,' said Imani.

They kept going.

'Here,' said Elli eventually. 'Found something. It's Gemma Adderley. Look.' She pointed to the date on the transcript, then to the missing persons report on the screen. 'They match, give or take a day or two.'

'Brilliant,' said Imani. She looked at the other two. Knew they were experiencing what she was: that copper's thrill of knowing you were on to something. 'Keep going.'

They did.

'I think . . .' said Patel, after a while. 'Have a look at this. This woman here. Gives her name as Mandy. Then here ...'He looked at his laptop screen. 'Missing persons report for the beginning of September. Amanda Harrison. Small Heath address. Still flagged as open. Never found, never turned up. Anywhere, never mind Safe Haven.' He looked at Imani, frowned. 'So where is she?'

'Or where's the body?' said Imani.

Elli shuddered. 'You think we've got a serial killer?'

Imani kept staring at the screen, the unsmiling face of Amanda Harrison gazing back at her.

'Let's not be hasty,' she said, 'But we could be on to something.'

'What would that be, then?'

The three of them looked up. An untidy, overweight man was standing before them.

'Detective Sergeant Hugh Ellison,' he said. 'From down in Digbeth. Just passing through.'

Imani stood up, positioned herself instinctively in front of the laptop. 'Detective Constable Oliver,' she said. 'What can I do for you?'

'Oh,' he said, trying to look over her shoulder at the screen. 'Just seeing how you're doing.' He gave up and looked round the room. 'Nice place. Well funded. Always liked it here.'

Imani looked at the other two. They seemed equally uneasy, as well as clueless as to why Ellison was there.

'Is there something I can do for you, DS Ellison?' said Imani once more.

'Oh ...' He shrugged, tried to make his enquiry casual. Failed. 'I headed up the Gemma Adderley missing persons case. Heard it was murder now. Just seeing how you were getting on.'

Imani hesitated. She was naturally disinclined to share information unless she was getting something in return. But there was something shifty and unsavoury about this man that made her even more reluctant to do so.

'Spoke to your CIO. Phil Brennan?' said Ellison. 'He can vouch for me. Worked with his missus, too. Just seeing how you're getting on.'

'We're—'

'Still at the evidence-gathering stage,' said Patel.

Clearly, thought Imani, he was feeling the same as she was.

Ellison nodded. 'I know you lot think that us in Missing Persons do nothing all day. Just fill in forms, do a few internet searches and leave it at that. But we don't, you know.'

'I'm sure no one thinks that,' said Imani.

Ellison nodded, looked round the room once more. 'Well,' he said, 'I can see you're busy. I'll leave you to it.'

'Thank you.'

'But if you find anything, I'd appreciate being kept in the loop. First dibs, and all that.'

'I'll see what we can do.'

'Oh, by the way, can I get a lift back to Digbeth? Any cars going that way? Mine's in for an MOT. Had to walk up here. Don't want to do that again.'

'Sorry,' said Imani. 'Not my department, I'm afraid.'

Ellison, clearly unhappy, turned and walked out. None of them were sad to see him go.

With a mixture of anticipation and dread, they went back to work.

38

'Oh my God . . .'

Marina was at home. Josephina had been picked up from school and they had survived another day. Now her daughter was playing in her room and Marina was sitting in the living room, the files on the arm of her chair, notebook and pen beside them, the local news in the background. The sounds and pictures filling the empty space in the room.

Suddenly the TV had Marina's full attention. The reporter was talking about a siege at an evangelical church in Handsworth. The camera showed the scene, and there, caught fleetingly in shot standing by an ambulance with a blanket around his shoulders, was Phil.

Marina stared, open-mouthed.

The reporter continued talking. Told the viewers of the siege by an unnamed man, and his two hostages. It was understood that the actions of a lone police officer had defused the situation.

'Phil . . .' Marina kept staring. 'You're soaking . . .'

The camera had moved on now; DCI Cotter, her name displayed on the screen, was talking about the bravery of the officer.

Marina kept staring in shock.

The news changed, went back to the studio. Marina kept staring. She didn't know what to think, how to feel. Seeing Phil on her TV was the last thing she would have expected. And to see him the way he'd looked – bedraggled, spent – made it even harder.

Immediately she wanted to go back to the home gym. Another session on the bag – pound it, pummel it, get rid of all the conflicting emotions she was harbouring. Ache and tire them out of her system. But she couldn't. She had Josephina to look after. It was bad enough that her daughter was being deprived of her father's company without her mother being absent too.

She looked down at the folders once more, unable to concentrate. That made her feel angry. She had been making good progress on them, had reached some interesting conclusions about the two cases and definitely needed to speak to Imani first thing in the morning. But Phil's appearance had put paid to that. So she just sat there, staring at the screen.

Phil. He had looked so alone, so . . . forlorn. And the way he had been in her office earlier . . . She felt her heart break just thinking about him.

I miss him, she thought. *I miss him being here, being with us . . . I miss . . . I miss how it used to be.*

So do it, she told herself. *Go back. Be a family again.*

She shook her head. *No. She'll take it away. I know she will. She'll wait until we're happy again, until we've let our guard down, and then, wham. She'll be there. And everything'll be gone. And I can't let her do that.*

Then another voice in her head: *She has taken everything away from you. She's taken your happiness. Is that what you want? To keep going on like that?*

Marina sat still. Said nothing, thought nothing

Her chest rose and fell with her shallow breathing. Then tears – heartbreakingly small – began to fall silently down her face.

Something had to be done, she thought. They couldn't go on like this.

She looked at the TV once more. The news was continuing. DCI Cotter was back on again, this time talking about the death of a young woman in West Bromwich.

Marina looked at the files once more, her own notes. She dried her tears.

Yes, she thought, something had to be done. And something would be done. But right now she had work to do. Cotter's appearance on TV had reminded her.

She picked up the folders. Began working again.

39

'What the hell do you think you were playing at?'

Cotter sat behind her desk. All traces of the smiling woman from the local news praising the brave actions of one of her finest officers had completely vanished. She was now flushed with rage and indignation.

Phil sat opposite her, still wrapped in the blanket. His clothes were drying on him. He smelt like he'd been swimming at a petrol station. He was exhausted beyond tiredness.

'He was bluffing.'

She stared at him. Not a good sign. Phil knew that shouting was one thing, but when his superior went quiet, matters had become serious.

'Bluffing. You've had a couple of hours to think about it, to come up with a convincing story, and that's the best you can do?'

'He ...' Phil shrugged. Even he had to concede that the gesture seemed futile. 'I called him on it. I knew he wouldn't do anything.'

'He had two hostages.'

'They could have got up and left at any time. He wouldn't have done anything. They were just scared. When I told them to leave, he didn't try and stop them. People can do a lot with fear. I just ...' he shrugged again, 'burst his balloon.'

Cotter leaned forward, her slow, patient voice at odds with

192

the unblinking, angry stare. 'You knew he wouldn't do it. Did you really?'

'Yeah.' He couldn't meet her gaze and instead pretended the blanket was slipping from his shoulders. 'Copper's intuition. He's not the type. Doesn't fit that kind of profile.'

'And what about you, Phil? What profile do you fit?'

He didn't know whether to answer or not. Suspected that whatever he said would be wrong.

Cotter sat back, still regarding him levelly. 'Phil, you were overheard. We had a long-range mic trained on you.'

Phil said nothing.

'Talking about your wife and daughter. And then pouring petrol all over yourself?'

He shrugged.

'You ignored the hostage negotiator's advice,' said Cotter. 'You were abusive and confrontational over the phone while you knew the suspect had hostages and was in a volatile state of mind. The negotiator in question, fearing the worst as a result of your actions, then refused to have anything to do with the operation once you'd entered the church.'

'I got the hostages out, didn't I? And Adderley?'

'The response team did that. You were ready to set him on fire, and yourself too.' Cotter stared at him. 'I should sack you right now for what you did. On the spot.'

Phil sighed, head down. 'I agree.'

Cotter leaned forward. 'So why shouldn't I? Give me one good reason.'

'I'm ... I'm a good detective.' He felt his voice starting to break.

Cotter picked up her pen, twirled it in her fingers. It seemed to be occupying all her attention. She spoke again. 'Can you remember one of the first things I said to you when you came to this department?'

193

Phil thought. He knew exactly what she was going to say. 'Not offhand, no.'

Cotter didn't call him on it. 'Then I'll remind you. I was told you had a certain reputation for unconventionality in your previous force. I was prepared to tolerate that as long as it got results and didn't make my department look bad.' She leaned forward, eyes unblinking once more. 'But I also told you I would not tolerate any maverick or reckless actions. Especially from an officer whose competence I now have serious doubts about.'

Phil nodded, eyes downcast.

'Phil, take some time off.'

He felt himself beginning to shake. 'I don't need to take time off. I'm fine. I'm . . . focused.'

She shook her head. 'No, Phil, you're not. I asked you to be focused on this one but not fixated. You weren't. As a result of your fixation, an innocent man has now . . . ' She shrugged. 'Well, you were there this afternoon; you know.'

'Innocent?' said Phil, finding his voice belatedly. 'He's got a history of violence and he's a wife-abuser. He's not innocent. And he still has no alibi for Janine Gillen's murder.'

'No,' said Cotter, 'perhaps not. But this is a high-profile case. We're getting a lot of media attention. They're linking the two murders, calling him the Heartbreaker now, for God's sake. The pressure to get a result is increasing. And I need someone who can handle it. I want you to go home, take some time off, think about things. Talk to someone. See a doctor. And when you're feeling better we'll talk.'

Phil opened his mouth to argue, but didn't have the strength to form words. In any case, he knew they would be useless.

'I'm sorry, Phil. You're no use to me as you are. Please get yourself well again.'

Phil, broken, stood up and left the room.

40

Cotter waited until the reverberation from the closed door dissipated before letting out the breath she hadn't been aware she was holding. Phil Brennan. One of the best DIs she had ever worked with. Jesus. When they went off the rails, they really went off the rails.

She could see the incident room through the half-glass panelling of her office. The nearly empty board that was the touchstone of the whole investigation. Photos of two dead women and not much else. She shook her head.

With Phil regrettably gone, she needed help with this one. And fast. She couldn't just draft in a new DI. High-profile or not, there wasn't the budget for that. She would have to promote from within. Fair enough. She knew who that would be. But would it be enough?

She thought of something Imani had said to her earlier. And the more she rolled the idea round in her head, the better it sounded. Might be just what the case needed.

She picked up her mobile, scrolled through her contacts, dialled a number.

'DCI Cotter here. How are you?'

She waited, listened to the response.

'I know. Yes. Listen. Are you interested in some work?'

'Funny you should say that,' said Marina on the other end of the line.

41

*You? No. I don't love you. I mean, I like you, but not like that.
Not that way.*

He was gone, lost to reverie and memory once more.

His first real job. Some dead-end agricultural supply company. Everyone passing through on the way to other things, hopefully better, sometimes not. His work colleague, Charlotte. Always looking at him flirtily, that back-over-the-shoulder look she did, hair sprayed out, eyes dancing with promise, lips red and wide. Always getting too near him to ask him something, bending over him, letting him see down her top, knowing he was doing it. Smiling all the more.

So he had asked her out. One night after work, all of them round the corner at the pub, making their meagre cash go as far as possible.

And she had laughed.

Let's not spoil everything, she had replied at first, laughing at him. *Let's just keep it as friends.*

He had tried to grab her, just playfully, but she had twisted away every time. Not unpleasantly, always smiling. Sometimes waggling her finger in mock-admonishment. Like it was all a game to her.

Just a fucking game.

And still day after day she persisted. That smile, those eyes, the bending down . . . He wasn't to blame for the way he felt. It was all her fault. He was innocent. She was doing it deliberately, leading him on. Stringing him along for weeks. Cock-teasing.

He couldn't help it, he had to respond. He thought about her when he wasn't at work. Woke up thinking about her. Went to sleep thinking about her. Talked to her when she wasn't there, imaginary conversations in his head. All different kinds. Sometimes they would be sitting on the sofa after work, just chatting. She'd be thanking him for the dinner he had made, praising his culinary skills. Sometimes they would be out together. Strolling through the park arm in arm, or in the cinema, where she was thrilled and astounded by his knowledge of foreign language films. And sometimes in bed. Where he would make her pay for all the times she had led him on and not gone all the way. He liked those scenarios the best.

So he asked her out again. But this time it felt different. He had been living with her in his mind for all that time, built up a relationship. Asking her out was just a formality really.

What? No, I told you before. Let's just be friends.

And then he said it. That he loved her. And she gave her response. *Not that way.*

He had felt like walking out of the pub there and then, never coming back, never seeing any of those people again, the humiliation too much to take. But he didn't. He stayed. And he was glad he did.

Because he saw Charlotte get friendly with Guy Winterburn. Friendly in a way she had never been with him. Never intended to be with him. And when they left together, arm in arm, he thought his head would explode.

He had been let down again. By a woman. Always by a woman. All his life they had let him down, ridiculed him, patronised him, belittled him. And he had begun to hate them. But this time there was something else. Another man. He couldn't let them get away with it. He would have his revenge. Oh yes.

The next morning he woke expecting to have forgotten about his plans for revenge, put it down to the beer talking.

But he hadn't forgotten. They were there in his mind, sharper than ever.

Over the next couple of weeks, Guy and Charlotte became closer. She didn't flirt as much with him then, just smiled occasionally. Made no real attempt to talk to him.

Guy came to work on a motorbike. His pride and joy. The Heartbreaker didn't know anything about motorbikes. But he was clever. He could learn.

One night, after they had been to the pub, Guy had had a couple of pints and got on his bike to ride home. Charlotte, with her own helmet by now, climbed on the back with him. And off they went.

They never made it.

When Guy needed his brakes, zipping between two slow-moving buses and misjudging the space, they weren't there.

He lost his right arm and both his legs from the knee down. Charlotte lost an arm.

He never saw either of them again. Which was a shame, he thought, because he still had imaginary conversations with her. Only this time he was telling her who was responsible for the crash, who had looked up motorbike maintenance on the internet, who knew which cables to cut. Who really loved her the most.

He smiled. Perhaps he should forget about her. She had learned her lesson. Or had she? She was still there, in his heart; still needed purging. Like the rest of them. He had always thought of her in a good way, really. The turning point. The one who taught him about revenge. But she was still there . . .

Yes, he thought. *Another one. Make up for that aborted operation in West Bromwich. Yes. Another. Do it right this time.*

He had to get home. Needed to be in his room. Among the

boxes. Couldn't be away from them too long. And scanning the airwaves.

He had to find the next one. Things were moving quickly. The police were getting close. He couldn't let that happen. Not before he was finished.

PART FOUR

SAFE HAVENS

42

Imani couldn't believe what she was hearing.

No warning, no preparation. Not even being pulled to one side and given a heads-up. Nothing. From experience she knew that wasn't how things worked; there was always consultation. But not now, not today. That, she decided, was an indication of just how much pressure Cotter was under.

The morning briefing had started as always. Cotter at the front of the team in the incident room, standing before the murder wall, bringing out people to contribute as and when they were needed. The board was mainly white space at the moment, waiting for the details to be filled in. Pictures of the two dead women, names and information beside them. Lines linking them to their partners, photos of them too. Different-colour lines linking them to Safe Haven. And that was that. For the time being.

Marina Esposito was next to Cotter. They hadn't had time to say hello, so Imani could only assume she knew why the pro-filer was there. The second difference that she and everyone else noticed was the absence of Phil. And Cotter wasn't about to gloss over that.

'Thank you,' she said, while the team settled themselves, notebooks before them, cooling takeout coffees and pastries beside them. 'As you're all no doubt aware, Detective Inspector Phil Brennan has unfortunately had to take some time off for personal reasons. We wish him all the best and hope he'll be back with us very soon.'

Imani saw Marina look towards the floor at the mention of Phil's name, keep her gaze rooted there.

Cotter continued. 'DI Brennan's absence gives us an opportunity to try a new approach to this investigation. Focus on several avenues that may not have been previously explored.

'Now, I'll come to the question of his replacement as CIO in a while. Before that, I want to introduce you to a couple of new additions to the team.' She gestured towards Marina. 'Some of you may know her already, but for those of you who don't, this is Marina Esposito. She works for Birmingham University and she's to be our consultant criminal psychologist.'

Marina looked up, seemingly unsure whether she should speak or not. She settled for a single 'Hello', then fell silent once more. That was apparently what was expected of her, as Cotter made no attempt to engage her in further conversation.

'Ms Esposito will be going through all the available data we have on the two murders so far and hopefully coming up with a profile of the offender that we can then work from. I'm sure you'll all extend to her every courtesy.'

No one replied.

'The other new face you see is DS Avi Patel from West Bromwich.'

Patel put his hand up, waved, smiled. The team responded in kind. They knew how to react and interact with one of their own, thought Imani. Much more comfortable on home ground.

Cotter smiled. 'Now we've promised Avi that we'll go easy on him since he's from out in the sticks, so I want you all to respect that.'

A few laughs.

'But don't be too surprised if you have to help him out with a few things. Electricity, cars, stuff that West Brom probably think is witchcraft.'

Louder laughs this time, a few jeers. Imani was sitting next to Patel. He was shaking his head, full of mock affront but grinning broadly.

'Moving on,' said Cotter, 'Forensics haven't as yet come up with anything we can use from either crime scene, but they're still looking into them. Similarly, we don't expect anything imminent from Pathology. The preliminary post-mortems have been done and further tests are being carried out. In the meantime, it's down to good old-fashioned legwork. And I'd like DC Oliver to address the team with her findings. Imani?'

At Cotter's gesture, Imani stood up, moved to the front beside the board. She turned to face the team, notebook open in her hand. This was the kind of thing Phil usually did, she thought, and he was good at it. She, however, was just nervous. She swallowed hard, tried to conquer her nerves. Not look at the negative expression on Sperring's face. She began.

'Thank you,' she said. 'DS Patel and I have been looking at similarities between the two victims. Both were in their late twenties, early thirties, both married, both with children. The important thing here, I believe, is that they were both in long-term abusive relationships. Elli' – she gestured towards her – 'has been cross-referencing information on the two women and we have discovered that they both contacted this place here. Safe Haven.' She pointed at the board, then turned back to the team. 'This is a glaring similarity and one that really needs exploring.'

She glanced at her notes. Realised she didn't need them.

'They both contacted the refuge with a view to moving in there.'

'Any similarity in their husbands?' asked Sperring.

'Not really,' Imani replied. 'Different kinds of men but the end result was the same. Like that Russian writer said about

205

everyone being happy in different ways but everybody's sadness being the same.' She glanced round the room once more, realised she might have slipped and let her university education show too much. 'Think I've got it the right way round,' she said with a self-deprecating laugh. 'Anyway. They both called Safe Haven. The refuge said they would send a car for them. Neither of them ever arrived.'

She pointed to the board again.

'Gemma Adderley disappeared a month ago. Her body was found two days ago in the canal at Saturday Bridge. Janine Gillen was found dead in Oakwood Park in West Bromwich. Both women had had their heart removed. That's too coincidental not to be the same perpetrator. We're currently working on a new theory. Looking for other potential victims. Women who called the refuge, were sent a car but who never turned up. We think he may have been intercepting calls somehow.'

'What about Janine Gillen?' asked Sperring. 'Was he disturbed?'

Patel cleared his throat. Everyone turned to him. 'I'll have a go at this one. I was the CIO on that case. There were no signs of disturbance. Apart from the obvious. Nothing seen in the surrounding area, nothing suspicious; no one's come forward with anything. At the moment we're thinking that maybe she realised what was happening and tried to get away. Or even changed her mind about wanting to go.'

'Or,' said Sperring, 'she recognised the driver?'

'Could be,' said Patel. 'We're looking into her background at the moment. Any similarities between the two women, mutual friends, stuff like that. Nothing so far, though.'

Imani took over once more. 'It'll be a long job. Lot of cross-referencing.'

'Can I just ask something?' said Marina before she could continue.

Imani shrugged. 'Sure.'

'You're looking for other victims. Or potential victims. Previous ones. D'you think he's done this before? Is there anything you've found so far to indicate that?'

Cotter jumped in before Imani could answer. 'It's a definite possibility. We're hoping that you may be able to shine some light on that for us, Dr Esposito.'

'Sure,' said Marina and fell silent.

'Safe Haven is run by a woman called Claire Lingard,' continued Imani. 'I've spoken to her and she's as concerned as we are about what's happened, offered to do everything she can to help, put all her resources at our disposal.' It hadn't quite gone that way, thought Imani, but it didn't hurt to embellish somewhat. Especially now that Claire Lingard was fully onside. 'Her husband's name is Keith Bailey. He's a counsellor for Relate.'

'Bet it's great to be at their dinner table of an evening,' said Sperring.

Some laughter.

Imani continued. 'These two might be an angle worth pursuing. Someone might have a grudge against one of them, or both of them: some disgruntled ex-husband blaming them for what happened to his relationship, something like that.'

'So is Roy Adderley definitely out of the frame for this?' said Sperring.

Cotter jumped in. 'He has no alibi for the time of Janine Gillen's murder. No. He's not off the table. No one is.'

'So that's where we are,' said Imani.

'Good,' said Cotter, standing up. Imani took that as her cue to sit. 'Thanks for bringing us up to speed, Imani.' Cotter looked round the team again. 'I think that's all fairly comprehensive. The focus of the investigation, as you can tell, is shifting. Bearing in mind what we've just heard, I'm coming to the question of the new CIO for this inquiry.'

Imani saw Sperring perk up at the words.

'Because of the sensitive nature of this investigation, because it now concerns murdered and abused women, I think it only natural that a woman should be put in charge.'

Here we go, thought Imani. Cotter stepping back into the fray herself. A quick glance at the faces round the room confirmed that she wasn't the only one thinking that.

'That's why I want DC Oliver to be the new CIO.'

Imani's heart skipped a beat.

'She's proved herself already with her discoveries and I believe she has the necessary qualities to take this investigation forward. I realise some of you may not be happy about this because of her relatively low rank, but I don't want that to cause any consternation. We're still working together on this and everyone's contribution is equally valid. I hope you'll recognise that she is in charge and treat her accordingly.' She looked straight at Imani and smiled.

Imani tried to return the smile. Managed only a grimace and a stare.

She was aware that everyone in the room was looking at her. Especially Sperring, and he wasn't happy. She was also aware of Patel's eyes on her and she noticed him wink. That went some way to make up for the expressions of the others.

'Right,' said Cotter. 'I think we've all got enough to be going on with. Can I just remind everyone that this case is high-priority. We need to get a result and quickly. The media have got hold of it, they're camping on our doorstep and whipping everyone up into a panic. They're calling him the Heartbreaker. But I don't want anyone here using that name, right? Not on this team, not in my hearing.'

She looked round. No one dared to contradict her.

'Right,' she said. 'Specifics. Another chat to Claire Lingard. Marina, you got enough to be going on with?'

Marina nodded.

'Good.' Cotter smiled at Imani again. 'Sensitivity. That's what we need. And a result.' She addressed the room once more. 'Let's go, people.'

They all got up from their chairs.

As Sperring passed, Imani was sure she heard him mutter something about shoving your sensitivity up your arse.

Patel appeared at her side. 'Congratulations,' he said. 'A promotion without being promoted.'

'Thanks,' she said. 'Hope I can do it justice.'

And just at that moment, with a sudden jangle of nerves, she wondered whether she actually could.

43

The ringing in Phil's head woke him up. He slowly pushed open his heavy eyelids, tried to focus.

Sleep hadn't come easy to him the night before. He had just slipped into a kind of alcoholic mini-coma. The fact that he had made it to bed surprised him. The last thing he could remember was sitting in an armchair in the living room, the usual balm of music and booze not working. Neil Young singing about how only love could break your heart certainly hadn't helped. Another bottle of bourbon had been devoured and all he had to show for it was a swirling head, a nauseous stomach and an acid-bitten throat.

He had started examining the events of the day – and the last few days and weeks – in the minutest detail. Wondering if there was anything he could have done differently, trying to see if there was a tipping point, an indicator of when everything had started to go wrong. And he always came back to the same one: Marina leaving. No matter which route he took in his mind, it always led back to the same place.

Marina left me. Because she thinks I can't protect her.

His eyes were open now but the ringing continued. He realised it was coming from outside his head, not inside. The front door.

He managed to throw the duvet off and slide his feet to the floor. Immediately the room began spinning and tilting.

'Oh God . . .'

He flopped back down on the bed again. Maybe if he waited, whoever it was would go away.

Another ring. They were going nowhere.

Trying again, he managed to get to his feet. The bedroom felt like one long swirling, rotating corridor that he had to brave in order to reach the other side.

A thought struck him. Was it Marina? Had she come back? Something quickened in his chest. Gave him the strength to grab his towelling robe from the back of the door, make his way down the stairs.

Better not be fucking Jehovah's Witnesses, he thought.

He opened the door, heart in his mouth.

'Hi. Sorry for calling early. Did I wake you?'

It took him a few seconds to focus properly, to lose the image of the person he wanted to see there and replace it with reality. Esme Russell.

He sighed. 'Oh. Hi. Sorry. Slept in.' And to emphasise the point, a yawn.

Esme looked embarrassed. 'Oh. Right.' She glanced from side to side. 'Is this . . . is this a bad time?'

Phil could have laughed at her choice of words.

'Erm . . .' He tried for something witty, couldn't even find coherent. He shrugged. 'What can I say? You know what's happened.'

She nodded. Looked at him. Silence fell between them.

'Look, d'you . . . d'you want to come in?'

He opened the door wide; she nodded and entered.

Closing it behind her, Phil realised how bad he smelled. Stale body odour, stale breath and stale alcohol. And how bad he looked. 'Sorry,' he said, finding he had to mention it, show her he was aware of it. 'I must look and smell something awful.'

She smiled. 'I've experienced worse.'

211

'Yeah, but you work with corpses.'

She laughed, desperately trying to break the ice between them. 'True.'

'Come through,' he said, hoping that the living room was in a fairly reasonable state.

It wasn't. Newspapers, old takeaway containers, empty bottles. And that, he knew, was just from the previous night.

'Sorry about the mess,' he said, trying to bend down and pick up the worst of it, giving himself an even worse headache.

'Have you been subletting to students?' she said, trying to laugh again.

He laughed too. But not too deeply and not for long. 'Please,' he said, once he had cleared a space on the sofa, 'sit down.'

She did so.

'Can I get you a tea? Coffee?'

'Whatever you're having.'

He went to the kitchen and made a cafetière of coffee, trying all the while to pull himself together.

'Here we go,' he said, returning to the living room and setting the tray down on the table, hoping it would hide most of the booze rings left there.

She watched him as he poured, then moved along the sofa and made space for him next to her. Phil pretended not to have noticed, went and sat in an armchair.

'So,' he said, aiming for cheerful and missing, 'what brings you here so early in the morning? Haven't you got work to go to?'

'I heard what happened yesterday,' she said, taking a sip of coffee, setting it down beside her.

Phil nodded, said nothing. There was nothing he could find to say.

'I just wanted to say I'm sorry.'

'Thank you,' he said. 'But it's not your fault.'

'No, I know it's not, but I wanted to let you know that . . . you've got a friend.'

Phil looked at her from behind his coffee mug. The concern in her eyes, on her pretty face. She really was pretty. Extraordinarily so. Beautiful, even. But . . .

'Thank you,' he said. 'I really appreciate that.'

She nodded. 'I know we left things on something of a . . . well, I don't know what. But I just wanted to tell you that I'm . . . I'm here. If you . . . you know.'

Her head was bowed as she spoke. It had taken a lot for her to come and see him, he realised, a lot for her to open up in front of him. And he felt bad because, beautiful though she was, and clever and funny and perfect, she just wasn't the one he wanted to be with right now.

He looked at her again. And could sense that she knew it too.

The silence stretched between them until Esme broke it.

She drained her mug, stood up. 'I . . . I'd better go. Bodies to cut up, and all that.' She tried to smile. It didn't take.

He stood up too. It still hurt. 'Thanks,' he said. 'I'm not much company at the moment.'

'I . . . Well, you know where I am.'

She leaned in to him, unsure of whether to kiss him or not, and with Phil offering nothing in the way of guidance, settled for a peck on his cheek.

'Thank you,' he said.

She nodded, turned and left the house without once looking back.

Phil walked back to the living room, sat down in the armchair once more. His coffee was cold now. He could make another. But in the meantime, all he had to do with the day was pick up where he had left off the previous night.

Working out what the greatest thing was he had lost.

44

Claire Lingard was trying to behave as if it was just a normal day. But given what she did, there was no such thing as a normal day. Safe Haven was exactly that. Claire was proud of what she and her colleagues had achieved. The refuge, along with other such places in the city, provided a vital resource. Don't judge, just help. That was the mantra she instilled in all of her co-workers and volunteers.

Don't judge, just help.

She sat in her office, looked at the things piling up on her desk. Risk assessments. Legal documents. Social services papers. Shift rotas. All needing her attention. All vital to the running of the refuge. She sat back, closed her eyes. The events of the last few days, the murders, had made her think back to a time when she was someone else. Someone on the other side of the counter.

Help. Me.

Her old mantra, repeated over and over again. And that was what she had needed, what she had found eventually. But it hadn't been easy.

It had started at university. Exeter. Shaun, his name was. She had been aware of him for some time. With a Venn diagram of mutual friends, they saw each other at parties, bars and clubs. He was her total opposite, the total opposite of Graeme, her previous boyfriend, too. Graeme had been on the same course as her, English literature plus social sciences. Loads in

214

common. Too much, ultimately. They stifled each other. Then she met Shaun.

A rugby-playing IT and electronics student. Couldn't have been more dissimilar. But in the way opposites attracted, they fell for each other. Hard.

At first it was purely physical. Rough, animalistic sex. Like their bodies couldn't get enough, devouring each other in every way possible. Then, as the initial spark faded, as it always did, something else took its place. A deeper, more abiding thing. Love, Claire would have called it. She presumed Shaun called it the same.

She was wrong.

After their finals, they prepared to set a course for the real world. Claire wasn't sure what she wanted to do. Shaun was. He had been offered a place at a huge electronics firm outside Reading. Good prospects, excellent starting salary. He was going to take it. He asked Claire to join him. With nothing else in her life, she did.

The first few months were wonderful. Like it had been at university when they had just met. Great sex, optimistic about the future.

But.

Claire began to feel more alone as Shaun started to work late. Not only that, but she was expected to have dinner on the table for him when he came in. At first she had done it – ironically, she thought. Shaun the breadwinner, Claire the little housewife. A game they shared. But gradually she began to feel that Shaun wasn't playing. This was what he expected of her.

All through university she had prided herself on being a strong woman. A feminist like women should be if they wanted any kind of decent life. She was ashamed at how far she had fallen from that.

One evening, down on her hands and knees cleaning the

toilet while Shaun was out God knew where, she realised things didn't feel right in her body. She was pregnant.

Shaun was delighted. As long as it was a boy, he said. She thought he was joking. He wasn't. Luckily it *was* a boy. She wanted to call him Graeme but Shaun wanted Edward, after his father. Shaun got his way. And then Claire was a stay-at-home mother.

She loved Edward, but it wasn't enough. He was often the only other human being she saw for days at a time. She had to do something. She had a degree. Time to use it.

She applied for a job with social services. Got an interview and, despite being underqualified, was accepted as a trainee social worker. She was elated. This was it. Her chance to do something for herself rather than exist day-to-day as Shaun's shadow. She told Shaun. He pretended to be pleased but she could tell he wasn't really. He went along with it at first. But things soon came to a head. One night there was no dinner made.

'Thought we could have an Indian,' she said. 'I've had a really rough day.'

But Shaun had had a rough day too. Didn't she realise that? How hard he worked? And what did she think she was doing, getting a job for herself? Wasn't his good enough for her? Didn't he bring in enough for all of them? Anyway, a mother should be at home with her son, not working and paying for childcare, letting some stranger bring him up. What kind of a mother was she?

And that was when he hit her for the first time.

Both of them were in shock. Shaun sobbed, begged her forgiveness, pleaded with her not to leave, to give him another chance. He'd never done anything like that before, didn't know what had come over him, would never, ever do it again.

So she forgave him.

But he did do it again.

The pattern was established. And Claire changed completely from that strong woman to a timid, quaking shadow, terrified of being late home, knowing he was going to ask her where she had been and who with. She dealt with abused women in her job. Was fascinated and appalled at how they could turn into doormats for some angry, weak man. And then she realised. That was her.

He told her to give up her job. She was scared, agreed that she would. But she couldn't. That was when he gave her her most severe beating. The one that put her in hospital. The one that got the police involved.

The female police officer who talked to her told her there were places she could go. Claire laughed. I know, she said. I refer people to them every day. The policewoman wasn't impressed. Told her it was time she went there herself. With her son. Because there might not be a next time.

Claire felt like an alcoholic at an AA meeting, acknowledging what she had become. She went to a refuge, taking Edward with her. She never went back to Shaun.

Gradually she regained her strength. Pressed charges. His barrister tried to tear her apart but she stood firm. He got three years. The only thing she felt as she watched him go down, in tears, was: I wish I'd done it sooner.

And that was what led to her new career.

She looked round her office once more, at the mounting paperwork on her desk that wasn't going to deal with itself. Her life was different now. So much better.

But the last few days . . . She kept the flashbacks at bay, her life with Shaun. But murder on her doorstep had a habit of bringing them back.

She would have to try even harder not to let the past take hold once more. And not just for her sake.

45

'This is a surprise,' said Keith Bailey. 'Wasn't expecting another visit from the police so soon.' He leaned forward, frowning, serious. 'Have there been developments?'

DS Sperring shook his head. 'Not as such, sir. We're just talking to people again. Seeing if there are any more details we can get. That sort of thing.' Affable, easy.

Bailey nodded. 'Right, of course. So.' He put his hands on the desk, smiled. 'How can I help you?'

'Can you tell us again about your relationship with Janine Gillen?'

'Relationship?' Bailey frowned. 'She was my client. She and her husband at first, then just her. I told all this to the other officer, DC Oliver, was it?'

'Just double-checking, sir. Like I said, you might remember something while we're talking that you forgot yesterday. No doubt you've been thinking about this.'

'I've barely thought about anything else.'

'There you go, then. Your relationship. What was it like?'

'Fine. Professional, if that's what you're insinuating.' Sperring didn't reply. Bailey continued. 'She was a . . . broken girl. Like so many we get here.'

'What was her state of mind?'

'Upset. Distressed. Naturally, given what she'd been through.'

'And you recommended she go to a refuge.'

'I did, yes. She was at her wits' end with her husband, no way out and no future. She was scared of him. I thought the best course of action would be for her to remove herself from the family home. I gave her a card for somewhere to go.'

'Safe Haven.'

'That's right.'

'Your wife's place.' Sperring leaned forward, smiled. 'You on commission?'

'Sorry?' The natural good humour in Bailey's face turned to puzzlement. 'What . . . what are you trying to say?'

Sperring gave an expansive shrug. 'Just a joke, Mr Bailey. Sorry.'

Bailey sat back, eyed Sperring warily. He didn't speak.

'Do you have a list of all the women you've referred to Safe Haven?'

Bailey frowned. 'I'm sure I could find one for you, yes. Either Safe Haven or one of the other refuges, is that what you want?'

'Just Safe Haven for now.'

'Well, it's . . . it'll take some time. I can't remember offhand. I'll have to go and physically check through my files.'

'Thank you.'

'Although I should warn you, Detective Sergeant, that that list is confidential. My work involves dealing with a lot of vulnerable women. Women who have experienced some of the worst things another human being can do to them. They tell me things in confidence. If I were to hand it over . . . '

'It'll be treated as confidential by us.'

'I see people from all walks of life. Even yours.'

'You have my word.'

Bailey nodded reluctantly. 'I'll get it to you as soon as I can.' He looked around, towards the door. 'I'm expecting a client soon. Was there anything else?'

'There was, actually,' said Sperring, gaze not shifting from Bailey's face.

Bailey looked puzzled once more. 'Oh? What was that?'

'Did a bit of digging on you, Mr Bailey,' said Sperring.

Bailey looked at him in surprise.

'Background, that sort of thing. Just routine.'

'On me?'

'Fancy yourself as a bit of a property tycoon, don't you?'

Bailey tried to laugh. 'What?'

'You inherited a block of flats, didn't you?' said Sperring. 'Or at least a couple of old houses that had been turned into flats. That right?'

'That's correct.'

'From a . . . grandparent? Aunt? Something like that?'

'A friend of my grandmother. She left the houses to me in her will.'

Sperring smiled, nodding, as if his memory was coming back to him and he hadn't been looking on the police computer only an hour ago. 'Right,' he said. 'Bit of a kerfuffle at the time, though, wasn't there? Didn't her family claim that she'd been tricked out of them?'

Bailey stood up. 'That's ancient history, Detective Sperring. I don't see what it has to do with—'

'They went a bit further than that, though, didn't they? In their insinuations. Claimed you'd actually killed her. Forced her to sign the flats over to you, then poisoned her. Have I remembered correctly, Mr Bailey?'

Bailey stared at him, mouth open. 'Oh, come on, Detective Sperring. That's absolute bullshit. Her family had had their eye on those flats for years, so naturally they were angry when they never received them. They tried their best to smear me, but it didn't work. They took me to court and lost, it cost them a lot of money, and that was that. What has any of it got to do with Janine Gillen's death?'

Sperring shrugged. 'Don't know. Perhaps nothing.' He

smiled. 'Just wanted to check you were the same Keith Bailey, that's all.' He stood up. 'Now, about that list.'

Bailey stared at him, seemingly undecided about what to do. Eventually he said, 'I'll get it sorted for you. It may take me a few days to go through the records.'

'Sooner the better, Mr Bailey. Thank you.'

Sperring left. No handshake, warm or otherwise.

Outside, it had started to rain once more. Sperring walked towards his car. His questions had been legitimate, valid. It was a murder inquiry, after all. But his dislike of liberals was well documented. If he had managed to annoy the *Guardian*-reading hippie in the process, just a little bit, then so much the better. That made him think about Phil. He smiled. He actually missed the leftie bastard.

Shaking his head, he hurried on, out of the rain.

46

'These are the phone transcripts from women who called Safe Haven.' Elli pointed to the pile on her right. 'Next to that, a list of missing women fitting the profile of the two victims. Goes back a year. Trying to cross-reference.' She gave an uneasy smile. 'Not a simple task.'

Marina looked at Elli. She had met her before; Phil had introduced her socially. She had intrigued Marina then and continued to do so. Small, Asian, with multiple piercings and tattoos, and her own idiosyncratic dress sense. Tolerated, Marina knew, because she got results. She could see why Phil liked her.

'What does that mean?' She pointed to Elli's chest.

Elli looked down. Smiled, blushing a little, but also proud to get the chance to talk. 'My T-shirt? It's Hank Pym.'

'Right.'

The design showed various superheroes of differing sizes, with a suited, shadowed man at the centre.

'That's him there. All the rest are his incarnations. He's a superhero who's not content with having just one secret identity. Down there at the bottom, that's Ant Man. He can shrink. Then Goliath – tall, obviously. Then Yellowjacket, then Giant Man. Biggest of the lot.'

'And who's the robot behind him?'

'Ultron. Evil. He created him too.'

'So how does he get these . . . powers?' Marina wasn't really interested, but she wanted to get Elli talking.

'Pills, initially. Pills to make him feel small, pills to make him feel big.' She laughed. 'He'd make a good case study for you, I reckon.'

Marina smiled too. 'I could build a career on him. If he was real.'

If Marina's final words upset Elli, she didn't let it show.

'Right,' said Marina, 'onwards. What have you turned up so far for me to work with?'

Elli looked at the desk once more. 'Just what was said in the briefing, really. I can fill you in on what's been done in the investigation so far, if you like.'

'I know a bit of that. I've already done some preliminary work on the two cases. Imani asked me. Haven't had a chance to talk to her about it yet.'

'Yes, but Phil—' Elli froze, eyes panicked. 'The previous CIO thought we should concentrate on Roy Adderley, the husband of the first victim. Phi— He thought that—'

'You can say his name, you know,' said Marina.

Elli looked embarrassed. 'Sorry.'

'Don't worry about it. He's my husband. And he was in charge of this investigation until recently. Don't feel you can't mention him.' Marina wished she felt as calm and composed as her words and the delivery of them made her sound.

Elli nodded, head down. She didn't continue.

Marina leaned forward. 'Elli? You were saying?'

'I . . . It's not really my place to talk about this,' Elli said.

'But he works here. You can mention him.' Hoping that her voice wasn't shaking as much as she thought it was. Hoping that the heaviness inside her wasn't showing.

'It's just . . . ' Elli looked round, checked to see no one was eavesdropping. 'He's been . . . really out of sorts recently. Not himself. I know he's been suspended, but don't judge him harshly for that.'

Marina smiled. 'I won't. I don't.'

Elli nodded. They sat in silence.

Marina opened her mouth, almost spoke. Closed it again. *I'll regret it if I do*, she thought. She wanted so much to talk about her situation, about Phil. And here was someone new, someone who would listen.

No. She was here to work, and that was what she would do. But she had to admit to herself that every time she heard Phil's name, something broke inside her. Something she hoped wouldn't stay broken for ever.

'Do you . . .' Elli was looking once more at the desk, 'do you think that's it? Or will the two of you get back together?'

Marina was floored. The last question she'd been expecting from someone she didn't really know. But then Phil had told her he suspected Elli was somewhere on the spectrum, so it wasn't so out of the ordinary.

'I . . .' She didn't know how to answer. 'Never say never, eh?'

Elli nodded.

'Now come on. Back to work. We've got a murderer to catch.'

47

'Back again?' said Claire Lingard, attempting a smile. 'Keep this up and we'll have to get a room ready for you.'

Imani smiled in return. 'Sorry to trouble you again. Could I have a word? Couple of things I wanted to go over.'

Patel had once again been left in the car. He was very understanding about it, which Imani appreciated.

'Sure,' said Claire Lingard, 'come in.'

Imani stepped through the doorway. The refuge was beginning to feel familiar. And, bare and institutionalised as it was, it had something about it. She could imagine how some women came to call it home.

Claire again led her to her office. Once inside, with tea on the way, she sat in an armchair, beckoned Imani to join her.

'I keep these two chairs for when someone wants to talk. The desk can get in the way of that sometimes. Well, quite a lot of the time, actually.'

'I can imagine,' said Imani.

'So has there been any progress?'

'We're examining a few leads,' Imani said diplomatically. 'In fact that's what I wanted to talk to you about. Plus get a feel for the place, how it works. That sort of thing.'

Claire smiled. 'You thinking of volunteering? You wouldn't be the first policewoman we've had here. On either side of the counter.'

'I'm sure. So tell me . . . how does it run?'

'You mean financially? Local council funding, mainly. We get a grant, donations. We're a registered charity.' She looked at Imani. 'That wasn't what you meant.'

'Not exactly.'

The tea arrived. The woman who brought it in was small, round, with her hair scraped back to make her as sexless as possible. She smiled nervously, as if she was asking for permission to do so.

'Thanks, Alice,' Claire said as the woman made her way to the door.

'She looks familiar,' Imani said, once the door had closed behind her.

'The case is public knowledge so I don't mind telling you. Husband was a banker. Tried to hire her out for sex to his friends. Used to hurt her if she refused. Eventually she hit him back. He's up on his feet now, and the police thought it would be safer for her to come here. Been with us a while now.'

'Yeah, I remember that. Not my case, though. How's she settling in?'

'Well. Still needs a lot of help, therapy and such. The risk now is she gets too dependent on us. Too institutionalised. Still, goes to show that class isn't a barrier to domestic abuse.'

Imani sipped her tea.

'Did the list I gave you help at all?' asked Claire.

'Thank you, yes. We've got someone going through it at the moment. Hopefully we'll get somewhere with it.'

'Glad to help. So what can I do for you now?'

Imani put her tea down on the small table between them. Noticed the box of paper tissues, the bottle of water and two glasses for the first time. She could imagine Claire having a heart-to-heart here. Since the woman had dropped her guard, realised that Imani was here to help, she had become a different person.

'Can you take me through the procedure after someone calls you?'

'It's watertight, the whole thing.' Claire stiffened slightly.

'I'm sure it is. But he's reaching these vulnerable women somehow, so we have to look at every angle.'

The word 'vulnerable' once more struck a chord with Claire. *Must be the key to unlocking her*, thought Imani.

'What d'you need to know?'

'Take me through it. Someone phones the refuge. They're desperate, at their wits' end. They need to leave their husband, need to come here. What happens next?'

'I thought I'd told you this.'

'You did, but I need detail now.'

'Well, they'd be assessed on the phone, as I said, and then if they had to come here we'd start to make arrangements. If they phoned during the day it wouldn't be a problem. We'd find out where they were, give them a location to wait in. A café, somewhere like that, if there's one local to them. But somewhere they'd feel safe.'

'Then you'd send someone from here to get them.'

'That's right. Or if we were busy, we'd ask them to get a taxi. Give them a number of a firm we trust. Or even the police. If they haven't any money and they're in immediate danger. Or – and again, this is if they don't have money but have a little time or need to travel some distance to reach us – we get them to contact social services, get a travel warrant arranged.'

Imani was writing it all down in her notebook. 'And that's all during the daytime.'

'Right.'

'What about night? Out of office hours?'

'That's when the emergency service comes in.'

227

'And how does that work?'

'The line's manned by volunteers, usually. The call will come through to here. Then it's a judgement call, really. The procedure's the same. Go to a safe place, wait to be picked up.'

'Now, would this safe place ever be a street corner?'

'No. We'd still aim for a café, somewhere like that. If everywhere's closed, then somewhere well lit. People about. Street corners are usually too conspicuous.'

Imani nodded. She wanted to drink her tea but didn't want to lose the momentum of the conversation. 'And then it's the same – a volunteer driver goes to get them, or a taxi.'

Claire nodded.

'And the driver would be a woman?'

'Yes.'

Imani frowned. 'Could the call be intercepted?'

Claire shrugged. 'I . . . don't know. I would have said not, but . . . in theory anything can be intercepted, can't it? Look at all those celebrities with their hacked phones.' She looked right at Imani, a half-smile playing on her lips. 'And I'm sure you lot have done enough of it.'

Imani laughed. 'Believe me, you have no idea the red tape you have to go through to set up an intercept or a wire tap. And then you run the risk of it not being admissible in court. Not worth the hassle, usually.'

Claire smiled, drank her tea. Imani closed her notebook. 'Thanks, Claire, I really appreciate it.'

Claire looked surprised. 'That's it?'

'Just about. Could you give me the name and contact details for the volunteer who would have taken Janine Gillen's call? And the driver she would have called?'

'Sure.'

She went to her desk, looked through some records on her computer screen, printed out a sheet of A4. 'Here you go.'

Imani thanked her, made to leave. As she reached the door, Claire put a hand on her sleeve, stopped her.

'Please,' she said, and there was something in her eyes, something that went beyond professional interest and looked like real hurt, 'please tell me. When you catch him, please let me know.'

Imani gave what she hoped was a reassuring smile. 'I will,' she said.

She turned and left the refuge, feeling Claire Lingard's troubled gaze on her back all the way to the car.

48

Roy Adderley opened the door of his house, pushed it closed behind him. The noise made him jump. Reminded him of the cell he had until recently been locked up in. He imagined all doors would carry the echo of that one for a very long time.

It felt like he had just got it out of his system from the last time. Back in his old, godless, violent life. Following his release then, he thought it would never go away, the clanging behind him as a door slammed shut, any door, anywhere, but he had gradually overcome it. With God's help, of course. Or so he told himself.

He walked into the living room, reliving the last few days over and over in his mind. Like a film he couldn't get up and walk out of because he hoped against hope that every time he saw it, it would have a different ending. A better ending.

A temporary moment of madness. Police bail. Own recognisance. The terms he was allowed home on. He closed his eyes, breathed in, out. Tried to forget.

'Roy? Is that you?'

A short, fat silhouette came down the darkened hall towards him. Something in Roy Adderley's heart sank. Trudi was here. On seeing him, she ran towards him, jewellery rattling cheaply against her flesh. She flung her arms round him, pulled him close to her.

Adderley's first instinct was to push her away, and he put his hands on her, ready to do that. But he managed to stop himself. Unable to respond in any way, he just stood there, allowed her to hug him.

'God, I've been so worried about you . . .'

Her voice all cranking and screeching. He flinched at the sound of it. Noting his unresponsiveness, she pushed her body closer in to his. He could smell her sweat mixed in with her perfume, feel her hot, wet skin pressed up against him.

What had he ever seen in her? Why was he even with her? This ugly whale of a woman, with her fake blonde hair, fake nails, fake tan, fake everything. Even faking her orgasms, probably, just so she could move in with him. Find somewhere stable to live. He knew her type. The Bible was full of them. Jezebel. He knew a better name for her.

Whore.

She pulled away from him, let her eyes rove all over his face. She looked concerned. Or scared. He couldn't tell which.

'What have they done to you? Oh Roy, you look terrible . . .'

Then she was hugging him again, stroking his face, and he felt like he wanted to throw up.

He'd had enough. He pulled himself away from her, walked into the living room, looked round.

'Where's Carly?'

'Social workers came for her. They wanted to take her away. She's at her grandma's for now. They won't let her come back here and they want to see you. Oh Roy, what are we going to do?'

Roy closed his eyes once more. Now this. No Carly. He opened his eyes, looked around. The room was different. Different things in it, different smells. Perfume. Sweat. Stale air. Trudi's smells. Trudi's things. A trashy magazine on the arm of

231

the sofa. A coffee mug leaving a ring on the glass-topped table. An open packet of cigarettes, an empty Coke can acting as an ashtray.

He turned to her. 'What have I said about smoking in the house?'

She stared at him, dumbstruck, like he had just said something that needed translating.

'Mm? What have I said?'

She looked quickly at the offending cigarette packet, back to him. 'I . . . Sorry, Roy, I was worried about you. I've only had a couple. Didn't think you'd mind.'

Adderley felt anger rising within him once more. Like a huge red tidal wave, building and building, looking for a shore to crash down on.

'Well, I do mind,' he said, voice calm and controlled. 'If I didn't mind, I'd say you could smoke in here all the time, wouldn't I?' The last few words rising in volume, his control slipping.

She backed away from him, hurt and confusion on her face. 'I'm sorry, Roy, I was worried about you . . . '

He looked at her once more. Properly looked at her. Short, fat, ugly. How could he ever have let her into his bed? Ever allowed her to tempt him into sex? That was what she had done. Tempted him away from his wife, who wasn't perfect but he was working on her, training her. And then look what happened. And what did he have to show for it? Nothing. Just this painted whore.

'They're going to lock me up,' he said, moving slowly towards her. 'Put me on trial and lock me up again . . . '

'I'm . . . I'm sorry,' said Trudi, now with no idea what was going on but not liking it. Not knowing who this stranger was in front of her. She reached out to him once more. 'Come on, come and sit down with me. I'll—'

232

'Get your filthy hands off me.' The words hissed at her. 'Whore.'

She just stayed where she was, too scared to move.

'I was weak,' he said. 'I should have resisted. God told me to. And I didn't listen. If I'd only listened to him, then none of this would have happened, would it?'

Moving towards her all the time.

He pointed a rigid finger at her. 'You. Your fault. All of it.'

'Me? Wh-what have I done? What have I ever done except be there for you, Roy?'

'Shut up.' He looked round, saw the Bible on the shelf. The one that Gemma had tried her best to tear up. God's word was stronger than that. He took it down.

Trudi kept backing away, inching towards the dining table, talking all the while. 'Remember when you used to come and confide in me, tell me that Gemma wasn't being a good wife to you? Remember?'

'Shut up . . . '

'You did, Roy. You talked to me all the time about her. About what she was doing wrong. And you remember what I said, Roy? Do you? Course you do, you must do.'

'Shut up . . . '

'I said I wouldn't be like that. I'd make you happy. That's what I said. And I did, Roy, didn't I? You told me I did . . . '

'*Shut up* . . . '

He swung the Bible hard at the side of her head. The force of the blow spun her round. She landed face down on the dining table, hitting it with a thud, the impact breaking her nose, sending blood pooling.

She moaned, tried to get up.

Adderley hit her again. Then he dropped the Bible on the table beside her, picked her head up by the hair.

'Whore,' he said, smashing her face into the table once more.

'Jezebel.' And another smash. 'This is all your fault, all yours . . . '

Smashing away, screaming at her all the time.

'They're going to put me away again . . . again . . . '

She died long before he stopped.

Adderley stared down at her lifeless, pulped body, and as the angry red wave broke and dissipated, leaving him suddenly exhausted, he finally realised what he had done.

49

Phil wasn't going to answer the phone. Probably just a sales call. Or one of his colleagues asking how he was. Saying they were all behind him. That he didn't deserve what had happened. Well, he did. He'd thought about it and had come to the conclusion that this was exactly what should have happened to him.

And then another thought: *Marina*.

He picked up the phone. 'Yeah?'

'Phil Brennan?'

The voice was familiar, but not too familiar. Heavy, Brummie. Words spoken through a lifetime of booze and fags.

'Yes?' Getting impatient now.

'Hugh Ellison. Digbeth. DS Ellison.'

'Oh. Right.' Phil carried the phone over to the sofa that Esme had previously been sitting on. He had showered since she had left, forcing his body under the hot water, standing there until it ran cold. Then dressing in whatever was to hand. A Neil Young and Crazy Horse T-shirt, old jeans. 'What can I do for you?'

'Just heard about what happened.'

'Right.' *Should have let it ring*, he thought.

'I went in there, the incident room. Just to see if there was anything I could do. Help, you know.'

'Right . . . '

Phil was becoming slightly confused now. Why was Ellison telling him this?

'They weren't very friendly, I must say.'

'Well, DS Ellison, I don't know what to say. I'm not in charge any more . . . '

'They've got your missus back working for them.'

Phil's stomach flipped. And again.

'Right,' he said, mouth suddenly dry. 'I see.'

'Just giving you the heads-up.'

Phil felt that ache, that yawning chasm opening up inside him once again. That sense of vast emptiness. The feeling that he wanted to be anywhere else but where he was at that precise point in time and space. That there was somewhere else – someone else – that would fill that void for him. He knew what it was. Work. Marina. And now to make everything worse, Marina had taken his place at work. It felt like an almost phys-ical blow.

'Why . . . ' He struggled to find his voice. 'Why are telling me this?'

'Like I said, just letting you know.' Ellison sighed. 'Sounds like the women have taken over on this one. That black lass, Oliver? She's in charge, I hear.'

'Imani's the CIO?' Phil was genuinely surprised. But pleased, too. She was going places. 'Well, if it has to be someone . . . '

'I'd have gone for your oppo, Sperring. But they don't want a bloke. It's political correctness gone mad, that's what it is. There'll be no place for the likes of you and me in this job soon. And they didn't want me anywhere near it. They made that quite clear.'

Phil's head was reeling. 'But . . . I still don't understand. What's it got to do with you?'

'My case first, wasn't it? Taken away by the glory boys. Or girls, rather.'

The last thing Phil wanted to hear was some bitter old has-been copper whose career had stalled for whatever reason sounding off to him. Not today. Not when he felt like he did. 'Well, thanks for the call.'

'They've stopped looking at Adderley.'

'What?'

'New focus, and all that. Talking to the marriage guidance bloke. Looking at the refuge. Not what we would do.'

Phil wasn't sure who he was talking about. That just made him realise, guiltily, how closely he had become fixated on Adderley. It was like he was hearing about a totally different investigation. 'Right,' he said.

'That's the way it's going now,' said Ellison.

Probably needed it, thought Phil. *After the blind alley I led everyone down.*

'Well,' he said, 'nothing to do with me. And nothing to do with you. Not any more.'

'Yeah, well. Just wanted to let you know about your missus.'

Phil hung up. He'd heard enough. Ellison's call had left him angry.

And, he reluctantly admitted to himself, more alone, more bereft, than ever.

50

'Can I come in this time?'
    'If you behave yourself. And be quiet.'
Imani and Patel had rolled up outside the address they had
been given by Claire Lingard. West Bromwich Library. The
building was old, late nineteenth century or early twentieth, all
ornate red brick and curling stone. It looked like it had been
built by philanthropists, belonging to a time when reading was
considered a valued part of social improvement. It was shabby-
looking, soot-blackened, but still stood out in a street of charity
shops, kebab houses and closed-up store fronts.

Patel looked at her, smiled. 'This is going to be a bust, you
know. Tenner says she never got the call.'

'You and your bets,' said Imani, returning the smile. 'Of
course it is. Or at least we think so. But here's one for you.
How's he doing this?'

'Well,' said Patel, stretching back in his seat, puffing out his
chest, 'I do know about electronics and stuff.'

'You're a bloke. Of course you do.'

He smiled, puzzled. 'I never know whether you're bigging
me up or putting me down.'

'And that's just the way it should be. Go on.'

'Well, I had a mate who used to work on details like that. Said
it was really easy to hack a phone. Divert calls, listen in. All of
that. Had another mate who used to be a journalist. Started off

on a national tabloid. A Sunday one. Said one of the first things he was shown was how to hack a phone. Common practice.'

'We know that.'

'So maybe this guy could be a journalist.'

Imani shrugged. 'Keeping an open mind.' She took the keys from the ignition. 'Come on.'

They entered the library, walked up to the desk, showed their warrant cards, introduced themselves. 'We're looking for Sophie Shah. Can you tell us where we can find her, please?'

The woman behind the counter looked nervous.

'It's nothing serious,' said Patel, with what he hoped was his most charming, winning smile. 'We just need to talk to her about something.'

That seemed to reassure the woman slightly. 'I'll go and see if I can find her.' She went off to do so.

Imani and Patel looked around. The building was even more impressive from the inside, all porcelain tiling and curved arches, high ornate ceilings, large double doors of glass and wood. The shelves were more modern; the space dwarfed them, made them seem slightly out of place.

'Should have shelves going to the ceiling,' said Imani. 'That's what this place needs. Ladders against them for the librarians to scoot along on.'

Patel nodded, not really interested.

A woman walked towards them. Small, neat, either light-skinned Asian or dark-skinned Caucasian. Her face was blank, unreadable. 'I'm Sophie Shah. Claire Lingard said you'd be coming. Didn't expect you this quickly.'

She led them to the staff room, depressingly like every other staff room, and sat down on a sofa that might have been on its last legs but wasn't giving up without a fight. She perched on the edge, palms together, knees together. She didn't offer them any refreshment.

'What can I do for you?'

'You work as a volunteer for Safe Haven, is that correct?'

She nodded. 'When I can.'

'And you sometimes pick up women who need to be taken there?'

Another curt nod. 'I do.'

Imani nodded herself. Sophie Shah had a hard carapace, she thought. She must have been through something to make her that way. And the fact that she volunteered at the refuge was a massive clue as to what that might have been.

'Were you working on Tuesday night this week?'

'I was on call.'

'And did you receive a call from the refuge?' Patel this time.

She looked at him, gave her answer. 'No.'

'Nothing at all?' he asked.

'I said no.' Slight tetchiness in her voice.

Patel continued. 'It's just that someone called the refuge that night, needing to go there urgently. And you didn't get the call?'

'No.' Irritation threatening to spill over into anger now.

Patel went on. 'Would they have called anyone else?'

'No, I was on call that night. And I didn't hear from them.'

Patel sat back, sighed. Sophie Shah caught the movement. 'I'm sorry I can't be any more help.' She sounded anything but.

'Okay then,' said Imani. 'If you think of anything else, please let us know.'

They stood up. Sophie Shah did likewise.

'We can see ourselves out,' said Imani, heading towards the door.

In the corridor, Patel turned to her, shook his head. 'Bit of a man-hater, that one,' he said.

'Detective Patel.'

They turned. Sophie Shah was standing in the hallway behind them. Neither of them had heard her leave the room.

'I know it's none of my business what you think of me, but yes. When men treat me the way they have in the past, I do hate them.'

Patel frowned. 'Yeah,' he said, 'I understand that. But not all men ...'

She laughed. 'Not all men. There's a hashtag on Twitter, Detective Patel. You know what that is?'

'What, Twitter? Yeah, course.'

'Right. Well, I know this isn't a scientific test, but there you go. Not All Men, it's called. It's where men – and women – report non-sexist activity. Fine. Good. There's also one called Everyday Sexism, where women report their daily harassment. By men who don't even realise how horrible they're being most of the time. Guess which one is used the most?'

Patel said nothing.

'Think about it. About what someone might have gone through. What she might have endured. And then laugh and call her a man-hater.' Her voice began to quaver.

'Thank you for your time,' said Imani.

Patel didn't reply. He couldn't find any appropriate words.

They said nothing more until they reached the car, drove away.

Then Imani received a call asking them to return to the station. Urgently.

Marina Esposito had something to tell them.

51

'Right, listen up.' Cotter, standing at the front of the incident room, made sure she had everyone's attention. The lights were down low. 'This couldn't wait until morning. I want you all to go away thinking about it.'

Imani stood on one side of her, Marina on the other. *We probably look like the worst girl band in history*, Marina thought.

But it was just nerves making her think such things. She had enjoyed the day, getting back on the horse, feeling the blood pumping, doing what she should be doing. What she believed she was meant to be doing. This case had just reminded her.

'Okay,' said Cotter. 'I'm going to hand you over to Dr Esposito. She's come up with some preliminary findings that you all need to keep with you. I believe this is how we're going to catch this guy.' She looked at Marina. 'Over to you.'

Marina took her place beside her laptop. She had rigged a projector on to the murder wall. An appropriate place for the team to focus on. She looked round. Felt energised. She had arranged with the departmental secretary, Joy, to have her lectures and seminars covered. More importantly, Joy was also picking up Josephina. And Joy's boyfriend was a tae kwon do black belt. She was sure her daughter would be safe there for a while. And Josephina loved Auntie Joy.

She began her PowerPoint, feeling as if she was addressing a room full of students.

'I've narrowed down the variables and come up with a pro-file of the person who I believe is our perpetrator. This is where we start. White, male, mid-thirties.' She looked round the room, tried a smile. 'I'm sure you've all watched enough films to reach the same conclusion. Intelligent, articulate. Likeable, even. Or at least doesn't pose a threat. Knows how to blend in, adapt. A good predator is an expert at camouflage.'

'Doesn't that rule out Roy Adderley?' asked Sperring.

'Not necessarily. Apart from the fact that Sperring has no alibi for Janine Gillen's murder, he may be playing a double bluff. Being too obvious, attracting our attention. The old hiding-in-plain-sight thing.'

She looked round the room. No more questions.

'Right. Evidence for this. He has to persuade a vulnerable young woman to get in the car with him. There's a password the driver has to give and he knows it. Must have got it through hacking the phones – not my department, I'm afraid – but he still has to be plausible.'

Next screen.

'Does he work alone?' The words appeared as she spoke them. 'Answer: yes. What he's doing is a very personal act. Intimate, even. Something that has meaning only to him.'

Key pressed again.

'And how do we know that?' The words once again appeared. 'Hearts. He takes out their hearts. Cuts them from their bodies.' As she spoke, the word *hearts* appeared on the screen. By chance, it covered the photo of Gemma Adderley's face.

'And that's where the intimacy comes from. Because that act isn't accidental. It's not an afterthought. It's specific, it's tar-geted.' She looked round the room once more. Continued. 'Taking the heart is an attempt to bond with the woman he's killed.'

'Can I just ask . . . ?' Sperring.

'Yes, Ian?'

'His victims. You say there's a bond. Does he actually know them?'

'Not as such,' said Marina. 'Not personally. Or rather, not necessarily personally. We don't know that for sure. But it's the type he knows, or wants to know. The type, or even the archetype. These women all had one thing in common. They were all abused by men. But not just any men. Not randomers in the street or work colleagues or trolls on Twitter, no. Very specific men. Their partners. The men who were supposed to love them. Protect them, even.'

Marina stopped talking. An image of Phil had entered her mind. With a pang of regret, she let it go, continued with her presentation.

Another click, another slide.

'He targets these women when they're at their most vulnerable. They've all suffered. And he makes them suffer some more. Or he certainly did in the case of Gemma Adderley. She was in agony for a long time before she died. He knew what he was doing.'

Marina clicked on to the next slide. 'This is a man who's been grievously hurt by women. Or believes he has. Now by this I don't necessarily mean physically. I don't think he'll bear any visible scars. It's more emotional. He's suffered in terms of his relationships with women. Or believes he has.'

'He's had his heart broken?' asked Imani.

'Exactly,' said Marina, continuing. 'And it's that, I believe, that makes him want to take their hearts. The hearts of damaged, suffering, vulnerable women. This is the important bit in understanding what he's doing, and why. These hearts are his . . . ' She searched for the right word. 'His trophies. His mementoes. But of what? Of what happened to him. Of what he believes women have put him through. His agony. His pain. Transferred on to them.'

She had their rapt attention now.

'He's a man on fire. He's burning. With rage. With hatred. And it's all directed towards women. Vulnerable women. Women he thinks of as weak. Who probably are weak, at their lowest ebb. But he's clever. He's cunning. Let's not forget that, not lose sight of it. And he hides his rage very, very well.'

'Like most men,' said Imani.

The women in the room laughed. The men looked either angry or uncomfortable.

'Like some men,' said Marina, smiling. 'But this one is cleverer than most. Or thinks he is. What he does takes planning. A lot of planning. And a lot of technical expertise. But with Janine Gillen he made a mistake. So he's not infallible. Let's not lose sight of that. Which leads us on to the next question.'

Another click.

'Gemma Adderley's body was found near Saturday Bridge, by the canal. Or rather in the canal. What does that tell us? Lots. And that's without even going into forensics. The first question we have to ask about this is did he intend us to find the body? And find it as quickly as we did? Or is he getting too clever, starting to make mistakes? And the answer?'

She shrugged.

'The location was specially chosen. Not so much for its geographical location in the city centre. Although, again, we have to think of the logistics of getting a body there and leaving it without being noticed. But that's not the concern here. I believe he left her body where he did because it meant something personal to him. This was a place where something significant happened to him. Something involving a woman. A woman who hurt him in some way. And he works through this – exorcises it, even – by leaving a dead, heartless body there to mark the spot. It wasn't a location chosen at random. But did he mean for us to find the body, and as quickly as we did? Did this methodical thinker miscalculate, or was it all part of his plan? Either he was panicked while leaving the body – somebody saw him, although no one's come forward – or he was in a hurry and didn't have time to secure it in place. The other option is he left it for us to find deliberately. So the answer: I still don't know. It depends where he is in the cycle. We'll come to that later.'

'So how many times has he done it?' asked Sperring, looking impatient.

'I'm coming to that too, Ian,' said Marina as calmly as she could. 'Now.' Another click, another screen. 'Let's look at Janine Gillen. She was a mistake. I don't mean choosing her was a mistake. She very definitely fits into his victim profile.'

She noticed that most of them were sitting forward now. Good.

'He went to pick her up, charm her, use his schmooze, whatever, and it went wrong. So he killed her there and then. Botched job. Now, the question we have to ask here is why did it go wrong? Well, again there are a few possible answers. Maybe she got cold feet, decided she didn't want to go to the refuge after all. Wanted to stay and sort things out with her husband. But she'd seen him, and more to the point, could identify him, so she had to be killed. One possible explanation. Another is that she recognised him already. Maybe she knew him.'

Sperring, Marina noticed, was leaning forward in his seat, listening intently. He nodded. To himself, thought Marina.

'Or maybe,' said Imani, 'she had been told it was going to be a woman and wouldn't get into the car with a man.'

'Maybe,' said Marina. 'Whichever you decide, one thing is certain. This is where he went wrong. No doubts, or shadows of doubts, like with Gemma Adderley. He went wrong.

'I believe that his pattern up until this point was to abduct the women, keep them alive, torture them, subject them to God knows what, and then eventually kill them. And afterwards take their hearts. To do with . . . ' she shrugged again, 'whatever he does with them. Whatever his ritual is. But he couldn't do that here. It went wrong. And the thing is, we might not even have recognised this as one of his if he hadn't done that one thing. That one thing he had to do – take the heart. His compulsion, the thing that drives him to do this in the first place, wouldn't let him behave any other way. Right, Ian.' She pointed to Sperring. 'The bit you were asking about. How many other victims.'

Another click, another screen. 'Answer? I don't know. But given what I've seen and read about Gemma Adderley, I'd say she definitely wasn't the first. Why? Because serial killers – and there should be no doubt that we're dealing with one of those – have a cycle. They go through phases. The initial phase is the getting started. Finding their voice, so to speak. Their . . . thing, for want of a better word. The one indefinable thing that motivates them. They might make a few missteps on the way. Sometimes they're caught before they have the chance to set out. But if they get past that stage, they move on to the next one. That's where they realise what they want and how to achieve it. When they refine their methods, their approaches. Hone their skills. This is their most successful phase.'

She paused, hoping this was all going in.

'The next phase is one of . . . well, boredom, really. They've achieved what they want. But they want more. This type of killer is, among other things – all of them sexually motivated in some way – an egoist. A narcissist. They want the world to be aware of what they're doing. How brilliant they are. Or how brilliant they think they are. And that's when the trouble starts for them.'

247

Another click.

'That's what I believe has happened here. To Gemma Adderley. And in a way, the answer to the question I asked earlier is the same. Did he let us find her body because he wanted to, or did he make a mistake? It's a moot point. He wants to let us find the body, say. He wants us to know how brilliant he is. It's also his downfall, leading to the next part of the cycle. The one where he makes mistakes. Janine Gillen is proof enough of that. And that makes him easier to catch. In fact, it's when most serial killers are caught. And usually for the stupidest of reasons. But it can also make him more desperate, quicker to lash out. Not so choosy with his potential targets. There's even the temptation to go out with a bang. A big blaze of glory. All these things have to be considered.'

She looked round the room once more.

'So to sum up, I believe there are other victims out there. Ones he's hidden, managed to cover up. And we have to find them. Then we'll know what we're dealing with. But more to the point, this Heartbreaker, as the media's calling him – and I apologise for saying that – is going to kill again. And it's up to us to stop him.'

52

He stared at his boxes. Lined along the walls, all around him. Every one a specially – lovingly – prepared final resting place for his darkest, bitterest, most disappointing and hurtful memories. Individually thought out, the trappings to match the memory, the shelf positioning matching the severity of pain. It was a room of loss, of failure, of harm, but also of hope. For the future. Strip the damage and the anger away, store it up here. Emerge a new man. A happy man. A perfect man.

But that wasn't what he felt now as he looked on his work. All he felt inside him was rage. And fear. One feeding and stoking the other.

The police were circling ever nearer. He could feel it, sense it. He had tried to enquire as to where they were with the investigation, what they were doing, how much progress had been made. There was a limit to what he could ask without giving himself away, though. And he was careful to skate along that line. As careful as he could be.

How could he stop them? Or at least hold them off until he had finished what he had set out to do? He didn't know. He had to think. Think hard.

Anger and fear roiled inside him once more. No. He couldn't be stopped. Not now. Not yet. He hadn't reached the point he needed to. Become the person he wanted to become. The good person. No.

So what, then? How could he stop them? Could he kill them? No. That wasn't part of what he was doing. His work didn't extend to something of that nature. That would just be murder. Pointless, senseless murder. And that wasn't what he did. Who he was. Murder was for lesser people. For those who couldn't help themselves. Who solved arguments not with rational discourse but with brutality. Not at all like what he was doing.

This was a calling. An experiment. And a successful one too. It was working. He was becoming a better person the longer it went on, the nearer he came to achieving his goal.

But . . .

Something would have to be done. If not killing, then . . . what? He walked round, stared once more at the empty boxes, more empty ones than filled ones. So many memories still to be locked away . . .

He knew what he had to. Escalate his plan. Find the next one straight away. Tonight, even. Weigh up the risks, of course, but keep moving. Only that way could he—

He heard a noise from outside. A voice.

Cunt.

Time to go back, he thought reluctantly. Time to put his emasculated mask in place once more, rejoin the rest of the world.

For now.

53

'Where you going?'
        'Just out. For a bit.'
'Where?'
'Just . . . ' Ellison sighed. He hated being questioned like this.
'Just out. Seeing someone from work. That's all.'

Helen stared at him. God, he hated the woman. Didn't know
why he'd married her. There she sat, in the same chair she was
always in, her arse wedged in permanently, too fat to get up and
do anything. The house was a tip. She never cleaned. And he
was always having to bring in takeaways because she wouldn't –
or couldn't – cook. Christ. What had he done to end up with
her?'

'Who?'
And he hated her voice. Probably that most of all. Even
above the sound of the TV, some inane chat-show thing, she
could always find the right frequency to screech into his brain.

Hate wasn't a strong enough word for what he felt about
her.

'You don't know them. No point in telling you. Christ, it's
like living with my bloody mother.'

'Don't swear. I won't have you swearing in this house.'

'Fuck off,' he mumbled under his breath.

'When are you coming back?'

'Later. I don't know.'

'Don't be too late. There's that murderer on the loose. It said so on the news.'

'I'm sure you're safe from him.' Too bloody right, he thought. Bastard would want his head examining going after her.

She kept talking but Ellison wasn't listening. He slammed the door, breathed in the damp evening. It smelt of freedom.

He walked to his car, plans for the night already taking shape. He kept a few things in the boot for such occasions. Playthings. A dress-up box. A few drinks first, to get him in the mood, then that.

Fun.

He got in the car, drove away.

54

'God, what a day . . .'

Claire was opening a bottle of red when Keith walked into the kitchen. 'Want a glass?'

'Lovely,' he said.

She poured one for him, handed it over with a kiss and a smile. 'Cheers,' she said.

He returned both the words and the smile.

She walked into the living room. He followed her.

'Where's Edward?' she asked, looking round before sitting down.

'Went to a friend's after school. Something involving computer games, I think. *Call of* . . . I don't know. Something.'

She nodded, took a sip. 'More violence. Anyway.' She put her glass down, leaned back in her chair. 'Had the police back in today,' she said.

'You too? Lot of it about.' He didn't look at her while he spoke.

'Oh.' She looked surprised. 'What for?'

He shrugged. Kept his voice light. 'Oh, Janine Gillen. Had anything slipped my mind, had she said anything, all that. The kind of things you see on TV but real. All the clichés. What about you?'

'Same, really. Nice girl, though. DC Oliver?'

'Oh yeah. Spoke to her yesterday. Knows her stuff. Had a

different one today. A bloke. Sperring.' He forced a laugh. 'Old-school. More at home in *The Sweeney*, I think. The dinosaur type.'

'Lovely,' she said.

'Anything planned for tonight?' he asked.

'Just want to chill,' she said. 'What with everything that's been going on and that. See if we can find something on Netflix?'

'Great,' he said, and picked up the remote, pointed it at the TV in readiness.

'So when can I see them, then?' She had got used to living in only one flat in the building. She sometimes forgot that the rest of the flats lay beyond the door Keith had just come through.

He looked up, startled. 'Sorry? When can you . . . '

'The flats.' She smiled. 'Surely they're ready for inspection by now. I mean, you've been doing them up for ages.'

'The flats? Soon,' he said, 'when they're ready. Really good and ready.'

'And then we can start renting them out, thank God,' she said, taking another mouthful of wine. 'Making a bit of money.'

He stood up. Smiled at his wife. 'Why don't I cook dinner?'

She had her head back, eyes closed once more. She opened them at his words. 'You sure? We could get a takeaway. Save us both cooking.'

'It's not a problem,' he said, sounding like it really wasn't. 'You just sit there, find something for us to watch and leave it to me.'

She grabbed his hand as he walked past. 'You're like a little island of tranquillity in a sea of . . . I don't know.'

'Rage?' he suggested.

She laughed. 'Rage. Yeah.'

He dropped her hand, walked away.

55

Josephina was playing contentedly on the floor with her Polly Pockets, making up elaborate worlds for them to inhabit. Marina had picked her up from Joy's, where she'd inflicted *Frozen* on them for what felt like the three hundredth time, complete with singing and dancing. Marina had laughed, wished life could be as simple and as happy as that all the time.

Now she stood at the window, gazing out at the darkened street, sodium light illuminating only patches, making hidden shadowed swirls out of everything else. And for the first time in a long time, she wasn't scared by what those shadows might be harbouring.

She had actually wished Phil was there to talk to about her day. She was pumped, energised by what she was doing again, and wanted to share it with someone. But not just anyone. Him.

So now she stood looking over the city, or her part of it. Watching the lights both near and far, trying to imagine all those lives out there. All those people behind locked doors living their secret, private lives. The joy and hatred, the boredom and excitement, the life and death. All going on around her.

She felt she had absented herself from it, gone into her castle, pulled up the drawbridge behind her. Walls of stone and brick, imaginary and real, to cut her off from the rest of humanity.

And now here she was, thrust back into the middle of it again. Hunting a killer.

In the midst of life we are in death. The old Bible quote. She smiled to herself. Roy Adderley would be familiar with that one. But for her it was different.

In the midst of death was life.

She kept looking. Seeing the shadows, seeing beyond the shadows. Knowing what to look for, but tired of looking. Wondering whether she could live the rest of her life waiting for someone to jump out at her. Wondering what alternatives she had.

Wondering about Phil. Where he was now. What he was doing.

And for the first time in ages, she allowed herself to acknowledge something to herself, admit something and listen to it. She missed him. Really, really missed him.

And more than that.

She wanted him.

Now all she had to do was decide what she was going to do about that.

56

Darkness had fallen. Roy Adderley hadn't noticed. The street lights had come on outside. He didn't care. All he cared about was his world. And his world was right here in this tiny little living room.

Or dying room.

'Trudi, Trudi, I'm s-sorry . . . '

He cradled her head, or what was left of it, in his arms, blood and other matter covering his sleeves, hands and chest. Her body lay lifeless, half on the floor, half on him. Tears and snot all over his face.

As soon as he realised what he had done, the anger had left him. He had held her body, tried to bring her back to life. But it was no good. There was nothing left of her. Not even a face.

He had prayed. Continuously. First for the breath to return to her body. Then, when he realised that wasn't going to happen, for forgiveness. Both prayers had been met with a resounding silence. Not even the ticking of a clock to mark the passage of time.

And now it was dark. And Trudi was still gone. Her heart, that seductive, Jezebel's heart, the one that had enticed him away from his wife, was no longer beating. He had heard it stop. Seen it stop. *Made* it stop.

God had a plan for Roy Adderley. But this wasn't it.

And now Roy Adderley was crying. For him, for her.

Forever.

PART FIVE

LIVE BAIT

57

He stood before his shelved boxes once more. Waiting for the hours to pass, hoping that there would be one tonight. *Needing*. That desperate yearning inside him, that ache for ritual, for closure. But she had to be the right kind of victim.

There had to be one. *Had to be*. His plan had to move forward, get back on track after the recent setback. And with the police circling, the sooner the better.

He kept staring at the box he had chosen. A jewellery box. It was empty. But soon it would be filled. And then he could move on.

Because this was going to be a special one. A really special one. He had someone – and a memory – reserved for this one. And it would be a huge turning point in who he had been, who he was now, and what he would become. Critical, in fact. So he had to get it right, make it work. Ensure everything was perfect.

The box, to start with. He had had this one in mind for a while. Had brought it down for just this memory. It was covered in shells, like something a child would make. And in fact a child *had* made it. That seemed right, somehow. Apposite. Especially for the memory he was going to summon up.

He was twenty-one. Her name was Hannah. And she was beautiful. Long blonde hair, which he didn't usually go for, quite tall, curvy. Very well proportioned. The kind of figure that got stared at on the street. That got her into places – from buses to nightclubs to stadium gigs, to anywhere she wanted – for free. And she would dress to match this. Cut-off jeans, halter tops. Everything clung, was accentuated, exposed. But – and he wouldn't have believed it if he hadn't got to know her so well – she wasn't aware of any of it. Her looks, her figure, anything. She wasn't scheming, calculating, didn't get men – or women – to do things for her. She didn't need to. She was pleasant and honest. Happy being who she was, with her place in the world. She smiled a lot. And when she did, it felt like she'd made your day.

Like most people, he fell in love with her. But unlike the rest, he actually got to do something about it.

He met her at a nightclub. She was with her friends, politely fending off unwelcome enquiries, happy to accept drinks from boys she either knew or liked.

He thought he had no chance.

And then he bumped into her on his way to the lavatory. An actual bump. He apologised for not seeing her. She said it was her fault entirely, and they got talking. Soon they were seeing each other, then they were an item.

And he couldn't have been prouder.

At first things went well. He was always happy to be seen out with her, to show her off like she was an item of jewellery or designer clothing that someone like him wouldn't have been expected to be able to afford. But the thing was, he loved her. Really, really loved her. Probably more than she loved him, if he thought about it. But he never did. Never, ever did.

And then it happened. She found out she was pregnant. She had put off telling him, asking him out somewhere special, somewhere that meant something to them both, to break it to him. An Italian restaurant on Queensway. No one else they knew went there, preferring the chain restaurants. But they liked it. Or he did. Made him feel more sophisticated, less of the herd.

Listen, I've got something to tell you. It's . . . really difficult and there's . . . Oh God. I'm pregnant. Leaning in close, ensuring no one would be able to overhear.

He just stared at her. Unable to speak. She stared back, waiting.

Eventually he found his voice. *How . . . how long?*

A couple of months. I wasn't well. Did a test. Then another. Then when I was sure, I went to the doctor's. And yes, I'm pregnant.

He looked at her over the weak flickering light cast by the candle in the Chianti bottle. Her eyes, normally so full of life, of joy, now seemed full of fear and uncertainty. As if childhood had come to a sudden horrific end and she was realising what it was like to be an adult.

He smiled at her. *It'll be fine,* he said, taking her hand in his. *We'll manage. Don't worry.*

They talked some more – lots more – about what was happening. He would stand by her, she needn't worry about him, he would be there for her. He told her all that.

And when he left her, he began to think. He was going to be a father. Have a child of his own. In the days that followed, he planned in his head what course his life would now take. What he would do to provide for Hannah and the baby. He kept calling her, but she never seemed to be around. Probably sleeping, he thought. Until she called him about a week later.

How's my little mother to be? he said, laughing.

Silence.

Hello?

I'm . . . I got rid of it.

He stood there, unable to take in what she had said. *You . . . you . . .*

I got rid of it. Had an abortion. The words harder now, slightly more shrill.

Got rid of it? he said. *But . . . but we talked about it. What we were going to do. How we were going to make ends meet. Manage. Our future. With our child.*

A sigh on the line. *That's just it. We don't have a future. I've done a lot of thinking. And I realised a few things. I don't want a child. I don't want to be a mother. Not yet, anyway. Not for years. And . . .* She paused. Another sigh. *Not with you. I don't love you. I don't think I ever did. But you were kind to me and you liked me. You treated me well, which is more than a lot of guys have done. So thank you. But I don't . . . I'm sorry . . .*

She put the phone down.

He tried to call her, to see her, but he wasn't able to do either. It was like she had disappeared from the face of the earth. Gone. And taken his child with her.

He had heard from her years later. Facebook. Married with three children. Happy and smiling. Her figure no longer as it had been, but she didn't seem to care. She seemed totally content with who she was now.

And he hated her for it.

He snapped back to the present. Looked at the shell-decorated box once more. Felt that gnawing yearning in his guts again. Soon, he thought, soon. It had to be. Tonight.

He stood back, checked his watch.

Waiting. He hated waiting.

But it wouldn't be long.

Until he found a heart to atone for the crimes Hannah had committed against him. To be finally free of her memory.

58

You'll be wondering why I called you all here . . .

That was what Marina wanted to say, but she knew she shouldn't because she didn't know these people well enough yet. And also it seemed too flippant a thing to do. Plus she hadn't actually called the meeting.

But she couldn't help it. She felt if not happy, then giddy. That was the best word she could find. Giddy. Back at work, doing what she loved, all of that. But there was something else, something overriding all of that. She didn't feel scared any more.

She was in the Six Eight Kafé on Temple Row and it was stupidly early. Or at least it was for her. The other two people with her seemed more used to the hour. Imani Oliver sat opposite her, but this time she was joined by DCI Cotter.

Joy had once again rearranged her lectures and Josephina had gone to the early breakfast club at school. Marina had hated to do that, to let her go, but she had no choice. She had looked over the security arrangements at the school, satisfied herself that no harm would come to her daughter and said goodbye. Josephina seemed quite happy to be there early: more time to play with the friends she couldn't often see after school.

A pre-briefing briefing, Cotter had called it on the phone. Marina was intrigued. And also pleased: clearly she had done something right the previous day.

'Thanks for coming,' said Cotter, once everyone had ordered what they wanted and sat down, small talk opened and stowed away once more.

Cotter had gone for coffee and a piece of cake. While Marina had nibbled at her almond croissant, Cotter's cake lay untouched. Not just untouched, avoided.

Marina took in the DCI's trim, gym-honed figure and surmised what she was doing. She remembered reading about Aleister Crowley, the infamous occultist. He believed that the human spirit could conquer any kind of temptation. One of Crowley's particular vices was drugs. She had read that he used to sit in his chamber surrounded by bowls of heroin and cocaine, fighting the urge to partake of them, nurturing his strength of spirit. She imagined Cotter doing something similar with that slice of cake. The fact that Crowley died a hopeless drug addict was the one part of the story she didn't want to dwell on.

'I've been doing some thinking,' said Cotter, 'and I wanted to run something by you both. See what you thought.'

Marina exchanged a glance with Imani, said nothing. Having been hooked, they waited for Cotter to reel them in.

'Imani, how d'you feel about being a Judas goat?'

Imani frowned. 'Sorry?'

Marina understood immediately.

'If he's intercepting calls to the refuge and picking up his victims that way, we need someone on the inside. Someone who can play the part of an abused woman.'

'And you think I can do that?' Imani's eyes were wide.

'Yes,' said Cotter. 'You phone the refuge tonight – Marina can coach you, make you sound convincing. Then, once you've been accepted, you'll be given a place to be picked up. When he arrives, we'll be waiting for him. What d'you think?'

Imani looked between the two of them. Marina could understand her trepidation.

'You're sure you'll be there?'

'We'll have prepared hours in advance. The whole team will be behind you. Armed response, the lot. All we have to do is wait for him to turn up, then bang. We've got him.' She took a sip of coffee. 'You game for that?'

Imani looked thoughtful. Marina could tell that whatever reservations she had were being tempered by the excitement of the opportunity. 'Sure,' she said.

Cotter smiled. 'Good.'

Imani frowned again. 'One thing. How d'you know he'll be listening tonight?'

Marina leaned forward. 'May I?' she said.

Cotter gestured: the floor was hers.

'From everything I went through yesterday, he'll be restless. He messed up with Janine. Botched it completely. That means he's only conducted an incomplete ritual with the heart. No preparation time to do whatever he does. And he'll hate that. He'll want to get back on the horse as quickly as possible. Because that incomplete ritual will be burning him up. He won't be able to think properly, concentrate on anything, until he's done it.'

'Sounds plausible,' said Imani.

'And also,' continued Marina, 'because of where he is in his cycle, he's much more likely to make mistakes and be in a hurry.'

'So that should, theoretically, make him easier to catch,' said Cotter.

Marina nodded.

'Or it might make him more dangerous,' said Imani.

'He'll be more prone to making mistakes,' said Marina. 'That's a certainty.'

'Well,' said Cotter, 'it's a calculated risk. A chance we'll have to take. We'll be there, we'll be ready for him. Worst-case scenario, he doesn't show. Best case, we've got him.'

'What about the refuge? Do they know?' asked Imani.

'Not yet,' said Cotter. 'Perhaps you could deal with that, Imani. You seem to be building a rapport with the woman in charge there.'

'Will do.'

A faint smile flickered on Cotter's lips. 'Take DC Patel with you again, if you like.'

Imani looked at her coffee. 'Yes, ma'am.'

Cotter looked towards Marina as if seeking a co-conspirator. Marina gave a professional smile in return.

'Right then,' said Cotter, looking at her slice of cake, 'let's finish up and go to the morning briefing, let the rest of the team know what's happening.'

They drank up, made ready to go. Marina looked at the piece of cake.

'You not eating that?' she asked Cotter.

Cotter looked slightly shamefaced. 'I'll ... take it with me. Have it later.'

Marina smiled. 'Course you will,' she said.

59

At first, Roy Adderley was going to go as he was. Dressed in the clothes he had been questioned and held in, covered in Trudi's dried blood and bodily fluids. He felt it was important to do that. A pilgrimage. Wearing his version of sackcloth and ashes.

But wiser counsel prevailed. A calmer, saner voice. And he knew who it was who had spoken to him. The thoughts, the words hadn't come from inside himself, from his own inner man or conscience. No. It was God. Jesus. The guv'nor.

He had sat all night on the living room floor. Crying at first, then praying, then crying some more. Then another bout of frantic praying. Until at last he had nodded off, come round with his head slumped down on to Trudi's. And with the wakening, acceptance of what he had done. He had sat unmoving, waiting for the coming of dawn, silently mouthing prayers and sections of scripture he knew by heart – even inappropriate sections, just as long as he said something – preparing her soul for the journey across. It was, he felt, the least he could do for her.

And then, job done, as God spoke to him, he listened, nodding in places, taking in the words, receiving his instructions and the reasoning behind them. Eventually he stood up, let Trudi's head fall gently to the floor, walked to the bathroom and got into the shower.

Now he was ready to go. Sunday-best suit, polished shoes, even a collar and tie. Hair neat and parted. Shaved.

Ready.

But it was a still to be a pilgrimage. That aspect hadn't changed. He was still going to walk. And walk he did. All the way into town, his shoes pinching his toes, hurting and rubbing his heels. His collar chafing at his neck, half strangling him, cuffs too tight round his wrists. But it was fine. All part of his suffering.

He called in to a petrol station on the way, selected a bunch of forecourt flowers. He didn't know what they were. Wide-headed, different-coloured bright petals. They looked fragile, as if they wouldn't survive the journey. But they would have to do.

And he walked on.

Until he reached his first destination.

Saturday Bridge was still cordoned off, the forensic teams not yet finished working the area. The white tent was still in place, the canalside path unpassable.

Adderley walked as far down the slope as he could, as near to the tent as he could get. Nobody made any attempt to stop him. Nobody even noticed him. There was a very small collection of wilting flowers at the side of the tent. Cellophane-wrapped and dying. Adderley knew who they were from. One bunch from Gemma's parents, one from them on behalf of Carly. He laid his pathetic, over-coloured flowers next to them, stood up, looked around.

He tried to work out what he was feeling. Remorse? Sadness? Loss? He didn't know. He was tempted to tell himself that he was feeling too many conflicting emotions to actually settle on something he could recognise. Something would hopefully reveal itself, define itself to him. Tell him what to say, how to feel. But that wasn't the truth. Because what he really felt – truthfully felt – was numbness. A void where there should be emotion of some kind, any kind. An absence of thoughts where prayers and eulogies should have been. His wife's body had been found there, mutilated, tortured and dead. And he could no longer feel anything for her.

He turned and made his way back up the path, on to the main pavement once more.

The route was memorised in his head. Besides, he knew where he was going. The inevitable place. Where he was always bound to end up.

The main central police station on Steelhouse Lane.

He stood on the street now, gazing up at the building. Behind the courts, it shared a lot of the same Gothic style, looking like an urban idea of an old Hammer horror film. But the cars, vans and uniformed officers wandering around in front dispelled that idea. Still, it looked appropriate to Adderley. As though some kind of old-style, truthfully physical justice went on in there.

At least he hoped so.

He found the main entrance, walked up to the desk. There were a couple of people before him so he calmly waited his turn. Eventually he stood before the glass partition. The desk sergeant looked up at him, waited expectantly for him to speak.

And the words deserted him.

'Yes?' said the sergeant, trying not to let irritation and weariness slip into his voice.

Adderley moved his mouth, hoped that the exercise would eventually produce words. It did.

'M-my name's ... Roy ... Adderley. Adderley.' He cleared his throat while the desk sergeant waited.

'Good,' said the desk sergeant. 'And what can I do for you, Mr Adderley?'

'I want to report a murder.'

The desk sergeant looked taken aback. 'Oh yes? Whose?'

'My girlfriend. And I'm only going to talk to Detective Inspector Brennan.'

'I'll see what I can do,' said the desk sergeant.

'No,' said Adderley. 'I'll only speak to Detective Inspector Brennan.'

'Fine. Okay. I'll get him. In the meantime, can you tell me, do you know who killed her?'

'Yes,' he said.

'Who?'

'Me.'

And Adderley gave a smile so radiant it was like he felt the sun streaming from his face.

60

'So,' said Imani, 'how d'you like it in the big city?'

Patel, in the passenger seat, laughed. She had hoped he would. They were driving back into the city centre, negotiating the roundabouts down from Balsall Heath through Edgbaston.

'It's not that different, you know,' he said. 'We've got mosques in West Bromwich.' He pointed to one through the right window. 'We've got roads, just like this one, we've got . . . oh, everything you've got here.'

'Including crime.'

'Well, that happens everywhere.' He looked out of the window, then back to her, still smiling. 'Scenery's prettier here, though.'

Imani tried hard to keep her eyes on the road, but glanced at him in mock surprise and admonishment. Or at least she thought it was only mock. She wasn't sure.

'Any more sexist comments like that, Detective Constable Patel, and you'll be walking back to Steelhouse Lane.'

He looked away from her, seemingly genuinely embarrassed. 'Sorry,' he said. 'Just trying to give you a compliment.' His words sounded clumsy, his body shifting like he was itching all over, hands gesturing impotently. He looked like someone trying not to lose their balance and fall downstairs.

'I know you were,' she said. 'Or I think you were.'

'I was,' he said. 'Honestly. That was all.'

Imani said nothing more. Just looked out of the opposite window and smiled to herself, hoping he wasn't watching her reaction.

She turned on to Bristol Road, heading into the city.

Patel had stopped talking. Imani risked a glance at him. He was looking out of the window, away from her. Something seemed to be on his mind, troubling him, furrowing his brow. It was a nice brow, she thought. Too handsome to look troubled.

She stopped herself. What was she thinking? Did she really fancy him? Well, yes. That much was obvious. And he fancied her. She knew that. Didn't have to be Psychic Sally to work out what he was thinking and feeling.

But why was she falling for it? It wasn't like her. She had spent a large part of her career fighting against the lazy, institutionalised sexism that was inherent in the police force. Batting away the wandering hands of senior officers, wondering whether to ignore or complain about the jokes directed at her. Knowing that she shouldn't have to stand for that kind of treatment, but that if she complained too much, stood up for herself, someone, somewhere, would be marking her down as a troublemaker. And if that happened, no matter how brilliant she might or might not be, her career would be less than stellar.

But Patel seemed different. Not like the usual rank and file, not treating her the same way. He had accepted her promotion to CIO, shared her concerns about domestic violence and even demonstrated that to her. It couldn't all be bullshit.

She found herself smiling once more. Risked another glance at him. He was still staring out of the window. She did like him. Admitted that much to herself. Even though she had told herself she would never end up with a copper. Because she knew what they were like. Not just from experience. Not just from working with them. Because she was one herself.

'Maybe . . .' Patel started, then stopped just as quickly.

'Yeah?' she said. Keeping her eyes on the road, negotiating the Queensway underpass.

'Well, I dunno,' he said. 'This investigation. I'm enjoying it. Better than we get in West Brom, you know what I mean?'

'I know,' she said. 'But we are the Major Incident Squad, don't forget. We don't do run-of-the-mill.'

'Yeah, I know that. But . . .'

Imani waited. 'Yeah?'

'I was thinking . . . maybe I should put in for a transfer.'

'To Birmingham or MIS?'

'MIS.' He looked at her, then quickly away. 'If, you know. If you think I'll be good enough. If you'll have me.'

'Well . . .'

'I mean, how would you like that? If I was on your team?'

'Don't know,' she said, trying and failing to keep a teasing tone out of her voice. 'We only take the best, you know.' She looked at him. 'You the best?'

He smiled. 'Oh yeah.' And there was a cockiness, a swagger she hadn't seen before. Not unattractive, she thought. He nodded. 'I've got some moves. Just wait and see.'

'I'll bet you have,' she said, and smiled all the way back to the station.

61

'Change of plan,' said Cotter, striding into the incident room and beckoning Imani and Marina towards her. They looked at each other, confused. The three of them huddled together in a corner.

'I've spoken to Claire Lingard, ma'am,' said Imani. 'She's ready to go tonight.'

'Well,' said Cotter, 'it may not come to that.'

The two of them looked at her quizzically.

'Roy Adderley's just walked in and confessed to the murder of his girlfriend.'

Marina and Imani stared at her. She continued.

'We've sent uniforms round to his place, and her body's there on the floor of the living room. It looks like he beat her to death.'

'Jesus . . . ' Marina stared.

Cotter turned to her. 'Could it be him? For the other two? Could it?'

Marina, put on the spot, shrugged. 'It's possible. As I said, he could be hiding in plain sight. So I'd say all bets are off.'

'Where is he now?' asked Imani.

'Interview room one.'

Imani looked at the door, back to Cotter. In a hurry to go. 'Who's handling it?'

'Well that's the thing,' said Cotter. 'He'll only speak to one person. Phil Brennan.'

Marina's mouth fell open. Before she could reply, Cotter continued.

'That was the deal. Phil's on his way into the building now.' She turned to Marina. 'I'm sorry.'

Marina recovered some of her composure. 'No, it's . . . it's all right. Had to happen some time. If that's what . . . It's fine.' She was breathing heavily.

'So if we can get him to admit to the killing of—' Imani stopped in her tracks, eyes drifting to the door.

'What is it?' asked Cotter.

The other two followed her gaze. DS Hugh Ellison was once again in the incident room. He spotted the three of them and began walking towards them.

'Doesn't he have any work to do in Digbeth?' said Imani.

'You've met him?' asked Cotter in surprise.

'Came in yesterday. Wanted to know if there was any progress on the Gemma Adderley case.'

'I worked with him on that,' said Marina. She gave an involuntary shudder.

'He's as slimy as they come,' said Cotter. 'We'll have to disinfect this place after he's gone.'

He reached them. They gave no indication that they had been discussing him.

'DS Ellison,' said Cotter, unable or unwilling to keep the dislike from her voice. 'What brings you here?'

'Is it true?' he asked. 'He's come in? He's admitted it?'

'Who are you talking about?' Cotter's face was blank.

'Adderley. Heard he'd copped for it.'

'Roy Adderley is in for questioning, yes. I'm afraid I can't say any more than that.'

'Oh, come on,' said Ellison, lip curling nastily. 'I worked that

277

case. I'm not some sodding reporter that you're trying to fob off. Has he copped to it or not?'

'No,' said Marina, sensing that Cotter was becoming angry, jumping in to save a confrontation. 'He's come in but he hasn't been questioned yet.'

Ellison turned, looked at her. Didn't bother to disguise the leer on his face as he gave her a head-to-toe appraisal. 'Hello, Marina. Good to see you again.'

She nodded, not trusting herself with words.

Ellison reluctantly took his eyes off her, turned back to Cotter. 'So when and where?'

'When and where what, DS Ellison?'

'When's the interview? I want to watch.'

'That's out of the question, I'm afraid. We're—'

'Oh, come on,' he said, in what he clearly assumed was a charming voice but which came out thin and wheedling. 'I was there at the start, I should be there at the end. Want to hear him admit it.'

'Sorry, but no. You're not part of the investigating team. I won't allow it.'

Cotter held firm. Ellison stared at her. She returned his gaze. Hard, steely. He glanced at Marina.

'You're letting her watch,' he said petulantly.

'Dr Esposito is a valued part of my team,' Cotter said. 'She's allowed to.'

He stared at Marina once more, mouth open to speak, then closed it again, apparently thinking better of it.

'So that's it, then, is it?'

'I'm sorry, DS Ellison. I can't allow it.' Cotter reached across, shook his hand. 'But thank you for making time in your busy schedule to come in. We'll let you know what happens.'

Realising he was getting nowhere, he made to leave. But

before moving off, he turned back again. 'Nice to see you again, Dr Esposito.' He made the words sound like an insult.

The three of them watched him go.

'I'm going to wash my hand now,' said Cotter. She turned to the other two. 'Horrid little man. Used to work Vice. And from what I hear, wasn't averse to helping himself to freebies. He's with MisPers now. I think it was either that or early retirement.'

'Oh well,' said Imani. 'I'm sure it's the force's gain.'

Cotter gave a smile of relief. 'Glad we're all on the same page as far as he's concerned. Now. What are we going to do about Roy Adderley?'

62

'Good to have you back, boss.' Sperring was the first to greet Phil as he returned to the station.

It felt strange to be back. He had only been away for a relatively short time, but the experience of walking into the building again was disconcerting. He had been suspended from an inquiry once before, at the behest of his then DCI, but that DCI had had a hidden agenda which Phil had then gone on to expose, so he had been reinstated immediately. This time was different. He would have done the same as Cotter in her position. Now he was back, uncertain as to when his next appearance here would be, and under what circumstances. So just do what he had to do and get it over with.

To say he'd been surprised by the phone call was a massive understatement. Not just at being asked back so soon, but the manner of the invitation. The one thing that hadn't surprised him was hearing what Adderley had done. He felt vindicated in his actions.

He reached the interview room. No other members of his team – should he keep thinking of them as his team? – were about apart from Sperring. And for that Phil was grateful.

Especially where Marina was concerned. Just knowing she was in the same building was disconcerting enough. Enough to put him off what he was here to do. Enough to send him spiralling downwards once more.

Focus. He had a job to do.

'Thanks, Ian.' Phil looked at his DS, then at the door. He didn't know if he should say anything further, or indeed if he could think of anything further to say. Sperring made the decision for him.

'Just go right in, boss. He's waiting for you.'

Phil managed a smile. 'I'll soften him up for you to take over.'

Sperring managed to return the smile. 'I'll be watching.'

Phil entered. Adderley sat alone at the table. Phil motioned to the uniform standing by the door to leave, then crossed to the table, sat down opposite.

'Just the two of us,' he said, hoping that he would quickly fall back into the rhythm of things. 'How quaint.'

Adderley was wearing a suit, but his tie and belt had been taken from him. He stared at Phil. 'You look terrible,' he said, face filled with compassion.

'So do you,' said Phil, automatically. Before Adderley could speak, he continued, 'That what you brought me in for? To say that?'

Adderley frowned slightly.

'Oh yeah,' said Phil, 'I should say before we go any further that anything you say to me doesn't count. I'm suspended.'

Adderley shrugged.

'And also,' said Phil, 'anything I say to you doesn't count. This isn't an official interview.'

'I don't care about any of that,' said Adderley, his voice strangely, almost disconnectedly, calm, his gave level. Too level. 'I know what I've done, I know what will happen to me. That's not what this is about. I wanted to talk to you. Just you.'

Phil shrugged, kept his face impassive. 'I'm here. So talk.'

Adderley stared at him for a long time before speaking. Phil waited, his face giving nothing away. Adderley's expression was bland but his lips were moving, like he was having a secret conversation. Or saying a prayer. Eventually he smiled.

'This . . . ' He gestured round the room, his arms stretched out expansively. 'This. Is all your fault.' Dropping his arms, looking straight at Phil. Waiting.

'No it's not,' said Phil, suddenly feeling back in the swing of interrogation, muscle memory taking over.

Adderley nodded, still smiling, face gravely serene. 'Yes it is.' His voice low, sure. 'Yes it is. You see,' he leaned forward, explaining a point, making sure it was understood, 'nothing would have happened. Nothing at all. If you'd left me alone. Nothing.' Leaning back, nodding to emphasise his point.

Phil folded his arms. 'Bullshit,' he said. 'It would have happened. All of it.'

'Really?' More amused than anything else, letting a lesser intellect have their fun before spoiling it with a killer argument.

Or at least that was the impression Phil received. And even though he shouldn't have let it, that rankled.

'Oh yeah,' he said. 'So you say you didn't kill your wife. Well, the jury's still out on that one. But you would have ended up here anyway. Maybe not like this, maybe not on this day. But you would have been sitting here, looking across the table at me, or someone like me. It would have happened eventually. Definitely.'

'Really?' Adderley still smiling, still not taking in Phil's words.

Denial, thought Phil. Work on that. 'Yeah. Because that's what you're like. This . . . ' he gestured round the room, 'is who you are. A criminal.'

'A criminal. I see.'

Phil leaned forward. 'Not only that, but a coward.'

Adderley flinched, blinked. Phil, sensing a glimmer of breakthrough, of victory, kept going. Ramped it up a notch.

282

'A coward,' he continued, 'who's terrified of the world. And what he thinks it's done to him, or could do to him. Who hates and fears it because it makes him feel powerless. So what does this coward do? What do you do? You bottle up all this hate and fear inside you. And because you're too pathetic to let it out any other way, you take it out on someone else. But this person has to be weaker and smaller than you. And if this person also has the bad luck to love you, even better. It makes all your hate and fear hurt them more. All that rage you pummelled out, transferred to Gemma. Your wife. And what was her crime? To fall in love with you.'

Phil sat back, not bothering to disguise the disgust he felt at Adderley. *Something to be said for being suspended*, he thought. *I can say what I like. Or rather, what I feel.*

The endorphins were firing up, the righteous anger coming out. The old Phil, back again. He was actually starting to enjoy himself.

63

'Good, isn't he?'

Sperring turned. He was in the viewing suite, watching Phil interview Adderley. And he was pleased with what he had seen. His boss had his old fire back, not like the angry, moping individual of recent times, shooting off his anger and despair at the most misplaced of targets. This was Phil back to what he did best.

'Didn't hear you come in,' said Sperring, hiding the fact that he had actually jumped on hearing Marina's voice. 'He is. Much as I hate to admit it.'

Marina gave a tight smile, moved closer to him, looked at the screen.

The room was small, almost a store cupboard, with a desk, an old chair and a monitor. But sometimes, especially if there was a big case on and an interview was going to blow it open, it took on TARDIS-like dimensions, somehow accommodating all the officers who wanted to see and be part of the outcome.

'Has he confessed?' asked Marina.

'To his girlfriend's murder,' said Sperring. 'That's all.'

'So why did he want to see only Phil?'

'I think we're coming to that.'

They continued to watch the screen, Sperring throwing surreptitious glances across at Marina, trying to work out what she was seeing, how she was feeling.

284

She looked proud, smiling a little, even.

'Hope he's back soon,' said Sperring, not taking his eyes off the screen. 'Properly.'

'So do I,' Marina said, the words coming out on a sigh.

Sperring took his attention away from the screen, focused on Marina. 'Why not wait till he gets out? Have a word?'

Marina looked round, suddenly flustered, like she was trapped and couldn't find an exit. Startled by her own words. 'I'd . . . better go. I . . . I've got work to do.'

'Marina . . .'

'I've got to go.' She turned, made for the door.

Sperring put his hand on her arm. 'Just wait. What's the matter with you?'

Marina stared at the hand, hard, until he released her. 'Look, I just don't want to bump into him.'

'Why not?'

'Because I don't feel . . . I'm not ready to see him yet, that's why not.'

Sperring shook his head, gave a bark of a laugh. 'Jesus. Why can't the pair of you behave like grown-ups and talk to each other? What's so bad you can't sort it out between you?'

Marina turned away from him, not wanting him to see her face. 'You don't understand.'

Sperring moved to her, turned her round to face him. 'I do understand.'

'He . . . If she comes back, he won't be able to protect me. Or our daughter. It's better if we're apart.'

'Better for who? Look, Marina, I've been working with him all this time. I know exactly what he's been going through, I've had it every day. It's been like hauling round the Incredible Sulk. It's hit him hard. And I'm sure it's been hard on you too.'

'Yes.' Looking straight in his eyes. 'It has.'

'All the more reason to talk, then. Sort it out.'

She broke the connection, turned away from him. 'I'm not ready . . .'

'Oh, Jesus Christ.' Sperring shook his head once more. 'Honestly. You two. Like dealing with a pair of kids sometimes.'

She glanced at the screen once more. Sperring thought she looked torn: part of her wanting to go, part of her wanting to stay. He said nothing, waited to see which part would win.

'I really have to go,' said Marina.

Sperring knew there was nothing more he could say.

'Whatever you think's best.' He couldn't look at her.

He heard her leave the room, close the door behind her with a soft click. He went back to watching the screen.

He wasn't alone for long. The door opened once more and Cotter entered.

'Has he got a confession yet?'

'Only for the girlfriend,' said Sperring once more. 'Not the wife. Think he's going in for that now.'

Cotter nodded, watched. 'So now we get to it,' she said. 'Now we see once and for all if it's him or not.'

The atmosphere in the room was suddenly tense.

64

Phil was back in the groove now, like he had never been away. Like he had never lost his focus.

Or Marina.

'So you killed Trudi,' he said, ploughing on in to Adderley. 'That much you admit.'

Adderley nodded.

'But what about Gemma? Your wife?'

'No. I didn't kill her.'

Phil gave a sad smile, shook his head slowly. 'No point in lying now, Roy. You're here. You're going down for this. You may as well admit it. You've got nothing to lose.'

Adderley leaned forward, eyes wide, unblinking. 'I didn't kill her.'

'Just admit it,' said Phil once more, but he could sense – reluctantly – the truth in Adderley's words.

'I didn't do it. I didn't kill Gemma. Or that other woman.'

'So where did you go the night I watched you? Where did you drive off to?'

Adderley shrugged uncomfortably. 'Just . . . drove.'

'Where to?'

Another shrug.

'Okay,' said Phil. 'Let's say I believe you about Gemma and Janine Gillen. Just tell me where you drove to and we'll leave it at that. Satisfy my curiosity, if nothing else.'

Adderley was clearly unhappy at being asked to deviate from what he wanted to say. But Phil was insistent.

'Tell me, Roy.'

'I . . . had sex.' His head dropped with shame.

'You had sex. What, someone you knew?'

He shook his head.

'A prostitute? That what you mean?'

Another nod of the head. Much more reluctant this time.

'So where did you go to pick this woman up? Balsall Heath, round there?'

Adderley mumbled something under his breath. Phil leaned closer to hear it.

'What was that?'

'I said, it wasn't a woman.' Adderley looked up. Shame burned in his eyes.

'A man?' Phil was stunned. 'You visited a male prostitute?'

He nodded once more.

'So that's it. Right. Why you hate women so much. Even why you turned to God. You feel like you should be doing one thing, living your life one way. But your family, your . . . I don't know, culture, whatever, tells you you should be doing something else, is that it?'

Adderley looked up, eyes filled with tears, face twisted with self-loathing. 'You know nothing. Nothing about me. I'm not gay. I'm not. That was . . . an accident.'

'You've done it before, though. That wasn't your first time.'

Adderley stared.

'And you always felt bad afterwards, right? Always felt sorry for yourself. Ashamed. You probably prayed, promised it wouldn't happen again.'

Adderley's head dropped once more, shoulders shaking as he sobbed.

'But eventually you felt the urge to do it again. That right?'

Adderley looked up, angry this time. 'No. That's where you're wrong. I wouldn't have done it again. Because I've got God's help. He keeps me strong. He helps me when I'm feeling ... tempted.'

'So you didn't kill Gemma.'

'No. I didn't.'

'But you would have done. If she'd stayed with you.'

'I wouldn't.'

'You would. You would have made it impossible for her to leave, no matter how much she wanted to. Scared her so much that she had to stay. And all it would have taken would have been one blow too many, and it would have been her you beat to death.'

Adderley said nothing.

'Or it could have been the next one. After Trudi. Maybe Trudi wouldn't have waited around to find out what you were like. One slap from you and she'd have been off. But you'd have found another. And you'd have killed her. It was going to happen, Adderley. The way you are, you were always going to kill someone. It was only a matter of time.'

Adderley's face looked like it had been repeatedly slapped, Phil's words having their effect. He wiped the tears from his cheeks, then sat still, his lips moving in silent, secret conversation, eyes closed. Eventually he opened them and that same stupid, beatific smile appeared on his face again. Back in control. Or what passed for his control.

'It's all your fault,' he said once more.

Phil shook his head, about to start again, but Adderley beat him to it.

'It is,' he said, 'and that's all right. Really.' Nodding now, still smiling. 'You know why?' Leaning forward, as if about to let Phil in on some great secret. 'Do you? Mmm?' He sat back, arms out. 'Because I forgive you.'

'Oh, for fuck's sake . . . '

'And Jesus forgives you. I forgive you. And Jesus forgives you.'

Adderley put his arms down and fell silent. Staring straight ahead, nodding to the words of a voice only he could hear, the vapid grin still in place.

'That it?' asked Phil.

No reply from Adderley.

'You've said your piece now, yeah? You've brought me all in the way in here when I could have been sitting on the sofa with a cup of tea watching *Homes Under the Hammer* and *Deal Or No Deal* just so you, a murderer, wife-abuser and repressed homosexual, can forgive me.' Phil gave a short, harsh laugh. 'Brilliant.'

Adderley said nothing, but the smile, Phil noticed, became more fixed.

Phil hadn't finished, though. 'Well, that's nice. How fine and dandy. Lovely.' He leaned forward once more. 'But it's you who should be worried about being forgiven. Don't you think?'

'God will forgive me,' said Adderley. 'Jesus has redeemed me.'

'I'm not talking about God,' said Phil. 'Let's put him aside for one minute. And I know that you religious types can twist anything to make your holy book say the things you want it to say, so let's also put aside the bit about "Thou shalt not kill". Not to mention the lying down with other men your lot seem to have such a problem with. That's for you to deal with in your own time. Of which you're going to have plenty.'

Adderley stared at the wall. Phil continued.

'No,' he said, 'not God. Much nearer to home. And a lot more real. I'm talking about Carly.'

Adderley flinched, as if expecting a blow.

'Carly. You must remember her. Little girl, very trusting,

290

very hurt now, of course. Hopefully she'll recover, but it's going to be a long road. Living with her grandparents, last I heard. Her mother's parents, of course. But then she has to, because you sent her mother, the one good and positive thing in her life, away from her. Forced her away from you. You should have been loving Carly, protecting her, nurturing her. Instead you made her home a battlefield. You terrified her. Now, when she has nightmares, it'll be your face she sees.'

Adderley shook his head, hoping to dislodge Phil's words. 'No . . .'

Phil kept on. 'You couldn't bear the fact that your wife and daughter were leaving you, so you killed Gemma, made it look like a madman was on the loose.'

'No . . .'

'Then you killed Janine Gillen. Why, Roy? What for?'

Adderley stared at him, eyes imploring. 'I didn't kill Janine! I didn't! I never even knew her, honestly! Why . . . why would I lie? I killed Trudi, why would I lie?'

Phil sat back. He had been in enough interrogation rooms, heard enough confessions to know when someone was telling the truth. Adderley wasn't the killer. The Heartbreaker. But that didn't let him off the hook.

'Fair enough. You didn't kill Janine Gillen. But you sent your daughter and her mother off into the arms of a madman, who abandoned Carly and tortured and killed Gemma.' He pointed at Adderley. '*You* did that. You. Not me. I don't need to be forgiven. Just you. You should be asking Carly to forgive you.

'And then there's Gemma herself. Gone. Dead. Her parents now have to bury their daughter. D'you think that's right? That parents should be the ones to bury their children? D'you think they'll be forgiving you any time soon?'

Adderley's bottom lip started trembling.

'Ask Trudi's parents for forgiveness while you're at it. Tell

291

them what you've done to their daughter. And her two sons. They knew their mother was with you because you'd put a roof over her head, give her a safe place to bring up her kids. What about them? Going to their mother's funeral? Will they want to forgive you?'

Phil sat back again, finished. And in that moment he felt more alive than he had for a long time. More sure of who he was and what he was supposed to be doing in the world. Confident of himself and even of his future.

Adderley stared straight ahead, his face impassive. An alabaster death mask. Tears formed and rolled from his eyes.

Phil stood up, made for the door, turned back.

'There's a special place in prison reserved for the likes of you. A special wing. It's where the rapists go. The child-abusers and killers, the wife-beaters and murderers. Even in prison there's a hierarchy. And you're going to be the lowest of the low. The scum. Hated by everyone, staff and inmates alike. That's your life, what you've got to look forward to. Where you'll get ...'

'What?' Adderley's voice was small, tremulous. 'What? What will I get?'

'What's coming to you. What you deserve. See how many of your new friends want to forgive you.'

Adderley's head dropped, shoulders heaving. Uncontrollable sobs.

'I'm going now,' said Phil.

Adderley looked up. 'Why? B—because you have to?'

'No,' said Phil, his voice calm and ice cold. 'Because I can't stand the fucking sight of you.'

He left the room.

Sperring was waiting outside the door.

'All yours,' said Phil, and walked away.

65

'It's back on.'

Cotter strode into the incident room. Imani, Patel and Marina all looked up.

'Adderley didn't kill his wife. He's not the Heartbreaker. And yes, I know I said never to use that word in here. But we're back with Plan A. Let's go.'

66

Marina was back in the incident room, working through a pile of files, at the temporary desk they had assigned her. Trying not to think of Phil, of how he had been when she had just seen him. Trying and failing.

He had looked like the man she'd fallen in love with. Strong, in command. And handsome. Very, very handsome.

She tried to put all that to one side, concentrate on what she was supposed to be doing. She couldn't think about him at the moment. Maybe they did need to talk. In fact they definitely did. But not here, not now. She had work to do. Finding matches between the killer's victims and previous missing women.

Even though some on the team had taken to calling him the Heartbreaker, Marina refused to do that. She hated the way serial killers – or multiple murderers, as she preferred – quickly had a nickname attached to them. And it always stuck. Something dramatic, heroic or romantic, even. Very Hollywood.

In Marina's experience, multiple murderers were among the most banal, boring people she had ever met. Worse even than golfing enthusiasts and UKIP candidates. They killed because there was something lacking in them. Because their hard-wiring was twisted. There was nothing romantic, dramatic and certainly not heroic about them. Their brains were like hotel breakfast-buffet eggs, fried or scrambled, and their motives a collection of sad, and often harrowing, life experiences that went beyond psychological causes and explainable, dramatic tropes to become tiresome clichés. They had all suffered abuse as children. Not all abused children went on to abuse, but all adult abusers had once been in that situation. They had probably also suffered some serious head trauma that had sent their neural pathways down different routes. Combined with an already twisted pathology due to the abuse, that created a serial killer. Sorry, multiple murderer.

Marina knew all that. But it didn't help get her any nearer to finding him. So she hoped the list that Elli was going through could provide some help.

'Marina?'

Speak of the devil. Marina got up, crossed to Elli's desk. 'How you getting on?'

'I think I've come up with a shortlist of other potential victims. Women who've gone missing under similar circumstances.'

Marina felt that thrill she always felt when a discovery was about to be made. 'Show me.'

Elli pointed to the screen. 'Okay. I started on the list of missing persons, narrowed down by the parameters you gave me. Age, background, marital status. Missing in the last few months. That was a start. Then I narrowed it down further. Had these women ever been for marriage guidance counselling? Had they ever been involved in incidents of domestic violence, even if it was only reported and not taken any further? Then I checked the geographical area. And this is what I came up with.'

She pointed to the screen. Marina saw several files, all profiles of missing persons.

'Five matches,' said Elli. 'Here we go. Bethany Worth.

Known as Beth, it says here. Twenty-nine, married with two kids. Lived in Stirchley with her husband, Peter. Been missing for seven months now.'

'Domestic violence?' asked Marina.

Elli nodded. 'Police called to reports of a disturbance last April. She was found on the kitchen floor, bruising about the face, holding her ribs. An ambulance was called, taken to A and E. Patched her up, let her go. Tried to take the husband in for assault but she refused to press charges.'

Marina nodded. 'Right. And she's been missing since then?'

'Shortly afterwards. May. I've managed to get hold of her file. The husband was questioned but had an alibi. Cast-iron. Away in Glasgow for work. The investigation got nowhere. Still open but on the back burner. Apparently she had relatives in the north. The supposition was that she'd gone to stay with them.'

'Children?'

'Left behind. Lot of name-calling, bad mother, all that.'

'Right. She fits. Next one?'

'Ludwika Milczarek. Polish. No children. Lived with her boyfriend, Marek Chociemski. Both immigrants. Had a flat in a high-rise in Handsworth. She worked as a cleaner and barmaid in a local pub. Doesn't say what he did.'

'Working off the books, probably.'

Elli nodded. 'Apparently Chociemski didn't like Ludwika working in the bar. Accused her of flirting with other men, according to the police report. When she came home, he used to question her then beat her.'

'That's all on the report?'

'It's what she told the investigating officer. Said she didn't flirt with anyone. That he was out drinking nearly every night and God knew what he got up to.'

'Did it go any further?'

'She was given information about refuges by the uniforms, and that was that. Said she didn't want to take things further because she was scared of being deported.'

'And then she disappeared. Nearly a year ago.'

'Right.'

'And the boyfriend?'

'He kind of disappeared too. For a bit. Came back on to our radar a few months later, living with another girl, causing another domestic disturbance. Didn't seem too upset at the loss of Ludwika.'

'And of course the police didn't exert themselves looking for her?'

Elli shook her head. 'Says here they did everything possible. Checked the airports, ports, all of that. Released a description in the Polish community. But no. I doubt they knocked themselves out on it.' Her hands played over the keys. 'Right. Next one.'

'Just a minute. Thinking.' Marina looked at the screen. There had been photos attached to the reports and she was scrutinising them, trying to see if there was any common factor between them, any similarity that would trigger something in the killer's mind. She couldn't see it.

So what did that mean? There was a trigger, there must be. Had to be. She looked at the pictures again. Nothing. Young women. Some white, some black. Hurt, vulnerable young women. That was his trigger.

'Go on,' said Marina.

Elli put the next one up on the screen. A young black woman. Pretty, Marina thought. Hard eyes. But looked nothing like the first two.

'Elizabeth Thompson. Thirty-one. Three children. Used to stay with their grandmother a lot. She went out. Had a number of gentleman friends.'

'A prostitute?' asked Marina.

'Doesn't say so, not in so many words,' said Elli, 'but that's the implication. Had a boyfriend, though.'

'For that I think we can read pimp,' said Marina.

Elli nodded. 'He's the one that beat her up. And then she disappeared.'

'I bet the boys in blue went to town on him.'

She scanned the report on the screen in front of her. 'Oh, yes. Or at least they tried. Turned up nothing. Had to let him go. Now.' She pressed more keys. 'Number four. Gail Simpson.'

Another pretty black girl appeared on the screen.

'Different kind of background. Kings Heath. Middle class. Husband's business went bust, started drinking.'

'And got a bit handy with his wife.'

'Looks like it.' Elli gave a grim smile. 'But you know one of the golden rules of policing? Or at least one of the great unspoken ones.'

'Tell me.'

'Don't fuck with the middle classes.'

'So nothing was reported.'

'No domestic violence reports, no. Or if there were, they've been dropped. No trace. But they went for marriage guidance counselling. Seemed to be doing pretty well, according to the husband's statement. And then she disappeared.'

'Anything from marriage guidance about them?'

Elli nodded. 'Apparently Gail was scared of her husband. Wanted a list of refuges. Case is still officially open, but ... ' She shrugged. 'And the last one that fits the profile. Jusna Kamdar. Originally from Pakistan, but had been living in the UK for ten years.'

Marina nodded. All vulnerable women with low self esteem. All isolated in some way. Her hypothesis about what his triggers were was strengthened.

298

'Disappeared three months ago. Recently married. But apparently unhappy. Her husband was a distant cousin who came over from the old country.' Elli looked up. 'We know what that means.'

'Arranged marriage?'

Elli nodded. Shuddered. 'Hateful. And she was having marriage guidance counselling. But not her husband. He wouldn't go.'

Marina frowned. 'Was she Muslim? Wouldn't she try to go to a Muslim refuge?'

'By all accounts she didn't want to be Muslim. Hated it. Saw herself as a Western girl. Went to university. But couldn't escape her family's clutches. Poor girl.'

'And disappeared,' said Marina.

Elli nodded. 'All of them.' She pressed another button. Another screen appeared. 'These are the notes from Safe Haven. Phone calls corresponding to the dates these women went missing.'

'So they all called Safe Haven and then all disappeared? And no one noticed because ...' She shrugged. 'How can you? What are you looking for?'

'Seems that way.'

Marina straightened up. 'Brilliant work, Elli. Really, really brilliant.'

Elli smiled.

'I'll go and tell Cotter. Confirm her worst fears for her.'

'Rather you than me,' said Elli.

But Marina was already out of the door.

67

Marina didn't reach Cotter. Not straight away. She went barrelling round a corner and ran straight into the last person she wanted to face.

Phil.

They both stopped dead, stared at each other. It seemed as if all those around them in the building, the building itself, the brightly lit corridor, the hubbub of voices and clacking of computer keys, echoing footsteps and ringing laughter, just melted away. There was only the two of them. Alone.

No running away now. Marina felt her body go into fight-or-flight, adrenalin pumping round her system. She couldn't help it: it was a physiological response. But even as it happened, she allowed her mind to take over and tried to override her body's response. After all, here was a man she loved, a man she had pledged the rest of her life to. A man who had seen her naked on every possible level.

And from the look in his eyes, she was certain that Phil was experiencing something similar.

'Hi,' she said, for want of anything else.

'Hi yourself,' he said, trying for nonchalance, attempting a smile. It died on his face.

'So,' she said, after an expanse of silence that seemed to last years, 'how are you?'

He shrugged. 'Fine,' he said, voice aiming for lightness, missing.

She nodded. 'Good. I . . . ' Should she tell him? Admit it? She didn't know. But she couldn't stop herself. 'I saw you. In the interview room. From the observation suite.' She gave a laugh, forced and high. 'God, whoever named it that had a sense of humour. Cupboard, more like.'

'You saw me?' he said, not joining in with her brittle laughter.

She stopped laughing. Her face became serious once more. 'I . . . yes. I watched you.'

He nodded, head down, eyes averted. Said nothing.

'You were . . . good.'

He gave a smile, a short laugh, as if he had just won a pointless, pyrrhic victory. 'Thanks.'

'You . . . ' She didn't know what to say next, felt she was talking for talking's sake. Just to be saying something, just to be communicating. 'You really nailed him. Good work.'

Phil nodded once more. Then he stared at her. And in the moment of their eyes connecting, she felt naked all over again.

She quickly looked away.

'Just what I do,' Phil said, distractedly. Like his words no longer mattered after looking into Marina's eyes. Like he had seen something there that made more sense than words.

She looked at him once more. Really looked at him this time. Saw beyond his usual battle armour of leather jacket and plaid shirt, took in the stubble, the messed hair, the black rings round the reddened eyes.

'You look terrible,' she said, the words out before she could stop herself.

His eyes widened slightly, as if he was taken aback a little. But only a little. She felt like he agreed with her.

'You don't,' he said, gulping the words like a drowning man struggling for air. 'You look wonderful.'

Her hand went instinctively to her hair and she smiled involuntarily. She felt herself blushing. 'No I don't. I'm ... I'm at work ... '

'Anyway,' he said, filling the void so she didn't have to respond further, 'you're not the first person to tell me I look terrible today. Getting used to it now.'

She looked like she was about to ask him who else had said it, so he continued talking, silencing her.

'You're back, I hear.'

She nodded. 'Yes.'

'On my case.'

She nodded again.

'Well, what was my case. Until recently.'

'That one, yes,' she said, as non-committal as possible, not going into detail, not picking up the thread from his words.

They stood in silence again. Staring at each other, looking away.

'How's Josephina?' asked Phil eventually.

'She's ... good. Yeah. She's safe.'

'Good.' He nodded. 'I'm glad. Safe. No, really, I'm glad. And you're safe? You feel safe? You can do this?'

Marina sensed something building within Phil, and while she couldn't blame him, she didn't want to go into it. Not here, not now. 'Please, Phil. Time and a place.'

He moved closer to her. 'Is there?' he said, voice a ragged whisper. 'When? Where?' As though everything he had stored inside, kept bottled up, was threatening to spill over. 'You tell me, because ... ' He sighed, stepped away from her once more, shaking his head, face twisted.

'I'm sorry,' Marina said. 'I really am.'

No response from Phil.

'Look,' she said, 'we need to talk. Properly talk.'

He looked up. 'You didn't want to talk a couple of days ago. What's changed?'

Marina sighed, shook her head. 'Look, Phil, we can't go into this here and now. I've got work to do.'

Phil nodded, composing himself. Glancing round to see who was walking past, suddenly aware that, no matter what they might be feeling, they weren't actually alone.

'Right,' he said, nodding once more. 'How's ... how's it going?'

Marina frowned. 'How's what going?'

'The investigation.' Phil's voice small, his eyes blinking, unfocused.

Marina was glad to be on safer ground, to have something she could actually talk to him about without him getting angry or upset. Well, not too angry or upset. 'It's bigger than we thought. We may have found more potential victims.'

'Confirmation that we're dealing with a multiple murderer?' he asked.

She nodded. 'That's about the size of it.'

She looked at him again and she could see it in his eyes. That hunger. That need to be there, to be involved. It was part of him, a defining part. It was who he was.

But there was more to it that that. Yes, he wanted to be back on the team, leading the team, involved, in the thick of it. But there was something more crucial. He wanted to be doing it with Marina. She could see that in his eyes, and it was a whole other level of pain for him.

'Look,' she said, 'I'd ... I'd better go. I've got to ... ' She gestured down the corridor.

He nodded, as if in acceptance of the situation. 'Yeah. Good ... good luck.'

She didn't know what to do. Kiss him, hold him, touch him ... She did none of them. She just gave an embarrassed half-smile, turned and walked off.

She knew, as she went, that he was standing there watching her.

68

'You ready? You know what to say and how to say it?'

Imani nodded. 'You coached me well, master.' She was aiming for levity, but the tightness in her throat, round her chest, betrayed her.

Marina took her hand from the other woman's shoulder. Looked down at her, then stood back.

Night had fallen. The incident room felt overlit, a lighthouse against the darkness outside. Imani had asked to be alone, or as alone as possible, when she made the call. She had Marina with her. Cotter, Sperring and the rest of the team were waiting nearby, out of earshot.

Imani had practised all afternoon. One-to-one sessions with Marina, getting the words right, and more importantly, the inflections, the sense of what she was saying. The emotions behind the words.

They had found a room, just the pair of them. Closed and locked the door. Marina had looked tense, shaken even, Imani thought. But then she had just discovered five other potential victims of the Heartbreaker, so in Imani's mind she had every right to be a little distracted. A little upset.

'Okay,' Marina had said. 'How d'you feel?'

'Good,' said Imani, feeling anything but. Trying to take it one step at a time, not think about what she was about to face,

just make sure she got through things as they presented themselves to her. Not rushing.

'Really?' said Marina. 'If it was me, I'd be terrified.'

Imani laughed then. 'Yeah, that too.'

They went to work. Going over the words, using the script
Marina had written for her.

'You have to sound like who you are,' said Marina, 'who they
want you to be. You have to be convincing. You ever done any
acting?'

'Nativity plays at school,' said Imani. 'I think I was a shepherd once. Wore a tea towel and a dressing gown.'

'Well, this is a bit different. Let's do it again.'

They did it again, Marina playing the person from the
refuge. And the more they did it, the harder Marina tried to
make it for her. At first Imani just stopped talking, said that
what she was doing wasn't in the script. But as Marina
explained, there wasn't a script for the person on the other end
of the phone. All she had was Imani and her voice. And that
had to be convincing. 'You have to know who you are and why
you're calling. You have to be desperate. You have to be in fear
of your life.'

That was the part Imani had found the most difficult. She
spent such a large part of her life trying to be in charge, to make
sense of things, to appear competent and commanding, that to
behave in the opposite manner was totally against her instincts.
She said so.

'Lie,' said Marina. 'Come on, Imani, you encounter liars
every day. You sit there looking across the interview room table
knowing the person opposite is lying their arse off to you. So all
you have to do is take a bit of that on board.'

'I know, but . . . ' She hadn't found the right words of encouragement from Marina yet, the one phrase that would unlock
her reticence, show her the way forward.

'Be weak,' said Marina. 'Or appear weak. When he goes for it, when you're out there confronting him, bringing him in, you've got all the time in the world to be strong.'

That made sense. That was it. A couple more run-throughs and she was ready.

Now she sat in front of the phone, Marina at her side.

'Ready?'

Imani nodded.

'Go.'

Imani picked up the phone, made the call.

'Safe Haven.'

She hesitated as she had been coached to do. 'Hello? I . . . ' She brought a quaver into her voice, her breathing, like she was fighting tears. 'I need help.'

'I'm Alice. What can I do to help you?'

'My . . . I . . . my husband, he . . . ' And then she broke down. To her surprise, she found that she was actually crying real tears. This buoyed her. She kept going. 'My husband, he's . . . I think he's going to kill me.'

'Okay,' said Alice. 'What makes you say that?' Her voice calm, professional, yet warm too.

'He . . . hits me. For the slightest thing. When I'm late, when I'm . . . out. He says things to me, he's always angry with me . . . '

And on she went, finding her strength, her voice. Or the voice she was pretending to have. The more she talked, the easier it became. And the more convincing she felt she was.

Marina, listening in on the other line, knew it was working, gave her a thumbs-up in encouragement.

But Imani didn't need it. 'Please,' she sobbed into the phone, 'please. I just need . . . I need to get away. Please. You have to help me . . . '

On the other end of the phone Alice said, 'Would you like to come here?'

Imani's eyes lit up. But she kept in character. Didn't want to lose it now, in the final few lines. It would be like a survivor at the end of a disaster movie slipping and falling on the way to the helicopter.

'Yes,' she said. 'Yes please . . .'

'Right. Whereabouts are you?'

Imani told her the name of the place the team had agreed on, and a fake name. Alice gave her directions where to go to meet the car.

'How . . . how will I know it's the right car?'

'You'll need a password. Ask the driver for it. The password's clementine. You got that?'

Through her sobs, Imani said she had.

'We'll see you soon.'

She put the phone down. Sat back and breathed a huge sigh of relief. 'Jesus, that was hard work.'

'You did brilliantly,' said Marina.

Imani smiled. 'Lot harder than playing a shepherd.'

Marina laughed. More out of relief than anything.

Cotter re-entered the room. 'We on?' she asked.

Imani stood up. 'We are.'

69

He couldn't believe it. The first night back listening in and here it was. Perfect. *Perfect.*

He could have leapt up, danced round the room with joy, but he controlled himself. Because he wasn't finished. The Heartbreaker still had something important to do. He watched the screen again. Saw the number being called. When it was just about to be picked up, he intercepted.

'Hello?' he said, his most passive voice.

'Hi,' said the voice, 'it's Alice from Safe Haven. Is Jan there?'

'She's . . . just nipped out. Shouldn't be long. Can I help at all?' As non-threateningly as possible.

'Oh, we need someone picked up and she was on call tonight. Don't worry, I'll try someone else.'

'It's no problem. As I said, she shouldn't be long. I'll tell her you called. She'll only be a few minutes. Shall I take the details?'

'You sure it's no trouble?'

What did I just fucking say, you thick fucking bitch?

'Absolutely. No trouble at all. And she'll be there. She won't keep your new charge waiting.'

'Well, if you're sure . . . ' Alice gave out the information about where Jan was to go. 'And her name's Melanie.'

'Melanie, right.' Talking like he was writing this down. 'Same, what is it, password, secret word, whatever as last time?'

309

'Same one.'

'I'll let her know.'

He said his goodbyes and hung up.

Same password as last time . . . He laughed to himself. Alice obviously thought she was being clever by not giving out the password. But in fact all she had done was confirm it for him.

He stood up, stretched. Eager to get going, excited that at last he was back in action. And this time there would be no mistakes. No fuck-ups. This time he would do things properly.

70

Claire Lingard was sitting at the dining room table, having commandeered it as her home office desk, papers spread out in front of her. She hated the idea of having a home office, wanting to compartmentalise her working hours and her leisure hours, her family hours. But unfortunately there were times when she had no choice but to combine the two, and this was one of them. She disliked working from home at the best of times, and completing grant forms counted as one of the worst.

Her phone beeped beside her. Grateful for any distraction, she picked it up, checked the screen. A text message from Imani: *It's on.*

She put the phone down, looked at it. Should she reply? If so, what should she say? She didn't know the etiquette of this kind of operation. She picked the phone back up again, answered.

Keep me posted.

That should do it.

She put the phone back on the table, took a mouthful of wine, looked at it.

A murderer. An actual murderer. Preying on the kind of women she helped on a daily basis. She still couldn't quite get her head round it. A murderer. Not in a film or a book, but here. Real. In her life. She shook her head. Took another drink.

Maybe it shouldn't be so hard to believe, she thought.

Murders did happen. Some of the women she had worked with were testament to that. But that was always an enraged, maddened husband or partner. This was different. A deliberate killer choosing his victims, targeting them. Killing them. A Hannibal Lecter. Here. On her doorstep. That was the hard part to work out.

The door opened.

'Hiya.'

Keith. Back from working in one of the other flats. Rubbing his hands together, shaking the dust from his clothes.

'Not in here,' she said.

'Sorry,' he replied with an apologetic grin. 'I'll go to the bathroom.' He set off down the hall, stopped, turned, came back. 'Oh, by the way. Just to let you know, I'm popping out for a bit.'

'What, now?'

'Yeah,' he said, scratching the back of his neck, face pulled into an awkward expression. 'Call from Brendan. Needs a chat.'

She sat upright. 'Brendan? What's wrong?'

'Dunno. You know what he's like. Him and Cath having problems, probably. Just needs a sympathetic shoulder.' He gave a small laugh. 'Or at least an ear. He does most of the talking.'

'But ... didn't you see him the other day?'

'Yeah, I know, but ... ' He gave a helpless shrug. 'What can you do?' He turned away, began walking towards the bathroom once more.

'But you've had a drink,' Claire called after him. 'You won't be able to drive.'

'Just one glass of wine,' he said. 'A small one. With dinner.' He laughed. 'Officer.' He came back into the room. 'I'll be fine. Don't worry.'

He pulled on his jacket, kissed Claire on the forehead and left.

She looked at the door to the other flats, the ones he was renovating. Where he spent all his spare time. Doing them up, preparing them to rent out. Bring in a bit of money. Or if everything went to plan, a lot of money.

She nodded to herself. Then looked at her phone, back to the door. She gets that text, he leaves. Coincidence? Of course. Of course it was.

She kept looking at the door. Unable now to concentrate on the grant forms.

Had she ever seen the flats? The work Keith had done? No. Wait until they're finished, he'd said. See them all at once. She'd be impressed.

She kept staring at the door.

Just a coincidence, that was all. Just a stupid, ridiculous coincidence. Not Keith. Not her husband. Rubbish. She couldn't believe it. Didn't want to believe it. Because if that was the case, if he was . . .

No. He couldn't be. No.

On her doorstep . . .

Claire kept staring at the door.

71

'Where to this time?'

'Just out,' said Ellison, pulling on his coat. He turned to look at his wife, still in the same chair, the TV turned up as if she was deaf. He hated her. 'For Christ's sake, woman, what business is it of yours?'

'I'm your wife, Hugh. I should know where you're going. Every night it's like this. I have to sit here while you go out.'

'You don't have to sit there. You could get up and do something.'

'Other husbands take their wives out places. Other husbands ask their wives if there's anywhere they want to go and take them. Not you. Oh no. Out with your friends.' She gave a snort of derision. 'Friends.'

'Yeah, friends,' said Ellison, turning from the front door, walking back into the lounge. 'Work friends. Colleagues. That's the only way to move up in this job. Networking. You know that.'

'Oh yeah,' she said, almost standing. 'I know that. There was a time when you used to take me with you. When there were parties and nights out with other coppers and their wives. Remember them? I know all about networking.' She stared at him, a cruel, unhappy look in her eye. 'I know all about the kind of networking you do.'

Ellison felt his hands shaking. He stuck them in his pockets so he didn't do something with them that he would later regret. 'What are you talking about?' he mumbled. 'You're talking rubbish.'

'I know your networking. I know who your friends are. Networking on their backs, is that what they do? Your friends?'

He stood over her, hands itching to come out of his pockets. He had never hated any woman as much as he hated her.

'You're a miserable, ugly cunt. Go fuck yourself.'

She was too stunned to reply.

He turned and walked out.

Trying to feel good about himself, about how he had behaved and what he had said. Trying not to hear the tears coming from behind him.

72

The Moseley Road Baths was a historic landmark, looking more like a church than a swimming pool.

An ornate Gothic Renaissance building with terracotta stone, red bricks and an imposing bas-relief coat of arms over the main entrance, the baths had been standing for over a century and was part of the city's rich Victorian and Edwardian heritage. But it had seen better days. Some of the square leaded windows were broken; moss and mildew grew on the brickwork. If it had been in a more secluded setting rather than a main road in Balsall Heath, it would have made an imposing haunted house.

Imani stood in front of it, checked her watch. Ten fifteen. The car was late.

It had been a struggle to organise things so quickly without making the driver suspicious. If indeed it was the Heartbreaker. Operations like this were usually planned well in advance, with areas chosen only after risk assessments had been done, negotiations conducted with all departments and permission granted from on high. But the speed of this one meant that no such action could be taken.

They had done the best they could given the time they had. The Moseley Road Baths wasn't a bad location. Somewhere public, somewhere it would be possible to make a scene if things went wrong. Hopefully.

Imani stood by the bus shelter before the baths. She shivered, even though the night wasn't particularly cold. But it had started raining again. Pouring. She was glad of the shelter to keep her dry.

The rest of the team hadn't been so lucky.

They were secreted all about the area: the junction with Edward Road, Moseley Road itself, even the back alley opposite. With an armed response unit stationed nearby, waiting for the word. The cavalry. Avi Patel had been elected personal back-up. Out of all of them he had the most recent firearms training, so he was armed. He was across the road, hood up, sitting on the bench of the bus shelter opposite.

'Anything yet?'

Imani heard his voice in her ear. She was in radio contact with all of them, but they were trying not to use it in case the Heartbreaker was watching, saw her talking to herself and put two and two together.

She sighed. 'No,' she said, trying not to move her lips. 'I'd let you know if there was.'

'You sound like a ventriloquist,' he said, laughter in his voice.

'Get off the line, Avi,' she said. Not unkindly.

She waited.

Just because you can't hear them, she told herself after a while, *doesn't mean they're not there. Just because you can't see them doesn't mean they're not there.* Her team were close. She knew they were.

Knew it.

But that still didn't stop her from shaking.

She waited. A bus came along, stopped. She made no move to get on it. It pulled away again, the driver giving her a less than friendly look. She waited some more.

Two youths walked down the street, coming towards her. Hoods up, gangster roll. Probably in their teens, she thought. Sixth-form kids trying to look tough. They saw her.

Please, she thought, *please don't start anything. Please don't make me start anything . . .*

They approached the bus shelter. One of them, the taller of the two, eyed her up, letting his gaze wander all over her body. Instead of playing meek, like her body language was doing, as Marina had taught her, she hardened her stare in return. Gave them cop's eyes. They looked away. Kept walking.

Imani sighed.

But whatever relief she felt was cut short. Her phone rang.

Heart pounding, she pulled it from her coat pocket, answered it.

'H-hello?' Still keeping in character.

'Hi,' said a cheerful male voice. 'I'm your pickup. I'll be there shortly. Traffic's terrible tonight.'

'Oh,' she said, as non-committally as she could. 'Right. Thought you'd be a woman.'

'Couldn't come. Sent me instead. I'm her husband.' Then, before Imani could answer, 'You there? Outside the baths?'

'Yeah,' she said. 'I am.'

'Could you just cross the road for me, please?'

Her heart skipped a beat. 'What?'

'Sorry,' he said. 'I'm on my way but the traffic's been terrible, like I said. If you could meet me over the other side of the road, I'd much appreciate it.'

Imani looked round. No cars slowing or stopped. Just the hiss and swish of passing vehicles in the rain. She scanned the nearby streets. No sign of a parked car with someone in it, even hidden in shadow.

'What's . . . what's the password?' she asked.

'Oh,' he said. 'Clementine.'

She nodded, even though he couldn't see her. Or maybe he could.

'I'm genuine,' he said, and gave a little laugh.

318

She nodded once more, thinking. Was there something familiar about that voice? Had she heard it before? Coming over her mobile in the rain, it was hard to tell.

'So can you meet me over the road? It's not far to go.'

Imani looked over at Patel. He was standing up now, looking across at her. Aware that something was happening, waiting for an order. She felt good knowing he was there. Safe.

'Oh . . . okay. Where will you be?'

'You see straight over the road from where you are? There's a road. Lime Grove. Dead end, leads nowhere. I'll park down there. That way I can just scoot round and get you to the refuge quicker.'

She looked across the road. Lime Grove was a narrow, shadowed, tree-lined lane with an old redbrick building on the corner and industrial units behind. It was a dead end, like he had said, mainly used for fly-tipping. *Dead end,* she thought. *Only one way out.*

'Right,' she said. 'I'll be there.'

'Good. Don't worry, soon have you out of the cold and the wet.'

He hung up.

Imani looked round. Patel was ready to go, but she didn't want him to accompany her. Too suspicious. Too obvious. She didn't know what to do.

She heard Cotter's voice in her ear. 'Imani, what's happening?'

She didn't want to talk, to say anything aloud in case he was watching, in case he saw her lips moving and suspected a trap. She tried speaking with her mouth closed.

'Got to . . . move . . .'

'Move, move where? Was that him, Imani?'

'Yeah.'

'Where do you have to move to? Tell me, Imani.'

319

'Just ... round the corner ...' She picked up her phone again, called Claire. Just to check that protocol was being followed. That there was no chance her driver would change the pickup spot.

Engaged.

She tried the refuge. Same story.

'Imani? What's happening?' Cotter again.

'Got to go over the road,' she said. 'Meet him there. Get Patel to cover me, follow from a distance.'

Without waiting for a reply, she picked up her bag, stepped into the road.

73

Sperring stood up. He had been crouching behind a railing at the side of the Moseley Road Baths. He had heard everything that was happening.

'Ian,' said Cotter.

'Here, ma'am.'

'On my signal, get ready to move. Imani's gone down Lime Grove. Wait a few seconds, then we follow. I'm not going to delay any longer. We can't have him driving her away.'

'He's changed the plan already,' Sperring said. 'Made her more vulnerable.'

'I'm well aware of that, thank you,' she said.

He heard her next call, to Patel. 'DC Patel. Go after her now.'

'Right, ma'am. She's just gone down the street. Lost visual contact with her.'

'Then go. I'll call the backup team, get them in place. Stop him from coming out.'

Sperring watched as Patel walked away from the bus stop and, moving as quickly as he could without drawing attention to himself, slipped down the darkened side street.

'Right, DS Sperring. Go. Now.'

Sperring made to cross the road but didn't make it. Another bus hove into view, slowed in front of him, stopped.

'Christ,' he said, ducking to the side of it.

Checking for traffic, visibility cut down because of the rain and the dark, he crossed the road. He was just at the entrance to the lane when he heard a sound. It could have been a car backfiring, but he knew exactly what it was.

Then he heard it again.

'Shots fired . . .' he shouted, and ran as fast as his overweight frame would take him.

A car screeched towards him, headlights on full, temporarily blinding him, making him stop, put an arm to his face. He moved to one side but the car did the same. To the other side; the car followed him once more.

He threw himself into a metal railing and the car sailed past him. Rounded a corner and away, before it reached the main road.

He watched it go, trying to make out the registration number. The rain and the dark stopped him. Plus the fact that it had been obscured by something – mud, or paint.

He looked round. At the far end of the lane there was a lump on the ground. Not the usual mattress or full bin bags that got dumped. He knew what the shape was immediately. He ran towards it.

'Get an ambulance,' he called, 'now.'

As he spoke, he hoped it wasn't too late.

The body of Avi Patel lay there, the life bleeding out of him.

PART SIX

HEARTS TO HEARTS

74

Phil was awoken by a knock on his front door. Not the bell; a knock.

His first thought: *Marina. She's back.*

He got quickly out of bed, pulled on his dressing gown, made his way downstairs. Then stopped, halfway down. Through the bevelled, coloured half-glass of the front door he could see a silhouette, and it wasn't Marina.

The small amount of hope he had been holding in his heart dissipated immediately and he resumed his downward journey, trudging now, in no hurry to answer.

Another knock.

Better not be UKIP canvassers, he thought. He was in just the mood to let them know what he thought of them.

He stopped again. What if it was the woman who had called before, the one claiming to be Fiona Welch?

Looking round, he tried to find a weapon. Couldn't see anything.

Another knock. Accompanied by a voice this time: 'DI Brennan . . . '

He relaxed. Not Fiona Welch.

He made his way down, opened the door. There stood DCI Cotter.

'Morning, ma'am,' he said, defensiveness creeping into his voice. 'To what do I owe this pleasure?'

Cotter looked directly at him. He saw the strain on her face, the dark circles beneath her eyes. He took in her rumpled, creased clothes. It didn't look like she had slept in them. It looked like she had been too busy for that.

'Can I come in?' she said.

He stood aside, let her in. Closed the door behind her.

'Coffee, please,' she said once inside, and Phil, unquestioningly, went into the kitchen and put the kettle on. He emptied the cafetière of the previous day's grounds, filled it once more.

'Black,' she said. 'And strong.'

He told her to go and sit in the living room, busied himself in the kitchen. He had slept well. His body and mind were fizzing with misplaced energy after the interview with Adderley, the accidental meeting with Marina. He had thought of using alcohol to help him relax, as he had the previous nights, but decided against it. Instead, he had gone for a run, pounded the streets of Moseley, earthing all that muscular and mental electricity as he went. He had returned home exhausted but strangely refreshed. He had eaten a decent meal – not takeaway junk – and listened to a couple of Band of Horses CDs. After that, sleep had come relatively easily.

Coffee made, he took two mugs into the living room. Cotter placed hers on a side table, barely glancing at the design on the mug: Hammer Films' *Countess Dracula*. A little in-joke between himself and Marina.

He took a mouthful of coffee, found it too hot, put it down. He waited for Cotter to speak.

'I'll come straight to the point,' she said eventually, her voice sounding as worn out as she looked.

Phil waited once more.

Cotter almost laughed. 'I can't believe I'm about to say this to you, DI Brennan.'

DI Brennan. Not Phil. That didn't sound good.

She took a mouthful of coffee. Liked it. Took another one. Replaced the mug. 'I've . . . got a proposition for you.'

Phil imagined the worst. This was obviously some way to get him to leave quietly, without any fuss. A way of brushing his recent behaviour under the departmental carpet, avoiding any unwelcome or difficult questions. Hush money. Or at least a hush pension.

'Go on,' he said.

'I . . . want you to come back.'

Phil wasn't sure he had heard her correctly. 'You . . . what?'

'I want you back.'

'In the department? MIS?'

She nodded. 'Yes. Well, need you back would be more accurate.'

'I thought Imani was in charge?'

Cotter looked at him levelly, holding his gaze for an uncomfortable length of time, then glancing away.

'What's happened?'

She looked up once more. 'This investigation needs a new CIO. I want it to be you again.'

'What?'

'Just what I said.' She was snapping, her voice rising in anger. She sat back, composing herself. 'Sorry. Lack of sleep.'

'What . . . what's happened?'

Cotter sighed, took another mouthful of coffee.

Told him.

'Twenty-four hours,' said Cotter. 'That's it. No more, no less.'

Phil sat back in his armchair, coffee long gone cold. He had listened to everything Cotter had said, made no comment, taken it all in. And now this. He still said nothing.

Cotter waited for his response.

'The Assistant Chief Constable wasn't happy,' she said, by

way of explanation. 'And that's putting it mildly. After everything that's happened in the last few days, with you, with DC Oliver, with DC Patel . . . ' She sighed. 'It was a tough ask. I had to go out on a limb for you. He only did this grudgingly. After that, it's handed over to another team and they can start afresh. And no doubt we'll be tainted throughout the West Midlands. Untouchable.'

Phil nodded, eventually spoke.

'Why?' he said.

'Because it's been one cock-up after another,' she said.

'No,' he said, leaning forward. 'Why did you go out on a limb for me? Why d'you need me back so soon, so badly? Why me?'

'Because you're good. Because you know the case. Or part of it, and it won't take you long to come up to speed on the rest.' She leaned forward also, her coffee forgotten. 'I need you on this. And I need an answer quickly.' Seeing he didn't speak straight away, she sat back again. 'Twenty-four hours for you to come up with something. To break the case. That's all. Then it's taken off our hands. For good.'

Phil smiled. 'So, damned if I do, damned if I don't, is that it?'

Cotter reddened. 'It was the best I could do, under the circumstances.'

He thought some more. 'And . . . Marina. She was the one who asked you about this? About me?'

'She suggested you, yes. She saw you yesterday. Talked to you.'

Phil neither confirmed nor contradicted her words.

'Can you work with her?'

'I've always managed to do so in the past,' he said.

'I mean can you work with her now,' said Cotter, irritation and exasperation taking over her voice, 'after everything that's happened recently between you?'

328

Phil shrugged. Aimed for nonchalant; didn't know if he'd managed it. 'If she doesn't have a problem, then I don't either.'

Cotter looked relieved. She reached for her mug, realised the coffee had turned cold and the colour of a dredged canal. Left it where it was. She stood up.

'So,' she said. 'Shall I wait for you?'

'What?'

'You're giving the morning briefing. We've got to go.'

Phil stood too. He was trying to keep his face as blank as possible, devoid of emotion, but inside it was a different story. He was squirming, champing at the bit to be going.

He was ready for the front line again.

75

He'd *known* it. Known it was too good to be true. Or should have known, should have suspected at least.

He'd recognised her voice. Not entirely, not enough to turn and run, just enough to proceed warily, with caution. As soon as he'd called her, as soon as she spoke, he felt something wasn't right. He should have just turned then, driven away, tried another night. But he had stuck with it. The need, the hunger inside him had been so strong that he couldn't fight it. It went far beyond desire, anything so rational as that. He *craved* another victimised woman, had to have her, no matter what.

No matter what.

Now he looked down at the bed where Imani Oliver lay stretched out. He had secured her wrists and ankles at each corner of the bed, spread-eagling her body tightly over the metal mesh frame as he had done with all the others. She wouldn't be going anywhere.

After securing her, he had begun cutting off her clothes. At the start, embarking on this course of action, it had been something that had to be done, an expedient task. But as time had gone on, this part of his work had taken on aspects of the ritual, become a mini-ritual in its own right, even.

First the top half, the scissors – huge and sharp, dressmaker's scissors – gliding smoothly through the fabric like an ocean-going liner through a becalmed sea. Sliding all the way from neck to waist, shoulder to wrist. Then repeated again for the bottom half, waist to ankle. Then the clothing removed, folded and destroyed. Like her old shell, her old identity, being removed, revealing the real person, the woman he wanted to see, beneath.

She was naked, yes, but that didn't mean he was going to do anything sexual to her. Play with her, anything like that. He wasn't some creepy pervert, doing this because he enjoyed it, derived some twisted pleasure from it, he told himself as he cut. This was work. It had a purpose. And yes, he would look at her naked body lying there when he had finished, and yes, he would feel some arousal within himself at what he saw. But that was obvious, to be expected. He was a red-blooded heterosexual male. It was only natural. That didn't mean he would do anything about it. He wasn't an animal.

He had gagged her, too. Not that he thought anyone could hear – the soundproofing on the walls should have seen to that – but it wasn't worth taking the chance. Besides, he had left the first couple of women without their gags and couldn't bear the absolute drivel that came out of their mouths. So the gag it was.

He stared at her, ignoring the growing erection he could feel in his trousers, focusing his mind on the body before him. But he couldn't stop himself from travelling back to the previous night, going over what had happened once again, trying to work out what had gone wrong and how he could put it right.

He should have just driven away. As soon as he saw that policewoman walking towards his car, he should have just turned and gone. But he hadn't. And he knew why. He had thought about it enough times. At first, he was ashamed to admit, he had sat there unable to move, paralysed by indecision. If he drove off, she might see him, recognise him. If he stayed where he was, he ran the risk of her having already identified him. So he did nothing. Waited.

But he had learned something from his previous attempt. He had come to this meeting armed. An untraceable gun. There were gangs all over Birmingham. Easy enough to get if you knew which pub to go into, who to ask. That had been simple. And the other thing he had with him had been just as simple to obtain, in its own way. An electric stun gun. Easy. Bought from a mail order company in America, no questions asked. Sent to a false American address, then forwarded on to him. People offered that service. Again, if you knew the right people to talk to.

What he held in his hand as Imani Oliver approached looked like a large door handle. He waited until she came right up to the car before extending his hand and pressing the trigger. One point two million volts coursed through her, changing her expression from near triumph – she had recognised him and was about to speak, alert the rest of the team – to extreme agony.

Then he had to move fast. He was out of the car, catching her prone body, bundling her into the back seat. And that should have been that. But as he got back behind the wheel, his heart froze. Another police officer was running straight towards him.

He had reacted so fast it was like he hadn't thought at all. He picked up the gun from the passenger seat, leaned out of the window and fired at the approaching figure. Once. Twice. Three times. The man spun round, twisted and dropped. He didn't want to waste any more time. Throwing the gun down beside him, he drove away as fast as he could. Avoiding the main road in case there were more of them, taking the side streets like he had planned, until he was away and free.

It was only when he got back to the flats, running on adrenalin, that reptilian part of his brain having taken over, that he stopped to think. Had he just killed a man? An innocent man? Well, a police officer, but still. Someone who had no business to be there, who wasn't part of his plan. And he had sat there in the car, Oliver still out of it in the back seat, and wondered why he wasn't feeling the remorse, the doubt, the guilt he had expected to. He felt nothing, didn't even need to rationalise his actions to his conscience. Collateral damage, he had thought. Either wounded or dead, that was all he was. A necessary casualty for the greater good. *His* greater good. If he hadn't been there trying to interfere, he would still be alive. But he had been and he wasn't. So that was that. And yes, he had decided, that was something he could live with.

He stared down at the body on the bed once more. Wondered what to do next. She had come round a couple of times but he had successfully stunned her once more. Now she lay there staring at him, eyes wide in terror, pleading silently. Would the ritual still work? Even though she wasn't who she had claimed to be? Could the programming still be done? He didn't know. He would have to wait and see.

He stared at her some more. Tried to form answers in his head. Something came. He smiled. Why not? he thought. Why not give it a go? If she wasn't in that state of release to begin with, he would just have to work harder to put her there. Why not treat it as a challenge and relish it? He nodded. Yes. That's what he would do. It wasn't perfect. But he would give it his best shot. Whatever happened, things would work out better than the last one.

But that was something to look forward to later. There were things he had to do first.

He looked down at the prone woman. Smiled. Knelt beside her.

'Soon,' he said, whispering close to her ear. She tried to pull away but he ignored her. 'Soon.'

333

Then he stood up, and, mask in place once more, left the room.

Imani Oliver would keep. She wasn't going anywhere.

Ever again.

76

'It's good to be back,' said Phil, scanning the tired, drawn faces before him. 'Just wish it was under better circumstances.'

He looked round the room. It felt like an age had passed since he was last there. But it also felt like no time at all. He glimpsed Marina standing off to the side, slightly apart from the group, not wanting to be directly in his eyeline. He felt his stomach turn over, those familiar pangs once more. Tried to rationalise: she was his wife. The woman he'd shared his life with until recently. Why was he so nervous about being in her presence? He looked at the other faces again. No time to think about Marina now. This was work. And he had to treat it as such.

Apart from that private bubble of tension between him and Marina, in the rest of the team weariness was competing with tension.

'You don't need me to tell you what's happened,' he said. 'Or who we've lost. I know how you're feeling. But we have to pick ourselves up and carry on. These next twenty-four hours are crucial. For us, for Imani, for catching whoever did this. And I appreciate how tired you all are. But we still have to keep going. Right.'

He looked round once more. His words seemed to have perked them up. A little, at any rate.

'Also,' he said, that familiar tension once more creeping into his voice, 'we have the services of Marina Esposito for a few days longer. She'll be staying on to help us catch him.' He looked at her, wanting to say more but unsure what those words would be. She caught his eye; contact flared, then she turned away. He did likewise.

'Right. Let's get on with it. We need to move as quickly as possible. I appreciate you've all been doing that while I was sleeping, so let's have some updates. Where are we? Ian?'

'Preliminary ballistics report says it was a Glock automatic,' said Sperring. 'They're seeing if it's been used before for anything, but they're quite common among the gangs. The gangster's handgun of choice.'

'You think he's a gang member?' asked Phil.

'No,' said Sperring. 'But they also supply guns. Would be relatively simple for him to buy one off them.'

'Right. Time to get the confidential informants out. See if anyone's heard anything about someone buying a gun, or being seen with gang members when they don't look like they belong.' He paused. 'How many shots were heard?'

'Three,' said Sperring. 'And Patel had three shots in him. He's currently fighting for his life in hospital.'

'So we can assume – dangerous word – that Imani wasn't shot. He got her into the car some other way. I suppose, until we learn otherwise, we should be grateful for that. What about forensics from the scene? Anything?'

'Not yet,' said Cotter. 'The rain took care of most of it. The teams are still out looking, though.'

Phil nodded.

Sperring pushed himself away from the desk he had been leaning against. 'We've been looking for the car all over the city. Uniforms, patrols, everyone's been informed. A description's gone out, CCTV checks, the lot. So far we've come up with nothing. He was clever. Changed the location to what we thought was a dead end. Except there was another way out through that industrial estate and he knew it. Sneaky bastard. I saw the car but didn't get the make and model of it. It looked like a saloon, a Toyota Avensis, something like that. But I wouldn't want to say. And the registration plates were obscured too. There were dents along the side, though, so that makes me think it was the same car used to run down Janine Gillen.'

'Same guy, then,' said Phil. 'Not much doubt about that.'

'I don't think we'd be jumping to conclusions to think that,' said Sperring. 'The car was last seen heading towards the Kings Heath area. We're getting uniforms to concentrate their search there. See if it's been stashed, garaged, whatever.'

Phil nodded. 'Good. Thanks, Ian.' A thought struck him. 'Isn't that where this refuge is? Kings Heath?'

'It is,' said Cotter.

'Well, forgive me if this has already been done, but shouldn't we be looking into people there? See if there's any chance one of them was involved? Or even behind it?'

'We are looking into it,' said Cotter. 'We can't rule anything – or anyone – out at this stage. We called them and asked who was on duty for pickups last night. Someone called Jan Melville. The refuge called her and spoke to a bloke who said he was her husband. Said he would give Jan the message.'

'Let me guess,' said Phil. 'Jan Melville doesn't have a husband.'

'Exactly,' said Cotter. 'Claire Lingard's been great at helping us, but I think now's the time to look a bit harder at the rest of them.'

'What about Lingard's husband?' said Phil. 'The marriage counsellor. Would it be worth talking to him again?'

'I've turned up something about him,' said Elli, blushing as she spoke. The whole room turned towards her. 'DS Sperring asked me to look into his background.'

337

Phil looked at Sperring, frowned.

'I found out that he'd come into property a few years ago,' said Sperring. 'Some dispute about how he got it. Just thought on the grounds of that he might be worth another look. With everything that's been going on, it got pushed to the back burner.'

'Fair enough,' said Phil. 'What did you find, Elli?'

'Keith Bailey's not his real name. Well it is, but he used to be known as Michael Bailey. Keith's his middle name. He started using it after university. That's why it took so long to find this out. He's originally from Manchester. There was something when he was at university in Hull. An allegation of date rape. Well, two, actually. Nothing was proved, only alleged, and no charges were ever brought. That's it, really.'

'Nothing else in his background?' asked Phil. 'Sexual assault, robbery, anything like that?'

'Nothing,' said Elli. 'Well, nothing directly involving him.'

'What d'you mean?'

'Again, more digging,' said Elli. 'When he was a child in Manchester he was taken into care repeatedly. Abuse in the family.'

'Father?' asked Phil.

'Not according to this,' said Elli, pointing to the screen. 'Mother. Pretty bad stuff, too.'

The atmosphere in the room changed. A crackle in the air. The team were still tired, but a mental adrenalin and caffeine shot had just been administered.

'So how does a suspected rapist get to work as a marriage counsellor?' said Sperring. 'That's like Jimmy Savile working with school kids.'

'Which he did do,' said Phil. 'Bad analogy.'

'Person of interest?' asked Cotter.

'I'll go and see him today,' said Phil.

'I'd like to come too,' said Marina. 'Get a psychologist's view.'

Phil looked at her, not knowing whether to be excited or nervous. He was aware that Cotter was watching him, waiting for his response, so he continued. 'Good,' he said. 'Let's do it. But let's not jump to conclusions. Look what happened to me when I did that recently.'

'Can I say something before we all go?' asked Cotter.

Phil gestured that the floor was hers.

'Just before the briefing I heard that Detective Constable Avi Patel has died. They tried, he fought to hold on, but ...' Cotter looked close to tears. 'I know he wasn't with us long, but he was one of us. And he didn't deserve that. None of us deserve that. Will you join me in a minute's silence for our fallen colleague, please.'

They did so.

When it was over, Phil looked round the room. He noticed that plenty of eyes were glistening.

'Come on,' he said. 'Cases like this are solved by footwork. Paperwork. Database work. But by teamwork above all. We've taken big losses. We've got one of our own down and another out there. The clock's ticking. Let's find that bastard.'

77

Imani opened her eyes. Everywhere hurt.

All she could see was ceiling. Dark and soft, a single bulb hanging from a cord. It hurt to move her neck, but she did so. Plastic sheeting on the floor. Stained. She looked to the side. Walls similar to the ceiling: thick padding with soft peaks. No windows. She realised what it was: soundproofing. Her heart skipped at that, panic racing through her body.

She tried to calm down, think logically as she had been trained to. She looked round once more. Took in her surroundings, herself. She was naked. That much she knew. Could feel cold air on her body, making her shiver. She felt vulnerable. Alone and afraid.

She pulled on her arms, testing her bindings. Firm. No give at all. Metal handcuffs, chains. She managed another look round. She was secured to an old metal bed frame. Solid, heavy. She tried jumping her body up from it. No movement. Secured to the floor. She felt uncomfortable. Metal chain link digging into her back. Tried to move away from it. No good. She was tied too tight.

She tried to shout, but whatever she had been gagged with, something hard and unyielding, was too tight for her. No sound would come, just little whimpers at the corners of her mouth. She hoped she wouldn't vomit, because that would be that. She didn't need to worry about him; she would just choke to death.

She closed her eyes, tried to focus on her breathing, concentrate.

Don't panic, don't panic, don't panic . . .

Think, Imani, think. How did she get here? The car. Walking towards it. A flash of recognition as she saw the driver and . . .

Nothing. A searing pain in her chest, her whole torso, like something simultaneously sharp and painful yet dull and probing had been forced into her body, reaching bone deep and shaking her until she passed out. She surmised what that had been. Electricity. Some kind of stun gun.

She had woken up again later, felt the same kind of impact when she tried to move. And then finally here. Wherever 'here' was.

But she knew who he was. *She knew who he was.*

And that knowledge was both satisfying and dangerous. Because she wanted to let the rest of the team know – needed to let the rest of the team know – but couldn't. And because she knew what was coming next. She had seen the other bodies. It was only a matter of time.

Don't panic, don't panic, don't panic . . .

Calm. Calm. Think. Think.

She couldn't scream, couldn't move. What could she do? Smell. She did so, analysing the contents of the room. Not good. Human waste, only to be expected. But something else. Like old copper. A butcher's shop smell. Dried blood. Dead flesh. No, not a butcher's shop. An abattoir.

Oh God . . .

Think. Think.

He had been furious when he realised who she was and had administered a severe beating. On and on it went, like he wanted to just keep hitting her. The rage in his eyes horrific. Even worse to be on the end of. She knew it was just because he had been duped, but a beating administered out of desperation and

341

anger was still a beating, and in her shocked state her body had taken about as much as she could bear before it collapsed, her mind shutting down again too.

And waking up once more to find herself here. Alone.

She listened. Nothing.

She pulled at her wrists again. They wouldn't budge, the metal cuffs too tight.

She had to get out, she had to—

Avi. Oh God, Avi . . .

She remembered then what had happened to him. She had heard the gunshots from inside the car, sounding like a sonic boom up close. Glimpsed his body jerk, spin and fall. No time to scream, shout. Warn him. Her body closing down, pain-addled from the stun gun. She had passed out then.

She just hoped he was okay. That someone had called an ambulance, got him to the hospital in time. That someone had saved him.

She pulled harder on her metal cuffs. Got only a pain in her wrists. She lay back on the metal frame, sighed. She wondered how many women had died on this bed. Been tortured, hurt, had their hearts removed . . .

Stop it. *Stop it.* That wasn't helping. *Concentrate. Come on. Focus. Don't lost it, don't . . .*

Think. The team. Cotter. Sperring. One of them. All of them.

She prayed that someone had worked out who had taken her, where she was. That they were coming for her now. She felt her spirits rise at the thought.

She clung on to that thought as she lay there. Desperately, as if her life depended on it.

Because she couldn't think about the alternative.

She really, really couldn't think about that.

78

Phil and Marina drove in silence. Not because they had nothing to say to each other but because they had too much.

Phil pulled the Audi in to the kerb in front of the Relate offices.

'How appropriate,' said Marina.

Phil was unsure whether she was joking.

He locked the car; they walked towards the centre. Still neither of them spoke. As soon as they entered, Phil felt something change within him. He didn't know if Marina was feeling it but reckoned she probably was. A dropping-away of professionalism. A sense of the true function of the place. It wasn't lost on either of them.

They walked to the desk. The woman sitting behind it smiled. Tolerantly, putting them at ease. Phil introduced himself.

'DI Brennan to see Keith Bailey, please.' He showed his warrant card.

The receptionist's eyebrows raised. 'Oh,' she said. 'I thought you were a couple. Sorry.'

Neither of them spoke.

'D'you have an appointment?'

'We don't,' said Phil. 'But it's important.'

Realisation began to dawn in the woman's eyes. 'The police have been in to see him a couple of times already this week.' She was frowning, thinking the worst.

Phil headed off her thoughts by giving her what he thought was a disarming smile. 'Just routine. If you could . . . '

'Yes,' she said. She checked a register in front of her. 'I'm afraid he's busy with a client at the moment.' She gestured to a room behind them. 'Would you like to wait?'

They did so, sitting down on two spectacularly uncomfortable chairs. Still they didn't speak. Phil looked round the room. Shelves full of books, all on the subject of healing relationships. Coping with infidelity. Sexual problems. Keeping relationships together. Marina was also looking.

'Nothing about being hounded by a homicidal woman,' she said.

Phil didn't reply.

At his side was a large hard-bound scrapbook. He picked it up, opened it. It was full of handwritten letters and testimonials. He flicked through them, read a few. All told variations of the same story. They stated the gratitude couples and individuals felt for the counselling they'd received. How their relationships, their lives, even, had been saved. All of them, over and over, pages and pages. Some with more detail than others. All the same outcome.

Marina looked also. 'Like online reviews,' she said. 'They only put the good ones up.'

Phil looked at her. Properly, for the first time that day. She was almost smiling but it was a tight, controlled smile. 'Cynic,' he said.

'Oh, come on,' she said. 'You're the same as me. You don't like counsellors either. Isn't it always the people who are most messed up who decide to be life coaches?'

'But this seems to work,' he said, gesturing towards the book. 'Counselling.'

'Yes,' she said. 'I'm not saying it doesn't. But there are other ways.'

Phil didn't answer. 'The receptionist mistook us for a couple in trouble,' he said eventually.

'Not much of a mistake,' said Marina.

Something dark shuddered through Phil at her words. 'Is that what we are?' he said. 'In trouble?'

Marina looked at him. Straight in the eyes. Her gaze was completely naked, nothing hidden. 'What d'you think?'

'I asked first.'

She shook her head.

'Just answer,' he said. 'Please.'

'I think . . . we've got things to talk about. Things we need to talk about.' She looked at him, waited for his answer.

He thought. 'We've got a problem. But it's not the usual kind that couples have.'

'No. But it's still a problem. It still stops us from being together.'

'Does it?' Phil turned to her. His voice more intense, urgent. 'Because it needn't. We're stronger together. You know that. Why can't you see that?'

Marina was facing him fully now, voice also hushed but intense. 'You want to do this now? Really? Here and now?'

'We have to do it some time. We can't keep ignoring it. If we've got to work together, we should at least know where we stand with each other.'

Marina shook her head. Said nothing.

'You think this is good?' asked Phil. 'A good way for us to live? To bring up our daughter?'

'Well, it's better than pretending nothing's the matter, isn't it? That we don't have a crazed psychopath just lurking around somewhere, waiting to attack us, to . . . I don't know, kill us? Kill our daughter? We don't know who she is. Or what she wants. So I'm not taking any chances.'

Phil nodded. 'So that's it. Do her work for her, yeah? Split us up. Make us miserable.' He leaned in even closer. 'Have you ever stopped to think that this might be what she wants? The two of us at each other's throats, separated. It would be so easy for her to move in, don't you think? Do whatever she's going to do.'

Marina said nothing. Phil continued.

'You can't live your life like this. Neither of us can. We have to—'

A throat being cleared. They both looked up.

Keith Bailey was standing there watching them. They didn't know how long he had been there. Long enough, Phil imagined.

'Detective Inspector Brennan?' he asked.

'Er, yes . . . ' Phil stood up.

'You wanted to see me?'

'Yes, I . . . I did.'

He looked at Marina. 'And this is?'

'Marina Esposito,' said Marina, also standing.

'You're not police.'

'I'm working with the police. Psychologist.'

Bailey's eyebrows raised. He smiled. 'Really?'

Phil looked round the waiting room. 'Could we go somewhere . . . '

'Of course,' said Bailey. 'Please follow me.'

They did so.

Neither looking at the other as they went.

79

Keith Bailey ushered them into a room, closed the door behind them. It had two easy chairs facing a third, a small table with a box of paper tissues. He gestured for Phil and Marina to sit in the two chairs. He took the single one. Crossed his legs. Looked at them.

'Now,' he said, concerned, 'what can I do for you? Is it about Janine? Have you found her killer?'

Phil started. 'We just have a few questions, Mr Bailey.'

Keith Bailey frowned, confused. 'What about?'

Phil ignored the question. 'Where were you last night, Mr Bailey?'

Bailey looked between the pair of them, mouth open in surprise. Phil's features were impassive, Marina's likewise. Something she had picked up from her husband as they had worked together over the years.

'Erm . . . At home.'

'All night?' Phil.

'Yes.'

'And could your wife confirm this?' Marina this time, leaning forward.

'Yes, she could,' said Bailey, then, in a louder voice, 'Can you tell me what this is about, please?'

'So,' continued Phil, taking out his phone, 'if we were to ring your wife right now, she would confirm that?'

Bailey, still looking between the two of them, relented. 'I ... did pop out to see a friend. Brendan. Brendan Hewson. He's got a bit of trouble with his ... Well, let's just say that when you're a marriage counsellor, your friends always seem to be asking for advice. Rather like a GP, I suppose.'

'Your friend Brendan.'

Bailey nodded.

Phil held up his phone once more. 'And if I were to call him now?'

Bailey looked confused, and slightly scared. 'He'd confirm what I said.'

'He would?'

'Yes. Can you tell me what this is about, please?' Angry now.

Phil replaced his phone. 'I'll need his full name and address,' he said.

'I'll write it down for you.' Another look between the two of them. Neither of them returned it.

Phil was finding it hard to disengage from the conversation he had been having with Marina in the waiting room. But he was trying not to bring his personal baggage into his work and hoping he had succeeded. A quick glance at Marina. She was giving nothing away.

He kept going. Ploughing on through his questions. 'What kind of car d'you drive, Mr Bailey?'

'A Toyota. Avensis. Why?'

Phil stiffened, sat back. Beside him Marina did the same. Bailey looked between the pair of them.

'It's off the road at the moment,' he said. 'In the garage for repairs. Been there a while now.'

'How did you get to work, then?' Marina asked.

'My wife gave me a lift as far as the bus stop. Public transport the rest of the way.'

'Can we check with the garage, Mr Bailey?' Phil again.

Bailey looked at them both once more. Eyelids fluttering like a caged bird's wings. 'Can you tell me what this is about, please? I've asked you four times.'

'Keeping count?' asked Phil. 'It concerns the murder of a police officer and the abduction of another.'

Bailey tried to answer; Marina jumped in. 'And the abductions and murders of several vulnerable young women. Including at least one you had a connection with.'

Again he looked between the two of them. Settled on Marina, since she was the last to have spoken.

'You're a psychologist, is that right?' he asked.

Marina looked surprised at the question. 'Yes,' she said.

'What kind?'

'The criminal kind.'

'Oh.' Bailey looked surprised, then gave a tight smile. 'And are you here to psychoanalyse me?'

Marina kept her face still, stony. She leaned forward very slightly. 'I don't know. Are you a criminal?'

Bailey laughed. It seemed to break the tension in the room for him. 'Very funny. Good.'

'Are you going to answer the question?' asked Marina.

'Which question?'

'Your car,' said Phil.

'Oh, that.' Bailey sat back, scrutinising them once more. 'In the garage. I said.' Getting angry.

'I know you said that. So can we check with—'

Bailey cut Phil off. 'Of course.' He turned back to Marina. Pointed. 'You interest me,' he said. 'You being here. I didn't think this kind of thing happened outside of TV dramas.'

Marina ignored his words. 'What made you become a counsellor, Mr Bailey? A marriage counsellor in particular?'

Bailey smiled. 'Because I'm good at it,' he said.

'Are you?' asked Marina.

349

'Yes,' he said, warming to the theme. 'I am. Or at least I like to think so.'

'How did you find out that you were good at it? At advising people about their marriages? What made you go into it? Was there a specific incident? Some trigger?'

Phil sat back, didn't interrupt. Let her go.

Bailey gave a self-effacing shrug. 'I . . . It was just something I was always good at. Friends were always telling me their problems. I must have that kind of face. I was always sought out.' He laughed. 'Sought. Funny word, that, isn't it?'

'And an interesting choice, too,' said Marina. 'Implies that you had all the answers. Your friends had all the questions.'

He smiled. *What can I say?* Still trying to be self-effacing, but his body language spoke the words for him.

'Because,' continued Marina, 'most people come to do this kind of thing through personal experience. A bad marriage, rough relationship. A counsellor helped them, inspired them to retrain. Happens with Samaritans too. Nurses, even. An involved response. But you're not saying that. Your motivation was because you were good at it.'

'Yes. What's wrong with that?'

Marina nodded, as if his words confirmed her theories. 'Dare I say it, that's quite an arrogant thing to believe, don't you think?'

Whatever traces of affability had been on Bailey's face dried up. He stared at her. He didn't get the chance to respond. Phil spoke first.

'So let me get this straight. Your friends were coming to see you for advice about relationships,' he said, as innocuously as possible.

'That's right. Nothing wrong with that.' Bailey sounded hurt.

'Nothing at all,' said Phil. 'But I just want to be clear. Was this before or after the rape allegations?'

Bailey froze. Stared.

Phil kept at him. 'Before or after? Just clarifying.'

'You've done your homework.' A small, dry voice.

'We have. University, wasn't it? Hull? Not just once. I mean, once and it could have – possibly – been swept away as a misunderstanding. Possibly. But twice? Two allegations? From different women? That's more than just coincidence, don't you think? That seems to me like a pattern emerging.' He turned to Marina. Making eye contact with her fully for the first time since they had entered the room. 'What would you say? Your professional opinion?'

Marina nodded. 'A pattern, definitely.'

Bailey still said nothing, just stared.

Phil continued. 'So what happened? What turned this fledgling, wannabe rapist into someone doling out relationship advice.'

'*Sought* for relationship advice,' Marina said.

'Thank you,' said Phil, making eye contact with her once more, 'Sought. What happened?'

Bailey still stared.

80

Hugh Ellison stared at his desk. The room seemed smaller and shabbier than ever.

He was finding it hard to concentrate. He knew he shouldn't be there. Somewhere else had a stronger call on him. The investigation into Gemma Adderley's death. That was where he should be.

That was his chance. His last chance, possibly, to be taken seriously, to get back on the ladder. If he could have just managed to squeeze a confession out of Roy Adderley, got him to admit what he had done, he would have been happy. Not just happy, vindicated. That would have shown the higher-ups what he was made of. That he didn't deserve to be stuck in this backwater, that he should be out and about, in MIS, high-flying with the other high-flyers. That was what he should have done. And it had been playing on his mind all morning.

Even if Adderley hadn't done it. Didn't matter. That wasn't the point. There was circumstantial evidence, a false statement He could have worked on that, built it up. For Christ's sake, the CPS had brought things to trial that had a much slimmer chance of a conviction.

But no. The case had been taken off him. Given to the golden boys. And girls. His stomach curdled at the thought. Bile rising. *And girls.*

Brennan had got Adderley to confess to his girlfriend's

murder but not his wife's. Well, great for Brennan. But Ellison should have been in the room with him. He should have been the one to get him to open up. To take the acclaim for that.

And then there was Brennan's wife. But that was a whole other part of his mind. He pushed her away from his thoughts: that wasn't what this was about.

But it was hard to do. He'd seen the way she had looked at him when he walked into their offices yesterday. They way all those bitches had looked at him. The black one, that dyke Cotter and Marina herself. They'd made him feel unwelcome even before he had spoken. Looked at him like he was a piece of shit. And having to turn round, leave the room while he knew they were all watching him had been fucking humiliating.

Fucking humiliating.

That hurt too. All wrapped up with everything else. Turning him into a ball of spite and rage.

He sat back, sighed. Tried to bring himself under control. Thought of last night. Smiled.

That had been good. Revenge. Sweet, sweet revenge. He felt his body tingle once more at the thought of it.

Hadn't been so much fun when he got home, though. The arguments that had followed, the tears. The abuse hurled at him, all his years of failings laid bare. In the end he had walked out. Gone to a Travelodge. He didn't have to take that shit. Not from anyone. Especially after the night he had just had.

Sublime.

He sat there thinking of what he could do. How he could relive the delicious thrills of the night before over and over in his mind, keeping him going for the rest of the boring day until he was free to do something about it once more.

Living for later.

353

81

'**Y**ou're a couple,' Bailey said. 'Together.'

Phil frowned. Not the answer he had been expecting. 'Nicely deflected,' he said with a grim smile. 'Are you going to answer the question?'

'You're a couple,' continued Bailey, 'but ... you're *not* together. Am I right?' A small smile of triumph.

'You were listening to us talk in the waiting room,' said Marina. 'You'll already know the answer to that one. Try again.'

'Or try answering my question,' said Phil, his voice hard, flinty.

'You're separated,' said Bailey, continuing as if they hadn't spoken. 'Living apart, at least. But it's not ... ' He gestured towards them. 'There's eye contact. You looked at each other. That's good, that's a positive sign.'

Phil sighed. 'I've had enough of this. If you don't—'

'Eye contact,' said Bailey, 'yet your body language is all wrong. Look at you.' He pointed towards Marina. 'You're stiff, pulling away from him. Arm on the opposite side of the chair. You softened slightly when he looked at you. There was depth in that look. Softness and warmth. You returned it, too, didn't you?'

Phil stood up. 'Mr Bailey—'

'This won't take a moment,' said Bailey. 'Please sit down.' He smiled, attempting to regain control.

Phil looked down at Marina. She wasn't looking at him; she was studying Bailey. Recognising that she was up to something, Phil sat once more.

Bailey seemed to take the gesture as an indication that he had won a battle of wills. Emboldened, he continued. 'And your body language, Detective Inspector, it's just as indicative. You aren't pulling away. You're leaning in, reaching towards her. Attempting to draw her back. But she won't come back, will she? She's pulled away and she's staying away. I wonder why that is?'

Anger welled inside Phil. He could feel it rising, looking for escape. Marina reached across, placed her hand calmly over his. Startled, he sat back.

Bailey noticed the gesture. Smiled. 'Touching now. That's progress, isn't it? Very quick.' He laughed. 'You've only had one session with me. And it isn't even over yet.'

Phil was trying to stand. Marina increased the pressure on his hand, stopping him. He stayed where he was. For now.

'So why are you still separated?' Bailey made a play of stroking his chin, thinking. 'No, don't tell me.'

Neither of them answered.

'Not infidelity,' said Bailey. 'I think we can rule that out. Unusual, though. That's generally the reason.' He sat forward. 'This is becoming interesting. I think we can rule out work, because you work together. Or you are in this instance, so you know what the other one has to go through. Hmm . . . '

'Something came between us,' said Marina.

Bailey's eyes lit up. 'I knew it.'

'Not hard to work out,' said Marina. 'Given that you've established we're separated and it's not one of the other two things.'

'Yes,' said Bailey, 'but what was it that separated you? That's the interesting bit.'

Marina glanced at Phil. He was staring straight ahead, looking like he wanted to attack the counsellor. She returned her attention to Bailey.

'Something threatening,' she said. 'Something big and threatening. Something we had no control over.'

Bailey sat forward. 'I'm intrigued.'

'Marina . . . ' Phil's voice held a warning.

Marina ignored him, sat back, the ghost of a smile on her face. 'That's as much as you're getting.'

Bailey also sat back, thinking. 'Big and threatening . . . Must have been very big, very threatening to split you up.'

'Oh, it was. It is.'

'And it's still there? Still hanging over you? Stopping you from getting back together? Not infidelity, not pressure of work or lack of it, not illness, not money troubles, not falling out of love with each other. An outside influence. Big enough to split you up.' Eyes fluttering, his head went back.

Marina was aware of Phil trying to look at her. She kept her gaze firmly on Bailey.

Eventually his head snapped forward. 'Fear,' he said.

'Fear,' repeated Marina.

'Yes, fear.' Bailey nodded as if he had just solved Fermat's Last Theorem. 'You see, it doesn't matter what it was, this big and threatening thing; all I need to know about it is what it did. What it caused to happen between you. Fear. That's all. That's what split you apart. Fear.' He looked at them, jubilation in his eyes. 'Am I right? I am, aren't I?'

Marina glanced at Phil. He returned the look. Marina felt something comforting in it, something she hadn't allowed herself to feel for a long time. Hope.

Bailey noticed it too. He smiled. 'Fear. What's that? Really, what is it?' He leaned forward, making sure neither of them missed the importance of his next few words. 'Nothing. That's what it is. Nothing. Fear is . . . ' He shrugged. 'What? Ourselves, or part of ourselves, holding back the rest of ourselves, the bigger and better parts. That's all it is. Feel the fear and do it anyway? A cliché, but it's true.' Still leaning forward, hands clasped together, eyes on the pair of them. 'You have to face your fear. Confront it. Only then can you . . . ' his hands became agitated; he turned one into a fist, hammered it down into the palm of the other, 'destroy it. Dismiss it. See it for what it is, get rid of it.' He frowned. 'What is it you fear? No, you don't have to tell me the actual thing. Just what it involves. The physical process of this fear. A fear so horrendous that it separated the two of you.'

'A sudden attack,' said Marina. 'One we're not prepared for.'

Bailey nodded, expression sympathetic. 'I see. Right. Of course.' He looked at her once more. 'But you can't live your lives like that, can you? It's not helping. What will you have if you do that? I'll tell you. Regrets. For not taking chances. For not conquering your fear, for not taming it, for letting it dictate and ruin your lives. So face it. Embrace it, even. And live.'

Marina nodded.

But Bailey wasn't finished. 'Because only then can you fully be yourselves.' He nodded, pleased with himself. 'Only then can you be the people you want to be. Should be. Deserve to be.'

He sat back. Finished.

Marina nodded as if she had taken it all in, was digesting his wisdom.

'Thank you,' she said.

'You're welcome.' Bailey was beaming.

'Just one thing,' said Marina, face innocently quizzical.

'Yes?' he said.

'What is it *you* fear? Is it those women who said no all those years ago?'

The smile faded from Bailey's face. 'What . . . '

357

'Are they still after you?' Marina kept going. 'Do they still haunt you? When you close your eyes, do you see them? And what are they saying to you? No, Keith, please don't, Keith, I don't want to, Keith . . . something like that?'

Bailey's eyes widened. He began looking round the room as if frantically seeking an exit. His face became a mask of fear.

But Marina wasn't letting go. 'Is that why you do this, Keith? Really why you do this? Not because you're good at it, or people *sought* you out, none of that. You speak to people at their most vulnerable, try to fix them. Am I right? Is that a fair description?'

Bailey didn't reply.

'Are you really just trying to fix yourself, is that it? Trying to find out what went wrong? With them. With you. Trying to find it and fix it?'

Bailey said nothing. He seemed close to tears.

Marina leaned forward, eyes locked on to his. Never leaving them no matter how hard he tried to pull away. 'Are you still trying to put the ghosts to rest, is that it, Keith? What other ghosts do you see?'

She sat back. Glanced at Phil. He nodded.

'What do you know about the murder of Detective Constable Avi Patel last night?'

Bailey shook his head.

'What do you know about the abduction of Detective Constable Imani Oliver?'

Bailey clamped his eyes shut.

'Or about the murder and abduction of Janine Gillen, and Gemma Adderley, and—'

Bailey stood up. 'Get out. Get out now . . .' gesturing, pointing frantically at the door. "How dare you, how . . . fucking dare you . . .'

Phil opened his mouth to speak again. Bailey jumped in first.

'You want to talk to me, you do it through my solicitor. Now get out.'

He grabbed Phil, tried to hurl him towards the door.

Phil and Marina stumbled through, heard the door slamming behind them. They heard a further noise as Bailey slumped down against it.

As they walked away, they were sure they could hear sobbing.

82

Phil and Marina got back into the Audi. Neither spoke or even looked at each other as they left the building.

Phil put the key in the ignition, made to turn it. Stopped. Looked at Marina.

She seemed to consider looking away, but something stronger won. She turned, looked at him too.

'You were great in there,' he said.

She smiled. 'You weren't so bad yourself.'

Their eyes were locked. Eventually Phil pulled away. Her gaze made him feel naked.

'What d'you think?' he said.

Marina frowned. Puzzled. 'About what?'

'Him. Keith Bailey. Reckon he's our guy?'

'I'd say he goes straight to the top of the leaderboard. Evasive, narcissistic, delusional . . . all the boxes ticked.'

'Still wouldn't answer a direct question,' said Phil. 'Hardly a criminal mastermind.'

'Doesn't need to be,' said Marina. 'He's got away with it until now.'

'Right,' said Phil. 'Back to the station. Get the wheels in motion. Talk to Cotter. See about bringing him in.'

'You going to charge him?'

Phil hesitated. 'I'll talk to Cotter. Last person I charged, well . . . that didn't go too well, did it? I have to make sure all the t's and i's are crossed and dotted.'

Marina nodded. 'No time for that. If it is him and he thinks we're on to him and he's got Imani, then we should move quickly. Like I said, he's coming to the end of his cycle. If it seems like he's not going to get the chance to complete it, he might step things up a gear. Or two.'

'Tell that to Cotter, then. Back me up.'

Marina smiled. 'Always.'

Phil turned, looked at her. And before he knew what was happening, his arms were round her, hers around him. They held each other tight, neither speaking. Phil's hands stroked Marina's body through her coat, feeling the familiar contours. Slow. Reverential. Privileged to be doing it, savouring it, like it was an experience he thought he would have again. She was doing the same with him. He knew what she was thinking.

They pulled apart slightly, looked at each other. And there was that gaze again. That naked gaze.

'I've missed—'

'Sshh,' said Marina. 'Talk later.'

She moved her face closer to his. Opened her mouth.

They kissed.

Deep. Hard. A kiss of life. Their mouths breathing a new cycle of existence into each other.

Eventually they pulled apart. Smiled at one another.

There was so much Phil wanted to say. So many emotions threatened to spill out of him. Marina sensed this. Put her finger to his lips.

'Later,' she said. 'Let's catch a killer first.'

Renewed, Phil turned on the ignition. The stereo came on. He drove away, The War on Drugs singing about how they were lost in the dream.

83

They're closing in. That was all he could think. Those three words. *They're closing in.*

He had pulled himself up off the floor after they had left – the angry-eyed copper and that bitch who though she was so clever, so fucking, *fucking* clever – and tried to get himself together. He paced his room, measuring the footsteps. The width. The length. Thinking, thinking all the time.

They're closing in. *They're closing in.*

He wanted to scream, to shout. To rend his clothes and grind his teeth. There were things inside him that were too big to stay inside. Feelings. Emotions. The way his mind was working, his heart. They should be let out, *needed* to be let out. He imagined them as if they were Hollywood special effects in the final reel of a film, shooting from his body, wraiths and ghosts, memories and previous lives. Filling the room, the city, the world. Exorcising himself. Ridding himself of them. So he could go on. Complete the ritual he had set out to do. Be the perfect man he knew he could be.

But that wasn't going to happen. Not here, not now.

Because they were on to him.

He knew that. Knew it from the way those two had talked to him. He had been playing her and she had been playing him. The bitch. Rage welled up inside him once more at the memory. He had reached her – both of them, but mainly her.

He knew their problems. Not that it had done him much good. Because she had turned it back on him. Got inside his head. And no one had ever done that before. Never even come close.

It was only a matter of time before the police arrived. Before his house was raided, his workroom, his ritual room. Before he was stopped. He knew it. Could sense it. He had to do something about it.

But what?

Pacing. Pacing. Thinking. Thinking.

He could cry again, tears of rage and self-pity. But he had done that and it had got him nowhere, so it was time to think. *Think*.

He weighed up his options. What to do?

Run. Take what he could. Get out. No. Not an option. They would find him. He wasn't equipped for escape. Besides, his work wasn't finished. And that was the important thing. His work.

So he had no choice. Not really. He had to go back. Home. The ritual room. Complete his work.

Just move the schedule forward, that was all.

But what about the woman? The police detective? Would she do?

She would have to. She wasn't perfect; he had been duped into taking her. But he would have to make her perfect. Or at least as perfect as he could manage. She would have to do.

He would *make* her do.

He grabbed what he could, left his room. Ignored everyone on the way out.

Headed home.

He had work to do.

84

Imani had never known such agony.

She stretched and pulled her hand once more, felt the flesh and bone grinding against the metal cuffs, knew from the wetness round her wrist, the ragged, pulpy squelch she felt, not to mention the pain that accompanied it, that the only thing she had done was drive the metal further in.

She had tried to escape, but he had been too clever for her. The cuffs were tight round her wrists. If she kept on doing what she was doing, pulling at them, she risked disfiguring her hands. She had tried squeezing her thumbs into her palms, pressing them into the flesh as tightly as she could and pulling against the cuffs like she had seen in films. No good. The hero or heroine always happened to be double-jointed or could shrink their wrists or something. Imani could do nothing like that. Except pull as hard as she could, try to wriggle her hands free. It was no good. She couldn't do it.

Then she had tried to grip the chains that held her, attempting to twist her fingers round the links, pull against the bedstead. She had hoped that the bedstead, being old, would be weak in places. It was up to her to find those weaknesses, exploit them. There was rust on the frame. At least she assumed it was rust; it was dark brown in colour. But the more she pulled and heaved at the metal, the more she realised that the bed wasn't going to give. And it wasn't rust. It was dried blood.

She flopped back on to the metal mesh. Felt the sharp edges rip and tear at her once more, work their way into fresh wounds. But tetanus was the least of her worries.

Imani sighed. She had always been so self-sufficient, so driven. Refused to let anyone else dictate how she lived her life. She had never felt so helpless as she did now.

She felt herself giving in to panic and self-pity once again. She had held it off so far, tried to concentrate, focus on escaping. But the longer she spent there, the more she realised she wasn't going anywhere.

Possibly ever again.

No. *No. Don't think like that.* They would be looking for her. The team would be looking for her. They had to be. They had to be . . .

She looked round once more. She had lost all concept of time. With just that one bare bulb shining down remorselessly on her face, she didn't know how long she had been there or whether it was day or night. It shone on and on, like its own special kind of torture. She was hungry, that much she did know. But that was it. She couldn't even trust her own body any more.

She sighed. Thought once more of Avi.

Oh God, Avi . . .

No. No. Don't think about him. He was all right. He was sure to be. She had enough to think of without worrying about him too. Right now he was probably tracking down where she was, joining the team in hunting for her. Finding her.

Yes. That was it.

She sighed once more. Shook her head. Felt tears well at the sides of her eyes. No. She wouldn't give in. No. They were looking for her. They had to be.

She thought of all the cases she had worked on. All the times they had been hunting some missing person, knowing

365

that the longer the hunt went on, the less likely they would be to find them. Alive, at any rate. Knowing all too well that moment that a hunt for someone missing turned into a hunt for a murderer.

She just hoped it wouldn't happen to her. But she knew that every victim of every crime thought that.

She tried not to give in to tears.

85

Claire Lingard hadn't gone to work. She had got Edward ready for school, taken him in, then come back home. After everything that had happened recently, a killer migraine had put her back to bed. After a few hours' sleep, however, the worst of it seemed to have passed and she felt able to get up. If not strong enough to go to work, then guilty enough to try and do something productive with the remains of her day.

Head still throbbing, she moved slowly round the flat, like she was a reluctant ghost, haunting it.

And saw the door to the other flats.

With that, she remembered the night before.

She had heard Keith come in. Creeping round, trying not to wake her. She heard him showering, coming to bed. She had checked the clock: past three a.m. And she was sure she had heard him in the flats before that.

'Bad stomach,' he had said when she had moved, looked at him. 'Been up for hours. Don't worry about it, go back to sleep.'

But she hadn't gone back to sleep. At least not until the safety of the morning had crept round the bedroom curtains.

So where had he been? With Brendan, he had said. Until that time? Was he seeing another woman? Or was he the serial killer, even? She felt ridiculous thinking such a thing.

And now she looked at the door to the other flats. She was sure she had heard noises from there last night.

It couldn't hurt . . .

She went back into the bedroom. Found Keith's clothes. Taking a deep breath, she started looking through the pockets. Trousers, jackets, nothing. The bedside table drawer held nothing out of the ordinary either. She went into the room Keith used as a study. And there, hidden amongst documents and files, she found the keys for the rest of the flats.

Not hidden, she told herself. No. Just . . . buried under all these papers by mistake. That was all. A mistake. Yes.

She took the keys and walked towards the door that joined them to the rest of the block. She'd never ventured further. A whole two houses that had been converted into flats. Keith had told her it wasn't safe. Too many loose or rotting floorboards. She had taken him at his word, stayed in the downstairs one they lived in, treating it like a bungalow. But now, fingers trembling, heart and head pounding, she put the key in the lock, turned it. Opened the door.

And stepped into the hallway.

She found the light switch, flicked it on. And sighed. Relief. She didn't know what she had been expecting to find, but this wasn't it. Building supplies lined up against the wall. Lengths of wood. Coving. Skirting. Pots of paint piled at one side. An opened tool box. All pointing to ongoing work being done.

She looked around. Except, she thought, that it didn't look like much had actually been done. Not considering the time Keith had been taking.

She tried to dislodge the thought from her head. He said himself he wasn't good at DIY, that he was learning as he went. He was probably going as fast as he could.

She walked on. Everywhere was less than half finished. As if any attempts at renovation were cosmetic, just there to show that something had been done.

She came to a door. Tried it. Locked.

Her heart skipped a beat. Why a locked door? Why here? She rationalised her anxiety, tried to calm herself down. Maybe this was where Keith kept his expensive tools. An extra deterrent if the flats were broken into.

She took the key ring out, tried the keys on it until, hands still trembling, she found one that fitted. She turned it, felt the lock open. Slowly she pushed the door.

She looked round before she entered. Like she was expecting to see someone there, some friend of hers, or Keith himself, even, laughing, telling her that there was nothing to worry about. But there was no one there. No reassuring, consoling voice.

She stepped into the room.

Found a light switch on the wall. And frowned at what she saw.

A desk and chair. On the desk, a laptop, one she had never seen before. It was set up with some unfamiliar equipment: a headset, earphone and mic. She had no idea what any of it was, what it did. Then, with a shudder that almost threatened to tear her apart, she understood.

This was where he must have intercepted the calls to the refuge. This was how he did it.

Claire's legs felt weak, her head spun. She needed to sit down, grabbed the chair and almost fell into it. As she did so, she touched something and the screen of the laptop lit up. Numbers scrolled there. She looked closely, recognised one.

Safe Haven.

Oh God . . .

She didn't know what to feel, how to think. It was as if she had realised her whole world was built on a lie – a succession of lies – and it was crumbling away. She stared at the screen feeling like she had been physically attacked.

She didn't move for a while. Couldn't move.

Then she noticed another door, at the end of the room.

Oh God . . . Oh God . . . Oh God . . .

Standing up, like her body was hollow, being controlled by a puppet master, she made her way to the door. She'd found this room, she thought; what could be worse?

Numbly, she tried different keys until she found one that fitted. Turned it. Opened the door.

Stepped in.

And realised just how much worse things could be.

86

In front of Claire were shelves. All round the room, rows and rows of them. And on those shelves were boxes. She looked closer. Beside some of the boxes were other things. She walked over to one, picked up the things beside it. Photos. She looked through them. Keith when he was much younger. With another woman. Pretty, long curly hair. Not at all like Claire, she noted. Underneath the photos were a couple of sheets of writing paper. Taped to the first one was a lock of hair. It matched that of the woman in the photo. The paper had writing on. Keith's handwriting. She started to read:

I found you. Or someone like you. Near enough like you. You didn't think I would, did you? Not after the way you left it with me. Well, I did. And I told her – or you – everything you'd done to me. I got you back for all the hurt . . .

She read on. And wished she hadn't.

Feeling physically ill now, she let the papers drop to the floor. Her head was spinning. She was nauseous, as if she was going to throw up or faint. She grabbed the side of one of the shelves to steady herself.

The boxes. There were still the boxes.

She didn't want to open them. Really, really didn't want to open them. But knew she had to. Like Pandora, she didn't know what she would let out, but she knew it wouldn't be good.

She reached for the nearest one. Dark carved wood. Took it off the shelf, flipped the lid open.

There was a heart. In formaldehyde.

She was physically sick then.

She dropped the box, the heart and the liquid going all over the floor, mixing with her own vomit.

Tears in her eyes, pain in her heart – pain like she had never experienced before – she spun round, desperately trying to get away, knowing there wasn't really anywhere for her to go.

She ran through the room with the laptop and radio equipment, back out into the hall. She flung herself against the wall, sliding down to the floor, sobbing all the while. Eyes screwed tight shut, knowing that all her worst fears were confirmed. She didn't think she could have felt worse if she'd been diagnosed with a terminal disease.

Eventually she opened her eyes. And saw another locked door ahead of her.

Oh no, no, no, no, no . . .

She put her head back down, closed her eyes once more. She didn't know what horrors that room would contain, what could possibly be worse than the room she had just been in.

Get out. Now. That's what I need to do. What I should do. Get out.

She looked at the locked door once more. There was a smell emanating from it. Creeping under the wood, around the frame. It wasn't good.

Claire stood up. Keys in hand. She had to do it. Had to see what was behind it. She had no choice. She knew that now.

She found the right key. Opened the door. And entered.

Jesus . . .

Imani Oliver was chained to an old metal bed frame, gagged and naked. She stared at Claire, eyes wide with shock, infused with just the slightest bit of hope.

'Imani . . .'

The room stank like an abattoir, old blood and animal waste. Claire wanted to be sick again, but seeing the other woman there in the state she was in, she knew she didn't have time for that, couldn't think about herself. She got the key ring out once more, went through the keys looking for the one that would fit the handcuffs. Couldn't find it. She threw the useless keys to the floor, undid the gag.

'Thank you . . .' Imani was gasping in air, trying to speak at the same time. 'Thank you . . . Oh God, I thought . . . I thought . . .'

Tears welled in the corners of her eyes. She struggled not to give in to them.

'Get a . . . get your phone. Call Cotter. Tell her . . . tell her . . .'

Claire understood. She took her phone out of her pocket, made ready to call.

'I'll have that.'

A voice from behind her. She turned.

There, looking like someone she had never seen before, a malevolent stranger, was Keith.

87

K eith tried to grab the phone from Claire, but she moved out of the way.

'Don't do anything stupid,' he said. 'Well. Anything more stupid than you've already done.'

'Keith, I . . . ' Claire stopped. She had no words.

'You dared to enter my trophy room,' he said, face contorted with rage.

She had never seen him like this before. It was his features, his body, his clothes. But his expression . . . it looked like a demon had entered him, possessed him.

'You . . . *fucking* . . . dared . . . to go into my trophy room . . . '

'I . . . Keith, what have you done?'

'That room isn't for you. It's for me. *Only* me. You've . . . defiled it. Spoilt it. Spoiled the ritual . . . '

He kept moving towards her. She backed away. Glancing down as he advanced, she noticed he was holding something in his hand. It looked like an overlarge door handle.

Imani saw it too.

'Claire,' she managed to call, 'that's a stun gun he's holding, be careful . . . '

Keith turned to her. 'Shut it, bitch.' Spitting the words. He turned his attention back to Claire. 'And you . . . ' Pointed at her with his free hand. A long, accusing finger. 'You are going to do what I tell you.'

Claire found her voice. 'Why did you do it? Why? I can't . . .'
She shook her head. 'I don't understand . . .'

'No,' he growled, 'you don't. You wouldn't. You're too . . .' He
searched for the word. 'Thick. Unambitious. Useless. You think
because you wrote poetry that made you special? Fuck you.'

Despite the fear she was experiencing, Claire was still hurt
by his words. 'Keith . . .'

'Fuck you.'

'Keith, this . . . this isn't you. You're a good man. A kind
man. Why . . .'

His eyes flared. 'I'm not good, I'm not *kind* . . .' He said the
words like they were alien, hateful objects in his mouth. Then,
having rid himself of them, he smiled. 'But I will be. Soon.'

'What d'you mean? What are you talking about?' Real
incomprehension in Claire's voice.

'Perfection. All the damage women have done to me, all the
hurt, the broken hearts . . . soon it'll be gone. Cleansed from
me. And once my rituals are completed, I'll be perfect. The perfect man.'

'I don't . . . Keith . . . please—'

Claire's words were cut short. Her phone rang.

She froze. So did Keith. He stared at it. She knew what he
was about to do, and in the split second before he moved, she
answered the call, put the phone to her ear.

'Hi, Claire? DS Sperring here. I just wanted to check
someth—'

'He's here!' she screamed. 'It's him, he's here, in the flat, in
here—'

The phone fell from her hands. Pain like she had never experienced passed through her. Like a thousand dull blades ripping
her flesh, hitting every nerve in the process. She screamed. Fell
to the floor.

Unconscious.

375

88

The phone in Sperring's hand was screaming. Then it abruptly stopped.

He stared at it, then looked round the incident room. He hadn't expected that.

He put the phone to his ear, tried again.

'Claire? Claire Lingard? This is DS Sperring. Hello?' He waved at Cotter as he spoke, tried to attract her attention.

A voice answered. 'What d'you want?'

He could guess who it was. 'I'm Detective Sergeant Sperring. Where's Claire? Is she all right?'

The only answer was breathing. He could hear a raised voice in the background, whimpering and gasping.

'Keith Bailey, is that you? Am I talking to Keith Bailey?'

Nothing.

'Hello?'

The voice came back, speaking slow and low. 'Why don't you just fuck off and leave us alone?'

The phone went dead.

Sperring stood up. Cotter had reached his desk.

'We've got trouble,' he said.

89

It didn't take long for the circus to roll up.

The road in Kings Heath was cordoned off, police tape unrolled at either end, makeshift barriers erected, uniforms posted on duty. The mobile incident room had been set up outside the flats. Phil and Marina entered.

'Oh God, not you again.'

Mike Battersby, the hostage negotiation expert, looked up. Did a double-take. Phil gave him a nod of acknowledgement by way of greeting.

Battersby stood up, finger pointing. 'Right,' he said. 'I don't care what you say, you are not having anything to do with this negotiation. You go nowhere near it. You got that?'

Phil held his hands up in mock surrender. 'Fine by me.'

Cotter interjected, leading Phil away by the arm. 'I'm sure DI Brennan has plenty of other duties to take care of.'

Battersby resumed his seat.

'Where are we?' Phil asked Cotter.

She told him about Sperring's call.

'Anything else? Any movement from inside? Attempt to contact him?'

Cotter shook his head. 'Waited until you got here.'

'And you're sure it's him? Keith Bailey's the guy we're looking for?'

Cotter looked quickly round as if being overheard. 'We don't know. We can only assume so at the moment. But it seems like a strong assumption. I think we have to proceed as if he is and that he has Imani in there as well as Claire Lingard. And hope that Imani's still all right.'

'Right,' said Phil. 'Think it's time for a phone call, don't you?'

Cotter nodded.

Battersby dialled the number of Claire's phone. Put it on loudspeaker. They waited. Each ring seeming to get louder. Eventually it was answered. No one spoke.

'Hello?' said Battersby.

No response. Just breathing.

'Hello, is that Claire Lingard?'

'Who's this?'

Phil recognised Bailey's voice. Nodded at Cotter, confirming it.

'This is Detective Sergeant Battersby. Mike Battersby, if you prefer. What's your name?'

'If you're calling this number then you already know who I am.'

'Keith Bailey?'

A snort. Laughter?

'Right, Keith. Listen. I just want to know who you've got in there with you and whether they're all right.'

'I'm not talking to you. I don't want to talk to you.'

'Why not, Keith?'

'Because you're going to try and talk me out of it. Try and make me let them go when I haven't finished yet.'

'Haven't finished what yet?'

'My work.' Said as if it was the most obvious thing in the world. 'What I have to do. You don't think I do this for fun, do you?'

'I don't know, Keith, you tell me.'

'You don't know. You don't know . . .'

They felt he was about to explode. Cotter sat forward, ready to order in a response team.

'Well, you'll have to help me, Keith,' Battersby continued. 'If you talk to me, I can—'

'Oh, fuck off,' said Bailey. 'I don't want to talk to you.'

'Well, Keith, I—'

'Is she there?'

Battersby looked confused. 'Who's *she*, Keith?'

'The psychologist. The one I spoke to this morning. Is she there?'

All eyes in the room turned to Marina. She stepped forward, moved close to the microphone.

The room held its collective breath.

90

'I'm here, Keith,' said Marina.

'Yeah. Thought you would be.'

Marina sat down to be nearer the microphone. Battersby moved along to let her in. Phil noticed – with dark relish – that he looked somewhat put out by that.

'What d'you want to talk about, Keith?'

'What I wanted to talk about earlier. I think you know. I think you would have talked about it – properly talked about it with me – if I'd said. Wouldn't you?'

Marina looked round slightly, as if she had missed a couple of pages in the script they were following. 'I would have talked about it?'

'Yes.'

'In your office?'

'Yes. If you'd known what I'm doing. And why I'm doing it.'

'Okay then, Keith, if you want to talk to me about it – all of it – then tell me all of it. I know what you're doing. You're taking women and killing them, is that right?'

'No,' he said. 'Well, yes, I suppose it is if you look at it in purely reductive terms.'

'And what way should I look at it, Keith? Just to get a handle on it, so we can talk about it.'

'It's not *what* I've done. It's *why*. You should know that.'

'Right. Well, as I see it,' she said, 'they're surrogates for women who've hurt you in some way, is that it?'

'Yes.' His voice cracked slightly on the word.

'And this is to make up for it?'

'Yes. For what those bitches did to me. All of them.'

'They hurt you, those women, did they?'

Behind them, one of the uniforms rotated his finger at the side of his head. Sperring knocked it away. The uniform dropped his head, stood in shamefaced silence.

'Yes. All of them.'

Beside Marina, Cotter scribbled a note: *Did he know all the women he killed?* Marina shook her head, continued.

'These women. The ones you took. You didn't know them, did you? They just represented the ones who had hurt you, didn't they?'

Silence.

'Keith?'

'Yeah. I said yeah.'

'So they let you down. The women in your life. They hurt you.'

'Every time.' His voice cracking once more. 'And they enjoyed it. All of them. That's the worst thing. They enjoyed it. Or just . . . didn't care. Treated me like I was nothing.'

'Surely that wasn't the case every time?'

'It was. Always.' The words sounded pained, forced out.

'What about your mother?'

Silence on the line. It lasted so long Marina thought he might have gone. 'Keith?'

'Don't mention my fucking . . . that fucking . . . '

'Right,' said Marina, responding to his raised voice by making hers even calmer. 'I see. Right. So you did what you did because of the hurt that had been done to you.'

'Yes.'

381

'But why these particular women?'

'Because ... because they were damaged,' he said, as if that explained everything, desperate to be understood. 'Hurt. Like I was. Just like I was.'

'Did you think you were mending their broken hearts? Was that part of it?'

'I took their hearts. And gave them to the women who had hurt me. Used their damaged hearts to help heal me. Don't you see? You should understand that.'

'I do, Keith,' said Marina, nodding, even though he couldn't see it.

Bailey continued. 'When I've done that, it's complete. That's the ritual done. For each one. The ritual gets rid of the ghosts. Makes them go away. And when they leave me, I become a better person. Well, obviously you can see that.'

'Yes,' said Marina. 'But what about Claire? Where does she fit in?'

'What d'you mean?' His voice hard once more. Wary.

'She's a good person, Keith.'

He made a sound like a wounded animal. Marina ignored him, kept going.

'She loves you, Keith.'

'No,' he said, the wounded howl tailing off. 'She doesn't. She can't.'

'Why not?'

'Because she doesn't know me,' he said, again desperate to be understood. 'Not really. She thinks she does. We all think we know someone else, love someone else. But we don't. None of us do. Because all we see is the mask. All she knows is my mask. She doesn't know what's behind it. She just fell in love with a mask. How stupid ...'

'But Keith,' said Marina, genuinely engaged with him, 'don't we all wear masks?'

'W-what d'you mean?'

'It's simple. We all wear masks. All of us. Every day. You know Kurt Vonnegut? The writer?'

Nothing.

Marina continued. 'He said we all had to be careful about the masks we choose to wear because in time we become them.' She looked up. Phil was staring right at her. She continued, eyes locked with his. 'Or they become us. You know, if we want to be brave, we pretend to be brave. If we want to be good, we act good. Or happy. Or anything. We find a mask for it.'

She saw Phil smile. Nod.

'And gradually,' she said, feeling encouraged by what she was saying, genuinely feeling she was making a breakthrough, 'gradually we become that thing the mask represents. Don't you think?'

Silence from the other end. Then slowly a scream built up. Deep and wailing at first, then ragged. Anger and pain vying for dominance.

'Shut up,' screamed Keith, 'shut up . . . '

Marina looked round quickly. She was losing him.

'I thought you would understand. You of all people . . . '

'I do, Keith, I do,' she said. 'Listen. There's something I need to know. Have you got Imani Oliver there with you? Detective Constable Oliver?'

'What?' Screaming again. 'What the fuck do you want to know about her for?'

'I just—'

'Her. That's all you were interested in. All this time. Her. Not me. You, you fucking liar. You fucking bitch liar . . . '

'No, Keith, I'm not. I swear I'm not. Please, listen to me . . . '

'Bitch . . . '

'Keith, please. What have I just said to you? What have we just talked about? If I wasn't listening to you, then what was all that for?'

'You . . . you just . . . ' He had calmed down slightly but she knew he was on a knife edge and could go either way. She had to be careful what she said next.

'We talked, Keith. And I meant every word. I'm trying to understand what you're doing. Why you're doing it. That's what you want, right? You want me to understand?'

Silence.

Marina continued.

'Listen, Keith. If you've got Imani Oliver there, why not let her go, eh? She's not part of your ritual. She's not damaged or hurt. Nothing like that. She's no good to you. You can't use her. Why not let her go?'

Silence. More heavy breathing. Then: 'Fuck you.'

The line went dead.

Marina sat back. Exhausted.

91

'You should have been closing,' said Battersby. 'All the time. Closing.'

Marina stared at him in disbelief. 'Sorry? Are we selling second-hand cars or something?'

'In hostage negotiation you're always moving towards that. Always trying to get the hostages out safely. Not . . . ' he threw up his hands, 'indulging him in his fantasies.'

Marina squared up to him. 'I was not indulging him. I was talking. He wanted to talk to me, not you. Maybe you'll get your chance later. *Close* him then.'

She turned to Cotter before he could answer. 'Alison, have you thought about what I said?'

When the phone had gone dead and Bailey had refused to pick up again, Marina had asked Cotter to go somewhere private, have a word. They had stepped outside, hidden round the back of the unit, away from long-range media lenses. There she had put her idea to the DCI.

Cotter, inside now, was shaking her head.

'But it's the only way,' said Marina. 'At least with such short notice.'

'No,' said Cotter. 'I won't hear of it. It's too dangerous.' She threw a glance at Battersby, then back to Marina. 'And you're not even trained.'

'It'll work,' said Marina. 'I go in. Claire comes out. I wear a wire. While this is happening, Phil leads a team in from the back.'

Cotter turned away. 'No. We've already got the stigma of this being some kind of maverick operation as it is. I can't allow a civilian in there.'

'After everything I've done, I'm hardly a civilian.'

'It's too dangerous.'

'It's the best chance we have. Otherwise this could drag on for . . . ' she shrugged, 'God knows how long. And we don't know what the situation is in there. What state Imani and Claire are in. I could provide information about that.'

Cotter sighed. 'It should be a member of my team.'

'Well, unfortunately, he doesn't want to talk to anyone on your team. Only me. That makes me an asset. Use me.'

'Marina's right,' said Phil.

They both turned, unaware that he had been listening.

'She's already established a bond with him. I think this is the best chance we have.'

Cotter looked at Marina, reluctantly relenting. 'Would you be armed?'

'No,' said Marina. 'No point. If I take a gun in there, it just makes it more dangerous.'

'But you wouldn't be protected. You wouldn't be safe.'

'Yes I would.' She spoke the words to Cotter but her eyes were on Phil.

Phil tried hard to hide his smile.

Cotter said nothing, thinking. Marina kept talking.

'And I'd be able to relay information back. Tell you which part of the building he's in.'

'We can do that with thermal imaging.'

'But you haven't got the equipment here yet. God knows how long it will take to arrive, or what he could do before then.'

386

'This is completely against protocol. If it goes tits-up, it could be the end of all our careers.'

'And if we do nothing,' said Marina, 'if we wait, it could be the end of Imani and Claire's lives. Which is more important?'

Cotter said nothing, looked at Phil. 'And you,' she said, 'how do I know you won't go in there and mess it up like last time?'

'Because I won't,' said Phil.

Cotter looked between the pair of them. Sighed.

'Do it,' she said.

92

The phone rang. They all looked at it. Waiting.

The tension in the room was palpable. Claire wanted to scream again, just to hear her own voice, to remind herself she was still alive. After Bailey had hung up, no one had spoken. Claire had pulled herself into a corner, arms round her bruised torso, gasping as the pain slowly subsided. Imani lay silently on the bed, spent. Bailey had put the stun gun down on a table, switched it for an automatic. Now he strode up and down, talking to himself, hitting himself in the temples occasionally, as if his head was hurting and it would alleviate the pain.

That was when the phone rang.

'Answer it . . .' Imani.

'Shut up, shut up . . .' Hitting himself in the side of the head once more. 'Shut up, I'm thinking . . .' Still pacing.

Claire had never seen him like this. Unravelling. She no longer recognised the person before her.

'Please,' she said, Imani's voice giving her the courage to speak, 'please just answer it.'

Bailey stopped moving, stood still in the centre of the room, threw his head back and gave a silent scream. The phone kept ringing.

Something had to be done, thought Claire. Ignoring the pain, she leaned forward, made a movement towards the phone. Bailey saw her, snapping out of his pose straight away, and beat her to it. Before he realised what he had done, the phone was to his ear.

'Hello? Hello? Keith? Is that you?'

Marina's voice again.

He groaned by way of response.

'Listen,' said Marina. 'I've got a proposal for you. Why don't you let Claire and Imani go and I'll come in instead?'

Bailey looked round, as if expecting a trick. 'What, I . . . '

'I think it's a good idea,' Marina continued. 'We can keep talking, like earlier. You can explain your work to me. How does that sound?'

He didn't reply.

'I won't be armed,' said Marina. 'I'm not police. Nothing like that. Just you and me. Talking. What d'you say?'

Keith closed his eyes. Thought. Just him. Alone with Marina . . . the two of them . . .

Then another thought struck him. He smiled at it. Felt excited by it.

Marina was damaged. Marina had been hurt. By her husband. Even better.

Yes.

Perhaps she was the one. The one to finish on. She could finally set him free.

Yes . . .

He nodded to himself at how clever he was.

But another thought entered his mind. A darker one. What if she was lying? Or what if it didn't work? He didn't have time, something like that? He would need insurance. A way to prevent that happening.

He looked round the room, worked out who was expendable, who was not. Who was useful, who was not. He made up his mind quickly.

'Claire can go,' he said into the phone. 'The other one stays.'

He hung up.

93

Marina put her arms up, let the technician thread a wire across her body, prior to pulling on a stab vest. Phil stood beside her, his own stab vest in place, anxious.

'You sure about this?' he said.

'As sure as you are,' she replied. 'You agreed with me.'

He leaned in closer, cutting off the rest of the activity in the trailer. Just the two of them. 'Well, yeah, it made sense.'

'So why are you asking if I'm all right with it?'

'Because . . .'

'Because it's me,' said Marina.

'Well, of course. I mean—'

'Do I ever stop you from doing what you're supposed to? Am I asking if you're all right with wearing a stab vest and leading a team in through the back?'

'Well, no, but—'

She turned to him. The technician had finished. 'Well what?'

'I just . . .'

'What?' said Marina. 'You want to keep me safe?'

'Course I do.'

She stretched out her arms, felt her muscles coil and uncoil. Spring-loaded, ready to punch out. She had changed into her gym kit and training shoes, the Lycra sculpting her body, helping her to move as freely as she wanted to.

'I don't want to lose you,' he said.

A smile spread slowly across her face. 'You won't,' she said.

94

The day was fading, dark creeping in, when Marina approached the front door of the house.

She felt alone, the distance between the incident room and the house seemingly immense as she walked, but she knew that was only an illusion. Time hadn't slowed down or speeded up. It only felt that way.

She was scared. She had agreed to do this, told Phil she was fine with it and smiled at him, but it was bravado. Out here, in this open space, she felt so alone. Like she was walking away from safety towards . . . what? Danger? Uncertainty? Both. She was doing this because it was the right thing to do. Facing her fear, trying to conquer it. Because there was something bigger at stake. But there was also that gnawing thought that she might enter that house and never emerge. She saw Josephina's face becoming more distant with every step she took.

She would see her again. She kept telling herself that. She had to believe it. Had to.

And Phil. He would be there. It was going to work. Ignore the fear, don't give in to it. She would be fine.

She would be fine . . .

She reached the door. Put her hand out to knock but didn't get the chance. It swung open slowly. Marina felt the telescopic sights of rifles on her back. She knew there was an armed response team waiting nearby, hoped they wouldn't be foolish enough to take a shot at him while she was in the way.

Claire Lingard was pushed roughly outside. She was holding herself, wincing with pain. Marina didn't have time to talk to her, ask her what had happened or even steady her. A hand holding a gun appeared.

'Get in. Quick.'

She did so.

The door closed behind her.

In the shadow she could make out the features of Keith Bailey.

'Hello, Keith,' she said. More for those listening in than because she was pleased to see him.

'Get through there,' he said, waving the gun at her.

She began walking. 'Down here?' she said. 'Down this hall-way?'

'Move.'

She kept walking until she reached a set of stairs.

'Upstairs.'

She did so. Moving slowly, deliberately, trying to make her trainered feet reverberate as much as possible, hoping that who-ever was listening would be able to count the steps.

'Left,' he said at the top of the stairs.

She turned left. *This bit's easy*, she thought. *He's doing my job for me. Hope the rest is the same . . .*

But she doubted it.

'Stop.'

She did so.

'I want to show you in here.' He opened the door wide, ush-ered her into a room with a laptop, kept walking, opened another door. The room was filled with shelves, boxes on shelves. 'This is where I keep them,' he said. 'The hearts. This is where the ritual takes place.'

Marina was suddenly terrified. More scared than she had been in a long time. The enormity of what she had agreed to suddenly sank in and she hit a new level of terror. The plan had been one thing. Now it was just her in a room of body parts with a dangerous maniac holding a gun. She knew he was waiting for a response from her. She had to find the right one.

Don't look appalled, she thought. *Don't show him you're scared.*

'And does it work?' she asked. 'The ritual?'

'Yeah, yeah, it works.'

'It gets rid of the ghosts?'

He nodded. 'It was doing, yeah. But that last one … that wasn't so good. I had to act quickly. In a hurry. That didn't feel right.'

'I see,' she said, quelling the screams she was hearing inwardly. 'But you're nearly finished now.'

He gave a smile that was the most frightening thing she had seen in a long time. 'Oh yes. I'm nearly finished.'

He waved the gun at her once more, gesturing for her to leave the room.

'Which way?' she said out in the hall, relieved not to have seen what was inside the boxes.

'Down there.'

'Left?'

'Just keep walking.'

She did so until they reached another room with a closed door.

'And this,' he said, reaching for the handle, 'is where the magic happens.' He gave out something that could have been a laugh and entered.

Marina followed him. There was Imani, chained to a rusty old bedstead. Again Marina felt screams within her. She tried to keep them down. Like increasing nausea, they were getting harder to swallow each time.

She turned back to Bailey. 'Come on, Keith,' she said, hoping her voice didn't sound as shaky and breathless as she thought it did. 'You've got me now. You don't need Imani as well. Let her go.'

Bailey, still smiling, was advancing towards her. 'I don't need her?'

'No,' said Marina, backing away. This was all getting out of hand too fast. She had to calm down, try to talk. Engage him. Give Phil and the team time to get in place. To make an entry.

'Come on, Keith,' she said, trying not to move any more, though his approach was hindering that. 'Let's . . . let's just talk. That's what you wanted, right? So let's talk.'

'We've talked, Marina. Haven't we? We've talked a few times now. Have you anything else to say? Anything I want to hear?'

'I must have. That's why you asked me here.'

He laughed. 'Is it?'

Marina was aware that Imani was trying to tell her something. She was looking at Marina, nodding in the direction of something with her eyes. Marina was confused at first, didn't know what she was looking it. Then she saw it. And understood.

She gave a small nod of acknowledgement. Kept moving.

'It's the end, Keith,' she said. 'Surely you realise that?'

Nothing. Just grinning.

'Why not let it go? Now?'

He giggled.

'There's other ways of getting rid of those ghosts, you know,' she said. 'Other therapies you can use. Ones that don't involve hurting people.'

Nothing. Just the slow advance.

'Come on, Keith. I know you don't enjoy hurting people. I know that's not what this is all about. You're not like that, are you?'

Bailey stopped, and for a single, blessed second, Marina

thought she had got through to him. But all he did was tuck the gun in the waistband of his trousers and replace it with a knife. He studied the blade, watched it glitter in the overhead light.

'It's too late for that,' he said, looking back at her. 'Much too late . . . '

95

'Here, boss. Look at this.'

Behind the flats that Bailey was holed up in, there was a row of garages, all with metal pull-over doors. Sperring had managed to open one of the doors and was standing inside. Phil turned to see what he had found.

'Toyota Avensis,' he said. 'Looks like it needs a bit of attention, too.'

'Good work,' said Phil. 'Best not touch it, though. Leave it for Forensics.'

He moved away. They were heading towards the back of the flats. They made their way past the garages and over the wooden fence, then edged up the garden, checking all sides.

Phil's team was augmented by a response unit. They were used to this kind of thing, knew how to effect a decent entry. They were carrying a battering ram, a heavy metal tube filled with concrete, handles on either end.

Phil glanced at Sperring. His DS was looking straight ahead. Determined. 'You okay? You ready?'

'Course I am,' Sperring said, not breaking stride. 'Why wouldn't I be?'

'Just thinking of your knife wound.'

He stopped walking, looked at Phil. Gave a grim smile. 'Take more than that to stop me,' he said.

Not the only one wearing a mask, thought Phil.

They reached the back door. Phil stood aside, let the guys with the battering ram get set up.

'In three,' called the lead officer. He held up three fingers. 'One, two ...'

The third was silent, just the folding down of his index finger.

The battering ram hit. One blow was all it took. And they were in.

'Upstairs,' shouted Phil. 'That's where they are.'

He found a staircase, took it two at a time, Sperring hurrying behind him.

He reached a landing. Looked left to right. Tried to orient himself from Marina's words. Turned left. Ran. Opened one door. A laptop. Some other equipment. Tried another. Boxes on shelves. Getting nearer, he thought. Tried another one.

That was it.

The door swung open. There stood Bailey, one arm round Marina's neck, the other holding a large and vicious-looking knife at her throat.

'Too late,' Bailey said, and began to push the knife in.

96

Marina felt what he was doing. She screamed and tried to push him away. Bailey stumbled backwards. His knife hand moved to steady himself but his other arm remained firmly round her throat. Marina also stumbled, but only as far as the table. Then Bailey had her once more, shoving her forward, the knife back in place.

'Let her go,' said Phil, trying to remain calm but failing.

'A stand-off,' said Bailey. 'Who has the power now, Mr Alpha Male Detective?'

'Let her go,' repeated Phil, calmer and more controlled this time.

Bailey gave out something that might have been a laugh. 'No,' he said. 'I won't. Because I have one more ritual, one more sacrifice to make. And you're not going to stop me.'

'And then what?' asked Phil. 'After you've done that, then what will you do?'

'I'll be complete, of course.'

'Complete. Right. But you can't escape, can you?'

'Can't I?'

'Look around you. Look outside. You're going nowhere.'

Bailey smiled. It had no connection with anything humorous. Or even remotely sane. 'Oh, I always had an escape planned. Of a sort.'

'Tell me.'

'You wouldn't understand.'

'Try me.'

'Well, it's very simple, really. Once I've achieved perfection, where could I go?'

Phil stared at him.

'Go on,' said Bailey. 'Answer the question.'

'I thought it was rhetorical,' said Phil, noticing that Marina almost smiled at that. 'Okay, where could you go?'

'Nowhere. I could go nowhere. Because once I've achieved perfection, there's no point in me being here. I'll use the knife on myself. Stop my own heart. Make my escape.'

'That's not an escape,' said Phil. 'That's getting away with what you've done. Not answering for all the murders you've committed. That's the coward's way out.'

Bailey just shook his head. 'We'll see, shall we?'

Phil took his attention away from Bailey, brought it to Marina. 'You okay?' he said.

She nodded.

'It's all right,' he said. 'Don't be afraid.'

And then Marina did something that took Phil completely by surprise. She smiled. 'I'm not,' she said. 'I'm not afraid of anything any more.'

'Well, you should be,' said Bailey, voice raised, not wanting to be ignored. 'Because I decide what happens next.'

'No you don't,' said Phil. Hoping his voice had conviction even though he didn't know what he was going to do.

Bailey laughed. 'You're not even armed,' he said.

'No,' said Marina. 'And I don't need to be.'

She stamped down hard on his instep. Bailey let out a cry, his knife hand loosening. She brought her head forward, then jerked it back sharply, making contact with the bridge of his nose. He screamed, stepped backwards, letting her go in the process.

Marina turned. Blood was pumping from Bailey's nose. He still had the knife.

'Bitch . . .'

He telegraphed a thrust with the blade and she neatly side-stepped it, bringing her leg up hard, her foot making contact with his thumb, bending it backwards. He screamed and dropped the knife. Staggered backwards.

Phil had made his way round the pair of them, picked up the stun gun from the table. He lifted it, ready to use it, but Marina brought her arm back and punched Bailey hard in the face. He went down. Just to make sure he wouldn't get up, Phil knelt and emptied the charge into him.

The voltage coursed through Bailey's body. He screamed, passed out.

Phil stood up, looked at his wife.

She turned to look at him.

And all hell broke loose in the room.

Police officers poured in. Picked Bailey up, dragged him out. Paramedics ran over to Imani on the bed.

But Phil and Marina were oblivious to it all. The calm at the eye of the storm, they stood there holding each other, letting everything happen around them.

Holding each other tight. Not letting go.

'I'm not afraid,' whispered Marina. 'Not of anything. Not any more.'

Phil smiled. Whispered back.

'Neither am I.'

They held on to each other like their lives depended on it.

PART SEVEN

BROKEN HEARTS

97

The rain was nearing torrential levels. Leaching what little colour was left out of the day, turning everything to a dull grey monochrome. The Sandwell Valley stretched down the hill and away, and Phil had to admit it probably looked beautiful in the summer. But this wasn't the summer. Now the trees just looked threadbare and apologetic, denuded and exposed.

The crematorium was behind them. He and Marina sheltered in the porch, keeping away from the rest of the mourners. They were both dressed in black, Phil with his Crombie overcoat pulled tight about him.

They didn't need to be there. Marina had said as much. It wasn't like they'd worked with Avi, or known him well. But Phil felt they should make an appearance. Avi Patel was, to all intents and purposes, one of their own.

The family had filed in before them, the parents still unable to believe that they were saying goodbye to their son. Phil found that shocked tableau depressingly familiar. He had seen it enough times. And it never got any easier.

Marina pulled in close to him. He still wasn't used to feeling her warmth near him again, didn't take it for granted. Almost a week since the events in the block of flats in Kings Heath. Since they'd caught Keith Bailey. Since they had come back together.

*

403

There had been the paperwork to take care of, but Cotter, seeing how close Phil and Marina were with each other, not to mention how exhausted they both looked, had sent them home.

Imani had been taken to hospital, Claire Lingard was receiving treatment, and Keith Bailey had been driven away to spend the first of many nights in a cell on his own.

'Where's Josephina?' Phil had asked.

'Joy's picked her up from school.'

Phil took his phone out.

'I already called,' said Marina, placing a hand on his wrist. 'She's fine.'

Phil returned the phone to his pocket.

'What about us?' he said, looking straight at her. 'Are we fine?'

Marina smiled. Phil saw tiredness etched in her features. 'We need to talk. About the future, about us. About that psychopathic threat hanging over us.'

'We do,' said Phil. 'Let's go home and do it.'

Leaving Josephina with Joy, they went home. It felt strange having Marina back after so long alone. For her part, Marina was appalled at the state Phil had allowed the house to get into.

'I was in a bad place,' he said. 'I didn't think anything mattered. If you weren't here.'

She smiled. 'I've always loved your honesty.'

He returned the smile. They put their arms round each other.

Kissed.

The next morning the sun came up, streamed through the bedroom window.

'Feels like a new start,' said Phil.

And Marina had to agree.

*

Things progressed smoothly after that. Keith Bailey was sent for psychiatric assessment. Marina made it clear she would be on hand for advice, but that was as much as she wanted to do with him. It was already looking like he might not stand trial, for reasons of insanity. He had admitted to other victims; all they had to do was find the bodies.

'That could go on for ever,' Phil had said to Cotter in the office a few days later. 'Depending on how much he wants to string us along.'

'Don't I know it. Still, at least there should be some anxious families who can put their minds to rest about their missing loved ones. Not in a positive way, though.'

'Closure,' said Phil. 'I hate that word.'

Cotter had nodded. Looked at him. 'So, DI Brennan, I believe you've had a change in your personal circumstances.'

'Things are looking up,' he said. 'Yeah. One step at a time.'

'Good. Well, with that in mind, are you ready to resume your place in the team?'

He grinned. 'I would love to.'

Claire Lingard had found it difficult to go back to work. She had found it impossible to stay at home. She had gone to her parents' place out in Oxfordshire, taken Edward with her. They had told her she could stay as long as she needed to.

One day while Claire was sitting in an armchair by the huge woodburner in the oak-beamed living room, trying to lose herself in a book, there was a knock at the door. She made no move to get it. Heard her mother talking to someone on the doorstep.

'Someone for you, Claire,' her mother said, coming back into the room, worry in her eyes.

Claire's stomach turned over. *He's found me. He's out. Oh*

God . . . She knew it was irrational, but she couldn't help but think that way. Not after what she had been through.

But it wasn't him.

'Hi, Claire.' Imani Oliver followed her mother in.

Claire stood up. She didn't know whether to hug Imani or shake her hand. Or just keep her distance. Keep contained. Imani made up her mind for her. She came over, took her in her arms. Claire had no option but to return the hug. Yielding as she did so, her defences dropping. Eventually they stood apart, looked at one another.

'How are you?' asked Imani.

Claire couldn't answer.

'Sorry, stupid question. Shouldn't have asked. I just wanted to see you.'

Claire nodded. She understood. When people went through an intense experience – good or bad – they could only talk about it with someone who had experienced something similar. As good as her parents had been, Claire hadn't been able to bring herself to open up to them about what had happened.

'I know,' she said. 'I was wondering how you were too.'

Imani nodded.

They sat on the sofa next to each other. Claire's mother excused herself, left them alone.

'It's . . . hard,' said Claire. 'Every day. You just can't . . . I just keep thinking back to . . . to what happened. What he was like. You know, whether I should have known, picked up on something. Some sign.'

'It's not your fault. Don't blame yourself. He had that mask firmly in place. He wore it well. There's no way you or anyone could have known.'

Claire just shook her head. 'I'm sure everybody's saying I must have known. Blaming me as well. But I . . . I . . .'

Imani placed her hand over Claire's.

'Sorry,' said Claire, starting to well up.

'It's okay,' said Imani.

Claire looked up, wiping her eyes. 'Sorry, I haven't asked about you.'

'That's all right.'

'How are you?'

Imani shrugged. 'Physically? Fine, really. No lasting damage.' She held up her bandaged wrists. 'Everything's on the mend.'

'And mentally?'

Imani tried to smile but couldn't. 'That'll take a little longer, I think.'

'Yes,' said Claire. 'You were very brave.'

'I was doing my job.'

'And it was a brave thing to do. The bravest thing I've ever seen.'

Imani looked straight at her. 'There's different kinds of bravery. You should know that.'

'I just run a refuge,' said Claire. 'There's no bravery in that.'

'You think not?' said Imani. 'You know what you had to go through to get there. Now you help other women to do the same. That's bravery.'

'I'm not sure I can go back there,' Claire said.

'Get yourself sorted first. That's the main thing.'

They talked on, well after day turned to night. So long that Imani accepted an offer to stay over.

Talking was good for both of them. There would be much more of it.

Together they had found their own personal refuge.

Hugh Ellison had heard what had happened. How Phil Brennan had been a hero once again, taken down that serial killer with the help of his wife. His *wife*. A psychologist, for fuck's sake. Confronting a killer. He felt sickened every time he heard

407

about it. And since it was still the main topic of conversation in the station, he heard about it a lot.

He sat on the pull-down bed in his studio apartment just off Hagley Road in Edgbaston and stared at the TV. His wife had finally kicked him out. Drinking in the Ivy Bush, meals from the chip shop next door. His life. And how he hated it.

He lay back on the bed. Thought again about the only thing on his mind. Phil fucking Brennan and Marina fucking Esposito. That case should have been his. *His.* He should have been the one to crack it, to find the real killer. He had gone over and over it. Marina should have done more when she was helping Carly. Should have gone further. All the brilliant stuff she came up with later, she should have done that with him. He hated her for it. *Hated* her.

But he knew what to do about that.

He checked his watch. Late. Good. It was time.

He took one last slurp from his bedside bottle of Bell's and made his way out. Drove to Balsall Heath. He knew where he was going. Rang the bell. She answered. Stared at him.

'Back again,' she said, and stood aside, allowing him to enter.

He was back where he always went to feel better about himself. To let off steam. The place his wife had continually complained about. Where he'd been when he told her he was out with friends. Networking, he had said.

He threw something at her.

'Put this on.'

She caught it, looked at it. 'Not again.'

'Just do it.'

She sighed, bracing herself. 'That's extra, you know.'

'I always pay, don't I?'

'For what you want to do, you should.' No attempt at seduction, no niceties. They both knew what he was there for. And what she was there for too. 'And go easy, will you? Bruises have just healed from last time.'

She walked away from him, pulling the long black curly wig on as she went. She reached the bedroom. It stank of stale bodies and cheap air freshener. She stood in front of him, bracing herself. Closed her eyes.

'I'm ready.'

He drew back his fist. 'Right, you fucking slut,' he said, building himself up for what he was about to do. 'Treat me like that, will you? Look at me like that, will you? I know what you're like. What you're really like. I know what you want.'

Rage built to a peak and he let go with his fist. It connected with her face, spun her round, knocked her down on to the bed. He was quickly on her.

'Right, you bitch. You're going to get it now. *Marina*.'

This was better. Now he was in charge.

Now he felt like a real man.

The rain was drying up as the service in the crematorium finished.

Phil and Marina had sat at the back, away from everyone else. They weren't family and they weren't strictly speaking colleagues. Just there to pay their respects.

The mourners filed out. They nodded and spoke. Phil noticed Esme Russell among them. She nodded at him, didn't speak. The family invited them back for something to eat. Phil declined. Waiting a decent amount of time, they made their excuses and left. Drove back to the city.

'We seem to go to a lot of these, don't we?' said Marina.

'Funerals? Line of work we're in, I suppose.'

Marina nodded. She drew in a deep breath, let it go. 'And I suppose also . . . that one day it'll be one of us.'

'You think?'

'Some things we just have to accept, don't we? It's what we do. Who we are. We've got someone after us who might strike at any time.'

'Or,' said Phil, 'might not strike at all.'

'True,' said Marina. 'But you know what? You're right. We're stronger together. If it happens, it happens. But we won't go down without a fight.'

He turned to her, smiled. She returned it.

They drove on in silence.

'So where are we going?' asked Phil after a while.

'You speaking philosophically or geographically?'

'Both,' he said.

Marina smiled. 'How about lunch?'

He laughed. 'That'll do nicely.'